Stone Mountain:
THE GRANITE SENTINEL

STONE MOUNTAIN:
THE GRANITE SENTINEL

George D. N. Coletti

Third Edition—Stone Mountain, Georgia

Summary: This historical novel, set in the little hamlet of Stone Mountain, Georgia, occurs just before, during and after the Civil War. The story revolves around a fictitious family, the Jernigans, and abruptly ends on July 4, 1865.

Cover Art: Wilbur Kurtz with permission from the Stone Mountain Memorial Association, Curtis Branscome, CEO.
Inside Front and Back Covers: Repinted with permission from Stone Mountain Memorial Association and Curtis Branscome, CEO.
Interior Photographs and Maps: Used by permission from the individual artists, photographers or owner of each image.
Cover Design: Julia Amirzadov
Interior Design: Julia Amirzadov

ISBN—Book: 978-0-9764895-6-2
ISBN—Supplemental CD: 978-0-9825370-1-5

Printed in China

This book is dedicated to the seventy known Confederate
Veterans and the approximately two hundred fifty-nine
unknown Confederate Soldiers and possible Union Soldiers
buried in the City of Stone Mountain Cemetery.[1]

contents

Part I

ACKNOWLEDGEMENTS   xi

FICTICIOUS CHARACTERS   xii

INFORMATIONAL   xiii

POEM BY LUCIAN LAMAR KNIGHT   xv

PROLOGUE   3

1.   APRIL 16, 1852   7

2.   MEET THE NEW SHERIFF—SPRING 1853   23

3.   FIVE YEARS LATER—A QUEST FOR THE BEST   35

4.   ENDEARMENT, ADVANCEMENT AND PROGRESS   49

5.   EMBRACING THE CHALLENGE   59

6.   HONOR AND TRUST   71

7.   EMOTIONS REIGN—NOVEMBER 1860   85

8.   JOE BROWN DRAWS THE SWORD   101

9.   LOST ON THE MOUNTAIN   117

10. THE SABER STRIKES   125

11. ADVANCED WEAPON TESTING   139

12. A NEW DAWN   157

13. A NEST ON THE RIVER   179

14. PANIC IN THE STREETS   197

15. MEDICINE, SURGERY AND HOPE   211

16. BACK IN STONE MOUNTAIN   221

17. THE STORK ARRIVES   239

18. DELIBERATING GEORGIA   251

19. HAPPY BIRTHDAY, LEGARE   263

20. THE SPIRIT OF MISTLETOE   281

21. PLUM PUDDING   299

22. HOME TO RECOVER   317

23. THE NOBLE AND THE VALIANT   329

24. DALTON TO RESACA   337

25. DEFIANT GENERALS   353

26. IN PURSUIT OF VICTORY IN WAR AND POLITICS   371

contents

Part II

	PROLOGUE	385
1.	THE MESSENGERS	387
2.	BRAGG'S DECEIT	401
3.	SURPRISE	419
4.	SAVING THE HOSPITALS	439
5.	THE BATTLE FOR DECATUR	451
6.	IN DEFENSE OF...	463
7.	THE FORTUNE OF WAR	475
8.	COLLEAGUES FOR THE UNION	487
9.	A FRIEND'S TALE OF WOE	499
10.	PREPARATION	515
11.	EYE WITNESS	529
12.	WITHOUT RESISTANCE	547
13.	TÊTE-À-TÊTE	557
14.	PASSING THROUGH	573
15.	PROUD AND STRONG	589
16.	AGAINST ALL ODDS	599
17.	SURRENDER OR DIE	617
18.	REFLECTIONS	641
19.	CHRISTMAS 1864	651
20.	QUESTIONS AND ANSWERS	663
21.	WHAT DO YOU THINK?	677
22.	POLITICS AND GENERALS	687
23.	SUDDENLY	699
24.	HOMEWARD BOUND	709
25.	IN THE SHADOW OF THE GRANITE SENTINEL	719
	EPILOGUE	737
	ADDENDUM	739
	MAPS APPENDIX	743
	ENDNOTES	751
	SUPPLEMENTAL CD	

acknowledgments

I could not have written this book without the genuine contributions of the following individuals.

My sincere gratitude cannot truly be expressed.

DESIGN AND LAYOUT EDITOR: Julia Amirzadov; ART AND ILLUSTRATIONS: My wife Susan Spickerman Coletti; CIVIL WAR HISTORIANS: Barry Leo Brown, Rusty Hamby, E. J. Seguin; FORMER MANUSCRIPT AND CONTENT EDITORS: Nancy Knight—Chief Editor, Mary F. Belenky, Kelli Watson Coletti, Dr. Wood E. Currens, Doc. Lawrence, Gerald T. Rakestraw, Jackie C. Reid; GULLAH TRANSLATION: Mr. Alfonso Brown, Charleston, SC; MASONIC CONTRIBUTION: James Payne and Charles Nash, Stone Mountain Masonic Lodge: no. 449, Will Simmons—Lithonia Masonic Lodge no. 84; MATERIAL CONTRIBUTIONS INCLUDING COPYRIGHT MATERIAL: Alabama Historical Society, Atlanta History Center, Cathy Colasanto—The Pirate's House, Curtis Banscome, CEO—Stone Mountain Memorial Association, Bob Cowhig—Stone Mountain Memorial Association, DeKalb History Center—Decatur, GA, Gary Livingston—*Cradled In Glory Georgia Military Institute 1851-1865*, Robert Niepert—*Samuel Moore Diary*, Gary Peet—Mayor of Stone Mountain, Professor Craig Symonds—*Joseph E. Johnston, A Civil War Biography*, Mr. Bill Scaife—*March to the Sea Maps*, Marietta Museum of History, Morgan County Records Archives, Anne Barnett, MD—Photographs of Congressman & Mrs. Dent, Larry Winslett—*Stone Mountain a Walk in the Park*, Mary Beth Reed, President—New South Associates.

fictitious characters

Buck and Betty Gail Jernigan

Polly and Norman (Wee-Bean)—The twin children of Buck and Betty Gail

Uncle Isaac and Aunt Sally—Two slaves belonging to the Jernigans

Little Joshua—Son of Polly and Hugh Legare Hill*

Georgie—Nephew to the Jernigans

Elias Mason—Freelance Writer

Buster Phillips—Neighbor of the Jernigans

Joe—Attendant at the Wayside

Richard and Charlotte—Cousins to Congressman Joshua Hill*

Marie, Keaton, Ian, Claire, Matthew, Jordan, Marcelle—Children of Richard and Charlotte

Al, Jemima, Jesse, Tot, Le Roy—Slaves belonging to Richard and Charlotte

Jodi—Social Friend of Charlotte

Katherine Turner—Friend of Congressman and Mrs. Hill*

Katherine Turner's Children—"Cannon Ball", Stephen Charles & Christopher Richard

Donald Lilly—Bank President

Dr. Frederick Daniel—Surgeon in Savannah

Jennifer—Niece of Thomas Purse,* Mayor of Savannah

Rooster—Confederate Soldier

Sharon & Beverly—Beautiful Young Maidens

Chip and Allen—Railroad Conductors

Antonio—Restaurant Owner

Jack & Ferry—Soldiers departing Savannah

Robin, Jane, Nan, Linda, Aunt Bess—Good Citizens

Any name resembling a living or dead individual other than the historical individuals listed is purely coincidental. All other names in this historical novel are historical individuals.

* Historical individual

informational

The Confederate army operating in Georgia was:
    The Army of Tennessee
The Union armies operating in Georgia were:
    The Army of the Tennessee
    The Army of the Cumberland
    The Army of the Ohio

In order for the reader who is not familiar with the names of individuals connected with either the Confederate or Union forces the writer is using the following table to assist in identifying whether the individual is a Confederate or a Union officer.

Abbreviations for military ranks:

Rank	Confederate	Union
General	Gen.	General
Lieutenant General	LG	Lieutenant-General
Major General	MG	Major-General
Brigadier General	BG	Brigadier-General
Colonel	Col.	Colonel
Lieutenant Colonel	LTC	Lieutenant Colonel
Major	Maj.	Major
Captain	Capt.	Captain
Lieutenant	Lt.	Lieutenant

Any rank not accompanied by an individual name can refer to either Confederate or Union. The "Captain" of any civilian ship is simply addressed as "Captain." When a new character is introduced his absolute rank, i.e. Major-General, Lieutenant General or Brigadier General is first used. Afterwards the form of address will be "General." For Lieutenant Colonel the form of address will be "Colonel."

informational

Unit Composition and Strength:

COMPANY: Captain, Two Platoons, 50-100 men
REGIMENT: Colonel, Ten Companies, 400-1000 men
BRIGADE: Brigadier General, Three-Six Regiments
DIVISION: Brigadier or Major General, Two-Four Brigades, 4000-12,000 men
CORPS: Major General or Lt. General, Two-Four Divisions, 25,000-40,000 men
ARMY: Major General or Lt. General, Two or more Corps, 120,000 men

Gray minstrel of the past, but monarch, too,
Of all the country-side, for many a league—
Unmated in thy Jovine gianthood,
A solitary pile, whose shadow vast,
Falls like a benediction upon the plain.[2]

prelude to the war

When the United States Government was formed, slavery existed in every state in the union. Slavery was distinctly recognized in the Constitution and its legality was reinforced by the Supreme Court's decision in Dred Scott v. Sanford which stated that slaves were private property, giving owners the right to carry slaves into any part of the United States or her territories. On two separate occasions, Congress enacted legislation regarding fugitive slaves. The Fugitive Slave Act of 1793 required the return of runaway slaves to their owners; however, it was rarely enforced by northern states which led to the more direct Fugitive Slave Law of 1850. Under this law, all United States Marshals and other Federal officers were required to aid in the capture and return of a fugitive slave or face penalties. Every Act of Congress and every decision of the Supreme Court had sustained the rights of citizens to own slaves. Additionally, the Senate of the United States adopted a resolution that "all of the states were sovereign and equal," and that Negro slaves were property. Therefore, Congress had no right to interfere with this kind of property in the territories, and each state had the sole right to legislate on the subject.

In Georgia, the fourth state to ratify the Federal Constitution and enter the Union, there had always been a strong Union sentiment. Conversely, under the leadership of "The Great Calhoun," South Carolina had resorted to nullification of the Constitution. New England had often threatened secession—first after the election of Thomas Jefferson, again during the War of 1812, and finally over the issue of slavery.[13] However Georgia had always set herself sternly against both. In 1850, the contest for governor in which the question of secession played an important part, the people of Georgia elected Howell Cobb, an ex-Speaker of the

United States House of Representatives. Cobb defeated a distinguished former governor, Charles J. McDonald, a secessionist, by the largest majority the electorate had ever given any man for governor within the state's entire history.

When Missouri was admitted into the Union as a slave state in 1820, a compromise measure was adopted. Under the terms of the compromise, all territories or future states north of thirty-six degrees and thirty minutes north latitude should be admitted into the Union as free states. All south of that line came in as either a free or slave state as the people of the territory would determine when the request for admission was submitted. This was an injustice to the South, because Congress, by this Act, assumed a right which had never belonged to it, to-1860wit, the right to legislate on a subject which belonged solely to the states.

It was at this time, because of this concession by the South, that the vexing question of Union with a constitution prohibiting slavery, one-half of her territory being North and the other half being South of thirty-six degrees and thirty minutes, the Missouri Compromise was abrogated. The status of the territories became the same as it was before The Compromise was adopted.

For the sake of peace and harmony, the South once again acquiesced. Four years later when Kansas and Nebraska were seeking admission into the Union, many Southern men had settled and others were settling in Kansas and Nebraska, especially the former. The abolitionists organized and sent into Kansas and Nebraska bands of armed men from the free states to drive the Southerners out. This would prevent the adoption of a state constitution recognizing slavery. A condition of civil war in essence resulted. Through this means, anti-slavery constitutions were adopted and both territories were admitted as free states.

So violent had the hostility to slavery and to the Southern slave owners become that a dozen Northern States enacted "personal liberty laws." These actions were considered by many to be a violation of the Acts of Congress, the Constitution and the decisions of the Supreme Court of preventing citizens of the South from going with their property into the territories with equal protection as provided by the various federal decisions regarding slavery. This equal protection was to slaveholders and their property as that accorded to citizens of all the other States. The people of the South could only be alarmed at the situation.

The Republican Party and the election of Abraham Lincoln as President in 1860, served to increase the agitation by seemingly trampling upon the Constitution, nullifying the Acts of Congress and defying the Supreme Court. It was not a party of fixed and well-defined principles but rather was believed to be a coalition of several parties and fragments of dead parties organized in its day to combat the principles of the party of Thomas Jefferson. This coalition agreed to nothing, except hostility to the party of Thomas Jefferson and the Southern States, the stronghold of Thomas Jefferson's influence.

None of these factions was within itself strong enough to be dangerous. However, united as they now were under the leadership of fanatical and unscrupulous partisans, every pronouncement made was a threat, an insult or a denunciation of the South. They became a menace to the peace of the entire country and to the material interest of the Southern States. Another factor in this coalition was a small but militant fragment of the old Federalist Party, aristocrats who favored a strong central government. The Federalist Party had opposed the adoption of the Constitution on the grounds that under it, the powers of the central government were too limited and those of the states were too broad.

The Federalist Party's leader was Chief Justice of the Supreme Court, John Marshall. Justice Marshall, by judicial construction, constantly amplified the powers of the Federal Government, and at same time, restricted those of the states.

Another factor in the coalition was the old Abolition or Free-soil Party which had existed since the establishment of the Union. The Free-Soil Party was perhaps more threatening because it was sincere in its fanatical desire to abolish Negro slavery. It had demonstrated that it would stop at nothing to accomplish its goal.

Still, another factor in the coalition was the northern wing of the old Whig Party which believed in protective tariffs and a national bank.

The last and most formidable factor in this coalition was made up of the army of manufacturers located in the middle and eastern states. The shipbuilders and the fishermen had for many decades fattened on subsidies, bounties and protective tariffs, all at the expense of the people of all other sections of the Union. They were not scrupulous about party alignment, but were willing and ready to coalesce with any party which would continue and increase the special privileges they had enjoyed.

The new coalition promised all of this. These factions joined eagerly, or rather were absorbed eagerly by the Republican Party, acceding to all of their demands for centralization of power in the Federal Government, creation of a national bank, granting special privileges to the favored few, and the abolition of Negro slavery. Thus, the coalition became all things to all men, North and East. The coalition arrayed a solid North bound together by sectional prejudice and the cohesive power of public plunder against a solid South, which asked nothing but equal rights in the Union.

The South asked nothing which was not guaranteed to them by the Constitution and continually reinforced by Congressional legislation. They had shown their attachment to the Union by sacrifices and concessions, never appreciated by their adversaries. These adversaries, in the meantime, had been successful in making a solid North, whose object was to deprive the South of equality in the Union and the rights guaranteed to them by the Constitution. So intense had become the hostility of the dominant party to the South and Southern rights and interests that every utterance of its press and of its leaders in the campaign of 1860 was a menace, a threat or an insult to the Southern people. The Southern people had foreborne with their fanatical enemies until forbearance had ceased to be a virtue.

For the most part, the five thousand Freedman Negroes who were slave owners in the South were simply darker copies of their white counterparts. To the Negro slave owner, slavery was an oppressive institution only when a beloved relative or trusted friend was a slave. Beyond these feelings, the Negro slave owner had the same feeling and thoughts as the white slave owner; slavery was a profit making institution. When Negro masters made use of their slaves for business reason, they would encounter similar problems which bewildered the white slave owners. Regardless of the race of the slave master, the oppressive nature of slavery was met with resistance and antagonism from the slaves.

1

The sun, rising from behind Stone Mountain bestows a beautiful spring morning on the inhabitants of the village and farms in the area. The perfume of flowers abounds, and the crowing of a rooster saturates the still air. The Jernigans are already busy, beginning their morning chores early in anticipation of a trip to town. Over by the barn, the rabbit box is closed, possibly concealing a successful catch inside. Uncle Isaac, one of the Jernigan slaves, peeks into the rabbit box, looks up, grins and calls out to Wee-Bean, "Mars Norman dis a fat-un!"

A lark darts from a fragrant cedar to an oak sapling, singing merrily. Standing in the front of the house the wagon is full of the last of the winter crops of greens and cabbage, ready for the trip to town. Jack, the pet mule, is harnessed and raring to go. Wee-Bean clatters out of the house and down the steps. He reaches down and pats their brown hound, Charlie, and tosses him a biscuit. His twin sister, Polly watches as Jack turns his head, swishes his tail and neighs for Wee-Bean to come over. Wee-Bean plucks a fresh clump of tall spring grass and delivers it to Jack's smacking lips. Betty Gail sits in the wagon, studying the bright and busy scene. She pulls her beautiful auburn hair away from her face, all the time, smiling at the familiar family scenes occurring on their little farm.

"Let's git. We're burnin' daylight," hollers Buck Jernigan, summoning their children, Polly and Norman, to hurry to the wagon.

Their darkies, Uncle Isaac and his wife Sally, climb into the back and the wagon rumbles off toward town. Jack heads up the hill and along the narrow dew-moistened trail toward the little Village of Stone Mountain.

Although the village is growing because of the newly finished railroad, it is still considered as an insignificant town, consisting only of several churches, a grocery, a grog shop, a tavern, a blacksmith shop, ten pin alleys and a few tumbled-down shanties. Yet this little hamlet stands in full view of the sloping side of the mountain. In contrast, Stone Mountain is home to Stone Mountain Academy, one of the finest education institutions in the state.[4] Arriving at the academy, Wee-Bean and Polly leap from the wagon.

"We'll pick you up after Mr. Johnson's funeral," Buck calls to his two children. Wee-Bean links up with one of his friends. Just as the bell rings, Polly, her brother Wee-Bean and his friend enter the school looking for their teacher, Miss Martha Tweedle.

"Giddy-up Jack," commands Buck. The wagon slowly turns as they head toward the depot track crossing. The plaintive sound of the train whistle can be heard in the distance. Peering over the tree tops, he sees the billowing clouds of smoke indicating the distance remaining before the train arrives. The engine rolls into view. "*Squeakkkkk*," echo the brakes, which slowly bring the train to a stop. The mail car door opens, and the railroad agent throws the mailbag to the waiting postal clerk.

"Thanks!" The postal clerk shouts as he grabs the bag and climbs onto his buckboard, heading to the post office. In passing, he shouts to the Jernigans, "Good morning to you, Buck. Good morning, Betty Gail."

"And a good morning to you! It's a fine day, ain't it?" Buck replies, offering a friendly wave. Betty Gail nods and smiles.

The engineer jumps from the fuming steam engine as it reaches the water tank. He grabs the handle of the waterspout and slowly lowers it, turning the valve to allow water to flow into the boiler. When the boiler is full, the engineer retracts the large metal nozzle and closes the valve. He climbs back into the engine cab and slightly releases the brakes on the engine, allowing the cattle car to roll where it needs to be. The car's agent raises his hand indicating to the engineer to prepare to stop. As the cattle car nears the proper alignment with the corral gate, the agent drops his hand. The engineer pulls the brake handle, stopping the cattle car precisely before the corral gate. The railroad agent unlocks the large sliding door. Around thirty head enter the corral. A flatbed rail car loaded with cut granite is parked on a sidetrack waiting to become a part of a southbound train due that afternoon.

"Hey, Buck!" James W. Goldsmith yells. "Can you help me a moment?"

Buck stops the wagon by the depot. "Might can. What do you need?"

"Jesse Lanford bought six heifers, but he isn't here to claim them. I don't mind doing it for him, but I need a witness. Would you sign the papers with me?"

"Anything for a neighbor." Buck takes the pen and signs the document willingly, knowing his neighbors would do the same for him.

Then, the cattle are driven into the corral. Buck hears the conductor shout, "All-aboard!" and watches as a few passengers approach the train. He places the "lady step" down to help board the train. Buck and Betty Gail exchange waves with some friends. In moments the old iron horse chugs out of sight, heading to Decatur and then on to Atlanta.

The Jernigans hurry to the church. Today is a sad day for the village and its residents. One of the town's founders and a good friend, Andrew Johnson, is to be buried in the afternoon. Betty Gail and some of her friends are going to prepare the family meal to be served after the funeral service. Other families providing food pull their wagons up to the church and begin to unload. Betty Gail, Sally and Isaac unload their contribution. Buck holds the halter of the lead horse while the other takes the fare to the basement of the church, and nods to Betty Gail as she retrieves the last of the vegetables. He takes a seat in the buggy and shifts until he finds a comfortable position. "I'm headed to the blacksmith shop. Jack sorely needs a foot trimming and to be shod. The wagon wheels need greasing, too. I'll be back in plenty of time for the funeral service."

❧

"Whoa, Jack." Buck climbs down and clasps the calloused hand of his old friend, Levi Hambrick, the blacksmith. "Nice seeing you and your wife at the laying out last night, Levi. I'm sorry Betty Gail and I didn't get to spend more time talking with you. There were a lot of folks there."

"Yes, so were we. There was a fine turnout there, Buck. We need to get together and have a long talk sometime. I

Andrew Johnson

don't believe anybody had much time to talk with anybody else at length. I know you and the Johnsons are very close friends. I'm sorry for your loss."

"Yes, we are," replies Buck. "Our families came from the Carolinas about the same time. My father and Andrew's father were very close." He chuckled for the first time since Andrew's death. "Talk about spinning tall tales, whenever those two gents got together, they could really mystify their listeners with Indian war stories. I'll pick my mule up after the funeral and will have Isaac get the other horse and buggy we left here yesterday."

"I should have everything ready in a couple of hours. Instead of having Isaac pick up the buggy, I'll leave it for you in front of the church." Levi released Jack from the wagon and looks back at Buck. "Please give my regards to the Johnson family. My wife will be at the funeral but I told the Johnsons I could not make it today."

"I'll be sure to do that, Levi." Buck left his friend and strode the two blocks to the church, focusing on his obligation. This isn't the way he would have chosen to spend his day. The loss of his good friend weighs heavily on his mind as he hurries the last few steps of his walk.

Around eleven o'clock, the friends of Andrew Johnson begin to gather outside the church. They greet each other somberly and, forming small groups, inevitably begin discussing local matters, and how Andrew has touched nearly everyone in the community. Buck is talking to Lewis Tumlin and Michal Winningham. "Michal, I know you dug the first grave in the new cemetery for the Guess child.[5] As I remember it, he is supposed to be a descendant of George Guess."

"You are right. George Guess's Indian name was Sequoyah. He was the man who wrote the alphabet for the Cherokee Indian Nation."[6]

"Yeah, exactly right. Did you prepare the grave site for Andrew as well?"

"Preacher asked me if I would do it and I did. Andrew will be buried on his family plot on top of the hill. Mighty purty spot."

"Yes, Betty Gail told me." Then Buck turns to Lewis Tumlin. "Has anybody started to dig in the Etowah Indian mounds you bought in '38?"

"Ever now and again some ask and some try and slip in. We can see the mounds from the house and try to keep everybody out. The mounds are an important archeological site and we hope to preserve them forever, if possible."[7]

Clusters of mourners talking in whispered tones wait patiently for the start of the funeral services. Some of Buck's Masonic Brothers gather to discuss local issues. Other neighbors mill around for a comfortable spot and talk that will momentarily free their minds of their grief. John

Beauchamp, who sold the mountain to Andrew, talks with the Veal brothers about his first impressive meeting with Andrew.[8]

Aaron Cloud and Thomas Henry are discussing Thomas's effort to build a new tower on top of the mountain after Aaron's blew down. "Thanks for the valuable information about building a tower, Aaron, and what I should do to keep it standing. I tell you, it's not as easy as I thought."

Aaron laughs. "Just be sure your tower is anchored better than mine was or the wind will make short work of it! I saw yours last week, and everything looks great. The anchors seem to be deep enough in the granite, but you never know. When do you think it will be finished?"

"Hoping by June. Mine is about half the size of yours, only forty square feet at the base and eighty feet high.[9] I hope to turn the tower into a popular observatory with the finest telescopes available in the South to exhibit the wonders of Heaven in their utmost glory."

"Professor Harper's astronomy lectures about the *Glorious Sun* during the day and the *Wonders of the Heavens* at night will draw a big crowd to the observatory, we hope. Should be a good attraction."[10]

"That's right. Thomas Johnson and John Quack are going to sponsor the lectures and observatory for me. Should be quite an enterprise."

"Anything to bring in the tourists will help all of us. Stone Mountain has become a very popular destination since the road[11] was completed."

Jesse Lanford is talking with a freelance writer in town to cover the funeral when he spots William Adair, Jr. who lives on the Lumpkin place outside Madison. "I see someone you should meet. He was in charge of laying the rail iron that brought the first train through our little town then to Decatur and on to Atlanta. William, I would like you to meet Mr. Elias Mason a freelance reporter. I thought maybe he could write an interesting story about you and the road coming through Stone Mountain."

"Nice meeting you, Mr. Mason. Be glad to answer most any question you have about the road through these parts. Help put the Georgia Road in place from Madison to Atlanta."

"Thank you Mr. Adair. How has the road helped this little place?"

"Why it's helped to increase the influx of tourists to Stone Mountain. Crowds are getting bigger everyday on the train, but hauling cotton and livestock is the biggest business." More locals gather to hear what William has to say to the reporter.

"Mr. Adair, tell me how you got started with the Georgia Railroad and how you took that first train through here to Marthasville."[12]

The clanging of church bells interrupts the conversations and everyone falls silent as they turn toward the church and begin to move in that direction.[13]

"Please, Mr. Mason, look for me at the mercy meal after the funeral. I will be glad to continue our conversation then," whispers William as he moves toward the church doors with the rest of the crowd.

"Yes, sir, Mr. Adair. I will look forward to continuing the interview after the funeral. Thank you, kind sir."

The crowd is silent as the funeral coach approaches. Friends form lines on each side of the path leading from the street to the front doors. Betty Gail, Isaac and Sally rush to join Buck just as others seek solace with their families.[14]

Two black horses slowly draw the shiny funeral coach up the gentle hill and come to rest in front of the Baptist church. Stable boys secure the horses and buggies as the family members and pallbearers step quietly from their buggies and wagons, gathering at the rear of the coach. Buck can't help but notice the large decorative windows of the coach that extend the full length of each side. The rear door's top half is glass with an upper border ornate with perfectly cut and beautiful stained glass. In the center of the stained glass border is a design depicting the crucifixion glistening brightly in the midmorning sun. In the simple, wooden coffin lays the body of Andrew Johnson.

The family and pallbearers silently assemble at the rear of the funeral coach. The minister opens the door. The pallbearers assume their positions. Men who had served with Andrew as Commissioners or Postmasters of New Gibralter, their current situation having taken a toll on each one. Aaron Cloud is the last to grasp his friend's coffin. The family escorts the coffin as Pastor Lewis Towers, proceeds in front.[15] Passing by the line of friends are William Edgar Johnson and Jane, both eighty years of age, the father and mother of Andrew. Each uses a cane and needs assistance upon reaching the steps of the church. Andrew's son, thirty-five year old William II, assists his grandfather. Andrew's other two sons, thirty-two year old Thomas and thirteen year old George, assist their grandmother. Next are Andrew's sister Lucretia and her husband James Goldsmith. Andrew's other sister Sara and her husband, John Ford, follow Lucretia. The last of the family to enter the church is twenty-six year old Mary, Andrew's daughter and her husband, Dr. John Hamilton.

After a prayer and the singing of two songs, Pastor Lewis Towers begins the eulogy for Andrew Johnson. "We are here to celebrate the life of the founder of the City of Stone Mountain Andrew Johnson. He was our loved one, our neighbor, our friend and our leader. He has gone to be with his wife, Elizabeth, who has been waiting for him in the hereafter for two years."

Betty Gail reaches for Buck's hand. As good friends of the Johnsons, they remember how painful it had been for Andrew to lose his wife. The pastor's words of reunion are a great solace to Buck as he glances at his beloved Betty Gail. He listens intently as the pastor gives a brief synopsis of his friend's great life.

"Andrew was born in South Carolina on June 4, 1800, and, as we all here know, he passed away on April 16 of this year 1852. Just short of 52 years, Andrew lived his life to the fullest. Around 1828, he and his wife, mother, father and three sisters moved here from the Indian territory of South Carolina. In 1830, he and his family owned and operated a general store on Killian Hill Road. Andrew, who always believed in a strong state militia, became a First Lieutenant in Captain Latimer's Voluntary Enlistment in the 4th Regiment of the Georgia Militia in 1836. When he realized the value of the mountain as the most popular tourist spot in our state, he decided to purchase the entire mountain. Andrew bought the mountain from his, and our, good friends Mr. John Beauchamp and William Meador.[16] In 1836, he built a hotel at the foot of the mountain, right at the spot where most people begin their trek up the mountain.

"When the first gold rush in America began in Dahlonega, his investment in his property around the mountain and in town begins to grow. Stagecoaches from Milledgeville stopped at his hotel. Passengers would spend the night and then travel on to Dahlonega the next morning.

"On December 21, 1836, Andrew was appointed to the DeKalb County Commission. With his influence, the Stone Mountain Academy was incorporated and approved by The General Assembly on December 31, 1838.[17] In 1839, he assisted in having New Gibraltar incorporated as our town and served as our first commissioner. The city limits ran from his house to three hundred yards in all directions.[18] He also served as our postmaster for seven years beginning in October 1839. Thanks to his persuasion, the railroad officials brought the Georgia Railroad through our city in 1845."

The sermon reminds Buck of the many good times he had with Andrew. The two of them watched the first load of granite leave Stone Mountain on the newly constructed spur line of the railroad, both laughing at how long it would take until the entire mountain had been hauled away. He remembers the time Andrew and John Graves announced that the Southern Central Agricultural Society would be holding a fair for all Georgians, right in Andrew's beautiful grove. Buck nearly laughs when he recalls the main feature of the fair: a traveling exposition complete with a run-away elephant. And there were the sad memories, like when Weldon Wright[19] used blasting powder to make a trail 25 feet long and two feet wide upon the steep side of the mountain. This was to be a tourist attraction for adventurers to walk on for a mere twenty-five cents. Then, while trying to extend the trail in 1846, he was blown off the mountain by a premature explosion. Buck squirms in his seat as he thinks of poor Weldon's remains at the base of the mountain. A brief pause in the pastor's sermon brings Buck's attention back to the moment at hand.

"Andrew's hard work and determination helped him become one of DeKalb County's wealthiest landowners. His two thousand acre plantation at the steep side of the mountain is a perfect example of cotton farming. His success and vision have become this community's success and outlook for the future. He took us from Rock Mountain to New Gibralter, and then to Stone Mountain. Andrew was the catalyst for developing our community into a rare pearl. We must all strive to protect and build upon the inheritance and vision given to us by Andrew Johnson. May his soul rest in peace and may his memory be eternal.

After a communal reading of the Twenty-third Psalms and the Lord's Prayer, the congregation stands. The pallbearers, with Pastor Lewis Towers leading slowly and solemnly, return the casket to the funeral coach. The family and friends form the funeral procession to the Johnson Cemetery. Betty Gail begins to cry as she sees the open grave and the four strong straps that will support the coffin and lower it to its final resting place. Buck pulls her into a close embrace and comforts her.

The pallbearers remove Andrew's casket from the funeral coach for the last time, placing it on the straps. After the family and friends gather around the grave, Pastor Towers delivers the final prayer. Then each pallbearer takes one end of the strap, lifts the coffin and walks on each side of the grave site, centering the coffin over the grave. In unison, they lower the body of Andrew Johnson slowly to its place of eternal rest.[20]

Isaac and Sally take Buck and Betty Gail to Levi's to get Jack and the buckboard. Buck assists Betty Gail from the wagon and into the buckboard. He holds onto the horse's bridle and turns the wagon. "Isaac, you and Sally head for home. Betty Gail and I are going back to the church.

After the family meal, we have to pick up some dry goods, several bags of chicken feed, corn, okra and pea seeds and some new plow heads. Then we will pick up Polly and Wee-Bean and head home."

Those who attended the grave side service are returning to the church for the mercy meal. This gathering is less solemn than the actual funeral. The people are more out-going and talkative. After a brief prayer, they eat.

Mr. Elias Mason and William Adair sit together and pick up their discussion about the railroad. Elias asks William, "When did you first start with the railroad?"

"In 1842 to be exact. We started working on the survey just as I was twenty-one. My pa gave me a dollar and told me to 'work out my fortune!'" William chuckles. "So I applied at the Georgia Railroad office and got a job as the assistant surveyor. John A. Wright was my boss. It took us about six months to finish the road survey from Madison to Covington. It was December 22nd and cold when we were finally done. You want exact dates if I remember 'em?"

"Yes, in fact, I do. Did you lay iron on the road right away?" asks Elias.

"Yep, as soon as possible. Although it was the middle of winter, a lot of farmers were holding their cotton. Anxious to get that cotton to Augusta for shipping to Savannah or to transfer the cotton to a connecting road. It wasn't until August of '43 that we began the survey from Covington to Marthasville. We followed the Stone Mountain-Sandtown Indian Trail from Stone Mountain through Decatur and to Atlanta.[21] L. P. Grant was hired to run the survey of the Georgia Railroad from Covington to Marthasville. F. C. Arms, who later became the assistant to Mr. Grant, carried the level instrument while I lugged the rod. We completed the survey to, what was then, Marthasville on December 23, 1843."

"How did you get to be the conductor and engineer?"

"Mr. Adams eventually became the superintendent in 1845 and hired me on full time. That's when I boarded with Mr. Melton at Yellow River."

"Yeah, and not long after that he married Mr. Adams daughter!" interjects Jesse clapping his hand on William's shoulder genially.

"Sure 'nough did. Got married on September 29, '47 just after she turned eighteen. Where was I? Oh yeah, I was surveying with Ezekiel Sanford at Latimer's Crossroads in February and March of 1844, staking out the road to Stone Mountain." William shakes his shoulder as if he has the shivers. "Real cold winter! When it got warmer in April and May, I was assisting Mr. Grant at Decatur in the survey from here to Marthasville."

"So what happened when you finished the survey?"

"I was stationed at Yellow River during June and July, receiving cross ties, string timber and mud sill for the railroad track from Covington to Conyers. The iron rails had been laid on the road to within three miles of Conyers and the first train crossed Yellow River on April 1, 1845. I continued supervising the laying of iron until we reached Stone Mountain."

"What about driving the train to Atlanta?"

"It was on August 15th, Mr. Arms promoted me to conductor and put me in charge of the construction train. My run was from Covington to where the track was being laid. I retained the position of conductor until the road was completed to Marthasville. Then, on September 14, 1845 while at Decatur, I was told that the track would be finished to Marthasville that afternoon and I was being ordered to go there that night. I had ten car loads of iron for the Western and Atlantic railroad brought up from Augusta."

"That's a heap of rail iron!"

"Sure was! My engineer, John Hopkins, took violently ill about that time, but my orders were clear. I must be in Marthasville that night!"

"Why the rush?"

"Big news event. Nothing daunted me as I mounted my engine, the 'Kentucky.'" Running his arm forward as if grabbing the throttle and pulling it back. "I pulled open the throttle and rolled out of Decatur at 8 o'clock PM. I halted the engine right where the car-shed now stands in Atlanta, a few minutes before 9 at night. The funniest thing was when Mr. John P. King, the president of the Georgia Railroad and Banking Company, disembarked from the train in the dark and fell into a well."

"Oh no. Did he get injured very bad?"

William laughs. "Only his pride."

"Whew. You had me worried for a minute."

"You have only to ask about the railroad construction from Covington to Atlanta. Do you know where the railroad really began?"

Putting his pencil down, Elias scratches his head thoughtfully. "Didn't it begin in Athens, or was it Augusta?

With a broad smile William tells the young Elias, "The Georgia Railroad Company was chartered December 21, 1833, by a group of Athens citizens led by James Camak. Their goal was to build a railroad from Athens to Augusta."

Elias picks up his pencil and begins scribbling notes. "I remember reading about that now. That was the first railroad in Georgia and I think the third in all of the United States. Right, Mr. Adair?"

"That's absolutely correct, Elias. Construction began in 1835, starting at Augusta. The company changed its name to Georgia Railroad & Banking Company in 1836 because the banking side of the business eventually proved more rewarding than the company leasing its railroad operations to others."

"So how long did it take to complete?"

"The thirty-nine mile Athens branch was completed in December 1841 and was operated with horse drawn cars until 1847 with a five foot gauge track." Elias leans back in his chair and places his coupled hands behind his head.

"So the Atlanta branch was completed in 1845, and soon the 171 mile Augusta-Atlanta rail connection became the main line in Georgia."

"Correct, and from early on, Augustans gained control from Athens interests, with Augustan, John Pendleton King serving as president of the railroad."

William leans over the table and pats Elias on the hand. "Come by and visit some time and bring plenty of paper. Then I'll give you the full story of the Western and Atlantic state owned road."

Andrew's father, William, and Buck are also engaged in reminiscing. "Buck, your Grandfather and my father fought the Indians together. It still burns me to think about how they murdered our neighbors, families and friends, the aged and young alike. Incarcerated our grandfathers and allowed them to perish in filth, famine and disease, knowing their mothers, wives, sister and young children had been robbed, insulted, and abused." He slowly shakes his head remembering the awful details. "If it hadn't been for Elijah Clarke ... I'm sure your pa and grandfather told you some of the horrible stories."

"They sure did. Several of my grandfather's brothers were held captive and murdered by the British and the Indians. Knowing things like that makes it easy to fight because it's the right thing to do."

"That's right. We were certainly glad to see you come to Stone Mountain after the Mexican War. Mexico got what they asked for ... Defeat! They should learn to keep their word. " William glances around at the thinning crowd as his wife signals him it's time to leave for home. "Well, it looks like the family is ready to head out. It's been a long day for all of us."

Buck shakes hands with William and the other members of the family as they leave. Other families follow suit, and soon the churchyard is empty. After tidying the church hall, Buck and Betty Gail leave to do their shopping. Once complete, they pull up to the Academy to pick up Polly and

Wee-Bean. As the two chattering children jump into the wagon, the sky begins to turn ominously dark.

Buck points toward the rolling clouds. "A storm's brewing and we best git." Wind ruffles the leaves on the trees as they pass revealing the lighter undersides. The temperature drops suddenly and thunder rumbles in the distance. The wind gains force—thrashing trees like whips.

"Let's git on Jack, only a half mile to go!" Buck calls out anxiously. Fat raindrops begin to fall. Lightning crackles across black clouds and thunder booms almost immediately. Hail pelts them as the dirt road turns to mud almost instantly. A bright flash and deafening boom knocks Jack over and carries the buckboard over into the ditch with him. Polly, Betty Gail and Wee-Bean are thrown into the mud. Blinding rain and wind cut into Betty Gail's face as she searches for her children. She hugs them close for a moment before they resume the search for Buck. She hears his cries for help.

"There," she shouts, trying to make her voice heard above the storm. "Merciful Lord, he's trapped under the buckboard." The muddy deluge floods over him. His shouts become garbled as the sienna colored water flows over his head. Jack lies motionless in the ditch, making no noise. They rush over to Buck and shield him from the rain and mud.

"Pa!" Wee-Bean scrambles down the bank, fighting a rising panic as he wipes water and mud from his father's pain stricken face.

Betty Gail assesses the situation as quickly as she can. "All right, Wee-Bean, help me lift the buckboard. Polly, help your pa slide out from under."

"No, no," Buck cries. "Don't touch my leg. It's broken!"

"Go get Doctor Hamilton and whoever else you can find to help!" screams Betty Gail to Wee-Bean amidst the chaos and wreckage.

He darts off up the muddy embankment and dashes towards town just as the clouds separate and the wind becomes a little calmer. Still muddy, he reaches the livery stable and throws open the door. Screaming and crying, he calls out frantically, "Lightning struck us, and Pa's trapped under the wagon! We need help!"

"Come here, Norman. Calm down son. What's happened?" Levi takes Wee-Bean by the hand and tries to settle him down to get more information. Wee-Bean rubs his eyes. "Pa, Ma and Polly are over the crest of the hill, and Pa is pinned under the load."

John Beauchamp jumps on his mount and goes for Dr. Hamilton, while others gather outside with their horses, wagons and ropes, ready to head toward the scene with Wee-Bean.

The storm disappears almost as quickly as it came. The sun is bright, and the sky sparkles blue once again. As the group led by Wee-Bean hurries toward the accident they encounter tree limbs, tin roofing torn from houses and water flowing on the red clay street. As the team tops the hill, Wee-Bean sees the overturned wagon Buck is trapped beneath.

"There it is," he shouts.

Buster Phillips hastens to the Jernigan's aid. The other men remove the harness from Jack. Then they line up on one side, push and return the wagon to the upright position. Wee-Bean scurries to his father's side.

"I'm okay." Buck says calmly. "Go check on Jack."

Wee-Bean, with tears running down his cheeks, slowly approaches poor mud-covered, unconscious Jack. Expecting the worst, Wee-Bean pats poor Jack on the head and then realizes that he is blinking his eyes. "Jack! You're alive!" bellows Wee-Bean as he scrambles to lift Jack's head from the mud. Buster and his companions pull Buck cautiously from the mud and place him on a waiting wagon.

"Betty Gail, you take Polly and Wee-Bean on home while I go to Dr. Hamilton's and get fixed up right," shouts Buck.

As the wagon is about to pull away, Dr. Hamilton rides over the hill. He stops by the wagon, dismounts and begins to examine Buck's leg. "Hello Buck. Looks like you had a little accident."

"Sure did Doc. Be careful with this leg. I know it's broken."

Cutting away the cloth of Buck's pants let, Dr. Hamilton shakes his head. "It's broken all right, but no tears in the skin. That's good news. Take him to my house so I can splint him up!"

"I hate to bother you on such a day, Dr. Hamilton. I know you and your family must be exhausted." Buck tries to find a comfortable position.

"No bother on my part at all, Buck. I'm glad I'm here to help."

Jack begins to neigh louder and suddenly rolls over for a brief moment. He kneels and then stands erect while Wee-Bean is holding tightly to the halter.

"Good boy. Good boy, Jack." Wee-Bean hugs and kisses his beloved animal. Polly hugs Jack and Wee-Bean together, trying to hold back the tears. As Polly turns to look back up the hill, she places her hand upon her chest and inhales quickly and deeply. She taps Wee-Bean gently on his shoulder.

Wee-Bean turns. "What Polly?"

With a grin and giggle, Polly answers, "Look at Jack's tail!"

Wee-Bean stares, speechless, eyes and mouth open wide. Finally, he mutters, "His tail. It's standin' straight up ... like a pole!" About the same time, Jack turns his head and flicks his tail but only the tip flickers in response to his attempts to place it in the inferior position. After their shock subsides, Polly and Wee-Bean walk Jack for a bit to check for other injuries.

Buster Phillips returns from Dr. Hamilton's with news for the twins and their mother. "The doc's splintin' yo pa's leg. Said he be good in 'bout six weeks. De men will bring him home soon," he says as he dismounts. Polly points to Jack's tail. Buster turns and asks with amazement, "W'at happened?"

"I guess it's still got lightning in it!" replies Wee-Bean.

The group begins to gather the remnants of the cargo. Polly, while surveying the scene, realizes that the birds are out singing again. It makes the drudgery of their work slightly more pleasant. All of the dry goods are now the color of the clay as are the garments she is wearing. The seeds and feed in the burlap are also wet. They load what they can salvage, and Buster hooks his horse to the wagon. Wee-Bean sits on the back of the wagon and holds Jack's harness tightly. The odd-looking animal trails behind.

As they approach the house, Isaac and Sally dash out to greet them. Betty Gail jumps from the wagon and relates the dramatic tale of the violent storm and its consequences. "What happened here, Isaac?"

Pointing and looking toward the hen house Isaac, still shaken, he says, "Mz Betty Gail, we's lost da hen house en some shingles on the 'zebo."

Betty Gail scans the farms, but nothing else seems amiss. "Looks like everything else is okay. No real damage."

"What matter whit Jack's tail?"

Wee-Bean replies anxiously, "Still got lightning in it!"

Uncle Isaac mutters, "Probly so! Probly so!" He begins to unload the now-wobbly wagon. "Got ter fix this 'un 'fore we uses it again."

Darkness is approaching as friends bring Buck home.

"Pa! You're home!" shouts Wee-Bean excitedly, rounding the corner of the house.

"Yep, everything's gonna be all right, son," Buck assures Wee-Bean.

Polly chimes in, "Pa, you got home just in time. Sally has fresh rabbit stew for us. It's on the table and waiting, so let's eat!"

Wee-Bean places a stool for his father to rest his broken leg on and they all gather for supper. Buck says, "Need to say a blessing." As the aroma of the rabbit stew fills the air the family joins hands and Buck bestows a gracious thanks to God.

With supper over Wee-Bean and Polly assist their pa to his chair nearest the small fire to warm him from the spring chill and dampness in the house. The funeral and the events of the afternoon move from a formal discussion to humor. Wee-Bean tells his pa the story about the effects of the lightning on the mule. "How long is the lightning gonna stay in Jack's tail?"

Buck laughs, imagining the sight. "Now that's what you call a real hair raising experience! I have no idea how much longer that lightning gonna stay in it, but what a sight he must be!"

2

MEET THE NEW SHERIFF—SPRING 1853

The early morning sun eases through the window on a clear and crisp day. Norman rubs his eyes and throws his sheets back. The aroma of breakfast and his mother's and father's voices inform him that the world is ready and waiting the arrival of his enthusiasm. The seven-year-old leaps from his bed, presses his nose against the window and peers out to check his rabbit box in the small garden near the house. The trap is still open, but there are plenty of rabbits nearby and one will soon become either a pet or a meal.

"Wee-Bean!" calls his father, using the nickname Uncle Isaac gave him years before. "It's time to eat. We gotta go to the new Sheriff's swearing-in ceremony today. Your mama is fixing rabbit stew for the affair."

Norman smiles, slips his straps over his shoulders and heads for the kitchen.[22] Polly is helping their mother gather the plates and serving utensils for the trip to City Hall. The family sits down for breakfast, and Buck leads the family blessing. "God we ask you to direct the new sheriff in all matters to relieve this place of the toxic consequences of the quarry workers round the Mountain. Eliminate their toxic qualities of drinking, fighting and womanizing. Amen"

After finishing breakfast, Uncle Isaac hitches Jack, to the wagon. Like most mules, Jack is a stout and headstrong animal. The only person he allows on his back is Wee-Bean whom he takes to school most every day. Anyone else attempting to ride on Jack is thrown instantly. Buck bought Jack when the price of cotton was down. When the price of cotton goes down, so does the price of a mule. Jack was a bargain at thirty-five dollars. Uncle Isaac has readied the horse and buggy for the trip and the festivities of the day. Everyone dresses in their Sunday best, though Betty Gail had to force Wee-Bean into his dress clothes. Polly was up early heating the irons on the stove so that his collar would be smooth and stiff. Wee-Bean dislikes dressing up as much as his father but takes the challenge with his well known smile and humor, declaring,

"Even the bluebirds are gonna laugh at me, Mama, with this here blue shirt on."

"Just you never mind," Betty Gail says. "You look fine. It's time to go."

Everyone loads into the wagon and off they go in a cheerful mood. The journey to town on the narrow trail is uneventful except for the few rabbits and squirrels skirting around. Main Street is crowded with horses and buggies. A festive mood prevails. Sniffing the air, Buck asks, "Can you smell that roasted deer, barbecued pork and beef steak?" Wee-Bean nods vigorously. "I sure can. I can't wait." Polly stands and holds to the back of the buggy seat and looks around at the festive scene. "Look at those cow brains, corn bread and biscuits."

"Look! There's Doc Hamilton, Henry Sampson and John Hicks." Buck parks the wagon, helps Betty Gail down and goes to join the conversation. All the men seem pleased that Mr. Perkerson was elected sheriff.

"My gosh, look at all the cheese. Must be fresh from the dairy farmers," says Polly with a broad smile. "Look, Ma. There's Miz Mary Gay. She told us she might be coming today." Polly and Betty Gail hurry over to welcome her.

"Well, hello there, Polly. My, you're about the prettiest young filly in these parts." Mary Gay hugs Polly. "How are you doing, Betty Gail?"

"Just fine, Mary. How are your mother, sister and brother?"

"My family is fine and our farm is the best it's been in several years. It's been a good rainy season for us, and Decatur is growing more crowded all the time. I hope you brought some of your roasted chestnuts and delicious pecan pie!"

"Sure did and it's right over there. Come get the first piece." Betty Gail takes Mary's hand and heads toward the dessert table. Polly follows behind closely but still manages to pull an aimless Wee-Bean along as well.

"Look, Ma. There's Mr. Maguire from the Promised Land Plantation. I hope he's brought me a fresh apple like he always does. His wagon is loaded with his corn, peas, beans, fried okra, and squash. Hello, Mr. Maguire!" shouts Wee-Bean as he rushes over to greet their friend from Lithonia.

Mr. Maguire reaches into a basket and retrieves two large red apples, "Here's an apple for you, Wee-Bean, and one for your teacher tomorrow."

"Thanks."

"How are your studies at the Academy, Wee-Bean? That's the place to be for the best education around these here parts, I hear."

"Making real good grades, so far, Mr. Maguire. Pa said he'd get me a squirrel gun real soon if I keep up the good work."

"Well, you're old enough now to have a squirrel gun, and I know your pa will get you a fine one. Just you be careful."

Wee-Bean moves along, admiring the apple, peach, and pecan pies. His eyes are wide open and his mouth is watering to taste whatever fragrant delight is teasing his nostrils. "Mmm. Smells real good."

The day is bustling with people, at least two hundred and fifty, there to celebrate the swearing-in ceremony. The new sheriff, Tom Perkerson,[23] is working the crowd, greeting and thanking all the citizens. He is especially enjoying sampling the food before others have the chance. His wide-brim hat complements what appears to be a new, store bought brown suit. His old brown boots add to the effect. Sheriff Perkerson stands about five feet ten inches tall and has a mustache and small goatee. His coat is open, revealing a pistol on his left side. Mr. Perkerson has the respect of just about everyone. He does not believe in the drinking and fighting going on with the rough necks from around the mountain quarry. His campaign promise was to "clean up the town."

Shortly before noon, the church bell rings and the citizens gather at the depot to witness Mr. Perkerson taking his oath of office. The city's officials are on the platform adjacent to the depot. The mayor introduces the former Inferior Court Judge and current Congressman, William B. W. Dent, his wife, Eliza, and two of their children, Joseph Hugh and John. Then the mayor introduces Samuel Dean, the Postmaster.[24] Filling the role as the former Inferior Court Judge, Sheriff-elect Perkerson had asked his good friend Congressman Dent to administer the oath of office.

Congressman Dent gives Mrs. Perkerson the bible to hold for her husband and asks Sheriff-elect Perkerson to place his left hand on the bible, raise his right hand and to repeat after him:

"I do solely swear, before God and the citizens, that I will uphold the laws of the United States, the State of Georgia, the County and the City. I swear that I have not been engaged in a duel, either directly or indirectly, either as a principle or second, or in any character whatsoever in this state so help me God." Sheriff Perkerson finishes his oath, smiles and waves to the crowd.

The Judge takes the bible from Mrs. Perkerson and hands her the Sheriff's new badge. She smiles, takes his coat lapel gently, pins the badge just above his heart and follows with a loving embrace. Hats are thrown into the air and the crowd cheers.

Sheriff Perkerson turns to the crowd. "If you wish to live among great citizens, drink crisp spring water, enjoy a long and healthy life, pray, and be free from crime, you need to live in Stone Mountain. Let the feast begin!"

After the ceremony, Congressman Dent meets up with Buck. "Hello Buck."

Buck clasps his hand. "Hello, Congressman. We're sure glad you could be with us today. How are you coming along with the purchase of the mountain?"

"We plan on closing the deal in November.[25] I have always loved this mountain and will be very proud to be the owner. It reminds me of some of the hard heads I have to deal with in Washington. The mountain listens to logic about as well as Congress does!" They both laugh. "Joshua Hill[26] and I are going to be climbing the mountain in a couple of days and would like for you to climb with us."

"I'd be honored."

About that time, Davis Wade approaches Congressman Dent and says, "I hope I am not interrupting, but if you're not real busy at the moment, I need to talk to Congressman Dent about some farm matters."[27] Buck excuses himself and begins looking for Drury Lee and Francis P. Juhan, the surveyor of Stone Mountain.[28]

It's nearing three o'clock when Buck finds his friend Drury Lee, looks around surreptitiously and asks.[29] "Do you have it?"

"It's in my wagon. Picked it up in Decatur the other day. It's mighty fine."

"Great! Let me fetch it and hide it in my wagon." They start out together and Buck pays Drury eight dollars. Once they reach Drury's wagon, Drury reaches in and hands over a squirrel rifle to Buck.

Buck examines it closely. "Mighty fine piece. I think Wee-Bean will like it. Thanks for picking it up for me. I see Mr. Juhan over there. I need to talk with him about doing some surveying for me. He did a great job marking the town boundaries. There's no question where the toll road starts anymore."

Buck rushes over to Mr. Juhan. The two converse as they return to the feast that is nearly eaten. After having a few final bites of roasted deer, they bid farewell to each other. The festivities are coming to an end and Betty

Gail gives Buck that familiar look that says it's time to go home. Before leaving, Buck presses the new sheriff's hands tightly, "Good luck to ya." The Jernigans climb into the buggy and head home around the mountain.

On the way back to the farm, Wee-Bean says to Uncle Isaac, "My teacher, Miss Tweedle, is going to be away next week and we are going to have a tutor." He continues "Miss Tweedle had Miss McCurdy come by the school and introduced her to my class. Miss McCurdy seems to be very nice and all of us are glad that she is 'tooting' all next week."

Uncle Isaac looks at the giggling Wee-Bean, pats him on the back and says, "I sure she do good job a-tooting" and laughs as they pull into the yard.

Wee-Bean jumps from the wagon and heads to his bedroom. Taking off his clothes, he peers out of his window once again. Still no rabbit in his box. "Something must be wrong," he thinks since he usually catches at least one each day. He changes his clothes and takes them out to the washtub. Uncle Isaac's wife, Sally, has the boiling water in the big black tub for the daily "washing." After dropping the clothes in the tub, Sally stirs them around with a long pole. After a good soaking, she removes each piece and scrubs them by hand on the old scrub board to remove all of the grime and dirt rinses the garments and then hangs them on the long clothes line to dry.

Buck changes his clothes and gets the squirrel rifle from the buggy. He's on the front porch spitting tobacco and reading the newspaper when Wee-Bean comes around the corner. "Hi Pa! That was a great picnic. Do you want me to feed the chickens now?"

Buck motions for Wee-Bean to come sit next to him. "I know you and your friends have been playing army and fighting the Indians and the British. So I got you a squirrel rifle so you can learn to shoot for real."

Wee-Bean looks down so as not to appear to be afraid. "Pa, that there squirrel gun might kick me clean to the ground."

"Don't worry none about that. This squirrel rifle carries a light charge and isn't that rough on you," Buck reassures him.

"I just don't think I'm ready to shoot it yet, Pa." Wee-Bean's eyes reveal the fear of disappointment that all young boys have when they feel they haven't lived up to their father's expectations.

Buck pauses for a few seconds and inhales on his pipe. "Now suppose you're out in the woods and a bear is a coming on you. Tell me what you'd do."

Wee-Bean looks back at his pa as he answers, "I'll just run and climb a tree!"

Buck shakes his head and places his hand on the gun, aiming it toward the fresh plowed yet barren planting fields. "Well, son, that's a fine idea except a bear can out climb all of us. Now, what if you're out in the corn field, no trees around, and a bear comes at you. What will you do then?"

Wee-Bean places his hand across his mouth and rubs his bottom lip, then looks his pa directly in the eye and declares, "Well, Pa, I guess heaven ain't so bad!"

Buck lets out a loud howl, smacks Wee-Bean on the back and places the squirrel gun against the wall. He spits out the remainder of the tobacco and says, "Let's go feed the chickens!"

Taking Wee-Bean by the hand, they head for the chicken coop. Their dog, Charlie, runs out to join them. His barking keeps the foxes at bay and the chickens don't seem to mind his presence. Wee-Bean and his father pluck about ten eggs from the nests and feed the chickens. Then they gather a few feathers to clean and use for cushions and bed pillows.

"Let's feed the hogs while Uncle Isaac milks Rosebud," Buck suggests. "We're out of slop so just get corn out of the barn. About a bushel will do." Wee-Bean rushes to the barn and drags out a bushel and dumps the corn into the trough. The snorting and grunting hogs fight and push for the right to have the first morsel.

While Wee-Bean watches the hogs fight for food, Buck sizes up his holding. The Jernigan farm covers about three hundred gently rolling acres. He looks toward his neighbor, Buster Phillips, checks out the pasture and cows and studies the new hen house and his plowed field. He is proud of their modest home. The shotgun style house has four bedrooms, a modest dining room and a sitting area. The high hearth inside is for cooking and houses a wood burning stove. Buck is proud to be among the very few who have the luxury of a hand water pump in the kitchen. The foundation is constructed from granite and completely encloses the underside of the house.

He envisions his grandfather's marble washstands in each bedroom. Each room has it own fireplace but they are seldom used since a huge draft occurs when the fireplaces are lit, chilling the room more that the fire can heat. Buck favors using the one big stove in the center of the kitchen. The fireplaces are used only during severe winter weather. He looks toward the outside cookhouse where Betty Gail and Sally prefer to do the cooking during the mild or hot weather. But his favorite part of the house is the wide porch that completely wraps around the house. Isaac walks up to help feed the hogs. Buck watches him study the hungry hogs. "I'm a lucky man Isaac. I have a good family, a great farm and we are well respected in his community. A man can't ask for more than that."

"That's rite, Mars Buck."

"Betty Gail and I depend on you and Sally to help us raise our livestock and crops. You and I fenced and crossed fenced the pasture and the house from those magnificent American chestnut[30] trees we cut on the place. Look at the corn, sorghum and cotton crop. It's a fine crop this year Isaac."

"I'se gettin the gin house ready fer da cleaning en bailing of da cotton."[31]

"We got a good price last year at the cotton exchange warehouse. It weighed good and graded good. Hope we have the same luck this year, Isaac."

In the evening, after supper, the family sits on the porch to enjoy the cool breeze. Betty Gail discusses Sunday school lessons with Wee-Bean and Polly while Buck is talking to Isaac and Sally about the next day's chores. Betty Gail and Sally are going to prepare delicacies for the church's annual homecoming day with "Dinner on the Grounds." The church serves as both the religious and social center of the community. Betty Gail relishes those Sundays when she, Polly and Wee-Bean can go and be with their friends. Buck seldom makes church a priority. He finds that most of the time the preacher is preaching to the wrong choir.

As the sun sets and the daily chores are complete, the lanterns and candles are lit. The warm glow radiates around the close family in the shadows of darkness. When it is time for bed, Wee-Bean takes his candle to his room, kneels beside his bed, "Thank you God for Your love and the love of my family and please God place a rabbit in the trap." He crawls in his bed, blows out the candle and drifts off to sleep. He rests quietly, dreaming of his rabbit box.

❧

Outside the gin house Buck wipes sweat from his brow and looks up as Congressman Dent and Joshua Hill ride into the yard. He motions and one of the darkies take the reins of the horses. Leaving the carriage with the stable hand, they walk over to meet Buck. "Good morning Congressman, Joshua. Mighty fine day to walk up the mountain." Buck stops at the front door of the house and yells to Betty Gail, "I'm heading up the mountain with Congressman Dent and Joshua. Wee-Bean is going with us."

Betty Gail pokes her head out the front door, wiping her hands on her apron. "We'll see you when you get back in a while. Y'all be real careful."

Buck approaches the men waiting for him and shakes their hands. "This is my son, Norman, but we always call him Wee-Bean."

"Nice to meet you, Norman." Congressman Dent shakes hands with Wee-Bean and smiles at Buck. "Mighty fine looking young man, Buck"

"I certainly agree with Congressman Dent, Buck. Norman's a mighty fine looking young man," says Joshua, ruffling Wee-Bean's hair.

"Thank you," replies the proud father. "It might get a little warm today. I have some canteens for us to take along." Buck hands out the canteens. Then he hands the bag of biscuits to Wee-Bean. "Would you mind carrying these, son?" Wee-Bean nods eagerly and ties the cloth bag to his belt.

"Well, let's start climbing," says Buck.

The group looks toward the mountain and heads up the silver hill. At the beginning of the climb from the foot there are huge slabs of granite that have split from the side by the winter's frost and ice. They now lay as in times past to disintegrate into sand and soil to support the surrounding vegetation.

After walking a short distance, they come to the carriage road, which Aaron Cloud built. "We can use Aaron's carriage road or walk straight up."

Buck stops and the others follow suit.

Joshua asks, "Which is the easiest route?"

Buck gestures toward the trail. "I think it would probably be better to walk right straight up. The carriage road winds around a good bit."

The men agree and continue taking the most direct route. As they climb the pass, the bank of the turbulent base of the great rock is lush with brilliant mountain laurels and radiant dogwood blooms. They see and smell the multi-colored honeysuckles. Wee-Bean grabs a few and sucks the juice out of them. As they climb higher, they see peach and pear orchards in the distance. Buck points to them. "Didn't get a freeze this spring and everything is in full bloom."

"It is a beautiful sight, all right," responds Congressman Dent.

As they continue their climb, bright plumaged birds fly among the tender leaves of the budding trees. Then a quarrelsome blue jay and a red-headed woodpecker announce their presence. Wee-Bean tries to catch a lizard as it darts beneath their feet to seek shelter in rocks and bushes. Butterflies paint the air with flying specks of color. Indeed, nature has combined to fill the senses with subtle feelings of delight. As they near the top of the mountain, the scene changes dramatically. Vegetation grows scant and then almost disappears. Stunted trees and pools of stagnant water become their view. The group continues gazing over the brilliant landscape while heading up to the gilded summit of the rock.

As they approach Thomas Henry's newly completed tower, Buck gestures to the scene around them. "Things have really changed around here. I remember how it was before Stone Mountain became a railroad town, before it moved out to meet the train."

"Yes," replies Congressman Dent. "Now the railroad reaches deep into the Southern forest. Generally speaking, it follows the narrow paths by which the daring hunter of our fathers and the enterprising trader used to travel to take their wares to rural markets."

"Taking our cotton to Atlanta took two days then. We'd load our ox carts, mule and horse team wagons and make the long journey to the warehouse. Now increasing prosperity has brought another change. Atlanta has become the haven for some of the ambitious youths in our village. The iron horse is bringing city ways and city vices to Stone Mountain. We regard the road with mixed feelings, some with awe and some with admiration. Others with disdain," Joshua replies.

"But the railroad sure does make selling cotton a lot easier. That's one good thing to come of it. Am I right, Buck?"

"That is definitely an advantage, but nevertheless life was simpler when the slow, plodding ox-teams carried our corn and cotton to the Atlanta market. Some of the deep woods farmers are still shaking their heads at the fashions their wives and daughters buy in Atlanta."

Congressman Dent listens quietly and nods. "We already have hideous vices among the men who quarry 'round the mountain. Let's hope that more of the big city follies don't catch on with them as well."

Walking around Thomas Henry's Tower, Congressman Dent tells Buck, "This tower should really benefit school children. They can learn about the stars and the heavens."

"Yes, my daughter Polly has been here several times with her teacher and classmates from the Academy. It's very educational. Lots of visitors come on the weekends. It's quite amusing to watch them climb the mountain and visit the tower."

"You see this old wall fortification here?" Buck points to a natural passage under a large rock. "This was the only entrance to the top of the mountain at one time. Only one person can enter at a time and only by crawling on all fours. The whole length of the wall is probably 'bout a mile. As you can see, what is left is nigh onto about breast high.[32]

"You should have been here when Thomas Johnson, John G. Quack and Thomas Henry had the grand opening last summer. The mountain had so many people coming and going to the tower that it looked like an ant hill."

"Really wished I could have been here. I read about the event in the newspaper," says Congressman Dent. "I read where Mr. Henry stood on his head on the top of the tower, just like he'd promised the kids," says Joshua.

"Yes he did and it was a very festive affair," Buck says. "Lots of free drinks and free food. But, it's just too high up to have a lot of parties. The old folks can't make the climb any more."

Congressman Dent asks Buck, "Tell me about the Cross Roads."

"Come on. It's right over this way." Buck leads them to the Cross Roads. "See these two fissures in the rock?"

"Sure do. It's kinda deep in some places," says Joshua.

"They start out as cracks and increase to a depth and width of five feet where they intersect. Now, you see where they cross each other at nearly right angles?" Pointing, Buck says, "The longest fissure is about four hundred feet. Here, where the fissures cross, is this flat rock. It looks to be about twenty feet across."[33]

"Wonder what caused this feature in the mountain?"

"It's the puzzle of the ages," replies Congressman Dent.

Buck and Joshua laugh. Congressman Dent and Mr. Hill remove field glasses from their carrying cases. Silently, they sweep the entire horizon. From this height, they see a wonderful panorama of field and forest. On the north side the mountain, a solid wall of granite rises abruptly from the plain. From this point on, the mountain is accessible to neither man nor beast. The edges of the mountain are round from the centuries of exposure to the elements. The lateral surface slopes slightly and is deeply weathered in many places. From the broad top, the mountain curves to meet the precipice. The top slopes severely, its bare surface an easy and treacherous fate.

Joshua hands Buck the field glasses. "That must be Decatur over there. That's the only town I can see from here."

Placing the glasses to his eyes and adjusting the focus on the white gleam in the distance, "Yes, that's Decatur. Not much to it from up here, just a few chimneys and a couple of stores. Almost as big as our town. Anything else you want to investigate Congressman?"

Dent and Hill look at each other and shake their heads. Congressman Dents says, "Guess not Buck. I've seen all I need to see. Let's go home."

After taking a drink from their canteens and sampling the biscuits Betty Gail sent, the group begins its long descent.

Buck is easing his way down the mountain. "What are your feelings Congressman?"

"That was a hard climb this time of day, but the view is fine and the place suits our purpose just fine, I think."

Buck comments enthusiastically, "I was hoping you'd say something like that. You know, around here you're well known as a staunch Unionist as well as an investor in real estate and railroads. The people of Stone Mountain have a lot of faith in you and your business dealings."

Congressman Dent raises his hat with a courteous gesture and takes Buck's welcoming hand, half way extended to meet his own. "Thanks for your confidence. I have traveled much of America, Buck, but I have rarely seen a lovelier view than meets the eye from atop this mountain. Joshua, what all do you have in mind for this rare beauty?"

"There are two important and lasting uses of this mountain. The first is the quarry business. The second is tourism."

Congressman Dent ponders for a moment. "Right now, visitors have nothing to see or do but climb the mountain. Just adding carriages to transport them from the train to the mountain will bring good revenue, but development around the mountain with hotels and natural pools with large meeting centers could help everyone's pocketbook. Farmers will have a ready market for their goods, selling to the hotels and tourists and some speculators might buy more land and develop it or sell it at a good profit later. The mountain is the over-seer to a huge pot of gold."

Buck nods his head and tightens his lips in agreement. He realizes that the kind of growth the congressman is talking about is a two-edged sword. He is not opposed to growth, but prefers that it occur slowly. The rays of the sun begin to play hide and seek with the mid-afternoon clouds cooling the end of their descent. They soon arrive at Buck's place and bid each other farewell. Buck stays up late that night, torn by the excitement and trepidation that stem from the new businesses concepts of Congressman Dent and Mr. Hill. He ponders quietly, "I'm not sure I like all of this intrusion, but it is their property."

CONGRESSMAN DENT'S FUNERAL—SEPTEMBER 1855

Buck is at the depot delivering the last bales of cotton of the season. "Have either you or Betty Gail seen today's newspaper?" asks James Goldsmith.

"No, just fixin' to buy one."

"Don't know if you folks have heard or not, but Congressman Dent passed away. His funeral was a couple of days ago."

"I hate to hear that. I heard a while back that he was not doing too well, but figured it was just a temporary sickness." Buck gives James five cents and picks up a newspaper.

Across the top the headlines read: "Congressman William Barton Wade Dent Dies at the age of forty-nine. The late Congressman William Barton Wade Dent passed away on September 7, 1855. Mr. Dent was born in Byrantown, Charles County, Maryland, on September 8, 1806."[34]

Laying the paper aside, Buck says, "James, Congressman Dent was a great statesman and the Dents are just getting started on the hotel on the mountain. I suppose Congressman Dent's death will delay the opening."

James replies, "I would think so. By the way, more news. George W. Latham came by today. He's getting ready to start construction on the Stone Mountain Seminary here by the railroad. He's going to be the principal and Judge Smith's wife is going to teach music, embroidery, ornamental needlework, and wax work."

Betty Gail looks in the direction of the building site. "Really."

"Miss Sayer's the assistant teacher in charge of the English Department."

"When do they expect the Seminary to open?" asks Betty Gail.

"Mr. Latham thinks the first session will be in January of 1858."[35]

"I'll have to look into that for Polly. We best get back home and write a letter of condolence to Mrs. Dent and her children. I hope you have a good day James and keep those trains on schedule." Buck mounts his wagon and he and Betty Gail head home.

FIVE YEARS LATER—A QUEST FOR THE BEST

EARLY 1860's

Buck and Wee-Bean are on the porch discussing the up-coming planting season when Uncle Isaac returns from town and delivers the newspaper to Buck. He nods at Wee-Bean and smiles. Taking a break in their discussion Buck scans the front page. "I see the Georgia Military Institute in Marietta is capturing the headlines again. It says here, 'The state-owned Institute has a new Superintendent and Commandant. The State is offering school grants to admirable and worthy individuals. One student from each Congressional District and two from the State at large may receive the grants. The individuals receiving scholarships will be required to teach in Georgia for at least two years upon graduation.'[36] Sounds good to me. What do you think, Wee-Bean? You talk about wanting to be a General someday."

Norman quickly answers, "Yes, sir. That sounds good to me!"

"Why don't we all take the train up to Marietta in a couple of weeks and check the Institute out? The whole family should go."

"Okay Pa," replies his excited maturing fourteen year old son.

"Well, then, that settles it then. I'll write a letter to the new superintendent for an appointment to visit the campus. Says here his name is Major Francis W. Capers[37] and he helped found the South Carolina Military Academy in Charleston."

VISITING THE SCHOOL—MARCH 1860

Buck and his excited family arrive in Marietta, board a carriage and heads to College Hill on Powder Springs Road. As the carriage approaches the one hundred and ten acre campus, Buck and Betty Gail smile as Wee-Bean and Polly show signs of being awe struck. The College Hill's panoramic view of Lost, Brush, Blackjack and Kennesaw Mountains is spectacular. The massive trees surrounding the campus offer an abundance of shade and sunlight. The landscaping at the entrance flourishes with rose gardens and beautiful shrubbery. Buck asks the carriage driver, "Tell us about these buildings."

The carriage driver points out various buildings on the campus and begins, "That two story building is the classroom building, and those fourteen over there are the one-story barrack buildings, each having two rooms. Each barrack has an adjacent steward's quarters with six rooms, a dining room, a kitchen and a gun house."

They approach Major Frances W. Capers' quarters, a grandiose three-story columned building which proudly flies a gigantic United States Garrison Flag.[38] He then reins his horse to a stop slowly. Two servants present themselves. "Yous is the Jernigans?" asks one of the servants.

"Yes, we are," replies Buck.

"We been 'pecting you. Major Capers will be back shortly. Please come inside." The servants assist Betty Gail and Polly from the carriage as Buck and Norman follow behind. One of the servants escorts the Jernigans to Major Caper's secretary who cordially introduces himself.

He welcomes the Jernigans. "Would you like some cool lemonade?"

"Thank you." Buck and his family readily accept the cool drink.

The waiting room's appointments consist of paintings and some fine china. A painting over the secretary's desk is of General Washington crossing the Delaware River on Christmas night in 1776. There's a large painting depicting the Battle of Bunker Hill. Buck points out to Norman. "That's one of the first battles of the Revolution." Another great oil illustrates General Cornwallis having General Charles O'Harn surrendering his sword in his behalf after the English defeat in 1781 at Yorktown. Buck proudly points to this picture, "This was the final battle for our independence and your great grandfather was there."

Before they can finish looking at the décor, Major Capers opens the mahogany door to his office, steps in and introduces himself. "Welcome. I am Major Capers. I've been expecting you."

Buck introduces his family. Major Capers invites them into his office, gesturing for them to sit. "How was your train ride from Stone Mountain?"

"Not too bad. The sky was a little cloudy, but not too much humidity, making for a mighty pleasant trip," replies Buck with a nod.

"Norman, I understand that you might have an interest in coming to GMI. We have a very regimented program here and expect a lot of studying and dedication to learn military tactics. This institution follows the same academic and military criteria as West Point Military Academy. You must be willing to devote your mind and body to the principle of the Georgia Military Institute and the principles of leadership and knowledge. Would you be willing to do this, Norman?"

"Yes sir. My pa lost his fingers in the Mexican War and my great grandfather fought in the American Revolution. They fought for our freedom and our homes and I want to be just like them. I want to be a leader."

Major Capers smiles, stands and extends his hand to Buck. "I'm pleased to know you're a veteran and survived your wound." Then he extends his hand to Norman as he invites the family on a tour of the campus. "Captain McGill, our Commandant of Cadets, is waiting for you in the reception area. He is also our professor of Engineering and acting professor of Drawing. He is going to be your escort for the campus tour."

They leave the Major's office and return to the reception area. Captain McGill introduces himself. As they begin their tour, Buck says, "The newspapers say the United States government gave the school a hundred and twenty short muskets, sixteen small swords, and a battery composing of four brass six-pounder field pieces.[39] Also the State Arsenal at Milledgeville issues muskets to the school. Is that true?"

"Sure is. We also get tents from the Chatham Artillery, the Savannah Guards and the Republican Blues.[40] Although the muskets are old, without these supplies, the Institution could not operate in the customary military environment. Let's visit one of the barracks first."

They enter one of the rooms of the barracks. "Each room is about eighty square feet. In your room you can have an iron bedstead, pine table, looking glass, foot tub, wash basin, water bucket and dipper, broom, washstand and a candlestick."[41]

"How about playing chess or backgammon?" asks Norman.

Placing his hand on Norman's shoulder, Captain McGill says "Sorry, but it is against GMI rules for cadets to play chess, backgammon, cards, or read any novel, poem, pamphlet or book that is not a part of their studies. No horse, mule, dog or waiter either. You just will not have time. At all times you'll keep your quarters clean and neat.[42] Let's head for the kitchen and Old Abe." Buck takes Betty Gail by the arm as Polly walks along. Norman follows close to Captain McGill. Standing outside Captain McGill explains, "The kitchen and dining room are attachments to the steward's quarters as is the gun house. This is 'Old Abe.' He is the steward in charge of these quarters." Betty Gail questions the steward about the meals. Old Abe shows her the storage room containing vast amounts of canned goods and cured meats. "We gets lots of fresh vegetables from what we grow an' meat from town. We git plenty good eats."

"I'll take you to the two story classroom building next," says Captain McGill as they depart the steward's quarters. "We follow the academics of the United States Military Academy at West Point as closely as possible. Freshmen and sophomores are on the second floor. In these classrooms, freshmen begin their studies with arithmetic, algebra, French, English grammar, literature and geography." The Captain escorts them to the next set of classrooms. "These classrooms are for sophomores. They study geometry, more French, rhetoric and drawing. As you can see, the classrooms have all of the equipment and books necessary for teaching and learning. Let's go downstairs now for the junior and senior classrooms.

"The juniors' studies include calculus, science, history and drawing and are conducted in these classrooms. Down the hall, the seniors study engineering, architecture, mineralogy, geology, ethics, philosophy, rhetoric and military tactics. We keep them mighty busy and expect their minds and bodies to become a proud part of GMI's soul."[43]

"Everybody likes a parade. When do you have parades?" asks Buck.

"It is 3 PM now and the cadets have a dress parade at 4 PM everyday, except Saturday and Sunday. Let's go by Old Abe's quarters. He is preparing an early supper for you before the parade begins."

"What time do the cadets get up every morning?" asks Norman.

"Reveille sounds at 6:30. Then we have morning prayers and the policing of quarters. This is when we inspect your room for orderliness and cleanliness. Finally, breakfast before classes which begin at 8 in the morning and end at 4 in the evening. At 4 in the evening just like today, the cadets have a dress parade. After supper you're expected to go to your room and begin studying. There's always a professor available to assist you if you have a problem. When taps sounds at 10:30, you'll extinguish all lights and go to bed. This ends the day."[44]

When they arrive at Old Abe's, there's a spread of fresh corn, beets, green beans and pork chops, ice tea and lemonade with apple pie for desert. "Hopes ye like me cooking," says Old Abe.

"He has to go now to prepare for the parade with the cadets. Old Abe is one of the drummers," says Captain McGill as he joins the Jernigans for the meal. "What do you think so far Norman?"

"I like this place. I can't wait to see the cadet's on parade. Like my pa said, I guess everybody likes a parade."

After they finish the sample meal, Captain McGill escorts them to the parade ground. "Sit under this big oak. This gives one of the best views of the cadets. I'll visit with you again after the parade." Several locals begin approaching the parade grounds. Norman sees all of the beautiful young girls gathering round, but stays quiet. Some drive up in their buggies while others walk, all looking for shady spots. Many of the locals come in full dress, complete with servants to hold their umbrellas.

As 4 PM approaches, more carriages, buggies and young girls line up to view the grandeur of the parade and handsome cadets. Many of them introduce themselves to the Jernigans and conversations begin about how proud Marietta is of GMI. Several of the spectators ask Norman if he is planning on attending. He simply smiles and says, "Maybe!"

The parade begins sharply. Old Abe is there with another drummer and a fife player. The cadets establish their ranks facing the viewing crowd and commanders of the Cadet Corp. The Cadet Commander begins barking a series of orders. "Order arms!" The entire Corps demonstrates the precision of moving their muskets from their shoulder to the ground, as if they were one. "Present arms!" Again, the cadets bring their muskets in a position in front of their breasts. "Present colors!" The Color Guard marches forward and renders the flags. Appropriate music begins to play. Everyone stands. All the men take off their hats, placing them over their hearts, while the women do the same with their hands. The crowd turns as one to face the flag quietly. This moment is for remembering the sacrifices of the past and the hopes for the future. With a resounding "BOOM," the two brass cannons fire, echoing the unsuccessful shelling of Fort McHenry on September 13, 1814, at the end of the War of 1812.

As the music ends, the Cadet Commander orders, "reduce arms!" and the cadets bring the muskets butts to the ground again. The colors march to a position to lead the parade with the accompanying drummer and fifer. "Shoulder arms!" Again the cadet's perform in unison and bring the muskets to their respective shoulders. "Pass in review!" The Cadet Commander and his staff position themselves in front of the Cadet

Corps and the march in review begins. The cadet commander and his staff lead the parade formation passing in front of the reviewing followed by the other companies in formation. As each company passes the reviewing stand, the cadet officers raise their sabers to a salute position, turn their heads to the right recognizing the GMI Superintendent, the Commandant and GMI Professors. At the same time, the Gideon Bearer lowers the Company flag to a horizontal position.

"What an incredible sight! Look at those uniforms, shiny buttons and shining emblems on their hats. Their uniforms are perfect! I stand here looking at our future soldiers, the defenders of America and freedom!" exclaims Betty Gail.

Buck puts his arm around Norman's shoulders. "Well, what do you think, Norman? Would you like to become a part of the Georgia Military Institute, the West Point of Georgia?"

Norman looks up at his father and smiles. "Yes, Pa, I'd like it!"

Last in the parade order are the two brass cannons. "Look at the two saddle horses! Solid limbs, full firm chest and sure-footed. They appear to have a good disposition," Polly says as she points to the horses.

Buck points too. "Those are the exact qualities the saddle horse needs to lead the team. See the riders? Look at their inside leg when they pass. They have a metal shield to protect their leg from sustaining an injury from the limber. Now look closely, again. That four wheel wagon is really two, two wheeled wagons."

"What do you mean a two wheeled wagon Pa?" asks Norman.

"See the limber is the front wagon which holds one ammunition chest. A two wheel caisson wagon hooks to the back of the limber wagon and also carries two additional chests of ammunition."

"I got it," replies Norman.

"Now look at the caisson. It also carries an extra wheel on the rear. The sponge, rammer rod, priming wire, vent pick, vent brush, lanyard, fuze punch and fuze saw all have places on the caisson, limber and field carriage. The bucket that hangs under the limber contains grease for the axle. The water bucket is hanging off the field carriage."

"Here comes the cannon," says Norman.

"Yep," says Buck as he continues. "The two wheels and frame which hold a cannon is called the carriage. The carriage is also hooked to another limber. That limber usually carries one chest of ammunition. Next to last is the battery wagon. It, as you can see, has a long body with a round top.

The battery wagon contains the saddler's and carriage maker's tools, spare parts, extra harness and other materials for making parts. At the end is the forge wagon which is a portable blacksmith shop."[45]

The parade lasts about forty-five minutes. The Jernigans are talking with some of the locals when Captain McGill returns. "Well, the decision is yours, Norman. Here is a petition for the admission examination." He hands it to Norman, who happily accepts the petition.

"Thanks, Captain McGill."

"You're quite welcome, Norman. Now, Mr. and Mrs. Jernigan do you have any other questions for me or Major Capers?"

"Not right now. We want to thank you for the tour and hospitality. Our train leaves at 7 PM so we must get to the train station," says Buck.

Captain McGill shakes hands with Buck and Norman and touches his fingers to his cap. He thanks them for their interest in GMI.

"My carriage is waiting," says Captain McGill. "I'll direct the driver to take you to the station. If you have any questions, telegraph or write to me or Major Capers. Have a safe trip to home to Stone Mountain and may God bless you."

TRAIN RIDE HOME

The conversation on the train ride home is punctuated with excitement, starting with Norman's question, "Tell me again about losing your fingers when you were fighting the Mexicans."

Buck begins the story again as Polly and Norman lean close and listen. "While Polk was president, I was a soldier in General Zachary Taylor's army. It all started when President Polk decided the United States should go from the Atlantic to the Pacific Oceans. Antonio Santa Anna, former president of Mexico, promised to give the land in the west to the United States, if President Polk would help him get re-elected. President Santa Anna won the election with the help of President Polk, but decided not to cede the territories. So, President Polk had no choice but to order General Taylor to move into a part of Texas which Mexico claimed as their own. President Polk also ordered General Winfield Scott to conquer Mexico City arriving through the port of Veracruz. General Scott took Mexico City.

"During the Battle of Palo Alto in May of 1846, my unit charged an artillery position. As I came over the embankment, one of the Mexican's swung his sword. I threw up my musket to protect myself but his sword sliced into my fingers which were supporting the barrel. I fell and rolled over, firing my musket as he was about to run me through. The ball hit him square under his chin and traveled right to his brain. I was bleeding so my comrade tied me off. It turned out that Matamoros became one of our main supply depots. We took care of the Mexicans that day, as we did every other day. Finally, on February 2, 1848, the Treaty of Guadalupe Hidalgo was signed. All of the West, including California, became part of the United States. After my fingers were severed, I kept covering the wound with salt bandages, knowing salt cured meat, I thought it would do the same for my wound. Maybe-maybe not, so I came back to South Carolina to be with my family."

Norman studies the half-fingers on his pa's hand and looks up in wonderment. Norman then reflects silently on his adventurous day at GMI as he watches the passing scenes and the setting sun from the train window.

The sun has long been down and the moon is peering over the mountain on this spring night as the train pulls into Stone Mountain Station. Mr. Goldsmith is still in his office at the depot. He waves to the Jernigans as he delivers a sack of mail to the mail car. The Jernigans walk over to the stable.

"I gots you buggy ready Mars Jernigan," says the stable hand as he hurries to bring it forward. They climb onto the buggy and heads round the mountain.

Everyone is exhausted from the exciting day. Buck yawns. "Bed time, I reckon." After his prayer, Norman climbs into bed. GMI, the boom of the six-pounders, and his papa's stories are in his dreams.

THE PETITION FOR THE ADMISSION EXAMINATION

Buck removes the papers given to him by Major Capers at Georgia Military Institute. After supper, the family settles in to fill out the petition for the admission examination. Previous and current education experiences are important. Proudly they list the Stone Mountain Academy as Norman's background for education.

"Listing Stone Mountain Academy should be in your favor, Wee-Bean. Now, here it says that you must take the standing examination at the

Institute on May 10th. It begins at one o'clock in the afternoon and lasts about two and one-half hours. It also says that you must come alone."

"I wish we could go with you!" declare his mother and sister.

"I am nearly fifteen and six feet tall, Ma, I can manage. I guess making the trip independently is part of the examination ritual."

The fees are one hundred, twelve dollars for each five month term. This includes tuition, board, washing, fuel, lights and other Institute charges. An additional charge of five dollars is for medical care.[46] Buck shakes his head. "Mighty steep."

Betty Gail nods. "We might could manage, but it would be cutting our finances close. Do you think we can get a scholarship?"

Buck studies the papers. "Maybe so. It has a place for the scholarship petition. Can't hurt if we reference Congressman Hill as Norman's possible sponsor. One section wants information, if any, on the family's military history." Buck takes the quill and completes the details of his grandfather's role in the American Revolution as well as his own role in the Mexican War.

When the petition is complete and in the envelope, Uncle Isaac takes it to the post office, and Norman tells his pa, "I guess I need to get ready for that examination. It's only two months away. I know my mathematic tables very well. My history and English literature should be good, but I probably need to get my French books out and study that a little more. You forget a language if you don't use it. Mrs. McCurdy taught us in French and she only would allow French to be spoken during class, but it's been awhile. Polly, are you going to take any language at the Seminary or an entrance exam?"

"I don't think they offer language as a part of their studies Wee-Bean. Mama said if I have good enough grades from the Academy, I don't have to take an exam to enter the Seminary."

"Then you shouldn't have any problems getting in."

Each evening, Norman comes in from working the farm, eats his supper and settles down to review for the examination. Hanging the lantern on the porch, he studies in the cool spring air. There are very few insects this time of year with the exception of an occasional moth. Charlie would at times bark at a far away coyote howl but usually slept at Norman's feet. After studying a while, Norman leans back, placing his hands on the back of his head and reflects on the things to come. "When I enroll in Georgia

Military Institute, my whole life is going to change. If my family needs help on the farm, I won't be here. At least Buster is nearby. And I'll be home for part of November, all of December and a few days in January. Still, I'm going to miss seeing them every day. Won't be able to hunt or trap." Then, he sighs and gets back to the French.

SUNDAY, APRIL 1, 1860

Betty Gail returns from church and puts away her hat and gloves. "The pastors are preaching the same sermon over and over."

"What might that be, Betty Gail?"

"The sermons all deal with the possible bad effects of the new hotel and other business enterprises coming to Stone Mountain."

Buck sits down in front of the fireplace, rubs his forehead, glances toward Betty Gail. "Yeah, these new business establishments are not only disagreeable to me and some of the old timers, especially those with deep religious convictions. I see it coming. These deep religious folks feel more strongly than I do that the railroad, which now brings prosperity, will also deliver more evil upon our little town."

Betty Gail lays a dish down and dries her hands on her apron. "Most of the women believe the new developments are going to bring more drunks, heathens, infidels, and the unconverted element to Stone Mountain."

Buck nods his head toward the quarry. "There are enough problems with the quarry workers whose conduct is worthy of the devil's smile, especially after payday. Though the quarry workers are basically honest and will help whenever one calls, their drinking, cursing and fighting on the streets is a disgrace to the community. When they land in the calaboose on the weekends, we have to feed them."

"I know, 'cause I take food to the jail. A part of their fine is for meals. But think Buck, those noisy and idle city folks will no doubt bring money to spend with our local merchants and buy produce from the farms around here."

Buck stands and walks over to the fireplace and throws on another log and while stirring the ashes tells Betty Gail. "I would be happy to sell them farm goods, but these same city folks will influence our young men to play cards, smoke cigars and drink whiskey. Following our young men's example, our young women will be led astray by the fashion and folly of the city folks. Why I think some will probably cater to the demoralizing attentions of these dissolute men."[47]

THE CONVENTION—APRIL 23, 1860

Rising early, Buck rushes to the telegraph office for the latest news on the opening day of the Democratic Convention. The train is running late, so the newspapers have not arrived at the depot. The Democratic Party is meeting in Charleston and, according to the most recent telegraph, they are deeply divided. It is apparent that most of the delegates from the Deep South are arguing that Congress has no power to legislate over slavery. The Northern Democrats disagree. The telegraph wires are clicking non-stop and everyone at the depot waits intensely for the latest news. "Southerners demand the Democratic Party come out with a platform in clear defense of slavery."

The telegraph receiver continues to click. Another telegram: "Senator Stephen Douglas and his supporters can not agree on the slave issue and many Southern delegates walk out of the Democratic convention in Charleston in protest." As the days pass more interest develops in the Conventions and the depot is the place to get the latest news.

May 3, 1860, a telegram arrives. "After 54 ballots, Stephen Douglas fails to get the required two-thirds votes … convention adjourns … plans to reconvene in June in Baltimore."

TAKING THE EXAM—MAY 10, 1860

An important day for Polly and Norman arrives. Polly will make a petition to the Stone Mountain Seminary for the session beginning on June 18, and Wee-Bean will travel to Marietta to take the entrance exams for GMI. He gets up early, and Betty Gail has his breakfast ready. Buck has already gone to the field with Isaac and the other darkies to plant before it gets too hot. Polly is out getting the horse and buggy ready for the trip to the train station.

Betty Gail sees the anxious look on her son's face and reassures him. "Pa said he's not worried about the examination. He said he knows you will do well, so don't worry. Polly and I are going to take you to the station this morning. I have made you a couple of turkey biscuits and some fresh cookies to eat on the way. Be sure to fill your canteen from the well before we leave."

"Thanks, Ma." Norman and his mother sit down to eat. "It's gonna be a long day. Two hours up to Marietta three hour examination and two hours back plus waiting on the train in Marietta" Breakfast is rather quiet.

Norman has a lot on his mind. He just wants to make a good score on the examination and not disappoint his family.

"Don't fret now Wee-Bean. We know you'll pass the examination and if you happen not to, it doesn't change our love for you one bit."

"Thanks. Ma," Norman finishes breakfast, picks up his canteen and leaves by the back door. "I'll see you in front. I'm gonna fill my canteen."

Reaching the well, Norman lowers the wooden pail. It drops about twenty-five feet and hits with a big splash. Norman lets the pail settle until it is full and slowly turns the crank handle until it reaches to the top. Ol' Charlie is standing by, tongue out and tail wagging.

"Want some of this cool water, buddy? Here you go." He pours some into a stone bowl next to the well. Taking the remainder, he fills his canteen and heads to the front of the house where Polly and Betty Gail are waiting. "Jump up here, Charlie." Norman pats the back of the carriage on Charlie's favorite riding spot. The old dog struggles and jumps aboard and with Polly at the reins and Betty Gail next to her they head toward town.

On the way, they pass John Rankin, a local stone cutter, riding his horse to the quarry. He waves them down, and they pull over. "Good morning Betty Gail, young 'uns. Norman is today the day you go to Marietta to take your examination?"

"Yes, sir."

"Eliza and I wish you the best! Everybody in town knows you'll pass the examination, especially Miss Tweedle. She brags on you all of the time."

"Thank you, sir, have a good day, Mr. Rankin. We gotta get on." Polly snaps the reins with a "gitty-up" and they are off to the depot.

The smoke from the locomotive is visible as they come over the short hill on the edge of town. "The train is early today. Just pull up to the depot and let me out. I already have my ticket so I can board." After kissing his mother and Polly and patting Ol' Charlie on the head, Norman jumps from the carriage. With his canteen and lunch box swinging, he boards the train.

Polly and Betty Gail wave good-bye. Cupping their hands around their mouths they holler, "Good-luck." Norman waves with a big comforting grin.

Betty Gail says, "It's your turn now Polly. Let's cross the tracks and get you enrolled in the Seminary. I told Mr. Latham we would come by today after seeing Wee-Bean off. It's just a short walk and a beautiful day so let's walk instead of riding."

In Mr. Latham's offices, Betty Gail and Polly complete the petition for enrollment. Mrs. George K. Smith greets them and assures Polly,

"Graduating from Stone Mountain Academy will make your studies here a lot easier.[48] So far everyone who has come from the Academy has done very well. We look forward to having you as a student."

Mr. Latham continues, "The first class begins on June 18.[49] Each class lasts twenty-two weeks. The first class studies will include the Alphabet, Orthography, which is the art of spelling, and Orthoepy, which is the study of correct pronunciation. You will also take Reading, Oral Arithmetic, Numbers, Tables, Weights and Measurements along with Mental Arithmetic and Penmanship. Penmanship is taught by the Hammond and Potter's System. During the course of each class, we will have guest lecturers and instruction in Vocal Music.

Mrs. Smith gives Polly a box of books. "These are your books for the First Class. The embroidery, fancy needle work, wax work, including the stock, will be kept at the Seminary."

"I'm excited about starting," replies Polly.

Betty Gail opens her small purse, "Here is the $12.00 for the First Class and the extra $8.00 for the embroidery and other materials.[50] Buck and I are so glad the Seminary is in Stone Mountain. We thank you for accepting Polly's petition for admission."

❧

Day after day, Buck and his friends gather eagerly at city hall or the depot to read the newspapers and the telegraph reports regarding the progress of the conventions.

May 15, 1860—The Decatur Watchman: "Representative John Bell of Tennessee with the new moderate Constitutional Union party forms from ex-Whigs and the (American) Know-Nothings has a vague platform that will pledge to find a way to protect slavery and the Union. The Constitutional Union party recognizes no political principle but the Constitution of the country, the union of the states and the enforcement of laws."

The new topic of conversation is about Alexander Hill Everett and John Bell and the Constitution Union Party. Representative Everett, against his personal feelings, permits his name as the Constitutional Union Party's candidate for the vice president position.

Buck awakens sharply at sunrise on May 16, 1860, the opening day of the Republican National Convention being held in Chicago. All of the citizens rush to acquire copies of the Daily Intelligencer and the Decatur

Watchman. The headlines read: "The nation is drifting toward war and the fate of the nation depends upon the outcome of this presidential election. Unfortunately there's no more room for compromise between the 'free states' and the 'slave states.' We now and must choose between the four candidates running for President! William Seward is the front runner but Lincoln is pulling ahead."

May 18, telegraph: "Senator Seward becomes too radical as an abolitionist. Third ballot … delegate from Ohio changed four votes to Lincoln and Lincoln is now the official candidate for President from the Republican Party. Pandemonium broke out … the cannon on the roof of the convention hall fires!"

Next telegraph: "Entire party supports Lincoln!"

The Decatur Watchman details; "The relatively new Republican party's platform led by Mr. Lincoln is not to attack slavery where it exists, but to prevent the expansion of slavery into the newly acquired western territories now up for homesteading."

Telegram June 18, 1860: "Democratic Convention reconvenes in Baltimore … fight over recognition of delegations."

Telegram June 22: "some delegations of the Democratic convention walk out … Douglas can not achieve 2/3 of the votes … party split into Northern and Southern factions."

Telegram June 23: "Northern Democratic convention votes to state only 2/3 votes required of delegates present … Douglas is nominee for President … former Georgia Governor Hershel V. Johnson nominated as Vice President."

The Daily Intelligencer: "The Northern Democratic party will sponsor the 'popular sovereignty' compromise from the 1850s which will allow the settlers of the new territories of Kansas and Nebraska to decide by popular vote whether or not to allow slavery."

"The Southern Democratic Party immediately convenes in Richmond to nominate United States Vice President John C. Breckinridge of Kentucky as their candidate for President. John Breckinridge is staunchly pro-slavery and believes in protecting the institution of slavery. John Breckinridge has no remorse in splitting the Union to ensure the salvation of slavery."

"It appears Lincoln and Douglas are competing in the North and Breckinridge and Bell in the South. Lincoln, according to reports, appears to be more concerned over the influence of Bell and Everett than any other candidate. Stephen Douglas has become the first presidential candidate in history to undertake a nationwide speaking tour."

ENDEARMENT, ADVANCEMENT AND PROGRESS

JUNE 1860

During these weeks of preparation for building the hotel, the Dents, Hills and even Thomas Johnson are familiar figures in the community. Spring and summer ring out with the pounding of hammers, and the voices of numerous workmen who break the silence on the mountain. Oxen pull heavy carts and trample up the carriage road, carrying loads of lumber, nails and other essential building supplies to the workers. Half-way down the sloping side, just where the forest dwindles to a scrubby growth of oaks and pines, the workers unload the last of the building materials.

The grand hotel on the mountain begins to take shape, and Hugh Dent stops by Buck's house to show him the drawings for the new hotel. On the dining room table Hugh unfolds the drawing. "Here's what the hotel will look like, Buck. It's a square wooden structure, two stories high with a broad, wrap-around veranda." Hugh points to drawing showing Buck where the two wide halls intersect in the middle of the building.

"Looks mighty fine." Buck looks over the plans, impressed by the details in the drawings and sketches.

"The plans for the interior call for a small parlor, a large ball-room, a spacious dining-room, and an ample kitchen. Mrs. Jernigan will like this drawing of the kitchen."

"I believe you're right. A woman could make a great supper in that kitchen." He continues to another drawing.

"There'll be around forty guest rooms. The attic of the hotel will be named 'Texas' and will be used to for the entertainment of single men and their poker games. These accommodations will easily be suitable for a hundred or more guests. What do you think about the drawing, Buck?"

"Good looking place. Might bring in lots of tourists."

"We're preparing drawings for other areas surrounding the mountain. There are plans for ten-pin alleys, barrooms, offices and private parlors."

"A site of more poker games right?"

"Right. Our partners expect this enterprise to reap their richest harvests. The grand opening is scheduled for June 21, 1860."

"The preachers are not taking to all this gambling and drinking very kindly, Hugh. We got enough trouble with the stonecutters already. Folks feel bringing in more of these sinful things could invite a lower kind of men and cause more crime."

"These places will not be for the average person. Gotta have plenty of money to visit the hotel and parlors. I don't see this adding any problems. It's just good business. Look for your invitation for the grand opening in the mail. I gotta get to the hotel and check on the finish work."

Shaking hands Buck watches in wonderment of events to come as Hugh rides off. Buck receives his invitation the next week, as do his neighbors in Stone Mountain and numerous dignitaries throughout the state. Some of former Congressman Dent's colleagues from Congress are invited, too. Buck looks forward to the evening, which promises to be quite an event.

Buck and Betty Gail arrive early. As the guests arrive Buck and Betty Gail admire the brilliant jewels and rare, old heirloom laces the ladies are wearing. Mrs. Dent and her son Hugh greet guests "Welcome Dr. and Mrs. Hamilton. Welcome Judge and Mrs. Smith," and the reception line continues as Alexander Stephens passes through.

Betty Gail's dress is very simple, but beautiful. Buck wears his best suit. They begin mingling with the crowd and soon spots Congressman Hill and his wife, Emily. Buck shakes Congressman Hill's hand. "Congratulation on winning the seat in Congress. We were pulling for you even though we are not in your district."

"Thank you, Buck. You know you can call on me at any time."

Betty Gail loops her arm around Emily. "We are very proud to have you and Joshua as our Representatives and glad you are a partner with the Dent's in this beautiful hotel. We both look forward to a great relationship."

"Thank you, Betty Gail. We will always be friends."

Joshua gestures magnanimously. "We always will need your support whether we are in the same district or not. Our country must come first. Allow me to introduce you to a few of my colleagues."

The leader of the band, a white-haired darkie announces the order of the dances, and of calling out the figures. Square dances are the only ones permitted. Polkas and waltzes are looked upon with great disfavor and confined to the larger cities. Standing on a high platform and tapping his bow on the back of his chair, the band leader calls out, "Gentlemen, git ye partners for the quadrille, partners for the quadrille gentlemen."

Buck smiles at Betty Gail and holds out his hand. "Our favorite dance."

They join the Winninghams and Hamiltons to form the routine sets. Then the dance begins.

"Salute yer partners," shouts the band leader. "Swing corners, fust four forward an' back, second two forward and back to yer places, ladies change balance to the right; right, gentlemen, right; don't yer know yet right hand frum yer left. Back to yer places now gentlemen, balance to de right hand's all round an' back to your places, ladies to de right, swing corners."

The night grows late, and Buck sighs as they take their seats after a vigorous set. "I'm wore plum out, Betty Gail. Glad they stopped this dance music." The musicians drift from dance music into familiar strains to which are set the plaintive lyrics peculiar to the South.

Excited by the brilliant scene and the rhythmic sound of dancing feet, the dusky orchestra burst into song. "'Twas down in the meadow, the violets were blooming, and the springtime grass was fresh and green. And the birds by the Brooklet their sweet songs were singing, when I first met my darling Daisy Dean.

"I'm dreaming now of Hallie. Sweet Hallie, sweet Hallie; I'm dreaming now of Hallie, for the thought of her is one that never dies. Listen to the mockingbird; listen to the mockingbird; The mockingbird is singing where she lies; Listen to the mocking-bird, listen to the mockingbird; The mockingbird is singing where she lies."

"Listen, Betty Gail. There's a whippoorwill a-singing with the rest of us."

Betty Gail laughs and nods. "It sure is a strange thing him being this close to the music and all. But it's a perfect end for the evening."

"That feathered songster of the forest must have awakened by the glare of the candles which he no doubt mistakes for the sunrise. So he bursts into a flood of melody such as can only come from the accomplished throat of a mockingbird, the king of song." Soon the sound of the mockingbird gets everyone's attention as his notes penetrate the quieting atmosphere and command attention even from the excited dancers.

Later in the evening the guests depart the grand ballroom, the broad galleries and take the torch-lit path to the grove below. Slowly the mountain returns to the sounds of nature leaving only the hungry fox and owls to complete their rounds before sunrise.

Buck rises early the next morning and takes to the rocking chair on the porch. "Good morning Mars Buck. Here iz ta paper."

"Thank you Isaac." Buck unfolds the Mountain Banner and reads, "Last night the spacious and elegant hotel at High Mountain, under the management of our distinguished and progressive fellow citizen, Hugh Dent, the son of our late Congressman William B. W. Dent, was resplendent with the beauty and fashion of the metropolis and DeKalb County. The great rock shone like a beacon light for the Grand Opening, so bright was the illumination, and the strains of bewitching music from our best string band awoke the birds and put them to the blush. Never in our history has there been a more delightful occasion nor a more distinguished gathering. The beauty, grace and elegance of our fair ladies have become proverbial, and the well-known gallantry of our gentlemen was never better exemplified. Dancing was kept up until a late hour, and the departing guests earned lasting impressions of the charms and beauties of this delightful summer resort. We predict a most successful season."[51]

✺

As the weeks pass, Norman grows anxious for GMI's decision. Whenever a family member returns from the post office, he would ask, "Any mail from GMI?"

"No news yet. Just have to wait till they make up their minds," becomes the monotonous response.

Finally, in late June, Polly picks up the mail. There are two letters: one letter from Congressman Hill and one from the Georgia Military Institute. Although filled with excitement, Polly dares not open the letters. She runs outside and holds them up to the light, hoping to get a glimpse of the messages inside. No luck! Polly exclaims excitedly, "Look Uncle Isaac, a letter from the Georgia Military Institute and one from Congressman Hill. They are for Wee-Bean! Let's get on home so Wee-Bean can open them and read what they say!"

Uncle Isaac whips the horses along at a trot, stirring up plenty of dust as they head round the mountain. Betty Gail and Sally are shelling peas on the porch as the buggy makes the turn into the yard. Polly raises her hand holding the letters high in the air. "Ma! Wee-Bean has a letter from Congressman Hill and the Institute!"

Uncle Isaac pulls the horses in to a walk and then to a halt. Polly jumps from the buggy as her mother meets her about half way. With a broad smile, Polly asks, "Where is Pa and Wee-Bean?"

"They're still in the field gathering the corn with a couple of Buster's darkies. Let's just wait and surprise them both at supper tonight. Now Isaac, you and Sally keep quiet about all this. I just know his acceptance is in this letter. They know his pa and grandpa were soldiers and they know Norman will make a great soldier and military leader, too. Now, how about we put the letter from Congressman Hill on the table so they can find it when they come in. Then, we'll give Wee-Bean the letter from GMI with his dessert."

"Great idea, Ma!" exclaims Polly.

Betty Gail continues with the plan. "We still have some of that deer Wee-Bean shot. It's in the meat house. Your pa and Wee-Bean would rather eat good, mild and tender venison than lamb or pork. We'll have fresh corn, squash, and the butter beans Sally just got through shelling. Isaac, go and get me enough venison to make four big steaks for supper and whatever you and Sally can eat."

Full of excitement, Betty Gail, Polly, Isaac and Sally start preparing the fabulous supper in the outside kitchen. While Sally and Isaac are preparing the meal, Betty Gail and Polly set the table, complete with a fresh apple pie in the center. Still warm, the aroma of the pie fills the room. "That's a happy smell, Ma. Wee-Bean and Pa will catch that scent before they even open the door. You wait. When they come in, they'll say, 'Where's that pie?' and we'll say, there on the table. We can have Congressman Hill's letter next to the pie for Wee-Bean to find."

Soon, ol' Charlie starts barking, a sure sign somebody is coming. Rushing to the window, Polly and Betty Gail peer out only to see two stray cows cutting across the near pasture. Somewhat let down, they return to the dining room and decide to shell the rest of the butter beans while Sally and Isaac finish up the supper. Betty Gail is pondering her children's future and asks casually, "How much do you like Buster Phillips, Polly?"

"I like him fine, Ma, but he is our neighbor and he is more like a brother than a boyfriend."

"He's going to make somebody a good husband someday and your pa and I would kinda like it be you."

"I know, Ma, he has a good farm and he's always been good to us. I just like him for a neighbor and friend. That's all. There goes Ol' Charlie again. Maybe it's them this time!" Polly runs to the window and sure enough

Norman and Buck are heading toward the house from the barn. Polly confirms, " They must have come in the back way this time. I guess they got the horses put up and the darkies are taking care of the harvest. Looks like one of those afternoon showers forming up over the mountain. The sky is getting cloudy. Let's sit back down and pretend to be shelling those butter beans."

Betty Gail and Polly sit quietly as Buck and Norman approach. "Smell that fresh apple pie, Pa?" questions Norman.

"Smells good as ever," replies Buck. Norman turns the knob, swings the door open, and quickly asks, "Where's that pie?"

Polly and Betty Gail can't help but laugh. "See, I told you, Ma! I knew that's what Wee-Bean was going to say."

Wee-Bean smiles and heads for the table. As he peers at the pie, his eye catches the letter.

> *Master Norman Jernigan*
> *Stone Mountain Post Office*
> *Stone Mountain, Georgia*

"A letter for me! It's from Congressman Hill! It must be about GMI!" Buck jumps to Norman's side as Polly and Betty Gail rush over to the table.

"Well, are you going to open the letter, Wee-Bean, or just stand there looking at it?" Buck asks excitedly.

"Why, this is my first letter ever!" Norman pulls his pocket knife from his pants. He opens the knife and runs the blade gently along the top flap of the cream-colored envelope, opens it and peeks inside. Using two fingers, he pulls out the contents.

Polly has lost all patience and demands, "Read it out loud, Wee-Bean, so we all can have the news!"

"Okay, Okay. It says:

> *Dear Master Norman Jernigan,*
>
> *It is with great pleasure that I have the opportunity to recommend you for a full scholarship to Georgia Military Institute. Of course, this scholarship is subject to your acceptance by the Institute. I know you are a graduate from the Stone Mountain Academy which has the recognition of a quality education program. I also know that your family is held in high regard by the community. I hope your petition meets the required standards of the Institute.*

Please give my regards to your family.

I am your obedient servant,

Joshua Hill
United States Congress"

Norman raises the letter in the air and shouts, "Wow! I have a chance to go to GMI!" Tears of joy and kisses from Polly and Betty Gail and a big hug from Buck round out the hopeful news from the congressman. Norman dashes outside to share the good news with Uncle Isaac and Aunt Sally. Finding them in the outside kitchen, he shows them the letter and reads it for them not once, but twice.

While Norman is outside, Betty Gail and Polly show Buck the letter from the Institute. "Both came in today?" Buck asks surprisingly.

"Yes, Pa. They were at the post office this morning. Uncle Isaac and I came on home right away. Ma and I made it a surprise for you and Wee-Bean. Now, how about we put this letter under the apple pie plate? When supper is over, you ask Wee-Bean to pass the dessert and he'll find it. No telling what his reaction will be when he sees this letter!"

Buck walk closer to Polly. "Let me have the letter." Polly hands it to him. He glances at the return address and places the light brown envelope under the pie plate. A loud clap of thunder breaks the excitement. "Looks like a good shower is coming and it might stay for a bit. How long before supper is ready? I can hardly wait to have Wee-Bean open that letter."

The back door bursts open and Norman enters, still embracing his letter from Congressman Hill. Taking off his hat, he slaps it on the side of his pants in an attempt to remove some of the rain water. "Uncle Isaac and Aunt Sally are thrilled to hear the news that I might make it to GMI. They said they would come to see me in a parade if you would bring them."

"Why, you know they'll be coming with us every time we come for a visit. It might be every weekend!" explains Buck proudly. "It's just 5:30 and already getting dark. Those are mighty thick clouds. Rain might stay a while. Best light those lanterns. We need to be able to see our supper and for Wee-Bean to be able to read that letter again," Buck tells Polly as he winks and finishes lighting the lanterns.

About the time the last lantern is glowing at its brightest, Sally and Isaac open the back door and start to bring in the special meal. "Cookin' that deer of yours, Master Norman! Gots fresh corn and squash to eats too," explains Sally happily.

Once the meal is on the table, the Jernigans take their usual seats. Everyone join hands and Buck offers grace. Buck says, "Wee-Bean, you gets the first cut of deer, then pass it to your Ma and Polly."

"You, Ma and Polly usually go first."

"You go first tonight, son."

Betty Gail interjects, "It's your night."

"Well, thank you, but I still need to hear from GMI,"

Buck redirects the conversation. "Sounds like the rain has settled down quite a bit."

Polly struggles to keep up the act and manages to asks, "Will you please pass that corn along with the butter beans and squash?"

As the last bit of gravy is soaked up, Norman grins and asks, "What about that apple pie, Ma? I'm ready for some!"

"Well, son, it's right in front of you. Have a slice and then pass the plate to your Pa!" Norman pulls the pie plate toward him but doesn't notice the envelope on the far side. He takes a slice of the pie and places it on his dish.

"Sure does smell mighty good!" Norman utters as he samples the remnants on his fork. Polly, Betty Gail and Buck look at each other in amazement. How could he miss the envelope? Everyone is silent. Norman notices the awkward moment and asks, "What's the matter? Did I do something wrong?"

Buck asks instantly, "Are you going to eat all the pie yourself or are you going to pass in on to me?"

"Sorry, Pa. It's just so good and you know it's my favorite. In fact, the piece I just cut was really for the rest of you. What's left in the pie pan is mine!"

Everyone laughs. Norman picks up the pie to pass it to his father and finally notices the envelope. After handing his father the pie plate, Norman turns his head to get a good look at the address on the envelope.

Developing a serious look on his face, Norman picks up the envelope says, "What's this? Oh gosh! It's a letter from GMI!" He leaps to his feet with excitement, his chair tumbling behind him as he grasps his table knife and breaks the seal. Everyone jumps up and surrounds him as Sally and Isaac come rushing over. Norman hurriedly takes out the letter and reads it to himself, "Yeah, yeah!"

"What does it say? Read it out loud, Wee-Bean, read it out loud!" his father demands.

"Okay, okay! Let me get my breath." He pauses for a moment and begins,

June 10, 1860
Master Norman Jernigan
Post Office
Stone Mountain, Georgia

"We know that part! Read the rest!" Polly urges nervously as Norman continues.

Dear Master Jernigan,

This is to inform you that your application for admissions to Georgia Military Institute has been reviewed by our Board of Governors.

I have been directed by the Board of Governors to inform you that the Board of Governors is granting you admission to Georgia Military Institute. Congratulations! You, and you only, are to report to my office at the Institute on the second Monday in July. Follow the rules in the Institute catalogue regarding allowable personal items.

Your obedient servant,

Frances W. Capers, Major
Superintendent

With a big "whoop-pee," Norman throws his head back and tosses the letter in the air. His mother hugs him tightly. Soon, they are all holding hands and dancing around the table. After a few minutes, civility returns.

"Now, where's the apple pie?" Buck asks.

"Who put the letter under the pie plate? That was a bona fide surprise, sure enough!"

"Not knowing is part of the surprise, Wee-Bean!" responds Polly.

The rain has stopped. The family settles on the front porch and can see the half- moon peeking through the separating clouds. Somewhat calmer, Norman reflects, "When I went to GMI in May to take my examination, I had a good feeling that my score would be satisfactory."

"Must have been. We are all very proud of you, Norman. We know you'll make a great cadet and soldier." Buck looks at his only son, pride shinning in his eyes. "Several days ago I read where Governor Brown spoke at the GMI Commencement. He said he is recommending an increase in the number of cadets by admitting one from each county. The governor went on to say that this would supply our people with a large number of highly trained southern born teachers who have too often been abolition emissaries in disguise."

EMBRACING THE CHALLENGE

JULY 1860

Full of excitement, Norman rises early, the hot July sun already making sweat beads across his brow. The aroma of his favorite breakfast is drifting under to door of his room. Betty Gail and Polly are preparing his favorite French toast and maple syrup along with hot cakes and fresh sausage. Norman is eager to head to the train station, but realizes his own personal need to hurry won't rush the train schedule.

Anxious though he is, he sighs and glances at his room. He double checks his personal items, packing only the items allowed by the Institute rules: two pairs of high quarter shoes, two pairs of white Berlin gloves, seven shirts, seven drawers, seven pairs of yarn socks, seven pairs of cotton socks, four pocket handkerchiefs, six towels, one each of: cloth bag, clothes brush, leather trunk, hairbrush, toothbrush, comb, single width mattress and mattress cover with bed strap, two pillow cases, two pairs of single bed sheets and blankets, six pairs of white pantaloons, one pair of shoe brushes and one iron bedstead. Some things are in a leather trunk while the smaller items fit nicely into his soft bag. Norman closes the trunk and ties the mattress to the trunk. Last he securely ties the bedstead with twine.

Polly walks to the kitchen door and calls, "Breakfast is ready Norman."

"Coming." He opens his bedroom door and hurries into the dining room, smiling with his modest belongings. Uncle Isaac and Aunt Sally are setting the table for breakfast. Buck looks at his children, realizing how quickly they're growing up.

"Let's all sit for breakfast. This is a great day for the Jernigan family. We are going to see a future general board the train today for GMI." Buck's eyes swell with pride.

Betty Gail takes the biscuits from the oven as Norman heads to the table. Polly grabs Buck by the hand as they find their familiar seats round the table. Staring smiles, "Sally, you and Isaac come and sit with us this morning."

"Ya mean at da table, Mars Buck?" asks Isaac.

"I sure do!" replies Buck. Sally and Isaac hesitantly pull up two more chairs to the large round table and sit silently. "Let's pray. Dear Lord, to-day is a special day for our family. Guide Wee-Bean, I mean our young man Norman, to follow your commandments. Guide him to become a leader among his peers. Protect him from evil and grant him good health. We ask this in God's name. Amen."

Everyone lifts their heads. "You start out passing the food, Norman," says Buck. "It's going to be four months before you get your Ma's cooking again."

"Okay, Pa," The clattering of the dishes, butter and jelly on the biscuits, sweet smelling French toast and fresh maple syrup covering the hot cakes make it a breakfast feast fit for any young fellow heading off to Georgia Military Institute.

"Are you sure you want to go alone to Marietta, Norman?" whispers Betty Gail.

"Yes Ma'am. That was the rule. I need to show up by myself. I can get settled quicker this way when I get to the College."

After breakfast, Isaac goes outside and brings the carriage to the front of the house. Polly helps Norman bring out his belongings and Isaac places them on the carriage. Norman walks over toward his pet mule, grabbing an apple for him along the way. Jack meets him at the fence and takes the tasty morsel. Norman pats Jack's head and says, "See you in four months ol' buddy!" He turns and gives Sally and Isaac a big hug. "Don't forget the rabbit box, Uncle Isaac! I'll see you around the end of November, Aunt Sally." Norman's voice has a slight quiver and he clears his throat to mask his emotion. Buck, Polly and Betty Gail are already on the carriage as Norman steps up and sits between his mother and sister.

"Gitty-up!" commands Buck and the horses pull away from the farm.

Isaac and Sally wave, and Norman returns their bidding until they are out of sight. They arrive at the depot early. It is a typical July morning, already around 80 degrees at 9:30. As they pass the hotel at the foot of the mountain, some folks are sitting on the porch while others have already started walking the trail to the summit.

"They are going to have a hot climb today. The saloon is probably open by now and I'm sure they'll make good use of the cool drinks. I saw a wagon full of ice going up there yesterday. The ice-man said that load came from Canada on the train," reports Buck as he points to the mountain.

As they pull up to the station, Norman jumps off of the carriage and ties the horses to the hitching post. He gives his hand to his mother and sister as they step down while Buck eases off the other side. They all go inside.

James Goldsmith, the railroad agent, sees Norman. "Today is a big day for you, Norman. We are all proud of you. Everyone knows you'll do well at GMI."

As he hands Norman his ticket for the train ride to Marietta, Buck gives him the one dollar to cover the cost of his tickets.

"Thank you, Mr. Goldsmith. I am going to do my best," replies Norman. Soon, he hears the train whistle coming from the direction of Lithonia. The noise and smoke grows closer and closer until he catches the chugging of the engine and sees the billowing smoke coming from the stack. Finally, the brakes squeak, and the engine seems to burp as it grinds to a halt. The Jernigans are outside now as Mr. Goldsmith rushes by in his usual manner, heading toward the mail car to deliver and pick-up mail bags for the postal clerk.

"Well, I guess it's time." Norman timidly turns to his family. Tears begin to flow from all of their eyes as they hug each other without saying a word. The scene of the pure bond of a family could never be more profound. Mr. Goldsmith watches with tears rolling down his cheeks as well.

"I love you, Wee-Bean," whispers Polly.

"I love you, son." cries Betty Gail.

Buck looks sternly at Wee-Bean. "I love you son. Take care."

"Thanks Pa. I love you, too." Norman tries desperately to hold back tears. He releases his grasp slowly, straightens his shoulder resolutely, turns and boards the train. He takes a seat next to an open window on the side where he can see his family. The sun glistens over the depot, reflecting in the shiny windows and polished brass hand rails. He sees his leather trunk and bedstead going to the baggage car. The porter lifts and pushes them inside. Polly and his mother clutch their handkerchiefs and his father lowers his head, slightly placing his hand in his pocket.

The train whistle blows, startling the solemn family. "Last call! All aboard!" shouts the conductor. He waits one minute, picks up the easy step, and waves to the engineer. The train jerks suddenly, the straining of the initial start on the engine, followed by a series of short bursts of smoke.

It pulls away slowly. Norman smiles and waves. As the train becomes more distant from Stone Mountain depot, he leans out of the window to catch one more glimpse of his family. Suddenly, the clack-k-de-clack of the rail and the surrounding wilderness are his only companions. He watches as the granite sentinel that has been a part of his life as long as he can remember slowly disappears behind a thick growth of trees.

Settling back into his seat, he holds on to his belongings as if he is holding on to his family. His mind begins to vacillate slowly between Stone Mountain and GMI. After the train departs the Atlanta mile-post one, Norman decides to eat the lunch his ma made for him. The first item that meets his fancy is a large apple from one of their trees. Biting into the apple reminds Norman of the smell of that fresh apple pie and the placing of the acceptance letter from GMI. With each bite, he laughs as he remembers that great evening and how everybody danced around the table. After the apple, Norman eats his turkey biscuit. Finally, he indulges in the homemade cookies. Content with a final thirst quenching drink from his canteen, he sits back and waits for the next twenty minutes or so to pass. He thinks, "After these next few minutes, my life will be forever changed. I'm no longer just a kid by the name of Wee-Bean. From now on I'm Norman Jernigan."

For the first time in his life he is thinking of himself as a man. He considers that for a moment and smiles, visualizing himself sitting on the porch with his pa and his friends. He laughs out loud, causing a woman two seats ahead of him to turn and glare briefly. He tries to act with more decorum, as befits a young man in his position, but can't as he continues to reflect on the fun events of his family.

Shortly, the train begins to slow as it takes a long curve before entering the straight-of-way into the Marietta station. The whistle sounds with a loud burst of steam and the train cars bump and jerk, coming to a sudden stop on the Western and Atlantic railroad track. The front of the now familiar depot reads Marietta, Georgia. Several wagons and carriages are parked at the passenger platform. A sign which reads GMI cadets report here catches his eye. Norman takes his cloth travel case and exits the train. Approaching the GMI carriage, he recognizes Charlie. "Hello Charlie."

"Hello, Mars Norman. I think you're the last one due from the south part. Lemme fetch yours trunk n mattress an' take you on in."

While Charlie is locating the trunk and bedstead, Norman climbs on to the carriage, stands and stretches a bit while looking around. After loading Norman's leather suitcase and mattress, Charlie unties the reins from the hitching post. He climbs aboard and orders the horses on toward Capitol Hill, just on the outskirts of town. "Your books is already en your room. Once ya register at Major Caper's office, de board of inspectors will guide you through da rest."

"Thanks, Charlie. I'm ready to start." Pulling up to Major Capers Office, Norman sees several other cadets are departing to the barracks. Norman is greeted as soon as he jumps from the carriage.

"I'm Major Black and you are?"

"My name is Norman Jernigan, Sir."

"Charlie, take his trunk to Company B. His roommate is going to be Cadet Paul T. Goldsmith.[52] I'll have him sign in."

"Goldsmith? I wonder if he is any kin to J. W. in Stone Mountain." Norman wonders aloud.

"Follow me, Cadet Jernigan," orders Major Black. Upon completing Norman's registration, Major Black and the new Cadet Norman Jernigan proceed to the barracks.

Once there, Norman meets his roommate. His items are being checked by another inspector. "Hello, my name is Norman Jernigan."

"Nice meeting you. My name is Paul Goldsmith. I hear we are going to be roommates."

"Looks that way. It's going to be a real adventure."

Major Black interrupts, "Open your trunk so I can examine your articles. In the meantime, Cadet Jernigan and Cadet Goldsmith, go to the commissary. Mr. Boyd will issue you the common use items there. Mr. Boyd has the list."

Norman and Paul head to the commissary, continuing to get to know each other. "I'm from Stone Mountain, Paul. Where are you from?"

"Just north of here in Cass County,[53] but I was born in South Carolina."

"In Stone Mountain, our railroad agent's name is James W. Goldsmith. He runs the depot. Any kin to you?"

"I hear we have some distant relatives down your way, but I'm not sure if he is or not. Most likely is, since there are not too many Goldsmiths around. I'll check with my ma and pa and let you know."

Mr. Boyd asks Norman and Paul their names.

"I'm Paul Goldsmith and this is Norman Jernigan."

Mr. Boyd strides toward them and says, "You are not Paul Goldsmith and Norman Jernigan! You are Cadet Goldsmith and Cadet Jernigan! And you always begin and answer questions with the word, 'Sir!'"

"Sir, yes, Sir," Cadets Goldsmith and Jernigan answer in unison.

"Now, stand up straight and listen. Here are your common items: one pine table, one looking glass, a foot tub, wash pan, bucket, dipper, and a broom. Cadet Goldsmith, here is the mattress you're purchasing. Put these items to good use! Now go over to the barber chair and have a seat. It's time to get your haircut. Crawford, they're yours."

Pointing to another area of the commissary, Mr. Boyd continues, "After you have your haircut, you'll receive your uniforms in that area. When you finish, take your common items and return to your quarters. A senior cadet officer will teach you the basics of formation and personal posture immediately. When he enters your room, stand up promptly. Any questions? And stand up before you answer."

Jumping to their feet, they respond quickly, "No, Sir!"

The young men sit quietly for their haircuts. As soon as they're done, Norman looks at the items issued by the school. Their common use items are on the pine table. They are able to place their uniforms and the mattress bundle on top of the table as well. Each takes a side of the table desk with one hand and balances their belongings with the other hand. He and Paul return to the barracks. A note is on their barracks room approving all of the personal items. The note also orders them to prepare to bring their empty trunks and clothing which they are wearing currently to the storage building before supper.

Around 5 PM, another senior cadet arrives. "I am Cadet 4th Corporal Thomas L. Bussey. I am your squad leader."

"I am Norman Jernigan."

"And I am Paul Goldsmith." Both extend their hands.

"It is a pleasure meeting you both. You are now Cadet Private Goldsmith and Cadet Private Jernigan. I know you'll enjoy the Corps. It's time to change into your uniform for the day: gray pants with black stripes down each side, the summer single-breasted, with a standing collar bleachless Russian drilling fatigue jacket. Put on this shirt and this blue forage cap with the patent-leather visor. Place your personal clothing and your cloth travel bag in the trunks. You have fifteen minutes to change. Then we'll take them to the storage building. Afterwards, there's a formation before supper. I'll teach you some of the basics in formations and stature. I'll be waiting for you out front. Don't be late. I would hate to issue demerits on your first day as cadets."

With great urgency, Norman and Paul relieve themselves of their last reminders of home and place the items in the leather trunks. Uniforms on and all buttons in place, they hasten to the storage building where another cadet greets them and places an identification tag on their belongings.

Dashing back to the front of the barracks, they find Cadet Corporal Bussey waiting. With several minutes remaining before assembly time, the old and the new cadets mix and become acquaintances. Suddenly, the bugler sounds assembly. "Fall in!" Commands Cadet Sergeant Todd.

When you hear the command 'Fall In' you will have a specific position to take in ranks. Upon taking your position, you will place your left arm horizontal to the ground like this. Then turn your head to the right and move until your right shoulder touches the left fingers of the cadet to your right. Drop your arms as the cadet to your left touches your fingers. Turn your head straight and then align yourself with the cadet in front of you. As your squad leader, I'll place my left arm forward to judge the distance between our squad and the squad in front of our squad. I will raise my left arm for the cadet on my left to attain the correct spacing. Next is the command 'At Rest.' This command authorizes you to move about, but keep your right foot in place and no talking. The next important command is 'Attention' … You will stand erect, facing the front, shoulders back, arms straight by your side with a slight cuff in your fingers. After falling into formation, immediately take the position of Attention."

After the demonstration, Cadet Corporal Bussey orders, "Fall In!"

Norman and Paul take their respective positions and, following the demonstration, complete their first official military formation. Corporal Bussey gives the other commands and the entire squad performance is satisfactory. He instructs his squad on the correct execution of "Attention," "Right Face," "Left Face," "About Face," "Halt," and the difference between "Fall Out" and "Dismissed" commands. "When the command Forward March is given, always start with your left foot. The distance between you and the cadet in front of you is the same one-arm length, but always align yourself to the right."

Cadet Corporal Bussey continues, "When the Bugler sounds meal assembly, you will form here within five minutes of the last note or receive corporal punishment in the form of push-ups or a demerit slip. Mealtime squads may vary from the regular military formation. Each meal squad will sit at a specific table in the mess hall. Each mealtime squad has what is known as a first carver and a second carver. I am the first carver and in charge of this squad. Not only do I march you into the mess hall but I am also in charge of discipline at the table. Any of you ever heard of square meals?"

"No, Sir," responds Norman and several other cadets.

Corporal Bussey continues, "I, as head carver, am the only person who may speak and call upon the waiters. The first and second carvers sit at the head of the table. When the entire Corps is in the mess hall and after the prayer, you may take your seat. You will sit erect. You will use the correct utensils and proper manners. The carvers will correct you on infractions of manners initially and issue demerits when appropriate. At the conclusion of the meal, fold your napkin. Then, on command the Corps rises. Place your chairs under the table and the Corps will march out of the mess hall. Between meals, there's a twenty minute period for you to take care of personal matters.

"Okay cadets, it's time for the first official meal of this session."

Paul and Norman follow the commands of Cadet Corporal Bussey and march to supper. "Hats off and under your left arm," instructs Cadet Corporal Bussey as they enter the mess hall. Once the cadets take their seats, they place their hats on special racks underneath their chairs. It is the quietest table Norman has ever sat at for a meal. The two waiters are Jake and Steve, two black men who serve the tables as the food is brought out by the cooks. First comes the pot roast, full of fresh beef, carrots, onions and potatoes. Creamed corn, turnip greens and corn bread follow close behind.

Following the protocol, Paul and Norman sit quietly as they finish supper. Soon, the Superintendent shouts "Attention!" Each cadet takes his hat from beneath his chair, stands, slides his chair under the table, and comes to attention.

Cadet Corporal Bussey leads the cadets of his table from the mess hall, "You are to report to your barracks room in twenty minutes. A senior cadet will come and detail the events of tomorrow's orientation. If he is a Cadet or Military Officer or a facility member of the Institute, you will assume the position of attention and remain such until otherwise given an order by the superior. Have the rules and regulations booklet available for the senior cadet. Dismissed."

As they walk into the barracks, Norman looks at Paul. "Not so bad. We came here to be soldiers and soldiers is what we're going to be."

"I'm ready," replies Paul.

Norman begins sorting his personal items and placing his uniforms in the closets. He opens the window to get a refreshing breeze. He and Paul assist each other in making the beds. As Norman and Paul are preparing to have a seat at the table-desk and review the academic books, a senior cadet walks into the room. Norman and Paul assume the position of attention immediately.

Acknowledging their demeanor, the senior cadet pronounces, "At Ease. I am the senior cadet to continue your orientation." Cadet Corporal Bussey looks from Norman to Paul. "Have a seat and let's go over some of the regulations. The bugler sounds Reveille which is the morning military summons at 6:30 on academic days. You have fifteen minutes to appear outside in your squad formation. At this time, the entire Corps assembles for the morning prayers. After the Reveille assembly, the mess hall squads form and march to the mess hall for breakfast. The same protocol applies to all meals. After breakfast, you have twenty minutes to prepare your room for inspection.

"Here is how the clothing is to hang in the closet. The loop of the coat hanger is to face the inside wall with the open end of the clothing facing to the left and buttons in place. The caps and hats are on the top shelf. The pants are to hang evenly, draping over the hanger with the fly facing outside with all buttons in place. After polishing your shoes, place them on the floor under the bed. The foot tub should be cleaned and placed between the shoes. The wash pan is in the center of the dresser. The dipper is to be hung on the right side of the mirror with the bucket beneath. The broom is behind the door in this corner."

Bussey continues and demonstrates the proper manner of folding handkerchiefs, white Berlin gloves, underwear, undershirts, socks, towels and wash cloths. The dirty clothes bag is to be hung at the foot end of each bunk, but may be removed at night. He demonstrates exactly how to place each item uniformly in drawers and on shelves.

"Heads are at opposite ends of the bunk beds. This is the proper manner to cuff the sheets. Each morning, remove the bed clothing, fold neatly, place on the mattress and roll up the mattress. Then, strap the mattress."

Paul and Norman are taking mental notes. "The cadet with the top bunk takes the left side of the dresser. The layout of the personal items will be: First, the comb at the top with the needles facing to the outside of the dresser with the hairbrush beneath and bristle up, handle to the outside. Place the toothbrush with the bristles facing toward the mirror. Soap dish open. Open pocket knife with blades facing to the inside of the dresser. Shaving soap, then the razor with the handle toward the middle of the dresser. The strap is to be hung next to the dipper. Clean the candlestick and holder each morning. An orderly will attend to the general policing of the room along with the arrangements of your arms and accouterments.

"Your room will stand inspection every day, each morning, noon and evening. You will be present for the morning and evening inspection. Look at your windows. The window at the top must be the same distance from the top as the other panel is from the bottom. Every Saturday morning, there's an inspection of the Cadet Corps consisting of room inspections and personal attire inspection. These inspections carry grades for the company. The company and squads with the highest points enter the mess hall first. It's getting dark. Light the candles."

Norman removes a match from the box. Striking it, he lights the first candle and then he and Paul bring the other three candles and light them from the first. Taking their seats again, they wait until Corporal Bussey continues, "No tobacco. No cooking or preparing food in the room. Profanity is strictly forbidden. No dueling. There will be no vicious, immoral, or irregular conduct between cadets. The regulation requires the enjoinment of each cadet where upon every occasion he is to conduct himself with the decorum and propriety of a gentleman.

"Classes begin at 8 AM and end at 3:30 PM. You march to each class unless your next class is in the same building. Silent and soldier-like deportment is mandatory. Ten minutes between classes. Demerits are given if you're late. You may not leave the classroom without the instructor's permission. Military drills begin at 4:00 PM every day, except Saturday and Sunday. In two weeks, the Corps begins dress parades every afternoon.

"You can check out one book from the library unless special permission is granted by the superintendent. A cadet cannot leave the campus without the superintendent's permission. When visiting Marietta, do not enter bowling alleys or billiard halls. Following supper, every night beginning at 7 PM except Friday and Saturday, cadets will stay in their rooms and study. There's one fifteen minute break from study hall at 8 PM. All candles out at 9:30 PM. If you're not on duty for demerits, then you can leave the campus on Friday and Saturday evenings. Still, you must wear your uniform at all times and return for candles out at 9:30 PM. Sunday morning at 10, the Bugler sounds assembly. This is for church. It is mandatory. Once assembly is complete, the Corps breaks into the various church groups and marches to the respective church.

"Tomorrow the superintendent will go over all of the regulations with the cadet Corps during morning assembly. This will include withdrawals from the student bank account your family has set up. Afterwards, a tour of your classrooms to meet your professors. After dinner, the supply officer will issue you a musket. Then, you'll begin instructions in the manual of arms and company marching. Remember, the course of studies and the rules of discipline prescribed for the United States Military Academy at West Point have been adopted for GMI. Do either of you have any questions?"

"Yes, I have a question," says Paul, leaning forward in his seat.

"Stand up when you ask a question and include the word 'sir' in your question," retorts Corporal Bussey.

"Yes, Sir!" Paul responds and stands up. "How about our laundry, sir? When does it get cleaned?"

"That's better. Next time you'll receive a demerit for this minor infraction. The orderly will collect the dirty laundry once a week. On the same day, he'll return the laundry from the previous week to your room. You will sort, fold and place the laundry in the appropriate location in your room. Any other questions?"

Paul and Norman both reply, "No Sir, no further questions."

"Complete your room arrangement and read the regulations in detail. Tomorrow, there's a morning room inspection. Candles out at 9:30 tonight. Since there's no study hall tonight, you can mingle with the other cadets but you are not to depart the campus or barracks." Cadet Corporal Bussey bids them good night, turns and leaves.

Peering down the hall toward the day room, Norman sees some of the cadets beginning to assemble. He and Paul head down the hall to meet some of them. Sam Goode, Edward Jordan, T. J. Hunt, G. A. and W. F. Patillo are a few. A general discussion begins. *Where you from? Do you know ...? No messing around here. Food sure is good. Rooms are a little small, makes it easier to keep orderly. Know any good jokes? Gonna really get busy tomorrow. I have a cousin living there. How big is your family farm? How many slaves? Gotta girlfriend? Like hunting and fishing? Ever been to ...?* Bonding was superb among the cadets as the first day comes to a close as the bugler sound Tattoo and fifteen minutes later sounds Taps. Then candles out.

"All present and accounted for," the sentry on duty shouts.

HONOR AND TRUST

SEPTEMBER 15, 1860

Buck, Betty Gail and Polly arrive at the parade grounds just in time for the four o'clock Friday afternoon dress parade. They find a seat in the shade of one of the large oaks. The leaves are just beginning to turn to an assortment of colorful shades of reds, oranges and yellows. A slight, cool fall breeze causes the flags to swing in the air. They introduce themselves to the other spectators and share in the delightful conversation of how proud all Georgians are of the Military Institute and the cadets.

"So, you're the Jernigans!"

"That's right Sir, Madam," replies Buck.

"We're the Goldsmiths. Our son, Paul, is your Norman's roommate."

"Why, yes! Norman has written us about Paul. We're going to take pleasure in meeting him today. It seems they have become good friends," replies Betty Gail.

Buck extends his hand. "My name is Buck; this is my wife Betty Gail and our daughter, Polly."

"It is a pleasure. My name is Turner Goldsmith and this is my wife, Maria Louisa. One of our daughters, also named Maria married Lewis Tumlin."[54]

"We know Lewis and Maria. Our railroad depot agent's name is James Goldsmith. Any kin?"

"Paul asked me about James. Yes, he is my cousin."

"We all know J. W. and Lewis. They are good friends to everyone. I guess Lewis still owns the Etowah Indian mounds."

"Yes, he'll never turn them loose. Stone Mountain is beautiful country. We might move there someday."

"Norman writes us that you're a physician. There's always room for a doctor."

Just as Betty Gail, Polly and Maria begin a conversation, they are interrupted by a long drum roll. They turn toward the drummers. The parade begins sharply at four o'clock with the military music. The three Negroes who are part of the staff lead the parade; pint-size Cornelius the drummer and Old Abe the other drummer, who also is the servant for the cadets. Then, there's ostentatious and tall Charley playing the fife. The cadet Battalion marches onto the field as the trio plays marching music. The companies take their positions facing the superintendent and faculty, as well as the spectators.

Buck knows Norman is in Company B and strains to pick him out from the rest of the cadets. Then the cadet commander begins issuing orders, and the Corps responds in unison. The Corps executes the manual of arms. Moving their muskets from shoulder to shoulder, from a position directly in front on their chest or placing the musket by their side was always in near perfect harmony.

"I have never seen this precision in movement and perfection in the manual of arms in all my years," says Buck with pride as he watches the cadets, particularly Norman go through the movements. Not a cadet makes a wrong move.

The Cadet Corps Commander turns and salutes the Superintendent. The superintendent issues an order to the Cadet Corps Commander, who turns and barks, "Pass in review."

The Color Guard immediately turns and takes position as the lead unit. The fife and drummers are next in the formation. As soon as the Color steps off, the fife and drummers begin their marching music. The Cadet Staff marches to a position behind the drummers and fife. Cadet companies A and B, each consisting of two platoon and four squads, follow the Cadet Staff.

As the cadet Corps pass in review, all families strain to see their "student soldier." Their tall caps with the shining brass insignia, muskets all in line on their shoulders, the snappy dress coat with the bright rows of buttons all come together to make a distinguished and proud looking cadet. Approaching the reviewing stand, the Company Commander shouts the order, "present arms" and the platoon leaders repeat the order. At this command, the Gideon Bearer lowers the Company Colors and all cadet eyes turn right. Company A passes and finally Company B approaches the reviewing stand.

"There's Norman." Polly points excitedly as Buck and Betty Gail peer by her direction with smiles on their faces.

"Look how he stands out. His gilt buttons shine, that stand-up collar and look how much taller he is with the dress cap. He's six feet tall and getting mighty stout and handsome." Betty gleams over her son.

"He's a fine and sharp young soldier, all right. His serious eyes even make him look like a commander." He takes Betty Gail and Polly's arms and begins to sniffle a bit. "We no longer have a Wee-Bean in our family. We now have a young man in uniform by the name of Norman." Betty Gail looks proudly at Buck,

"You so right my dear."

Polly wipes a tear from her eye as Buck regains his composure, points and says, "That is the artillery battery commander on horseback. It takes those two strong black horses to tow that roaring six-pounder cannon. Look how clean the pair of brass howitzers is."

"Look how bright they shine, Pa, as they roll past."

"Here comes the team of horses pulling the caisson. See how each of the horse teams is being led by two cadets in perfect dress uniform? How much better can it get?" Buck nods and smiles.

As the last, following the caisson, are the cadet battery gun crew. Loud cheers and applause from the spectators congratulate the Corps as the last caisson passes. Several members of the crowd have flags and begin waving them excitingly as a manner of salute.

Dr. Goldsmith proudly states, "These cadets performed with great honor and pride I can see that they are in every degree young soldiers."

The Corps marches from the immaculate green parade field to the armory. "Look! Here they come!" Polly shouts and they all turn in her direction.

Norman runs up and hugs his mother, Polly and Pa. Paul also embraces his mother and father.

"Why, you look every bit a general, Norman," Buck says proudly. Introductions of each other's families occur between Norman and Paul.

"We've all met," Dr. Goldsmith tells Paul and Norman. "Just needed to meet each other's son."

"Well, today is Friday and neither one of us is on restriction. The superintendent has given us permission to spend the evening with our families. Pa, remember meeting Captain McGill? He fought in the Mexican War like you. He's over there." He turns to the others. "Excuse us a minute."

Norman and Buck walk over to Captain McGill and wait until he finishes his conversation with another cadet. Captain McGill turns and says, "Hello, Mr. Jernigan." The two shake hands. "Hello, Cadet Jernigan, what can I do for you?"

"Sir, remember I told you that my father also fought in the Mexican War. I thought you might want to share stories."

"It is a pleasure having your son as a cadet here, Mr. Jernigan. He is going to make a fine soldier. Where were you during the Mexican war?"

"I was at the Battle of Palo Alto."

"I understand that was a nasty battle."

"Yes, Sir, we lost about two hundred men and I lost these fingers!"

Captain McGill offers his hand to Buck. "Allow me to shake the hand of a fellow soldier and a person who could have well lost his life for our country. I'm certainly glad your wound was not any more severe. I was with General Scott. We landed at the port of Veracruz. From March until August, we fought Santa Anna until we reached Mexico City. Taught Santa Anna a lesson for going back on his word!"

Buck nods his head. "Sure did teach him a good lesson."

"We sure did, thanks to soldiers like you. It is a pleasure meeting you, Mr. Jernigan. I must go now to ascertain that the armory is secure. Maybe we can talk in more detail again someday about our war experiences." They shake hands and Captain McGill departs for the armory.

Buck and Norman return to Betty Gail and Polly. Norman says, "Paul and I know a good hotel for a fine supper. Let us change from our dress parade uniforms to our regular cadet uniforms and we'll meet you at the carriage house."

They head off to the barracks and the Jernigans and Goldsmiths walk toward the carriage house. With permission from the superintendent, Norman has a double carriage waiting. The Jernigans and the Goldsmiths climb aboard and the driver takes them to the front of Norman and Paul's barracks.

The barrack's door opens and out comes a cadet, then another cadet, then another cadet. Finally, the door swings open and Norman emerges. "We had to be present for room and personal inspection, then sign the leave book before we could go off campus. There were a lot of cadets in front of us. Paul's right behind me."

Paul comes out and jumps into the carriage. He taps the driver on the shoulder. "Take us to the hotel near the depot. That way, when we finish supper you'll be near the train since we have to be back by 9:15. No one will have to rush back and forth."

The carriage ride to town takes about fifteen minutes. On the way to the hotel and during supper, the conversation tends toward the pending presidential election and states' rights issue. Lincoln has just selected Hannibal Hamlin, who is totally anti-slavery, as his vice presidential running mate.

"I'm strictly for keeping the Union in place. Breckinridge and Douglas have split-up the Democrats." Buck begins to expound on the topic he most enjoys discussing. "Then you got John Bell starting the Constitutional Union Party. I think he's the one Lincoln needs to look out for. If people don't come to their senses, I think a civil war is coming. Where do you stand, Dr. Goldsmith?"

"Buck, I prefer that you call me Turner. Personally, I really figure it doesn't matter who wins the election in November, war is coming sooner or later. It will be sooner if Lincoln wins in November. The Wilmot Proviso Congress passed in 1846 and 1847 not allowing slavery in any of the territory won in the Mexican War really added wood to the fire."[55]

"Henry Clay helped cool the fire down when the Clay Compromise bill made it through in 1850.[56] Our Representatives, Charles Murlhey, and Alexander Stephens and our Senator Robert Toombs, supported that bill." Buck looks around the table at the gathering of the two families and realizes how alike they really are. "California a free state, the New Mexico Territory can organize without restrictions on slavery … they had to pay Texas ten million dollars for some of their land, though. I think the last provision part was to protect slavery in the District of Columbia while abolishing the slave trade there."

"I think what really scared the members of Congress is when Ol' John Calhoun read Ol' James M. Mason's speech." Turner taps his fingers on the table to emphasize his words. "Remember, he said that if the South is not made secure on the slavery issue, she will probably leave the Union."

"It definitely brings the issue to our table now! Georgians need to look to our ploughboy Governor leadership." Buck laughs. "Those politicians who are anti-slavery call him 'ploughboy' because his family doesn't own slaves."

"Joe Brown has done well. He came from nothing and graduated from Yale Law School. He wants to provide for education for all free-white children. He believes education is the key for Georgia to develop faster. If the slave states start secession and bust up the Union, only a strong Governor can keep us out of the war." Turner glances around as if to ascertain the amount of support for his statement.

Buck sips from his mug and places it on the table. "I agree," replies Buck. "There were five candidates before the state convention. All were and still are well known." Pausing he takes another sip from his mug before continuing. "They all had, and still have, honorable reputations. There's John Lumpkin who comes from a powerful family He is an ex-judge and former congressman. And James Gardner, editor of the Augusta Constitutionalist, great newspaper. That's two. Hiram Walker, the New Englander and a former superior court, state judge and in congress. Then, there's H. G.. Lamar, also a former judge and congressman. And the last one 'Silver-tongue orator,' W. H.. Stiles from the Savannah aristocracy. Yes he's the former minister to Austria and former congressman."[57]

Turner contemplates for a few seconds. "But who comes along with a 'dark horse' candidate but this young politician Leander N. Trammell?[58] Brown's nomination finally in committee was by a quick viva voice vote by Linton Stephens before the counting of the ballots. Brown was recommended to the convention and accepted quickly.[59] They say that after he was nominated, the committee votes were actually counted and Alfred H. Colquitt was nominated by a one vote majority."[60]

"That's the same report I got, Turner. That's politics."

Turner acknowledges Buck's answer with a grin. "Lots of talk about that vote."

"Yeah, he was working in his harvest field when he got the news. We all were pleased, actually that a working man could rise up to be governor."

"I hear the way he got started was that he invested $450 in a piece of land in the mountains. He found copper on the land and developed a copper mine. Then he sold a one-half interest in the copper mine for $25,000 and started buying farms.[61] The most comical part of Governor Brown is his pronunciation of judgment.[62] That drives his opponents crazy. He accuses Ben Hill of lacking qualities of 'judgment', 'prudence', and 'sagacity', and that since he recognizes those qualities as missing in Ben Hill, then he must possess them himself. They were really at each others' throats. I think it is so bad that it will take them to their graves."[63]

Buck takes a sip of his drink then leans forward in his chair. "What we need now, as well as then, is a Governor who is for the Union and for States Rights. Of course, the old aristocrats are still unhappy with Governor Brown, especially when it comes to the banks forfeiting their charters. They are suspending payments and closing their doors. It's the law and the legislature does not want to follow the law and he does.[64] So far, he has stood by the people of Georgia."

"Well, when it comes to the railroads, I think he may make us a profit. Since last year, he has made the state $20,000 just on scrap iron he picks up along the railroad. I think this year is supposed to be even more. Not bad work." Turner shifts in his seat and slides his chair back a bit." Looks like the American Party thinks that Methodist minister Warren Akin can beat the Governor.[65] The Governor's record is too good, especially with that $35,000 coming into the treasury from the State Road."

Mrs. Goldsmith nods and says, "The governor got the Legislature to appropriate $75,000 for GMI in January of last year, and I expect he and the Legislature will do more this year for the Institute. It's proved to be a success."

"Well, what we must look for is who will be the next President of the United States?" Turner looks at Buck and leans his elbows on the table.

"Now that's a question we all want an answer to." Buck grins at Turner and then nods at the two cadets who are politely listening to the conversation.

"Paul, you and Norman are right about this here barbeque. It tastes as good as it smells. And the fresh corn and Brunswick stew goes mighty good with it. We need to finish up here and head for the depot. By the way, what is your favorite pastime activity?"

"Why, it's the Friday night 'hops,'" replies Norman.

"The girls show up, whether they have invitations or not. Lots of mighty pretty girls too . . . just for the pickin'," continues Paul.

They all laugh as they finish up the supper. Buck and Turner haggle for a moment but finally agree to split the check. Going outside, Buck inhales deeply. The cool evening breeze is like a kiss. The two families amble toward the waiting carriage. The driver has a throw covering his legs as he sits in front of the café in order to accommodate his passengers. "Gracious, it's such a lovely evening and only a short distance to the depot. I believe we should walk," says Betty Gail.

"Oh, you're right," agrees Mrs. Goldsmith. "I'm afraid I ate a bit too much of that wonderful meal."

A group of girls approach to enter the café. A beautiful young lady wearing a white rabbit fur jacket shouts, "Hi, Paul," with a sweet smile.

"Hello, Sharon." Paul grins at her and then glances at his parents.

"Hello there, Norman." The second young lady wearing a bright blue scarf and a colorful wool jacket waves.

"Well, hello Beverly, are you coming to the hop Friday night?"

"Sharon and I'll be there." The two girls wave and hurry into the café with their friends.

"So this is why the Friday night hop is your favorite past time. Now I understand," Buck says as he looks at Paul and winks.

"Gotta go, Pa," Norman tells Buck. He embraces his family, climbs aboard the carriage, and waits for Paul. After a second quick hug for his mother, Paul takes a seat beside Norman and bids another farewell and they head off.

While waiting for the train at the depot, Buck obtains a cup of coffee for everyone from the depot restaurant. They sit outside and chat a bit more. Soon the train whistle is heard in the distance and the train comes to a slow stop with its usual squeaky brakes. "All aboard for Atlanta, Decatur, Stone Mountain and other points South, East and West."

"I'm sure we will be seeing each other on many occasions," says Buck, returning the cups to the restaurant. Betty Gail, Polly and Maria Goldsmith embrace, while Turner and Buck shake hands and bid each other good-bye.

SATURDAY, OCTOBER 6, 1860

Congressman Hill invites Buck to the hotel for a political discussion on secession. On the way to the meeting they pass the burned down Stone Mountain House.[66]

Buck tells Congressman Hill, "Not much left of the place. Even the brick walls are ready to fall down. Mr. Alexander was in partnership with Josiah Clark from Social Circle. Lost it all."

"I'm afraid we all stand to lose a lot more, Buck, if we secede," replies Congressman Hill.

Politics is the all-absorbing topic of the day. Fierce discussions have, at times, ended in deadly duels fought in some secluded spot. Usually one of the hotheaded disputants stains the ground with his heart's blood, and forfeits a life of which his country was about to have sore need. Some such discussion is in progress as Buck and Congressman Hill dismount their horses and fling the reins to a waiting stableman. Buck looks at the new hotel, then, climbs the steps to the porch. To his neighbors' surprise, Buck joins the audience of newcomers even though he is deeply hostile to their invasion in the simple life of his community and generally shuns all intercourse with them.

The principal speaker, Congressman Lucius J. Gartrell, is a stately man of the planter class, a lawyer by profession and well known throughout the state. He rises to address the attentive listeners, and seems, indeed, to be carried forward rather by the impetuous current of his own thoughts than consciously addressing his remarks to any audience. Congressman Hill seats himself beside Buck, whose keen eyes become riveted upon the speaker.

"It is not of one aggression, or of many aggressions, that we complain," begins Congressman Gartrell, "but of a long series of aggressions, extending from the very founding of this government. We entered this Union with a full understanding that all our rights, including the right to hold slaves, would be respected. Who has profited more by the institution of slavery than the people of the New England States?"

"Nobody but the Yanks," shouts a man Buck doesn't know.

"Who is more largely responsible for it? Did they not have for many years a monopoly of the slave trade?"

"Absolutely," yell several others. Buck turns to see who was yelling, but fails to discover whom they were.

"Did they not sell their slaves to Southern planters when they ceased to be profitable for themselves?"

"Yeah, we got cotton ground and they ain't."

"In spite of constitutional guaranties, compacts and those so-called compromises, by excluding slavery from the territories, the North seeks to deprive us of the fruits of Southern statesmanship and valor. The vast territory of this country comes from the political wisdom of Jefferson and to the favorable issue of the Mexican War. That war was fought mainly by Southern soldiers under Southern leaders."

"That's true, Colonel Gartrell." Red-faced James Gozz stands with his fist in the air. "'Tis to the South that the country is beholden for them territories. But what about that John Brown fellow?"

"The North dignifies John Brown by the name of martyr," answers Col. Gartrell. "Yet his hands are red with the blood of his fellow-citizens in Kansas."

"Good thing he done dead," shouts James Elliott, another angry spectator.

"Also, in the name of humanity, John Brown has sought to deliver our wives and daughters to the brutal fury of a Negro insurrection."

"Only if they want to die," can be heard among the louder shouts.

"When heavily burdened with a protective tariff imposed just for the benefit of Northern factories, South Carolina declared nullification. Then, the North re-echoes with the cry of treason! Now the followers of this red-handed fanatic are protected by Northern governors, who disregard the laws of the general government. When these fanatics proclaim that they live under a higher law than the constitution, does the North cry treason. Nary time!" shouts the Col. with his fist high in the air. "All the traitors the North knows are south of Mason and Dixon's line."

"They best stay north of that line and live than come south and die," yells John Holmes.

"We, of the South," the Col. goes on, "are by force of circumstances an agricultural people, and agricultural we must for the most part remain. Ever since I could remember I have heard the institution of slavery referred to in the pulpit and in religious conversations. Although not so much as a thing that might be proved to be holy, but which was incontestably divine in its origin and character. Just as much as marriage or any other Christian institution. As sovereign states, we entered the Union. As sovereign states let us depart, peaceably if we may, forcibly if we must."

Buck angrily jumps to his feet. "Secession's a mighty bad remedy, Congressman," he shouts while giving his quid a turn in his capacious jaw, and sending a stream of amber over the railing. "A mighty bad remedy. I'd think a powerful long time before I'd say secede. I'm not a denyin' as how the facts are like you say, matter-of-fact they never make a right but two wrongs don't make a right. I'm clean against secession. If we can't get our rights in the Union in respect to those territories you're talking about, then we can't get them out of the Union except by fighting for them. As to the blackies, we hang the abolitionist fools now what circulates that poison among them and we can't ever do any more. Suppose we secede and have a Northern and a Southern Union. Then there might be another split and we'll have an Eastern and a Western Union. Where does it stop?"

There's mumbling among the crowd, some booing and some agreeing. Buck listens and decides the crowd is about evenly divided. "Then you propose to vote for Bell and Everett?" asks Congressman Gartrell.

"That's what I plan to do. The constitution of the country, the union of the States and the enforcement of the laws is a good enough platform for any man to stand on. Human nature is a sullen, obstinate, unreasonable brute. But it always has its own way with all of us and the results most always are disappointing."

"Mr. Jernigan is right." Judge George K. Smith rises and nods to Buck. "It is the fatal split in the Democratic Party that is about to ruin us. Oh, for a leader with the broad statesmanship and true patriotism of Washington, and the eloquence of Patrick Henry! You are hotheaded people, making the mistake of considering a fanatical minority to be the Northern people. The great majority of the thinking people of the North and South are opposed to extreme measures."

Congressman Hill stands and the crowd gradually gets quiet. "Allow me to explain how the Northerner and Southerner view one-another." He walks sedately to the podium. Most of the crowd sits back down. "The North and the South are two households living under one roof. Two nations under one name. The intellectual, moral, and social life of each has been utterly distinct and separate from that of the other. We do not understand or appreciate each other's feelings or development. It is true we speak the same language, use the same governmental forms, and most unfortunately, think we comprehend each other's ideas."

The spectators become quieter still listening for a key point. Buck leans back against his chair, glad for so gifted a speaker to have the floor.

"Each of us thinks we know the thoughts and purposes of the other better than the thinker knows his own. The Northern man despises his Southern fellow-citizen in bulk. The Northern man views the Southern fellow as a good-natured bragger, mindful of his own ease, fond of power and display, and with no animating principle which can in any manner interfere with his interest. Now most of the Southern men simply despise his Northerner as cold-blooded, selfish, hypocritical, cowardly and envious."

"That there's a real definition for a Yankee," spouts John Holmes with several others in agreement. A few men chuckle at his assessment.

"This is how the North and the South plays at cross-purposes, each thinking that he knows the others heart far better than he seeks to know his own.[67] That's all I have to say. Thank you, Judge Smith, for allowing me to speak." There's a little mumbling and Congressman Hill takes his seat.

Judge Smith hesitates briefly. "You are most welcome Congressman Hill. All the political conditions of today point to a like result. Let but this new party find its Cromwell, who under the pretext of war will set aside the Constitution to advance party interests. Then the parallel will be complete. The cry of a violated Constitution will unite the South; the cry of a broken Union will unite the North. When I contemplate our situation," continues Judge Smith in a more somber voice, "I think I see the green fields of our land stained red with blood, and the very flower of our young Southern manhood festering upon the hillside where the flowers of spring are happy today." The crowd becomes somewhat quieter. "Yes, the blood of our best and dearest, and what reparation could ever wash that stain away?" Judge Smith trembles with emotion, and put his hands over his eyes, as if to shut out the crimson vision. His audience is visibly impressed.

Then the hot-headed unknown spectator who, through it all is chewing vigorously and expectorating on the floor, missing the spittoon until a filthy puddle forms a malodorous puddle at his feet, leaps to his feet and exclaims, "Blood, did you say, Jedge? I'll drink all the blood that's spilt. Them fellers haven't got no fight in 'em. They're jest a blusterin' a little to let themselves down easy."

Judge Smith sternly replies, "Such unthinking men as you, sir, are the cause of these sad conditions. I heard you say you would drink all the blood that is spilled, but you're not willing to give of your own blood. When the armies of the North and South stand face to face, you and those like you will not be found upon the battlefield."

"That's an insult I'd not take from a younger man." Red-faced the unknown spectator raises his fist as he walks toward Judge Smith.

"I am always responsible for my words," replies Judge Smith evenly, "and at your service any time." Judge Smith bids the stranger and the gathering a courteous good-bye, mounts his already saddled horse, and canters away. The angry John spits out more of his tobacco, eyeing the Judge until he is some distance away.

That night, Congressman Hill and Buck sit together on the veranda, chairs tilted back to a comfortable angle, their feet upon the gallery railing. Congressman Hill takes up the thread of the morning's conversation.

"I have just come from Washington. If the South secedes, there will be war. Apart from mere sentiment about the breaking of the Union, of which there's no lack, the South has too much to lose in a business way. The South is a great and wealthy portion of the Union, and the North is dependent upon us for products. The North must have our cotton for their factories. With secession, all the present business conditions will be changed."

Buck responds, "Business reasons lie at the bottom of most wars."

"It's true. That topic does not find its way into spread eagle speeches, but down deep in the hearts of nations, the thought is there."

"In reality there is one of four modes by which the issue of slavery can be solved. The first and safest mode is the voluntary emancipation of the part of the slave owner and that is not about to take place."

"You're right Buck. What do you feel would be the second choice?"

"Political action in the exercise of assumed, not to say, usurped, legislative authority."

Joshua is quiet for a moment while he ponder that point. The he leans forward in his chair, looks directly into Buck's eyes and tells him, "Jefferson and Madison were against slavery, but in order to form our Union Jefferson and Madison presented as part of the Federal Constitution the Fugitive Slave law. Along with this came the right to exclude slavery in any of the territories or future states. These provisions were universally accepted by all of the signers of the Federal Constitution."

Buck listens intently as Congressman Hill leans back in his chair and continues, "With the acquisition of the territories of Louisiana, the Floridas and of Texas and the introduction of nine slaveholding States from those territories into our constitutional Union utterly nullified the fugitive slave law. This left the free States without the shadow of a political obligation to deliver up fugitive slaves. This is what has strengthened the abolitionist because the pact formed by the founding fathers has been abandoned. "

Buck leans over and spits his tobacco over the porch rail and onto the pine needles on the ground. "What you are saying is true and leaves only two other options."

"What might they be Buck?"

"The third mode is servile insurrection and war or the fourth, which appears to be where our country is heading, political disunion and civil war." Buck looks sternly at Joshua as asks, "And what chance has the South to win?"

"My own conclusion is against a population of twenty million in the North and set against nine million in the South with four million of our population slaves, and therefore noncombatants we don't stand a chance of winning a war. The North has nine billion dollars of estimated wealth. We in the South have less than three billion dollars in total wealth of which two billion dollars of our wealth is in slaves. Give the North the world for a recruiting office, the navy to blockade all Southern ports, and the better part of our military stores. I want to know what heroism could win against such odds."

Somberly Buck replies, "None at all."

"Buck, you need to make the best of your business opportunities this season, for it may be long enough before they come again."

EMOTIONS REIGN

NOVEMBER 1860

The day after Election Day November 6, 1860, Buck is among a large crowd gathering at the depot to get the latest news. Late in the afternoon a telegram comes through. "LINCOLN WINS! Lincoln 180 electoral votes; California, Connecticut, Illinois, Indiana, Iowa, Maine, Massachusetts, Michigan, Minnesota, New Hampshire, New York, Ohio, Oregon, Pennsylvania, Rhode Island, Vermont, and Wisconsin. Stephen Douglas (Northern Democratic) 12 Electoral Votes; Missouri, and New Jersey. John Breckinridge (Southern Democratic) 72 Electoral Votes; Maryland, Delaware, North and South Carolina, Georgia, Florida, Alabama, Mississippi, Arkansas, Louisiana, and Texas. John Bell (Constitutional Union) 39 Electoral Votes; Tennessee, Kentucky and Virginia."

"We're in trouble now! Governor Brown is going to take us out of the Union!" says Buck. Most of the citizens agree and the look of worry and concern is evident on the faces of most of the crowd.

Buck shakes his head wearily. "This is a sad day in America. We are in for hard times and a long and bloody civil war."

NOVEMBER 8, 1860

Governor Brown in his annual message to the legislature states, "The organization of several volunteer corps is now complete. These volunteer corps are now commanded by young gentlemen educated at the Military Institute in Marietta. These young commanders reflect great credit upon the Institute. The ranks of the Marietta Rifles, the Kennesaw Dragoons with the appointment of Captain Capers, and the McDonald Guards are filling up with volunteers from area alumni, current and former GMI faculty."

NOVEMBER 13, 1860

Robert Toombs and Alexander Stephens have been invited to address the Georgia General Assembly.

Honorable Robert Toombs Rises to the Podium
GENTLEMEN OF THE GENERAL ASSEMBLY:

I very much regret, in appearing before you at your request, to address you on the present state of the country, and the prospect before us, that I can bring you no good tidings....

The basis, the corner-stone of this Government, was the perfect equality of the free, sovereign, and independent States, which made it. They were unequal in population, wealth, and territorial extent—they had great diversities of interests, pursuits, institutions, and laws; but they had common interests, mainly exterior, which they proposed to protect by this common agent—a constitutional united government—without in any degree subjecting their inequalities and diversities to Federal control or action. Peace and commerce with foreign nations could be more effectually and cheaply cultivated by a common agent; therefore they gave the Federal Government the sole management of our relations with foreign governments. These powers made armies, navies, and foreign agents necessary—these could only be maintained by a common treasury....

The Executive Department of the Federal Government, for forty eight out of the first sixty years under the present Constitution, was in the hands of Southern Presidents, and so just, fair, and equitable, constitutional and advantageous to the country was the policy which they pursued, that their policy and administrations were generally maintained by the people.... No advantage was ever sought or obtained by them for their section of the Republic ... Mr. Jefferson acquired Louisiana, extending from the Belize to the British possessions on the north, and from the Mississippi to the Pacific Ocean—a country larger than the whole United States at the time of the acknowledgement of their independence. Mr. Madison vindicated the honor of the nation, maintained the security of commerce, and the inviolability of the persons of our sailors by the War of 1812. Mr. Monroe acquired Florida from Spain ... Mr. Tyler acquired Texas by voluntary compact, and Mr. Polk California and New Mexico by successful war. In all their grand additions to the wealth and power of the Republic, these statesmen neither asked nor sought any advantage for their own section; they admitted they were common acquisitions, purchased by the common blood and treasure, and for the common benefit of the people of the Republic, without reference to locality or institutions. This is our record. Let us now examine that of our confederates.

The instant ... the Northern States evinced a general desire and purpose to use it for their own benefit, and to pervert its powers for sectional advantage, and they have steadily pursued that policy to this day....

They demanded a monopoly of the business of ship building, and got a prohibition against the sale of foreign ships to citizens of the United States, which exists to this day.

They demanded a monopoly of the coasting trade, in order to get higher freights than they could get in open competition with the carriers of the world. Congress gave it to them, and they yet hold this monopoly....

When we acquired California and New Mexico, this party, scorning all compromises and all concessions, demanded that slavery should be forever excluded from them and all other acquisitions of the Republic, either by purchase or conquest, forever. This position of this Northern party brought about the troubles of 1850, and the political excitement of 1854. The South at all times demanded nothing but equality in the common territories, equal enjoyment of them with their property, to that extended to Northern citizens and their property nothing more.... The North understand it better—they have told us for twenty years that their object was to pen up slavery within its present limits—surround it with a border of free States ... and like the scorpion surrounded with fire, they will make it sting itself to death.... One thing at least is certain, that whatever may be the effect of your exclusion from the Territories, there is no dispute but that the North means it, and adopt it as a measure hostile to slavery upon this point....

They took up arms to drive it out of Kansas; and Sharpe's rifles were put into the hands of assassins by Abolition preachers to do their work. Are they mistaken? No; they are not. The party put it into their platform at Philadelphia—they have it in the corner-stone of their Chicago platform; Lincoln is on it—pledged to it. Hamlin is on it, and pledged to it; every Abolitionist in the Union, in or out of place, is openly pledged, in some manner, to drive us from the common Territories. This conflict, at least, is irrepressible—it is easily understood—we demand the equal right with the North to go into the common Territories with all of our property, slaves included, and to be there protected in its peaceable enjoyment by the Federal Government, until such Territories may come into the Union as equal States—then we admit them with or without slavery, as the people themselves may decide for themselves. Will you surrender this principle? The day you do this base, unmanly deed, you embrace political degradation and death.... For twenty years this party has, by Abolition societies, by publications made by them, by the public press, through the pulpit and their own legislative halls, and every effort—by reproaches, by abuse, by vilification, by slander—to disturb our security, our tranquility and to excite discontent between the different classes of our people, and to excite our slaves to insurrection....

I demand the protection of my State government, to whom I own my allegiance. I wish it distinctly understood that it is the price of my allegiance ... I say the time has come to redress these acknowledged wrongs, and to avert even greater evils, of which these are but the signs and symbols. But I am asked, why do you demand action now?

The question is both appropriate and important; it ought to be frankly met. The Abolitionists say you are raising a clamor because you were beaten in the election. The falsity of this statement needs no confirmation. Look to our past history for its refutation. Some excellent citizens and able men in Georgia say the election of any man constitutionally is no cause for dissolution of the Union.... Hitherto the Constitution has had on its side the Federal Executive, whose duty it is to execute the laws and Constitution against these malefactors. It has earnestly endeavored to discharge that duty... The Executive has been faithful—the Federal judiciary have been faithful the President has appointed sound judges, sound marshals, and other subordinate officers to interpret and to execute the laws. With the best intentions, they have all failed—our property has been stolen, our people murdered; felons and assassins have found sanctuary in the arms of the party which elected Mr. Lincoln. The Executive power, the last bulwark of the Constitution to defend us against these enemies of the Constitution, has been swept away, and we now stand without a shield, with bare bosoms presented to our enemies, and we demand at your hands the sword for our defence (sic), and if you will not give it to us, we will take it—take it by the divine right of self-defence, which governments neither give nor can take away.... He comes at their head to shield and protect them in the perpetration of these outrages upon us, and, what is more, he comes at their head to aid them in consummating their avowed purposes by the power of the Federal Government. Their main purpose, as indicated by all their acts of hostility to slavery, is its final and total abolition. His party declares it; their acts prove it. He has declared it; I accept his declaration....

But you are advised to wait, send soft messages to their brethren, to beg them to relent, to give you some assurances of their better fidelity for the future. What more can you get from them under this Government? You have the Constitution—you have its exposition by themselves for seventy years—you have their oaths—they have broken all these, and will break them again.... Twenty years of labor, and toil, and taxes all expended upon preparation, would not make up for the advantage your enemies would gain if the rising sun on the fifth of March should find you in the Union. Then strike while it is yet time.

But we are told that secession would destroy the fairest fabric of liberty the world ever saw, and that we are the most prosperous people in the world under it. The arguments of tyranny as well as its acts, always re-enact themselves.... The arguments I now hear in favor of this Northern connection are identical in substance, and almost in the same words as those which were used in 1775 and 1776 to sustain the British connection. We won liberty, sovereignty, and independence by the American Revolution—we endeavored to secure and perpetuate these blessings by means of our Constitution. The very men who use these arguments admit that this Constitution, this compact, is violated, broken and trampled under foot by the abolition party. Shall we surrender the jewels because their robbers and incendiaries have broken the casket? ...

We are said to be a happy and prosperous people. We have been, because we have hitherto maintained our ancient rights and liberties—we will be until we surrender them. They are in danger; come, freemen, to the rescue. If we are prosperous, it is due to God, ourselves, and the wisdom of our State government....

My countrymen, if you have nature in you, bear it not. Withdraw yourselves from such a confederacy; it is your right to do so—your duty to do so. I know not why the abolitionists should object to it, unless they want to torture and plunder you. If they resist this great sovereign right, make another war of independence, for that then will be the question; fight its battles over again—reconquer liberty and independence. As for me, I'll take any place in the great conflict for rights which you may assign. I will take none in the Federal Government during Mr. Lincoln's administration.

If you desire a Senator after the fourth of March, you must elect one in my place. I have served you in the State and national councils for nearly a quarter of a century without once losing your confidence. I am yet ready for the public service, when honor and duty call. I'll serve you anywhere where it will not degrade and dishonor my country. Make my name infamous forever, if you will, but save Georgia. I have pointed out your wrongs, your danger, and your duty. You have claimed nothing but that rights be respected and that justice be done. Emblazon it on your banner—fight for it, win it, or perish in the effort.[68]

Robert Toombs takes his seat.

⋙

Upon arriving at the depot in Milledgeville, Buck, William Sheppard and Jesse Lanford take a carriage to the Capitol building. As they walk up the stairs of the Capitol building, several State Representatives are departing while others are standing around in small groups carrying on conversations. Buck walks up to one of the representatives. "Excuse me, sir, is the session over for today."

"Yes sir. The General Assembly is in recess until tomorrow."

"Has Congressman Stephens spoken yet?"

"No, Sir, Mr. Stephens is scheduled to speak tomorrow evening. Mr. Toombs spoke today. Gave a mighty stirring speech for secession. You gentlemen have a good day."

"Thank you, sir, and you also have a good afternoon. Look there's Thomas Maguire." The three men walk over to talk with Thomas who is in a discussion with some of the Legislature. He sees Buck approaching and acknowledges him with a nod and raising his hand indicating he will be through with his conversation in a minute. Buck, Jesse and William continue to talk while Maguire finishes his conversation.

"Hello, gentlemen, I'm glad you are able to come to the session. It's been interesting so far."

Jesse gazes at Thomas Maguire. "What did Senator Toombs have to offer?"

"Well, he's one hundred percent for secession. He's always been hotheaded. Said he would not serve under Lincoln and for us to appoint someone else in his place."

Buck responds, "Sounds unreasonable to me. As smart as he is, he should know the South will be destroyed if we secede. There will be war. He has everything to lose … all his wealth, land, and fame. The Union should stand."

Interjecting in the conversation Williams states, "He's always acts like a spoiled child when he can't have his way. Mule headed fits his temperament. Georgia will be better off without him in the Senate."

Thomas smiles to his friends, "I feel like Congressman Stephens will counter Senator Toombs arguments tomorrow night. Right now I'm hungry. Let's go get something to eat."

NOVEMBER 14, 1860

Buck, William and Jesse take a chilly November evening walk to the capitol building. There are a number of spectators in the balcony to observe the speeches and debate, but they are able to find three seats together.

Soon Buck observes Congressman Stephens walking to the podium to address the State Legislature at the Capitol in Milledgeville. The Chamber of the State House becomes quiet as Congressman Stephens stands before the podium.

Congressman Stephens begins, "Fellow citizens: I appear before you tonight at the request of Members of the Legislature and others, to speak of matters of the deepest interest that can possibly concern us all, of an earthly character.…

My object is not to stir up strife, but to allay it; not to appeal to your passions, but to your reason. Let us, therefore, reason together … There is with me no intention to irritate or offend.

I do not, on this occasion, intend to enter into the history of the reasons or causes of the embarrassments which press so heavily upon us all at this time … The consternation that has come upon the people is the result of a sectional election of a President of the United States, one whose opinions and avowed principles are in antagonism to our interests and rights, and we believe, if carried out, would subvert the Constitution under which we now live. But are we entirely blameless in this matter, my countrymen? I give it to you as my opinion, that but for the policy the Southern people pursued, this fearful result would not have occurred.

"The first question that presents itself is, shall the people of Georgia secede from the Union in consequence of the election of Mr. Lincoln to the Presidency of the United States? My countrymen, I tell you frankly, candidly, and earnestly, that I do not think that they ought. In my judgment, the election of no man, constitutionally chosen to that high office, is sufficient cause to justify any State to separate from the Union. It ought to stand by and aid still in maintaining the Constitution of the country ... Would we not be in the wrong? Whatever fate is to befall this country, let it never be laid to the charge of the people of the South, and especially the people of Georgia, that we were untrue to our national engagements. Let the fault and the wrong rest upon others. If all our hopes are to be blasted, if the Republic is to go down, let us be found to the last moment standing on the deck with the Constitution of the United States waving over our heads."

The members of the Legislature give a spontaneous round of applause. Buck, William and Jesse join the Legislature's applause. Buck leans over to Jesse. "Congressman Stephens has always made good sense to me."

"Likewise for me, Buck."

"Let the fanatics of the North break the Constitution, if such is their fell purpose. Let the responsibility be upon them....

"But it is said Mr. Lincoln's policy and principles are against the Constitution, and that, if he carries them out, it will be destructive of our rights. Let us not anticipate a threatened evil. If he violates the Constitution, then will come our time to act. Do not let us break it because, forsooth, he may ... If he does, that is the time for us to act."

Most of the Legislators, as well as Buck, William and Jesse, are in agreement with Congressman Stephens and show their approval by another round of loud applause. Senator Toombs does not show any consideration for Senator Stephen's remarks.

"What ever may be his spirit to do it, for he is bound by the constitution checks which are thrown around him, which at this time render him powerless to do any great mischief. This shows the wisdom of our system. The President of the United States is no Emperor, no Dictator—he is clothed with no absolute power ... House of Representatives is largely in a majority against him ... there have been large gains in the House of Representatives, to the Conservative Constitutional Party of the country, which I here will call the National Democratic Party.

"In the Senate, he will also be powerless. There will be a majority of four against him ... Mr. Lincoln cannot appoint an officer without the consent of the Senate—he cannot form a Cabinet without the same consent ... Mr. Lincoln will be compelled to ask of the Senate to choose for him a

Cabinet … Then how can Mr. Lincoln obtain a Cabinet which would aid him, or allow him to violate the Constitution? Why, then, I say, should we disrupt the ties of this Union, when his hands are tied—when he can do nothing against us?

"I have heard it mooted, that no man in the State of Georgia, who is true to his interests, could hold office under Mr. Lincoln … Should any man, then, refuse to hold office that was given him by a Democratic Senate?"

Mr. Toombs loudly interrupts, and says, "If the Senate is Democratic, it is for Breckinridge."

Buck tells William, "Toombs has little respect for anyone who disagrees with him or shows him where he is wrong."

Mr. Stephens holds up his hands for quiet and continues. "Well, then, apprehend that no man could be justly considered untrue to the interests of Georgia, or incur any disgrace, if the interests of Georgia required it, to hold an office which a Breckinridge Senate had given him, even though Mr. Lincoln should be President."

The Legislature applauded again. Many of the members look toward Senator Toombs as he blushes with embarrassment.

"In my judgment, I say, under such circumstances, there would be no possible disgrace for a Southern man to hold office … My honorable friend, Senator Toombs, who addressed you last night and to whom I listened with the profoundest attention, asks if we would submit to Black Republican rule? I say to you and to him, as a Georgian, I would never submit to any Black Republican aggression upon our Constitutional rights … My countrymen, I am not of those who believe this Union has been a curse up to this time. True men, men of integrity, entertain different views from me on this subject. I do not question their right to do so; I would not impugn their motives in so doing. Nor will I undertake to say that this Government of our Fathers is perfect … But that this Government of our Fathers, with all its defects, comes nearer the objects of all good Governments than any other on the face of the Earth, is my settled conviction. Contrast it now with any on the face of the earth?"

This time Senator Toombs stands and shouts "England," looks around and takes his seat.

Congressman Stephens looks at Senator Toombs. "England, my friend says. Well, that is the next best, I grant; but I think we have improved upon England. Statesmen tried their apprentice hand on the Government of England, and then ours was made. Ours sprung from that, avoiding many of its defects, taking most of the good, and leaving out many of its errors, and from the whole our Fathers constructed and built up this model Republic....

"The next evil that my friend complained of was the Tariff... The tariff no longer distracts the public councils. Reason has triumphed. The present tariff was voted for by Massachusetts and South Carolina. The lion and the lamb lay down together-every man in the Senate and House from Massachusetts and South Carolina, I think, voted for it, as did my honorable friend himself...."

Still unable to win an argument and frowning Senator Toombs stands again and says, "The tariff lessened the duties."

Politely Congressman Stephens replies, "Yes, and Massachusetts, with unanimity, voted with the South to lessen them, and they were made just as low as Southern men asked them to be, and those are the rates they are now at ... If reason and argument, with experience, produced such changes in the sentiments of Massachusetts from 1832 to 1857, on the subject of the tariff, may not like changes be effected there by the same means, reason and argument, and appeals to patriotism on the present vexed question? ... I believe in the power and efficiency of truth, in the omnipotence of truth, and its ultimate triumph when properly wielded."

Buck, William and Jesse stand with the legislators as they give a very loud round of applause for Congressman Stephens.

"Another matter of grievance alluded to by my honorable friend, was the Navigation Laws. This policy was also commenced under the administration of one of these Southern Presidents ... It is not my purpose to defend them now. But it is proper to state some matters connected with their origin.

"One of the objects was to build up a commercial American marine by giving American bottoms the exclusive carrying trade between our own ports. This is a great arm of national power. This object was accomplished. We now have an amount of shipping, not only coastwise but also to foreign countries, which put us in the front rank of the nations of the world. England can no longer be styled the mistress of the seas. What American is not proud of the result? Whether those laws should be continued is another question. But one thing is certain, no President, Northern or Southern, has ever yet recommended their repeal. And my friend's effort to get them repealed has met with little favor North or South...."

Again Senator Toombs interrupts, "In spite of it!" There is mumbling among the legislators against Senator Toombs lack of respect for the speaker. Buck just shakes his head.

Politely Congressman Stephens addresses Senator Toombs, "My honorable friend says we have, in spite of the general government; that without it I suppose he thinks we might have done as well, or perhaps better than we have done. This grand result is in spite of the government? That may be, and it may not be; but the great fact that we have grown great and powerful under the government, as it exists, is admitted. There is no conjecture or speculation about that; it stands out bold, high, and prominent, like your Stone Mountain, to which the gentleman alluded, in illustrating some facts, in his record— this great fact of our unrivalled prosperity in the Union as it is, is admitted—whether all this is in spite of the government ... Our foreign trade, which is the foundation of all our prosperity, has the protection of the navy which drove the pirates from the waters near our coast, where they had been buccaneering for centuries before, and might have been still, had it not been for the American navy, under the command of such a spirit as Commodore Porter. Now, that the coast is clear, that our commerce flows freely, outwardly and inwardly, we cannot well estimate how it would have been, under other circumstances. The influence of the government on us is like that of the atmosphere around us. Its benefits are so silent and unseen, that they are seldom thought of or appreciated.

"It was only under our Institutions as they are that the natural resources were developed. Their development is the result of the enterprise of our people under operations of the government and institutions under which we have lived...."

A general applause by the members of the Legislature is given to Congressman Stephens with Senator Toombs remaining silent again.

"Why this sad difference? It is the destruction of her institutions that has caused it. And my countrymen, if we shall, in an evil hour, rashly pull down and destroy those institutions which the patriotic hand of our fathers labored so long and so hard to build up, and which have done so much for us, and for the world; who can venture the prediction that similar results will not ensue? Let us avoid them if we can. I trust the spirit is amongst us that will enable us to do it. Let us not rashly try the experiment of change, of pulling down and destroying; for, as in Greece and Italy, and the South American Republics, and in every other place, whenever our Liberty is once lost, it may never be restored to us again." Applause ensues again.

"I notice in the Comptroller-General's report, that the taxable property of Georgia is six hundred and seventy million dollars, and upwards—an amount not far from double what it was in 1850. I think I may venture to say that for the last ten years the material wealth of the people of Georgia has been nearly, if not quite, doubled. The same may be said of our advance in education, and everything that marks our civilization. Have we any assurance that had we regarded the earnest but misguided patriotic advice, as I think, of some of that day, and disrupted the ties which bind us to the Union, we would have advanced as we have? I think not. Well, then, let us be careful now, before we attempt any rash experiment of this sort. I know that there are friends whose patriotism I do not intend to question, who thinks this Union a curse, and that we would be better off without it. I do not so think; if we can bring about a correction of these evils, which threaten—and I am not without hope that this may yet be done. This appeal to go out, with all the promises for good that accompany it, I look upon as a great, and I fear, a fatal temptation ... When I look around and see our prosperity in everything—agriculture, commerce, art, science, and every department of progress, physical, mental and moral—certainly, in the face of such an exhibition, if we can, without the loss of power, or any essential right or interest, remain in the Union, it is our duty to ourselves and posterity to do so. Let us not unwisely yield to this temptation. Our first parents, the great progenitors of the human race, were not without a like temptation when in the Garden of Eden. They were led to believe that their condition would be bettered—that their eyes would be opened—and that they would become as Gods. They, in an evil hour, yielded—instead of becoming Gods, they only saw their own nakedness.

"I look upon this country, with our institutions, as the Eden of the World, the Paradise of the Universe ... if we yield to passion, ... instead of becoming Gods, we will become demons ... Now, upon another point, and that the most difficult, and deserving your most serious consideration, I will speak. That is, the course which this State should pursue toward those Northern States which, by their legislative acts, have attempted to nullify the Fugitive Slave Law.

"Northern States, on entering into the Federal Compact, pledged themselves to surrender such fugitives; and it is in disregard of their constitutional obligations that they have passed laws which even tend to hinder or inhibit the fulfillment of that obligation ... They have violated their plighted faith. What ought we to do in view of this? That is the question. What is to be done? ... By these principles, have the right to commit acts of reprisal on these faithless governments, and seize upon their property, or that of their citizens, wherever found.

"Now, then, my recommendation to you would be this: In view of all these questions of difficulty, let a convention of the people of Georgia be called, to which they may all be referred. Let the sovereignty of the people speak. Some think that the election of Mr. Lincoln is cause sufficient to dissolve the Union. Some think those other grievances are sufficient to justify the same; and that the Legislature has the power thus to act, and ought thus to act. I have no hesitancy in saying that the Legislature is not the proper body to sever our Federal relations, if that necessity should arise.

"I say to you, you have no power so to act. You must refer this question to the people. We, the people, are sovereign. I am one of them, and have a right to be heard; and so has every other citizen of the State. You Legislators—I speak it respectfully—are but our servants. You are the servants of the people, and not their masters. Power resides with the people in this country ... Our Constitutions, State and Federal, came from the people. They made both, and they alone can rightfully unmake either.

Should Georgia determine to go out of the Union, I speak for one, though my views might not agree with them, whatever the result may be, I shall bow to the will of her people. Their cause is my cause, and their destiny is my destiny; and I trust this will be the ultimate course of all. The greatest curse that can befall a free people is civil war.

As to the other matter, I think we have a right to pass retaliatory measures, provided they be in accordance with the Constitution of the United States; and I think they can be made so ... At least, let these offending and derelict States know what your grievances are, and if they refuse, as I said, to give us our rights under the Constitution, I should be willing, as a last resort, to sever the ties of our Union with them."

This time the entire Legislature and as Buck, William and Jesse stand to give applause of approval to Congressman Stephens. Senator Toombs reluctantly stands this time. Buck tells William and Jesse, "Toombs is standing because Congressman Stephens mentioned the possibility of secession."

"My own opinion is, that if this course be pursued, and they are informed of the consequences of refusal, these States will recede ... Another thing that I would have that Convention do. Re-affirm the Georgia Platform with an additional plank in it. Let that plank be the fulfillment of these Constitutional obligations on the part of these States— their repeal of these obnoxious laws as the condition of our remaining in the Union. Give them time to consider it, and I would ask all States South to do the same thing.

"I am for exhausting all that patriotism demands, before taking the last step. I would invite, therefore, South Carolina to a conference. I would ask the same of all the other Southern States, so that if the evil has got beyond our control ... which God in his mercy grant may not be the case, we may not be divided among ourselves." This time instead of applause, there are cheers of approval as well as applause.

"In this way, our sister Southern States can be induced to act with us; and I have but little doubt, that the States of New York, and Pennsylvania, and Ohio, and the other Western States, will compel their Legislatures to recede from their hostile attitude, if the others do not. Then, with these, we would go on without New England, if she chose to stay out."

"We will kick them out."

Buck learns over and asks Jesse, "Was that Toombs?"

"I don't think so."

Congressman Stephens again responds to the specific statement. "No. I would not kick them out. But if they chose to stay out they might. I think, moreover, that these Northern States, being principally engaged in manufactures, would find that they had as much interest in the Union, under the Constitution, as we, and that they would return to their constitutional duty—this would be my hope ... I am, as you clearly perceive, for maintaining the Union as it is, if possible ... conclusion, is for the maintenance of the honor, the rights, the equality, the security, and the glory of my native State in the Union, if possible; but if these cannot be maintained in the Union, then I am for their maintenance, at all hazards, out of it. Next to the honor and glory of Georgia, the land of my birth, I hold the honor and glory of our common country ... I am proud even of Georgia's motto, which I would have duly respected at the present time, by all her sons, 'Wisdom, justice and moderation...' But, if all this fails, we shall at least have the satisfaction of knowing that we have done our duty, and all that patriotism could require." Congressman Stephens's[69] returns to his seat as the Legislature stands, giving him a loud and long applause of appreciation."

Buck slaps his knee wearily. "These two speeches are only the beginning. I guarantee you Congressman Stephens's views have the support of Joshua Hill, former Governor Herschel Johnson and Benjamin Hill and you know Thomas R. R. Cobb and Governor Brown support the views of Robert Toombs."

To Alexander H. Stephens For your own eyes only.

Springfield, Ills. Dec. 22, 1860

Hon. A. H. Stephens My Dear Sir:

Your obliging answer to my short note is just received, and for which please accept my thanks. I fully appreciate the present peril the country is in, and the weight of responsibility on me.

Do the people of the South really entertain fears that a Republican administration would, directly or indirectly, interfere with their slaves, or with them, about their slaves? If they do, I wish to assure you, as once a friend, and still, I hope, not an enemy, that there is no cause for such fears.

The South would be in no more danger in this respect than it was in the days of Washington. I suppose, however, this does not meet the case. You think slavery is right and should be extended; while we think slavery is wrong and ought to be restricted. That I suppose is the rub. It certainly is the only substantial difference between us.

Yours very truly

A. Lincoln

JOE BROWN DRAWS THE SWORD

NOVEMBER 21, 1860

Buck keeps close eyes and ears to the regular 1860-1861 Georgia Legislative session in Milledgeville, anxious to find out what the state government's reaction is going to be to Mr. Lincoln's election to the presidency. Picking up the Decatur Watchman at the depot, Buck reads the headlines and rushes over to Liberty Hall[70] for coffee with Sheriff Perkerson and some other friends. Most of the men are sitting around the pot-belly stove taling about the same subject.

Buck and Sheriff Perkerson rush inside. Buck shouts out, "Hey guys, dang-gone, the legislature is having a special session January 16. And listen to this! Joe Brown has issued a proclamation." Everybody turns their head toward Buck. Some of the men take their pipes out of their mouths, while others spit tobacco in the bucket next to the stove.

"Read it Buck!" anxiously responds Jesse Lanford.

> *Executive Department*
> *Milledgeville, Georgia*
> *November 21st 1860*
>
> *A PROCLAMATION*
> *By Joseph E. Brown, Governor of Georgia*
>
> *The General Assembly of the State of Georgia, now in session, has passed unanimously an Act in the following words:*
>
> *Whereas, The present crisis in our national affairs, in the judgment of this General Assembly, demands resistance; and*

Whereas, It is the privilege and right of the sovereign people to deter-mine upon the mode, measure and time of such resistance.

Section 1. Therefore, the General Assembly do enact, That upon the passage of this Act, his Excellency, the Governor, be, and he is hereby re-quired to issue his proclamation, ordering an election to be held in each and every county in this State, on the first Wednesday in January, eigh-teen hundred and sixty-one, for Delegates to a Convention of the People of this State, to convene at the seat of government, on the sixteenth day of January, eighteen hundred and sixty-one.

Section 2. That said election for delegates shall be held and conducted in the same manner and at the same places as elections for members of the General Assembly are not held in this State; and all returns of such elec-tions shall be in the same manner forwarded to the Governor of this State, who shall furnish each delegate chosen with a certificate of his election.

Section 3. That the counties entitled under the last Act of Apportionment to two members in the House of Representatives, shall be entitled each to three delegates to said Convention;and the counties entitled under said apportionment to one Representative, shall elect each two delegates to said Convention.

Section 4. That said Convention when assembled, may consider all grievances impairing or affecting the equality and rights of the State of Georgia as a member of the United States, and determine the mode, measure and time of redress.

Section 5. That the members of said Convention of the people of Georgia shall be entitled to the same mileage and per diem pay received by the members of the present General Assembly, and said Convention shall, by vote, fix the pay of all their officers, and of any delegate or delegates they may appoint to any other Convention, Congress or Embassy; and shall provide for all other expenses incurred by said Convention.

Section 6. That said Convention shall have the power to elect all officers necessary to the organization, and to do all things needful to carry out the true intent and meaning of this Act, and the Acts and purposes of said Convention.

Therefore, I, Joseph E. Brown, Governor of Georgia, in obedience to the requirements of said Act, do issue this my Proclamation, ordering said election for delegates to said Convention, to be held in conformity to said Act; and requiring the managers of elections for delegates in the several counties of this State to certify and send up to this Department all returns of said elections, as in case of elections for members of the General Assembly.

And I do further require all delegates elected to said Convention to meet at the Capitol, in Milledgeville, on the sixteenth day of January, 1861, to consider of the mode, measure and time of resistance.

Given under my hand and the Seal of the Executive Department, at the Capitol, in Milledgeville, this 21st day of November, in the year of our Lord eighteen hundred and sixty.

Joseph E. Brown
By the Governor:
H. I. G. Williams, Sec'y. Ex. Dept.

"Let me see that thar newspaper Buck," insists Malcom Hamby.

Buck hands the newspaper to him. "Read it for yourself. We've got to elect delegates on January 1. I guess Judge Smith and Charles Murphy will be on the ballot." Raising his fist in the air Buck emphasizes his words, "That's who I'm gonna vote for! We know them both and they are against secession. Judge Smith served as our seventh Postmaster in 1848-49 when the town was named New Gibraltar.[71] Charles Murphy had been our State Representative. He is currently our State Senator as well as the Judge of our Inferior Court.[72] They both are pro-union. I'll bet Thomas Maguire is going to be a Representative for Gwinnett County. I think he is probably pro-union as well."

❦

Upon returning home, Buck hurries into the house, removing his hat as he goes through the door. "Betty Gail, all of the people I have talked to are going vote for Smith and Murphy."

"I hope they win," she says and sighs. "All this talk of secession scares me, Buck."

He slides his arm around her and hugs her close. "Let's don't borrow trouble, Betty Gail."

❦

Buck and his fellow Georgians head to the polls on January 1, 1861 to elect their representatives to the Secessionist Convention in Milledgeville.

At the same time Governor Joseph Brown is in Savannah to meeting with Col. Alexander Lawton the Commander of the 1st Volunteer Regiment of Georgia. The Governor informs Lawton, "I am gravely concerned about the current and dangerous political events taking place. We must capture Fort Pulaski from the Union in order to keep Savannah port open. Savannah is a key rail hub as well as a key port for Georgia and the South."

"We have the troops to take the Fort whenever you give me the order, Governor."

"It will come today because most likely the manufactured goods from the North will stop, but trade with the English and the French should continue. Europe needs our cotton. Fort Pulaski is an important port for the Union Blockade against the South. We must prevent this from occurring. I have received information that the Federals are preparing to heavily man this fort soon."

"Currently there are only two soldiers occupying the Fort and their removal is simple."

"Then take control of Fort Pulaski immediately," orders Governor Brown.

"Yes, Sir."

⋙❦

"Men, today we take Fort Pulaski." On a rainy January 3, 1861, Col. Lawton with one hundred thirty four state militia soldiers from the Oglethorpe Light Infantry, the Chatham Artillery and the Savannah Volunteer Guard boarded the Ida steamer for the seventeen-mile journey to Cockspur Island and the location of Fort Pulaski.

Around noon Capt. Francis Bartow commander of the Georgia Force arrives and marches through the gates of Fort Pulaski. The two Union soldiers offer no resistance. In moments, the Georgia State flag is hoisted to replace the Union flag and military operations begin under the auspices of Col. Lawton at the behest of Governor Brown.[73]

JANUARY 7, 1861

On a snowy winter day, Buck and Betty Gail take Polly to the Stone Mountain Seminary to begin her Second Class.[74] Polly sits between her mother and father on the journey. "We are very proud of the grades you received on the First Class examination," Buck says. "You and your brother are very bright, and we're very excited that you're entering the Second Class."

"The First Class was not bad except for the Mental Arithmetic problems. Once I caught on, they became simple for me. Some of my First Class instruction is going to continue with the Second Class. I'll pick up my books when you drop me off at the Seminary."

Betty Gail hugs her daughter. "Have you got the twenty dollar gold piece we gave you to pay the tuition and supply fees?"

"Yes, Mama I do. Right here in my pocket."

When the Jernigans reach the Seminary, Polly gives her mother and father a hug and leaps from the wagon. Buck tells Polly, "We'll pick you up after school. I hope the snow will end before the day is out."

Inside the warm Seminary Building, Polly reports to Mrs. Smith to get her books and schedule.

"We're so glad to have you back Polly. You are a wonderful student and set a good example for study habits for your classmates."

"Thank you, Mrs. Smith. I am anxious to get back to the studies. I really enjoyed my First Class."

"How did your brother do at GMI?"

"Very well, thank you, and he loves it. Mr. Goldsmith's cousin is his roommate. They have become close friends."

"I'm glad to hear that news."

Polly looks at her schedule. "The Second Class Schedule includes advanced Penmanship, Orthography, Mental Arithmetic and Reading. New instruction will begin in Elocution, Analysis, Written Arithmetic, Mensuration, Descriptive and Political Geography, History of the United States, English grammar, Composition and Declamation. Looks like a busy schedule Mrs. Smith. Here's the twenty dollars for my tuition and supplies.[75] I guess I best get my books and go to class."

"Thank you, Polly, and keep up the good work."

SECESSION CONVENTION—JANUARY, 1861

As the Secession Convention draws near, Buck rides to town for a newspaper and heads home. Sitting by the fireplace he has a taste of his hot coffee and begins to read. "Dang-it-again! Betty Gail, listen to this." Betty Gail comes to his side as Buck reads, "Senator Murphy died on us just when the state special session is about to begin. Paper says he died of pneumonia shortly after his election this month. He had said many times during the campaign that he prayed he never would live to see Georgia leave the Union. His prayer has been answered,"[76] Buck mutters to himself and with disgust lays the paper aside.

Betty Gail picks up the paper and reads a few lines. She sighs and shakes her head sadly. "Another strike against Georgia for staying in the Union."

The delegates are divided sharply over the issue of secession. United States Senator Robert Toombs and former United States Secretary of the Treasury Howell Cobb and his brother Thomas R. R. Cobb, along with Governor Brown, favor immediate secession from the Union. Congressman Stephens, a close friend of President Lincoln, argued that his election could not by itself harm Georgia.

Alexander Stephens stares at the men gathered around. "Lincoln's election could not harm Georgia and as Georgians, we should be patient and observe what Lincoln will do as president before pursuing any dangerous course."

Buck heads back to Milledgeville again to sit in on the secession convention of the legislature. He, William Sheppard, Marvin Minor, and Mark Beauchamp having arrived on the Central of Georgia train. They are anxious to hear Congressman Stephens' speech, speculating openly about what may happen.

William Sheppard says, "It is a singular fact, however, and as true as it is singular, the Northern conscience never became quickened to a realization of the enormity of slavery until after the Northern slaveholders had converted their own slaves into gold. Then the gold found a lodgment deep down in their pockets and the abolitionists changed the name of the Jefferson Party to the Republican Party."

"I agree," replies Marvin. "The Republican Party has declared 'a higher law' than the Constitution and denounces the Union as 'a covenant with hell' and the Constitution as 'a league with death,' and who derisively points to the flag of the Union as 'a flaunting lie.'"[77]

Mark Beauchamp jumps into the conversation. "Yeah, you're right. It's the triumph of this coalition which is denying the Southern people equal rights in the Union and heaping upon us insult after insult with the objective to humiliate and destroy three thousand million dollars worth of our accumulated wealth which is invested in slaves."[78]

Buck has listened quietly until now. "Yep, and many of the slaves were bought from the people of the States now waging this political war against us."

⁂

In their seats in the balcony of the State Capitol, Buck, Marvin and Mark listen to the last plea from Congressman Stephens. He concludes, "We should wait and see what Lincoln does as president before we take any drastic action such as secession."

Buck leans over and whispers to Marvin, "Mr. Stephens's views do not have the support of former Governor Herschel Johnson or Benjamin Hill. Remember Former Governor Johnson and Benjamin Hill ran against Joseph Brown for Governor."

⁂

On the 19th of January, the vote for secession is taken at the Capitol in Milledgeville. By a vote of the delegates, a resolution at the convention appoints Peter Fite Hoyle, a physician from Decatur to fill the vacancy of the late Senator Murphy. Dr. Hoyle arrives several days after the Ordinance for Secession is adopted, but is given permission after he arrives to sign the document. Dr. Hoyle officially registers his nay vote. George Smith also votes against the Ordinance for Secession. The vote is 208 to 89 in favor of secession.

Outraged Buck exclaims, "I can't believe we have 208 idiots in the Georgia Legislature! This is the end for Georgia. The South will never survive a war." The three disgusted men head back to Stone Mountain.

The next day the headlines read:

AN ORDINANCE
TO DISSOLVE THE UNION BETWEEN THE STATE OF GEORGIA
AND OTHER STATES UNITED WITH HER UNDER A COMPACT
OF GOVERNMENT ENTITLED "THE CONSTITUTION OF THE
UNITED STATES OF AMERICA."

WE, THE PEOPLE OF THE State of Georgia in Convention assembled do declare and ordain, and it is hereby declared and ordained,

That the ordinance adopted by the people of the State of Georgia in Convention on the second day of January, in the year of our Lord seventeen hundred and eighty-eight, whereby the Constitution of the United States of America was assented to, ratified and adopted; and also all acts and parts of acts of the General Assembly of this State ratifying and adopting amendments of the said Constitution, are hereby repealed, rescinded and abrogated.

We do further declare and ordain, That the Union now subsisting between the State of Georgia and other States, under the name of the "United States of America," is hereby dissolved, and that the State of Georgia is in the full possession and exercise of all those rights of sovereignty which belong and appertain to a free and independent State.

GEORGE W. CRAWFORD, PRESIDENT
Attest: A. R. Lamar, Secretary
Passed January 19, 1861

JANUARY 20, 1861

Norman writes home.

Dear Ma and Pa,

"There is great anticipation on campus about war with the North. We read about the secession vote. Although a lot of the cadets may be leaving to join the service or to become drillmasters, the faculty is advising us to stay and train the different units as they organize. Until then, our studies and drills go on."

JANUARY 23, 1861

Congressman Hill refuses to withdraw from the United States House of Representatives as directed by the Georgia Convention. Instead he regretfully submits his letter of resignation from the United States Congress to the Speaker of the House of Representatives.

MARCH 23, 1861

During assembly, Capt. McGill stands before the Corps. with his waiter, Jake, by his side with a wheel barrow full of newspapers. Capt. McGill orders each Company Commander forward and instructs them to insure each cadet receives a copy. "This is a historical speech by Confederate Vice President Alexander Stephens and each of you must read and understand the concepts set forth."

Upon dismissal each Company Commander has each squad leader secure enough copies for distribution. Norman and Paul take their copies and read the headlines before class begins:

> *On March 21, 1861, Confederate Vice-President Alexander Stephens, of Georgia, gives an extemporaneous speech at the Athenaeum in Savannah.*

Norman and Paul go directly to the barracks. They both have about forty-five minutes before class. Norman sits in his chair, placing his feet on his desk while Paul chooses the bed. He adjusts the pillow, "Let's read what our Vice President has to say."

Norman begins reading in silence and suddenly realizes that there are really two separate nations in America: The United States of America and the Confederate States of America. He looks over the top of his newspaper at Paul and then hears the shouts of some of his fellow cadets who are happy with secession. He wonders if they've really stopped to consider what it means. He sighs and continues to read.

At half past seven o'clock on Thursday evening, March 21, 1861 The Honorable Alexander Stephens addresses the largest audience ever assembled at the Savannah Athenaeum. They were waiting in the house, waiting most impatiently for the appearance of the orator of the evening, Hon. A. H. Stephens, Vice President of the Confederate States of America. The committee, with invited guests, was seated on the stage, when, at the appointed hour, the Hon. Charles C. Jones, Mayor, and the speaker, entered, and were greeted by the immense assemblage with deafening rounds of applause.

The Mayor then, in a few pertinent remarks, introduced Mr. Stephens, stating that at the request of a number of the members of the convention, and citizens of Savannah and the State, now here, he had consented to address them upon the present state of public affairs.

Mr. Stephens rose and spoke as follows:

Mr. Mayor and Gentlemen of the Committee, and Fellow-Citizens: For this reception you will please accept my most profound and sincere thanks ... We are in the midst of one of the greatest epochs in our history. The last ninety days will mark one of the most memorable eras in the history of modern civilization.

[There was a general call from the outside of the building for the speaker to go out, that there were more outside than in.]

The Mayor rose and requested silence at the doors, that Mr. Stephens' health would not permit him to speak in the open air.

Mr. Stephens said he would leave it to the audience whether he should proceed indoors or out. There was a general cry indoors, as the ladies, a large number of whom were present, could not hear outside. Mr. Stephens said that the accommodation of the ladies would determine the question, and he would proceed where he was....

Seven States have within the last three months thrown off an old government and formed a new. This revolution has been signally marked, up to this time, by the fact of its having been accomplished without the loss of a single drop of blood.

This new constitution or form of government, constitutes the subject to which your attention will be partly invited. In reference to it, I make this first general remark: it amply secures all our ancient rights, franchises, and liberties. All the great principles of Magna Carta are retained in it. No citizen is deprived of life, liberty, or property, but by the judgment of his peers under the laws of the land. The great principle of religious liberty, which was the honor and pride of the old constitution, is still maintained and secured. All the essentials of the old constitution, which have endeared it to the hearts of the American people, have been preserved and perpetuated ... Allow me briefly to allude to some of these improvements. The question of building up class interests, or fostering one branch of industry to the prejudice of another under the exercise of the revenue power, which gave us so much trouble under the old constitution, is put at rest forever under the new. We allow the imposition of no duty with a view of giving advantage to one class of persons, in any trade or business, over those of another. All, under our system, stand upon the same broad principles of perfect equality. Honest labor and enterprise are left free and unrestricted in whatever pursuit they may be engaged. This old thorn of the tariff, which was the cause of so much irritation in the old body politic, is removed forever from the new.

Again, the subject of internal improvements, under the power of Congress to regulate commerce, is put at rest under our system. The power, claimed by construction under the old constitution, was at least a doubtful one; it rested solely upon construction. We of the South, generally apart from considerations of constitutional principles, opposed its exercise upon grounds of its inexpediency and injustice. Notwithstanding this opposition, millions of money, from the common treasury had been drawn for such purposes. Our opposition sprang from no hostility to commerce, or to all necessary aids for facilitating it.

The true principle is to subject the commerce of every locality, to whatever burdens may be necessary to facilitate it. If Charleston harbor needs improvement, let the commerce of Charleston bear the burden. If the mouth of the Savannah River has to be cleared out, let the sea-going navigation which is benefited by it, bear the burden. So with the mouths of the Alabama and Mississippi rivers. Just as the products of the interior, our cotton, wheat, corn, and other articles, have to bear the necessary rates of freight over our railroads to reach the seas. This is again the broad principle of perfect equality and justice, and it is especially set forth and established in our new constitution.

Another feature to which I will allude is that the new constitution provides that cabinet ministers and heads of departments may have the privilege of seats upon the floor of the Senate and House of Representatives and may have the right to participate in the debates and discussions upon the various subjects of administration....

Under the old constitution, a secretary of the treasury for instance, had no opportunity, save by his annual reports, of presenting any scheme or plan of finance or other matter. He had no opportunity of explaining, expounding, enforcing, or defending his views of policy; his only resort was through the medium of an organ ... In the new constitution, provision has been made by which our heads of departments can speak for themselves and the administration, in behalf of its entire policy, without resorting to the indirect and highly objectionable medium of a newspaper....

Another change in the constitution relates to the length of the tenure of the presidential office. In the new constitution it is six years instead of four, and the President rendered ineligible for a re-election ... The new constitution has put at rest, forever, all the agitating questions relating to our peculiar institution—African slavery as it exists amongst us—the proper status of the Negro in our form of civilization. This was the immediate cause of the late rupture and present revolution. Jefferson in his forecast had anticipated this as the "rock upon which the old Union would split." He was right. What was conjecture with him is now a realized fact. But whether he fully comprehended the great truth upon which that rock stood and stands, may be doubted. The prevailing ideas entertained by him and most of the leading statesmen at the time of the formation of the old constitution were that the enslavement of the African was in violation of the laws of nature; that it was wrong in principle, socially, morally, and politically. It was an evil they knew not well how to deal with, but the general opinion of the men of that day was that, somehow or other in the order of Providence, the institution would be evanescent and pass away … They rested upon the assumption of the equality of races. This was an error. It was a sandy foundation, and the government built upon it fell when the "storm came and the wind blew."

Our new government is founded upon exactly the opposite idea; its foundations are laid, its corner-stone rests, upon the great truth that the Negro is not equal to the white man; that slavery—subordination to the superior race—is his natural and normal condition. This, our new government, is the first, in the history of the world, based upon this great physical, philosophical, and moral truth … They were attempting to make things equal which the Creator had made unequal. In the conflict thus far, success has been on our side … It is upon this, as I have stated, our social fabric is firmly planted; and I cannot permit myself to doubt the ultimate success of a full recognition of this principle throughout the civilized and enlightened world.

As I have stated, the truth of this principle may be slow in development, as all truths are and ever have been, in the various branches of science … It was so with Harvey, and his theory of the circulation of the blood. It is stated that not a single one of the medical profession, living at the time of the announcement of the truths made by him, admitted them. Now, they are universally acknowledged … It is the first government ever instituted upon the principles in strict conformity to nature, and the ordination of Providence, in furnishing the materials of human society. Many governments have been founded upon the principle of the subordination and serfdom of certain classes of the same race; such were and are in violation of the laws of nature. Our system commits no such violation of nature's laws. With us, all of the white race, however high or low, rich or poor, are equal in the eye of the law. Not so with the Negro. Subordination is his place. He, by nature, or by the curse against Canaan, is fitted for the condition which he occupies in our system … It is not for us to inquire

into the wisdom of His ordinances, or to question them. For His own purposes, He has made one race to differ from another, as He has made "one
star to differ from another star in glory." The great objects of humanity
are best attained when there's conformity to His laws and decrees, in the
formation of governments as well as in all things else. Our confederacy is
founded upon principles in strict conformity with these laws. This stone
which was rejected by the first builders "is become the chief of the corner"—the real "corner-stone"—in our new edifice … We hear much of
the civilization and Christianization of the barbarous tribes of Africa. In
my judgment, those ends will never be attained, but by first teaching them
the lesson taught to Adam, that "in the sweat of his brow he should eat
his bread," and teaching them to work, and feed, and clothe themselves.…

But to pass on: Some have propounded the inquiry whether it is practicable for us to go on with the confederacy without further accessions? Have
we the means and ability to maintain nationality among the powers of the
earth? On this point I would barely say, that as anxiously as we all have
been, and are, for the border States, with institutions similar to ours, to
join us, still we are abundantly able to maintain our position, even if they
should ultimately make up their minds not to cast their destiny with us.
That they ultimately will join us—be compelled to do it—is my confident
belief; but we can get on very well without them, even if they should not
… we take this occasion to state, that I was not without grave and serious
apprehensions, that if the worst came to the worst, and cutting loose from
the old government should be the only remedy for our safety and security,
it would be attended with much more serious ills than it has been as yet.

But to return to the question of the future. What is to be the result
of this revolution? Will every thing, commenced so well, continue as it
has begun? In reply to this anxious inquiry, I can only say it all depends
upon ourselves … We are a young republic, just entering upon the arena of
nations; we will be the architects of our own fortunes. Our destiny, under
Providence, is in our own hands. With wisdom, prudence, and statesmanship on the part of our public men, and intelligence, virtue and patriotism
on the part of the people, success, to the full measures of our most sanguine hopes, may be looked for.…

We have intelligence, and virtue, and patriotism. All that is required is
to cultivate and perpetuate these. Intelligence will not do without virtue
… Our growth, by accessions from other States, will depend greatly upon
whether we present to the world, as I trust we shall, a better government

than that to which neighboring States belong. If we do this, North Carolina, Tennessee, and Arkansas cannot hesitate long; neither can Virginia, Kentucky, and Missouri. They will necessarily gravitate to us by an imperious law. We made ample provision in our constitution for the admission of other States....

The process of disintegration in the old Union may be expected to go on with almost absolute certainty if we pursue the right course. We are now the nucleus of a growing power which, if we are true to ourselves, our destiny, and high mission, will become the controlling power on this continent ... The prospect of war is, at least, not so threatening as it has been. The idea of coercion, shadowed forth in President Lincoln's inaugural, seems not to be followed up thus far so vigorously as was expected. Fort Sumter, it is believed, will soon be evacuated ... All I can say to you, therefore, on that point is, keep your armor bright and your powder dry.

The surest way to secure peace is to show your ability to maintain your rights. The principles and position of the present administration of the United States—the republican party—present some puzzling questions. While it is a fixed principle with them never to allow the increase of a foot of slave territory, they seem to be equally determined not to part with an inch "of the accursed soil." Notwithstanding their clamor against the institution, they seemed to be equally opposed to getting more, or letting go what they have got.

They were ready to fight on the accession of Texas, and are equally ready to fight now on her secession. Why is this? How can this strange paradox be accounted for? There seems to be but one rational solution—and that is, notwithstanding their professions of humanity, they are disinclined to give up the benefits they derive from slave labor. Their philanthropy yields to their interest. The idea of enforcing the laws has but one object, and that is a collection of the taxes, raised by slave labor to swell the fund necessary to meet their heavy appropriations. The spoils is what they are after—though they come from the labor of the slave....

...That as the admission of States by Congress under the constitution was an act of legislation, and in the nature of a contract or compact between the States admitted and the others admitting, why should not this contract or compact be regarded as of like character with all other civil contracts—liable to be rescinded by mutual agreement of both parties? The seceding States have rescinded it on their part, they have resumed their sovereignty. Why cannot the whole question be settled, if the North desire peace, simply by the Congress, in both branches, with the con-currence of the President, giving their consent to the separation, and a recognition of our independence?

At the conclusion Mr. Stephens takes his seat, amid a burst of enthu-siasm and applause, such as the Athenaeum has ever displayed within its walls, within "the recollection of the oldest inhabitant."

"Wow! This is some speech! I knew all along the Confederacy meant business, but this truly means war!" exclaims Norman. He stands and ap-proaches Paul with the newspaper in his hand.

"Give me about five more minutes to finish and I probably will give you two Wows!" Norman takes his seat at his desk and combs over some particular parts of the speech. Norman finds the "peculiar institution" portion the most interesting and he takes his pencil and underlines that section of the speech.

"What do you think about African slavery being named the 'peculiar institution,' Paul?" asks Norman.

Paul pauses for a moment then replies, "It is a 'peculiar institution.' What else can it be called?"

"No doubt! It's like the Vice President said and President Jefferson forecasted and anticipated. Slavery is the rock upon which the old Union would split."

"Well, we have Georgia, Alabama, Mississippi, Louisiana, Florida, South Carolina and Texas forming the Confederate Republic. His speech makes it easier for North Carolina, Tennessee and Arkansas to join us."

"Yeah, hopefully Kentucky, Virginia and Missouri will also join the Confederacy." Suddenly their attention shifts as the bugles sounds first class. Laying the newspaper aside, they fetch their math text books and head for class.

LOST ON THE MOUNTAIN

APRIL 6, 1861

The clock on the kitchen mantel has just struck 8:00 in the morning on Saturday. Betty Gail's favorite nephew, ten year old Georgie, rubs his sleepy eyes, awakening in Norman's bed. Up high on the huge dark mass of granite rock, which towers above his humble home, Georgie hears the tinkle of a bell whose musical sound had long been familiar to the Jernigan's ears. Georgie knows that the bell hangs from the neck of Rosebud. Rosebud is a favorite white heifer with a wandering disposition, which leads her out of the pasture and has cost Uncle Buck many a tramp. The tinkle, tinkle, seems to come from the lazy clouds, floating so high up in the blue. Georgie hears his uncle's voice.

"Darn her white hide! Rosebud's out and climbing the mountain again. Isaac, I cannot figure out how she gets through the fence and away with that yoke still around her neck."

Rushing outside, Georgie hurries over and tugs on Buck's elbow. "I'll go 'long an' help you, Uncle." With his blue eyes and rosy cheeks, the cute child slips a chubby fist into his uncle's hand, with all the confidence of eight years of timeless indulgence.

"No, not this time. We've got to move fast so she won't get hurt. Besides, I've gotta meet Hugh Dent and Congressman Hill. We're going to walk the mountain together. They want me to check the new hotel carriage road. Stay home and help your Aunt and Polly. I'll send Uncle Isaac after Rosebud."

With a sigh of discontentment, Georgie walks away, and Isaac seizes his heavy walking stick and starts up the mountain, grumbling to himself as he goes. Unnoticed, Georgie slips in behind. Isaac isn't aware that a small but resolute boy was toddling manfully behind him.

This energetic youngster is also going out to find the absent heifer. There are many winged creatures in his path that claim him for a playmate. Georgie stops and lingers aimlessly at the chirp of an insect or the call of a bird. By this time, Isaac is long out of sight and hearing. A brilliant butterfly rises slowly in the air almost within the grasp of Georgie's fingers. A shriek of delight and a chase greets the butterfly. He rushes through thorny clumps of blackberry vines and stubby thickets of oak and pine. He stumbles over boulders, wounding his bare feet with sharp rocks and cruel briars until the chase ends and the butterfly disappears.

The path grows gray and steep. He looks up at the clear blue sky. Far in the distance, he can see Aunt Betty Gail's home. Georgie strains his eyes and can discern the familiar forms of Aunt Betty Gail and Polly standing at the garden gate. He is tired, scared, and has sore feet. Looking around he cannot see Uncle Isaac and feels helpless and lost.

"Aunt Betty Gail, Polly come help me!" he screams.

Seeing they do not hear his cry for help, he rushes forward. As he waves his hands and begins to shout out again, his foot slips. The scared lad rolls over and clutches frantically at a scanty bush as the sliding moss carries him downward. After the first wild shriek of fear, he is too frightened to cry out. Consciousness deserts him long before his downward course ends.

Up the sloping side of the mountain, Isaac toils over a carpet of green grass, pine needles, and dandelions. He stops, and shading his eyes with a rough hand, listens to the tinkle of the cowbell. Isaac mumbles, "What, cazy cow want ter climb dis rock?" Isaac continues his gaze impatiently over the brilliant landscape and up to the gilded summit of the mountain.

Soon Hugh Dent, Congressman Joshua Hill and his son, Legare Hill, arrive at Buck's. Buck is at the gin house and sees their arrival. One of the darkies takes the reins of the horses. Leaving the carriage with the stable hand, they walk to meet Buck. Waving at Congressman Hill, Buck stops at the front door of the house and yells to Betty Gail, "I'm heading up the Mountain with Congressman Hill and Hugh Dent."

"Okay we'll see you when you get back. I'll have some hot cornbread ready for all of you then."

Buck approaches and shakes hands. Joshua Hill introduces his son to Buck, "This is my son, Legare."

"Nice to meet you, Legare." Buck turns to Joshua Hill. "Mighty fine looking young man you have there, Joshua."

"Thank you, Buck."

"I have a stray cow on the mountain, but I sent Isaac to fetch her back. For some strange reason, she loves to climb the mountain. She breaks out of the pasture whenever she gets the urge to go up there. She even has her favorite spot. It might get a little warm today. I have some canteens for us to take along." Buck hands out the canteens.

"Well let's start climbing." They turn and head up the silver slope.

Isaac locates Rosebud at her favorite spot, yoke and all. He places the rope around her neck and leads her back down the mountain to the house. Isaac ties Rosebud to the fence post and goes to the kitchen. "Miss Betty, me got de cow."

"Good job, Isaac. Did Georgie go with you?"

"Nos 'um." Appearing somewhat puzzled, Betty Gail thinks, "Maybe he is with Buck," and returns to her work.

After about an hour of looking over the carriage road to the hotel, the gentlemen begin their descent. Buck says, "I guess by now Isaac should be down to the farm with Rosebud." In the distance, dark forms are floating lazily, high up in the air.

"Look over there. Turkey-buzzards," says Legare as he points up and they stop to watch their flight. They draw near to the distant edge of the precipice, and seem to circle there. "Must be a dead animal nearby," continues Buck.

As Buck nears his home, he sees Betty Gail standing at the garden gate. She shades her eyes with her hand to protect them from the sun. She and Polly are anxiously peering up the road.

Behind the two is Uncle Isaac, leaning on a hoe, and looking eagerly in the same direction. Betty Gail asks as he came within speaking distance, "Isaac said Georgie did not go with him to get Rosebud. So I figured he must have gone with you. Where is he?"

With a blank look on his face, Buck exclaims, "Didn't go with me! You sure he's not around anywhere?"

Betty Gail and Polly approach Buck and the others. "Nowhere to be found. Jack is still here too. Georgie's shoes are by the bed so he is barefooted. He must be lost! Lost on the mountain!"

Buck shouts to Isaac," Rally the neighbors! Sally, go get the Sheriff! Tell them we need a rescue party. Georgie is lost on the mountain."

Isaac and Sally each take buckboards and head in opposite directions. Buck gathers rope from the barn. Betty Gail and Polly gather the canteens and fill them with water. Buck has a carriage ready to ascend the mountain as far as possible. Within a half an hour, the neighbors and the new Sheriff William Wright with his deputies, assemble at Buck's gate.[79] They are equipped with ropes, lanterns and every necessary appliance for a thorough and protracted search for Georgie. Sheriff Wright, a resolute man, takes the lead.

Legare stands a little apart from the group and listens as the Sheriff develops a plan of action before starting. He takes his field glasses from the case around his shoulder and begins scanning the gray precipice. Shortly, Legare lowers his field glasses. Pointing, he shouts, "Mr. Sheriff, look there where the buzzards are circling," as he points to a spot on the steep mountainside.

The crowd turns and looks. Silently, they remember the pitiful fate of a stray dog that tumbled and became caught by a projecting rock. The poor dog fell too far down to be rescued and cried until death silenced its pitiful howls. Then, the awaiting buzzards feasted upon its still body. Betty Gail sees her motionless nephew on the sheer side of the mountain. Clutching her chest and grasping Polly and Buck, she barely is able to stand. This horrible recollection prompts everyone to rush up the path, some in carriages, some on horseback and others running.

Buck, Betty Gail and Polly hastily climb onto their ready carriage. Joshua Hill and Legare join them. Hugh Dent goes with Sheriff Wright and one of his deputies.

While the others organize, Legare has been carefully examining every detail of the steep slope. Legare hopes to choose a route, which could offer the greatest chance of a successful rescue. He is an athlete with a daring spirit. He now possesses a stronger motive. He only sees the face of Polly in his mind, her Venus shape made more perfect because of her marble pallor. Her long curling lashes, wet with tears, shade her dark brown eyes like the morning dew on a rosebud and captivate his heart.

Every detail of that flower-like face and perfect form fills his mind. As the carriage reaches its distance, Legare leaps down. He gathers rope as he and Buck rush ahead of the rescuers. His father, Betty Gail and Polly hasten to keep up with them as they race up the path to the top of the mountain. Stopping, Legare looks around.

"Those trees there are the ones that I saw above your nephew with the field glasses." Legare takes his rope and ties it around the base of a tree.

Buck takes the other end of the rope. "Best tie the rope around two or three trees. Legare. The roots are shallow up here and one tree won't hold."

As Buck finishes tying off the rope to the other trees, the sheriff appears on the scene. Legare takes the rope and prepares to ease down the side backwards. At the proper time he'll allow the rope to slide slowly through his hands. From the edge of the cliff, Georgie is plainly visible, lying near where the hound had lain earlier. Georgie is too exhausted to cry out. With Polly restraining her, Betty Gail leans over the rocky edge, calling to Georgie with appealing pleas. Georgie does not respond in any way to the tearful appeals of his distraught aunt. Polly holds her mother sympathetically but securely as she continues to lean over the rocky edge begging her nephew to whisper any reply.

An impulse moves sweet Polly and she turns her eyes towards Legare. Their eyes meet and she silently begs Legare to save her cousin. Not a word is spoken between them. Legare turns and says, "Mr. Sheriff, I am Legare Hill. Though young, I am physically fit and am accustomed to daring ventures."

Joshua nods to the sheriff. "He is physically able to carry out this feat!"

The mountain at this point has been worn into a deep furrow. Georgie had slid a distance of one hundred feet or more. A rock ledge which slants upwards from the mountainside prevents him from further peril.

Sheriff Wright replies, "So be it!"

Polly rushes over to Legare and hands him a shawl. "I brought this shawl as bandage. Take it with you!"

Legare smiles, placing the shawl in his shirt. "Don't you fret, Polly, your cousin is safe with me."

Sheriff Wright places his hand on Legare's shoulder. "You take the end of the rope and we'll go down together. About halfway of the descent, I'll stop and relay word to those on top."

Holding the rope securely the men begin to let the rope to Legare and the Sheriff. It is a perilous undertaking, and only possible because of the youth of Legare and the leadership and skill of the sheriff. Cautiously treading backwards, and slipping hand over hand along the supporting rope, Legare finally reaches the boy. Georgie looks up, but can barely speak.

Legare softly tells him, "You're going to be all right. Just be very still and I'll lift you." Georgie gives a weak but assuring smile and does not move.

Sheriff Wright shouts, "Hold tight. Legare has reached the boy!"

The deputy relays, "Hold tight! Legare has reached Georgie!"

Legare eases to the side and then maneuvers below Georgie. A slip, the wavering of nerves, or an error in thought, could now mean two lives might fall upon the cruel rocks below. Legare sees that Georgie's feet, hands and arms are badly skinned. Though not bleeding profusely, there's still some oozing. Legare ties the rope around his waist and leaves about four feet dangling. Then Legare gently lifts Georgie in his arms. He pulls the injured boy close and binds him tightly to his person with Polly's shawl. Then he indicates with an upward motion of his head and tells the sheriff, "Pull slowly!"

The sheriff relays the message to a man at the head of the ropes, who turns and gives the "Pull slowly" signal to the other rescue team members. The ascent is even more difficult than expected. Georgie lay like a dead weight upon Legare's chest. In breathless anxiety the party watches him from above, as he and his precious burden slowly ascend the steep incline.

As Legare approaches Sheriff Wright, he says," Take the short piece and help pull."

Sheriff Wright reaches the four-foot length dangling from Legare's waist. While still holding to the main rope, Sheriff Wright pulls Legare along to reduce the strain on his body. Soon, the head of the precious human cargo is seen by the assembly at the top. At last, the trio reaches the safety of the top. The men seize Legare and the sheriff by their shoulders and arms and deliver them to a place of safety. A great shout rises from the crowd gathered on the mountain as Legare places Georgie in his aunt and uncle's arms.

Words fail the grateful Betty Gail. She tries to speak, but cannot. Sweet Polly, coming forward quickly, overcome by conflicting emotions, almost falls at Legare's feet.

Legare reaches to support Polly when a voice at his side says, "Give her ter me, stranger."

Legare turns as the young man takes possession of his precious flower with the air of one whose claim cannot be in dispute.

"Yes, Buster, take the girl," says Buck, "she's wore out with worry. Her cousin's been in mortal danger, and to this young man, Sheriff Wright and all of these folks, we're beholden for his life." Buck turns to the Sheriff and Legare with unconscious dignity and tears, and says, "Sir, I'd thank you if I could, but it's all there," and he strikes and rubs his rugged hand upon his chest.

⁂

It is late that night when Joshua Hill tosses the stub of his cigar into the handsome garden, which surrounds his home in Atlanta. He rises to go to where the strained and blistered Legare is resting. "Legare," he says to his son, "Your deed today was exemplary. I know the look that now possesses you. It is all about beautiful Polly Jernigan. Mind your manners, for the Jernigans are eternally grateful to you and the sheriff."

Legare laughs lightly. "Very true father. You recognize her loveliness as I do. She is beautiful just like a thoroughbred filly!"

Then Legare follows his father up the broad stairway to their rooms. In spite of fatigue, he sleeps very little, continuously thinking and dreaming of the fair face of Polly Jernigan. The Cherokee rose of a girl and her brown hair lingers in his memory like magic in the sunshine. He sees the wind gently blowing her soft ringlets around her beautiful face, framing as if in gold. She stands shading her deep dark brown eyes with her small pure white hand.

Betty Gail feels the thoughts in Polly's mind and heart. Betty Gail prays that night thanking God for the life of the darling boy. She also prays that the rescue does not cost her the soul of her daughter.

But Polly, dreaming of a sweet future, sees Legare reaching for her. In her dreams, she responds by stepping into his protective embrace. Love quickens in her heart.

THE SABER STRIKES

APRIL 12, 1861

Governor Brown issues the first call for volunteers to assemble at Camp Brown in Smyrna no later than April 22 for training. From every corner of the state, Georgia patriots report to Camp Brown. Under orders from the Governor, GMI faculty and cadets train the volunteers.

At the afternoon parade and with the permission of Maj. Capers, a group of Marietta ladies present the GMI cadet corps with a new "Star and Bars" flag. The new flag has Stars for each Confederate state on the blue canton and the three stripes of red, white and red. Maj. Capers expresses his gratitude to the ladies as they present the flag to the cadet commander who in turn salutes the ladies and presents the flag to the color Guard Commander. The flag is placed on the new staff as the Cadet Corps commander orders, "present arms." The flag bearer takes his position with the Color Guard. A slight spring breeze unfolds the new Stars and Bars. The fife and drummer begin. The appropriate command leads the corps as they "pass in review." Norman thinks, *A new era is upon us.*

※

The first Confederate recruits assemble for training on April 23rd, at Camp Brown. Maj. Capers gathers the GMI staff in his conference room. Once everyone is seated he opens the letter and reads to the staff,

"We have orders from Governor Brown to train volunteers at Camp Brown, four miles south of Marietta. The officers and non-commissioned officers of Phillip's Brigade are already regularly encamped for some weeks. All ranks are surrendered. I am in command, and the cadets acting in such capacity as he assigns them. Our general schedule will be: One day is sufficed to fix the separate company ground and train them to assembly. The second day the organization is in one company with the cadets acting as commissioned and non-commissioned officers. For several days afterwards the main instruction will be in guard duty. After the first week, the encampment is by battalion. The drills are in different arms, infantry, artillery and cavalry. The officers of the various regiments, then forming or formed, shall find a place in ranks and profit by the practical instruction and the drills of the encampment."[80]

⚓

Norman takes a few moments to write home. "We have very little time for studies. All of us camp with the troops we are training. Tents as far as you can see. We are training about thirty five companies. It is still real cool at night and chilly during the day. Just right for training. Food is good, plenty of bread, beef and bacon. Reveille sounds at 5:30, and I am lucky to get to my tent by 10:30 at night. The troops have to have training in guard duty so a cadet has to be with them. Love to all, Norman"[81]

⚓

"On April 30, 1861, Governor Brown went up to review the training of the Phillip's Brigade at GMI." Buck shows it to Polly and Betty Gail. "Read this about GMI and what the Governor has to say about the training."

Taking the newspaper Polly reads, "Major Capers, elegant in his manners and thoroughly fitted for his duties, aided by his cadets as they are detailed by him to drill the various squads, prove the absolute need in times such as these, of military educated men." Turning to the next page, "Here's another article on GMI." She begins reading out loud.

"The GMI cadets vote to recognize the Phillip's Brigade as GMI's first contribution to the training of Georgia's army. For this occasion, the cadets elect to present the 'Stars and Bars' given to them by the Marietta ladies to the Phillip's Brigade.

"A full dress parade is routine at the completion of training. During the 'Presentation of Colors' the Cadet Corps Color Guard marches to a position in front of the Phillip's Brigade Color Guard. The Phillip's Brigade commander orders 'Present Arms.' At this time, the GMI Cadet Battalion

Adjutant Jack Crutchfield and the Cadet corps Color Guard bearing the 'Stars and Bars' steps forward. At the same time, the Phillip's Brigade Color Guard Sergeant and the Color Guard Corporal who would normally bear the United States Flag step forward. They are facing one-another. On command, the Color Guard Sergeants salute each other. Then the cadet Flag Bearer sharply passes the 'Stars and Bars' to the Phillip's Brigade Flag Bearer. Presenting the 'Stars and Bars' to the Commander of the Phillips Brigade is a very proud moment for the corps and the brigade. Then the Cadet Color Guard marches off the field." Paul Goldsmith writes home, "It was like passing a part of us to them."

As the Phillip's Brigade Color Guard takes the appropriate position for the "Presentation of Colors" with the new "Stars and Bars," a gentleman walks to a position in front of the drummer and fifer. On command, the drummer and the fifer begin to play what sounds like the Star Spangled Banner and the male vocalist begins to sing. The music is the same but the words are different.

> *Oh, say can you see, through the gloom and the storm,*
> *More bright for the darkness, that pure constellation?*
> *Like the symbol of love and redemption its form,*
> *As it points to the haven of hope for the nation.*
> *How radiant, each star, as the beacon afar,*
> *Giving promise of peace, or assurance in war;*
> *Tis the Cross of the South, which shall ever remain,*
> *To light us to Freedom and Glory again!*
> *It is the new national anthem for the South; The Southern Cross.*[82]

❧

The night following the presentation Paul tells Norman, "Chills raced up and down my spine when I heard the new words to the Star Spangled Banner. It was as if I was listening to the soul of the Union and the spirit of the Confederacy."

"I found myself speechless as well. The men of Phillip's Brigade came here ready to fight, but know very little about tactic. Some think fighting a war is like hunting squirrels … not much to it. Now Phillip's Brigade knows discipline, and tactics."

"I only hope they are all successful and return home safely."

❧

Beginning in early April, President Lincoln has strategy meetings on the national military situation with General Winfield Scott, the Commanding General of the Union Army. President Lincoln directs General Scott, "To devise a strategy which will hasten an end to the rebellion of the Southern States and bring the Southern States back into the Union."[83]

LATE MAY 1861

General Scott returns to President Lincoln's office with his complete military strategy to end the rebellion. President Lincoln and General Scott sit at a conference table with their respective staffs. "I'm ready for your briefing, General."

"Sir, I believe that the majority of Southerners desire a complete union with the United States. In order to restore the Union with as little bloodshed as possible, I have developed a relatively non-aggressive policy against the rebellion in the South for your approval."

"Show me your specific plan on the map, General Scott."

General Scott places a large map of the southeastern United States on the conference table and continues," The primary strategy of my plan to persuade the South back into the Union is to create a complete naval blockade of the Southern states.[84] The major component of the naval blockade includes cutting the South's supply lines to the outside world."

"How sound is the plan and do we have enough ships to not only perform the blockade, but defend against any foreign assistance to the South?"

"Yes sir, the plan is militarily sound. The South has no naval force whatsoever not even a single ship and Europe is not ready to enter this conflict." Pointing to the map, General Scott continues his presentation, "This is an ambitious strategy and to be successful, will involve a naval blockade of more than 3,500 miles." Using a pointer, General Scott shows the area involved in the blockade as President Lincoln and his staff observe. "The blockade will extend from the coast of Virginia to Mexico and up the Mississippi from New Orleans. Then from New Orleans to New Madrid Bend."

"How long in time do you feel it will take for the blockade to be effective?"

"The naval blockade plan will require time and patience to succeed and will save many lives in the North and the South. The South will slowly feel the economic effect. Again, Mr. President, I must emphasize patience is an essential part of the strategy. The naval blockade does not allow supplies to reach the South from the sea, and the South will begin to suffer severely economically."[85]

"Give more details concerning the effect on the Mississippi River." President Lincoln continues to listen as General Scott explains the blockade strategy further.

"There are two parts to the strategy. The first is to prevent the exports of cotton, tobacco and other cash crops and to prevent the import of goods especially from Europe. The second part of the strategy divides the Deep South by controlling the Mississippi River, cutting of the southeastern states from the West. Again, Mr. President, once the blockade is complete, neither imports nor valuable exports of cotton and rice will be possible. With the South in economic disaster, then not only can the Union Army invade from within but also the Marines can invade from the coast inflicting a defeat upon the South rather quickly."

"How many troops are we talking about?"

"The Union army will require 60,000 troops to move down the Mississippi with gunboats in order to secure the river from Cairo, Ill, to the Gulf. This military action that, in connection with an effective blockade, will seal off the South."[86]

"So you feel that we should wait before invading the South."

"Rather than invade the South, Mr. President the federal troops should only threaten an invasion. The Union should wait for the Southern Union sympathizers to turn on their Confederate Governors and compel them to surrender. I believe that sympathy for secession is not as strong as it appears. The isolation and pressure can make the 'fire-eaters' back down and allow calmer heads to take control." General Scott considers his words carefully. "I also do not recommend a military action against the Confederate Capital of Richmond, Virginia. The cost in lives will be extremely high."[87]

President Lincoln hesitates thoughtfully for a moment. "I have diplomatic concerns about adopting the Isolation Plan. The risk of committing diplomatic suicide is ominous. Since a nation would never blockade its own ports, I am effectively recognizing the Confederacy as a sovereign nation. To avoid this diplomatic view, I must again proclaim the war is merely the suppression of a rebellion. This should make foreign interests think twice about forming diplomatic relations with the Confederacy and offending the United States. The blockade certainly poses the risk of offending other nations attempting to trade with the Confederacy, but I am to preserve this Union first and foremost." General Scott nods. "Of course, Mr. President."

"I like your plan and will elect to adopt this Blockade Plan, without alterations."

"General Scott, The blockade will remain central to the Union strategy."[88]

The Northern newspapers title General Scott's plan "Anaconda" and General Scott receives considerable public criticism especially from the abolitionists who want all out war against the South.

President Lincoln orders a blockade of the South on April 19, six days after the fall of Fort Sumter. The job of creating and maintaining a true blockade of the South falls on the shoulders of Secretary of the Navy, Gideon Welles. He informs his naval commanders, "To meet this new challenge the navy must begin a massive expansion of its fleet. The Union as well as the South, is aware the most strategically important coastal region is Hampton Roads in Virginia where the wide mouth of the James River pours into the Chesapeake Bay. For the North, Hampton Roads is our doorway to the Confederate capitol at Richmond. For the South, this is the passage to the sea and potential European allies. Fort Monroe, the massive stone fortress that guards the inward approaches to Hampton Roads, is solidly in our hands. We must insure that Fort Monroe remains in Union control. It is key to Union expeditions into the South, as well as an anchor for the blockade of the Atlantic coast." In the spring of 1861, the navy consisted of eight-two largely obsolete ships.[89]

⁂

In response to General Scott's Anaconda Plan, Gen. Robert E. Lee and President Jefferson Davis meet to determine the effect of General Scott's naval blockade and conclude, "that all of the forts along the coast are beyond the reaches of the federal artillery."[90]

Since secession, former United States Congressman and now Col. Lucius J. Gartrell,[91] is a fiery advocate for war. He prides himself with military ado and hastens to organize the Seventh Regiment, Georgia Volunteer Infantry in May.[92] Col. Gartrell plans to be among the first to take the field against the North. The fall of Sumter early in the spring sends an electric thrill through North and South and from both sections comes the call to arms.

PROPOSAL BY BUSTER—JUNE 1, 1861

Buster Phillips' patrimonial acres join the Jernigan farm. The Jernigans consider Buster well-to-do, good-looking, and above all else, kind. Buster is a most desirable match from every standpoint for Polly. Therefore, when Buster set his eyes upon Polly, her father gave a glad consent and Betty Gail claimed him as a son. Buster finishes his regular Saturday night supper with the Jernigans and invites Polly to sit outside with him.

"Polly, 'afore my very eyes you're a fadin' from me, an' it looks like unless you marry me, I must jest stand by and see you die. Let's fix the wedding day. Polly, please give the man what's loves you the right to care fer you until death."

Polly looks across her father's farm and sees the white cypress vie with the morning glories in a laudable attempt to cover up unsightly stumps and fences. The Cherokee rose, now in full bloom, shuts in this paradise of scent and color with a snowy hedge.

As Buster speaks, he takes her hand in his and presses tenderly. She does not encourage his grasp. Instead she allows her hand to lie unresisting in Buster's.

"Your pa's mighty stirred over politics these days. He reckons how there's gonna be great trouble in the land. It 'pears he's about right. Who'll protect you then, Polly, like a husband can? Let da preacher marry us right away, an' give the old folks another son to lean on."

As Buster speaks, Polly's gaze roams listlessly over the lovely scene before her. She hears Buster's voice as one hears in a dream, wishing that it were the voice of Legare. She sees the frantic struggles of a brilliant butterfly entangled in the lace-like meshes of a spider's web. Her feeling prompts her to remove her hand from Buster's clasp and go to the assistance of the butterfly. However she does not yield to the impulse. She leaves her hand hidden in the clasp of the young fellow at her side. She, too, is tangled in a mesh, which circumstances are weaving around her. She sees her struggle as unable to break the silken threads of the web of Buster's love.

"Speak, Polly," says Buster. "Shall I tell your ma an' pa we've set da day?"

Polly, not desiring to offend Buster or her parents, answers, "Yes."

JUNE 11, 1861

With the increase in volunteers, the necessity for a larger camp which can accommodate a brigade becomes a necessity. The governor sends orders to close Camp Brown and establish a larger camp at Big Shanty in order to address to the growing armies requirements for a larger training area.

During the months of June and July, the cadets move to Camp McDonald located six miles up the Western and Atlantic state road to Big Shanty. The camp is named in honor of Charles J. McDonald, a past Georgia Governor. The cadets move the base of operations from Camp Brown and establishment to Camp McDonald at Big Shanty.

"I understand two good reasons why Big Shanty's such a good location for a training camp," Norman says to Paul. "Plenty of fresh water and the Western and Atlanta Road."

Gen. William Phillips of the Georgia Militia is the commander of the camp and treats the cadets as if they, too, are generals. Paul and Norman inspect the camp together. "Looks like everyone lives in tents," observes Paul. "Those must be the two parade grounds over there, Norman."

After further inspection, he says "Smart move by the governor. There's room for infantry, cavalry, and artillery training."

"No contact with the outside world. There's no telegraph," Paul notes.

The camp surrounds the depot. There are more spectators on Sundays to view the drills, dress parades and mock battles than there were at GMI. During the mock battles, there are at least 5000 spectators to see how the military conducts war. After watching, Norman tells Paul, "These simulated battles are our payment for our instruction and furnish us with an object lesson in the evolution of troops in line of battle. We could never hope to have seen this elsewhere."[93]

Norman and Paul's company continues to direct all of the exercises, but the senior cadets do the tactics and artillery training. The governor visits regularly to review the various brigades and always takes time to talk with the staff and cadets.

MONDAY, JUNE 17, 1861

Polly is up early and on her way to start her Third Class in the Seminary. Her ma, pa, Uncle Isaac and Aunt Sally wave to her as she takes the horse and wagon, heading towards town.

Polly is excited to be trusted for the first time to drive herself to school. She takes care not to overtax the horse as she reaches the edge of town. Proud of herself, she drops the horse and wagon by the stable and dashes to school.

"Good morning, Mr. Latham."

"Good morning, Polly. I see you're ready to start your Third Class."

"Yes, sir." Polly reaches in her purse and takes out a twenty dollar gold piece.

"Here's the twenty dollars for my Third Class tuition and supply fees."

"Thank you, Polly. Your books are in Mrs. Smith's room. I believe you already have a list of the courses, but here is another one for you. You were among the top of your class again. Congratulations!"

"Thank you, Mr. Latham. I really like the Seminary." Polly takes the list and reads it over: Advance studies in Penmanship, Arithmetic, Mensuration, Composition, and English Grammar. New studies include Book keeping, Plane Trigonometry, Logarithms, Physical Geography, Physiology and Botany.[94]

AUGUST 1861

On a beautiful summer morning, Isaac has the buggy ready for the Jernigans. "When I get back, Isaac, we'll grease the wheels in the ginny house and replace the bellow.

Giddy-up Jack!" commands Buck. The wagon turns and the family heads toward the depot. Betty Gail and Polly are going to Atlanta to have dinner with friends and hopefully buy some cloth for new frocks. Shortly, the whistle of the train is heard in the distance, and peering over the trees, the billowing clouds of smoke connects with the whistles and the familiar sound of a train running on the tracks. The brakes squeal as they are applied, and the train comes to a stop. The mailbag is delivered to Henry Sampson, the mail coach driver who climbs onto his buckboard and immediately heads in the direction of the post-office.[95]

The engineer jumps from the fuming steam engine and reaches the water tank. He grabs the handle, slowly lowers the spout of the water tank and turns the valve allowing water to fill the boiler. When the boiler is full, the engineer retracts the large metal nozzle, closes the valve and returns to the engine cab. A flatbed loaded with fresh cut granite is on the sidetrack waiting to be coupled to the main line.

The fare to Atlanta is twenty cents round-trip. Polly and Betty Gail hear the Conductor's "all-aboard." They approach the "lady step" and board. Buck returns their waves and smiles. The old iron horse is soon out of sight, heading to Decatur and Atlanta. Buck turns the buggy about and heads back to the farm. He and Uncle Isaac have to get the gin ready to render clean cotton.

Uncle Isaac is waiting at the gin house when Buck returns from town. Buck pulls up to the two-story building and ties off the horse to a hitching post. "This old gin has been mighty good to us, Isaac. It has never failed to give us the two bales a day from the time we put it into operation."

Isaac nods, indicating the cotton is out of the way. "Got de grease fer de wheels."

"Let's check the main power wheel first," Buck suggests. They walk over to the large horizontal power wheel to which the mule will be attached with a harness. The mule will have a bucket of feed on the halter to keep him happy as he walks the circle to keep the gin in motion. Climbing onto the wheel, Buck looks over at Isaac "Hand me the bucket of axle grease, Isaac."

Isaac hands Buck the grease and climbs up on the power wheel with him. Isaac pries open the axle cap. Buck cleans out the old grease and Isaac fills the empty axle cavity with fresh grease. "Isaac, go ahead and remove the grease cap from the vertical wheel. Clean out the old grease and then fill the axle cavity with the new grease while I check the cogs on both wheels."

Shortly Isaac tells Buck, "I through with da grease."

"The cogs are all in good shape. Let go upstairs and check the saw and doffing brush." Buck inspects the apparatus carefully. "Still clean after finishing last years crops, the saw blades and doffing bush assemblies look almost like new. Did you bring the new bellow from the barn, Isaac?"

"Me go fetch hit now." Isaac descends from the second floor and goes to the barn. While Isaac is gone, Buck checks the lint chute attached to the bellow. The chute is clean and clear all the way to the lint room at the back of the gin house. Soon Isaac returns with the new bellow. He and Buck attach it to the chute. Now the seed-free cotton lint can be blown to the lint room for baling.

"Everything is in working order, Isaac. Probably next week we will start picking cotton. I sure hope we get mostly 'fancy' grade like we did last year. It looks like this year's crops should be as good as last year's. I remember how they had the trains loaded last year with the cotton. Each flatbed was for each grade of cotton: 'stained,' 'tinged,' 'ordinary,' 'good ordinary,' 'low middling,' 'middling,' 'good middling,' and 'fancy.' We had just the right amount of rain this year. Plenty of corn and plenty of good clean cotton."

꽃

As the train pulls to a stop in Decatur, Betty Gail shouts, "Here we are Mary!" As she and Polly wave to their dear friend, Mary Gay, she climbs aboard. Dressed in her usual black attire, she finds a seat near Polly and Betty Gail.

"I hear someone is getting married!" says Mary. Polly blushes and smiles back. Mary sees Polly is somewhat shy about the announcement and continues, "Let's have dinner at the eatery on Luckie Street. This is the day for barbeque, ham hocks and vegetables and they make the best cracklin-corn bread."

"Fine with us," replies Polly. It is just a short ride to Atlanta, arriving a little after 9:30. Upon disembarking, the three immediately set their sights on the ladies fashion stores. Rushing to the first store near the terminal, peering in the window they see the latest fashions. Silk parasols, colorful Sunday hats full of feathers, shoes of highly polished leather and dresses for any occasion.

As they enter, Mary asks, "Where are your black dresses?"

"Are you in mourning madam?" asks the clerk.

"Shucks no! I just like black."

"Follow me please, madam." The clerk shows Mary the modest selection of black dresses. Polly and Betty Gail shift through the ladies silk attire. Polly picks out a silk scarf and blouse with hummingbird designs. Betty Gail finds a lace-lined bonnet with a silk tie that fits her perfectly. Paying for the merchandise, the happy group departs for the next store. It is here that Mary finds the black dress of her dreams, and Polly, new shoes for church.

It is now noontime and there are no shadows cast by the trees. "There's the eatery and I can smell the barbeque," says Betty Gail.

"And crackling-corn too!" exclaims Polly. Once inside, they find a table near a window. The mid-day sun feels better with a breeze on this hot August day.

"Hello, Betty Gail," says the owner's wife who is also the waitress. "We have not seen you in a while. How have you been?"

"Doing just fine. Been busy getting ready for the fall crops ... and how are you and your husband?"

"Everything is good. What are you going to have today?"

"A big plate of ham hocks and streak-a-lean with green beans on the side."

"Make it two," says Polly.

"No, make it three," says Mary.

After dinner, the trio can hear the concert at the city park. They decide to attend the event while they digest their delightful meal. The afternoon is sweet and soft. Every now and then, a massive cloud hides the sun, but for the most part, it's a beautiful day.

"The day is perfect for Mozart's music; lively, vigorous in spirit and beautiful melodies that always sound fresh," comments Betty Gail.

The concert area is surrounded by large oaks and magnolia trees offering abundant shade for the seated guests. To their delight, wine for sipping along with fresh cheese is being served by the waiters. After sampling the wine and cheese and listening to the music for about an hour, Betty Gail looks at her watch. "Time is running out. And we haven't paid a visit to the dry goods store. We best go so we can make the next train."

With the purchase of several yards of fabric for new draperies and a bed spread, a quick bag of licorice for Georgie, who has fully recovered from his fall on the mountain they need only make one more stop. Polly tells her ma, "Gotta get new socks and straw hat for Pa," as they stop on their way to the train station. They barely make it back to the station in time.

"All aboard." The train pulls away slowly from the Atlanta station mile post number one and heads to Stone Mountain, stopping at Decatur. Mary energetically jumps off to the station platform. She waits until the train departs and waves Betty Gail and Polly along.

When the train reaches Stone Mountain, Buck is waiting for them at the depot reading the newspaper. He sees Betty Gail and Polly sitting by a window as the train squeals to a stop. They wave to him as they get out of their seats to get off of the train. Soon they are in the buggy and chattering about their exciting day.

"Looks like y'all had a good time in Atlanta. What's in the bags?" Polly reaches in one of the bags and says, "Got you a new straw hat Pa." Polly takes off Buck's old one and puts the new one on his head. "Looks good!"

Slightly adjusting the hat Buck says, "Feels good too! So how was Atlanta?"

"It was nice. All of the stores were open. Mary Gay bought her typical black dress and then we ate a big lunch. We were so full after lunch that we went to the open-air concert at the park. All in all it was a great day." Betty Gail looks in the back of the buggy, "I see you got two big bags of salt. Are you killing hogs?"

"Probably will in a day or so. Looks like salt might get scarce. A lot of speculating going on. Isaac and I have been working on the ginny today making sure all of the wheels are greased and ready for the cotton crop. Been reading the paper. Didn't realize so many of our boys have gone off to the war." Buck hands Betty Gail the newspaper. "Read the names, Betty Gail."

Betty Gail takes the paper from Buck. Polly looks over her mother's shoulder as Betty Gail starts to read the names, "In March, William J. Lee enlisted with Billepique's Battalion. In April, Michal Winningham and his son Oliver enlisted with the DeKalb Militia 34th Military District Georgia Militia. In May, Hiram J. Holley enlisted with the Stone Mountain Volunteers. In June, John Wilson McCurdy, John Rankin, George Riley Wells all enlisted for Murphey Guards, 38th Regiment Georgia Volunteer Infantry. On August 5, James R. Smith enlisted as a Capt. in the Georgia 36th Regiment Georgia Infantry for the Stone Mountain District."[96]

"Hiram Holley, John Wilson McCurdy, John Rankin, Michal and Oliver Winningham, are my Masonic Brothers. Hope this is the last of our folks to go. James Goldsmith is going to post a list of the enlistments from Stone Mountain at the depot."

Betty Gail puts the paper down and stares straight ahead.

Buck watches her for a moment. "Are you all right?"

"All right?" Betty Gail echoes. "I don't think so, Buck."

"Tell me what's wrong. Are you hurtin' somewhere?"

She sinks into a chair and shakes her head. "No Buck. I don't think I am." She turns suddenly as if coming out of a dream. "Oh, I'm not in physical pain."

"Then what is it?" Concern scores Buck's forehead with wrinkles. "Talk to me. You got me worried."

"It's all true, Buck." Betty Gail closes her eyes briefly as if in prayer. "We're at war, really at war."

ADVANCE WEAPON TESTING

OCTOBER 11, 1861

About mid-morning, Buck observes several military and civilian wagons passing by his farm. They are pulling several cannons and appear to be heading for a clearing in front of the eastern steeper side of the mountain. Curious, Buck mounts his buckboard and arrives at the clearing as the men begin unloading and setting up camp.

"Hello, I'm Buck Jernigan. Kinda curious about what's going on."

The solider replies, "That man over there with the wide brim brown hat, he is in charge. His name is Rushton."

Buck walks over and extends his hand. "Howdy neighbor, my name is Jernigan. I own the farm just over yonder. Wondering what's going on?"

"My name is William Rushton[98] and I own an arms manufacturing factory near Atlanta. The government has obtained permission to use this side of the mountain for some test firing. The army will test the quality of the trajectory, the range and the accuracy of these new and improved breech-loading cannons. Then some tests will be run on the new swivel which I have also manufactured."

"Where is the government planning on placing these new cannons?"

"Hopefully this new cannon will be a great asset in the coastal defense of our state. That's Capt. G. W. Lee over there. He is the chief artillerist and a highly skilled gunner. His troops are mostly from Wright's Legion, 38th Georgia Regiment Volunteer Infantry. His company commander is Cornelius Hanleiter, of the Georgia Light Artillery."

"Where is their camp?"

"They are currently stationed at Camp Kirkpatrick, here in DeKalb County."

"I thought so. I'm familiar with Kirkpatrick's place and have seen soldiers there in his grove."

"That's the campsite all right."

"I hope these tests prove successful."

"If they do then Cornelius will be at Savannah setting up the defenses of that city."[99] Pointing toward the mountain, Mr. Rushton continues, "There is a mule team going to the top of the mountain. The crew will place the targets on the north face. Then the testing will begin."

"How long is the testing going to last?" asks Buck.

"Probably just for today. The cannons will prove their worthiness in a very short time."

Buck removes his hat and tips his head so he can see better. "Reckon I'll stay and watch for a while if you don't mind."

"Not at all, Mr. Jernigan," responds Mr. Rushton. Shortly, Capt. Lee points to the soldiers at the target site. The target is approximately ten feet by twenty feet and constructed from some type of thin cloth. It is fastened to the top of the mountain's north side. A huge black dot identifies the center of the target. A dot directly in line with Thomas Henry's eighty-foot tower.

Capt. Lee informs Mr. Rushton, "The targets are ready. As soon as the men return to safety we will begin the testing."

Buck asks, "How far away are these cannons from that target Mr. Rushton?"

"The target distance is 1500 yards," replies Mr. Rushton.[100] Thirty minutes later, the soldiers return with the supply wagon from the mountain. Capt. Lee orders the men to prepare the cannon for the test. "You best place your hands over your ears Mr. Jernigan. Things get loud, even at the distance we are from the cannon."

"I know." He places his hands over his ears. The first three shots from the cannon almost hit the target and are within inches of each other. Then the fourth shot strikes the target within a few inches from the center. After each shot the breech action assembly is inspected for metal stress before firing the cannon again. About thirty minutes pass between each firing. For the last three shots, the cannon's elevation is set at over fourteen hundred feet.

Buck looks surprised and asks, "Why the elevation?"

Mr. Rushton glances at Buck. "The next three shots will confirm the accuracy at a greater distance. These shots are going directly over the top of Mr. Henry's Tower."[101]

"Aren't you concerned that someone might be in the tower or on the other side of the mountain?"

"We have all that taken care of. The army has permission to clear everyone off of the mountain and out of the tower. Also, the area where the cannon balls should fall is under military guard. If by accident we hit the tower, the army will pay Mr. Henry under the contract they have with him. If successful, these shots will go slightly over the top of Thomas Henry's tower which is approximately one and one-quarter miles from the position of the cannon."[102]

With the elevation checked, re-checked and the range twice confirmed, the command "fire" is shouted. Smoke bellows and the cannon recoils. Deafening thunder is produced from the barrel. Then silence. Capt. Lee removes his cap and along with the gathering crowd of soldiers all eyes follow the cannon ball as it ascends in to the sky and begins to form the peak of its arching path. As the cannon ball approaches the high point of Thomas Henry's Tower the cannon ball begins its decent as it crests not more than thirty feet over the top of the tower.[103]

The soldiers shout, jump and shake each other's hands. Buck smiles and nods his head in approval to Mr. Rushton. "Looks like a successful shot to me, Mr. Rushton."

"Exactly what we were hoping for, right between twenty and thirty feet from the top of the tower." The remaining two shots are as successful as the first.

The sun is beginning to set beyond the crest of the mountain and the swivel has not yet been the subject of any test. A somewhat modified and hurried trial is performed on its power, range and accuracy. All of the tests are successful.[104]

Buck turns to Mr. Rushton. "Well, it appears that you have developed an advanced gun. Probably unsurpassed by any gun in use today. Congratulations are in order, Mr. Rushton."

Mr. Rushton walks back to the wagon with Buck. "Thank you. You know, Cornelius Hanleiter owns the Franklin Publishing Company."

"Yes, he sold the Atlanta Intelligencer to a group of investors so he could buy the new printing equipment for the Franklin Publishing Company. He is also against secession and so am I, Mr. Rushton. The South cannot be victorious against the North."

"Let's hope that Georgia is prepared for whatever happens."

Buck shakes Mr. Rushton's hand. "Thanks for an enjoyable and educational afternoon." He climbs on his wagon and heads home. Arriving at the house, he sits on the porch and stares at the mountain. Buck raises his fist toward the mountain and shouts, "What are you bringing us next?"

Betty Gail, in the garden, sees him and rests her hoe on the fence. She gets a bucket of water from the well. She enters the house, gets a glass, goes to the porch and sits next to him. "What's all that ruckus going on at the east side of the mountain? I saw all those mules, wagons and cannons heading that way."

"A fellow named William Rushton owns an arms manufacturing company near Atlanta. He was there testing some new cannons. They used the mountain as target practice with the cannons."

"Well, we are at war and the war is gonna get closer to us."

"Yep, I'm already worried about killing and burning. Governor Brown needs to come to his senses and make peace. After supper we need to make plans on how to hide food. First of all, we will fly the Union Flag. This county voted against secession."

NOVEMBER 2, 1861

Betty Gail shifts in the seat and waved to a friend. "Two more stops, Uncle Isaac, and then we can head home. First is the post office to mail this letter to Norman and then to the depot to get a newspaper."

Betty Gail, Polly, and Uncle Isaac have been shopping in town for flour, sugar and salt. The fall day is clear and crisp. The colorful leaves on the trees are holding well this season due to the lack of heavy rain. There's a lot of dust on the buildings in town, so most of the merchants have been keeping the doors and windows closed. When Uncle Isaac stops at the post office, Polly jumps from the wagon and delivers the letter to Mr. Browning, the Postmaster.

"Got a letter for you to mail to Norman, Mr. Browning. You can write a note on the back if you like. I know he would like to hear from everybody in Stone Mountain."

"Thanks Polly, I'll write a line or two and let him know how proud we all are of him at GMI. What else are you and your mama doing in town today?"

"We had dropped off about a half-hogshead of muscadine wine and one barrel of corn syrup at the hospital.[105] Looks like there's about twenty barrels of syrup at the hospital now."

"Hopefully the war will end quickly, and we can close the hospitals around here."

"Ma and I need to get to the depot and pick up a newspaper. You know how much Pa likes his newspapers!"

"Sure do, your pa is really keen on current events. I always enjoy talking with Buck. That man is a walking history book. Say hello to him for me."

"I sure will, Mr. Browning. He's home today salting beef and has some of the other hands picking the last of the peas. I think he is going to put a couple of hogs up to fatten so he can slaughter them before Christmas." Polly waves good-bye and returns to the wagon where her mother and Uncle Isaac are waiting.

Uncle Isaac snaps the reins and turns the wagon toward the depot. As Uncle Isaac pulls up to the entrance of the depot, Polly holds her hat on and jumps off. She goes inside, "Good afternoon Mr. Goldsmith, Pa wants me to buy his regular newspaper."

Mr. Goldsmith points behind himself. "Got a stack of them over here, Polly." He turns, retrieves the top paper and hands it to her.

Polly places a nickel on the counter. "Thanks Mr. Goldsmith. See you in a day or two!"

"Good-bye Polly."

As Polly prepares to board the wagon, she hands the paper to her mother. Betty Gail unfolds it and begins reading intensely. As Uncle Isaac begins to pull away, Betty Gail places her hand on Uncle Isaac's arms, "Hold up a minute. I want to read this about Fort Monroe and General Scott."After a minute or so, she says, "Head on home Isaac, I'll finish the article with Buck at home."

Polly looks over her mother's shoulder. "What are the articles about?"

"General Scott is retiring. Your pa served under General Scott in the war with Mexico. The other is about the blockade. I'm sure we'll discuss the articles after supper."

Polly finds her pa in the barn when they reach home. Uncle Isaac and a couple of other hands help unload the bags of salt. "Pa we could only get two bags of salt.

One fifty pound and one twenty pound. Mr. Winningham said salt is getting scarce and may run out. Got plenty of flour and sugar, though. Ma got you the newspaper. Said there are some good articles, especially one about General Scott."

"It's time to quit for the day. Sally should have supper ready when we get to the house. Let's go, Polly." Buck and Polly head to the house while Isaac puts up the wagon and horse.

Inside the house, Buck glances at his wife. "Hear you got the newspaper, Betty Gail. There's an article about General Scott on page two."

She points to the fireplace where the paper lays. "There's a couple of good articles. Supper is ready."

"We'll sit down after supper and study the news together," replies Buck.

As soon as supper is over, Buck rakes the newspaper from the chair and he and Betty Gail sit next to the fireplace. Polly sits on the floor in front of them. "Well, let's read about all of the excitement you have been telling me at the dinner table." Pausing as he reads the article, he chuckles, "Looks like that ex-governor, Claiborne Jackson, of Missouri, is at it again. He was kicked out in July and now he is trying to have a special meeting of the Confederate Legislature in the Masonic Hall in Neosho. Didn't have a quorum, so the meeting will be held at a later date. He's still trying to get Missouri out of the Union. Those people from Missouri are going to be fighting each other before this war is over. Instead of it being the 'Show me State,' it will be the 'I'll Show You State.'[106] Not much else going on with the war right now."

Turning the page, Buck finds an article concerning Fort Monroe. "This is an interesting article about the navy fleet leaving Fort Monroe, at Hampton Roads. The article says there was a large sea expedition involving seventy-seven ships with several ships carrying twelve thousand Marines for land expedition. The fleet was headed for Port Royal and the Carolina coast. This armada is the largest ever assembled by the United States. The fleet encountered a sudden and violent storm. The storm caused the sinking of a troop transport and the U.S.S. Sabine and damaged several of the other vessels. No Marine lives were lost in the encounter."[107]

Reading a bit further silently, Buck mumbles and then turns to another page. "Here's the article on General Scott you were telling me about."

"Ma said you served with him Pa."

"Yes, I did. Fine man."

"Well read it out loud so we can all know what happened."

On October 31, 1861, General Scott is physically incapacitated and writes President Lincoln;

> *HEADQUARTERS OF THE ARMY,*
> *WASHINGTON, Oct. 31 1861.*
> *The Honorable SIMON CAMERON, Secretary of War.*
>
> *SIR- for more than three years I have been unable, from a hurt, to mount a horse or to walk more than a few paces at a time, and that with*

much pain. Other and new infirmities—dropsy and vertigo—admonish me that repose of mind and body, with the appliances of surgery and medicine, are necessary to add a little more to a life already protracted much beyond the usual span of man.

It is under such circumstances, made doubly painful by the unnatural and unjust rebellion now raging in the Southern States of our so lately prosperous and happy Union, that I am compelled to request that my name be placed on the list of army officers retired from active service. As this request is founded on an absolute right, granted by a recent act of Congress, I am entirely at liberty to say it is with deep regret that I withdraw myself, in these momentous times, from the orders of a President who has treated me with much distinguished kindness and courtesy, whom I know, upon much personal intercourse, to be patriotic,without sectional partialities, or prejudices, to be highly conscientious in the performance of every duty, and of unrivaled activity and perseverance. I remain, Sir, with high respect,

Your obedient servant,

Winfield Scott[108]

President Lincoln and his Cabinet regretfully agree with General Scott's request, "Under the circumstances of his advanced age and infirmities, he cannot be declined." President Lincoln notifies General McClellan, "With the unanimous agreement of the Cabinet, the command of the army is devolved upon you."

At four o'clock in the afternoon the Cabinet again waits upon the President, and attended him to the residence of General Scott. After being seated, the President reads to the General the following order:

THE WHITE HOUSE

On the first day of November, A.D. 1861, upon his own application to the President of the United States, Brevet Lieutenant General Winfield Scott is ordered to be placed, and hereby is placed, upon the list of retired officers of the army of the United States, without reduction in his current pay, subsistence or allowances.

The American people will hear with sadness and deep emotion that General Scott has withdrawn from the active control of the army, while the President and unanimous Cabinet express their own, and the

*Nation's sympathy in his personal affliction, and their profound sense of
the important public services rendered by him to his country during his
long and brilliant career, among which will ever be gratefully distinguished his faithful devotion to the Constitution, Union, and the Flag,
when assailed by parricidal rebellion.*

ABRAHAM LINCOLN
PRESIDENT

General Scott thereupon rose and addressed the President and
Cabinet, who had also risen, as follows:

"Mr. President, Sir, This honor overwhelms me. It overpays all services
I have attempted to render to my country. If I had any claims before, they
are all obliterated by this expression of approval by the President with
the support of the Cabinet. I know the President and this Cabinet well. I
know that the country has placed its interests in this trying crisis in safe
keeping. Their counsels are wise, their labors are as uniting as they are
loyal, and their course is the right one."

"Mr. President you must excuse me. I am unable to stand longer to give
utterance to the feelings of gratitude, which oppress me. In my retirement
I shall offer up my prayers to God for this Administration and for my
country. I shall pray for it with confidence in its success over all enemies,
and that speedily."

President Lincoln responds, "General Scott, you will naturally feel so-
licitude about the gentlemen of your staff, who have rendered you and the
country such faithful service. I have taken that subject into consideration.
I understand that they go with you to New York. I shall desire them, at
this earliest convenience after their return, to make their wishes known to
me. I desire you now, however, to be satisfied that, except the unavoidable,
privation of your counsel and society, which they have so long enjoyed,
the provision, which will be made for them will be such as to render their
situation as agreeable hereafter as it has been heretofore." Each member
of the Administration then gives his hand to the veteran, and retires in
profound silence.

Buck lowers the paper and rocks a bit. He leans over and tells Polly
and Betty Gail, "When I served under General Scott, during the War
with Mexico I knew he would go down in history as one of the greatest
generals in America and by far the greatest general up to now! He served
America for around," Buck starts figuring on his fingers, "forty-seven years.

That's longer than any other person in American history. His first tour was under President Jefferson and his last, President Lincoln. That means he has served under," Buck and Polly begin counting the presidents.

Polly says, "Lincoln makes fourteen presidents, Pa!"

"Let me think Polly, General Scott was the commanding officer in the War of 1812, the Mexican-American War, the Black Hawk War, the Second Seminole War and started out in this war. I guess if you count this war that is a total of five wars in which General Scott was the commanding officer.[109] If Norman comes halfway to General Scott, America, or the Confederate States, will have another great soldier. I think Norman is made of the same stuff."

"So do I, Pa! Norman is a mighty calm person with lots of self-confidence. He studies and it takes a lot to shake him up!"

ELOPING NOVEMBER 8, 1861

Legare and his father arrive by train to Stone Mountain. Congressman Hill has some business to attend to with the Dents concerning the new furnishings in the hotel. Legare and his father go inside the depot while waiting for their baggage.

"Good day!" exclaims James Goldsmith, the station agent, as he waves to the Hills. Continuing William asks, "Have you heard the news?"

"What news, William?" asks Congressman Hill.

"The news about Polly and Buster. They are to be married."

"Well I'm proud for them. I'm sure we have an invitation at home. We've been staying between Atlanta and Milledgeville most of the time, trying to deal with this terrible war. I know Buck and Betty Gail are very proud and happy."

The news of Polly's approaching marriage to Buster Phillips is not what Legare wants to hear. His face flushes angrily, and the blood receding leaves it deadly pale. He's just returned from a trip to Milledgeville with his father, and came to Stone Mountain to visit Polly.

As Congressman Hill and Legare pass by the Jernigan's, they see Buck at a distance. Buck waves for them to come over. Congressman Hill and Legare are always welcome with the Jernigans, as well as every Stone Mountain home. The small farmers of the district and the wealthy owners of broad plantations appreciate the work their Congressman has done. In particular, the Hills are frequently seen at the Jernigan's. The grateful heart of Mrs. Jernigan has banished every doubt of conflict, and she lavishes the hospitality of her simple home upon Legare. Georgie has long since claimed Legare for his own. Old Uncle Isaac's never failing, "Howdy, Mars' Hill and Mars' Legare, des xpecting you," is a most familiar greeting.

"I understand congratulations are in order for an upcoming wedding."

Buck nods. "Yep, coming up soon, Polly and Buster."

Buck and Joshua have engaged in many long and anxious talks about the political questions of the day and today is no exception. The mutterings of the coming storm of civil war is disturbing to even this secluded spot.

Polly, always sweet and gentle, seems to be avoiding Legare. She flushes and pales beneath his inviting and loving gaze. During each warm summer day, Polly has been drooping like a wilted flower and goes listlessly about her household tasks. Buck cannot figure out why Polly is so quiet and temperamental.

"What ails the gal? She gets punier and punier every day."

"I think it might be the birds and the bees!"

"So long as it is Buster bee, that's okay!"

Buck is on his porch when he sees Congressman Hill and Legare enter their yard. He steps from the porch. "What brings you and Legare to these parts today?"

"Gotta meet with Eliza and Hugh Dent. Had a little work done on the hotel, and I need to pay my part of the bills. Business is getting slow though and all of us have concern for keeping it open."

Buck admires the horse Legare is riding. He dismounts and hands the reins to Uncle Isaac. Buck takes Legare's hand. "Good to see you son. Mighty fine mount you got there."

"Thank you, sir," and smiles at Buck's words. Legare closes his eyes briefly and imagines himself sitting with the Jernigan family—as a real part of the family. He could hardly breathe for a moment. If only that were possible. Nothing could make him happier.

"Legare and I better mosey along to the hotel before dark. Have a good evening."

Legare takes to his mount and his father to the carriage. Buck tips his hat and, reining the horses, Legare and his father canter the horses up the mountain.

As they ride to the front entrance of the hotel, the odor of fresh paint overpowers the sweet smells of the forest. The building stands resplendent in a fresh coat of white with crimson facings. The green shutters compliment the changing forest leaves. John and Hugh Dent are on the veranda talking with some of the guests when Congressman Hill and Legare arrive. The Dents are delighted and eager to visit them. Hugh and John jump from the porch to greet their friends, taking the reins and securing the horses.

"Hello, Congressman Hill, Legare. I hope your trip was good," says John with a smile. Hugh summons one of the stablemen over to take the horses as Congressman Hill and Legare dismount from the buggy.

"Glad to see both of you." Hugh extends his hand. "I hope you like the new paint job on the hotel. It was almost too late in the year to paint but the weather has been warmer than usual."

He gestures at the hotel edifice. "Brightens the place up a lot and the color of the shutters really makes the hotel stand out. How is your mother?"

"She is just fine and making sure supper is ready for the guests and us, of course. There are a few guests, men from the neighboring city, playing cards. They hope to make expenses by fleecing the inexperienced gentlemen from the plantations."

"Most of the plantation owners have great self-confidence. The gamblers will bet against the plantation owner's inexperience and self-confidence. I hope you make them check their guns when they arrive." They both laugh.

Some of the guests recognize Congressman Hill and engage him in a conversation about the war effort. Congressman Hill gladly shares what he knows and then moves inside to visit with Mrs. Dent.

"It's good to see you, Joshua." Eliza approaches, wiping her hands on her apron. "Where is Legare?"

"He's outside talking to John. They are catching up."

Eliza and Joshua make their way to the sitting room, take comfortable chairs and continue their conversation. "And, Emily, how is she? I was hoping she would come along and stay a few days."

"We still have five children at home younger than Legare. Keeps her plenty busy. I figured you would have the boys looking after the place."

"I just came up a couple of days ago to see how they were doing with the paint job. I plan on departing tomorrow or the next day."

"Well, after supper we can talk about how much money I owe for the expenses of the hotel."

"It's not very much. Hugh keeps a good set of books and watches the money closely. Just not many visitors this summer like last year. The war and all, you know. If it doesn't do better next year, we probably should close the hotel down for a while."

"Hugh has good business sense like his father. Whatever the two of you decide will be satisfactory with me. Let's hope the war is over by then and peace returns to our country."

"Amen to that."

After supper Legare excuses himself and strolls out into the moonlight. He looks toward the mountaintop, now bathed in a flood of silver light. Far down below, Legare sees the twinkling of a light in Polly's house. He wonders if she is still awake. Thinking of his love, the one woman whom the wide world holds for him, Legare drops onto the bare rock, still warm from the sun, and buries his face in his hands. Honor forbade him to interfere with her upcoming marriage. Prudence whispers that their social spheres are different. At the close of every one of Legare's arguments, Polly's radiant face smiles at him. Her lovely brown eyes seem to shower love into his own. Words are not necessary, although he has not spoken a syllable which could betray his feelings. Legare knows Polly loves him. All he needs to do is figure out how to get her to admit it and break her engagement.

Exhausted from his sleepless night on the mountain, Legare finally lays his head upon the warm granite with his last thought. "Come what may, Polly shall be mine." And then he falls asleep. Strange fancies vex his slumber, the outcome, no doubt, of the depressing events of the past days and his hope for the future. So realistic is the dream that it lingers in his mind long after he awakens. Legare arrives at the hotel as daylight is peaking on the Eastern horizon with a pink and gold sunrise.

Sitting on the porch Joshua watches his son approach from the mountain path. "Where were you last night, son?"

"Took a walk and fell asleep on the mountain," answers Legare. Even though he and his father are close, he doesn't feel he can discuss his feelings about Polly.

"You have been mighty quiet since we arrived in Stone Mountain. Is something bothering you?"

"Nothing I can't handle, Father."

"Anything I can help you with?"

Legare looks at his father. "No, sir, this problem is all mine to solve!"

Legare goes to his hotel room to take a short nap. After awakening, he spends the day with John and Hugh. They climb the mountain together and gaze out over the beautiful forest joking and laughing, but Legare's thoughts are focused on Polly as he sees her little farm house in the distance. The fall colors are exceptionally bright and fill his mind with the grandeur and beauty of nature as well as his love. He won't soon forget these moments on the mountain, thinking of Polly.

John points to an area on the mountain. "Legare, isn't that the spot you rescued Polly's cousin?"

"A little more towards us is where we came up."

"Everybody was really proud of you that day."

"Just glad I could help." Seeing Polly for the first time flashes in Legare's mind. Soon the afternoon shadows begin to elongate and the young men head back to the hotel for supper.

Supper is a jovial occasion with his friends, but Legare feels he has to get away alone. He waits for an opportunity and then steals away from the hotel. He wanders onto a path through the woods and surprises a fox along the way. Lost in the tranquility of the evening, he is all the more eager to find a way out of his dilemma. He's wandering where his feet lead him when he reaches a crystal clear creek at the base of the mountain. He sits quietly and, after a while, stretches himself full length upon its mossy bank, imagining what life with Polly might be like. Closing his eyes, he tries to shape some kind of plan for him and Polly. He comes to no definite conclusion, but realizes he must see her. He feels an urge to follow a tugging at his heartstrings and walks in the direction of the Jernigan's farmhouse. As Legare begins to walk the path from the creek, to his surprise he finds Polly standing on the other side of the creek.[110]

His heart pounds as he leaps the small creek and rushes to Polly's side. Now that he's with her, he has no idea what to say. Finally, he manages to speak. "Some kind angel must have sent you here in answer to my prayers."

"I've just come from a neighbor's." She takes his out-stretched hand, looks at him with her beautiful, but sad, brown eyes. "Have you heard the news about my wedding?"

"Yes, Polly," he answers with a low voice. "Shall I congratulate you? "

Polly's lips turn down. She takes a deep breath and tears begin to flow, glistening on her checks.

"If you love Buster and wish to marry him, I'll leave Stone Mountain tomorrow morning." Legare musters all his courage and takes her hand. "But something tells me—something here." He places his and Polly's hand upon his heart. "Oh, Polly don't you know how much I love you! Can't you tell when you look into my eyes?" He gathers her in his arms as her tears turn into an uncontrollable weeping. She rests her head on his chest in silent acknowledgement of their love for one another.

Legare's heart breaks to see her in such distress. Their situation seems hopeless. The honorable approach would be for him to escort her home safely, wish her happiness on her upcoming marriage and walk out of her life—forever. He simply cannot do that. His own heart is breaking, and he knows hers must be. But to act any differently would bring shame to both families.

He looks down at her and lifts her chin. In the soft moonlight, she stares up at him, her love apparent in her gaze. "Polly, I consider myself an honorable man, but I cannot just wish you well and walk away. I adore you and would have you rip my still-beating heart from my chest before I would see you marry another."

Polly reaches up and caresses his cheek. "Oh, Legare … what answer is there for two people in our situation? What can we do?"

Sobs wrack her cheeks as she buries her face against his chest. "Shh … Polly, my love. We will be together. I have a plan."

All of the emotional obstacles evaporate. Polly regains her composure and the two sit on the mossy creek bank. She wipes away her tears. "Legare, what will Pa and Ma say if I let them know I don't want to marry Buster?"

He rises and walks a few steps away. The anguish in her voice is enough to break his heart. She has always been a good daughter and, what he's asking of her, will make her view herself otherwise. But to ignore their feelings is something he cannot do. He returns to her side, takes her hand and helps her to rise. They walk slowly through the woods, fearful yet solemnly discussing their dilemma as they approach her home. Together, they stand on the edge of a clearing under a wide spreading oak, sheltered by beautiful fall leaves. Moonlight drifts through the falling leaves as he kisses her, an enduring kiss that holds promises of more.

"Good-night, my darling, Polly. Bring your necessities, dress as a boy and meet me here tomorrow at midnight." They embrace again, much longer this time, with a kiss full of fire. Reluctantly, he releases her and watches her graceful form until she enters her father's gate. With the heart of a cupid, Legare sprints like a deer up the mountain, scurrying back to the hotel to make final preparations.

The following morning, Congressman Hill finds Legare on the porch, deep in thought. "I am departing for Atlanta and will return sometime tomorrow. You're welcome to come along or stay in Stone Mountain to visit with your friends."

Unable to believe his luck, Legare replies hastily, "I'll stay!"

⚘

Around midnight, Polly and Legare approach the small one room log cabin of Uncle Isaac and Aunt Sally. Uncle Isaac and Aunt Sally are awakened by a quiet knocking on their windowpane. Uncle Isaac jumps up, lights his candle and rushes to the window. Seeing Polly, he opens his window and places a stick to hold the window in place. "Miss Polly what is you doing up dis late?"

"Uncle Isaac, I'm running away with Legare. I have loved him from the moment I first laid my eyes on him. I just want you and Aunt Sally to know that I am all right. I know Ma, Pa and Norman will worry, but I hold your word not to speak a word to them or anybody else about this."

Aunt Sally looks on, and Uncle Isaac tells Polly with a loving smile, "O, Lordy, me know'd all 'long 'bout des. What took you so long? Now jus' git. Wes ain't saw nuffin! God bess you!" Polly reaches through the small window and hugs and kisses Uncle Isaac and Aunt Sally good-bye. Legare grasps Uncle Isaac and Aunt Sally's hands and squeezes them gently. Then, without saying another word, Legare and Polly, holding hands, slip off into the dark.

As they approach Legare's horse, Polly turns to view the dark outline of her home and begins to weep. She takes a last look of the surrounds of her happy childhood and family, then Legare whispers, "Come, dearest, we've got to ride, or we'll miss the train. You'll see them all again another day, I promise."

Polly sobs quietly. "Never again. Ma and Pa will be changed, or they will be indifferent to me." Legare places her gently in the saddle, climbs on himself, and the horse soon takes them out of sight.

Finally, they reach the stables near the depot. Legare leaves a note on the horse for Mr. Levi. "Please deliver the horse to my father when he returns to town. Legare Hill." They hurry toward the depot where the train is waiting to depart. It is late and no one is at the ticket window. Polly, dressed in her "young man outfit," and Legare board the train. They should be in Augusta by morning.

Legare hands Polly some money. "When the conductor ask you for your ticket, just give him two dollars and just say, 'Augusta please.'"

"I have money. Hold on to yours."

There are only a few other passengers on board, so Polly and Legare take separate seats across from each other. Soon the conductor gives the lantern signal to the engineer that all are on board. With several strong chugs from the engine boiler, the train eases from the depot, on its familiar journey to Augusta.

Once the trip is under way, the conductor passes through the car and asks Polly, "Where to young man?"

Polly hesitates for a moment and says in her deepest voice, "Augusta."

"That will be seven dollars and seventy five cents please, sir."[111] Polly hands the conductor a ten dollar gold piece. He gives her change and a paid ticket to Augusta. "My name is Allen; if you need anything just let me know."

Polly smiles and nods her head. She smiles and gives Legare a little wink. They begin their lives together, a daring chapter of love and adventure. Polly knows the future holds a reckoning ahead for her. One day, she and Legare will have to face their parents. But, for now, life is wonderful and exciting—and full of promise.

⟩⟨

The Jernigan family is astir early in the morning. Around 9:00, Buck is excited about the day's events and is anxious to see his daughter. "Why is Polly sleeping so late?"

"Let the child alone," replies Betty Gail. "I'll wake her shortly."

Soon Sally has breakfast on the table, and Betty Gail goes to Polly's room and taps on the door. There's no answer. She taps again a little louder and calls, "Polly, breakfast is ready. Remember Buster is coming over to have breakfast with us this morning." Still no answer. Suspiciously, she opens the door and peeks inside. She does not see Polly, but the bed is made. Betty Gail throws open the door and shouts for Buck. "Come quick! Polly's gone."

Anguish and surprise renders Buck speechless. Uncle Isaac and Aunt Sally stay quiet in the kitchen. Almost at the same time, Buster knocks at the front door. Uncle Isaac answers the door, and Aunt Sally is standing still and quiet in the dining room.

Buster, not taking notice of their stoical posture, smilingly says, "Good morning Uncle Isaac and Aunt Sally. Mighty fine day. Where is everybody?"

"'orning Mars Buster," replies Uncle Isaac while pointing to the back of the house. Looking in the direction which Uncle Isaac has just pointed, Buster sees Buck come rushing to the kitchen with Betty Gail not far behind. Standing still, Buster takes in the situation at a glance.

"Whoever he is, and I think I know," Buck shouts, shaking his fist in the air. "Let him take my curse and as for this unthankful and disobedient daughter—"

"Oh no! No! Mars' Buck," cries Uncle Isaac, "Don't curse da little gal. Me carried in these ol' arm."

Betty Gail puts her hand upon his lips to keep back the dreadful words, and weeps aloud.

Shocked and pale Buster screams, "If he's wronged her, if he wronged de gal I love and we live to meet, one of us shall die!"

Aunt Sally and Uncle Isaac look at each other sadly. Uncle Isaac says nervously, "Vengeance belongeth to de Lord. You turn de other cheek, Mars' Buster."

Immediately Buck takes his rifle, mounts his horse and gallops up toward the hotel. At the front entrance, Buck dismounts and spots Hugh Dent on the verandah. "Where's Legare Hill? Is he with Polly?"

Mrs. Dent hears the commotion from the hotel study where she is examining the day's receipts and rushes onto the porch. "What's troubling you, Buck?"

"Polly's missing. Not home all night. I think she and Legare done run off somewhere!"

"Legare was not here all night. His father is in Atlanta, and we expect him back sometime today to finish up some business here. I'll tell Joshua you need to see with him as soon as he returns."

"Do that for me, Mrs. Dent. Much obliged to y'all. If you see my daughter or Legare, best warn them I'm a disturbed man!" Buck turns his mount and heads down the mountain, still in search of his daughter and Legare.

"Hugh, you best high tail it to the depot and wait for Joshua. Let him know what's happening. Mr. Jernigan is not a happy man right now."

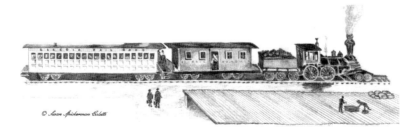

© Susan Spickerman Colelli

Hugh is waiting at the depot as the afternoon train arrives in Stone Mountain. He sees Congressman Hill standing in the passenger car and greets him as he steps from the train. Looking somewhat puzzled, Congressman Hill asks, "Hello Hugh, what brings you here? Is something wrong? Is everyone all right?"

"Well, sir, as far as I know everyone is all right, but Mr. Jernigan came to the hotel this morning. Looks like Polly and Legare ran off sometimes during the night. Mr. Jernigan is mighty upset. You probably should stop by his farm. He wants to see you as soon as you arrive."

"I was afraid something like this was going to happen. Legare has loved Polly since he laid eyes on her. Let me fetch my buggy and try and smooth Buck's feathers a bit. I know he and Betty Gail are, or were, excited about Polly and Buster's upcoming wedding. "

Congressman Hill and Hugh rush to the Jernigan farm. Buck sees the dust from the buggy and steps from the porch as Congressman Hill pulls to a stop. Hugh takes the reins as Joshua steps down from the carriage. "I hear we are missing two young 'uns."

Looking sternly at Joshua, Buck replies, "Yep ran off during the night. I've searched these woods, been all over the mountain and creeks. Not a sight or sound of them anywhere."

"I am heartily sorry and share the strain and anxiety caused by the actions of these two children. If we all think about it, we all have been bearing witness to the romantic looks Polly and Legare have given each other."

"If your son has violated my daughter, he is going to be full of buck-shot!" replies Buck with Betty Gail austerely gazing at Joshua and Hugh.

Joshua, in a neighborly manner looks straight at Buck. "Buck, my son would not violate your daughter, for he has the utmost respect for her as well as respect for you and Betty Gail. There's no telling where they are right now. They are going to have to show up sooner or later and face the consequences. I'll share with you any information I obtain and will count on you to do the same."

12

A NEW DAWN

The train reaches Covington and stops at the station. Legare watches the conductor talk to another conductor on the platform. The two conductors shake hands. The conductor, Allen who was on the train with Polly and Legare, disappears into the depot. Only Polly and Legare are in this particular passenger car. Legare quickly moves over next to her. "Let your hair down now. A new conductor is coming on board."

Polly removes her straw hat quickly. She then removes the hairpins and her beautiful long hair falls to her back. Now Legare and Polly are sitting next to each other as the new conductor, Chip, waves the lantern to the engineer. As the train departs, Legare holds Polly's hand, looks her directly in the eyes. "Polly, I'll always love you!"

"I have loved you from the moment I first laid eyes upon you, Legare."

As the train continues toward Augusta, the monotonous clickety-click of the train wheels passing over the track produces a hypnotic effect. Holding each other's hands, Polly and Legare fall asleep with her head resting on his shoulder.

The jerking of the train stopping in Augusta suddenly awakens the two lovers. Legare opens his eyes. "Looks like we are in Augusta, Polly."

She raises her head up, places her hand over her mouth, and yawns. She and Legare stand up and stretch their arms upward and out to relieve their bodies from the stiffness of their sleep. Placing their hands on the window sill, they peer outside into the morning sun to investigate their Augusta surroundings.

Picking up the luggage, they move to the back of the passenger car and descend the steps and face a chilly Augusta morning. Chip, the conductor, assists Polly as she places her foot on the ladies step and onto the station platform. Polly tightens her coat to keep the cool morning air from filtering through her clothes to her warm body.

As she studies the crowd, Polly sees young couples probably the same age as she and Legare. She wonders if any of those young couples are eloping. If they are, she hopes they love each other as much as she and Legare.

Legare steps from the train with a broad smile and takes Polly's hand. "There are several hotels on Broad Street. The best one is the Augusta Hotel. Augusta has private baths and running hot water. We'll stop by there first and, if you like it, we'll stay there. If not, we'll find a hotel you like. Then we will find the local Baptist preacher and get married! How does that sound to you, Polly?"

She blushes. "Let's go take a look at the Augusta. I need to freshen up a bit before our wedding."

"The hotel is a couple of blocks from here. We probably can walk just about as fast as waiting to get a carriage. What do you want to do Polly?"

Polly takes his hand and glances at their strange surroundings. A sense of adventure fills her and she can't wait for events to unfold. "Let's walk. The fresh cool air feels good and will help wake us up."

Legare picks up their luggage and they depart the Georgia Railroad platform and head for the hotel. As they stroll down Broad Street, the city is still quiet. Tall, stone buildings line both sides of Broad Street, some probably five stories in height.

"People say that Broad Street is the widest street in all of America."[112]

"Well, it is plenty wide for sure. Nothing like it in Atlanta!" replies Polly.

They pass by the principle office building for the cotton merchants. The banks have not opened. Several darkies are out early sweeping the sidewalks in front of various buildings. As Polly and Legare pass by, they render a good morning to each other. The theater marquee displays the latest stage production, a concert featuring many of Mozart's works.

"Here's the Georgia Railroad Bank Building. My father owns stock in the Georgia Railroad. Look at the twin stone columns on each side."

"They are beautiful. The Greek architecture all along Broad Street is beautiful."

"Isn't Augusta where Lyman Hall and George Walton are buried?" asks Polly. "Two of Georgia's three signers of the Declaration of Independence."

"Yes, I believe so." Legare stops and glances around. "Here we are. Let's see if you like it or not."

Polly looks at the stately exterior as they climb the several steps to entrance. As they reach the door, a butler wearing a red velvet coat and top hat opens the door for them. "Good morning."

Polly and Legare exchange greetings with him and enter the lobby. The lobby has marble floors covered with oriental rugs. Grand gas light chandeliers sway from the ceiling. The walls have large beautiful oils depicting scenes of early America, early Augusta and Georgia. Legare and Polly approach the front desk and observe paintings of Washington and Jefferson hanging on the wall behind the desk.

"Could I help you, sir?" asks the clerk.

"Yes," replies Legare. "My wife and I would like to view one of your suites if possible." Polly turns her head toward Legare, smiles and takes his hand.

"Yes, sir. Just give me a moment while I look over the room list. There's one on the second floor with a private bath and hot water. Here is the key sir. The stairs to the right will take you to the second floor. Then turn right. The suite is the last room."

Taking the key, Legare asks the clerk, "May I leave my luggage here?"

"That will be fine sir."

"Thank you. We will be back in a few minutes." Polly and Legare climb the marble staircase to the second floor and turn right and find the suite. He unlocks the door and allows her to enter first. The suite is large, probably twenty by thirty with the bath additional. The bathtub is copper and has a little side-arm gas furnace attached at one end. It has the shape of a shoe like the French and English models. The water in the tub flows and circulates backwards until the entire bath is heated to satisfaction.

There's a table and four chairs, two comfortable cushion chairs, a coffee table and a large wardrobe. The headboard of the bed is massive with beautiful designs and constructed from maple. The wooden floors are accented with small oriental rugs. Legare walks with Polly and they open the tall blue cotton draperies partially covering a large window. The view overlooks the Savannah River and the many steamers full of cotton.

"I like the suite, Legare. Let's take it."

He kisses her. "I'll go down, check us in and bring the baggage up." Legare dashes downstairs and informs the clerk that the suite is satisfactory. He signs the registration card.

A bellman approaches. "Would you like for me to assist you with the luggage sir?"

"Please." Picking up the luggage, Legare and the bellman go to the room. Legare is a little embarrassed. He knocks on the door. Polly opens it and smiles. "I left the key in the room by mistake."

The bellman places the luggage on racks. "Is there anything else I can assist you with sir?"

Legare hands the bellman a tip. "Thank you. That will be all for now." The bellman departs. "Polly while you freshen up, I'll go down the hall to the common bath to shave and wash up."

"I'll see you in a few minutes." They kiss lingeringly, and Legare leaves the room. He hastens down the hall to the common bath to bathe.

Returning to the room, Legare finds Polly combing her hair. "Almost ready Legare, just a few more strokes."

Legare approaches Polly from behind and places his arms tightly around her waist. Pushing her hair away from her cheek he kisses her and whispers, "I love you, Polly Jernigan and I'm hungry and we need to get a set of rings and we need to find a preacher—straight away."

"Straight away is the word of the day! Let's get started!" She kisses Legare again.

They go to the hotel dining area. The hostess escorts them to a table near a window. "Is this satisfactory sir?"

"All right with you, Polly?"

"Fine, thank you."

After breakfast, they walk down Broad Street looking for a jewelry store. Not too far away, they find a small one with a window displaying a large assortment of engagement rings and wedding bands. They study the display, and Legare hugs her close. "Do you see a wedding band you like?"

Polly tucks her hand in his. "This is a gift from you. You pick. You're a gift to me, and I'll pick your wedding band. How does that sound?"

"Well, Polly, you already have me wrapped around your finger for life. A wedding ring you pick out for me will give me two beautiful objects to look at and cherish for the rest of my life." He hugs her, tasting her hot breath, feeling her soft body nestled in his arm, her heartbeat strong and fast. With a smile he opens the door for her and follows her in.

A well-dressed gentleman pops out of a door in back. "Good morning to my first customers of the day. What can I do for you?"

Legare and Polly respond, "Good morning sir!"

Legare continues, "We're getting married today and would like to purchase a set of wedding bands."

Looking at them the salesman smiles. "You are a beautiful couple. I think I can help you. Follow me down to the other display case." Upon reaching the display case, the jeweler removes several trays of wedding bands. "Now you take your time deciding. You'll have to wear these for the rest of your lives, so I want you to be happy with your decision."

Legare and Polly each picks up and examines several different styles while the jeweler silently attends to some of his paper work. Soon Polly finds a ring she feels suitable for Legare. "I have chosen this gold ring for you, Legare. See it has a bold gold ridge border around both edges. To me the ridges represent your sound and honest character."

Legare examines the ring and tries it on. "I love it. I picked the ring I like for you immediately. This one stood out like it was calling me to pick it up." Legare hands Polly the gold band. "See how the exceptional width magnifies the beautiful and strong design of the band and at the same time compliments your strengths and beauty. This is why I chose this band for you."

Polly slides the ring on and gazes at it for a moment.

"Fits perfect." Polly admires her ring with a broad smile.

"We've made our choices sir and are ready to settle up."

The jeweler comes over and takes the two rings. "Beautiful choices. You both have good taste."

"How much do we owe you?" asks Legare.

"Six dollars each."

Polly looks at the jeweler. "He'll pay for mine, and I'll pay for his. That way they are gifts from each of us and we never can ask for them back."

The jeweler nods his head in agreement. "May your life be filled with happiness, success and good health. God bless you both." Legare shakes hands with the jeweler, thanks him for his kind words, and they depart.

Outside, Augusta seems to have come to life. Horses and carriages are moving along Broad Street, and pedestrians are becoming more apparent. "It's around 10:30, Polly, and the Baptist preacher should be up and about by now. The church is on Green Street. Let's take a carriage there."

Shortly, a carriage passes in their direction and Legare waves to the driver. "Are you for hire?" asks Legare.

"Yes sir. Where would you like to go?"

"Take us to the Baptist Church on Green Street." After a short ride, they arrive. Standing in front of the rectory, they read a plaque; On May 8-12, 1845 the Southern Baptist Convention was founded at this Church. Its first president was William B. Johnson. The mission of the Southern Baptist Convention was to preserve the religious foundation for human slavery.[113]

"Well, looks like we are getting married in a historical place," says Legare.

"Our historical moment in a historical place."

They enter the rectory. "May I help you?" asks a lady sitting at a desk.

Legare hugs Polly and nods. "Yes, we would like to know if the pastor is available to marry us this morning."

"Why I'm sure he'll be delighted to marry such a lovely couple. Just give me a moment, and I'll locate him for you. His name is Rev. A. J. Huntington.[114] Have a seat if you would like."

In a few minutes, Rev. Huntington appears, and the receptionist introduces him to Polly and Legare. "My receptionist has notified me you would like to be married this morning."

"Yes, sir, we would," replies Legare.

"Are any family members coming? Do you have a best man and maid of honor?"

"No, sir, just me and Polly," Legare informs the pastor laughingly. "I'm the Best Man. That's why Polly is marrying me and Polly is the maid of honor and that's why I'm marrying her!"

Rev. Huntington and his secretary laugh at Legare's comments. "I guess you're right on that matter, son. If you would please give us your names and addresses so your marriage can be placed in the Church Records."

"My name is Hugh Legare Hill. I'm from Madison."

"My name is Polly Jernigan. I'm from Stone Mountain."

Rev. Huntington studies Legare for a moment. "You wouldn't be kin to Congressman Hill, would you, son?"

"Yes sir. He's my father. Polly and I are eloping."

"Your father is a courageous man, and so are you. Well, let's go into the Chapel for the wedding ceremony. If it is all right, I'll have my secretary as the witness to your marriage."

"It will be a pleasure to have your secretary as our witness."

The four enter the Chapel and approach the altar. The sun shines brightly through the windows of the chapel, producing a very enlightening atmosphere. Rev. Huntington starts the wedding ceremony with a prayer. Polly and Legare bow their heads. As Rev. Huntington prays, Polly's wish is her Ma, Pa and Norman, and Legare's family, could be here and be happy for them. She silently prays they will forgive her for running away to be married.

Tears begin to flow down Polly cheeks as Rev. Huntington ends the prayer. Seeing Polly's tears, Rev. Huntington, asks, "Are you all right, Polly?"

"Yes, sir, one eye is shedding tears of joy, and the other eye is shedding tears of sadness for I wish our families were here with us." Legare wipes away Polly's tears. Teary eyed and yet smiling they stand hand in hand placing rings on each other's fingers. Repeating the eternal love vows, Polly and Legare end with, "to love and to cherish till death do us part." Then they seal their vows with a kiss.

Legare thanks Rev. Huntington and his secretary, and offers to pay the Rev. Huntington, but he refuses to accept any money. "It is my gift to you for being the son of a great statesman."

Thanking the Rev. Huntington, Polly and Legare depart the chapel and begin walking back to the hotel, hoping to wave down a passing carriage. When they reach Broad Street, Augusta has turned into a busy town.

Passing by a cafe Legare suggests to Polly, "It's dinner time Polly. I think we should eat before returning to the hotel."

Smiling Polly takes Legare's arm and pulls him closer. "Yes, I want a full meal, because I doubt if we get any supper."

Following their dinner, they decide to walk the four blocks to the hotel. They arrive around three o'clock and Legare goes to the front desk and orders two steak suppers with champagne to be delivered to their room around 7:30. They go up the stairs, and he unlocks the door. He picks up her in his arms. She smiles and places one arm around his neck and one hand on his shoulder as they enter their honeymoon suite. He closes the door with his foot and carries her to the bed. Gently laying Polly on the bed, he kisses her with deep emotion and passion.

"I'll be back in a moment." Polly gets up and goes to her luggage. "I have a special gown I want to wear for our honeymoon." Polly turns and enters the separate room with the claw foot bathtub.

Legare takes his fresh clothes from the luggage and departs for the common bath area down the hall. In a few moments, he returns to the room and awaits Polly.

As Polly emerges from the dressing room, Legare takes her hand. "Polly, I love you. Our life together will now begin."

Legare gently takes her hand, looking down into her face. They embrace and touch their lips together, melting their souls together in their first real kiss as a married couple.

"You are mine, Legare, and I am yours." Polly snuggles closer to him than she has even been.

"Forever, Polly." Legare inhales the soft, sweet scent of her hair. "We have a lifetime before us. This moment is just the first of many beautiful memories we will make together."

Throughout the night, Polly and Legare, share themselves in the dreamy state of their wedding night until the sunlight beckons them to rise. They awaken to an Augusta that has already begun its day. From the hotel window, Legare see the four hundred ton steamer Talamicco at the docks on the Savannah River.[115] "Polly, Let's take that steamer rather than the train to Savannah. The trips on the river are very scenic, even this time of year. We probably can eat on the steamer as well."

At the dock, he seeks out the captain, Captain C. R. Powell. "Sir, my wife and I would like to purchase a ticket to Savannah if you have room on board."

"Why sure, there are ten cabins for guests. Most of them are empty this time of year. Take cabin number five. The keys should be in the door. It has a private bath and is the largest cabin on the steamer. We make a couple of stops and should arrive in Savannah about this time tomorrow. We serve hot meals and have plenty of duck right now. The Petersburg boats are docking and we have several hundred more bales of cotton to load, so if you want to come back in about an hour, we'll be ready to depart. I'll give three long blasts of the horn to let you know the steamer will be leaving in fifteen minutes."

"Thank you, sir."

"Leave you luggage with me for now. You can put it in the cabin when you board."

Legare hands over the luggage to the Captain. "Thanks again, sir."

After the newlyweds leave their belongings on the steamer, they walk along the riverfront. "See those long, open-face boats, Polly? They are the Petersburg boats. From what I understand, the Petersburg boats transport the cotton from further up the river. The Savannah River is navigable for shallow draft and barge traffic from its mouth to Augusta but ocean vessels can only travel five miles above Savannah,"

"I've heard of the Petersburg boats, but never even seen a drawing of one."

"It's kind of slow on the river and the wharf right now, being it's winter. Even the cotton warehouses are not weighing much cotton. Let's go ahead and board." He takes her hand and they walk onto the gangplank. The side rails are solid, but the gangplank shakes a little as they walk to the main deck. They locate cabin five and enter.

"Watch your step, Polly. There's a high ledge under the door. Helps keep the rain water on the deck from entering the cabin." She steps into the cabin and is surprised at the small fixtures and furniture.

"This almost looks like a doll house! It's so cute and quaint and really pretty." She walks over to the porthole and peers to the other side of the river. She decides to have a seat at the small table in the cabin. When she sits down she attempts to move the table a bit and finds that it is bolted to the floor. "Why is the table bolted to the floor, Legare?"

"Everything on board a ship is secured in case of a storm." He takes her hand. "Come over here. Try to open this drawer." She places her hand on the drawer handle and pulls, but to no avail.

"Lift up the drawer handle and then pull."

Polly follows his instructions. The drawer comes open. "Pretty good trick! Come over here and sit with me a minute Legare. I need to talk to you." She takes his hand and they sit on the side of the small bed. "Where are we going to live?"

"My mother and father have a beautiful home on the river in Savannah. I thought we could live there."

"Think about it, Legare. We are in a pickle. There's no telling what is going on in Stone Mountain and Madison. Might even be a lynch mob looking for both of us. Now I love your mother and father, but we have just eloped. You're taking me to live in your parent's river house without their permission. I don't think that is a wise move. I feel that we would be insulting your family if we did that. Moving there without their permission would not make them at all happy. Think about it for a moment. I have all my money with me. We need to find our own place to live."

Legare is silent for a few seconds. "You're absolutely right, Polly. We will stay at the Pulaski Hotel, if you like it, in Savannah until we rent our own place. I have money in the bank in Savannah from my working with Uncle Richard every summer. He always told me to save my money for a rainy day. So that's what we will do." Legare pulls Polly close, feeling her warm body against his as he hugs her tightly and kisses her lips.

"I love you, Legare, but we best get breakfast before we have dessert! I'm starving."

Still holding Polly, Legare whispers in her ear. "I love you, too, Polly. Let's go to the cafe across the street from the docks. It looks like a popular place to eat."

Just as Legare is paying for the breakfast, Polly turns her head toward the wharf. "Is that the steamer's signal?"

"Yep, that's our fifteen minutes call to board."

Standing on the main deck of the streamer, Polly and Legare watch the shore man release the large anchor ropes from the pier. The deck hands draw in the heavy rope and stow it in a designated area. The paddle wheel slowly begins to turn, moving the giant ship from the pier as if she was a baby.

"This is going to be a beautiful day, Polly. We should see some grand sights on the river."

The steamer picks up speed as she slowly moves away from the congested area of the docks. Most of the crew is engaged in the routine duties of maintaining the equipment and cargo. Standing at the rear of the steamer, Polly and Legare watch the paddle wheel push the boat farther from Augusta until Augusta disappears into the mist almost as if by magic. Now, only a few Petersburg boats and small boats with fisherman can be seen on the river.

Yawning and taking a deep breath, Polly whispers, "I need to take a nap. Let's go to the cabin." Holding hands, they stride to their cabin as the November sun begins to break through the mist. Once inside the cabin, Legare hears the inarticulate sound of the machinery operating the paddle wheels. The sound flows like a sleepy hum throughout the cabin. Legare places his hand near the radiator,

"This radiator sure makes a comfortable cabin." Polly acknowledges Legare with a sweet smile as she closes the curtain over the porthole. Then they undress and pull the covers back from the bed. Polly eases in between the warm wool covers. Legare lies next to Polly and they draw as close as

possible to one-another, embrace and kiss. Exhausted and in love, they fall asleep in each other arms.

A loud blast from the steamer's horn five hours later instantaneously awakens them. They are in the same embrace as they were upon falling into their idyllic sleep. They dare not move, fearing that they'll lose their ideal and romantic embrace. Polly and Legare spontaneously enter into an amorous and blissful state, repeating the rapture of the honeymoon and then fall back into a peaceful slumber. Later a strong wave from a passing ship startles and awakens them. Legare sits up and pulls back the curtains. The bright sun causes him to shield his eyes for a moment.

Polly kisses Legare's hand. "I'm hungry again. It must almost be dinner time."

Departing the room for dinner, Polly and Legare seek out a deck hand. "Where can we find some food?"

"Down those stairs over there. That will take you to the captain's mess. Just let the cook know what you would like for dinner. I know we have some fresh roast duck and roast vegetables. The cook makes a great wine sauce to go with the duck for our guests."

"That's what Captain Powell said to us earlier. Want to try the duck, Polly?"

"I'm so hungry I could eat the feathers and the quack right now!"

"Thanks for the recommendation. We are going to try the duck—quack and all!" The deck hand laughs and nods his head.

Polly and Legare locate the Captain's mess. Inside there are several waiters. One of them approaches. "I assume you're the passengers in cabin five?"

"Yes we are," replies Legare. "How did you know?"

"You're the only passengers on board today. You can sit anywhere you like, but I recommend the table by the window."

Taking their seats, Legare informs the waiter, "Thank you. We already know what we would like for dinner. The roast vegetables and the roast duck cooked in the wine sauce everyone has been telling us about. Also, two glasses of red wine with the entree, please."

After dinner, Polly and Legare stroll the main deck, observing the ship's cargo. They eventually make their way to the helm of the boat. Captain Powell is steering the steamer as she gently runs the Savannah River.

"Are the two of you going any place else after you get to Savannah?" asks Captain Powell.

"No sir, that is our final destination," replies Legare. "My Uncle Richard owns the Magnolia Plantation in Savannah. I believe your steamer has carried his cargo before."

"Oh sure, I know Richard. I've hauled cotton and rice for him on many a trip. He's a really nice man."

"Thank you, sir," replies Legare.

"The duck you recommended for dinner was splendid. I would like to have the recipe for the wine sauce before we leave the ship, if that's possible," asks Polly.

"It's really a very simple wine sauce. I'll write the recipe down for you and leave it on your door when my relief for the wheel arrives."

"Thanks, Captain Powell," replies Polly.

Legare adds, "We are going to check out the bow. I'm sure we will see you again."

Finding a comfortable seat at the bow of the boat, Polly and Legare get a first hand look at Mother Nature on the river. Turtles are sunning on the logs along the river. Frightened by the steamer, alligators plunge into the water and disappear only to surface in a moment to study the intruder. Kingfisher birds fly by, plucking small fish and salamanders from the water. A bald eagle departs his high perch and dives into the water. Grasping a large fish in his talons, he flaps his wings gracefully to gain speed and altitude. Soon the majestic bird is over the tree line, heading for his nesting site.

The river banks are scattered with woolly headed darkies with their cane poles, fishing for the large river cats. Their clothing is constructed from patches of every color of cloth available to them. The women sit, smiling and playing with the children in their sack-like apparel. The women adorn themselves with beads and dress their heads with handkerchiefs.

As the sun begins to set and the evening gets cooler, Polly and Legare return to the cabin. On the door is the recipe for the wine sauce. It reads:

For the duck and sauce:
1 duck breast
10 oz beef stock
½ glass red wine
olive oil, to drizzle

For the roast vegetables:
2 tbsp olive oil
½ red pepper, de-seeded and sliced
½ courgette, cut into wedges
½ onion, peeled and sliced

2 garlic cloves, peeled
½ sweet potato, peeled and cut into wedges

"This recipe is simple. I can make this for you whenever you want, and we can recall our first boat ride as husband and wife." Once inside the cabin, Polly and Legare lie facing each other on the bed. "What are we going to do in Savannah to make a living, Mr. Hill?"

"I have worked for Uncle Richard during the past two summers overseeing the darkies and managing three hundred acres of cotton. I hope when we see Uncle Richard and Aunt Charlotte he'll still allow me to work on the plantation. If he doesn't, I'll get employment at either a bank or as a clerk in one of the courts. I want to study law but that might have to wait until the war is over. Don't you worry. I'm not concerned about employment." Leaning closer to Polly, he kisses her gently on the forehead. "I know I have skills that can be useful to someone."

"I can work, too, teach school maybe, Legare. I have some gold with me from home. We'll be able to make it, I'm sure. Just might take a while. So long as we are together, we will be all right. We just need to get to Savannah and settle down."

"We'll be there tomorrow and start our new life together. Of course, we may not live in splendor for a while."

Polly interrupts. "I've never lived in splendor. You know what a modest home I come from, so don't think I'm in a rush, honey. A hayloft with you is just fine for me. The Augusta Hotel was like a palace to me, but my splendor is being with you."

"What makes you happy, makes me happy, too." Holding each other near, they drift into a slumber until the steamer's horn awakens the two lovers once again. "Look! It's dark already! We must have slept for a couple of hours. Let's freshen up and get some supper. I could really eat another steak! How about you, Polly?"

"Steak and wine. I wonder if they have any muscadine wine."

After dinner Polly and Legare meander around the main deck in the fresh river air. She pulls her shawl tightly around her shoulders and arms, and Legare is wearing a light jacket. They find the seat at the bow of the boat. Peering into the night sky, as the quarter moon rises over the horizon, they talk about the wonder of the universe. "What do you think is really out there?" asks Polly.

"That's hard for us to know. I'd like to meet the Creator and have at least a thirty minute conversation with Him to find out."

"That would be a most interesting conversation all right!" They both laugh. "What would be your first question?"

Studying the star silently for a moment, Polly takes Legare's hand. "I would ask Him where he came from."

"Mighty good question. And your second question?"

"Depends on how he answered the first one!" Legare wrinkles his forehead.

"Mighty good answer." Polly kisses Legare sweetly on the cheek and whispers in his ear, "It getting mighty chilly sitting on the deck. So my next question is, are you ready to go to bed?"

"You bet." The newlyweds enter their cabin and light a candle. Soon the warm glow fills the room. They prepare for another night filled with the bliss of love.

The next day, following their mid-morning breakfast, they stand on the main deck. "Look, Polly, the Savannah docks are in sight."

Shading her eyes with her hand, Polly looks in the direction the boat is heading. "Yes, I can see the outline of the buildings. How far is your father's river house from the docks?"

"Only a mile or so. We'll take a carriage to Antonio's for dinner and then to the Pulaski Hotel."

The stores and warehouses on the riverfront grow larger. The tall masts of large sailing ships and paddle wheels of steamers come into view as they approach the docks.

"I never knew this many ships could be in one place. Look at all of this cotton! What's in those large sacks over there?" asks Polly.

"Those are sacks of rice. It would be hard to calculate how much cotton and rice are in the warehouses and aboard the ships. There's no way to export the cotton and rice from here any more. The Yankees have all of our water routes in and out of Savannah blocked. The last time my father and I saw Uncle Richard, he told us that he has been transporting rice by train to other southern cities, but the cotton stays here."

Captain Powell steers the steamer cautiously towards the dock. At the appropriate moment, the crew throws the large tie down ropes to men on the dock. Slowly the steamer draws next to the dock and the paddle wheel stops. The crew lowers the gangplank to the awaiting hands. The dockhands secure the gangplank and the captain gives the go-ahead for disembarking. After thanking the captain for allowing them passage to Savannah, Polly and Legare disembark.

Taking her by her hand, Legare leads her down the gangplank onto the dock. She is amazed at the number of ships on one side and the large cotton and rice warehouses on the other side of the riverfront. It is a busy place. Men are moving the large bales of cotton to the warehouses for sorting and grading.

Strolling up the steps to Bay Street, Polly observes the granite steps, "This rock looks like Stone Mountain granite." She stops, kneels and runs her hands over the granite steps. "Feel Legare, what do you think?"

Legare kneels down next to Polly and feels the stone. "I think you could be right. The mica pattern is the same. We can always come here and visit when we miss the mountain. Look, there's a carriage." Picking up their baggage, they rush up the steps. They wave at the driver to get his attention. The horse and carriage stop. Legare helps her climb aboard and asks, "We haven't eaten since breakfast. How about some dinner?"

"I'm hungry all right!"

"Wehr fuh go suh?" "Where to go sir?" asks the carriage driver.

"Let's go to the Pirates' House.[116] You'll like this place, Polly. My family eats there when they are in town."

Puzzled by the carriage driver's dialect, Polly asks, "What language did the carriage driver speak?"

"Oh, that's the Gullah dialect.[117] You'll catch on to it fast."

"I thought you said we were going to Antonio's."

"We are. Antonio is the owner of the Pirates' House." Legare and Polly sit close to one another, holding hands and exchanging an occasional kiss with a tender "I love you."

All the while, Polly studies the landscape. "What are all those gray stringy plants hanging from those willow leaf and oak trees?"

"It's Spanish moss. Almost like mistletoe, but it's not a parasite and isn't attached to the tree. Spanish moss has air roots that picks up moisture from the air. The city of Savannah's an old place. Look at the houses. Most of them are brick or frame structures."

"We studied Savannah in Seminary. I know Savannah is larger than Atlanta and its streets are laid out nice and square. Atlanta's streets are more like cow paths. Look at the large yards and beautiful ornamental shrubbery and at this time of the year."

They pass several parks on their way to dinner. "These city parks are absolutely gorgeous. Look at the beautiful trees and statues and the mansions surrounding the squares."

"One day soon, we'll tour all of the parks in town."

"Yah de Pirates hous' Mistuh." [Here is the Pirate's House, Mister.] Legare reaches into his pocket and hands the driver ten cents.

"If you don't mind waiting until we finish dinner, I would like to ride down to the shore before going to the Pulaski Hotel. Of course I'll pay you for your wait as well."

"Happy fur suh." [Happy to sir.]

Legare assists Polly from the carriage. He places his arm around her waist, and they go into the Pirates' House.

Antonio recognizes his old friend as they enter. "Hello, Legare." Shaking hands, Antonio continues, "Glad to see you. And who might this beautiful young lady be?"

"Antonio, you have the pleasure of being the first person I know to meet my wife, Polly."

Smiling, Antonio takes Polly's hand and kisses it. "My dear lady, it is a great pleasure to meet you and have you dine at my establishment. You have married a wonderful young man." Looking to Legare, he inquires, "What do you mean I am the first person you have introduced your lovely wife to?"

"We eloped two days ago."

Clasping his hand and with a broad smile Antonio looks at the newly weds. "Love is mighty powerful. Only those truly in love know how deep and boundless it can be. May your life forever be wonderful! I am honored to be the first to meet your wife. You're always welcome here."

Legare takes Polly's hand. She smiles and holds back her tears of appreciation as she says, "Thank you Antonio." Sensing her sincerity, Antonio gives the couple a good Italian hug. "Dinner is on me today! Follow me to my most special table." Seating the newly weds, Antonio lights the candle in the center of the table. "I'll order for both of you."

"Thank you again Antonio. I did not expect this, but thank you."

"You are very welcome my friends." Soon Antonio returns with a bottle of white wine. "From my family vineyard in Italy, comes this wine that I share with the two of you." Removing the cork, Antonio pours three glasses and offers a toast. Legare pushes his chair back and stands while holding Polly's hand. "Long life, love forever, healthy children and prosperity, I toast to Legare and Polly." The three glasses click.

"Thank you, Antonio." Polly wipes her tearful, yet happy eyes.

Legare shakes Antonio's hand. "Thank you so much, Antonio. Your toast will always be true for us."

A familiar voice from across the room asks, "Is that you Legare?"

Legare turns and sees a family friend and neighbor, Mrs. Turner, sitting at a nearby table. "Excuse me a minute, Polly, while I speak to Mrs. Turner. She is widowed. She owns the house next to us on the river." Legare excuses himself and heads over to Mrs. Turner's table. He takes her hand, leans over and gives her a tender hug around her neck.

"I have a surprise and good news to tell you, Mrs. Turner. First, are you eating alone today?"

"Why, yes I am."

"Then please come over and join us. I want you to meet someone special."

"Well, that's mighty nice of you, darling. I would love to meet that beautiful, young lady sitting with you. Are you sure she won't mind?"

"Not at all, Mrs. Turner." Legare assists Mrs. Turner from her seat and escorts her over to their table. "Mrs. Turner, I want you to have the pleasure of meeting my wife, Polly."

"Well, my-oh-my. Darling, it is a real pleasure to meet you." Mrs. Turner looks at Polly, smiles and extends her hand. "I'm Katherine Turner. A good friend of the Hills."

"Thank you, Mrs. Turner. It is a pleasure to meet you as well."

"When did this happy event take place?"

"Just two days ago."

"A big wedding I hope. But Legare, darling, I'm disappointed that I didn't receive an invitation."

"Don't feel badly. There were only four invitations. One to Polly. One to me. One to Pastor Huntington, in Augusta and one to his secretary, our witness. We eloped!"

Being caught completely by surprise, Mrs. Turner places her hand on her chest, "Well! My-oh-my, darling, you could not have picked a more beautiful bride. But why did you elope?"

"To make a long story short, it was love at first sight and to prevent an unfortunate event from occurring, we decided to elope."

"What unfortunate event could cause you to do such a thing?"

"Polly's marriage to another man."

Mrs. Turner laughs and hugs Polly. "Well, well, my dears ... I'll wager that put the tongues to wagging."

Polly blushes, but can't help smiling at the affable woman. "We didn't stay around long enough to find out, but I'm sure it did."

"When did you arrive in Savannah?"

"About an hour or so ago."

"And are you going to stay at your father's house?"

"Oh, no. We are staying in the Pulaski Hotel until we find our own place."

"Darling, Legare, you must have really stirred the embers when you ran away."

"Probably so, Mrs. Turner," responds Legare.

"To say the least," says Polly with a chuckle.

"What does your family do Polly, darling? Oh, and where are you from?"

"My folk's have around three hundred acres of farmland in Stone Mountain, raising cotton, corn, hogs, and a few dairy cows. I have a twin brother, Norman, who is enrolled at the Georgia Military Institute in Marietta."

"Have you been to Savannah before, Polly, darling?"

"No, Ma'am. This is the farthest I've ever been from Stone Mountain."

"Are you glad you ran away to get married?"

"I could not be happier if I had the wedding of the Queen of England. I love Legare. A wedding would have been nice with our families and friends there. Having the blessing of our families is important, but … I hope … I know that will come later. The circumstances just did not permit that to happen."

"Is there some kind of a family scrap going on darling?"

"No Ma'am. My folks had their heart set on me marrying our neighbor, but I never had my heart set on marrying him. The first time I saw Legare, I knew he was the man I was to love forever."

"I like you, Polly, darling. You don't put on any airs! You are a very honest person and that look in your eyes when you glance at Legare let's me know you really love him."

Polly smiles and blushes at the same time. "Thank you Mrs. Turner."

Hesitating for a moment Mrs. Turner continues, "Not going to move in your father's place, right?" Polly and Legare nod in agreement. "Truly an act of good judgment and respect. I have known you all of your life, Legare. I am concerned about this war. My boys, 'Cannon Ball' Connon and Christopher Richard, are in the Union Navy."

"What about Stephen Charles? Is he staying in Savannah to   practice medicine?"

"No, Stephen Charles is a medical doctor in Nassau now. None of us are sure what's going to happen to Savannah, being it's such an important port. Polly, my husband was a very successful cotton broker. He built us a place in Nassau several years ago and I have decided to move there. In fact, my trunks are on the ship already."

"When do you expect to leave for Nassau?" asks Polly.

"Probably in a day or two. The captain suggested that I stay at the Pulaski Hotel so as not to delay the ship's departure." Taking Legare and Polly's hands, she winks conspiratorially. "So here is my wedding present for both of you. I have put my river house up for sale, furniture and all. Polly the same builder constructed your in-laws' house and my house."

Polly smiles and looks at Mrs. Turner. "How interesting."

"Well dear Polly, they are nearly the same style and plan. My banker has all of the papers at his office to handle the transfer." Polly and Legare look at each other as if to ask "What is Mrs. Turner talking about?" Reaching into her purse, Mrs. Turner pulls out her set of keys.

"Here are keys to the house. Take Polly over there and spend the night. I'll go by and tell my banker you're staying there. A carriage will pick you up at ten o'clock tomorrow morning and take you to the bank. If both of you like the house, it's yours for half of what I'm asking. The other half is your wedding gift."

Totally caught by surprise, Legare squeezes Mrs. Turner's hand. "Mrs. Turner, I can't believe you're making us such a wonderful offer as our wedding present."

Polly smiles and softly says," You are very kind, Mrs. Turner, and most generous. This is too good to be true. We will pay you full price for your house if we like it, even if I must work to earn more money."

"A young lady who is not afraid of work. Unusual. I like that. Now both of you listen. It's my house and I can sell it to whomever I want and for whatever price I decide. I won't have to worry about the house that I love. No more discussion. Simply say 'thank you.'"

Polly becomes teary eyed. "Thank you, Mrs. Turner. This wedding present means more to both of us than you'll ever know. We will be happy to spend our first night together in Savannah at your house."

"Now if you don't like it Polly, darling, don't let Legare talk you into buying it. All right?"

"Legare and I have pretty much agreed on everything so far. We tend to think alike."

"Good, keep it that way! Just one more matter. While I am alive, you cannot rent the house. If you decide to sell, I must have first refusal to buy it back at the same price plus any major expenses. Deal?"

"Deal," reply Legare and Polly. "Now let's eat!"

The waiter comes from the kitchen with Antonio's famous Italian salad and homemade bread. Another waiter serves a huge platter of beefsteak and potatoes. "This is Mother's recipe for the salad and bread. I leave you to eat and enjoy. Let this be your wedding feast from Antonio."

"We cannot thank you enough for dinner. This truly was our wedding feast and we shall forever remember your friendship and thoughtfulness."

Polly concurs. "Thank you, Antonio. You and Mrs. Turner have made this day even more special for us." Antonio and Mrs. Turner walk to the carriage with Legare and Polly.

As the carriage drives away, Antonio waves and shouts, "Bon Voyage!" and Mrs. Turner throws a kiss. Riding out of town, the carriage driver takes the direct road to the beach.

They stop at a large sand dune. Legare holds Polly's arm. "Let's take off our shoes so we can walk on the beach."

They remove their shoes, and Legare assists Polly from the carriage. There is a somewhat chilly breeze as they climb to the top of the sand dune. Polly listens to the murmur of the rippling waves crowned with their whitecaps rushing on each other. The silver sand sparkles against the bright afternoon sun. The happy couple holds hands and stares out at the horizon. As the gentle wind blows and partially releases the ribbon from Polly's hair, it begins to ebb and flow with the changing wind.

"I cannot get over Mrs. Turner selling us her house."

"There's no doubt that she thinks a lot of you and your family, Legare. She considers you as part of her own family."

"You're probably right. She's known me from birth and has always admired my father. I think she secretly loves him. Look over there, Polly. That tall structure is the lighthouse on Tybee Island. It shows ships where the mouth of the Savannah River is located."

Holding hands, they stroll to the ocean's edge. Polly lifts her skirts just in time. A cold wave rushes in and wets their warm feet. They bounce up attempting to avoid the cold seawater. Legare squeezes her hand. "Mighty cold." Sea gulls fly overhead, begging for food.

Watching the gulls, Polly notices that some are motionless in the air, moving neither forward nor sideways. "Look Legare." They watch the gulls for a moment before movement in the water catches their attention.

Mullet dash along in the shallow water. Occasionally, one springs into the air as another fish follows in pursuit. Fiddler crabs dart in and their burrows. Polly stops on several occasions to pick up various seashells. She places the prettiest ones in her jacket pocket. Returning to the carriage, Legare gives the driver directions and the carriage pulls away from the beach.

A few moments later, Legare taps the driver on the shoulder. "Stop here, driver. Polly we must get groceries for the house. I almost forgot we'd need food." They step down from the carriage and enter the grocery store. He finds the clerk. "Do you have a chicken you can kill and dress?"

"Yes, sir. How many do you want?" asks the clerk.

"Just one," replies Legare.

They gather various food items including bacon, eggs, bread, grits, fresh greens, wine and butter along with the fresh chicken. After paying for the goods, Polly and Legare are again on their way to the river house.

13

A NEST ON THE RIVER

"There's the river house, straight ahead on the right! Do you see it?" Holding onto Legare, Polly stands up in the moving carriage.

Smiling and full of excitement, she says, "Yes, I see the house. It's beautiful! I had no idea how nice this would be!"

Polly and Legare remain standing as the horse and carriage stops in front of Mrs. Turner's river house. He jumps from the carriage and gently assists her. She hesitates for a moment and admires the beautiful house and the surrounding gardens, which will be their first home. The carriage driver, having already tied the horse to the hitching post, removes the groceries and luggage from the carriage.

"Just place the groceries and baggage on the steps." Legare settles his debt with the driver. Soon the carriage is out of sight and the only sound is the mild cool breeze migrating through the trees surrounding the house. "Polly, you wait here while I open the door. I must carry you over the threshold and into our new life." They hug and kiss lingeringly.

Legare climbs the stairs to the front door of the river house. Searching his pocket, he finds the key and anxiously slips it into the lock. He turns the key several times but the latch does not release. As his heart races, he realizes that he is trying the key to the back door instead of the key to the front door. He hastily places the second key into the lock and it releases. Legare turns the doorknob opening the door and leaves it slightly ajar while he returns to his wife.

"Are you ready?" Polly kisses Legare and places one arm around his neck.

He bends over, placing one hand behind her knees and the other arm to support her back. As he lifts Polly to the level of his chest, she chuckles and gives him a sweet kiss on the cheek. When they reach the door, he pushes it open with his foot and steps across the threshold. He carries her to the bedroom and gently lays her on the bed. He lies next to Polly and they embrace passionately as the joy of the moment rushes over them. Their warmth is eventually compromised by the cooling temperatures in the house.

"Go ahead and put up the groceries while I get the fires started." The fireplaces and stoves had been cleaned and made ready. Legare lights the fire in the parlor and the stoves in the bedroom and the bathtub room. Lastly, Legare goes out to a storeroom on the side of the house where the water heater is located. Here he lights the charcoal underneath the huge boiler sitting high off the ground. Gravity sends hot water to the bathtub room and kitchen. Mrs. Turner's room has an English tub similar to the one at the Augusta Hotel.

Returning to the kitchen, Legare finds the chill in the river house is subsiding. "Come, Polly, let me show you around the house." Taking her by the hand, he begins the tour. "Of course, this is the kitchen."

Polly studies the kitchen layout. "Very similar to my home with the high hearth and fireplace."

"Outside there's a cookhouse, carriage house and two cabins for the servants."

Entering the parlor, Polly observes the beautiful Oriental rug on the floor and the rosewood table with eight beautiful chairs. She rubs her hand across the table and then observes, "Look Legare how the drapery blends with the Oriental rug, wing back chairs and sofa."

"It is very elegant Polly."

She then looks at the chandelier hanging above the dinning room table and walks over to the tables besides the sofa and chairs. She picks up a candleholder. "That four-branch oil chandelier matches these beautiful crystal candleholders." She feels the cuts in the crystal and then returns it to the table. She them turns her attention to the wallpaper. She runs her hand over the scene of well-dressed, polite society riding through the woods in beautiful carriages. Legare is still silent as Polly continues to study the luxurious decor of the house. With Legare by her side and holding her hand, she silently studies a large oil painting of a Savannah Plantation hanging over the rosewood sideboard. Sconces hang from the wall with beautiful figurines resting on their pedestal.

"Let's go upstairs Polly. I think you will find the view beautiful from the cupola." Still holding hands they climb the stairs to the second bedroom. "This is one of the guest rooms. It also has a bath."

"A high post bed Legare. I've always admired how pretty they are. This one is perfect for this room." Resting at the foot of the bed is a large steamer trunk. "Look Legare, a slipper chair. I have my grandmother's in my bedroom in Stone Mountain. She releases his hand and gently sits in the slipper chair. "Sits just like my grandmother's. You sit in the armchair and let me how you like it." Legare sits in it and leans over the inlaid table separating them.

"This chair is as comfortable as you are beautiful, Polly."

She gets up and goes over to Legare, sits in his lap and kisses him. "I love you Legare. You make my life beautiful."

They tour the remaining two bedrooms. Polly stands in the last guest bedroom for a moment at the edge of the ornate Oriental rug, smiles back at Legare and takes a step. The plush carpet cushions her steps as she strides to the trestle table. She rubs her hand across the gleaming mahogany surface, noticing her reflection in the lustrous finish.

"Now, Polly, for one of my favorite spots. The cupola."

"I heard you say that earlier. I'm not sure what that is."

"The cupola. The little house on top. Follow me." They climb the narrow staircase to a trap door. Lifting the trap door, Legare takes hold of the handrail in the cupola and climbs onto the platform. He reaches for Polly's hand as she climbs onto the platform to join him. Standing in the cupola, she is amazed at the view across the river.

"It's beautiful up here. You can see the ocean, the river, and some of the city, the forest and even the universe."

"Over in that direction is Fort Pulaski."

"I've studied about General Pulaski."

"Look out toward the river. We have a small dock to fish from. There's a row boat that we take out in the summertime, but it's too cold to get on the river now."

Polly looks into her husband's eyes and smiles. "We're already in a boat! Or maybe in a pickled boat, but as long as I am in the boat with you, I really don't care about the season." She kisses Legare, and he draws her close and tight. She embraces him passionately. With her arms still around him, Polly peers over his shoulder. "The sunsets and sunrises must be beautiful from up here."

"There are some mighty striking ones, especially in the early spring and fall. We'll come back up here and check out the view at sunset." Now standing next to each other, he stares out across the river, suddenly thinking of his family back home. "Like my father's property next door, this property is about three acres on the river. Over there's the barn for the carriages and horses. Father's horses are kept at Uncle Richard's. Jesse and Al are the darkies that care of our horses, and Tot is our cook, but they stay at Uncle Richard's as well. We bring the horses and darkies over here when we're in town."

Descending the stairs from the cupola, Legare asks, "Well, what do you think, Polly?"

"Mrs. Turner has to be an angel. Who could not love this place? To me, this house is a palace. I promise I'll take good care of it."

"You just take care of me. Let the servants take care of the rest!"

Polly smiles. "I have nearly $325 in gold remaining. I wonder how much Mrs. Turner is going ask us to pay."

"Don't really know, but I think I have enough in the Bank in Savannah to pay her if it's not over $2,900 Right now, let's get a bite to eat and then go back to the cupola and watch our first sunset together."

"Let's have cornbread, chicken, greens, rice and tea for supper."

"Great, I'll get the fire going in the wood stove and high hearth kitchen fireplace."

Polly removes the whole chicken and cuts it into sections. "Legare you like your chicken battered, or roasted over the open fire?"

"Let's cook the chicken over the open fire. I saw the skewers on the high hearth over the kitchen fireplace." Legare grabs the skewers and hands them to her.

"You skewer the chicken and start cooking it and I'll prepare the cornbread, greens and rice." He places the skewered chicken on the rack over the hot coals in the kitchen fireplace watches the process of the chicken. He rotates each skewer occasionally to insure the chicken is cooked thoroughly. Soon the house is alive with the aroma of fresh cooked food. They place their first home cooked meal on the table.

"This is our first official home-cooked meal together, Polly. I'll always remember this moment and how it came about."

Taking her hand, he prays, "Thank you God for protecting and delivering us together. Always be assured that the love Polly and I share is enduring and everlasting … and by all means, thank you for giving Mrs. Turner a heart of kindness, love and generosity. Protect her and grant her a long and happy life. Bless our families and may we be joined again someday soon. Please bless and protect our soldiers. Amen."

With tears in her eyes, she squeezes Legare's hand and hugs him tightly. "I love you more than you'll ever know. You are my heart and soul."

Legare draws Polly around to his lap and kisses her deeply.

She snuggles against her husband's chest for a moment before returning to her own chair. "You are my heart and soul too, Polly. We are going to be very happy together." They enjoy their first meal in their new home.

After the meal, Polly clears the table. "Legare, I'll clean the dishes if you get the heater going in the tub and light the fireplace in the bedroom."

"I'll do that. Are you sure you don't need help with those dishes?"

"No, I don't mind at all." She busies herself scrubbing the dishes and hums to herself. She can't remember ever being this happy.

Returning from the bedroom, Legare watches her for a moment. "Mrs. Turner is right. She left everything. All of the towels, soap, washcloths and robes are in the bathtub room. All of the sheets, blankets and pillowcases are in the bedroom chest of drawers. The house is completely furnished."

"I'm just about finished with the dishes. Is the water in the tub hot?"

"It's beginning to warm up. I think we have time to see the sun set."

Polly folds the dishcloth and turns. Legare takes her hand as they climb the stairs to the cupola. They walk to the side, which faces the river. Although the sun is not setting directly along the river, the red sky is reflecting in the rippling waters. The sky darkens and the beauty of the full moon averts total darkness. The moonbeams turn the ripples of the dark river into a mirror. Occasionally, a distant splash is seen in the river as a fish attempts to escape a pursuer. A cool November breeze carries the sound of an owl declaring his territory, completing a beautiful first evening in their new home.

"The bath water should be hot by now, Polly. Let's go down and I'll get more wood for the fireplace while you bathe."

She returns to the warm bathtub room, undresses and steps into the comfortable tub of hot water. Legare finds a hefty mound of coal and decides to burn it rather than wood. As he places the large lump of coal in the parlor fireplace, Polly calls out, "Legare this tub is large enough for the two of us!"

Legare hurries to the bathtub room. He opens the door and leans in. "Are you inviting me to bathe with you or do you just need someone to scrub your back?"

"Why don't you come on in and find out?" responds Polly as she lifts and spreads her arms to invite him to join her. He closes the bathtub room door and then sits on the rounded lip of the tub and begins disrobing. She has a washcloth in her hand and stirs the water. Then she soaps the cloth and begins to wash Legare's back as he slides backwards into the tub. He takes his hands and splashes his face and head. She takes his arms and turns his back to her.

"Turn around and I'll wash your handsome face and chest for you." He turns see Polly's radiant smile that takes over the commands of his emotions. Silently she washes his face, shoulders, chest and arms.

"Turn around, Polly; I need to hold you tight against my body."

She turns her back to Legare as he places his arms under her breasts and draws her soft derriere tightly against his body.

Legare holds her tenderly and kisses her warm neck. "I love you Polly."

"And I love you, Legare." They stay motionless, comfortable together as they enjoy these quiet moments. "Let's go to the parlor, Legare. I'll get the blankets and pillows and have a cozy spot ready in just a few minutes."

Slowly they stand together. Polly's wet body drips upon Legare, her breath reaches the lips of her lover. Forcing himself to move, he steps from the bathtub and secures towels and robes for the two of them. "I'll be waiting for you in the parlor, or we may never leave this bath."

Grinning broadly while retrieving her towel and robe Polly taunts Legare. "I'll be in front of the fireplace before you have the blankets and pillows on the floor."

Legare gathers the quilts and pillows from the bed and takes them to the parlor. Then he removes several other quilts from the trunk at the end of the bed and places these along with the other quilts on the floor. Spotting the leftover bottle of wine from dinner he swiftly takes two glasses and begins pouring wine as Polly enters the parlor. She walks up behind him and places her arms around his waist.

"I won. I beat you to the fireside bed! Plus I have two glasses of wine on the way." He turns and gives her one of the glasses of wine.

She offers a toast. "With you Legare, I'll always be a winner and my love for you … I don't know how it can grow to any greater heights than heaven."

"You're already my Goddess." And they drink their wine together. Taking off their robes, they lie on the quilts in front of the warm fire.

The next morning, they look from the parlor window as the carriage arrives at their door at the appointed time of ten o'clock. They ride to the bank in the carriage sent by Mrs. Turner. "I hope we can afford this house, Polly."

The twenty-minute ride seems like an eternity. The driver stops the horse and carriage in front of the bank, and Polly and Legare get out.

Taking a deep breath, Polly looks around as if to get a sign from his countenance that everything is going be all right. All that is visible is the clear, November sky and a few birds soaring high above the trees. Other citizens walk by unaware of what the future might hold for Polly and Legare as they enter the bank.

"Come on in, you two!" Legare and Polly turn around and see Mrs. Turner standing in the open bank door. She takes Polly by the hand. "Well, Polly darling, how did you like my little house on the river?"

"To be honest Mrs. Turner, I am reluctant to tell you."

Looking somewhat bewildered, she leans back and stares. "Darling, what is it you don't like about the house?"

Legare also stares at Polly in amazement.

"Because if I told you how much Legare and I truly fancy your house, you would no doubt double the price."

"Oh darling, I thought for a moment … you simply had me scared blue." She turns to Legare. "Legare darling, I consider myself a good judge of character. Your wife has a confident mind and a quick wit about her. She sets the example of a beautiful, independent, Southern countrywoman! You best hold on to her. I knew from the first time I met her she was a special person. Come on inside and let's close this deal. The captain informed me that the boat leaves for Nassau in about an hour."

They walk into the bank president's office. He rises and extends his hand to Legare. "How are you today, Legare?" Legare takes his hand firmly.

"Fine, thank you, Mr. Lilly. This is my wife, Polly."

"How do you do Mrs. Hill? I'm Donald Lilly. It is a pleasure to meet you. Please, let's all take a seat at the conference table. Mrs. Turner directed me to draw the deed on her river house for you. I put Legare's name on the deed. Is that the way you wish to have it?"

"Yes, please." He looks to Mrs. Turner, "I am almost embarrassed to inquire how much are you asking for your house? Polly and I need to know the price."

"Well, darling Legare, how much money do you have in the bank here?"

"I have about $3,000." He glances at Polly and squeezes her hand.

"And I have about three hundred twenty five dollars in gold with me, Mrs. Turner."

Smiling, Mrs. Turner takes and holds Polly and Legare's hands. Love is worth much more than gold. Legare, you have always been like a son to me and I have always loved and admired your mother and father …

and Polly, you would make me a wonderful daughter. You are unassuming, very intelligent, although it is somewhat masked by your accent, and you're very beautiful."

Polly blushes. "Thank you, Mrs. Turner, for the compliment."

"The house is yours for nineteen hundred dollars."

Polly and Legare are unable to suppress their stunned emotions and indisputable gratitude to Mrs. Turner. A huge lump forms in Legare's throat as tears of appreciation flow from Polly's eyes.

"Now, now! I've already signed the necessary papers, and Mr. Lilly will transfer the money to my account. The ship is waiting and so is my carriage. I know you two will always be happy. God bless you, both."

Polly and Legare, almost unable to speak, stand and hug Mrs. Turner together. Finally Legare and Polly are able to say their good-byes as they escort Mrs. Turner to her carriage. "Your thankful tears mean more to me than all the words in the dictionary." Boarding the carriage, Mrs. Turner directs the driver to the dock where her journey will begin. Polly and Legare return to Mr. Lilly's office and finalize the deed. Then Legare has the money transferred from his account to Mrs. Turner's.

"Mr. Lilly, I may be in need of employment. I don't know if my Uncle Richard will hire me to work the darkies in the cotton fields as he has in the past."

"Well as a matter of fact I can use you part-time. Your family banks with me, and I always like to help my clients. I need a teller three days a week since one of my employees takes vacation this time of year. Probably for two months, maybe three. Could you start next week?"

"I'll go ahead and say yes! Cotton field work doesn't start until February. I'll see you on Monday at nine o'clock." Legare stands and shakes the hand of his new boss. "We need to buy two horses. Is the stable still nearby?"

"Yes, and he has some quality carriage horses. I'll get my carriage driver to take you there."

"Thank you, sir."

After procuring two horses, Polly and Legare ask Mr. Lilly's driver to take them to their new home on the river. They sit very close to one another, and Polly is still full of emotion and gratitude for Mrs. Turner. "I still cannot believe that Mrs. Turner sold us her house for nineteen hundred dollars. It is a dream come true. Just think, we will raise our children and grand children there."

Legare smiles at Polly's enthusiasm. "Yes, Polly. We'll grow old together there."

Executive Department
Nov 9 1861
Milledgeville, Ga.
Proclamation

To the Volunteer Military Companies of the State: The invaders having landed a force upon the soil our sister State of South Carolina near the borders of Georgia, where they now hold position and menace the City of Savannah; and it being thought advisable to increase our force for the defense of the coast, I issue this my Proclamation, giving notice that I'll accept, in addition to the number of volunteers already accepted, the services of the thirty companies which will first tender their services and report to me their readiness to march. These companies will be received for six months, unless sooner discharged. Each Company, to be accepted, must consist of not less than fifty nor more than eighty members, rank and file, unless the statute shall, in the meantime, be changed so as to permit a greater number to compose a company. Each man in each company must be armed with a good country rifle or double-barrel shot gun, or with a good military gun, fit for immediate use. As unarmed troops could be of no service in the defence (sic) of the State, while they would be a heavy expense, I here state, to prevent all misapprehension, that any volunteer going to the coast without such arms as I have mentioned above, will not be received, but will be sent home at his own expense. It will also be necessary for each volunteer armed with a country rifle to carry with him his bullet moulds, pouch and powder horn or flask; and those armed with double-barrel shot guns must each take with him a powder horn or flask.

As our homes are in danger, it is hoped that no citizen of the State having a good gun will hesitate a moment to carry or send it into the service.

Given under my hand and Seal of the Executive Department the 9th day of November A.D. 1861.

James E. Brown[118]

Governor Brown issues another order on the 9th:

I hereby place at the disposal of Gen. Robert Y. Harris and Col. Robert H. May, of Augusta, the guns now in possession of Col. May and the Fire Companies of Augusta, also the guns in the hands of Rogers and Bowen;

*also those in possession of the Volunteer Company at the Sand Hills, and
of the Oglethorpe Company B., subject to my order at any future time.*

*Said persons are authorized to place said guns in the hand of ten
Volunteer Companies of not less than fifty each, rank and file, to form a
Regiment, if the Companies can be reported with in a very few days. As
soon as each of the Companies is ready, it will proceed to Savannah, and
report to the BG Francis W. Capers, for orders, and an election will be
held for field officers, so soon as all the companies arrive. The Regiment
will be accepted for six months, unless sooner discharged. If the proposed
Regiment fails, the guns are to be subject to any other order that I may
pass for their disposition.*

Joseph E. Brown[119]

Phillip Buford McCurdy mustered in on the sixteenth of November.
Phillip is commissioned First Lt. of militia for the Stone Mountain
district.[120] One week after his friend Phillip McCurdy musters, Buster decides to follow the example of his neighbors and proceed to the seat of war.
Buster has come to spend this last evening with his dearest friends, Buck
and Betty Gail. During supper, Buster seems unsettled and his attitude
toward life is much more morose.

After eating, he hands a letter to Buck. "This here gives you power o'er
my property, Buck."

Buck opens the letter and reads. "I hereby entrust all of my worldly
affairs to Buck Jernigan until my return." Buck passes the letter to Betty
Gail, "We expect you to come back home when the war is over ... just like
we look for Norman to return home. There's to be no worry on your part.
We will care for your place as if it is ours."

Standing sternly and with a serious, yet hurt expression Buster says,
"Look after de place since I ain't here to tend to it myself—an' if I never
comes back hit's your'n— leastways, hit's your'n in trust fer Polly. Keep
my place till she comes a creepin' home in shame ... fer the one what loved
her best. An' tell her ... tell her ... how much I cared fer her, an' dat I never
blamed her when she chose another—an' don't be hard on her, fur my
sake, don't be hard on her."

Buck eye's meet Betty Gail's as Buster speaks his confused thoughts. A
painful silence follows the reading of Buster's letter and hearing his verbal
wishes. Betty Gail wipes her moist eyes with the corner of her apron. Buck

clears his throat, acting as if the evening air suddenly affects his voice. Gathering his composure, Buck stretches his hand to Buster and with a warm clasp, seals the unspoken compact.

In truth, Buck is thinking about Polly, about how she has broken his heart. Pain seizes his chest and he can hardly breathe as he recalls her innocent girlish face. For just a moment, he would give anything to see her, but the shame of her action rushes over him like a tidal wave.

"Good night," says Buster. "I must go to bed. I gonna be a stirrin' by day-light tomorrow mornin.'" He strides rapidly outside, toward his farmhouse. Buck and Betty Gail walk out to the porch and stand together for some minutes, gazing at Buster until he disappears into the darkness.

Concerned about Buster's mental state, Betty Gail rises at dawn and travels the path to his house. She presses her hands over her throbbing heart. She knocks gently and a servant soon opens the door. "Mornin' Miss Betty Gail. Mars Buster still sleeps."

Betty Gail quietly enters Buster's abode and pauses irresolutely before his sleeping form. Buster's damp locks have fallen back from his broad forehead, revealing a look of peace and dignity. Her heartaches from the thought that she must rouse this dear son of her adoption from his peaceful sleep and send him forth, perhaps to death.

"Wake-up, Buster, wake-up! The day is here!" Sitting on the bedside, Betty Gail burst into tears. He opens his eyes and takes her hand.

"I am de one who needs to cry, fer I am 'parting my parents, and maybe dis here life. Thank you fer coming to wake me, fer I must depart soon."

"You will always be in our prayers, Buster. May God protect you and send you back to us." Kissing Buster on the cheek, Betty Gail tearfully departs.

❧

Buck and Betty Gail travel to town to see Buster off. A large crowd is assembled at the depot to bid farewell to the departing troops. Mothers, sisters, wives and sweethearts struggle vainly to repress all signs of grief so they can give their heroes a brave send-off. A small band composed of town folks and children from the Academy and the Seminary make the great rock echo with martial strains. At length the music of the fife, flute, and drums play a soft and familiar tune. Suddenly, all is quiet until the long roll of the drum thunders through the hearts of everyone. The women draw their veils more closely over their tear-stained faces.

Buster notices Betty Gail and Buck. He nods solemnly as he joins the other men.

"Fall in!" calls the sergeant. Each soldier takes his assigned spot in the formation. The long gray line blends with the backdrop of the gray mountain in the distance. The roll is called. The sergeant turns and salutes his captain. "All present or accounted for, sir!"

Capt. Johnson returns the sergeant's salute and the former takes his place at the head of the column.[121]

The parting moment has come. "Right face! Forward, march!" and on to the waiting train whose smoke seems to be anxious to carry these brave men north.

The little band plays again.

> *What air comes floating back upon the summer breeze?*
> *It is the song of the mockingbird.*
> *I'm dreaming now of Hallie, Sweet Hallie, Sweet Hallie;*
> *I'm dreaming now of Hallie,*
> *And the mockingbird is singing where she lies.*
> *A flash of bayonets in the morning light—the tramp of*
>   *marching feet*
> *Keeping time to the melody—and they are gone.*

TUESDAY JANUARY 14, 1862

During breakfast, Legare thinks about the day and glances at his wife. He can hardly keep the smile from his face, knowing that every time someone mentions her name he breaks into a broad grin. He's more in love than he ever thought possible. "Polly the bank is closing at noon for a Board of Directors meeting. Mr. Lilly told me I didn't have to stay after closing, so I think I'll go over to Uncle Richard's and Aunt Charlotte's. My visit should be a surprise since they don't know I, or rather we, are in Savannah."

"What are you going to say to them?"

"Probably that I have someone special I want them to meet. I'm not going to let the cat out of the bag regarding our marriage and Mrs. Turner's gift. We can surprise my cousins by divulging those details when I take you over to meet the family."

Polly walks out to the carriage in front of the house with him. He gives her a loving embrace before he boards and heads for the bank.

After a short day of work and a short surprise visit with his family, Legare returns to his new wife and home. "Well how did your visit go with your family today?"

"Only Uncle was home. So I got to visit and we had dinner together. He wanted to know what I was doing in Savannah."

"And?"

"I just told him I was checking on some business matters for my pa. As I was leaving I told him that I had someone special I wanted him, Aunt Charlotte and my cousins to meet. Of course I had taken off my wedding band. He tried to pull more information from me, but I told him that he would just have to wait."

"Then what?"

"He got enough to know that there's a special girl in my life and invited us over for supper tomorrow. He also seemed excited about meeting you. Then he asked me where we're staying."

Polly takes his hand. "How did you answer that question?"

"That also was a surprise."

"So you didn't tell him we eloped?"

"No, just that I have a special person I want the family to meet. I didn't say much else except that he'll be impressed when he meets you tomorrow evening." Legare kisses her and she smiles.

"I'm looking forward to meeting your Savannah family. Did you tell me they have seven children?"

"Yes, but only four will be with us for supper. Jordan and Matthew are in England studying to be mercantile brokers in Europe. Marcelle is there studying medicine."

"Why do you call your cousins, Uncle and Aunt?"

"I guess because they're so much older than I am. I was taught to address them as Aunt and Uncle at an early age. Let me warn you, Aunt Charlotte can be curt at times. She's like a big rock in the road. You can't change the position of the rock, so you just have to go around it. Enough about them for now."

"I've been promising to buy us a couple of guns so I bought two pistols today. They're the new Colt revolving type. Got some cartridges so we can practice." Legare pulls out an article that is included with the pistols and holsters. "This article is real interesting. It the history about Samuel Colt and how he came up with the idea for a revolver."

Legare hands Polly the article. "It's interesting. You might want to read it later."

Polly glances at the article and places it in her pocket. "I'll read it later. Let's shoot."

"Right now?"

"Yep."

Legare reveals the chamber and places six cartridges in the empty slots. "Have you shot a pistol before, Polly?"

"Why, of course. Simply pull the hammer back, aim and squeeze easy. See that stump over there Legare."

"That small one by the barn?"

"That's the one. Watch now."

He is surprised because she is not hesitant in showing her skill with a pistol. He backs away. Polly takes the pistol in both hands, aims quickly and fires once, twice, three times.

"Hit it three out of three." She lays the pistol on the ground. Smiling she turns to her astonished husband. "It's your turn now honey."

The next evening, Polly and Legare depart for Uncle Richard and Aunt Charlotte's. The ride is a leisurely twenty minutes. They soon pass a long row of fencing. "This is one corner of Uncle Richard's property. This tract extends about one mile square. He has another larger tract near the river for flooding the rice fields."

Polly looks amazed as she views the ground, although barren in the winter, she can visualize the tall corn and the cotton growing as far as one can see. "How many slaves does your Uncle Richard have?"

"Not real sure, but probably around a hundred or so."

"This plantation is enormous. Larger than the Johnson's. How many acres are here?"

"Covers some six thousand acres."

"Is Uncle Richard or Aunt Charlotte your blood kin?"

"Uncle Richard is a relative on my mother's side of the family. My Aunt Charlotte is from England. That's why my cousins are in England studying."

"Is this the only place they have?"

"No, they have a home in Florida as well. Since my childhood, we've always visited Aunt Charlotte and Uncle Richard. For the last two years, I worked on the plantation learning to manage one of the cotton sections. Uncle Richard paid me good wages."

"So what are your other cousins like?"

"Let's see." Legare grins at her. "There are seven children: Marie, Claire, Ian, Jordan, Matthew, Marcelle and Keaton. Ian is closest to my age and Uncle Richard used to take us hunting and fishing when all of our work was completed. During the first summer, Uncle Richard taught me the techniques of the daily business of planting and cultivating, grading, and ginning cotton."

"Did Ian help you?"

"No, Uncle Richard put him to work with the darkies so he could learn about rice cultivation." He points at a stately mansion. "There's the big house." They turn onto a lengthy dirt trail. A wooden, split-rail fencing lines both sides of the trail. She sees a scattering of cattle on one side and the open winter fields to the other.

"What a beautiful house."

"It is a three story Savannah type. See it sits around fifteen feet above the ground and has the typical large, wide stairs ascending to the porch."

Although the plants are dormant, Polly visualizes the landscape is full of beautiful azaleas, numerous varieties of roses, camellia, the yellow flowers of Chinese juniper plant, perennial iris flowers in white, blue, violet, and purple.

"Look honey, there's a witch hazel plant. Ma and Aunt Sally use the bark, leaves, and twigs once they're distilled in alcohol and water. It makes an all-purpose astringent for use on bruises and swellings." She passes the gardens and feels as if she is a humming bird, observing and studying the details of each flower that is yet to bloom.

"The porch, look how wide it is and you can walk around the whole house just like Ma's and Pa's in Stone Mountain. Look at that beautiful, pure white furniture. I'm kinda scared about meeting your family in such a grand place. It's so overpowering."

"Just think of this place as if you were at home. You will be fine," Legare reassures her.

At the instant the carriage pulls in front of the mansion, an elderly stable hand appears and takes the reins of the horse. "'ello, Mistuh Legare!"

"Hello Jesse! Polly, this is Jesse. Remember, I told you about him?" Jumping from the carriage, Legare shakes Jesse's hand. "Jesse, this is my wife, Polly, from Stone Mountain."

Jesse removes his hat and nods his head. "Ya'as, Ma'am."

Polly and Legare walk up the wide stairs to the large front door. A shiny, brass plate about two inches long and one inch wide protrudes from the front of the door. Legare twists the plate several times. A bell rings on the other side of the door each time Legare turns the brass plate.

"Oh, my! Let me try it!"Legare smiles and removes his fingers and Polly takes her turn and twists the bell plate. Almost at that instant, the knob turns and the door opens.

"'ello, Mistuh Legare!"

"Hello, Jemima!" Legare and Jemima hug each other. He whispers to Jemima, "This is my wife, Polly, we want to surprise Aunt Charlotte and Uncle Richard." Jemima giggles and renders a slight bow to Polly.

"Nice to meet you, Jemima."

Uncle Richard sees Legare and Polly at the front door and hurries down the hall to greet them. "Hello, Legare, and who might this young lady be?"

"This is the special person I was telling you about. Are you ready?"

"I certainly am."

"This is my wife, Polly. We eloped to Augusta in November."

"Well, congratulations to both of you! You certainly picked a beautiful young lady to marry. Come on into the back study. I think everyone is there. I just happened to see you in the hall."

Richard leads the way and Legare places his arm around Polly's waist as they follow him to the back study. Richard enters the mahogany paneled study where the family is gathered. Some are standing and talking. Two of the younger children are playing a game of checkers, and Charlotte is talking to Marie. Richard steps forward, "Guess who I found at the front door?" Everyone becomes silent and looks as Legare and Polly enter the study.

The eyes of each family member fall on Polly with her small, delicate features. Her sweet, morbidezza appearance is that of a pure southern beauty and is so perilously fascinating that everyone is clearly in awe of her. The kids jump up and run over to Legare, giving their usual Southern hugs, followed by Charlotte. Polly stands quietly by as Charlotte approaches.

Legare takes Polly's hand. "Everyone listen. I want to introduce someone special to the family. This is my wife, Polly."

Taking a deep breath, and placing her hand on her large bosoms, Charlotte appears almost faint. "Well mercy me! When did all this take place?" The rest of the family is somewhat shocked as well and a silence temporarily comes over the room.

Uncle Richard instructs the waiter. "Bring in champagne for everyone. We must toast the newlywed couple."

"Aunt Charlotte, Polly and I eloped in November and were married in Augusta."

Recovering from the shock and excitement of the news, the children come over and begin welcoming Polly to the family.

"I'm Marie"

"I'm Claire."

"I'm Ian."

"I'm Keaton."

Talking all at once, the excited children begin to ask questions.

"Now, now children. I've got to meet the beautiful blushing bride." Charlotte strolls over to Polly and extends her hand. "I'm Legare's Aunt Charlotte, but really, I'm Legare's cousin by marriage."

"It's nice to meet you." Polly's polite yet deep Southern accent causes Aunt Charlotte's eyes to widen in shock.

"It's nice to meet you as well, Polly. Welcome to the family. Excuse me while I go and check on supper."

The servant comes in with the champagne and pours everyone a glass. Uncle Richard begins a toast but notices Charlotte is missing. "Hold on a minute and let me find Mother." He goes to the kitchen and finds Charlotte talking to one of the cooks. "Charlotte, come back to the study, I am giving a toast to Legare and Polly."

"I can't right now, Richard. That girl scared me to death when she opened her mouth with that accent! Just let me get my breath. I can't believe poor Legare would marry someone who talks like that."

"Now, Charlotte. She is purely Southern and has a beautiful accent! Get over it and come in the study so we can toast and have supper."

Charlotte begrudgingly returns to the study and takes a glass of champagne. Richard raises his glass and everyone else also lifts their glass. "To the health and happiness of Polly and Legare. May their lives be long, full of love and prosperity." Everyone, including Charlotte, clicks their glasses against Polly and Legare's. During supper Polly displays her simple social graces as she and Legare disclose how they met, fell in love, eloped, and ran into Mrs. Turner. "Then we returned to Augusta and spent Christmas Eve and Christmas on a steamer."

Claire walks over to Polly and Legare. "If there was ever a true love story, this has to be one of the best, certainly the best I ever heard. I think you should write a book."

After dinner, Polly and the children tell stories and laugh genuinely. Marie leans toward Polly with a warm smile. "I love your accent. Listening to Gullah all the time dilutes our Southern accent. It just sort of begins to blend together. It's great to hear pure Southern again."

Aunt Charlotte turns a deaf ear on the children's conversation. At the evening's end, the children and Uncle Richard have accepted Polly, but Aunt Charlotte is unable to see how Polly will fit in with her social groups. In her own fashion, she welcomes her none-the-less.

On the way home, Legare tells Polly, "Uncle Richard is allowing us to use Tot, Al, and Jesse."

"Doesn't he need them to work in the fields?"

"He says they are getting too old to do any field work and they'll be coming over in a couple of days."

"What about Tot?"

"According to Uncle Richard, Tot is going to be permanent while Al and Jesse will switch off every three days."

"Well, can we just buy Tot from Uncle Richard?"

"I offered to buy Tot and Al, but Uncle Richard said they are too old to sell and, if the truth is told, I believe he's too fond of them. They've been with him for a long time. If you don't care for them after a few days, we can send them back."

"We'll see."

"So, how do you like my cousins?"

"You have a great family. All of your cousins are wonderful. I just love them, especially Maire. I hope I get to visit with them often. And what a beautiful home! I should say what a beautiful castle. I've only seen drawings of homes so lovely."

"It is spectacular in its own way."

"I bet the flower gardens are spectacular in the spring and summer. I can't wait to see them in full bloom."

PANIC IN THE STREETS

Tot, Al and Jesse arrive at Polly and Legare's modest river house. The darkies have known Legare since he was a child. Polly is rearranging the furniture in the living room when she sees them enter the turn-about driveway. The three are in a beautiful, white carriage drawn by two horses. Polly goes to the front door and walks down the steps to greet them. Tot is already out of the carriage as Polly approaches. "Hello, I hope the trip in was nice. Jesse, you and Al take the carriage and horse around back then come inside. Tot, you come on inside with me."

"Yas'um."

Polly has some hot water boiling for tea. She pours a cup of water for the two of them. "Have a cup of tea with me, Tot, so we can get a little better acquainted." Polly notices that Tot is a little hesitant. "It's all right Tot, come on and sit down. Have some tea."

Tot pulls the chair from around the table and has a seat across from Polly. Tot is about five feet two inches tall and has coal black eyes. She is slender, has a strong mind and has always been a very capable servant. "Have you always lived in Savannah Tot?"

"No-um [no Ma'am] I bin trade fum uh man in Decaytuh fuh two cow 'n uh mule when I bin fohteen. I had fuh leeb muh mudduh 'n fadduh, uh brudduh 'n uh udduh sistuh. Dat duh gwoin on obbuh thirty-five yea'. I duh paat Cherokee'n paat Niggruh." [No, I was traded from a man in Decatur for two cows and a mule when I was fourteen Years old. I had to leave my mother and father, one brother and one other younger sister. That is now going on thirty-five years. I am part Cherokee Indian and part Negro.]

"How about Jesse and Al. Where are they from?"

"Dey two fum Suhwannuh. Jesse 'n Al wuk fuh Massuh Richud 'n Congressman Hill." [They both from Savannah. Jesse and Al both work for Mars Richard and Congressman Hill.]

"Do you ever hear from your family in Decatur?"

"I scarcely git word ob muh sistuh 'n brudduh from Massuh Richud when 'e trabbul to 'Lantuh on bidness, but I ain' 'llow fuh go to 'Lantuh." [On rare occasions I receive some word of my siblings from Mars Richard when he travels to Atlanta on business, but I am never allowed to go.]

Polly asks Tot, "Do you have a husband?"

"I husbun John bin dead sebbrul yea' when 'e git shoot 'n kill." [I lost my husband John several years ago when he was shot and killed.]

Polly leans across the table, "Shot and killed! By who? What happened?"

"One affuhnoon John bin een de big bahn by 'e self when 'e eye ketch de hoss getting' res'les. 'E look fuh see wha' bin bottorin dem hoss den two buckrah man jump out de empty stall 'n 'tack em. John duh big skrong man. When deh grab John, 'e able fuh hit one een de face 'n knock um to de groun'. Dah buckrah hit 'e head on uh stone pilluh 'n git knoc' out cohl. De udduh buckrah man had uh gun. On de way gwoin out de doh John grab uh pitch fork. [One afternoon John is in the big barn alone when he notices the horses are getting restless. As he goes to discover what is bothering the horses two white men jump out of an empty stall and attempt to attack him. John is a big and strong man. As the two grab John he is able to hit one man in the face knocking him to the ground. That white man hit his head on a stone pillow and got knocked out cold. My John turns and runs and the other white man has a gun. On the way toward the door John grabs a pitch folk and quickly turns.]

Polly's eyes grow wide with anticipation. "Tell me what happened next Tot?"

"My John turn fas' wid de pitch fork. De buckrah run right into de pitch fork 'n 'e gun shoot. De musket ball hit John een 'e chest. Wen de odduh daakie yea' de gun deh all mek hays to de bahn. Dey swing de bahn dooh opin 'n dey al see poh John lay still n' de blood pour fum 'e ches'. De buckrah wid de pitch fork, 'e eye bin opin wide 'n 'e han' bin hol' tight tuh de handle ob de pitch fork, E gun bin on de groun' nex' to 'e body. De odduh buckrah man bin still layin' by de stone pilluh when Massuh Richud git deh. Com' tuh fin' out dese buckrah bin hoss teef." [My John turns around fast and the white man runs directly into the pitchfork and his pistol fires. The musket ball strikes John in the chest. The shots are heard by the other darkies and they all come a-running to the barn. They swing open the barn doors and they all see my poor John laying still and blood gushing from his chest. The bandit with the pitchfork… his eyes are still wide open and his hands are tightly grasping the handle of the pitch fork. His pistol is on the ground next to his body. The other white man is still laying by the stone pillar when Mars. Richard arrives. Come to find out these two white men were horse thieves.]

"What did Uncle Richard do with the man who hit his head on the stone pillar?"

"'Bout two week' laytuh dah buckrah wha' hit 'e head on de stone pilluh bin hang fuh teefin' haw'ses. My poh son Scott, leeb yah een uh moh peaceful way. John bin lay fuh res' next to we son een de slaybe graybyaad. [About two weeks later that white man who hit his head on the stone pillow was hung for stealing horses. My poor son Scott, passed in a more peaceful way. John was laid to rest next to our son in the slave cemetery.]

"You had a son. Tot?"

"Yas um."

"Tell me about your son. What happened to him?"

"I had uh son whne I bin sebbinteen. When time fuh slip de suckuh de wrsp 'roun' de baby neck. De doctuh dem say 'e caus' brain damage." [I had a son when I was seventeen. During birth the cord wraps around baby Scott's neck. The doctors say this caused brain damage.]

"Oh that's so sad Tot." Polly rubs her stomach hopefully feeling for her and Legare's baby. "How did you take care of Scott?"

"Massuh Richard 'n Congressman Hill bin always unnuhstan ob Scot 'n ghee me de bes' job so I kin tek kayuh ub my 'flicted son. Keppin up they hous' bin paat ob my job." [Master Richard and Congressman Hill was always very understanding of Scott and gave me the best possible duties so that I could attend my afflicted son. Keeping up their house is part of my duty.]

"How did Scott pass away?"

"One mawnin when Scott bin 'roun' ten yea' ol'I gon' to 'e bed 'n find um stil' 'n col'. I pit my ears puntop 'e nose 'n een bin uh breeze. Poh Scott troubbul body had turn loose 'e soul so 'e kin walk noe 'moung de cloud." [One morning when Scott was around ten year old I went to his bed and found him still and cold. I laid my ear upon his nose and there is no breath of life. Poor Scott's tormented body had released his soul so he could now walk among the clouds.]

Polly slides her hands across the table and holds Tot's hand in hers.

"Uh place bin set fuh Scott een de slayb graybyaad . Massuh Richard had uh 'spectubul headstone fix wid de wuud, "Here his body lays and his soul is committed." Now I een got no chyl' 'n no husban". [A place was prepared for Scott in the slave cemetery. Master Richard had a respectable headstone prepared with the inscription "Here his body lays and here his soul is committed Now I have no child and no husband.]

Al and Jesse enter through the back door directly to the kitchen. They take off their stocking caps and stand in the kitchen silently. "Al, you and Jesse can come and sit down with me and Tot. I just want to find out about you and what you usually do around the river house." Tot turns and with a diminutive smile, looks at Jesse and Al signaling all is well. With great humility, Al and Jesse walk over to the table and take a seat as they continue to clutch their stocking caps.

"Tot informs me that both of you are from Savannah." Al and Jesse look at each other.

Jesse squeezes his hat in his hands. "Yas'um we two bin bohn on Massuh Richard plantashun. We duh brudduh." [Yas'm both of us born on Mars Richards plantation. We are brothers.]

"What are your duties at Congressman Hill's house?"

This time Al answers. "We keep de groun' n' de flouwuhs. We clean de stall 'n pretty up de 'n feed haws' when deh deh yah. Sumtym' we ketch fish fuh Tot fuh cook. We help inside we deh need we. We keep de two wadduh tank full. We keep de fuh on de one tank gwoin for de hot wadduh. We do wha' ebbuh else de tell we fuh do." [We keep the grounds and flowers. We clean the stalls and groom and feed the horses when they are here. Sometimes we catch fish for Tot to cook. We help inside when we are needed. We keep the two water tanks full. We keep the fire on one tank going for the hot water. We do whatever else you tell us to do.]

Polly turns her attention to Jesse. "How many horses are generally kept there?"

"Shree haws 'n two carriage Ma'am." [Three horses and two carriages ma'am.]

Polly is satisfied with her new servants and asks Tot to start supper while Al and Jesse help relocate furniture. Like a good wife, Polly hopes to have the house neat and supper on the table when her husband arrives home.

FEBRUARY 2, 1862

Governor Brown, after deep deliberation, sends for his clerk. With pen, paper and ink his clerk enters. "Yes sir, Governor."

"Have a seat and take down these directives as a draft. To send troops to the Confederate Government's call, either through volunteers or via conscription. However do not include officers or cadets at GMI in this draft."

Norman is instructing in the manual of arms on March 10 when a familiar voice calls to him. "Is that you, Norman?" Norman turns and there stands an old acquaintance, Milton Herndon, from Jackson County. "Hi, Milton. Hold on a minute. Stand at ease," Norman commands the troops. He hurries over to where Milton is standing and they exchange a firm handshake.

"You sure look sharp in your uniform."

"Thanks. We have to keep them looking nice."

"I know you're busy right now, but I saw your folks a short time ago when passing through Stone Mountain. They are doing fine. I told them I was enlisting at Camp McDonald in a couple of weeks, and they said you're a cadet at GMI. Your pa told me that the cadets are instructors at the camp and to be sure and look you up. Your mother gave me a package just for you and your roommate, Paul. They're in my tent. Come on by during dinner and I'll give them to you."

"Great! I can't wait to see what she sent!" says Norman. "Let me get back to the troops now. I'll see you later." They shake hands again and Milton stays to watch his friend instruct the soldiers.

As soon as the sound of the dinner drum rolls, Norman dismisses his trainees and runs down Paul. "Hey, we gotta package from mother. A family friend who just enlisted has it in his tent." They hasten to Milton's tent. He sees them coming, gets the package from inside and hands the taste of home to Norman, who in turn introduces Paul to him.

"I hope it's Ma's corn bread and country ham!" They all take a seat and Norman methodically open's the package. "Sure 'nough! It's corn bread and country ham." Using his knife, Norman starts carving pieces of ham and shares the feast with his friends. "Half of this is yours, Paul, so don't let me eat it all!"

Paul laughs, "Eat all you want, it's your Ma's cooking."

They eat all the ham their stomachs will allow and top it off by drinking plenty of water from the nearby spring. Milton describes to Norman how many people have left his home to join up and that a lot of folks from Stone Mountain are joining up as well. "Nobody wants to be taken by conscription. It would kinda make you feel unpatriotic."

Soon, the drum roll begins, marking the start of assembly. "Thanks for delivering the food, Milton. Maybe your platoon will train under either me or Paul."

About that time, another cadet approaches. "Are you Milton Herndon?" questions the cadet.

"Yes sir, I am."

"Follow me please. I am going to be instructing your platoon in the basics of drill today."

VALENTINE'S DAY

Polly is settling in her home in Savannah and is comfortable with her role as Legare's wife. For the past few weeks she has been feeling very tired and suspects she might be with child. She has confided in Tot about her changing feelings.

Polly wakes up before Legare with a "butterfly" feeling in her stomach. She places the palm of her hand against her belly in anticipation of feeling the life which she and Legare have created. She kisses her dear husband on the cheek and awakens him with her heart bursting with love. "Legare, dear, happy Valentine's Day."

Legare enjoys a last moment of drowsiness and then opens his eyes. He can't resist teasing her a bit. "Good morning, darling. Is it really Valentine's Day?"

Polly is too excited to rise to his jibe. "I have something important to tell you. Something very important."

He snakes his arm around her, pulls her close and kisses her. "And, what, dear Polly, could be more important than the two of us ... snuggled up together in bed on this fine morning?"

"Legare! Stop teasing me. This is important."

"Nothing is more important than kissing my wife good morning."

She pokes him in the ribs. "Legare, listen to me for just a moment and then—"

"And, then?" he asks suggestively.

"Oh, you. You're incorrigible." She turns aside in mock anger. "Maybe I should just keep my secret."

Legare laughs, pulls her back into his arms and gazes into her eyes, observing the sparkle and adoration so evident there. "Polly, I adore you. It's a beautiful morning and I can't resist teasing you." He kisses the top of her head and assumes a serious demeanor. "Now, what's so important that can't wait?" He turns her onto her back and raises his upper torso above her so he's looking down into her eyes again. "I demand that you tell me now, temptress, or I'll devise—"

"Oh, Legare … I do love you." She kisses him and then lays back on the bed to look into his eyes. "I'm so happy and need to tell you our exciting news. We are going to be parents!"

Speechless for a moment, he stares at her, trying to comprehend what he's just heard. His eyes widen with excitement and his smile beams from ear to ear. He wraps Polly in his arms. "Polly darling, how wonderful! I love you. You will be a wonderful mother to our child. This is the best Valentine's news I have ever received, or ever could receive. When did you find out? Tell me the details."

"I have suspected I was with child for the last couple of weeks and dear Tot confirmed that the dream of bearing your child has now come true."

APRIL 10, 1862

The tranquility of the early morning is shattered with a series of loud blasts. Polly opens her eyes wide and her hearing becomes keener. She wonders if she is awakening from a dream. Suddenly a second blast is heard from the direction of Fort Pulaski. Nervously she throws her cover back, scrambles into her robe and dashes into the hall to see what is happening. "Legare!"

At 8:15 AM Captain Quincy Gillmore, a brilliant engineering officer, gave the order to open fire on Fort Pulaski.

Since February, he has been devising a plan to capture the fort. During the months of February and March 1862, he hid his operation on Tybee Island, operating only during darkness and utilizing the deep grass and bushes for concealment. Without detection, he transported thirty-six siege guns and mortars, weighing a total of eight and one-half tons, into position on the north shore of the island. He is discharging the new rifled guns and the new high speed conical shells used by the Union onto Fort Pulaski.[122]

Legare rushes to Polly just as she is coming out of the bedroom. Another huge blast causes a vase to crawl from the sideboard and smash to the floor. Windows rattle and a mirror in the dining room crashes. The shelling is relentless. For a moment, Polly fights the panic rising in her. "Tot, secure the other mirrors. And glassware. What's happening, Legare?"

"Sounds like it's coming from Fort Pulaski. Let's go up to the cupola, Polly." With Polly still in her robe, Legare practically drags her up to the cupola. "Damnation! The Yankees are shelling the fort."

The scene is both grand and awful. From every sound of the cannon, a white curl of smoke floats high in the air, forming countless smoky ribbons and rings. In moments, the acrid smell of the smoke reaches them.

Holding Legare tightly around his waist she nervously stares at the evidence that the war has, at last, come to Savannah. "Seems those rumors we've been hearing must be true. Those Yankee ships been sitting on the river since December."

"Listen Polly, do you hear that strange noise?"

"Yes I do. It sounds like some sort of a crowd or something."

Polly looks slightly in the other direction. She claps her hand over her mouth and grabs Legare with the other. "Oh my, look there in the distance."

At first, they have to strain to see the throngs of people pouring through the streets, a stampede of panic-stricken humanity. Legare shakes his head sadly. "It seems nobody knows where they're going; they're just running from the danger they perceive."

They watch in silent awe as mothers drag screaming children along behind them, slaves run with dogs on leashes and others shove people to one side in their haste to leave. Yet others pull carts of household goods. Some, on horseback, seemingly with no remorse, trample through the crowd, leaving injured and dead in their wake. Hysteria rules Savannah.

Appalled by the sight of a mob where yesterday there had been only peace and tranquility, Polly dashes down to the bedroom. Legare follows close behind. "Legare, I had best get dressed in case there is trouble. Maybe you'd better check the pistols and be sure they are loaded. See to it that Tot is safe."

"Calm down, Polly. We are safe here."

She rips her nightgown over her head and stares at Legare. "I'm as calm as you are, honey. Just wanna be ready in case trouble comes around." He nods and leaves the room to do as she asks. Her hand flutters to her abdomen protectively. "You're safe, little one. Never fear. You have a mother and a fine father to take care of you."

Legare soon returns. "Tot's just fine. She's taken down the rest of the mirrors, but the one over the buffet is in shards as we suspected. She's going to clean that up and then start dinner. Let's go back to the cupola and have another look around."

From the cupola Polly looks at the countryside and town. "Honey, the shelling is still going on but looks like the crowds are beginning to diminish. I guess everyone got to where they were going."

"These people should stay home and guard their belongings in times like this. Seems like the Yanks are only after Pulaski."

When they return from the cupola, Tot is in the kitchen preparing dinner and Polly inhales the aroma. "What's for dinner, Tot?"

"Cornbread, fish, rice and spring greens, Ma'am, Polly."

As suddenly as the ruckus from the streets began, it ends and the city is eerily quiet. Polly and Legare are preparing to sit for dinner, when there's a sudden, loud knock on the door. Between this loud knock and the resumption of the shelling, Polly's nerves are jolted more than before. She and Legare jump from the table. Without a word, they rush to the desk and take the pistols from the drawer.

"Stand back Polly." He peeks through the side of the curtain. With an audible sigh of relief, he holds up his hand. "It is Aunt Charlotte and Uncle Richard."

Richard spots Legare and waves frantically. "Let us in! We've come to check on you."

Polly unlocks the door. "Come in, come in."

Uncle Richard stops just inside the door. "Put the pistol down, you're safe for the time being. The Yankees are shelling Fort Pulaski." He pauses and asks, "You wouldn't really shoot anyone would you, Polly?"

She responds with a look of firm conviction. "In the blink of an eye!"

Aunt Charlotte appears nervous. She changes the subject quickly. "We're preparing to depart if conditions continue to deteriorate. The slaves are packing our silverware, clothing, food and other necessities of the moment. If the Yankees invade Savannah, we will certainly leave."

Polly asks, "Why are the Yankees shelling Fort Pulaski?"

Richard glances at Legare and then grimaces. "It guards the river's entrance to the ports of Savannah. Without the river available, we cannot ship our cotton to Europe or receive supplies. We have a smaller plantation further south and will be leaving tomorrow afternoon if matters get worse. You're welcome to join us."

Legare ponders his uncle's invitation but does not answer immediately.[123] He eyes Polly for a moment. "Uncle, I feel that I must remain here, but Polly cannot. Her condition … well, I must think of our child. Polly will go with you."

Polly jumps to her feet. "No, Legare. No, of course, I can't leave you."

Aunt Charlotte rises and puts her arms around Polly. "Now, dear, you must listen to Legare. He's right. You must think of your child."

Polly gazes for a moment at Aunt Charlotte and then turns back to Legare. "If you stay in Savannah, I will. You cannot force me to leave." She shifts her gaze back to Aunt Charlotte. "I have a responsibility to my husband and to my home. I ... Do what you must, Aunt Charlotte, but do not expect me to leave without Legare."

Legare opens his mouth to speak, but, seeing the determination in his wife's eyes, decides that the discussion has—for the moment—ended. Perhaps, he can reason with her later, but he's well-acquainted with her stubborn resolve. For her safety and that of their child, he would prefer her to go, but for his own comfort, Legare wants nothing more than to have her at his side. He is a man at a crossroads and paralyzed with conflicting desires. He needs time to think ... and time is the one commodity which may not be afforded him.

Later in the afternoon, Uncle Richard and Legare climb back into the cupola. The firing hasn't abated in the least. Smoke rises from the Union cannons on the north side of Tybee Island. Shells strike the walls of Fort Pulaski, which is only one mile away. Shouting down into the house, Uncle Richard calls, "Charlotte, you and Polly come up and look at the battle. The Union must have some type of new cannon. Every shell is hitting the fort."

Aunt Charlotte and Polly scurry up to the cupola and watch the continuing bombardment. Uncle Richard gestures widely, indicating the area near the fort and the river. "I don't see any troop vessels, so I don't think the Yankees are going to try and take Savannah. Probably just going to starve us out if they are successful in taking the fort."

"From what I can see, Uncle Richard, our cannon fire is not making any marks on the Yankees on Tybee. Looks like the Yankees are better shots than we are. Pray our troops are all safe." Polly closes her eyes briefly and utters a silent prayer while Legare squeezes her hand gently.

Uncle Richard tries to comfort the ladies, but can say little to achieve that. "I've been counting the cannon shots. They are averaging seven shots a minute. That's around four hundred shots each hour. I don't see how the fort can stand much longer."

Looking around from the cupola, Legare sees the streets are still crowded with people moving in all directions, but the initial panic seems to be subsiding. "Everyone seems a little more at ease since there are no troop ships in sight."[124]

The shelling progresses through the day but begins to slacken at nightfall. Only periodic shelling continues during the night. Polly sits in her comfortable chair in front of the fireplace and falls asleep, while Aunt Charlotte follows suit on the sofa. Legare bids Uncle Richard good night as he departs quietly for the plantation. Al and Jesse watch for activity outside while Tot stays half awake to ensure no one tries to break into the house.

Before sunrise the next morning, Polly awakens to the enticing aroma of brewing coffee. Upon opening her eyes, she is almost unaware of where she is. She realizes she slept in the chair all night. She stands and stretches, noticing Aunt Charlotte sleeping on the sofa. Polly smiles as Aunt Charlotte grunts an occasional snore. Tot is in the kitchen having a cup of fresh coffee and greets Polly as she walks in.

"I hab some fres' coffee mek. Would ya wantuh, Ma'am?" asks Tot.

"Sure smells good," comments Polly as Tot pours her a cup and gives her a warm muffin. Polly takes her cup of coffee to the bedroom and sits next to Legare on the bed. She rubs his back gently. He awakens and rolls over. "Good morning, honey. I had a sleepless night without you next to me."

He places his arms around her waist. "You looked so peaceful sleeping in the chair, I would have felt guilty to awaken you just to have you by my side."

"I missed you, too. Maybe Tot's coffee will warm your spirits a bit." Polly holds the coffee cup as Legare sits up. She places it to his lips, and he takes a long sip. He and Polly share a good morning kiss and briefly escape the chaos that surrounds them. Once out of bed, he leads her to the front door. He opens the door slowly and visually investigates the misty morning. No sooner than the door opens, than the shelling begins again. Aunt Charlotte awakens and looks around, startled as if she isn't certain where she is. Legare closes the door quickly.

Unaware that Aunt Charlotte is awake, Polly looks out a window as Tot refills the cup. "The streets are quiet. I bet most everyone has already scattered from town. Just a few stragglers and lots of litter is all that's left. Look, the police and militia are making rounds."

Aunt Charlotte yawns, stretches her arms and looks around to let everyone know she is awake. "Oh my goodness! I fell asleep on your sofa. Just look at me! I am mess!" She begins to straighten her clothing and hair, obviously embarrassed to be caught with her appearance so disheveled.

"Aunt Charlotte, you're welcome to use our wash basin in the guest room to freshen up. Tot has some hot tea waiting for you. Legare and I are going to the cupola to see what else is going on."

"Thank you darling, but where's Richard?"

"He went to the plantation last night to check on the children but will be back soon to pick you up." Legare smiles at his aunt. He's seldom seen her in such disarray. "He didn't have the heart to awaken you."

Appearing somewhat disgusted, Aunt Charlotte goes to the guest room to gather herself a bit before breakfast.

When she returns Tot asks, "Wantuh some breckwas?"

"Yes Tot, eggs, grits, cured ham and muffin with hot tea."

"Yas Ma'am." Tot turns and heads to the kitchen.

Shortly, Polly and Legare return from the cupola. He reaches down and plants a soft kiss on her cheek and, simultaneously touches her belly where his son or daughter rests.

"What time did Richard leave last night?"

"A little after dark. He said he'd be back for you around noon. The shelling is still around seven rounds per minute like Uncle counted yesterday. Still no signs of any Yankee troop ships."

Polly, Legare and Charlotte take seats at the table. "Is Tot preparing your breakfast, Aunt Charlotte?"

"Oh yes, my standard muffin, tea, eggs, grits and cured ham."

The smell of the ham fills the air as Tot serves the steaming breakfast. Aunt Charlotte inhales the aroma briefly before attacking the ham with gusto. Polly meets Legare's eyes and both smile. After eating, they return to the cupola to witness the continuation of the shelling.

As she studies the area, Aunt Charlotte recognizes her husband's carriage. "Look, there comes Richard. Let's see what he has found out."

Legare and Polly follow Aunt Charlotte down into the parlor. As Charlotte and Polly rush to the door and swing it open, the shelling stops. All three look at each other in amazement. Polly says, "First this morning, we open the door and the shelling begins. Now, we open the door and the shelling stops! Is this some kind of magic door?" They laugh as Uncle Richard walks up to the house.

Charlotte, unhappy, glares at her husband. "Why did you leave me here last night to sleep on the sofa?"

He smiles. "Because that's the quietest and most peaceful I've seen you in ages." Polly and Legare turn their heads to hide their amusement at Uncle Richard's humor.

Aunt Charlotte retorts, "Rubbish!"

Richard notes the sudden end of the shelling and suggests a trip back to the cupola. Once there, silence falls over the group. "Look there," shouts Legare as he points in the direction of Pulaski. "There's a white flag flying over the fort."

Uncle Richards cocks his head slightly and turns an ear toward Fort Pulaski. "Listen. Be quiet. Can you hear those faint cheers? Must be the Yankees on Tybee." Uncle Richard reflects quietly on the sad situation. "Col. Charles Olmstead[125] is a friend of mind. He told me the story of when he and Gen. Lee met in November of last year at Fort Pulaski. They stood together there on a rampart. Gen. Lee told Charles, 'Upon graduating from West Point in 1829, due to my high standing in my class, I qualified for the highest rated branch of service in the military—the Corps of Engineers.' His first assignment was to build the dikes and a drainage canal for the future site of Fort Pulaski. He assured Charles that, 'The Union guns could not breach the seven foot thick walls from Tybee. Fort Pulaski is the strongest point to control access to the port of Savannah.[126] Looks like Lee was wrong."

After standing silently for a few moments, they descend from the cupola and gather in the parlor. Quiet, order and stillness return to the town. Legare and Uncle Richard begin discussing what they believe will happen.

Aunt Charlotte, on the other hand, seems to want some type of diversion, as if she can't stand to think about the war. "So, dear Polly, what are you going to name your child?"

Polly wrenches her attention from the discussion of the war and stares at Aunt Charlotte. "Pardon?"

"I asked what you're going to name your child."

"Name … oh. We haven't decided." She glanced back at Legare.

"Nonsense. You must begin thinking about it right away. A name is awfully important to a child. For instance—"

Aunt Charlotte's words are cut off by a commotion in the street. All of them rise and dash to peer out the window. Legare is the first to react. "Looks like a messenger."

He rushes to the door and flings it open. "Hello! You, there. What news do you bring?"

Winded, the young man stops and faces the doorway where Legare stands. "Morning, sir. Fort Pulaski has fallen, but the Yankees are not attacking the town. Yet."

Nodding, Legare waves the messenger on. "Thank you. Continue on your journey. God speed."

Uncle Richard expresses his disgust about the war. "Polly, the South entered this conflict because it allowed emotion to over-ride logic. We must be prepared for defeat." He turns his attention to Aunt Charlotte. "I am going to continue gathering most of the valuables and have them transported to the smaller plantation in Florida. They'll be safer there. We need to head home now."

With a sense of foreboding, the families hug. Aunt Charlotte and Uncle Richard hurry out to the carriage and leave. Polly and Legare watch until the carriage is out of sight. For a long moment, they stand arm-in-arm on the verandah, looking up and down the street.

Legare hugs her close and sighs. "Polly, dear Polly. What am I going to do with you? You must—"

"Stop right there!" Polly pulls out of his embrace and gazes up at him. Tears rim her eyes and begin to slide down her cheeks. "I know what you're going to say, Legare. You must believe me when I tell you that I have thought of nothing else since the shelling began. I will not leave you and our home to the ravages of war. Fort Pulaski may have fallen, but the Hill family will stand united against those Yankee invaders. We will fight them together or flee together, but I will not ever leave you."

15

MEDICINE, SURGERY AND HOPE

MID-APRIL 1862

Within a day, the populace returns to a more normal demeanor from the shock of the fall of Fort Pulaski. Polly hears of a church and school that have been turned into temporary hospitals to help with the numerous casualties suffered by the Confederate soldiers at the fort. She feels there must be something she can do to help, but for the moment, she can think of nothing. A vague sense of uselessness seems to override everything she does.

APRIL 11, 1862

The harrowing scenes at Fort Pulaski are somewhat relieved and lightened by the heroic bearing, cheerful resignation, and wonderful fortitude with which the wounded bore up under their afflictions. This is especially conspicuous in the younger soldiers. These mere striplings are wounded badly. Many of the youth are mutilated or mortally injured yet attempt to ignore their pain. The older wounded manifest far greater anxiety toward the character of their injuries, having experienced the sad outcome of comrades wounded in the past.

The wounded men begin appearing at the hospital, some hobble along while others are brought in the ambulance wagons. Many are stripped nearly naked, displaying the bloody dressing of their wounds. The hospitals rapidly become overcrowded and many who arrive late remain in the wagons exposed to the cold and damp night.

Chief surgeon, Dr. Blair, and the other surgeons work diligently and unrelentingly. By dim lights and in the open air, the surgeons perform countless delicate operations. The air stinks of blood. The halls and rooms become crowded. Anguish, death, blood and mounds of body parts become a haggard in and around the operating rooms.

A universal spirit of brotherhood and an absence of selfishness are displayed by everyone attending of the wounded and dying. The groans of the suffering and the cries of those undergoing surgery are oppressive. The distinct gurgling sounds of soldiers shot through the lungs, waiting to meet their maker, resonate throughout the compound.

Row after row of soldiers wait for their time on the dreaded operating table. Many are already under the influence of morphine, but still cry out in the agony of life-stealing injuries. The assistant surgeon and Dr. Blair labor intensely with this never-ending chaotic ordeal. As soon as one surgery is complete, another patient is placed on the bloody table. The smell of blood and piles of arms and legs overflowing from baskets near his station greet each new patient. Flies swarm everywhere. The overwhelming presence of hopelessness cannot fail to touch each soldier as he is brought into surgery.

"Doctor, can you save my arm?" The latest young man on the table looks up, his watering eyes imploring.

"I'm afraid not, son," replies Dr. Blair as the chloroform begins to drip on the soft cloth covering the soldier's nose and mouth.

Sleep comes quickly. The assistant surgeon passes Dr. Blair the knife. Grasping the bloodstained tool, Dr. Blair carves away the tissue to the bone, tying off arteries and veins as he goes. Then comes the saw. In a brief moment another arm is thrown upon the pile of lifeless flesh. With a bloody, long and curved needle, the doctor uses horsehair to close the wound. His assistant wipes his hands with a wet towel and takes a three-inch long straight needle threaded with silk thread, completing the task which but a few hours ago was dreaded. Now, it seems little more than routine, something that must be done to save a life, however distorted it may have become by the war and injury.

The life altering surgery takes less than twenty minutes to complete. The chloroform stops and the soldier awaken with one limb less than his last memory recalls. His constant companion for the next few days is pain and, if he's fortunate, the nightmares of a morphine-induced trance.

For ten hours, one soldier after another suffers a similar consequence, the amputation of an arm, leg, or finger. When a wound is in the gut, a bare probing finger attempts to find and remove a foreign material from that part of the body. Finally, the long line of soldiers awaiting surgery ends.

Exhausted, Dr. Blair and his assistant assist the nurses in making their rounds to the dying, authorizing medication to reduce the pain and suffering. There truly seems to be no rest awaiting those who tend the injured.

APRIL 13, 1862—THE GREAT LOCOMOTIVE CHASE

The Superintendent at GMI retires early after the excitement of the chase between the stolen General and The Texas. Around midnight on the 13th, the superintendent of the Institute is awakened by a messenger from the Commander of the Confederate provost guards at Big Shanty.

"To: Maj. John M. Richardson, Superintendent of Georgia Military Institute. Accordingly, four of the Union prisoners are in prison in the Marietta City jail. There's a restless crowd of several hundred gathering about, and I fear an attempt to overtake my guard and render vigilante justice. At all speed, sir, I request that you send cadets with arms to aid in securing the prisoners aforementioned."

Maj. Richardson hastily scrolls on the bottom of the request and writes, "I'll comply with your request. Maj. J. T. Richardson." The messenger salutes and takes to his mount and hastily heads toward the jail.

Maj. Richardson wakes up Cornelius. "Play the 'long roll' for assembly."

Upon being awakened by the bugle, Norman tumbles from his bed. "Get up, Paul. Quick. Something serious is going on for Cornelius to call us out at this hour!"

Paul peers out of the window and sees Maj. Richardson pacing on the assembly ground. In moments, the two cadets are dressed and dash outside. Within ten minutes of the bugle call, the entire cadet corps is in formation with their muskets.

Maj. Richardson paces the formation as the last cadet joins the others. "The Provost Guard needs our assistance protecting the prisoners at the jail. Your companies are to proceed to the armory and draw ammunition. From there, we will march to the jail and assist the Provost Commander as the need arises." As they procure their weapons, the excitement of the coming action sends the morale high in all the cadets.

Paul glances at Norman with a grin of excitement. "We can keep the order at the jail without any problem."

"Probably a bunch of drunks trying to make trouble. But you can't really blame them too much. After all, those Yanks tried to burn eight bridges between here and the border." Norman can hardly contain his emotions. On the one hand, uncertainty colors his thoughts. But, on the other hand, he realizes that he will, at last, make a contribution to the war effort. He realizes this is only the beginning. For better or worse, the GMI cadets have entered the war.

The Provost Commander sees the cadets as they approach the jail near the depot. He greets Maj. Richardson, "Take the cadets and have them completely surround the jail. Have them load their weapons and stand tall."

Maj. Richardson surveys the cadets. "Load weapons!"

The precision movements of loading the weapons are impressive to the mob. The mob's angry shouting lessens as they begin to realize these cadets most probably mean business. After loading is complete, he commands, "Single file around the jail and hold your positions."

Maj. Richardson and the Commander speak to the crowd in no uncertain terms, "Any person or persons attempting to enter the jail will be shot. The cadets, as well as the provost guards, are armed and ready to respond. We advise you leave the area. Let the courts handle these criminals with true Southern Justice."

The cadet corps maintains a stoic attitude during this "reasoning conversation." The locals are accustomed to the cadets and realize they have been trained to kill or capture. They become very reluctant to challenge them on this issue and the unruly crowd begins to evaporate slowly, easing the tense situation enough for the cadets to settle into a pleasant night of guard duty.[127]

⁓

Several days after the capture of Fort Pulaski, Uncle Richard and Aunt Charlotte decide not to depart for Florida, and Polly receives an invitation from Aunt Charlotte inviting her to their townhouse near the hospital. After supper, Polly shows Legare the invitation. "I received this from Aunt Charlotte today. She has invited me to assist her and her friends in scraping lint, cutting material for bandages and sending culinary delicacies to the hospitals. I would like to help out with the war effort. Would you mind if I accepted the invitation?"

"Why, of course, I would not mind. You have a lot to contribute. Your knowledge of herbs would be of great interest to Aunt Charlotte and her friends, although most of them are society conscious."

"I'm going on six months with child now. Women generally stay to themselves at this stage, but I would like to go."

"I don't feel Aunt Charlotte would send the invitation to embarrass you in front of her friends. Besides, I'm certain most of her friends already know all about us and would love to meet you. So give 'em your best shot which is better than any of their shots, I promise you that!"

Polly hugs Legare and he pulls her around to his lap. "I sure do love you, Legare!"

"And I sure do love you, Polly!"

The following day, Al takes her to Aunt Charlotte's townhouse. Polly is glad to participate in the lint scraping, however, she feels extremely uncomfortable because of the air of a "social occasion" of tea and gossip. Al escorts Polly to the front door and knocks. A house servant opens the door. "'ello, Al."

"'ello Jemima. 'ember Ma'am. Polly? Ma'am Charlotte is expecting her."

"I be back een de carriage hous' wen you ready fuh go, Ma'am Polly."

Jemima conducts Polly to the grand sitting room. Aunt Charlotte sees Polly entering and greets her. "I'm glad you could join us today, Polly."

"Thank you for the invitation."

"Come, Polly. I'll introduce you to my friends." Entering the sitting room, she announces, "Ladies, this is my cousin Legare's wife, Polly Hill."

Each lady present warmly introduces herself, and Polly acknowledges each introduction with a kind smile and "Nice to meet you as well," then finds a chair. She casually studies the elegant surroundings of the grand room. There are seven marble top tables, beautiful vases and numerous antique lanterns. A thick bright red and green oriental rug covers the floor. The drapery is gold in color and ascends to the twelve feet high ceilings.

The servants serve hot tea, finger biscuits, confections of all sorts, and fresh fruits in a liberal manner. As the servants offer the delicacies, Polly graciously accepts and leaves it to her palate to determine if she'll accept another dose of the same delight. As Polly chooses a piece of fabric to scrape, one of the ladies asks, "Have you scraped lint before Polly?"

"Many times, ma'am. Why do you ask?"

"Charlotte passed on to us that your family only has several hundred acres to farm. So I am curious if you scrape lint at home or if you hired yourself out!"

Polly eyes the lady directly and calms herself before she speaks. This woman is, after all, a friend of Aunt Charlotte's and Polly doesn't want to offend her hostess. "I don't hire out and to answer your next question, Legare and I have been married long enough for me to be with child. Do you have any other personal questions?"

Another lady in the group intercedes, "Pay Jodi no attention, Polly. She is just an ol' nosey gossip. If you're good enough for Legare, you're good enough for me!"

"Why I did not mean any harm Polly, I just ..."

"Just be quiet Jodi, you have said more than enough!" Aunt Charlotte cuts off her friend before the situation can escalate.

"No bother, Aunt Charlotte, scraping the lint is more important."

The women begin their around town gossip. Polly is well aware that scraping the lint is secondary to the social gathering. "Aunt Charlotte, I will be glad to deliver the lint and bandages to the hospital."

The ladies become very quiet as Polly receives a Victorian stare from the group. Aunt Charlotte smiles woodenly. "The hospitals are no place for ladies. The doctors and the nurses will notify us when they need bandages for the patients."

Polly hears the words and knows Aunt Charlotte speaks the truth, but Polly is a young woman with a strong sense of duty. "Do y'all not care? If you had a loved one there, you certainly would."

"Yes," replies one of the ladies. "But we will see them in time and especially when they come home."

Polly offers a simple response. "I see." *What kind of love is this?* She wonders. She simply smiles and continues to scrape lint and partake of the sweet delights, tea and light conversation.

⚘

Doctor Samuel Moore, the Chief Medical Officer for the Confederate States, foresees how the shortages in drugs, hospital supplies and medical instruments will present a dilemma to the treatment of patients. He has purchased supplies from Europe and has medical supplies from captured Union hospitals. Dr. Moore also has an indigenous drug manufacturer in Macon. Aunt Charlotte has a copy of a book distributed by Dr. Moore. The book details the native herbs and other plants that grow wild in the South. These plants are believed to provide curative qualities to certain ailments and diseases.

Aunt Charlotte glances around the room full of ladies. "The newspaper reports show that quinine, morphia and calomel which normally came through New Orleans are no longer as plentiful. Shortages of medicine are already noticeable since the surprise capture of Fort Pulaski. Richard has several of our slaves harvesting as many of the herbs in Dr. Moore's book as they can find."

Aunt Charlotte picks up the book and begins showing it to the other ladies. Polly listens eagerly for a moment. "Aunt Charlotte, may I take the book home and read it?"

Jodi chimes in again. "My dear child, do you think you can read well enough to understand what the book contains?"

Polly, being of a more simple and pleasant nature, pauses for a long moment. Knowing herself to be very well read, she replies directly to Jodi. "I'll do my best and surely call upon you or Aunt Charlotte for what I can't read and understand."

Another lady, embarrassed by Jodi's comment interjects, "There you go again, Jodi, minding everyone's business but your own!"

Aunt Charlotte hands Polly the book indignantly and continues her conversation with the other ladies. When there's no more lint to scrape or bandages to prepare, Polly bids the ladies farewell, summons Al, and with Dr. Moore's book, heads home for the evening.

Sitting by the fireplace after supper, Legare wonders why Polly hasn't mentioned her outing. "How was your day with Aunt Charlotte?"

"It went just fine. I met some interesting people and Aunt Charlotte gave me Dr. Moore's book on herbs. One of Aunt Charlotte's friends by the name of Jodi asked me if I could read."

Looking surprised, he studies his wife a few seconds. "What did you say back to her?"

"Told her if I had any problems I would check with Aunt Charlotte and about that time another lady somewhat chastised her for her comments. Nothing to be concerned about though."

"You're a better person than I am, honey. It's a good thing I wasn't there."

"Thanks, but it's all right. Please forget I mentioned the incident. I know a little about herbs from Mother and Aunt Sally. They were good at identifying and picking the right plants."

"Well, I'm glad you sorta enjoyed yourself today." Legare places his hand on Polly's enlarged stomach.

She places her hand on top of his. "Feel our baby kicking?"

"Sure do," replies Legare. "Must want out of there!"

"Well he or she is more than half-way to freedom," replies Polly as they snuggle close to one another in front of the fireplace. "When will you see Uncle Richard again?"

"Tomorrow. Why do you ask?"

"I want to talk to him about selecting and collecting herbs with a couple more of the darkies if he can spare them. Ask him when I can meet him."

"I will. This might be the last year for cotton. Uncle Richard said he has word that Governor Brown is going to demand a reduction in cotton production. Food is getting scarce. Corn and syrup are bringing more money than cotton right now."

The next day Polly reads the book and discusses herbs with Tot. Some of the plants are familiar to both of them. Polly's parents, Tot's parents and Uncle Isaac have used herbs for treatment of their family's ailments. "When the blackberries are plentiful, we can produce blackberry cordial. This has been recognized as a good treatment for upset stomach. I know painkillers are getting in short supply so we can make some from the jimsonweed. I see there are a lot dogwood trees in the woods. So we can produce an appetite stimulant or medicine to relieve stomach discomfort from its bark."

Early the next morning, Polly departs with Tot to seek out Uncle Richard at the plantation. It is planting season and as far as one can see, there are mules and plows working the fields. The slaves are singing a popular Gullah song, *De Fox en de Crow*, all in unison as they plow and plant.

The song conveys the story of a crafty fox who manages to trick a lady crow into dropping a piece of meat clenched firmly in her jaws. The fox sees the crow steal meat from a white man, who is going to give the meat to his dog. Once the crow has the meat, she flies safely to the limb of a nearby tree. The crafty fox reasons that, as a woman, the crow must like to talk. So the crafty fox figures if he can persuade the crow to open her mouth and speak, she'll have to drop the stolen meat. The crafty fox flatters the crow, praising her theft of the meat, her flying abilities, and her "stylish" plumage. The crow pretends not to listen and says nothing and continues to hold tightly to the meat.

> *Den, Fox staat fuh talk. E say to eself, e say,*
> *Dish yuh crow duh ooman, enty?*
> *Ef a kin suade um fuh talk,*
> *   him haffa op'n e mout, enty?*
> *En ef e op'n e mout, enty de meat fuh drap out?*

[Then, the fox started to talk. He said to himself, he said,
    This here crow is a woman, not so?

If I can persuade her to talk,
she has to open her mouth, not so?
And if she opens her mouth, isn't it true the meat will drop out?]

> Fox call to de Crow: "Mawnin tittuh," e say.
> "Uh so glad you tief da meat fum de buckruh,
> cause him bin fuh trow-um-way pan de dog,
> E mek me bex fuh see man do shishuh ting lukkah dat."

[Fox called to the Crow: "Morning girl," he said.
"I am so glad you stole that meat from the white man,
because he would have thrown it away to the dog,
It makes me vexed to see a man do such a thing as that!"]

Crow nebbuh crack e teet! All-time Fox duh talk, Crow mout shet tight pan de meat, en e yez cock fuh lissin.

Crow never cracked open her teeth! All the time Fox was talking, Crow's mouth was shut tight on the meat, and her ears were crooked to listen.

Finally, the fox discovers the crow's weakness when he praises her singing voice, which to the fox, is notoriously bad. Flattered, the crow tries to impress her admirer, lets out a long, ugly screech, and drops the meat to the ground. The fox picks it up and says, "Tengky fuh de meat, tittuh." ["Your voice is very good because it's my breakfast bell, but, as for your common sense, it ain't worth much," says the fox.]

The mid-April day is overcast, relieving much of the sweat and toil of the laborers. Cook stations are abundant and water bearers are running the rows to quench the throats, dry from the dust, hard work and songs.

Polly looks at Uncle Richard and begins to explain her purpose for her visit. "I think scraping lint and rendering bandages are an important part of the war effort for the ladies, but I feel I can be more useful in gathering herbs."

Uncle Richards listens intensely. "I see. Go on."

Polly continues to present her reasoning. "Throughout my life, my family has relied on herbs for treatment, and I am very familiar with their identification and formulation."

Uncle Richard realizes from his recent conversation with his wife that Polly feels uncomfortable among Charlotte's friends. He sincerely comprehends and appreciates Polly for her subtle values, dedication and love to

Legare. Without hesitation, he consents to her request. "I'll give you two or three of my older slaves to assist you and Tot with the herbs. Besides, even if we have a good cotton crop this year, I don't see it going any further than the cotton warehouse now that the river is blocked. Probably will have to start planting corn and peas for the soldiers. Come back tomorrow and I'll have my workers who know herbs ready to assist you."

"Thank you, Uncle Richard. You made my day! Just one more request."

"What is it, Polly?"

"Could you set me an appointment with the doctor at Bartow Hospital?"

"I'll be happy too. That would be Dr. Blair."

Polly smiles and gives Uncle Richard a hug before she and Tot depart.

BACK IN STONE MOUNTAIN

APRIL 22, 1862

"Ha! Ha! Ha!" Nearly overcome with laughter, Buck gets out of his rocker on the porch. He holds the newspaper in his hand and goes to the front door. "Betty Gail, come out here. I want you to hear this!"

"Hear what, Buck?"

"About this double barrel cannon[128] a dentist in Athens invented!" Betty Gail comes to the front porch and sits next to Buck on the front porch steps.

"Listen to this, 'For a cost of $350 subscription raised by thirty six interested citizens, the Athens Steam Company cast a double barrel cannon for John Gilleland, who is a dentist, a builder and mechanic. Thomas Bailey supervised the casting of the cannon. The two barrels have a divergence of three degrees. The cannon is designed to shoot two cannon balls simultaneously connected with a chain to mow the enemy down like scythe cuts wheat. The gun is four feet-one inch long. The bore is three and thirteen-hundredths inches and the gun weighs about thirteen hundred pounds. Each barrel has its own touchhole so it can be fired independent of the other. Then there's a common touch hole in the center designed to fire both barrels simultaneously.' Now this is where the story really gets funny. Are you ready for this Betty Gail?"

"I'm ready Buck!"

"The double barrel cannon was taken out to Newton Bridge Road near Athens for test firing. The test was, to say the least, spectacularly unsuccessful. The cannon was set and aimed at a target of two upright poles. However when fired, one ball left the muzzle before the other ball and the two balls pursued an erratic circular course. The balls and chain began plowing up an acre of ground, destroying a cornfield and mowing down some saplings before the chain broke.

Then each ball adopted a separate course. One ball killed a cow and the other demolished the chimney on a log cabin at which point all of the observers scattered in fear of their lives."

Betty Gail chuckles. "I would have liked to have seen that Fourth of July display myself."

"The last sentence says, 'shooting cannon balls connected with a chain is commonly done in naval warfare, but these chain-shots are fired from a single barrel.'"

"I need to get back and finish helping Sally with the washing or whatever it was that I was doing."

Buck kisses Betty Gail and gently wipes her tears from her eyes. "I'm gonna read the article again. Then I think I'll mail Norman a copy at GMI. Those cadets will really get a kick out of this one!"

Betty Gail goes back inside and Buck returns to his rocker to read the article once again and laughs as he imagines what a sight the firing of the double barrel cannon must have been.

MAY, 1862

The GMI bugler plays "parade assembly. "Norman picks up his musket and turns to Paul. "It's great to have Maj. Capers back from Savannah. Today's parade will show him how much we really appreciate his return."

"Yeah, Norman. I can't believe he's been gone for six months. I'm anxious to hear some stories about the defenses of Savannah during our military tactics class."

"I understand he's been plenty busy going through the big stack of applications for admission, Paul. His secretary says the Institute now has more applications than it has space for potential cadets. He also said Maj. Capers' first order of business is to protect us from the dark cloud of the Confederate Conscription Law."

"He doesn't seem to understand that we want to fight."

"Well I think Governor Brown will put us in the state militia sooner or later to reduce the criticism from the press about GMI becoming a hiding place to avoid conscription."

"According to the newspaper, Maj. Capers communicated with Governor Brown and the State Adjutant General, suggesting, that we should be allowed to muster into service as officers of the corps." Just before Norman and Paul take their place in the ranks for the parade, Paul places his musket by his side and looks at Norman. "The governor is considering Maj. Capers offer, however he informed Maj. Capers, that he is developing another alternative to exemptions. Probably something safer since his son is a cadet now."

JUNE 1, 1862

Uncle Richard informs Polly of her appointment with Dr. Blair and Madame Cazier at Bartow Hospital. Madam Cazier is the Vice President of the Ladies' State Military Association and the principle Lady Manager of the Bartow Hospital. Bartow Hospital is a part of the Oglethorpe Medical College. Madam Cazier is a well-respected homeopathic ladies' physician in Savannah. She and Madam Young are in the process of preparing the hospital in anticipation of the arrival of more wounded troops.[129]

The hospital's location is almost in the center of town. It is an old, Grecian style building adorned with thirteen columns, each one at least twenty feet tall. Polly enters the foyer, immediately recognizing the odor emitted from mixtures of indigenous herbs. She approaches a slender, sickly young man who is sitting at a desk in the foyer. As she reaches the desk, she notices the clerk has only one arm. She introduces herself politely and tries not to stare. "I am Mrs. Legare Hill and I have an appointment with Dr. Blair and Madam Cazier."

He is stoic and rises slowly from his chair. "Follow me, ma'am. Dr. Blair is expecting you." He escorts Polly to the open ward where there are at least twenty beds lining the walls on each side of the large room. He approaches a middle age lady who is about five feet four tall and has a delicate, slender form. Her face is round and pleasant. She and a gentleman are having a conversation with a patient who is stricken with some type of illness.

Upon Polly's approach, the lady turns and says with a strong French accent, "You must be Polly!"

"I am."

"Please give us a moment and then we can talk about your project in Dr. Blair's office."

The doctor approaches and introduces himself. "Hello, my name is Hugh Blair. I am the Chief Surgeon at Bartow. It is nice to meet you. We have been expecting you. Just give us a moment more and wait for me in my office."

"Follow me please," says the clerk and he escorts her to an oval table in Dr. Blair's office. Polly notices a stand-on scale as she looks around the office. There is an extension rod that can be extracted in order to measure one's height extending from the scale. In one corner, there's a human skeleton. All bones are intact as it hangs from a slender pole with arched wire at the top, attached to the center of the skull.

Lining the walls are several shelves of books that immediately catch Polly's attention, including *Materia Medica* and a copy of the book Dr. Moore has written. Other shelves have numerous bottles containing what appear to be notions and potions from indigenous plants. The labels on the bottles read, "Quinine Sulphatis, Colomel, Laudanum, Morphiya, Alcohol, Cactus, Eucalyptus, Cod-liver-oil, Chloroform, Charcoal, Quinine, Turpentine, Opium, Iodine, Iris, Borax, Mercury, Bismuth, Camphor, Hydrochloric Acid and Hydrogen Peroxide, Asparagus, Attar of Rose, Bear-berry, Blackberry Brandy, Honey, Carrot-fruit, Cinnamon Powder, Corn silk, Corn-Husk Meal, Dogwood Extract, Garlic, Raspberry Vinegar, Turkey Corn, Wheat flour, Whale Sperm, and Whiskey." In another corner of the room, there's a woven basket full of fresh lint for packing open wounds. There are two oil lamps on his desk, several pens and numerous stacks of papers as well as a broken in meerschaum smoking pipe. A portrait of Hypocrites healing the sick hangs over the mantel of the large fireplace. The mantel also holds bandages, dressings and an array of silk thread and oddly shaped needles for bringing torn skin together. Thermometers and a couple of stethoscopes call the mantle home as well.

Soon, Dr. Blair and Madame Cazier enter the room. Dr. Blair is an older man and, like most of the doctors of his era, learned his "science" through an apprenticeship. They take a seat at the oval table with Polly.

Dr. Blair observes her a moment. "We are glad you have come to offer your assistance. Your Uncle Richard is a very close friend of mine and speaks highly of you."

"Thank you for taking your time to talk with me today Dr. Blair."

"Madame Cazier and I understand you and Tot are familiar with herbs and how to convert them into medicine."

"Yes, sir, Dr. Blair. I learned from my parents. I brought some Rhubarb Syrup and Dogwood Extract for y'all to try." Polly removes a few bottles from her woven basket and places them on the table in front of Dr. Blair and Madame Cazier.

Dr. Blair twists the cork and removes it from the Rhubarb Syrup bottle. He raises the bottle to his nose, sniffing the syrup and samples a small amount of the mixture by using his finger as a spoon. "Mighty good." He passes the bottle to Madame Cazier, smiles and leans back in his chair.

Madame Cazier removes the cork from the Dogwood Extract. Passing the bottle beneath her nostrils, she inhales to detect if the mixture is complete. She places some of the extract on her finger and touches her tongue to it. The three sit quietly for a moment. Madame Cazier stands and locates a spoon on the nearby shelf over the sink. Polly watches patiently as Madame Cazier fills the spoon and swallows a complete dose. She licks her lips and returns to her chair at the small round conference table. "I could not have made it better myself!"

With a warm smile, Polly gives a sigh of relief. "Thank you."

Dr. Blair looks from Madame Cazier to Polly. "The Yankee navy has Pulaski. Lord knows when the ground troops will enter Georgia. I'm afraid the affairs of war are going to involve Savannah. From where the Yankee ground troops will come none of us knows. But when they arrive, it will cause chaos all around. There will be an abundance of sickness, disease, death and destruction. For the salvation of the state, it would be better if Governor Brown comes to terms with himself and raises Old Glory again. The impact of the recent blockade on our port is going to prevent medical supplies and food from entering, as well as preventing our crops of rice, cotton and other agricultural commodities from being exported. This will render our economy useless."

"I understand your husband, Legare, is not in uniform yet, and you and your husband are planning on staying in Savannah until the war ends?"

"Yes, sir, that is correct."

"Would you like to go on a tour of the hospital wards and facilities with Madame Cazier?"

"Certainly."

"There are several younger physicians on duty who have been in practice for nearly two years. If you're ready, Madame Cazier, you may take Polly on the hospital tour now."

Madame Cazier and Polly stand as the doctor continues, "I am looking forward to working with you, Polly. We are going to need a lot of medicine. The disaster at Fort Pulaski is taxing our ability to care for these brave soldiers."

As the women enter one of the wards, Madame Cazier directs Polly's attention to several patients with bowel disorders. "Their treatment involves salts, castor oil and laudanum. There are seven patients who are back from the war with amputated legs. One poor man is missing part of his jaw from a shot to his face. There have been forty soldiers transported here by ship and all have died except these seven. "

The air has a sour odor, and the floors are dark red from the seeping bloody bandages. Outside in the washing area, slaves are cleaning wash pots and hanging sheets. On the other side of the building there's a small plot of ground where several wooden coffins are stacked. "This is where we place the amputated limbs and dead. The grave detail buries them in a separate plot in the cemetery."

Returning inside, she introduces Polly to female nurses who bathe, bandage and comfort the patients. "Matters are going to get worse, I'm afraid, Polly, as the war grows."

Dr. Blair is in the kitchen, inspecting the quality of the food being prepared when Madam Cazier and Polly enter. "I should be finished in a few minutes and will meet you in the operating room."

Acknowledging Dr. Blair, Madam Cazier informs Polly, "This time of year, mostly greens and meats are available for the patients. The stoves and ovens use prime oak and hickory, which is stacked in the woodshed. Now let's go to the second floor."

On the second floor, there are no empty beds. "Those with known infectious diseases, such as syphilis, malaria, measles, typhoid fever and so forth are kept separate from the soldiers with wounds on this floor."

Polly notices the netting on each bed is a vain attempt to ward off flies and mosquitoes. In the middle and ends of the wards are large, potbelly stoves. The oil lanterns hanging from the ceiling afford little light during darkness so there are candles at each bedside.

The last stop on the tour is the operating area. It smells of stale cloth and mildew. Blood stains the floor. They see long flat tables where the surgeons use the knowledge, skill and instruments available as they try to save lives. Chloroform bottles and small bundles of cloth line the walls. Silk thread and horsehair suture material and a large assortment of needles lay on joining shelves, tables and cabinets. There are odd-looking instruments all about the room used for surgery and treating wounds.[130]

Fanning his hand in front of his face, he says, "Flies are a nuisance. Even now, in the early spring, they crave the dried blood and secretions left behind. Sometimes we operate outside because the lighting is better."

Polly absorbs all of the information and feels a bit ill. They return to Dr. Blair's office to talk about compensation for her herbal medicines.

Polly takes the conversation back to her herbals. "Payment would be minimal, just for the alcohol, ether and acetone, but in gold coins rather than silver would be ideal. Also, I'll be glad to volunteer in some capacity if you ever need me."

They agree to the terms and Dr. Blair and Madame Cazier bid Polly good-bye. On the way to her carriage, Polly passes the new prison adjacent to the hospital. The prison wagon is parked next to the gate of the stockade. "Go ahead and unload the prisoners." The stockade commander directs the guards. Polly stops to observe the prison induction. As the prisoners climb down from the calaboose wagon, they appear starving, weak and ill from their stay in the over crowded prisons of Richmond.

Although sobered by the sight, Polly is full of excitement as she boards her carriage. "Jesse, take me by the bank. I want to give Legare the good news!" Before the carriage comes to a complete stop in front its destination, Polly hops to the ground and enters the bank with a broad smile. Legare sees Polly and rushes to hug her.

"Good news from Dr. Blair, right, Polly?"

"Yes, Dr. Blair and Ms. Cazier seem to be satisfied with my samples. They want me to make more and are willing to pay for them. I told them like you said, I prefer payment in gold and that was all right with them."

"It's just about time for my break. Let me check with Mr. Lilly to see if it's all right for me to leave ten minutes early for lunch." Legare goes to Mr. Lilly's office and returns quickly. "He said I could leave early, but not to be away for more than an hour. How about the Pirates' House?"

Taking Legare's hand, she smiles happily. "Sounds good to me. That seems to be our place for celebrations!"

After lunch and upon arriving at the river house, Polly finds Tot in the kitchen. "Tot, Dr. Blair and Ms. Cazier said my herbs were satisfactory and my processing would fill a need for the herbal medicine at the hospital. So, we need to begin making plans for the gathering of more herbs. Strange as it may seem Tot, when I was at the hospital I could not help but notice that many of the slaves have become surly. I guess they are waiting for the Union Army to arrive in Savannah and set them free. At supper the other night, I heard several folks have slaves running away. I cannot keep you from running away either. I hope you don't and if you're free when the war ends, Tot, you can surely work for me, if you like. If you aren't freed, I will buy you from Uncle Richard and set you free myself."

"Dohn fret none Ma'am Polly. I een hab no plac' fuh go but yah." [Don't you fret Ma'am, Polly. I have no place to go but here.]

"We'll just have to wait till the time comes," says Polly.

The first order of business for Polly is to have the slaves gather the various plants to extract the necessary ingredients for her mixtures. On his days off, Legare assists in gathering large quantities of alcohol, acetic acid and ether for use in the processing. The materials and plants are taken to the river house where the processing of drugs begins. Al and Jesse have arranged several large black pots that are sitting over open pit fires in an area behind the river house. The first extract processed is the bark from the root of dogwood trees. Legare scans the area. "This is a new experience for me. Show me what you want done, Polly."

"Here's how to select the best bark." Polly selects several pieces of dogwood bark. "Take bark that has moisture and no bugs." Then Polly bends a piece to show that the bark does not break. "That's all there is to the selection process, honey."

Legare watches his wife a moment. Her belly is beginning to show her condition. "Polly, dear, I'm concerned about your … well, your condition."

"My condition? Whatever do you mean?"

"You are carrying our child, Polly." Legare hugs her close and snuggles against her sweet-smelling hair. "Are you sure this is safe?"

"Oh, Legare! Is that it? I am a healthy woman." She places her hands on the bulge on her belly and smiles. "Our child will be fine. In fact, he'll be all the better for having a mother who continued to be active."

Shaking his head, he grins, once again feeling an almost overwhelming pride in his wife. "I must believe you, but you must promise that you will rest if you feel the least bit tired. I am aware of your value to the Confederacy, but I assure you, it is of little consequence when compared to your value as the mother of our child."

Realizing she'll get no work done until he's satisfied, she puts down the bark and slides her arms around his neck. "I promise, Legare. I promise to be as careful of my health as possible. But, you must also promise to be careful of your health. I can't stand the thought of. …" Words fail her. Polly simply can't articulate her fears.

He kisses the top of her head, lifts her chin and brushes her lips with his own. "Then don't think about it, Polly. You promise to look after yourself, and I'll promise to look after myself. That's the best we can do, don't you think? We will leave it unspecific. Is that all right?"

"Oh, thank you, Legare." She hugs him and then pushes away. "Now, back to work."

Legare takes Polly's lead and fills a large black pot with the selected bark. Then, the darkies pour boiling water from another large black pot over the bark, stirring as it boils for several hours over an open fire. Cheesecloth is placed over buckets to act as a filter. The tainted water is poured through the cheesecloth and then cooled.

"Tincture of dogwood" is ready for use as a substitute for quinine.

After refining several barrels of tincture of dogwood, the bark of the alder tree is processed in a similar fashion. The resin, tannic acid and oil are extracted.

In a separate process using alcohol, alnuin[131] is extracted from the resin. This diluted extract is to be used to treat sore throats and swollen gums as well as an ointment for ulcers and chronic wounds of the skin, which generate pus. Sassafras root bark can be stored in a cool place for an extended period of time and remain fresh. When chewed, sassafras root bark acts as a carminative.

JUNE 2, 1862

Several days later when Legare arrives home, he finds Polly in the back yard. Polly sees Legare and rushes to give him his daily "home from work" embracing kiss. "I'm glad you're home. I missed you all day. How was your day at the bank or did you go to Uncle Richard's?"

"Went to the bank today, Uncle Richard's is tomorrow. Guess who came by to see me this morning?"

"Let me guess. Mrs. Turner?"

With a broad grin, "Nope. One more guess."

"Mrs. Cazier?"

"Close. It was Dr. Blair."

Polly looks surprised. "It must have been a good visit or you wouldn't be so happy."

Legare reaches in his vest pocket and removes an envelope. "Read this."

Polly takes the envelope addressed to both of them and removes the note card.

> *Mr. & Mrs. Hugh Legare Hill,*
>
> *My wife and I have been asked by Mayor and Mrs. Purse, to invite you to the upcoming concert featuring the works of Beethoven at the Athenaeum on July Fourth.[132]*
>
> *Formal dress.*
>
> *Dr. & Mrs. Hugh Blair*

"Legare! We get to meet Mayor Purse and his wife. I sure am excited about meeting them but right now our unborn baby and I need a break. Let's go inside and have some tea. Al, let's finish up for the day." Al nods his head. Placing their arms around each other's waist, Polly and Legare head for their house.

JUNE 15 1862

Aunt Charlotte and Uncle Richard attend the concert as well. The evening is warm and humid as the carriage stops in the circular driveway to pick up Polly and Legare at seven o'clock. Aunt Charlotte is wearing her red gown with a blue waist band, bowed in the back and beautiful white leather shoes. An elegant diamond set from her marriage is on her ring finger. She wears another ring with a large, blue, solitaire gem on her right hand. Around Aunt Charlotte's neck is a pearl choker necklace with four stands of matching white pearls. Her hair is set around a beautiful gem stone studded hair-comb made of ivory. Uncle Richard is wearing his best black suit, complimented with a red bow tie and cummerbund.

The carriage driver and Uncle Richard climb the short staircase and the latter knocks on the door alerting Polly and Legare of their arrival. When the door opens, the evening sun strikes the glow of an angel over Polly. Legare looks at his wife and sees a Grecian beauty with classic expressions and a noble manner. Polly is tall in figure and supple with a willowy motion. Wearing only a simple broach on a thin, satin ribbon around her neck, Polly is the embodiment of feminine Southern grace.

Uncle Richard stands speechless at first, and then offers Polly his hand to the carriage. "My, dear, you look lovely tonight."

Aunt Charlotte compliments Legare as he takes his seat in the carriage. "How handsome you are, Legare."

"Thank you, Aunt Charlotte."

"Polly, you look lovely as well. Did you take a beauty bath today?"

Polly smiles sweetly. "Yes, Aunt Charlotte, and I also cleaned my fingernails!"

Legare looks firmly at Charlotte. "Now, Aunt Charlotte!"

"I did not mean that the way it sounded. I thought maybe Polly used some special type of lotion for her skin to be so soft and radiant."

With that, the carriage driver whisked the horses on their way. Legare takes Polly's hand and the two lean back to enjoy the short ride.

Upon arriving at the Athenaeum, Mayor Purse has arranged for a staff member and his niece Jennifer to escort Polly and Legare to their box seats. The mayor and his wife are running a little late, due to a conflicting event. As Legare and Polly depart, a jealous Aunt Charlotte gives Richard a disgusted looks. "Richard, take me to our seats! I assume we'll have to find them ourselves!"

Mayor and Mrs. Purse arrive minutes before the concert is to begin. "Hello, I'm Thomas Purse and this is my wife, Elizabeth. Please excuse our tardiness, but my wife and I had a minor conflict of schedule. I see you have already met my niece, Jennifer. Please pardon me for a few more minutes. I have some announcements to make before the concert begins."

The mayor stands and the audience becomes quiet. After several civic announcements, Mayor Purse concludes with, "Finally, ladies and gentlemen, I would like to introduce Mr. & Mrs. Hugh Legare Hill, the son and daughter-in-law of our distinguished United States Representative Joshua Hill. Mr. and Mrs. Hill are now living in Savannah. Mrs. Hill has volunteered to produce medications for the hospital in cooperation with Dr. Blair and Mrs. Cazier. Any ladies, who wish to assist her and her noble cause, please contact my office or my wife." The audience stands and gives Legare and Polly a modest and respectable applause. Shortly thereafter, the gas lights dim and the music begins.

During the concert, Polly's emotions drift back home to memories of the afternoon concerts with her family and friends. She remembers the comfort of the warm fire in her bedroom and the aroma of her mother's food. She smiles as she thinks of how Norman was always concerned about his rabbit box. Her fond memories, her love of Legare and their child, and the melodious orchestra comfort her as the sad realization of her father's predictions for a defeated Georgia creep into the otherwise peaceful moment.

As Polly and Legare leave with Mayor Purse and his wife, numerous citizens acknowledge Polly by taking her hand and squeezing it gently to show their appreciation for her volunteer role with herbal medicines. Mrs. Purse informs the group, "We can only chat a few minutes this evening, but my husband and I are having a Fourth of July reception at our home around 6:00 PM. Would you please join us there?"

Legare replies, "Thank you, Mrs. Purse, I'm sure we will be able to attend."

Mrs. Purse takes Polly's hand. "You're a doll, Polly, and I can't wait to talk with you at length."

Polly responds, "Thank you Mrs. Purse for your kind words. Legare and I will be at your home on the Fourth of July."

Legare and Polly thank everyone for a delightful evening and bid Mayor and Mrs. Purse good night. Before leaving, they look around for Richard and Charlotte. They find Aunt Charlotte and Uncle Richard in the front of the Athenaeum, sitting in the carriage, waiting for their arrival.

On the way to the river house, Charlotte feels the need to inform Polly of previous events. "I have sat in the mayor's box on many previous occasions, but I guess tonight he only invited new guests to share the box seats."

"The view was excellent. Mayor and Mrs. Purse are very gracious people." The remainder of the ride is silent. As the carriage stops in front of Polly and Legare's house, Polly asks Aunt Charlotte, "Would you and Uncle Richard like to come in for some tea and pastries?"

"Not tonight. It's late and I know you must be exhausted, being in a delicate condition and all," replies Aunt Charlotte. Bidding each a good night, Aunt Charlotte and Uncle Richard depart for the plantation. Tot is waiting with hot tea and pastries ready when Polly and Legare enter the house.

"I'm sorry Aunt Charlotte acts the way she does around you. She's just a little bit jealous."

"Don't let Aunt Charlotte's attitude bother you. It certainly doesn't bother me. I kind of think she's funny in a sort of weird way. Besides, if there's any jealousy, it's because I have you!"

"And I have you!" responds Legare with a kiss for her.

After finishing their tea and pastries, she places her hand across the small of her back, "It's time for me to get to bed. My back is beginning to bother me a bit."

"How about I give you a great back rub? You certainly earned it tonight!"

JULY 1, 1862

Norman writes home:

> *"I have finished my exams and passing all of them is a great relief. Paul has done well on his exams also. We are still recovering from the excitement of Andrew's Raiders and guard duty at the jail. We even got to talk*

to some of the prisoners after the crowd broke up. The cadet corps is still
performing drill master duties at Camp McDonald. When we aren't
drilling or having instructions in marksmanship and artillery training,
we usually are singing and dancing. One of our favorite songs is "Dixie":

SOUTHERONS, hear your Country call you!
Up! Lest worse than death befall you!
To arms! To arms! To arms. In Dixie!
Lo! All the beacon-fires are lighted,
Let all hearts be now united!
To arms! To arms! To arms! In Dixie!
Advance the flag of Dixie!
To arms! To arms!
Hurrah! Hurrah!
For Dixie's land we take our stand,
And live or die for Dixie!
To arms! To arms!
And conquer peace for Dixie!

There are several verses to the song, but the troops sing this one over and
over. They say this is written by a fellow by the name of Albert Pike.
What's going on with Polly? Any more news? I feel Legare is very capable
of taking care of her and protecting her.

With love, Norman

Al is shepherding Legare and Polly to Mayor Purse's for the Fourth of July
reception. Legare surveys the festivities. "Polly, July Fourth is not what
it used to be! Lots of parades, picnics, and family gatherings. Ol' Glory
would be flying everywhere. I wonder why the mayor wants to have a July
Fourth reception."

"When we arrive, I'm sure we will find out plus see fireworks. Those I
saw on New Year's were my first. They were spectacular!"

Al halts the horse and carriage in front of the mayor's residence and
two stable hands assist Polly from the carriage. As Polly and Legare walk
to the porch, Polly spots Jennifer talking to Dr. Blair, his wife and Mrs.

Cazier. Polly and Legare stop to say hello and chat a bit with the group. Jennifer takes Polly's hand. "Come on, you two, the mayor and my aunt are looking for you."

Inside, Jennifer locates Mayor Purse and his wife on the veranda talking with some of the guests. Mayor Purse sees Jennifer and politely excuses himself. Mayor Purse and his wife turn toward Jennifer, Polly and Legare.

Legare extends his hand. "Good evening Mayor, Mrs. Purse. Thank you for inviting us to your reception."

"We are so delighted the two of you accepted our invitation. Legare, there are folks here who want to meet the son of Congressman Hill. Polly, if I leave you the charge of my wife and Jennifer, would you excuse your husband while I introduce him to our fellow citizens?" asks the Mayor.

"Of course, Mayor. We did not get to spend much time together at the concert and I was looking forward to doing so this evening."

Mrs. Purse interrupts, "I also want to get to know you better, Polly. Come; let's sit for a spell. I want to hear more about your herb recipes. Dr. Blair and Mrs. Cazier speak highly of you and your herbs. My grandmother use to make remedies as well. Will you share some of yours with me?" Jennifer, Polly and Mrs. Purse partake of the hors d'oeuvres and wine as the waiters circulate among the guests.

Mayor Purse tells Legare, "I really admire your father."

They begin a discussion on the politics of the South with some of the city councilmen. Charlotte and Richard arrive shortly and enter the mayor's house. Neither Polly nor Mrs. Purse notices their entrance.

Charlotte spots them and informs Richard, "Why, there's Polly, talking with Elizabeth, the mayor's wife. I did not know Polly and Legare were invited to this affair today." Charlotte and Richard walk over to Mrs. Purse to express their gratitude for the invitation.

Mrs. Purse looks up as Charlotte and Richard approach. "Why, hello Charlotte and Richard. I would like for you to meet—"

Richard interrupts, "Polly's husband, Legare, is my cousin. We know Polly."

Mrs. Purse takes Richard and Charlotte's hands, "I've met this young lady twice and simply love her and her accent. She speaks true Southern and makes it sound like the music of the South."

Charlotte's face turns as red as the fireworks and she is unable to articulate for a moment. Once composed, she answers softly, "Yes, her Southern accent is unique and does have a musical flavor."

Uncle Richard turns and looks at Charlotte's red face. "Would you like a glass of wine Charlotte?"

"Don't mind if I do, Richard."

Richard takes Charlotte by the arm. "Excuse us for a moment."

Charlotte and Richard turn and walk toward a waiter to retrieve a glass of wine. Charlotte continues to wave her hand in front of her face to reduce the flushing. Jennifer is returning from greeting another friend and is standing behind Richard and Charlotte and as they depart, she returns to sit with Mrs. Purse and Polly.

"Will you two excuse me for a little while?" asks Mrs. Purse. "I need to speak with some of the guests who have just arrived."

Jennifer asks Polly, "What happened to Charlotte? She's red as a beet!"

Polly replies, "I think her corset is too tight!"

Jennifer glances at Polly. "I'm glad that we met and hope to see more of you and Legare now that you live in Savannah."

"Likewise," responds Polly.

"Dr. Blair and Mrs. Cazier brag to everyone about your herbs. I'm a nurse and work at Guyton General Hospital.[133] In the month of May, the hospital had a five member medical staff, but the staff is growing rapidly. It's around thirty or so now." Polly and Jennifer continue talking about their work, hobbies and families.

"I have a question for you, Jennifer. Why is there a fireworks display on the Fourth of July while we are at war with the North?"

"My Uncle says this Fourth of July is for the country, North or South, and the freedom and Independence we gained from our split with Great Britain."

"That makes sense! Let's go find my husband. I know he is talking politics with everybody." Polly and Jennifer start looking through the crowd and locates Legare. Smiling, Legare places his arms around Polly's waist and introduces her to some of the city officials with whom he has been discussing the war. The band stops playing and a trumpeter plays several musical notes to gain the attention of the guests.

Legare whispers in Polly's ear, "I did not mean to leave you alone, dear,"

"I wasn't alone. I found me another man," Polly teases.

Legare looks at Polly out of the corner of his eye. "I see no humor in that statement!"

Squeezing Legare's arms and drawing him near, she whispers in his ear, "Fear not. No one has my heart but you, my love!"

Jennifer laughs. "She didn't find another man, Legare, but a lot of the same men continued walking by and speaking!"

Mayor Purse announces, "Ladies and gentlemen, may I have your attention? My message for this great day in our history is a simple one. Independence and freedom! That's what our forefathers fought for and what the Confederacy is fighting for!" Loud applause follows Mayor Purse's single remark. "The fireworks will begin in about thirty minutes. You may either walk or ride in your carriage to River Street. The display will take place over the Savannah River. The City police will direct you to hitches. There's an area marked off for our party tonight. I'll see you there!"

When Polly and Legare arrive at River Street, several thousand people have scurried about in order to claim the best vantage point for viewing the fireworks. Adding to the festivities on the street, a large band is playing the favorite melodies of the South. Confederate National flags line the river's edge. Strong moonlight facilitates easy travel, yet is not bright enough to interfere with the transitory pyrotechnic display. Thirteen ships, all lit up, represent the original thirteen colonies and are in the river facing each other as if a line of battle. The third ship has a large sail with "Georgia" painted across it, representing Georgia as the third state to sign the Declaration of Independence. A large Confederate States National flag is at the top of each ship's mast. Children and young adults are laughing and discharging small banging firecrackers among the crowds.

At the appointed time, a large cannon fires from the shore, one shot for each of the thirteen colonies. Another ship fires one shot for each of the eleven Confederate states. The crowd cheers and raises their beer in salute thirteen times and then eleven times in response to each cannon shot. Then suddenly, the shore artillery fires Roman candle like balls toward the ships and the water lights up beneath the flame.

Polly takes Legare's hand and places it upon her belly. "Feel the baby, it's responding to the fireworks. It's all excited!"

"I think you're right. Maybe it's trying to give a toast with the rest of the crowd!" The larger Roman candle balls are fired from the ships toward other ships and toward the shore artillery battery. The distance between the ships and shore is sufficient to prevent any close encounters. Suddenly, all of the ships begin firing Roman candle-like projections.

The noises of the fireworks resound. As if accompanying one another, the band plays louder as the displays become more stunning and grander. The grand finale is every cannon firing thirteen times as rapidly as possible.

The Signal Corps on Hutchinson Island sends up eleven squid[134] displays. When the last of the displays subside, the church bells begin to ring and continue to ring until midnight. Large bonfires begin to light the riverfront as the citizens begin to dance to the music and the new found light.

"I would love to dance with you tonight, Polly, as we did on New Year's, but it's hot and humid and you're one month from giving birth. In such a festive crowd, you might get bumped to the ground. We will dance alone on the dock when we get home."

"That would be the best way to finish out this wonderful Friday night, the Fourth of July, evening with my husband."

© Susan Spickerman Coletti

17

THE STORK ARRIVES

AUGUST 16, 1862

Polly is nearing the time for the birth of her child. The Saturday August day is clear, but sulky with a mild breeze. Polly's pregnancy has produced some back pains and of the usual, "Is this baby coming or not!" emotion. The windows are open in the house to allow the river breeze to afford some additional coolness to the shade trees surrounding the house. Polly and Legare are in the back yard where Polly has planted her vegetable and herb garden. "Legare, it's hard for me to bend over. Please pick a few of those tomatoes, cucumbers and peppers. Can use them in the dinner salad."

Legare obliges gladly. "Show me the ones you like, honey."

Polly walks through the rows and points to the tomatoes and peppers. Legare removes the vegetables of Polly's choice.

"Let me run these inside to Tot. I'll be right back." Kissing Polly, he turns and rushes inside and places the tomatoes and peppers on the kitchen table. "Tot, Polly wants these in the salad today. I guess we will have those fresh pole beans for dinner as well."

"Yas'suh, wif 'eef," replies Tot. [Yes sir and with beef!]

Legare returns to Polly and takes her hand, "Honey, it's such a beautiful day. Let's go sit on the pier. You look tired."

They walk hand in hand onto the pier. "Legare, the moon is full on Monday. That's when our baby is coming." Reaching the end of the pier, Legare helps Polly sit down so her feet can dangle over the edge. He sits next to her and she takes his hand, placing it on her rounded belly. "Feel our baby, Legare? It's kicking and really wants out to see its wonderful father."

"And more wonderful mother," adds Legare.

"The baby has dropped. See how low the center of my stomach is now. The full moon is gonna push our baby right on out." Polly is a familiar sight to the sea gulls. She has discovered that feeding the gulls gives her a sense of calm, so she brings crumbs of bread for them regularly. As the gulls fly overhead, Polly reaches in her pocket and tosses bread, sometimes in the air and sometimes in the water. "Here Legare, you throw some crumbs so they can get more accustomed to you."

Legare throws the crumbs high in the air. He and Polly watch as the gulls dive to snatch the crumbs before they reach the water. Demanding more, the gulls soar and squeak until they realize the food is gone. They disappear mysteriously, almost as fast as they appeared.

"You know Legare, we have written to both sets of parents explaining our marriage, our love for one-another, our where-about and how happy we are together. We have waited hopelessly for a letter from either family announcing that they are all well and have found forgiveness in their hearts for our sudden departure."

"I know Polly. I guess they feel betrayed or something like that … as close as we were to our parents and all … I would think they would respect our feelings. I miss my family and yours equally."

"We told them about our coming baby in our letter. I want them to be with us, not just for the baby, but to be together as a family." Pausing for a moment Polly continues, "Then again, I don't want to beg them since they have not written. Every girl wants her mother with her at childbirth. I dream of my mother and father often, as I work our small vegetable garden to resemble theirs in Stone Mountain. Oh, how I wish for my mother and father to be with us during the birth of their first grandchild."

"Polly, I'll go and telegraph your mama and papa right now and let them know you're about to deliver their first grandchild and we want them here. I'll beg them to come and be with us."

Sitting close to Legare, Polly takes his cheeks between her two hands, "Having you by my side gives me all the strength that I need. When either your parents or my parents respond to our letters, then we can notify them about the new grandchild. Until then, it's just our baby and us. I just wish they would understand that we are in love." Polly places her head on Legare's chest and begins to sob. He holds Polly close and begins to cry with her.

With a choking voice, he whispers to his wife, "I'll fulfill your every wish my love. I know childbirth must be hard physically and emotionally, Polly. We have fared well together, but the love from our families is missing and it hurts deeply. You truly are independent like Mrs. Turner said. You're the brightest example of firmness and courage I have ever known."

There are only a few anxious days remaining before the newest addition to the Hill family is to arrive. Polly is concerned about the safe delivery of their child because of Tot's misfortune with hers. "Are all the necessary preparations for the mid-wife, Dr. Blair and Tot cared for?" asks Polly. She imagines the baby in the cradle next to their bed. Polly's handmade quilt lies across the back of the crib. On top of the fresh linen sheets are the two new silk handkerchiefs. Polly visualizes how happy she and Legare are as they cuddle and hold their little angel.

Polly becomes restless during the day on Sunday, the 17th of August, the day before the moon will be full. Nervously, Legare comforts Polly. He does not allow her to move around the house. Tot encourages her to eat yams and drink as much sassafras tea as possible. In the early evening Polly holds her stomach with both hands as another small contraction occurs. "Legare our baby is coming tonight or tomorrow. Please send Al after Mrs. Cazier."

Legare jumps to his feet. "Yes, darling." He rushes to the back door to locate Al. He dispatches Al to let the midwife know of Polly's condition and ask her to come to their house right away.

Mrs. Cazier arrives and examines Polly. "Polly, you need to go to the bedroom and make yourself comfortable."

Legare escorts Polly to the bedroom, never leaving her side. Once she is comfortable, Legare encourages her to follow Tot's advice to keep her strength by eating and drinking. He hands another cup of steaming tea to his wife.

Mrs. Cazier then warns Polly, "You're going to need a lot of strength before the baby arrives. So please eat and drink." Legare is determined on attending to Polly's every need. Peering out of the window, he sees the August moon, full and bright. He sees the drowsy shadows of bats flying through the full moon's outline. The wild shriek of a nearby owl blends with the croaking frogs and chirping crickets.

Endeavoring to divert Polly's attention from the business at hand, Legare asks, "Polly, can you see the moon from your bed? It's so bright! It seems like it's smiling at us."

Polly turns her head toward the window. "It must be beautiful. I can see the bright shadows of the trees from here."

Shortly after midnight Polly cries out, "Legare, our baby is nearing!"

The midwife and Tot are in the bedroom. Tot checks the crib and stacks the extra towels. She brings in extra lanterns, candles and potholders. The midwife places the pans nearby. Some will contain the afterbirth and others will have fresh water for her and the Doctor.

Legare rushes from Polly and goes outside to wake Jesse and Al. He sends Al immediately for the doctor and tells Jesse, "Fetch Aunt Charlotte and Uncle Richard after the baby is born."

Tot and the midwife prepare the necessary cloths, water pitcher, and washbasin at Polly's bedside. The two fine silk handkerchiefs are ready as well. It is customary in the Hill family to tie the umbilical cord with two new silk handkerchiefs before separating the new arrival from the mother.

Although Polly is of a strong constitution of mind and body, she knows that childbirth is as close to death as a mother can come without actually dying. As the contractions strengthen and become closer and closer, the intensity of the pain grows. Legare is by her side and grasping her hand, asking her to squeeze his as hard against them as she can. Tot keeps Polly's head clear of sweat with a cool moist cloth. The midwife directs Polly to push with each contraction, while Dr. Blair checks to see when the head approaches for delivery. With each contraction, Polly rolls her eyes back, breathing heavily, whimpering and praying for a healthy child. Legare continually reassures Polly that everything will be fine.

"Breathe through your mouth and push hard," urges the midwife.

Polly does her best to comply as tears rolls down her smooth cheeks. How she deeply wishes for her mother and prays for the unborn baby.

After ten hours of labor Polly is totally exhausted. Her strength has withered and she is able only for one final, almost effortless push. Polly groans while Legare weeps helplessly. Helpless, naked, piping loud a new life dashes from its mother's womb and the loud cry heard throughout the house. The rooster sounds a shrill clarion of welcome, "Cock-a-doodle-do!" The sun delivers a gloriously bright and beautiful morning through the windows. All nature seems both lovely and joyful. The midwife clears the baby's mouth of fluid. Suddenly, the newborn Hill turns red faced begins thrashing at his newfound freedom and screams even louder.

"Good set of lungs on your baby boy!" says Dr. Blair.

Legare, still holding Polly's hand, now sits next to her. He is dizzy, and on the verge of passing out. While the midwife holds the newborn, Dr. Blair picks up the two new silk handkerchiefs from the crib and he firmly ties the umbilical cord. Then he reaches onto the table for the utility scissors and starts a new life by cutting the cord. Unable to speak with tears streaming from his eyes, Legare continues to squeeze Polly's hand.

Dr. Blair smiles, as the mid-wife cleans and wraps the screaming baby Joshua. She places the newborn on Polly's chest. Polly immediately kisses this new life and presses him gently against her breast. Tears continue to roll from her eyes as she softly whispers to their son, "I see your pa in you."

Uncle Richard and Aunt Charlotte arrive about forty-five minutes after little Joshua is born. Aunt Charlotte and Uncle Richard ask Dr. Blair anxiously, "How is Polly and the baby?"

"Everybody is just fine. Exhausted, but fine. You have a handsome new cousin. Polly and Legare named him Joshua."

Charlotte places her hands together. "Oh, how wonderful. After Legare's father, no doubt."

Richard nods. "A very strong name indeed! Can we visit with them?"

"Go ahead and peek in. All three are probably asleep now. The labor was as bad for Legare as it was for Polly. Tot and the midwife are still in the room.

"Thank you so much, Dr. Blair." Richard knocks on the bedroom door gently. In a few seconds, Tot cracks the door.

"Good morning, Mistuh Richard and Ma'am Charlotte." Tot opens the door further as Charlotte and Richard reverently enter the room. Polly has just let the midwife put the baby in the crib. Polly's demeanor is drained, yet when she sees Uncle Richard and Aunt Charlotte, she graciously welcomes them.

"Do you want to see a beautiful baby boy who looks like his pa? If you do, just look in the crib."

Charlotte and Richard ease over to the crib watchfully and look closely at baby Joshua.

"He is perfect. Look at those rosy cheeks," exclaims Charlotte.

Legare, who is lying next to Polly, opens his eyes and sees Richard and Charlotte. Legare gets up and his Aunt Charlotte and Uncle Richard embrace him. Turning toward Polly, Charlotte gleefully hugs her. "Congratulations! What a fine looking baby boy!"

Richard goes to Polly's bedside, takes Polly's hand and tells her, "You will be good parents. We know you both are exhausted and we will visit again later. Get some rest now for that baby will be hungry again before you know it!"

Polly renders a tired smile. "Thank you for coming by." She closes her eyes and falls asleep almost instantly.

Legare escorts Charlotte and Richard to the front door. He returns to the bedroom with barely enough energy to remove his slippers before lying next to Polly. Softly placing his arm over Polly's arm, he too falls asleep instantly.

BUSTER PASSES THROUGH STONE MOUNTAIN—FEBRUARY 1863

Buck is leaving the hotel across from the depot as a train heading north pulls into town. The train is loaded with troops, and they appear to be veterans. Upon further observation, Buck recognizes the unit as Buster's. To Buck's great delight, among the bronzed faces of the soldiers, the familiar and distinguishing figure of Buster Phillips steps from the train. The newly arrived regiment is returning from Augusta with several box-car loads of ammunition and new recruits. As the formation is dismissed Buck rushes to Buster, and catches him by surprise.

"Why I didn't think you would be here Buck."

"I just happen to come up for the mail run due on the south bound train. We're waiting to hear from Norman. I wish Betty Gail was here to visit with you, but she stayed at the farm today. You're looking mighty good."

"Been doin' lots' of fightin' Buck. Lots of killin' a goin' on. I'm lucky ta be alive. Fur myself I don't take no stock in such talk. But hit do seem powerful good that no bullet nor shell nor nothing never hit me. A many of 'em have come might near!

Buck claps Buster on the back, "Got time for something to eat at the hotel across the way? They got some fresh beef in this morning."

"I got thirty minutes."

The two men head across the dirt street. Shaking the dust from his feet on the wooden sidewalk, Buck enters the hotel lobby just ahead of Buster.

"How about Col. Gartrell? Do you ever see him? He was so much in favor of this war."

"Oh yes, I can see Col. Gartrell now, jest like he look they day of the big battle. Ours guns talkin' all day, and rippin' up the trees and rocks all round those Yankees. On the back of the ridge, where Longstreet's division was stationed, our boys were a formin' to meet a Yankee charge. Oh, but the Col. did look grand that day a settin' so straight an' proud on his white horse waiting for de word to move."

Buck nods thoughtfully. "That must have been a sobering time."

"With death a starin' me in the face so close? It's strange," says Buster, "but would you believe instead of seein' the ridge I was on and the long stretch that lay between us and the Yankees, where many of us was expecting to lay down our life … instead I saw Stone Mountain in her spring green so close, I smelt the honeysuckles on the mountainside. I heard that mockin'bird singing among de white blossoms of the dogwood tree. Not fer long, though. Longstreet nodded, and we blasted away at the Yankees. Luck was on my side, an' out of that Hell I survived—how, I never could tell—without a scratch. The next day they retreated, and we buried the Yankee dead with our own."

"That's the Christian thing to do. Their mamas couldn't ask for more," replies Buck.

"Sometimes I have my misgivings how this here war will end. If the South's whipped, there's no place better than de grave fer men like de Colonel." As the servant places plates of hot food on the table.

"I'm not a professor, but somehow I'm thinking in this case the good Lord knows best." Buck peers at Buster. "What about the judge's sons, two likable boys. They were in your regiment. What's become of them?"

"Dead," answers Buster." One fell on the battlefield an' one died of fever in the hospital at Petersburg." Buck makes no comment, allowing Buster to regain his composure. "I just was thinking about that shaded verandah of the Stone Mountain Hotel and the other days, happy days."

Buck takes a sip of cool milk. "Buster, sometimes that's all you can do to keep from going mad." A long silence follows as the men try to enjoy their meal.

Buster finally breaks the silence. "What bout Polly? Do you know where she be?"

"Nothing to tell, Buster." Buck watches the emotion play across Buster's face as he clinches and unclenches his hands.

"When this war is over, I think about moving to Tennessee… Sell you my place. Nothin' here fer me." Buster takes the last bite of his meal.

There isn't much Buck can say about Buster's feelings, so he just lets that comment pass. "Lots of our folks have gone to war, Buster. Some killed, some captured. Got the list posted inside the depot. You know most of them. Let's take a look before you get back on the train."

"Glad to Buck."

Inside the depot, the list has grown since Buster's departure over a year ago. There have been 13 more enlistments added, four wounded and three killed since his departure.

KIA
March '62
James Robert McCurdy-Orange Courthouse, Va
May '62
William S. Mehaffey-Chancellorsville, Va
Oct '62
Richard G. Thompson-Winchester, Va

WOUNDED
Jul '62-Benjamin Thomas Ivie
Aug '62-George Riley Wells-Second Manassas Va
Sept '62-John Wilson McCurdy-Sharpsburg, Md
Dec '62-W.F.A. Dickerson-Federicksburg

ENLISTMENTS
Phillip Buford McCurdy-Enl 11/16/61-McCullough Rifles
John Hendrix-Enl 3/11/62- Fulton Greys-1st Regiment Ga. Regulars
Isaac Newton Nash- Enl 3/1/62- Murphey Guards, 38th Regiment Ga Vol Inf
Solomon Gibson-Enl 3/24/62- Dekalb Rifleman
Luther Mason-Enl 4/9/62- Dekalb Rifleman
E.F. Camp-enl 4/14/62- Magruder Dragoons
Augustus T Cochran-Enl 4/10/62- Ga 36th Regiment Ga Infantry
Thomas P. Wells-enl 4/10/62- Ga 36th Regiment Ga Infantry
Wilburn Ransela Wells-Enl 4/10/62- Ga 36th Regiment Ga Infantry
John Thomas Willingham-Enl 5/1/62- Dekalb Rifleman
James A Mackin-7/15/62- Hutchins Guards
Isaac B Pope-Enl 7/29/62-Cobbs Legion
Edward Newton Nash-Enl 8/4/62- Ga 36th Regiment Ga Infantry
Andrew Jackson Thompson /Brother George- Enl 11/26/62 Ramson-12th Bat Ga Artillery
Elihu Paden Lanford-Enl 12/1/62-12th Battalion Ga Artillery

"These lists continue to grow, Buster. Never hope to see anybody else's name here." Suddenly the trains whistle blows. Buster leaves Buck with a simple handshake. "Good luck to you, Buster."

"Thanks, Buck." Buster boards the train and stares at Buck as his thoughts are framed in golden curls as he sees the image of Buck's daughter. Without a smile, waves good-by.

JUNE 1863

Dr. Blair summons the hospital administrator, the hospital staff surgeons, Mrs. Cazier and Polly for a scheduled Admissions Committee meeting. Today, the Committee is going to administer an oral examination to a new, young surgeon applying for privileges.

Dr. Frederick Daniel arrives at the hospital on time, reporting to the orderly at the front desk. "I am Dr. Frederick Daniel. I have an appointment with Dr. Blair."

"Yes, Dr. Blair and the staff are expecting you in the conference room. Follow me, please." The orderly leads him down a hall and knocks on the door.

"Come in," calls Dr. Blair.

"Dr. Blair, Dr. Daniel is here."

"Have the young doctor take a seat. The committee will be with him in just a few minutes." Everyone on the committee has read and reviewed Dr. Daniels' file. Notes from his professors suggest that he may be quick-tempered but his good clinical skills should balance this shortcoming.

Once the group is ready, Polly goes to fetch Dr. Daniel. "Dr. Daniel, the committee is ready to interview you. Please come in."

"Thank you … your name is…?"

"Excuse me for not introducing myself. My name is Mrs. Polly Hill."

"Come on in, Dr. Daniel," encourages Dr. Blair.

After a round of introductions, Dr. Blair begins the proceeding. "We want to start this exam early since the days are hot and humid this time of year in Savannah. Hopefully, we will finish before noon."

Dr. Blair and the staff begin with simple questions like: "What are your drugs of choice for heart burn?"

"Tincture of nux vomica. But with the embargo it's difficult to get the dried ripe seed from India. So, when that is not available, vegetable charcoal works very well. There's plenty of wood from the beech, birch or oak trees to make the charcoal from. When in season rhubarb is great." Dr. Blair nods his head in agreement.

"How about diarrhea?"

Dr. Daniel speaks with confidence. "Cinnamon is one of the best medicines for diarrhea. Then there's the hops flower blossoms made into a tea. Not only is it good for diarrhea, but can also be used in cases of nervousness, mild anxiety and sleeplessness."

"Thank you, Dr. Daniel. How about controlling fever?"

"Cold rags, turpentine, quinine, iris tea or the powdery green leaves of the sage plant."

"How about hemorrhoids?" Dr. Daniel squirms in his seat. "Do you have hemorrhoids Dr. Daniel?"

"Not now sir, but at one time."

"And how do you treat them?"

"By crushing the horse chestnut and making a paste. This gives great relief to the pain and inflammation of hemorrhoids."

"A couple more questions on medicine. How do you relieve the pain of a toothache?"

"Take the tooth out or chew on a poultice from the yarrow flower."

Dr. Blair leans back in his chair and looks over toward Mrs. Cazier. She smiles casually as Dr. Blair puts his hands behind his head and asks Dr. Daniel, "How would you control bleeding?"

"Of course a tourniquet."

Dr. Blair learns forward and asks, "What other way?"

"The shepherd's purse plant made into a bandage stops bleeding fairly quickly."

Dr. Blair takes his pen and makes a note on Dr. Daniel's record. Looking up he asks, "How do you know when a patient has enough chloroform?"

"By his breathing rate and his pulse rate."

At the end of the two-hour oral examination, Dr. Blair has the young man so nervous that he's afraid another question will throw him into a state of total confusion.

Finally, the last question from Dr. Blair, "What would you do if you found a soldier on the field of battle shot through the knee-joint?"

"There are several avenues to resolve a problem such as this, but your question is much too broad to give a specific answer, Dr. Blair."

"Then what would you do first to determine which avenue to take?"

Dr. Daniel remains silent thinking that Dr. Blair probably would like for him to recommend amputation. Instead, he responds, "Again, sir, my answer is the same."

Dr. Blair continues, "Now, Dr. Daniel, what would you do for me if you found me on the field of battle shot right through there." He holds up his own leg and points to each side of the knee joint.

Aggravated by the attempt to squeeze an incorrect answer out of him, the young Dr. Daniel replies, "Well, sir, if it was indeed you that was shot, I would most likely abandon you!"

Dr. Blair sternly informs Dr. Daniel, "You are excused to the adjoining room, Dr. Daniel, while we review your answers."

The young surgeon stands and departs the room in a gentleman-like manner. Taking a chair outside the office, Dr. Daniel ponders his future with the hospital. He shifts in his chair, realizing his answer many have sealed his fate. "I don't think I made them very happy with my last answer, but they have been needling me for over two hours," he mused, mutters, to himself. "Hopefully, they are not just testing my knowledge but rather how I will react under the stresses of war. Surely, they are going to judge me fairly."

⚜

"Although Dr. Daniel's last statement may have been reckless and somewhat vengeful, you brought that last answer upon yourself, Dr. Blair," says Polly laughingly. "You have been testing his nerves for two hours. Besides, he was already nervous about even having to come before the hospital board."

"You're right, Polly. I was trying to get him to say he would amputate, but he stuck by his guns. That's the kind of surgeon I want on this staff." During the next thirty minutes Dr. Blair and the other surgeons review all of the new surgeon's answers. "Polly, would you ask the young Dr. Daniel to come in please?"

Polly nods and goes to the door. "Dr. Daniel, Dr. Blair and the staff would like to complete your interview. Please come in."

Dr. Daniel rises, almost as if he going to face his executioner.

"Please take a seat, Dr. Daniel," suggests Dr. Blair. "Do you have any questions from me or the hospital staff?"

"Not at this time, Dr. Blair," replies the young man with a somewhat more relaxing tone.

"This Board has reviewed your answers and your credentials. I must say that your last answer illustrates your integrity to do what is right by your patient." Pausing for a moment, Dr. Blair stands as he extends his hand to Dr. Daniel. "The unanimous decision is that you have the qualifications to join the hospital staff. We are confident you will perform surgery well within the accepted medical standards. Congratulations!"

Smiling and with a breath of relief, Dr. Daniel stands. "Thank you for your confidence. I'll work diligently not to disappoint the staff or embarrass this hospital in any manner."

Dr. Blair chuckles."That's all fine, son, but we'd just as soon you work diligently to save our brave fighting men."

GENERAL ORDERS,
HEADQUARTERS STEVENSON'S DIVISION, Army of Tennessee
Numbers 33. Atlanta, Ga., September 14, 1863

I. The major general commanding has received official information of the exchange of the officers and men of his division. Relying upon the patriotism and courage of his officers and men, he assured the Government that immediately upon their exchange they would come forward with the utmost alacrity and soon be ready to take the field. Acting upon this belief, he has made every preparation for their speedy and complete equipment. Arms and clothing will be ready for them upon their arrival in camp, and there will be nothing to prevent them from soon joining their companions in arms and participating in the great struggle that is to preserve their native States from ruin and devastation. It now rests with them—soldiers of Georgia, of Alabama, and of Tennessee—to show whether they will respond promptly to the summons to duty and once more rally to the support of our cause, or be forced into the ranks that they should glory in filling. Let it never be said that men who cheerfully endured what they did in a far distant theater of operations, men who acted a heroic part in the siege that has rendered the heights of Vicksburg historic, will be recreant now, when they are called to gather in the defense of their kindred and their firesides.

II. The brigades of BG Barton and Col. A. W.. Reynolds will rendezvous without delay at Decatur, Ga.; that of BG Cumming at Stone Mountain, Ga., and the Alabama brigade at the places already designated for its different regiments preparatory to moving to this place. The artillery

*companies will be conducted to the places designated as the rendezvous
for their respective brigades.*

*III. The quartermaster's department will furnish transportation to the
points named on requisition by the commanding officers of regiments
and detached companies.*

By command of MG Stevenson:

*JOHN J. REEVE,
Maj. and Assistant Adj. Gen.*[135]

≫•

During the fall of 1863, the military engagements along the state line with
Tennessee become more personal with the cadets at GMI.

SEPTEMBER 17, 1863

A telegraph reaches Stone Mountain. Union forces and Confederate
forces are facing each other along Chickamauga Creek. Union forces are
on the west side. Confederate forces on the east side. For two days, the
thick forest conceals the movements of both armies as they attempt to
outmaneuver one another. At the end of the struggle, General William
Rosecrans seems to have the advantage.[136]

≫•

However, during the next two days, the complete Confederate army is
massing against General George Thomas. He is able to hold firm against
the overwhelming Confederate forces, saving the union forces from
a bitter defeat. General Thomas retreats through McFarland's Gap to
Chattanooga.[137] The Confederates are too exhausted to pursue the enemy.
There are more than eighteen thousand Confederates killed and sixteen
thousand of the Union. Thus, in reality, the battle is an irresolute success
for the Army of Tennessee.

Soon thereafter, the misfortunes of war begin to arrive in Marietta.
The civilian population fleeing from battles engulfs the city and surely
tests its ability to care for them. Many simply pass through on their way

to Atlanta. Marietta has sufficient hospitals to care for most of those who are wounded. Then the dead arrive by train and wagons. The cadet corps and the war weary surviving soldiers are temporarily assigned to bury the dead in the new cemetery across the road from GMI.[138]

Oct. 1863 Norman writes home:

Thanks for sending me the letter you got from Polly and Legare. It's great to be proud grandparents. I am just as proud to be an uncle. I will write Polly. I'm hoping you and the Hills are going to visit and show them how much you really care for both of them. Leave your feeling for Buster at home. Anyhow I like Legare better. When you decide to go, give my nephew a big whatever for me! The days are becoming cold and foggy. The trees are more beautiful than one can imagine with all of the different colors of autumn. These past two weeks have surely shown us the true and dark side of war. Yet we dream of our chance to prove ourselves in the defense of our homeland. We have been part of the Honor Guard for several Generals who were killed in the battle of Chickamauga. We lined up with several hundred regulars as the bodies were brought to their final resting place. The caskets are on a horse drawn bier with one stirrup upon the saddle. The Drummer and Fifer led the funeral brigade. Following the Drummer and Fifer was the Color Guard, then his military unit, usually consisting of about 500 men. And then the casket.

It is an awesome sight. It seems that the beauty of death is told in nature by the beauty of the colors of the dying leaves on the trees.

I'm sure you have read about our general, Gen. Benjamin H. Helms, being one of the casualties. Gen. Helms commanded Gen. Breckinridge's third brigade. His wife is Mary Todd Lincoln's sister, making him the brother-in-law of President Lincoln. His brigade was known as the "Orphan Brigade" due to the fact that it is made up of Kentuckians who chose to fight for the Confederacy. The story goes that on Sunday morning, the 20th of September, Gen. Helms was having a difficult time leading his Kentuckians against the Union breastworks of General Thomas when a bullet tore through his right shoulder. He was taken to the field hospital and died later.[139]

The Cadet Corps was also part of the Honor Guard for Gen. Preston Smith. He was killed on Saturday the 19th of September. The soldiers who were in the battle said the fighting became so intense in the thick forest that it was difficult to tell friend from foe. The fighting was desperate with hand to hand combat. Soldiers screaming with commands and well as screaming from the agony of ghastly wounds.

The third Gen's funeral which Paul and I were part of was for Gen. James Deshler. He was killed on the same day and near the area where Gen. Helm's received his mortal wounds. Gen. Deshler was struck directly in the chest by a piece of shrapnel. According to witnesses, the shrapnel ripped his heart completely from his body. What a horrifying sight that must have been. As soon as the roads are passable Gen. Deshler's body will be sent to Alabama. Gen. Smith's body is to be sent to Memphis, Tennessee, and Gen. Helm's body is to be transported to Kentucky.[140]

The entire cadet Corps dig graves daily, though not as many now as in the first week after the Battle at Chickamauga. It is now customary when an officer's body is to be honored; the cadet corps provides the Honor Guard.[141]

I'm worried about Polly. Have you heard anymore from her since the first letter to all of us?"

I hope everyone is well. Love to All.

NOVEMBER 1863

Polly rises early on November 11, starting off on a chilly Wednesday morning. The embers in the fireplace are still warm and glowing. Polly eases silently from the side of Legare and places two logs over the warm embers. She opens the door from the bedroom and sees Tot in the kitchen.

"Got de root tea 'n de popcawn cereal ready fuh uh good brekwas fuh you 'n 67 Massuh LeGree. Jes' need fuh put de egg on. Got de rice grits fuh de baba. [Got the root tea and the popcorn cereal ready for a good breakfast for you and Mr. Legare.[142] Just need to put the eggs on. Got the rice grits for the baby.]

"That fried ham sure does smell good! Is that part of the pork rump Uncle Richard brought over the other day?"

"Yass Ma'am!" replies Tot.

"It's still early, so wait a little while longer before putting the eggs on."

Polly enters the bedroom and quietly places a breakfast tray on a table. She sits on the side on the bed, next to the sleeping Legare. She whispers gently in his ear, "Wake up, my love." Without moving Legare opens his eyes. "Happy birthday, honey! I have breakfast in bed for you this morning." Legare pulls Polly close to him. He kisses her soft and warm lips, pulling her even closer.

"My life is perfect with you and little Joshua. No man can ask for anything more. I'm living in heaven." After lying together quietly for a few minutes, he looks at Polly. "Not only is today my birthday, but the day I have to volunteer for the army —a double sided sword." He tightens his grip around her. "Capt. Picquet expects me at Thunderbolt before dark. He said I am going to be in Company A of the 63rd Georgia Regiment, doing duty right here in Savannah."

Polly gives him another warm kiss and hugs him dearly. In her heart Polly knows their life is about to change.

Suddenly, little Joshua awakens and stands up in his crib. With his stretched out arms, he calls, "Mama, Pa--pa." Removing the large, warm down comforter, Legare walks around the bed and takes the little one in his arms. "I don't need to squeeze you too much because you stink! But I can give you a big kiss!" Laughing, Polly places a towel on the bed and the daily routine of the first change of the day is over in a matter of minutes.

"Your breakfast is going to get cold." Polly leans over and lets Legare kiss his son.

"I don't want to eat without you, Polly."

"Tot is bringing mine and the baby's in just a minute." Polly walks to the door. "Tot, bring my and the baby's breakfast."

Tot already has the food prepared and brings the tray into the bedroom. "Happy bertday Massuh LeGree. 'E uh bootiful 'n sunny day."

"Thanks, Tot!"

Tot departs and proceeds to the cookhouse. She has to prepare for the gathering in the afternoon when Richard and Charlotte come over for Legare's birthday. The sun is beginning to shine through the frosty glass, giving a little more warmth to the house. Polly, Legare and little Joshua sit around the table in the bedroom. Little Joshua is in his highchair staring at the food and ready to eat. Legare gives him the first bite of the warm rice grits.

Little Joshua smears his food over his face. Polly feeds him and Legare tries to keep his face clean. Soon Joshua is stuffed and satisfied.

"I've invited Dr. Blair and Mrs. Cazier over for cake and hors d'oeuvres this afternoon. It will probably be more like supper knowing Aunt Charlotte. She is making the cake and said it is going to be unusual since flour is hard to come by. Also, I think Mayor and Mrs. Purse and Jennifer are dropping by for a few minutes."

Legare responds, "I guess we best get moving and get this place in perfect order. You know how Aunt Charlotte is about neatness. I wish some of our other friends could be with us, but they are all off fighting. I'm lucky to be able to stay in Savannah. Capt. Picquet tells me I'll be close by on Whitemarsh Island some of the time, but furloughs are easy to come by right now."

"Tot has the place clean and neat. How about you, me and Joshua just take a carriage ride through town after it gets a little warmer."

"Sounds like a great idea. I'll tell Jesse to get the carriage ready for us in an hour. Maybe we can find a place to have dinner."

Around ten o'clock, Jesse has the carriage at the front door. He enters the parlor. "The carriage is ready and I have warm blankets and some hot stones in the wooden box to keep your feet warm."

The day is nearly perfect. Not even much of a breeze is coming from the water. Climbing into the carriage, Polly and Legare put little Joshua between them and cover his back and head with a thick blanket. Polly and Legare place their feet on top the thick and warm wooden box. Polly has a jar of pabulum wrapped in a small towel for little Joshua. She places it on top the rocks of the warming box.

"Your foot warmer is just right, Jesse!"

"Tink yuh Massuh LeGree," replies Jesse as he urges the horses forward. "Weh you want me fuh dryb you to?" [Where would you like for me to drive you?]

"Just take us through town and around the squares. We might want to stop and eat dinner if we find a place open."

As they ride through town, their mood is more melancholic. Polly notices the town is quieter. Most of the buildings are closed due to the blockade. Some even have for sale signs. She takes Legare's arms. "Normally this is a busy place. People are usually dreaming about Christmas and relatives coming and going."

Moving closer to Polly, Legare appearing somewhat depressed looks at the scene,

"The war has taken away most of the men from Savannah. The spirit of the city is sinking into a deep gloom. I can't help but feel this war is heading our way." Pausing for a moment he continues," I fear you and I will witness the gradual destruction of the Confederacy."

Polly squeezes Legare's hand. "If people would listen to the likes of your father and mine, we probably would not be in this war. Since the fall of Vicksburg and Gettysburg, the whole Confederacy feels threatened."

"Governor Brown is not our guiding hand toward peace, but toward the destruction of our state. He will not listen to anyone. I still have the Morning News article from February at home. People in Savannah want to reconstruct the Union. I have read it over and over and practically put it to memory. 'Uniting the Union again will occur when light has learned to dwell with darkness. When the truth has learned to dwell with false-hood. When honor has learned to dwell with dishonor and when justice learns to dwell with fraud!' That's the main part I remember."

"Mr. Hopkins was the only one of the three candidates for the Confederate Congress who wanted peace at most any price. Hartridge won. His platform was peace with recognition of Southern Independence."

Jesse maneuvers the carriage slowly along the dirt streets. The sun shines through the moss draped oak trees. Large Magnolias, oleanders and crape myrtles dot the squares. The beautiful azaleas lay dormant wait-ing for the first sign of spring to bring forth their colorful blooms. Soon the carriage reaches Chippewa Square. "This is the social gathering place in Savannah. Look at the vagrant whites and those darkies just trying to keep warm by their fires and homemade tents. There's one over there boil-ing something to eat I would imagine. I don't guess we will stop here and walk. Although I have the pistol, it could be dangerous."About that time several vagrants look seriously toward the carriage and begin talking.

"Head on to Washington Square, Jesse. That's where Polly and I spent the New Year's celebration last year. I hope we can get a pass to celebrate again this year. I don't recognize any of the vagrants as laborers from the plantation." In a few minutes, Jesse rounds the corner at Washington Square. "This does not appear to be the happy New Year's Square where we were back in January. Maybe Mayor Purse can get some of those Chinese fireworks in to heighten everyone's spirits. They were beautiful this past January and July. Let's get out and dance like we did on New Year's Eve, Polly." Legare takes Polly's hand and instructs Jesse, "Watch Joshua for us."

Jesse steps down from the carriage and ties the reins to the hitching post. He then climbs into the passage section and picks up smiling Joshua. Legare and Polly climb down from the carriage. While holding hands, he walks Polly several yards onto Washington Square. He releases her hand

and they face each other. Smiling, Legare folds one arm and places it across his belt line and then folds his other arm and places it along his back waistline. He bows and Polly gleefully returns Legare's bow with an inviting curtsy. She presents her hand and Legare accepts. He pulls her close, their joined hands extending outward. Legare draws Polly close by placing his other arm lovingly around his lover's waist. Polly closes her eyes as if to hear the wonderful music of the orchestra. Legare leads her in the waltz as they swirl around with a relaxed and genteel feeling. The gentle breeze and the leaves seem to move in harmony with their loving spirit. Soon a small group gathers and begins clapping.

"Nice dancing!"shouts Mrs. Gordon from the group of spectators.

Another happily says, "You brought the park to life today!"

Polly opens her eyes and she and Legare turn to see who the friendly crowd is.

"Why, hello Mrs. Gordon," says Polly as she and Legare walk over to return Mrs. Gordon's greeting.[143] "Today is Legare's birthday .We're taking things easy. We're getting ready to have dinner. Would you and your friends like to join us?"

Mrs. Gordon replies, "Thank you for the invitation, but we're heading home for some tea, and you need to spend the time alone. We'll dine with you on another day." Polly and Legare bid Mrs. Gordon farewell as they board the carriage.

Legare takes Joshua from Jesse. "Take us to town and let's find a place to eat."

"Yez, Mistuh Legare." Jesse turns the carriage toward town on the dusty street.

Little Joshua's eyes get heavy, and he falls fast asleep under the warm blankets. Some of the heat from the rock box flows under the blanket contributing to his perfect sleep. His head lies on his fathers lap, and Polly gently pats his small back.

Polly kisses Legare. "Little Joshua is going to grow up and be a fine man, just like his pa. You're going to be very proud of him." Polly leans to kiss Legare again with deep affection.

Legare replies, "You are the heart of the family and I am the head of the family. It is your heart that will lead the way for him to be loving and caring. Hopefully I'll teach him the good road of manhood."

"Look deh. Da Massuh Tonio Pirate House. You want me fuh stop deh?"

"Pull over. It looks safe enough here. What do you say, Polly?"

"I'm hungry so let's eat. Jesse, Joshua is still sleeping. Keep him covered and we'll bring you some fish for dinner."

"Yez-um." Jesse brings the carriage to a stop and ties the reins to the post in front of the Pirates' House. Little Joshua is still sound asleep. Legare gently removes the baby's head from his lap and makes a soft pillow from part of the blanket. Joshua squirms a little and returns to a sound asleep. Legare helps Polly down from the carriage, and they stroll down the walk. He opens the door and they enter the warm tavern. The big stove in the middle has a bright red belly and the glowing heat saturates the place.

"Hello, Antonio."

"Hello Legare. Hello Miss Polly." He shakes Legare's hand. "It's a beautiful day for November and even nicer, now that my two best customers have joined me. I just started cooking some freshly caught fish. 'Bout all we have this time of year is rice, fried or boiled. We also have fried rice and fish or boiled rice with fish or just plain fish! What would you like to have?" asks Antonio laughing.

"We'll have the fish with an ale to go with it," replies Legare. "Also, I'll need a dish for Jesse. He's outside in the carriage baby sitting sleeping Joshua."

"I'll fix you right up and have my cook take Jesse his dish. Go ahead and take any seat. The dinner crowd doesn't usually get here until about one o'clock."

Polly and Legare choose a table with a candle. Polly takes off her gloves and warms her hands above the flame. The lanterns hanging from the ceiling provide a restful glow throughout the tavern. Shortly, Antonio approaches with the tray of food. "Here's your ale, fish and rice. What are you doing off from work today, Legare?"

"Well, today is my birthday. I'm eighteen and I have to enlist at Fort Thunderbolt. Three events this week! My birthday and enlistment is today and the day after tomorrow is Friday the 13th."

Antonio looks somewhat apprehensive. "Happy birthday, Legare." He places his hand on Legare's shoulder. "In Italy, the number thirteen is a good luck sign. When a child is born, it is given a gold necklace and a gold charm. The charm is engraved with the number thirteen for good luck and prosperity. Not like in America where the number thirteen is bad luck. Did you know that part of the superstition in America comes from the last supper of Christ? Some of the faithful believe it is unlucky to have thirteen at a table or in a company because that was the number of people at the Last Supper, with the thirteenth guest at the table being the traitor, Judas. So don't worry. I know you'll do very well in the army. Just take plenty blankets to keep warm."

"Very interesting! Thanks for sharing that with us. I'm sure I'll be just fine, Antonio! How about two more ales? This home brew sure is tasty." Soon Legare and Polly finish the rice and fish dinner and pay Antonio. "The fresh fish was delicious, Antonio. Have a good day and I hope to see you again when I am on leave."

Joshua is awakening when Polly and Legare arrive back at the carriage. Polly picks him up, "Time to eat, my little man." Legare reaches down and retrieves the baby food. The hungry boy smiles and tries to grab for it right away.

"You sure are a hungry boy. Jesse, drive us down by the river at the docks."

The foursome leaves the Pirates' House behind. Soon little Joshua finishes his dinner. After a short jaunt, they arrive at the riverfront. Looking around, Legare tells Polly, "See all the cotton bales and rice sitting outside? There's not room for either in the warehouses or on the freighters. The blockade is preventing those ships in the harbor from going anywhere. There are only a few that can get around the blockade. The *Kate* is probably the best blockade-runner in these parts. Uncle Richard uses it to transport his cotton to the West Indies. Uncle Richard had around three hundred bales of cotton on the Oconee. She slipped through the blockade before springing a leak and finally coming to rest off St. Catherine's Island. Of course the, Union Navy took her over then."[144]

"Our navy in the Savannah River is like a mirror of the entire Confederate forces. We do not equal or surpass the Union in any category." Polly peers down the river front. "I don't think we even have as many naval vessels as the Union."

"Not nearly in number or quality. Since the Federals burned the Norfolk Navy Yard, we won't be building anymore, either."

"What's that we have in Pensacola?"

"That's the naval repair yard in Pensacola." Polly is still looking toward the river. "I feel like those ironclads will change naval warfare forever. That battle between the *Merrimack* and the *Monitor* at the Battle of Hampton Roads proves there will be no more wooden ships for battles at sea."[145]

"That's the way it really looks." Legare takes on a begrudging tone. "You know our army isn't any better, either. We are outnumbered, out gunned and out supplied. Plus, Governor Brown is out of his mind, and I gotta sign up to be a part of this mess today."

"We'll be okay. You're in Savannah and the war is far north of here." Legare kisses Polly on her cheek.

"Look over there Legare. There's an old merchant ship which looks like the *Fingal*. Remember the *Atlanta*? I read that it was converted from the *Fingal*, a merchant ship."[146]

"You're right," replies Legare. "The *Atlanta* ran around the Union blockade in June before she had to surrender to the Union Navy. Look over there. There's our 122 feet paddle-wheel boat, the *Everglade*. Poor old' navy and poor old' Commodore Tattnall. He has the awesome responsibility of ensuring the protection the converted *Everglade* to the flag ship *Savannah*, sitting right there in the harbor. I assume my duty will include defending the coast and rivers either at Fort Thunderbolt or on one of the islands."[147]

They sit and study the scene quietly for a while. Ready for happier thoughts, Legare says to Jesse, "Let's head to the house. It's nearly two o'clock and the guests will be arriving soon."

"Yaas'suh, Mistuh Legare." Jesse snaps the reins and heads for home.

Polly begins to tickle and play with their precious son on their journey home. Legare joins in just as Polly picks Joshua up to begin narrating the passing scenes. "Look at the big river. Polly points toward the river. Little Joshua looks for a moment and then turns to his pa.

"Come to your pa." Joshua stretches his arms for his pa to lift him over to his lap. Look that way. Look at the big oak trees, and there's our house down the road." Little Joshua peers over the front of the carriage while in his pa's lap. "Polly, I find it hard to imagine a better birthday present than spending the day with my beautiful, loving wife and sweet son."

"Happy birthday, Legare." She kisses Legare and pinches his cheek.

"Looks like some of the guests have already arrived," Legare notes as the carriage comes to a stop in front of the house. "The wooden box of hot rocks is still warm. That was really nice to have. Thanks Jesse."

Jesse smiles and nods his head toward Legare.

HAPPY BIRTHDAY, LEGARE

Legare jumps to the ground and takes Joshua from Polly as she steps down from the carriage. They see the familiar carriages of Mayor Purse and his niece Jennifer. Looking somewhat puzzled, Polly sees two carriages that belong to Uncle Richard and comments to Legare, "Why did Uncle Richard bring two carriages?"

Legare shrugs his shoulders and lifts his eyebrows. "Maybe one of them will have to leave early."

Polly opens the door for Legare and Joshua and the three walk inside their home. A great surprise causes Polly and Legare to stand completely still and speechless. Tears fill Polly's eyes. Polly catches her breath and forces her weak legs into motion. She runs with open arms. "Mama! Papa! I can't believe you're here! I've missed you so much and think about you and home all the time."

The reunited trio hugs each other tightly. As Buck hugs Polly, Betty Gail whispers, "We love you more than you'll ever know."

Simultaneously, Legare is barely able to contain his emotions and rushes toward his mother and father, grasping them tightly with one arm as he holds onto little Joshua in his other. Tears flow from Mrs. Hill's eyes. She and his father embrace him and the grandson they are meeting for the first time. Congressman Hill, like Buck, is quiet. Their actions speak volumes for their feelings. Mrs. Hill demonstrates her and Congressman Hill's feelings with the embrace only a mother can provide. Tot, Mayor and Mrs. Purse and Jennifer, Uncle Richard and Aunt Charlotte are also standing nearby quietly witnessing this emotional reuniting of families. Grandmother Hill takes the baby from Legare's arms. She hugs and kisses him in a manner befitting a new grandson as they walk over to the Jernigans.

She hands the baby to Betty Gail, "I guess it's your turn to kiss this beautiful little cherub." Betty Gail takes little Joshua and stands next to Buck. Buck still cannot speak, but holds the baby with Betty Gail as they admire him as though to ask for forgiveness for waiting so long to be together. Without hesitation, Polly goes to Mrs. Hill and Congressman Hill, giving them an embrace without thought of the past and only love for them, her husband, little Joshua and their future.

Legare goes over to Buck. Before he can get close, Buck grabs his hand and in a stern and sincere voice Legare, "Please forgive me for doubting your sincerity when you eloped with Polly. We couldn't ask for a better son-in-law or a father for our grandchild."

Legare's heart is swollen with emotion and can only respond in a whisper. "Thank you, Mr. Jernigan. I love your daughter and your family as much as my own."

Uncle Richard, Aunt Charlotte, Tot, Jennifer and Mayor and Mrs. Purse join in the celebration of bonding with everyone. After a while, everyone settles down. Legare is sitting between his mother and Polly as Polly asks her mother, "How'd you get here?"

"We came down with Congressman Hill and Emily two days ago.[148] Richard and Charlotte picked us up at the depot and we've had a wonderful visit with them. You see, Emily and I got together not long after you and Legare eloped, trying to figure out what to do next."

Polly starts weeping, wipes her eyes and turns to Mrs. Hill, "I don't know what to say. I am just so happy we are all together." Legare pulls Polly near.

Emily leans forward and takes Polly's hand. "When your mother and father received the letter you and Legare wrote to them, as well as to us, we contacted each other."

Excited, Polly asks, "So when did you visit each other?"

"Buck, Joshua, your mother and I have had several visits together."

"So Uncle Richard has been keeping you abreast of our well-being, I guess."

"Oh yes, Richard has been keeping us informed. It took us, especially your pa, time to get over you running away when you had promised Buster to marry him. So when your pa finally swallowed his pride, well, here we are."

"On Legare's birthday no less. What a great birthday present." Becoming more somber and lowering her head, Polly tries to regain her composure. "And the day he has to enlist."

Betty Gail takes and holds Polly's hand. "Congressman Hill talked with your father and told him that today is Legare's birthday and he has to enlist. So, we all agreed that today would be a good day to surprise the three of you."

"Where is Norman? Why couldn't he come?"

Betty Gail's expression shows her dismay. "We tried to get the school to release Norman for a few days, but they would not because the cadets are training the regular soldiers at Camp McDonald."

"I dearly miss my brother, Ma."

"He couldn't be better. We wrote and told him we were coming to surprise you. These next kisses are from him." Betty Gail gives Polly and little Joshua kisses from Norman. "He loves GMI and, like I told you, they are training the soldiers at Camp McDonald. We don't hear from him that much because paper is getting in short supply. Says he wants to see you and your family badly. He'll send us a telegram to Mr. Goldsmith at the depot. He always asks about his sister."

"And Uncle Isaac and Aunt Sally?"

"They're just fine." Betty Gail hugs Polly and squeezes her three times cementing their love with tears. "We have been more than anxious to see our wonderful grandson." Congressman Hill and Buck come over and take seats with the family.

Uncle Richard and Aunt Charlotte are with their daughters, Marie, and Claire. Mrs. Purse has taken over the care of the baby. Looking around, Legare asks, "Where are Ian and Keaton?"

"Not back from the Florida Plantation," answers Uncle Richard.

Aunt Charlotte goes quietly to Tot. "Go to the cook house and bring in the surprise birthday pies." Tot has been keeping the birthday treat warm in the cookhouse away from Legare and Polly. Aunt Charlotte then turns and announces, "Gather round, there's a birthday pie coming in the door!"

Everyone jumps to their feet and gathers in the small dinning room. The door to the cookhouse opens and Tot enters with two large pies. Legare and Polly stare at the two pies and Legare shouts, "It's a shoo-fly pie! My favorite!" He turns to his mother with a big smile and gives her another hug. "Thanks, Ma."

"I made it fresh this morning." Pointing to the other pie, Mrs. Hill whispers to Polly, "Look, Polly. Guess what your mama has made for you."

Polly leaves Legare's side and moves toward the table. Suddenly, she picks up a familiar sweet fragrance. "Ma, you made me a fresh pecan pie." Picking up the pecan pie, Polly places it close to her nose and inhales deeply. "Smells just like home!" She rushes over to her mother and father, embracing them both.

Betty Gail smiles and whispers to Polly, "I made it at Richard's and Charlotte's but the pecans are fresh from Stone Mountain!"

As if on cue, everyone begins singing, "For he's a Jolly Good Fellow,"[149] to Legare, followed by more embraces.

Polly takes Legare's hand. "It's time for your spanking, honey.[150] Bend over."

The entire group bursts into laughter. She takes his hand and places it on the table. "I told you to bend over, honey."

He slightly bends and looks over his shoulder. "Not too hard now, Polly."

"I'm giving you the first spank … the happy one." She spanks him on the fanny once. Everyone applauds.

"I'm next," says his mother, "I'll give you the one to grow on." She also spanks him on the fanny.

Uncle Richard walks up with Betty Gail. "Here's the smack for you to eat on," says Uncle Richard.

"Mine is for you to live a long life," says Betty Gail as she renders her spank.

"The last one is from me and Buck," says Congressman Hill. "It's a little late coming, but it's the spanking for marriage." Buck and he walk up behind Legare, and each takes his turn in giving him a spank.

Legare laughs. "I bet that relieved a lot of frustration for you, Mr. Jernigan."

"Everything's fine. You got what you deserved—my daughter!" Everyone applauds again. "And a good marriage it will be. Congressman Hill, I believe it's your turn now."

Congressman Hill walks over. "Now I get to give you the eighteen spanks, one for each year. With each gentle spank his father counts to eighteen."

Standing, with a broad smile Legare tells his family and friends, "Thanks for all your blessed spanks!" The group cheers again. "Time for the shoo-fly pie, Tot."

Tot begins cutting the shoo-fly pie. "Fuss piece ob shoo-fly is yourn Mistuh LeGree." Then Marie and Claire begin cutting and distributing the balance to the guests. Tot the cuts a wedge of the fresh pecan pie, "Dis duh yourn ma'am." Before Polly thanks Tot, she nearly ingests the entire wedge in one bite, barely allowing the palate to enjoy the wonderful flavor.

Aunt Charlotte turns to the gathering and says, "Don't worry; there are two more of each pie in the cookhouse. Congressman, would you please bless this food so we can get to the pork roast!"

The room becomes silent as Congressman Hill asks the gathering, "Let us hold hands." Each person takes their neighbor's hand and Polly and Legare place their hands tightly together. "Dear Heavenly Father, thank you for this blessed day. A day of rejoicing, a day of families uniting. I thank you for giving Legare the constitution to select Polly as his wife and mother of his child and our grandchild. .Bless our son, Legare, as he enlists today. Protect and return him to us upon the end of this terrible conflict. Protect our soldiers who stand to protect their family and property against our Union brothers. We beg you to bring reason and fellowship to our leaders of the Confederacy and the Union. And last, God bless the cooks! Amen."

Tot, Jesse, Al, and one of Uncle Richards's servants bring in the birthday feast. Al begins slicing and serving the pork while Jesse serves up the fresh greens and sassafras tea.

Soon, the fireplace begins to give more light to the surroundings as the sun creeps behind the crest of the large oak trees. Legare looks at Polly and takes her hand as they stand. Everyone turns his attention to the lovely couple. Legare stands silent for a few seconds. In a quivering voice, Legare says, "Folks, you know what time it is. Polly and I cannot thank you enough for your forgiveness and love. Antonio told Polly and me today that all Friday the 13th's are not bad luck. He's right. Day after tomorrow will be the greatest Friday the 13th on the face of the earth!"

"Capt. Picquet is expecting me before nightfall at Fort Thunderbolt. It's only about three or four miles from here, so I am going to have Jesse and Al take me there in the carriage. Please, do not make this any harder than necessary. Jesse already has my belongings in the carriage. Capt. Picquet said that furloughs are easy to get, especially if you have family in the area, so I hope to be in and out quite frequently."

Tears begin rolling down Polly's cheeks as the entire room swells again with another kind of emotion. The last to embrace Legare is his mother and with "God's speed," he and Polly depart for the awaiting carriage. Standing beside the carriage, Legare holds Polly tightly. "I love you Polly. There's no soul or heart on earth which could love you more."

Polly responds emotionally, "Only my heart and soul knows how your heart and soul feels."

They embrace tightly and kiss passionately as Al and Jesse reverently observe the farewell of lovers. Legare and Polly slowly separate as he turns and boards the carriage. Soon the carriage turns a corner beyond the house and Polly's tears go from warm to cold as they stream down her soft cheeks.

It's not long before Fort Thunderbolt and the command center flag are in sight.[151] Fort Thunderbolt and the flag grow larger as the carriage draws closer. Jesse pulls on the reins and the carriage comes to a halt in front of the headquarters building at the entrance of the fort. Al steps down and unloads Legare's satchel.

Legare steps from the carriage and faces Al and Jesse. "Thanks for bringing me to the fort. I hope to see you both again soon." He shakes Al's hand and Jesse leans over and shakes Legare's hand as he passes by the side of the carriage. Taking a deep breath, Legare opens the door at the front building, enters and approaches orderly. "My name is Hugh Legare Hill. Capt. Picquet is expecting me for muster this afternoon."

"Follow me, Hill. Capt. Picquet told me you were coming in today." He leads Legare to a nearby room. Legare notices the nameplate on the door: Capt. Lewis Picquet.

The orderly knocks and Capt. Picquet responds, "You may enter."

Upon entering, the orderly salutes. "Sir, this is Hugh Legare Hill reporting for muster."

Capt. Picquet dismisses the orderly and invites Legare to take a seat. "I see you made it, Legare. Welcome to the 63rd Georgia."

"Thank you, Capt. Picquet."[152]

"There are a few papers you need to sign and the oath you need to take. Here is a copy for you to read. Take a few minutes and if you have any questions, please ask me."[153]

Legare takes a few minutes to review the documents. "Everything looks in order to me sir."

"Good, then let me administer the oath to you. Please stand and raise your right hand and when I finish the oath, you can simply say, 'I do.'"

"I, Hugh Legare Hill, born in Madison in the State of Georgia, aged 18 years and by the occupation a farmer, Do HEREBY ACKNOWLEDGE to serve for the period of THREE YEARS OF THE WAR, unless sooner discharged by competent authority: Do also agree to accept such bounty, pay, rations, and clothing, are or may be established by law. And I, Hugh

L. Hill, do solemnly swear, or affirm, that I will bear true allegiance to the State of Georgia, and that I will serve her honestly and faithfully against all her enemies or opposes whomever; and that I will observe and obey the orders of the Governor of the State of Georgia, and the orders of the officers appointed over me according to the Rules and Articles for the government of the armies of Georgia, so long as I remain under the control of Georgia, and should I be transferred by Said State to the Confederacy of States, which have seceded, or may secede from the government of the United States, and may adopt a confederated Government, I will thenceforth, to the end of the term for which I have enlisted, bear like allegiance, and render like services to said Confederacy, by whatsoever name it may be known."

"I do."

"You may lower your hand now, Pvt. Hill." Capt. Picquet extends his hand and shakes Legare's hand. Capt. Picquet offers Legare a pen, lays the oath on the desk and points with his finger. "Sign here, Pvt. Hill." Legare takes the pen and inks in his name. "Congratulations! You are assigned to Company A of the 63rd Georgia Volunteer Infantry. Maj. Joseph Allen is the company commander. We will not be issuing you any uniforms for a couple of months. Did you bring extra clothing to wear?"

Yes sir. I also brought a couple of extra blankets as you suggested."

"Your squad leader will be a fellow called 'Rooster,' who is a Sergeant. Rooster is his first and last name."

Legare looks puzzled. "Did you say Rooster is his first and last name, sir?"

"That's right."

"Should I ask how'd that come about sir?"

"Rooster is from North Georgia. Some hunters found him in a covered wagon asleep when he was a baby. They came upon the wagon with the mules tied to a tree. The front and rear flaps of the wagon were tied closed."

Legare listens intensely. "Really."

"They searched for his parents in the woods and the nearby river, but couldn't find any trace of them. Soon the Sheriff became involved, but nobody could locate his family. There wasn't even a piece of paper in the wagon with any kind of address or name."

Legare appears very concerned. "No trace of his folks at all?"

"None. So one of the hunters and his wife took the baby and raised him to be a fine young man and soldier."

"How did he get the name Rooster?"

"Oh I almost forgot that part. There was a cage on the side of the wagon with a rooster in it that kept crowing. So they named the baby Rooster. He never took the family name of the folks who cared for him." Capt. Piquet looks straight at Legare, "So when he enlisted he had to have a first and last name. So he enlisted as Rooster Rooster."

"What a story. So his family was never found."

"Not a trace of evidence whatsoever as to what happened to them."

"His unit is from North Georgia and he was transferred to Savannah with his unit and some other units. These units were consolidated to form the 63rd.

"Tomorrow, you'll begin orientation and your drill instructions. Over the next couple of weeks, you will participate in musket drills and artillery drills. Afterwards, you will be assigned to Whitemarsh Island as infantry security. Like I told you several weeks ago, furloughs are easy to come by so long as there's no threat from the Yankees." Capt. Picquet leads Legare to the door. "Orderly, escort Pvt. Hill to his quarters."

"Follow me, Pvt. Hill," states the orderly.

Legare picks up his satchel and follows. They go from the headquarters and enter a barracks in the adjacent building. Once inside, Legare sees about fifty beds lining the walls. There are two large stoves, each about a third of the way from each end of the barracks, in the middle of the room. "Sgt. Rooster, here is Pvt. Hill. He mustered a few minutes ago and has been assigned to your squad."

"Welcome to Company A." Rooster extends his hand and he and Legare shake. "Call me Rooster or call me Sergeant, but do not call me sir. What's your full name, Hill?"

"Hugh Legare Hill, but I go by Legare."

"Where you from?"

"I'm from Madison, but my wife, baby, and I have been living in Savannah. Where are you from, Rooster?"

"I'm from the Cassville area of North Georgia. Let me introduce you to a few of the other guys " By now, most of the soldiers in the barracks have gathered around Legare, They all shake hands and introduce themselves to the newest member of their squad.

"I'm Adiel Blanchard. Welcome."

"I'm 7th Corporal Joseph Warren. Glad to have you with us."

"St. John Nimmo is my name. Welcome."

"A. T. Lyon is my name. I'm the Company Bugler."

"Hello, I'm David Blount."

"I'm Pleasant Barnett. Nice to meet up with ya."

"My name is Alonzo W. McCurdy. Welcome aboard." Shaking hands, Legare looks at A. W. and asks, "Do you have any kin in Stone Mountain?"

"I'm from Madison County, but my uncle Robert McCurdy lives there. Why do you ask?"

"There's a large clan of McCurdys living in Stone Mountain, and I am married to a girl from there. Her maiden name is Polly Jernigan."

"I've heard my uncle speak of the Jernigans. Owns a small farm, right?"

"That's them all right!"

Hugh Legare Hill's muster document, November 11, 1863, and uniform issue slip, April 14, 1864, Fort Thunderbolt, GA.

"Howdy. My name is John Carroll."

"Hello, my name is Legare Hill. Nice to meet you."

The round of introductions is briefly interrupted when a young gentleman approaches and taps Legare on the shoulder. "Hi Legare!"

"John Dent! I can't believe it! You're in the 63rd?"[154] John and Legare shake hands again, before sitting in two chairs nearby to talk about their families.

"I hope you're still married to that beautiful Polly!"

"Sure am and we are living in Savannah—just down on the river a short piece from here." The two old friends catch up on old times until the bugler sounds taps.

The following morning at 7:30 AM sharp, Sgt. Elijah Stowe sounds *Reveille* with his bugle. Everyone is up and in formation within ten minutes. Rooster pokes his head in. "Just follow along with Pvt. Dent, and after breakfast you'll get your drill instructions and orientation."

After breakfast, Rooster teaches Legare the proper method of military formations and marching. Later in the morning, they discuss the various ranks and the insignia associated with each rank, who to salute and how to address individuals. He also explains the election process of the officers by the troops. "Got any questions, Pvt. Hill?"

"Not yet. Pretty straightforward," replies Legare.

"Well, Pvt. Lyon will be sounding the bugle for dinner shortly, so take a break. After dinner, you'll meet with Maj. Allen.[155] He'll give you some history on the 63rd and explain our mission at Fort Thunderbolt."

Following dinner, Rooster walks with Legare over to Maj. Allen's headquarters. He reminds Legare to "stand at 'attention' and salute. Wait until Maj. Allen returns your salute before returning to attention. Then, remain standing at attention until Maj. Allen gives you an order otherwise." When they arrive at Maj. Allen's office, Rooster informs the headquarters clerk that Maj. Allen is expecting him and Legare.

"I'll tell Maj. Allen you're here." In a moment, the clerk returns. "Maj. Allen said for you to come into his office."

Rooster and Legare walk to Maj. Allen's office and knock on the door. "Come In!" They enter, stand at attention and salute. Maj. Allen returns their salute. "Stand at ease and have a seat. Rooster, if you have something else to do, you may go and I will send Pvt. Hill to the barracks when I finish with the orientation."

"Yes sir. There are a few items I need to attend to, sir." Standing, Rooster salutes and departs.

"How has your enlistment been so far Pvt. Hill?" asks Maj. Allen.

"Pretty busy sir, otherwise everything is fine."

"Military clothing is in short supply, but eventually you'll be given some uniforms. This afternoon, you'll pick up your musket and accoutrements: knapsack, haversack and canteen. Do you know how to swim?"

"Yes, sir."

"It is important that you know how to swim. We had a soldier drown this past April right here at Thunderbolt. Poor fellow fell out of the boat and never came up. The current was so strong that we never found his body. Probably carried him out to sea." Legare squirms a little in his chair. "I am going to give you a little history of the 63rd. Originally, we were the 1st Ramsey" Regiment Georgia Volunteer Infantry. After one year in March '62 the name changed to Company A, 12th Battalion Georgia Light Artillery. In November and December of '62 the unit is transferred to the Col. George A. Gordon's 13th Battalion Georgia Infantry and increased to Regimental size and another name change. This time to Gordon's Regiment and shortly to the 63rd Georgia Volunteer Infantry. So Company A is a part of the 63rd Georgia Volunteer Infantry under Col. Gordon and is known as the Oglethorpe Artillery Company. Now every soldier in Company A is not trained in Artillery. The 63rd is both an infantry and a heavy artillery unit."

"The 63rd ranks were greatly reduced due to sickness and casualties during the defense of Charleston. We were ordered to return to Savannah on August 2nd of this year. The strength of company "A" is around 150 soldiers. Our main mission is defensive in nature. We guard the coast of Savannah.[156] The entire outside coastal defense batteries were ordered by Gen. Lee to fall back upon the interior forts. For us, that's Thunderbolt and Fort Beulieu. There are two artillery batteries on Whitemarsh Island. The southern end is Battery Point and there are works at the northeast point. Turner's Battery is across the Wilmington River from Fort Thunderbolt and next to the Augustine Creek. The mission of Fort Thunderbolt is to protect against an attack by the Union Navy from Wassaw Sound. Thunderbolt has four guns located on the water approach from Wassaw Sound up the Wilmington River. If these guns at Fort Thunderbolt were controlled by the Union, the enemy could land 20,000 men and march straight into the South.

"The Whitemarsh Island Line is a bastion of gun batteries between Fort Bartow and Fort Gibson. Wilmington Island and Whitemarsh Island are the two islands prior to reaching Tybee Island six miles below

Savannah. So you will be stationed as a picket at, or near, one of the artillery batteries on one of the islands or at Fort Thunderbolt. I started out as a Lt. in Ramsey's and Capt. Picquet started out as 1st Corporal in Ramsey's … and as you can see, we both have been elected as a Captain and now I am a Major."[157]

"What about you, Pvt. Hill? Tell me about yourself. Where are you from?"

"Well, sir, I'm from Madison. My wife and I moved to Savannah about a year ago. We have a house on the river and a son named Joshua. I work for my Uncle Richard on his plantation and with Mr. Lilly at the Bank." Legare thinks it might be best to not give any more details , just in case Maj. Allen does not like his father's pro-union stand against the war.

"As long as the war is quiet around here, we are pretty liberal about furloughs. However, there are no furloughs while you are in training and furloughs can be stopped at any time. Furloughs help keep more food for the soldiers who have no place to go to for home cooking. If you don't have any questions Pvt. Hill, you are dismissed. Rooster will give you a tour of the fort."

"Don't have any questions right now, sir."

"Then you are dismissed."

"Thank you, sir." Legare stands, salutes and departs. Returning to the barracks, Legare goes to his cot and finds a haversack.

John Dent sees Legare inspecting his equipment. "Rooster left the haversack, knapsack and canteen for you. The cartridge boxes and musket will be issued to you next week. That's about all you are going to get right now. Supplies are running short."

"Thanks!" says Legare. Opening the haversack, Legare finds a metal plate, fork and knife. The Knapsack is empty.

John is sitting on the bunk next to Legare's and watches him as he checks his equipment. "I guess you know you have to provide your own clothing and blankets for now."

"Yes I knew that." Maj. Allen says. "Rooster is giving me a tour of the fort this afternoon."

"It's a pretty nice and quiet place. But we keep our eyes toward Wassaw Sound all the time. That's the direction from which the Yankees will attack. I guess you heard about President Davis visiting here last month. He disembarked the *Beauregard* to inspect our unit. He called us the 'Phoenix Riflemen.' He congratulated us for repelling the Yankees on May 19 last year and not losing a single man."

"Personally, I think President Davis makes a good cheerleader. He can really give an encouraging speech," Legare responds.

Soon Rooster returns. "I see you found your haversack, knapsack and canteen. Let's move on and take a tour of the fort before dark. Pvt. Harrison, you are the interior quarters guard today right?"

"That's me, Rooster."

"Okay Dent you can come along with us if you like."

John Dent replies, "Should see more action out there than in here!" The three depart the barracks and approach the highest point on the fort. Rooster points toward the river.

"From this position, along this high bluff, we have strategically built earthworks with these mounds, bombproof shelters and cannon emplacements. Now, lean over and look at the river below." Legare leans over as far as he safely can and looks toward the river. "See those large oaks in the river? We put them there as obstacles to slow down enemy ships if they attempt to move up the river towards Savannah. If the Union takes this fort, they can move thousands of troops into the interior of our state. You see, we have provost guards on duty here, always looking toward Wassaw Sound. Half of the artillery batteries are manned twenty four hours. Most of the ordinances have come from the outer perimeter costal forts." Pointing as he walks, he continues, "Here are several of the eight inch Columbiads and seven inch rifled guns. We even have mortars."

"How often do the guards and artillery crews change?" asks Legare.

"Generally every eight hours here. Out on Whitemarsh, it could be ten to twelve hours up to several weeks. At Whitemarsh, it depends on how many we can spare from Fort Thunderbolt. The 63rd performs primarily provost duty on Whitemarsh." They continue the tour. "Along this line, we have eight inch Navy guns, 18 pounders, 24 pounders, 32 pounders and 42 pounders. Most of these guns came from the Skidaway Battery."

"Attention!" shouts John Dent. Rooster and Legare turn and see Col. Gorgas[158] approaching. Rooster and Legare come to attention and salute as Rooster says, "Good afternoon, Col. Gorgas."

"Good afternoon, Rooster," replies Col. Gorgas as he returns their salutes. "Stand at ease. Is this a new soldier?"

"Yes sir, Pvt. Hill mustered yesterday. I am giving him a go round of the fort."

"Pvt. Hill, we have a total of fourteen big guns here. No Yankee ship dare come near and they are well aware of our ability to destroy any ship that attempts to traverse this river. Most of the artillerists are from the outer defenses. We have well trained soldiers manning these big guns. Congratulations, Pvt. Hill. You're a part of a great outfit. Carry on, Sgt. Rooster."

"Yes sir, Col.," and the three come to attention and salute Col. Gorgas as he departs. "Well, it is almost time for supper. Tomorrow is Sunday and usually preacher Sweat comes and leads us in prayer."[159] Next week, you'll receive your musket training and some more drills and instructions on provost duty. Then, you'll get basic training in operating the big guns. When all of your training is complete, you'll be stationed on Whitemarsh in rotation on provost duty around the first week of December. I'm going on furlough this weekend. If I hear any cannon fire, I'll return immediately. That is the standing order when you are on furlough. You cannot go out of range of the cannon sound. So, I'll see you Monday."

Legare turns to John, "Let's try to get our provost duty together with Alonzo McCurdy. That way we may be able to have a furlough at the same time and I can take you to our house for supper."

"Mighty generous of you. Rooster can arrange the schedule for us. He's pretty fair about scheduling everyone for furloughs. There are a couple of gals that hang around the fort that provide "favors" for the soldiers. They're here just about every evening. The guys come and go all night long once their duty is finished for the day!"

"Happy hunting to them! I'm happy to wait for my furlough!"

During the last week of training, Rooster summons John, Alonzo, and Legare for the scheduling. "I have your request for furlough for Christmas and have been reviewing the schedule. Most of the fellows are too far away from home to get furlough for Christmas. If you three are willing to provide provost duty on Whitemarsh from December 10th through the 21st, I can get you a furlough from December 22nd through the 26th. What do you think?"

"I'll be more than glad to serve two weeks on Whitemarsh to be with my family on Christmas," replies Legare.

Sitting around the camp fire, beneath the brambling underbrush, oaks, pines and Spanish moss on Whitemarsh Island, Legare reflects on his past few weeks. "Rooster, you, Alonzo, and John have really been helpful to me during my first month at Thunderbolt. I know I've just been here a short time, but it seems like everyone thinks we're already defeated. I hear talk about how many soldiers have left and gone over to the Yankees, especially when they are on duty on one of the islands."

Rooster stirs the fire with a stick. "Most of the deserters around here are Irish. They feel they are only defending the planter ruling class and desert. They are an unusual breed. As for us, our jobs are performing picket duty and alert the battery commanders of any Yankee gunboat patrols trying to come ashore. So long as one of us is on guard duty, then the other two of us can go into the bomb shelters and keep warm and sleep. It's comfortable in the winter time, but hotter than Hades during the hot months. At night we will rotate every three hours."

"We have to be on constant surveillance to alert the battery commanders if any of the water avenues to land is threatened."

John pours a cup of tea and forewarns Legare, "You'll find out that you're going to be bored stiff or suddenly under fire from Union gunboats or the Yankee pickets attempting to come ashore."

"When was the last time you had excitement out here?'

"Not too long ago, the Yankees burned off the marsh on some of the islands so they could observe our batteries and troops." Slicing a piece of cured ham and placing it in his mouth, Legare continues to listen.

"The government rations are not very good, but the cured ham your wife brought to you sure is going to come in handy for the next two weeks. Good for our morale!"

Legare finishes the slice of ham and asks John, "What's it like during the summer?"

"You're lucky you're not performing duty in the summer. The gnats, red bugs, heat, boredom, and mosquitoes will drive you nuts."

"That bad, huh."

"Yep, some of the soldiers get sick from the mosquitoes. So be sure to eat plenty of garlic when you're out here in the summer. Garlic is supposed to keep the mosquitoes away."

Rooster interrupts and instructs Legare, "Remember stay on the platform in the top of the pine tree. That's why this picket area is called 'Pinetree.'" Legare looks up at the platform eight feet above the ground, just high enough to see over the marsh. Rooster smiles. "It also keeps you above the alligators. Seriously be careful of the gators, but remember this post is really important because it has a perfect view of the mouth of the Savannah River, Tybee, and the Atlantic Ocean."[160]

Legare leans against his musket. "How should I alert you if I spot something suspicious?"

"If you see or hear anything suspicious, fire a shot. That's the signal for us to come running. I'll relieve you and McCurdy in three hours. Remember; fire a shot to alert us!" Rooster and John head for the bomb shelter to sleep until it's their turn on guard duty.

Slowly, silence sets in as Rooster and John disappear toward the bomb shelter. Only the occasional splashing of the alligators in the marsh disturbs the night. "Too cold for bugs, crickets and snakes. Just alligators and Yankees are what I need to watch out for," Legare thinks. A slight breeze begins to blow. Legare picks up a couple of warm rocks and places them in his knapsack. Legare and Alonzo climb the sapling ladder to the top of the platform. Legare places his knapsack on the floor. Leaning back, he turns his attention to the Savannah River.

There's a quarter moon on the tenth of December, as Legare begins his first night as a picket. The moon reflects off of the silent glistening Savannah River. Legare first peers toward the Atlantic, then toward Tybee Island. Occasionally, a shadow takes the form of a Yankee shore boat, but suddenly disappears as quickly as it appeared. Each time he prepares to fire his musket, but hesitates to be certain he is not issuing a false alarm. The damp cold breeze turns into a light wind and Legare begins to feel the platform sway. He wraps himself more tightly in his blanket and resets his knapsack to in order to get the full benefit of the warm rocks.

After what seems like days, he sees a faint light coming from the direction of the bomb shelter and nudges Alonzo. Alarmed, Legare takes his musket, lies flat on the platform and places his musket site on the approaching figure. Alonzo supports his weapon on a limb. Soon the figure is within range of Legare's musket. "HALT!" shouts Legare. The figure instantly stops, slowly raising the lantern to its face.

"It's me, Rooster."

"I see it's you, Rooster. Come on to the post." Legare waits until Rooster is at the base of the pine tree before saying anything else.

"You and Alonzo come on down. Your three hours are up. It's my turn now." Legare gets his knapsack and drops it down to Rooster. Then he climbs down the sapling ladder to the ground. "See anything exciting?"

"Nothing but shadows that disappear as rapidly as they appear."

"There's a good pot of hot charcoal in the bomb shelter to help warm you up again. The artillery battery duty officer will wake John up in three hours. Take the lantern and head to the bomb shelter. You remember the password right? You'll be stopped by the guard at the battery emplacement."

Legare takes the lantern from Rooster. "I'll hold the lantern while you get up to the platform. It's been swaying pretty good in the wind so you best hold on."

Rooster takes his knapsack and musket and climbs up the sapling ladder to the platform. "See you later."

"Later." Legare and Alonzo turn and head for the bomb shelter.

As they approach the bomb shelter, a voice shouts, "HALT!" Legare and Alonzo stop. The voice somewhat quieter says, "Sun!"

Legare responds, "Moon." The voice of the picket commands advance. Legare and Alonzo continue.

Suddenly the picket commands "Halt!" Legare and Alonzo stop. Very quietly, almost in a whisper the picket says, "Bay."

Legare responds quietly, "Clams."

"You may advance, but hold the lantern to your face," directs the picket. Legare and Alonzo advance while holding the lantern to their faces until they are near enough for the picket to recognize who they are. "Hello Legare, Alonzo. How was your first night of picket duty at Pinetree?"

"Cold, windy, quiet and I need to warm up!" Legare heads into the bomb shelter, followed by Alonzo. Inside, some of the soldiers are playing cards, while others are asleep. There are several pots of hot charcoal rendering the cold dampness more moderate. Legare takes his haversack and knapsack and locates a quiet spot, putting his blanket on the ground. He sits on the blanket and removes his shoes. Using his knapsack as a pillow, he lies down on his side, placing his shoes and haversack near his chest. Taking the blanket corner, he covers his chilly body, yawns deeply, and drifts off to sleep.

Fort Thunderbolt, 1864.

THE SPIRIT OF MISTLETOE

CHRISTMAS 1863

Legare's furlough begins at noon on December 22. Jesse, Polly and Little Joshua are at Thunderbolt headquarters waiting for Legare to leave his barracks. Polly is standing by the carriage holding little Joshua in her arms as he bounces around, looking at the sights of the fort. She constantly rearranges his blue blanket to keep him warm. The door to the barracks opens and Legare emerges. With him are John Dent and Rooster. Polly and Legare rush to meet each other. Little Joshua is squeezed between the two as they embrace and kiss.

Legare takes Joshua in his arms. "How's my little man?" asks Legare, as his arms remain wrapped tightly around his wife and son.

Rooster, Alonzo, and John approach and give Polly a gentlemen's hello. "How are you, Polly?"

"Just great now that Legare is coming home for Christmas. You're coming over Christmas Day, right?" asks Polly.

"Unless something strange comes up, we plan on being there," replies John.

"I'll have Jesse pick you, Rooster, and Alonzo up around two o'clock Christmas Day. Go look in back of the carriage. There are four hams from the smoke house. Uncle Richard wants the 63rd to have them for Christmas." Rooster, John and Alonzo smile and rush over to the carriage.

"Wow! Look at those hams!" Rooster, Alonzo, and John each pick up one. They turn it over and around, inspecting and sniffing as they wonder at the treasure.

Still playing with Joshua, Legare boards the carriage with Polly. "Jesse will help you take them inside." Jesse steps from the carriage and ties the reins to the hitching post in front of the headquarters building. Polly hurries onto the carriage and sits close to Legare. Jesse takes the ham and follows Rooster inside to the company kitchen.

"Look what Legare's uncle sent to Company A for Christmas! These four large hams!" Samuel Guy, the assistant cook, hurries over to view the prizes.[161]

Samuel points to Jesse, "You better bring those four hams over here." Jesse walks over with two hams and places them on the kitchen mess table. "Man, oh man, the guys are really going to appreciate this. Meat is a problem. Nothing but fish, oysters and crawfish with rice get mighty tiresome after a while."

Jesse asks Guy, "Iz dat duh suh?"[Is that do sir.]

Guy replies, "That's all, get on outside to your master!"

Jesse nods his head and leaves by the same door he entered. Returning to the carriage, he unties the reins and boards the driver's seat. Legare pats Jesse on the back, "It's good to see you, old friend."

Jesse turns, salutes Legare and says, "Wehkum home Mistuh LeGree" Jesse turns the carriage about and heads toward the river house.

Polly takes Legare's cheeks in one hand and squeezes his lips to a pucker and kisses him. "We've missed you dearly, Legare," and kisses him again.

"Legare, Tell me about your picket duty on Whitemarsh. Did anything exciting happen? Did you see or catch any Yankees coming on shore?"

Legare holds Polly close. "I can sum up picket duty on Whitemarsh Island in six words."

"Really, in just six words?" responds Polly, looking somewhat surprised.

"Yes. Boring, boring, boring and more boring! The only exciting event had to do with our new cook. His name is Pvt. Samuel Guy and he's in training so the meals have been interesting. All of the soldiers in the 63rd have our 'messes' together. Each company cook draws their company rations and brings them together. Then, the days are divided for cooking so that each company bears its share of duties of the 'mess,' one day for each day of the week. Our company drew rice one time and it was Pvt. Guy's day to cook. We did our boiling in a two gallon camp kettle. Pvt. Guy filled the kettle one-half full of rice to boil for dinner. When the rice began to boil and swell, Pvt. Guy would take out a dipper full and put the rice on a piece of pine bark. We started laughing. The more rice he took out of the kettle, the more the boiled rice filled it. Before long, Guy could hardly get to the pot for the piles of rice scattered around the campfire. What was left in the kettle didn't get cooked and the uncooked rice made us all sick. The next time Pvt. Guy cooked rice, he didn't put on enough to divide the 'mess.' Guy said the rice was the 'craziest stuff' he ever saw."[162]

"Well, I've got some real food cooked for you, Legare. Ma and Pa are arriving on the train tomorrow. Your folks have been over at Uncle Richard's and are coming over tomorrow afternoon after Ma and Pa get here. Your mother and father have really been enjoying a great time with little Joshua. Everybody is so glad to be together for Christmas. The only three that won't be here are your cousins Marcelle, Jordan and Matt. They are stuck in England. Norman can't get leave from GMI. Pa said the cadets are on alert. The governor suspects General Sherman is about to cross into Georgia at most anytime. Our state has been lucky in this war so far, but I think in a few months musket and cannon fire will filling the air over our soil. The other states in the Confederacy are suffering badly. Pray to God, Governor Brown saves Georgia from destruction." She takes Legare's hand. "I'll be so glad to see Ma and Pa again."

"Me too, my love. I always hoped that our families would be together and get along. They've liked each other since the first time they met. When this war is over, life will be generous to all of us, and the sooner the better! After all, we have wiggling little Joshua to raise. Who knows? He might become President someday."

Rubbing Joshua's little head she intently stares at him. "He would be another great leader for our country." She turns her attention back to Legare. "Looks like the wind is picking up and some clouds are forming."

Legare stares in the direction of the approaching clouds, "Yeah, look it's lightning over there. We should be home in about five minutes or so."

The house is in sight and grows larger as Jesse snaps the whip over the horses head and begins moving in a steady gallop toward the house. The carriage soon reaches the front door and the wind becomes stronger as Polly, Legare and little Joshua jump from the carriage. "Go ahead and take the horse and carriage to the barn Jesse before the storm hits," shouts Legare.

Tot holds the door open as Polly rushes inside with Legare holding little Joshua. Tot gives Legare a warm welcome hug with a "Wehkum home Mistuh. We gonna a mite 'ine Chrymus 'is year."

"Yes, we are Tot!" replies Legare. "What are you cooking for supper tonight?"

Suddenly, a loud crack of thunder sounds over the house. Everyone ducks as if to dodge the bolt. Little Joshua lets out an insecure cry as Polly draws him close. The wind whips up and throws the rain against the windows. As the wind moves across the chimney, a howling sound emerges in the parlor along with a gust of smoke.

"We saw this one coming, Tot, and made it home just in time. This storm may hang around for the rest of the day. I don't think there are any Yankees on the river today. Once the storm settles down, keep alert for any cannon fire towards Fort Thunderbolt. That's the signal for everyone to return immediately."

Polly hands little Joshua to Legare as she and Tot light the candles. The fire in the fireplace gives a bright glow in the dimly lit room. As occasional burst of steam spews from the fireplace as some of the rainwater finds a path to enter the top of the chimney. Soon, Polly and Tot have the room glowing again with the abundant candle light.

Legare is playing with his son, crossing his legs and bouncing little Joshua on his foot. He holds little Joshua hands and begins moving his foot up and down with a "gitty-up horsey." Joshua laughs and his cuteness forces Legare to grab him and hold him tightly, giving Joshua a big kiss. "Pa and Mama love you." Legare's eyes become misty from the joy of being with his family.

The severe thunderstorm begins to ebb and only a steady rain is falling. The thunder in the distance has reduced to a soft, rumbling sound. Little Joshua rubs his eyes and fusses. Legare holds him close. "Time for your nap, Mr. Joshua!"

Polly already has his bottle prepared and they take him to his bed. Legare sits in the rocker, and Polly hands him the bottle to feed little Joshua. Joshua grabs the baby bottle of Karo syrup mixture vigorously. Soon, his eyes become heavy and close tightly. His body goes limp and Joshua finds sleep in the comfort of his father's arms. Polly tenderly leans over and takes Joshua from Legare and places him in the crib.

Legare stands and blows out the candle. As Polly turns, he takes her in an embrace. "I love you, Polly!" He kisses her dearly.

Polly clutches Legare, holding him tightly and nibbles on his ear, "I love you the most!" Smiling at each other they gently kiss again. Peeking back toward Joshua, Polly and Legare ease out and return to the parlor.

"What is that delightful smell, Tot?" asks Legare.

"Pohk Rib" replies Tot. "On ob yoh faybrit!"

Legare goes to the sink and turns on the hot water faucet. "The water is just warm. I want to soak in the tub for a while." Legare opens the back door and goes to the stone building attached to the house. Opening the door, he sees that the fire under the boiler is just about out. There's a stack of oak logs outside the door, and he takes several of them. He places them on the hot coals, stirring the coals with a poker to stoke the fire.

Legare dashes back inside and takes a towel from the kitchen rack, wiping his face and head. "Still raining pretty good. Looks like the rain is going to stick around for a while. The cistern will be overflowing if this rain keeps up. The water should be hot in a few minutes. I am going to soak in the tub before supper. I'm clean, but I just want to be sure all of Whitemarsh is off of me! Have either Al or Jesse keep the fire going under the boiler."

"Yea' uh baah ob soap uh mek n da summer, Massuh LeGree." [Here's a bar of soap I made in the summer, Mars. Legare.]

Legare takes the soap. "Thanks, Tot."

He goes to his closet and removes some clothing better suited for home than for duty at Whitemarsh. He places them near the tub. The small stove in the bathtub room heats that area to a toasty temperature. Legare turns on the hot water and checks the temperature. Once the cold water is out of the pipe, the water begins to warm until it is finally hot. He removes his civilian uniform and steps into the tub. His body is immediately surrounded by the immensely comforting hot water. Taking a wash cloth, he scrubs his body and washes his hair. He ducks his head in the hot water to remove all the soap. Sliding down so his head is resting on the back of the claw foot tub, Legare closes his eyes for what seems like a moment until he hears a familiar voice.

"Wake up, my dear," followed by a tender kiss. Legare opens his eyes and finds Polly kneeling next to the tub. "It is time for supper, sleepy boy."

"I just got comfortable," replies Legare.

"You have been comfortable for over two hours." Placing her hand in the water, she whispers, "I've been heating your water for you. I declare you're beginning to look like a prune."

"I guess there's no place like home!" Legare takes his two hands and places them on each side of Polly's face. He pulls her to him and kisses her affectionately. Polly places her hands on Legare's cheeks and holds his lips tightly against hers.

"Miss Polly, you want me fuh go head 'n feed Massuh Joshua?" Tot shouts from the dinner room.

"I'm coming Tot. Here's your towel, honey. Those ribs smell mighty good!" Legare leans forward and pulls the plug from the tub. He sits for a minute as the water begins to drain. Placing his hands on the tub's rim, Legare pushes himself up and then out of the claw foot tub. Just as the last sound of water rushes from the tub, Legare dresses and heads for the dining room. Joshua sees his father and begins jumping and giggling in his high chair. Legare pulls his chair close and takes the spoon full of oatmeal from Polly.

"It's my turn now. Open up, big boy!" As fast as Legare can fill the spoon, Joshua is ready and waiting with his mouth wide open. "Let's say the blessing so Mama can go ahead and eat." Polly and Legare hold hands with Joshua. "Dear God, thank You for your many blessings. Protect this mother and child and continue to bestow your blessings upon them and this house. And God bless the cook! Amen."

Polly takes up the ribs and places them on Legare's plate. She scoops a serving spoon full of greens in a side dish. Legare finishes feeding Joshua as Tot comes over to freshen up the mess.

"Great ribs, Tot. You make the best around! The greens are not shabby either!"

"Tink you, Massuh LeGree."

Soon supper is finished. Joshua, Legare and Polly sit on the floor in the parlor. Polly and Legare take a small ball and roll it to Joshua. Little Joshua is able to pick up the ball but instead of rolling it back, he tries to chew it up. Legare gently takes the ball from him and rolls it to Polly. "See, Joshua? Roll the ball to Pa or Mama." Legare rolls the ball to Joshua again. He picks up the ball and tries to eat it again.

Polly is sitting close to Joshua. She presses her cheek next to his, "When your two papas and two grandmas arrive tomorrow, we're going to put up a Christmas tree. It's going to be pretty and Santa is going to bring you some surprises for being the perfect angel that you are. But first, we are going to the edge of town and cut a beautiful cedar tree." Polly reaches for a large box on the floor near the fireplace. She pulls the box close to her side. She reaches inside and removes some beautiful bows. "Look, Joshua. Tot and I have been making these pretty bows for the Christmas tree. Here's a big red one and a beautiful green bow." Polly looks in the box again, "Aw! Here comes Santa Claus!" She pulls out a big Santa rag doll. "This goes under the tree." Little Joshua reaches for the doll, putting it to his mouth for a "taste test."

"Ebbyting clean Miss Polly. Wantuh one ting mo tonight?" "Everything is clean Ms. Polly. Need anything else tonight?" asks Tot.

Polly replies, "Just be sure there's wood under the boiler. We have to bathe Joshua and I need to take a bath, also."

"Yez 'um. Goodneigh."

"Honey, watch the embers on the kitchen fireplace. I told Tot that we would drop the ashes through the trap and close the flu when they cool." Polly stands up and comes over to Legare. She kneels next to him and places her hand on his arm. Teasingly, Polly says, "I'm going to take my bath now, but I'm not going to fall asleep like you did for a couple of hours! I've got better things to do!" Legare smiles and they kiss. She leans over and kisses little Joshua. "See you in a bit!" and closes the bathtub room door.

Legare picks little Joshua up with both hands and holds him high. He quickly yet playfully lowers his arms, as if to drop him. Joshua giggles from the rush of excitement in his little body. Legare plays this game with Joshua until his arms tire. Legare lies over on his side and places Joshua on the rug next to him. He puts lips on Joshua's stomach and blows hard, making popping sounds. The little one laughs from deep within. Continuing his fun and games with Joshua, Legare holds his finger high in the air and spirals it down toward Joshua's stomach, making it buzz like a bee. Joshua breaks out with laughter again and again as his pa's finger tickles his side and stomach.

"What are you two boys doing? It sounds like you're having lots of fun out here!" says Polly as she emerges from the bathtub room.

Her adoring husband smiles. "Come over here. Joshua and I will teach you how the birds and bees can make you laugh! Right Joshua?"

"As soon as we get this little one to bed and the kitchen ashes are dumped, you can teach me all about the birds and bees by yourself, Pvt. Legare!"

Soon the ashes are dumped and Joshua is sleeping soundly. Legare removes his clothing and wraps himself is a warm cotton bathrobe. Only the warmth of the glowing fire and candles light the parlor. Polly and Legare gather the pillows from their bed along with two large comforters from the closet. They place the items on the beautiful burgundy Oriental rug in front of the fireplace. Legare goes to the wine cabinet and finds a bottle of homemade blackberry cordial. Polly grabs two cordial wine glasses from the china cabinet and brings them over, just as Legare removes the top from the bottle. The smell delights his nose as he sniffs the wine. "Gotta be your brew, honey! It smells as sweet as you, my love."

"I made it just for the two of us!"

Legare pours and fills each glass to the rim and places the bottle on the table. Taking Polly by the hand, he leads her to the inviting and alluring fireplace. He raises his glass to toast. "To the woman I love, whose smile always envelops me. She is the most beautiful and wonderful woman in the world."

"And to the wonderful man I love; whose arms, no matter how far away, are always holding me close, protecting and loving me." Polly and Legare click their glasses and sample the blackberry cordial. Polly draws Legare's hand upon her mid-drift and he eagerly pulls her silky body to his. There robes fall from their anxious bodies as their warm, moist lips bond. The world disappears as they indulge in the joy of their reunion before blissfully falling asleep by the fire.

The following morning, breakfast is finished and little Joshua is dressed as the young family waits for Legare's mother and father to arrive. The day is chilly with a slight breeze. The clouds are breaking away as the sun plays hide and seek with the ground below. There's a knock on the door and Legare rushes to it in anticipation of his mother's and father's arrival. As he throws the door open, he is greeted with a sweet and familiar. "Merry Christmas!"

Legare and his mother and father embrace in a big, three-way hug. Polly stands with little Joshua and points and the little one exclaims, "Gram-pa! Gran-mama!" The youngster holds his arms out in anticipation of one of his grandparents taking him into their arms. Gram-pa is the first to take the bait, squeezing his grandson's fat little body.

"Haven't seen you in two days, young man! Gram-pa and Granmama miss you."

Polly informs the Hills, "I have some hot oatmeal when you're ready. We've got about one hour before my folk's train arrives."

Joshua places his hand on Legare's shoulder. "Looks like the army is treating you well, son. You look mighty good!"

"Thanks to the extra food Polly brings to Fort Thunderbolt. The army rations are mighty poor. A lot of the fellows kill and eat alligator. The marsh is full of them. Had some myself and it's pretty tasty. Have you ever tried gator, Pa?"

"Yes, I have. As a matter of fact, your mother and I had alligator at Richard's and Charlotte's yesterday … and yes it's pretty tasty. Richard told us that the number of alligators is dwindling because so many are being killed for food."

"Well, that will make my job a little easier on Whitemarsh Island," replies Legare." Guess who's going to spend Christmas day with us, Pa? I wrote you about him in my last letter."

"Gotta be John Dent. It's a small world. Both of you in the same unit together and his pa and I were very close friends. It's been a couple of years since I've seen John and I'll be glad to have him here today."

Legare replies, "He and Rooster are coming to Uncle Richard's in the afternoon of Christmas day. We all have become good friends!"

"We should start heading for the train station. The train should be here in about forty-five minutes. Tot, have Jesse bring the larger carriage around front. There's gonna be six of us riding from the station."

Jesse shortly enters the front door alerting everyone the carriage is around in the front and waiting. Everyone gathers their coats and Legare fetches little Joshua's warm blanket while Gram-ma Hill puts on his coat and gloves. She takes little Joshua in her arms and they all go outside and climb into the carriage.

Emily glances around at her surroundings. "What a beautiful December day."

Polly asks Mrs. Hill, "If it meets your approval after we pick up Mama and Papa and eat a bite, Legare and I would like for you to go with us to cut a Christmas tree for the house. We wanted to wait until both of our families are here so we can decorate it together."

"Sounds like fun to me," replies Emily.

The carriage ride to the depot takes about twenty minutes. The road is still a little wet from the previous night's rain, helping to keep the dust down. The giant green magnolias add contrast to the barren gray of the Spanish moss and oak trees. Reaching the Union train station, Jesse ties off the horses and assists the ladies from the carriage.

Congressman Hill says, "Just as a point of interest Polly, this railroad building is among the most extensive scale and completeness in the United States."[163]

Polly affirms his statements. "I do admire this depot. It is as beautiful as some of the mansions in town, but I didn't know it is one of the best in the country. Would you like me to hold little Joshua for a while?"

He leans over to pass little Joshua to his mother but the two are quickly interrupted. "No you don't, Mrs. Legare Hill! It's my turn to hold this sweet bundle!" says Emily as she reaches for her grandson.

"You best enjoy him before the train arrives."

Polly and Legare laugh and he says, "We might have to establish a 'holding little Joshua schedule!'"

The group enters the depot where they are greeted by the warmth of several large glowing pot-belly stoves. Legare goes to the ticket agent. "Good afternoon, sir. Any idea how long before the train arrives?"

"The last telegram I got said the train should be here in about…" the ticket agent looks at his pocket watch. "In about four minutes!"

In just a few moments Legare hears a loud whistle in the distance and the group rushes outside. Excited to see her parents, Polly stands on the platform in front of everyone as the engine rolls to a stop. Joshua is scared by the noise and sight but is comforted by the look of excitement and joy on his mother's face. The spirit of the holiday season is in the air as the numerous families who have gathered on the platform strain to find their loved ones as they deboard from the train.

"There they are!" shouts Polly as she waves her hands vigorously. Her parents' eyes find her at the same time and they wave back with excitement. The group follows Polly as she rushes to embrace her parents.

After a round of hugs and kisses, Emily winks at Betty Gail and says, "I found this little fellow on the road side. Maybe you should take care of him for a while."

"Why I think I can handle that job!"

Buck, standing next to Betty Gail, seizes the opportunity. "Let me hold him for a minute so I can see how much he has grown," beating Betty Gail out of the first "holding."

After a few seconds, a no-longer-patient Betty Gail says, "Time's up, Buck! You can play with him later." She takes little Joshua into her arms.

Legare chuckles and turns to Buck. "Point out your baggage, and Jesse will put them into carriage."

Buck shakes Legare hand. "It's good to see you son." He gives him a gentleman's embrace. "Looks like the army is treating you well. There are our bags." Buck points to three travel bags.

Jesse gathers the three pieces of luggage and places them in the cargo area in the rear of the carriage. Everyone climbs into the carriage and they depart the depot, just as the locomotive that brought them there does the same. Little Joshua struggles to get one last look at the strange smoking machine, still unsure if he likes it.

Meanwhile, Tot has been on the lookout for their arrival. She sees Jesse through the window as the carriage comes to a stop in front of the house. Joshua is sound asleep in Betty Gail's arms. Tot meets the entourage at the door. "Welcome back Mistuh Jernigan and Ma'am Betty. De cohn cake 'n wittle spread on de table. Wantuh you like sassafras tea, hot cocoa, or watuh?" [The corn cakes and food spread on the dining room table. Would you like sassafras tea, hot cocoa, or water?]

"I'll have tea. What about you Buck?"

"Jest water for me, thanks. No, I think maybe something hot. Let me try the hot chocolate," replies Buck.

Betty Gail takes the baby and the two grandmothers lay him gently in his crib. "Most precious little angel I have ever seen!"

"Sure is," adds Emily. The two ease out of the room and join the others in the dining room. They have already sat down at the table and the conversation is lively.

"Don't forget when we are through eating, we are going Christmas tree hunting on the edge of town. After we return, you men can put it on a stand and then take care of little Joshua. We women are going to do the decorating."

Congressman Hill turns to Buck. "We might go fishing out back, right Buck?"

"We jest might!" replies Buck.

"Supper tonight is fresh fish, rice with a few greens from Tot's garden and, of course, corn cakes. Tot has made a great lime pie for desert, too."

"Weh you want dese bag, Miss Polly?" asks Jesse.

"Put them in the guest bedroom, Jesse."

"Now, Polly, we are staying here tonight but Christmas Eve, we are spending the night with Richard and Charlotte. We all agreed that you, Legare and little Joshua should spend Christmas morning together and alone," says Betty Gail.

"Emily and I are staying next door."

"Al has the house in order Pa. There's even smoke coming out of the chimney."

Congressman Hill tells Jesse, "Go ahead and take our bags to our house when you finish placing Mr. and Mrs. Jernigan's bags upstairs."

Legare anxiously begins to give the account to his pa and Buck about meeting John Dent and his squad leader, Rooster. Soon, the three men are off in a corner talking politics and the effects of the war on Georgia. Polly informs everyone, "This is a very casual dinner. Help yourself when you get hungry. After Joshua wakes up and eats his dinner, we'll load up and go cut the Christmas tree."

Over the course of the next hour, the family catches up on each other's activities since they last met. During the conversations, the women gather decorations for the Christmas tree. Emily tells the group, "When we leave, Tot is going to bake some fresh cookies for the tree. I've already made some candy sticks to hang and Aunt Charlotte gave us some beautiful crochet snowflakes and stars. While we are decorating, the men can fetch the mistletoe, ivy and holly from the trees outside."

Soon, a faint noise is heard from behind the door of little Joshua's room. "I think I hear someone calling us!"says Emily. Polly heads towards the room as Emily and Betty Gail follow close behind.

"Good afternoon, little man!" says Polly as she lifts her son from his crib. "You look more like you father everyday! You sure are going to be a handsome man!"Turning to Emily, Polly continues, "Don't you think he looks like Legare, Mrs. Hill?"

"Let me hold him and I can give you a better answer." Polly hands Joshua to his smiling grandmother.

"Yes, I think he looks a lot like his father, but also has your beautiful features."

"A good blend!" says Betty Gail.

"Tot has little Joshua's oatmeal ready if you'd like to feed him."

Betty Gail replies, "I think Emily and I can handle that!" They head toward the kitchen. Little Joshua finishes his oatmeal and milk with constant encouragement from his two grandmothers.

Jesse opens the front door. "De two carriage ready, Mistuh LeGree."

"Thanks, we'll be right there Jesse!" Everyone locates their warm coats and heads for the carriages. Legare takes two pistols and places them in his coat pocket. Outside, Legare asks Jesse, "Do you have the saw and ax?"

"Yaas'suh," replies Jesse.

With everyone on board, Jesse snaps the reins and the horse and carriage leaves the house. Al follows behind in the farm wagon. The afternoon is still bright and the temperature has become much more comfortable. "Just head toward Guyton, Jesse. Should take us about fifteen minutes. There's a grove of beautiful cedars at the edge of town." Feeling festive, they begin to sing Christmas carols: *Silent Night, O Come, All Ye Faithful*, and last, *While Shepherds Watched Their Flocks*. Even Buck chimes in with a very low, bass voice.

Jesse brings the carriage to a stop. "Good find Jesse, this looks like the spot," says Legare. "Look at this grove of cedars. It must cover ten acres. This year, Polly and I want to have a tall tree that reaches from the floor to the ceiling instead of a small Christmas tree for the table. Polly, you, Mama, and Mrs. Jernigan pick out the tree and Pa, Mr. Jernigan and I'll do the cutting." The ladies and Little Joshua begin their enthusiastic search for the perfect Christmas tree. Legare goes to the wagon. "Jesse, go ahead and cut a couple of trees for you and Tot and anyone else who needs one as well." Jesse jumps from the carriage and motions for the farm hand on the farm wagon to join him in cutting several small trees. They place the fresh cut trees on the farm wagon.

"Over here, Legare! We have found it!" shouts Polly.

Legare shouts out to Jesse, "Bring the ax and saw and let's find the women!" Legare, Buck and Congressman Hill amble to the site of the tree and excited women.

"Isn't this a beautiful tree? See how it forms a nice point at the top and is full all the way around?" Polly takes Legare's hand and walks around the tree.

"It's perfect. Let's cut it down and take it home. Since this is a family project, I'll make the first couple of cuts, and then Pa and Mr. Jernigan can make the final cuts." Legare removes his coat and takes the ax from Jesse. He studies the tree and then removes the lower limbs, exposing the trunk close to the ground. Legare gives the ax back to Jesse and takes the saw to his father. "Now, you and Mr. Jernigan can finish the job." The two grandfathers get down on their knees and proceed with the cutting.

After Congressman Hill strokes the saw against the tree several times, he passes the saw to Buck, "Finish it off!"

Buck smiles and takes the saw. In about ten strokes, the tree is laying on the ground. Jesse comes over and picks up the tree to load it on the wagon. He places the tree along side the other small trees that have been cut. Polly and Legare put their arms around each other's waist and stroll back to the carriage with the rest of the Christmas party. On the homeward journey, the women lead the men in singing more carols, *The Twelve Days of Christmas and finishing with Good King Wenceslas.*

As the carriage enters the circle drive and comes to a halt in front of the house, Tot meets the family at the door. "Welcome back! De sassafras tea, hot chocolate en watuh is ready." Everyone enters, removes their coats, and heads for the roaring fireplace. Jesse follows close behind with the prized Christmas tree.

"Weh you want de Chrymus tree Massuh LeGree?" asks Jesse.

"Prop it up in the corner over there and then we'll go to the barn for the bucket and rocks so we can stand it up. Jesse and I'll be back in a minute." Once in the barn, Legare spots the ritual bucket. It is about two feet wide and eighteen inches deep. They gather fist-sized rocks to fill the bucket to steady the tree. Before long, the two re-enter the back door and walk into the parlor with what will serve as the tree's stand.

The women have decided on a location for the tree. Polly stands in the center of the parlor. Soon, the gentlemen and Jesse have positioned the tree in the bucket. The rocks are used to wedge the tree straight and secure it in its new home. After passing the scrutiny of the women's expectations, Legare fills the bucket with water to keep the tree from drying out.

"It looks great!" Legare confirms. "Let me have a cup of tea and then Papa, Mr. Jernigan and I'll fetch the holly, mistletoe and ivy. Tot, that popcorn sure smells good. Make enough for us to eat and string for the tree."

Tot pours the cup of sassafras tea for Legare from the hot kettle. She places the cup on a saucer along with a cookie and warns him lovingly, "It's hot Mistuh LeGree."

Polly, Emily, and Betty Gail gather bowls of holly berries and popcorn. Each finds a comfortable seat. Little Joshua is placed on the sofa between his two grandmothers and falls asleep quickly. They remove his shoes and cover his little body with a small blanket. The ladies begin stringing the holly berries and popcorn, catching up on the latest gossip as they work.

"We're ready when you are, Legare," urges Buck.

"Well, let's go. There are some trees on the river with mistletoe on some low branches. There's plenty of holly bushes and English ivy on the trees on this property." The three men walk outside to the barn and locate two bushel baskets and some snipping shears. "Mr. Jernigan, these are for you and Pa. Jesse and I'll go to the river to get the mistletoe. We might have to do a little climbing."

Congressman Hill turns to Legare and says, "It's going to be dark in about an hour and a half so we'd better get going."

Legare and Jesse walk the short distance to the river and locate a tree with mistletoe." These limbs are low, Jesse. I'll climb up, cut the mistletoe and drop it down to you. I'd shoot it down, but ammunition is getting scarce." Legare takes off his jacket and jumps to grab the lowest limb on the tree. He pulls himself up and grasps the next limb. After getting his balance, he climbs up one more limb and is in the midst of a productive mistletoe growth. He cuts as much as he can reach and tosses it down to Jesse.

In a short time, Jesse shouts, "Mars. Legare, the basket is full."

Legare climbs cautiously from the tree and jumps to the ground. He checks the bushel basket. "Jesse, you and I could kiss every lady in

Savannah with all this mistletoe but I prefer kissing Polly as many times as there are ladies in Savannah!"

"Mistuh LeGree, Miss Polly duh true jewel."

Legare and Jesse head for the house as the sun is setting. Candlelight gives a soft, warm glow to the house. Legare sees Polly and their families inside, standing around the tree. "Looks like they have started putting on the decorations, Jesse. We'll slow them down when we bring in the mistletoe! There will be quite a kissing exchange going on for a few minutes!" Smiling broadly, Legare and Jesse throw open the back door and carry the basket into the parlor. Legare shouts, "All ladies get in a line. We've got the mistletoe!"

Laughter breaks out as everyone comes to inspect the harvest. Legare cuts the branches and presents a piece to Polly and his other loved ones. "Jesse, you and Tot get mistletoe as well. Come on over here!"

Polly holds her mistletoe over Legare's head as he holds his mistletoe over hers and says, "Thank you, Goddess Frigga." They exchange a kiss, a genuine hug, and a "Merry Christmas!" Legare moves to his mom and Betty Gail and finally. Simultaneously, Buck and Congressman Hill use their mistletoe for a kiss with each of the ladies.

"Legare," says Betty Gail. "Do you know what mistletoe means?"

"Can't say that I do, Mrs. Jernigan."

"It was observed in ancient times that mistletoe grew where birds would sit on a tree limb and leave their droppings. 'Mistle' is the Anglo-Saxon word for 'dung' and 'tan' is the word for 'twig.' So 'mistletoe' means dung-on-a-twig!" Everybody laughs.

Legare shakes his head. "I'd rather not know that!"

Buck climbs up a ladder and drapes the small chandelier in the dining room with the ivy and holly. "Take the ivy and twine it around and over the arms of the chandelier, Buck. Give it a little grace." Buck attempts to rearrange the ivy to the satisfaction of Betty Gail. "Kinda do it like you're hanging tobacco in the barn, Buck … nice and neat. Here, use this holly, too. Be sure to let the red berries show up good!"

"Yes, Ma'am. Whatever you say dear." Meanwhile Congressman Hill who is twinning ivy around the legs of the table in the dining room and following the instructions of his wife as well.

"Come on down here, Buck. Stand under the mistletoe for me, and I'll show Polly and Emily how to win an argument with your husband!"

Polly and Emily laugh as they continue to string the popcorn and holly berries around the tree. They tie the lace stars and snowflakes to the tips of the branches. Betty Gail ties a bow made of red or green ribbon to each. Tot brings over the fresh and sweet smelling but uneatable cookies. "Almost smells too good to put on the tree." They begin threading the cookies to hang on the tree.

Buck and Congressman Hill intertwine some Muscadine vines into an oval-shaped wreath. Then they lace the wreath with ivy. After arranging more holly with red berries and mistletoe, the task is complete. Legare shows the wreath to the women and they all approve.

The men go to the front door. "There's already a hook on the door from last Christmas," says Legare. "It should hang okay."

Buck takes the wreath and runs one of the back vines over the hook. He gives the wreath a slight tug. "That ought to hold jest fine." Shaking a little, he comments, "The air's getting chilly since the sun set. Let's get inside. I'm ready for another cup of hot chocolate."

Just then, Polly calls, "Supper's ready!"

Legare tucks Polly's arm over his, smiles down at her and leads the way to the dining room. His father and Buck follow suit. The men seat the ladies and then take their seats. Little Joshua is sitting in his highchair, flanked by a grandmother on each side. Everyone joins hands and Legare blesses the food, "Lord, thank you for the abundance of your gifts and the love of our families. Protect our soldiers, our families and loved ones. Amen."

Polly begins passing around the food. "This is fresh sea bass. Uncle Richard sent it over yesterday with some fresh lemons. A friend of his caught about fifty pounds of it. Tot put some fresh almonds in the rice."

Betty Gail says, "We've got to make Christmas pudding."

Emily laughs and explains, "Don't worry, Betty Gail. Charlotte is going to make it at her house. I'm sure she'll be more than glad to have us pitch in and add our touch to the delicacy."

"Mrs. Hill?"

"Yes, Polly"

"You know how particular Aunt Charlotte is about her food."

"Yes, but it's Christmas, and I'm sure she'll be on her best behavior. I've known Charlotte for a long time. She's a gracious hostess and lets everyone pitch in."

After supper, Polly leads everyone to the parlor for a final inspection of the Christmas tree. "Smell that fresh cedar! It has filled the entire room."

Everyone takes a deep breath of the enchanting cedar fragrance. After the addition of a few more red ribbons, mistletoe and a grand star on top, the Christmas tree passes the ladies' final inspection. The evening is growing late as the Hills and Jernigans take pleasure in each other's company. Polly excuses herself and takes little Joshua to his bedroom with the two grandmothers close behind. Little Joshua is practically asleep when his night clothes are put on and he is placed in the crib.

After returning to the parlor, Betty Gail touches Buck on the shoulder. "Buck, we're going to bed. We have had a long day. Polly wants to give us a tour of Savannah tomorrow while Legare stays here with Emily and the two Joshua's. Plus, tomorrow night is Christmas Eve and we are going to hear Handel's Messiah at the Athenaeum.

Buck stands and rubs his stomach. "It's late and I'm mighty sleepy after that great supper."

Congressman Hill follows Buck's lead, stands and looks at Emily, "Yes, it's time to go next door, Emily."

They bid each other a good night and head for their bedrooms. Polly and Legare stay up for a short time, enjoy each other's company in their comfortable parlor. The house grows quiet. The fireplace becomes the center of attention. Sitting next to each other on the sofa, Polly and Legare snuggle contentedly while gazing at the crackling fire.

Polly leans her head against Legare's shoulder. "Oh, Legare. Life is just perfect. Please don't let this horrible war ruin it for us."

"I cannot ever think of living without you. Everything is in place for us to have a good life when this war comes to an end and leave us alone!" Legare hugs her closer, recognizing her unspoken question in her statement.

"Your love is all I could ever ask for."

The two sit in silence for a short time engrossed in their own deep thoughts as the flames die to scarlet embers, Legare stands and walks over to the fireplace, placing a large, somewhat green, log over the coals in anticipation of it holding until morning. Replacing the fire screen, Legare leads her to their room. Joining each other under the down comforter, they bring their warm bodies together, cherishing the short time they'll have together.

PLUM PUDDING

Polly rises early the next morning and takes care of Joshua. She gives Tot directions for the comforts of their guests. After breakfast she and her parents leave to tour the city. Betty Gail takes Polly's arm. "What a beautiful Christmas Eve day to spend with our daughter."

The morning is perfect for a carriage ride through the streets and squares of Savannah. The drive provides some time for them to talk about some of their Stone Mountain friends. As they catch up, Polly points out some of the more interesting aspects of the town.

"The weather has been nearly perfect. That light breeze off the river chills a bit, but the sun warms you right back," says Buck as he continues to study the sights.

"What did you like best?" asks Polly. "Was it the City Exchange which houses the custom office, the post office, city hall or the newspaper offices? Or was it the squares in town and Tomochichi's grave or Fort Thunderbolt? Which one?" As their tour is coming to a close, Polly realizes what a gift the ride has been.

Betty Gail takes Polly's hand. "Savannah is really a beautiful town, but being with you was by far our favorite part!" The mother and daughter exchange a meaningful hug. "Mrs. Cazier really knows her herbs. I picked up a few good tips on some medicine. It was a pleasure meeting her, and she seems to be impressed with your ability to make concoctions. I'm sorry we didn't get to meet Dr. Blair, though."

"Dinner at the Pirates' House was really good. Plus we got to meet Antonio," comments Buck.

"I'm glad Antonio had fresh duck today. Last time we ate there, all he had was fish and rice for dinner." Polly peers at the street ahead. "Two more stops and we will head home. I want you to see the steps going down to the river at River Street. People think they're made of Stone Mountain granite. Every time I pass by I feel like I'm close to home."

Betty Gail studies her daughter for a moment. It's easy to see how happy she is. "What are your plans when the war is over?"

"Well, Mama, Legare wants to study law and become a judge and possibly go to Congress. I know he wants to come back to Madison, and I would love to be closer to home myself. We just have to wait and see what happens."

Buck stares at the steps and finally says, "Well we'd sure like to have you close to home."

On the way Buck tells Polly, "Your mother and I talked with Augustus Cochran and Emma Aurelia and told them we were coming to Savannah to surprise you and Legare and meet our new grandson. They were excited and told us to be sure and congratulate you and Legare and give little Joshua a pinch on the cheek for them. Then they begin to tell us about some letters from George Wells when he unit was in Savannah Christmas of 1861."

"You mean Mr. Wells was in Savannah?"

"Yes he said that he, John McCurdy and Jim Lankford took a boat out to an island and saw vegetation unlike anything you could ever see in Dekalb County."

"I can imagine how they felt Pa. The first time I ever saw the sea oaks I was really fascinated."

"George describes how they saw schools of fish swimming and jumping out of the water and how they watched they sea gulls following the schools of fish looking for scraps. Then George tells them about there being 25,000 Yankees on Tybee Island with their heavy guns pointing in the direction of Brunswick."[164]

Betty Gail tells Polly, "In February of '62 George Wells wrote home from Camp Bartow and the Modena Plantation on Skidway Island."

Polly is listening intently and replies, "Modena is a very large plantation on Skidway Island. John Milledge was the original owner."

"George tells Augustus that he and Lt. Rankin had been on picket duty for two days and had been fired upon by the Yankees. Oh, and they also expected Savannah to be shelled to death. The good news was that he had gained 12 pounds."

"Were they here when Pulaski was shelled?" Surprisingly asks Polly.

Buck continues, "They got a letter from Willis Wells dated the 13th of April. Willis told Augustus that he thought Fort Pulaski had been taken by the Yankees and predicted Forts Jackson and Thunderbolt would also suffer the same consequence."

"Lucky for us we didn't lose those two forts." answers Polly.

"In the last part of the letter Willis reports that George had a sore throat and cough and came to Savannah to the Bartow hospital. He was diagnosed with chtarrhal (sic) fever, but was fine when he wrote the letter."

"I'll be." replies Polly. "I bet he saw Dr. Blair."

"May have." Answers Buck as he laughs a little. "Said he like the doctor."[165]

"Look! There goes one of Uncle Richard's wagons. He's delivering turkeys and hams to the hospital, Fort Thunderbolt and to the church for Christmas dinner for the needy. He's very charitable and has been very nice to me. Aunt Charlotte is a very socially conscious person, and I understand her and her ways. We get along fine."

"I do declare Polly, these folks walk in mighty high cotton around here. Much higher than ours in Stone Mountain. I'm glad they are treating you so well. By the way, do you understand everything Tot says to you? I have a hard time with that Gullah talk."

Polly nods sympathetically. "It took me a while but I've got it down now. It was rough at first."

The carriage comes to a stop at the stone steps leading to River Street. "Here are those steps, Pa. Do they look like Stone Mountain granite to you?"

Buck steps down and takes a closer look. "I think so, Polly. The mica looks to be the same pattern." Buck turns and looks at the ships and freighters at the docks. "My word! Look at all that cotton and rice! Must be fifteen thousand or so bales." Buck studies the river quietly. "So this is the bulk of our navy as well. Not very impressive." Buck starts to walk down the steps.

"Better not go down there, Pa. Lot of riffraff folks with no work hang around there."

Buck returns to the carriage. "We probably need to head home and get ready for tonight"

"It promises to be quite an evening. All of the churches have their choirs together at the Athenaeum to perform in Handel's *Messiah*. We're going to the second performance this evening." Polly looks at Jesse and nods. "Take us home, Jesse."

❧

After supper, everyone dresses in their best evening attire. Polly gives Tot last minute instructions in caring for little Joshua.

Emily announces, "Richard and Charlotte said they'll meet us tonight around 7:15 at the Athenaeum. We should be leaving in a few minutes."

Betty Gail, Emily and Polly check their dresses in the petticoat mirror and give one last check to their husbands' bow ties. Tot and Al wait at the front door with warm garments for the ride to the Athenaeum. Everyone bundles up and joyfully takes a seat in the carriage.

After a quick ride, Jesse pulls into the line of carriages at the Athenaeum. They move slowly toward the main entrance, finally stopping. Attendants assist the guests from the carriage. Richard, Charlotte and their children are inside waiting for their arrival. Congressman Hill spots Richard and motions for everyone to follow him.

Richard and Charlotte are talking with Nellie Gordon. Richard and Charlotte cheerfully greet everyone. Emily takes Nellie Gordon's hand,

"Hello Nellie. How are you? It is delightful to see you here tonight."

"Charlotte told me you and Joshua were coming and I have been looking forward to seeing you again." Nellie looks over toward Legare and Polly. "Emily, I see Legare and Polly on occasions." Then she takes Polly's hand and brings her closer. "You're a wonderful couple and, it goes without saying, Legare you're as handsome as ever."

Legare blushes a bit as he takes a slight bow. "Mrs. Gordon, you and Capt. Gordon have always been two of my favorite people."

"Thank you Legare."

"Yes and thank you, Nellie. We're quite fortunate to have such a wonderful daughter-in-law," replies Emily.

Charlotte is talking with Buck and Betty Gail standing beside Nellie when Joshua interrupts. "Will you excuse me Nellie? I see Admiral Tattnall and would like to visit with him before the concert begins."

"Most certainly, Joshua. We can visit during the intermission." Richard looks at Nellie. "I would like for you to meet Polly's father and mother. This is Buck and Betty Gail Jernigan."

"Why it is indeed a pleasure to meet both of you. Everyone in Savannah has high praise and admiration for Polly and her work at the hospital. I understand she makes some of the best herbal medicines."

Before Betty Gail or Buck can say "Thank you," red-faced Charlotte intervenes, "You know, Nellie, my sewing circle does a lot of lint scraping for the hospital."

"Of course I know that. What would we do without your sewing circle working as hard as they do scraping lint? Everyone has to offer aid for this war."

Richard continues his conversation. "As I was about to say this is Nellie Gordon, wife to Capt. William Gordon. Nellie is from Chicago, and her family is close friends with the Ewing's. That's the family who adopted General Sherman. You probably know General Sherman married his step-sister, Ellen Ewing."[166]

Betty Gail extends her hand to Nellie. "It is a pleasure to meet you, Mrs. Gordon."

Buck simply says, "Nice to meet you ma'am," with a slight nod of his head.

As Nellie and Betty Gail are about to continue their conversation, the manufactured gas lights begin to flicker Richard begins to walk and urges everyone, "Let's head up stairs. The concert starts in a few moments and the children have already taken their seats."

As Betty Gail and Buck climb the stairs, he asks Betty Gail, "Did Richard say Sherman married his stepsister?"

"That's what I understood him to say."

Buck shakes his head. "Strange." At the top of the winding staircase is the entrance to the balcony.

"This way please." An usher escorts the family to their box seats. Just before the gas lights get more dim, Richard leans over to Buck and Betty Gail, nodding his head toward the side seats on the lower level.

"There on the lower level are the clergy from all of the Negro churches in Savannah." Betty Gail and Buck casually glance in that direction as the lights grow dimmer and the audience becomes quieter.

The curtains open and, according to the program, the Christmas concert begins the musical performance of the *Messiah*.

As the orchestra plays the final note of *God's Triumph*, the gaslights slowly brighten the dim concert hall. The audience stands, and Buck and Betty Gail join in the grand round of applause for the sterling performance.

Richard learns over to Buck and Betty Gail, "The kids can take care of themselves. Let's go down to the atrium and have refreshments during the intermission."

In the atrium the waiters appear with hors d'oeuvres and wine. Buck looks at the small black beads on top of the cream cheese on the cracker. Polly sees her pa studying the caviar and nudges Legare. Just as she begins to tell him, "I hope Pa doesn't try the caviar," Buck picks up a cracker with the cream cheese and caviar. They watch as her father's eyes grow large, his cheeks enlarge and his face turns red. Polly puts her hand over her mouth to conceal her laughter, eases over to her pa and offers him a sip of her sweet wine. Buck washes the bite down with a gulp.

Polly whispers, "It's caviar, Pa. Salty fish eggs."

Betty Gail turns to Charlotte, while trying not to laugh. "Charlotte, we cannot thank you enough for inviting us to be your guests tonight."

"Why, my darling, we would not think about spending this evening with anyone else and we all just adore Polly. Besides, tonight is a great opportunity for you and Buck to meet some of our friends." Buck takes another strong drink of wine to recover.

Observing Buck's ordeal, Joshua asks, "Are you all right?"

Laughing, Buck looks at Joshua, "Never knew a glass of wine could taste so good!" The lights flicker and everyone takes their respective seats again before the orchestra begins the next act of the Messiah.

When the concert is over, the audience stands and gives a long-lasting applause for the orchestra. Acknowledging the gratitude of the spectators, the maestro bows and invites the orchestra to also accept the generosity of the audience. Soon, the curtains close and everyone rises to exit. They gather their garments and wait to board their carriages. Bidding Polly and Legare good night, Buck, Betty Gail, Joshua and Emily ride to the plantation with Richard and Charlotte. Polly and Legare board their carriage and head home. "Did you see Pa when he bit down on that caviar, Legare?"

"Sure did and I had to turn around to keep from laughing. I know how he felt. The first time I had caviar I reacted the same way, if not worse! I spit the caviar out on a napkin and wiped my tongue!"

Snuggling close, Polly holds Legare's arm tightly and whispers in his ear, "I love you!" Legare turns and draws Polly close, kissing her with deep emotion.

"There's no way for me to ever show you how much I love you, Polly." Soon, the horse and carriage come to a standstill. Legare jumps from the carriage and invites Polly into his strong arms. She obliges and he carries her to the front door. Tot sees the carriage and rushes to open the door for Polly and Legare. "Thanks, Tot."

"You wehkum, Mistuh LeGree." Tot assists Polly and Legare with their coats.

"How did little Joshua do, Tot?" asks Polly.

"Jes fine, Miss Polly."

"We'll finish up for the night, Tot. I know you've got things to do for Christmas tomorrow. Have a good night." Soon the house is quiet again. Legare and Polly peek in on Joshua and return to the parlor. Polly settles down in front of the fire. Legare finds a half-green log and tosses it upon the fire before finding a comfortable spot next to his loving wife on the thick Oriental rug. The embers glow softly and soon a vision of Christmas Day enters Polly's mind. Both are exhausted from the busy day and evening. Legare leans his back against the sofa. Polly places a pillow in his lap and lays her head on it. They gaze into the fire, their eyelids become heavy. Feeling secure and surrounded by love, they mellifluously slip into a deep slumber.

Polly and Legare are startled awake by a thud near the fireplace. Rapid crackling sounds are coming from the fireplace as they open their eyes to see Tot putting more logs on the hot embers. The sun shines through the window and into their eyes. Polly sits up and exclaims, "Why, it's Christmas morning! Merry Christmas, Tot!"

"Mehey Chrymus, Miss Polly! Mehey Chrymus, Mistuh LeGree!"

"Merry Christmas, Tot," responds Legare as he stretches and yawns. "While you're getting breakfast ready, Polly and I will take care of Joshua. We have to bathe and get ready to leave for Uncle Richard's in a couple of hours."

By 10:30, breakfast is finished and the Christmas fun begins. The sweet smell of the cedar tree permeates the parlor. "Tot, get Jesse and Al and bring them in here. Saint Nicholas left a few gifts for each of you under the tree." Tot, Jesse and Al merrily enter the parlor. Legare reaches under the tree and hands Polly Tot's gifts.

Polly hands Tot her gifts and hugs her. "Merry Christmas, Tot." Then, Legare hands Polly the gifts for Jesse and Al. Polly hands each of them their gifts, with an embrace and a "Merry Christmas."

Tot, Jesse, and Al wish Legare and Polly, "Mehey Chrymus." They know Polly and Legare want to be alone with Joshua so they excuse themselves. Legare reaches under the tree and finds two gifts with Polly's name and one with little Joshua's name. Legare hands them to Polly and kisses her. "Merry Christmas, my love."

She sits on the floor next to Legare and little Joshua and gently unwraps her first gift. It is a small, somewhat square, package. After removing the wrapping, she eases open the red dome box. "It's so beautiful!" exclaims Polly as she lifts the necklace with a gold cross. The cross has two diamonds, one on each end of the horizontal bar. Legare's birthstone is at the top of the cross. Polly's birthstone is at the heart of the cross and little Joshua's birthstone is just below it. "I love it, Legare. Put it around my neck." Polly lifts her hair and Legare slips the necklace around her soft neck and secures the latch. Polly glances down at the shining symbol of their life and kisses her devoted husband.

Legare reaches under the tree. "Here is another one for you."

"That's too many. We said only one gift each, remember?" Regardless, she takes the gift and unwraps it. "This one is a little heavier, but I don't know of anything to better my necklace." After the ribbon and paper are removed, Polly lifts the lid from the box and stares into the box.

Legare smiles, "I whittled this from a cypress branch I found on Whitemarsh. It's my very first carving. Rooster got me a good piece of cypress and gave me some instruction on woodcarving." Polly continues to stare at the masterpiece: a carving of her and Legare holding little Joshua between the two of them. They are looking at little Joshua who is covered in a blanket. A small heart is carved into the center of the little blanket. Polly begins to cry and pulls Legare and little Joshua close.

Without wiping her tears away, Polly says, "I cannot match your gifts, but mine are from my heart." Polly hands Legare a small red and green package. He carefully removes the wrapping and opens the white square box. Inside is a thin layer of cotton covering an embroidered fine silk handkerchief and white wool scarf. Embroidered on one corner is "Legare," the other corner "Polly," the third corner "Joshua," and the fourth corner is a "heart." All the lettering is done in Old English style.

Polly watches silently as Legare feels the embroidery. He runs his fingers gently over the embroidery again and again. Looking up at Polly and holding up the handkerchief,

"This one is embroidered with your hair. You used your hair to embroider this beautiful design and," holding up the handkerchief to the light, his voice choking, "and Joshua's name is done with his hair. A treasure fit for a king! Nothing on earth could be more meaningful." No longer able to hold back his affection, Legare clings to Polly and Joshua for what seems to be an eternity. "There's one more gift under the tree. This one is for Joshua." Legare hands Polly a small box. She opens it and finds another gold necklace with a gold charm. Lifting the chain from the box, she reads the inscription of the charm.

"13." Polly looks at Legare, "So you took Antonio's advice. It's beautiful. If 'Thirteen' brings good health and prosperity for the babies in Italy then I'm sure it will do the same for Joshua on this side of the ocean."

After exchanging presents, they depart for Uncle Richard's and Aunt Charlotte's. Once they have arrived, Polly carries Joshua in, each wearing a necklace from Legare. Legare, decked out with his new scarf, gathers the basket of gifts and follows close behind. The circular drive is heavily decorated with ivy, holly, and large red and green ribbons. Inside, the mood is festive. Betty Gail and Emily meet Polly as she enters and quickly take charge of little Joshua. Aunt Charlotte, Marie and Claire are in the kitchen supervising last minute preparations for the Christmas feast. The house is festive in every detail for Christmas. The gifts are decorated handsomely with taffeta ribbons, fine flowers, and colorful paper.

Polly and Legare enter the parlor and find that Rooster, Alonzo and John have already arrived. Alonzo and Buck are getting acquainted, talking and getting caught up on all the happenings in Stone Mountain. Uncle Richard and the children have been occupying Rooster. They want to hear all about Fort Thunderbolt and how many Yankees Rooster has killed. John Dent and Rooster walk over to Polly and Legare, "We have thanked your Uncle and Aunt for the invitation, but we also want to thank both of you."

The men enjoy the hors d'oeuvres carried by the servants as they meander through the parlor. Smiling, Legare asks Buck, "Have you tried any caviar today Mr. Jernigan?"

Buck cracks a smile. "I've had my lifetime share of caviar. I even dreamed of the stuff last night! But the bakes and oysters are great! I'll probably fill up on those and not have enough room for supper."

Legare replies, "I wouldn't do that! Aunt Charlotte would pitch a real hissy fit if she thinks you don't like her cooking. This is the one-day of the year when she really gets involved in the kitchen. The Christmas plum pudding has to meet her every expectation."

"Oh, I'm just kidding. I can't wait to get into all of the good food. If it's as delicious as the smell, you're going to have to fight me for your share!"

Meanwhile, Polly had gone into the kitchen. "Aunt Charlotte, your house is decorated so beautifully."

"Oh, thank you, darling. I've been working on it since the first of the month! I'm so glad you appreciate it."

"It smells like your cooking instructions are being followed perfectly."

"I have acquired my 'culinary genius' over the years and that's what makes this the great feast of the year! The pudding was prepared on Advent Day and we all took turns mixing it, always stirring clockwise for good luck. And, we each made a wish and threw in a thimble, ring or coin into the batter. You know darling, the ring signifies marriage, the coin signifies wealth, and the thimble signifies a happy but single life. Now, who gets what is the question! The pudding has been hanging in a sack in the cellar until this morning. You know, without the perfect Christmas plum pudding, the entire supper will be lost. This year, I am using pears in the pudding. They seem to do better than apples. Your mother, Emily and I set the pudding in boiling beef broth for eight hours of cooking which was up at two thirty. It's a beautiful, walnut brown color and is in the cellar cooling. In about ten minutes, I'll have the servants bring the pudding from the cellar and set it for re-steaming."

"I can hardly wait. Just wanted to see you and say hello before supper." On her way to the parlor Polly hears the other family members singing Christmas carols. As she passes by the dining room she stops and observes the massive Chippendale table is set for sixteen guests. Marie is beginning to light the candles.

"Come help, Polly. We are all so excited to have the whole family together." Pausing for a moment, she sighs. "Except for Jordan and Marcelle."

"It would be great if they were here. I can't wait to meet them. I'll hold the candles while you light them, Marie."

"Just take the large one from the centerpiece." Polly leans over the table, careful to not touch the Christmas bows with designs of mistletoe and holly that flow from the center toward each place setting. She removes the large red candle so Marie can light it easier. Polly tilts the candle as Marie positions the small flame from the match to the wick which catches fire quickly. The napkins rings are sterling and hold either a red or green napkin. Each place setting has personal crystal salt and pepper cellars. "Polly, I need some help with the seating cards." Giggling, Marie looks around to be sure her mother can't hear her and quietly tells Polly, "Mama wants everything perfect, and I want to be sure I'm sitting next to Rooster."

Polly smiles. "Rooster would be a good one for you to sit beside." The green or red seating cards correspond with the color of the napkins and are in front of each plate.

"Well let's start with Rooster and me. We already know where our Ma's and Pa's are sitting." Soon Marie and Polly finish their mission. Marie looks around the room. "See anything we missed Polly?"

Polly studies the setting. "Don't think so Marie, let's get to the parlor and join the singing."

A short time passes and the servant says the magic words, "De Chrymus feast iz 'eady fuh be saeb." [The Christmas feast is ready to be served.]

Everyone smiles and excitedly heads to the dining room. As Rooster enters the dining room, Marie motions to Rooster. "Here's your name right here."

Rooster smiles and walks around the table locating his chair next to Marie. Uncle Richard is at the head of the table and Aunt Charlotte is facing him at the other end.

"Let us join hands and bow our heads," asks Uncle Richard. "Dear Heavenly Father, we thank You for Your gifts of love and protection. We ask that You protect our soldiers, especially Legare, John, Rooster, and Alonzo during this period of chaos in our nation. Bless all of our servants and bestow the blessings of Christmas around the world. And God bless the cooks! Amen."

Everyone chimes in, "Amen, Amen."

Two butlers deliver and place the grand, baked stuffed turkey in front of Uncle Richard. The platter is porcelain and matches the fine supper china. Before taking up the carving knife and fork, Uncle Richard offers a toast. "To good health and prosperity." Everyone clicks wine glasses.

Congressman Hill offers a toast as well. "To bring harmony and unity to our nation."

Betty Gail nudges Buck. He clears his throat, stands and turns to Polly and Legare, "May the marriage of our Polly and Legare and your marriages be as happy and as successful and loving as mine and Betty Gail's." Everyone raises a red Venetian glass with "Here! Here!" and then sips.

Buck takes his seat and Betty Gail leans over to him with affectionate eyes, "Those are some of the sweetest words you have ever said, Buck. I love you. You do pretty good for an old codger." She pats Buck on the leg.

Uncle Richard takes the carving knife in his hand and begins the celebration. All eyes are on Uncle Richard as he begins carving the grand turkey. Rooster takes his spoon and samples the hot turtle soup. "Wow this is great turtle soup, Marie."

Marie smiles and looks at Rooster. Patting him on the back, "I'm glad. I was hoping you would like it." Polly looks across the table and winks at

Marie. When Uncle Richard completes the carving, the butler takes the platter and begins offering the turkey to each guest.

Marie leans over to Rooster and asks, "Do you want some Giblet gravy and corn bread stuffing with your turkey?" Rooster turns his head and finds the waiter holding the giblet gravy and corn bread stuffing. "Keep on singing Rooster, I be sure you get plenty of both."

Uncle Richard slices up the roast goose with sage and onion dressing. Buck turns his head towards Betty Gail, "Mighty fine goose here. Wonder what kind of feed Uncle Richard fed these geese?"

"I'm sure he'll share his type of feed with you if you ask him. Put some of the marmalade sauce on the goose. It really tastes good." Buck moves his green beans with almonds, corn, and yams to make room for the marmalade sauce. Then he enjoys every bite as he joins in the festive atmosphere.

Almost, it seems, as with the blink of an eye, the main course is finished and the servants refill everyone's wine glasses. Aunt Charlotte motions for a waiter to assist her with her chair. As she begins to get up, all eyes turn toward her.

Legare leans closer to Polly and grins. "Guess what's next, Polly?"

"If I have to guess it's going to be Aunt Charlotte's Christmas pudding."

"I can feel the excitement in the room. Look, my cousins have their forks in their hands and the Christmas pudding isn't here yet. Look at Keaton and Ian. Even John and Alonzo are set. Look at them staring toward the kitchen with their mouths open." Polly pats Legare on his leg.

"You need to look at you own mouth. It's just as wide as the rest of ours."

"Bring it on, Aunt Charlotte! I'm ready."

The climax to the Christmas feast draws near as Aunt Charlotte excuses herself from the table to check on the prize Christmas pudding. In her absence, the guests chatter amiably. A hush comes over the room as Aunt Charlotte leads the cooks from the kitchen. The butler removes the centerpiece from the table and replaces it with the pudding. Aunt Charlotte takes the decanter of warm Madeira from the cook, pouring it with a religious intent slowly and methodically over the pudding. Everyone is silent as Aunt Charlotte ignites the Madeira. Once the glowing flame flickers and sputters, everyone gives a loud round of applause. Aunt Charlotte takes the knife from the servant and makes the first slice while the guests watch her every move closely.

Legare asks, "Who gets the ring? Is it going to be Claire or Marie? Maybe Ian or Keaton."

"Not me!" shouts Ian. "I rather have the thimble!"

"Not me either!" declares Keaton. "I rather have the coin. Let the girls fight over the ring!"

Everyone laughs and raises their glass of wine as if to toast Ian and Keaton. Each slice of Christmas pudding has a topping of egg custard. The servers deliver each guest a slice. Aunt Charlotte takes her seat and places her napkin in her lap, looking around to be certain no one has taken a bite of the pudding before her. She picks up her fork, cuts into the pudding and slowly slides the morsel between her lips. Her jaw moves up and down and suddenly a smile appears. "PERFECT!" The excited guests rush to begin to sample and please their taste buds while seeking one of the three charms.

"Found one!" exclaims John Dent. Clearing away the pudding everyone anticipates his discovery. "It's the thimble!" Everyone raises their wine glass to toast the discovery.

"Here's the second one!" cries out Keaton. All eyes turn to him. Removing the charm from the pudding with his fork, "It's the ring! I'm too young to marry!" Again, everyone raises their glass to toast Keaton on his great discovery and future.

"I have the last one … the coin!" yells Marie. "When can I expect my ship to come in?"

"No time soon," bellows Ian. "At least not as long as the Yankees blockade the harbor!" All the guests laugh and again raise their wine glasses, this time to salute Marie.

The empty platters, the swelling of the bellies and the fellowship from the pleasures of the Christmas supper directs all thoughts to the parlor's Christmas tree. They find seats and Uncle Richard takes the high back red French provincial armchair next to the Christmas tree. Buck, Betty Gail, Congressman Hill and Emily sit together on the large Chippendale sofa. Polly, Legare and little Joshua find a spot on the floor near their parents. Little Joshua begins playing with a small ball on the bright and colorful Oriental rug.

Aunt Charlotte reaches under the tree and hands a gift to Uncle Richard. He reads the name on the tag, "This one is for John Dent from Santa." John smiles while one of the children delivers the gift to him.

John accepts the gift and smiles. "Thank you all for a wonderful day."

Uncle Richard continues to call names until all the gifts are distributed. Excitement fills the room. Five pound bags of salt for the Jernigans and Hills from Aunt Charlotte and Uncle Richard. Alligator change purses to Aunt Charlotte, Betty Gail and Emily from Polly and Legare. Alligator belts for Uncle Richard, Buck, and Congressman Hill from Polly and Legare. Pillow cases for Polly with embroidered violets from Aunt Charlotte and Uncle Richard and lace handkerchiefs and a hair comb from the Hills. Polly opens a large package from her mother and father. A beautifully embroidered family quilt with the birthdays and names of Legare, little Joshua and Polly.

Only three packages remain. Aunt Charlotte hands one to Uncle Richard. "This one is to Legare." She picks up the second. "This one is also for Legare." He accepts the third. "This one is for Legare as well!"

Legare reads the label on the first package, "With love from Mama and Papa." Everyone except Polly and Legare knows what the packages contain. The family eagerly awaits the expression on Legare's face when he opens each package. He removes the outer wrapping and feels the squashy box. Removing the lid from the white box, Legare observes gray material. Polly is watching intensely as he lifts the gift from the box. First there is a collar, followed by a row of glistening buttons, and then he sees his monogram initials on the cuffs. Then Legare realizes that this is a Confederate uniform. Polly's mouth drops open as Legare removes the Confederate soldier's trousers and hat from the box. He stands and holds the shirt against his body.

"Ma! Pa.!"

"Son, every soldier needs a handsome uniform. Your father and I had it made especially for you."

Legare reaches his mother and father, hugs them. "We don't have uniforms yet, but when they are issued, you know I'll wear this one first."

"Open this one next," says one of the children, reading the label on the gift. "From Betty Gail and Buck."

"Another large gift." Legare shakes it a little and feels some slight movement. "It's heavy." He removes the outer wrapping and removes the top of the box, finding a new pair of boots, two pairs of wool socks and wool mittens. He lifts the boots and says, "Wow, Mr. and Mrs. Jernigan. These are great boots." He stands, walks over, shakes Buck's hand and hugs Betty Gail.

"Every soldier needs a good pair of boots, wool socks, and wool mittens," replies Betty Gail.

Buck continues, "We asked Mr. Maguire to make these boots for us to give you. He and his family send you their best wishes."

"Please let them know how much I really appreciate their work and wishes."

Polly hands Legare the last gift. "This is your last one."

Legare sits on the floor next to Polly and reads the attractive red and green label. "From Uncle Richard, Aunt Charlotte and the children."

He holds the package to his ear and shakes. No movement. Legare shakes again. Still, no movement. Everyone continues to watch as he begins removing the outer wrapping exposing a large white box. Legare lifts the top from the box and finds a new Confederate overcoat. Jumping up, he removes the coat from the box and holds it up for inspection.

Uncle Richard offers a proud broad smile. "Something to keep you warmer on Whitemarsh."

Legare shakes Uncle Richard's hand and gives Aunt Charlotte a hug and a thank you.

"Would you mind trying on your new uniforms, Legare?" Polly asks. "We want to see what a handsome soldier looks like."

Everyone else begins to encourage Legare to put on his uniform. He obliges and hurries to the bedroom to change into his new Confederate uniform, boots, overcoat, gloves and cap. Soon, the door opens and Legare enters the parlor.

"The Confederate Army has arrived!" announces Legare as he proudly enters the parlor. Everyone whistles and applauds.

"The troops have arrived, and we are all safe," shouts Alonzo. Legare opens his new overcoat and swirls around for everyone to see his new uniform. Polly, Betty Gail and Emily rush up to kiss him.

Polly reacts to her handsome Legare in uniform. "Can't lose the war with soldiers dressed in a new gray uniform with shining buttons."

"Thanks again Mama, Papa, Mr. and Mrs. Jernigan, Aunt Charlotte and Uncle Richard and thanks to all of my cousins."

Soon, everyone's attention turns to the delicious desserts that wait. Servers bring around the sundry collection while Marie and Claire begin leading the Christmas Carols. Marie has taken control over Rooster and Claire has John under her wing. Emily and Aunt Charlotte take over playing the piano while Betty Gail cares for little Joshua. Eventually, Emily changes the piano tune from carols to a waltz. Little Joshua curiously watches as the family sings and dances. Betty Gail stands, takes little Joshua in her arms and waltzes with Buck.

Buck, Congressman Hill and Uncle Richard are again speculating about the future of Georgia in this war. The festivities wear on and around 10:30 in the evening, the music, song and dance begin to fade. John, Alonzo and Rooster approach Uncle Richard and Aunt Charlotte. "We want to thank you for allowing us to spend this wonderful Christmas Day with your family," says Rooster.

"We also want to thank you for the wool socks. We will certainly use them on Whitemarsh," continues John.

Marie asks her father, "Would it be all right if Claire and I rode in the carriage to Thunderbolt?"

"That should be fine. But Ian needs to ride along and take a pistol. Leroy will be driving the carriage tonight."

The servants are waiting for John, Rooster, Alonzo, Ian, Marie and Claire at the door and assist them with putting on their coats. Once the young people are on board, Leroy heads the carriage toward Fort Thunderbolt.

Around eleven o'clock, the sound of music from the music box replaces the piano. Little Joshua is fast asleep on the sofa and Legare is still proudly dressed in his new uniform. Most of the wine glasses are empty and the pie plates contain more crumbs than pie. The servants offer eggnog or tea and cookies. A general discussion concerning the future of Savannah and the blockade ensues.

"Ian will be seventeen October 27 of '65. He'll have to muster in the military at that time. We all pray the war will end soon and that Legare will stay in Savannah until then," declares Uncle Richard sincerely.

Polly draws close to Legare and takes his hand and looks in his warm eyes. "He's a great father, a great man and a great soldier. Our love for each other is going to be with us forever," Then Polly leans forward and sets a kiss on Legare's cheek.

"Thank you Polly. We cannot ever thank our families enough for re-establishing our bonds." Legare picks up his wine glass and offers a toast, and the family members raise their glasses, "To our family bonds. They are our main world and have brought us happiness on top of happiness. God bless and protect us all this Christmas Day."

As Legare lowers his glass, the mantel clock strikes midnight. "It's midnight so soon! Polly and I must head home. We all know the story of Cinderella!" Everyone laughs.

Polly gathers their belongings, and begins to dress Joshua. Betty Gail says, "Leave little Joshua here for the night. He's sleeping sound. The train departs in the morning around ten o'clock. Just meet us at the train station and we just might give this little angel back to you. Right, Emily?"

"Just depends," replies Emily.

"What do you think, Legare?" asks Polly.

"They can certainly change his diapers in the morning!" Polly and Legare walk to the couch and gently pull the blanket from little Joshua's head. They quietly kiss the sweet baby goodnight.

Polly and Legare approach their house on the river and, from a distance, the soft flickering glow of the fireplace outlines the Christmas tree behind the parlor window. Jesse brings the horse and carriage to a halt in front of the house. The mare neighs a bit and whuffs steam from her nostrils. "I think she's ready for bed, too, Jesse," says Legare.

Jesse responds, "Yaas suh. Tink so! I tink yuh fuh Chrymus wid muh fam'ly at de plantation."

"You're welcome, Jesse. Merry Christmas again and I'll see you around 7:30 in the morning."

Jesse snaps the reins and directs the mare to the stalls. Inside the house, Polly removes her heavy fox fur coat, and Legare removes his new Confederate overcoat. They place the coats over the banister post and enter the parlor to look at the Christmas tree. The cedar fragrance still perfumes the air with the sweet scent of Christmas. Legare checks the water level as he slides from underneath the tree. "No need for water tonight. It's still high in the tub."

Polly takes Legare's hand and pulls him from the floor. "The embers are still bright in the fireplace. It's pleading for a fresh log. You stoke the fire and I'll get the blankets and pillows. I want to spend another night with you in front of the fire." Polly goes to the bedroom and dresses in a warm, pink, silk and wool bathrobe.

Legare enters the bedroom. Staring at Polly and smiling, he pulls her close, "You're the most beautiful and caring woman in the world. I love you."

Polly slides from his grasp teasingly and leaves the room. She peeks around the door frame and curling her finger to Legare, "Hurry up. There's a young maiden waiting for you in front of the hot fire and she has a glass of blackberry cordial for you."

Legare turns his head toward the door, "Tell the maiden that I'll arrive shortly and that I want more than blackberry cordial!" Legare enters the parlor clad in his blue wool robe.

Polly leans against the back of the couch, observing the mesmeric fire as the fresh wood steams and crackles. Her knees are against her chest and the quilt is pulled up to her neck. Polly's robe is slightly open and spread across the couch behind her. She smiles and looks up. "I see you found the maiden."

Legare begins to disrobe, "Sure did and she doesn't have to wait any longer." He finishes untying his robe and allows it to drop to the floor. She lifts the quilt and Legare accepts her invitation. They wrap their arms around each other and slide until their joined bodies are lying on the down comforter. She nibbles his ear. She holds him tight against her body as he traces his fingers across her silken back and kisses her. With a sigh punctuated by a shifting log, their bodies join in joyful abandon, followed closely by a few drowsy kisses and then sleep.

HOME TO RECOVER

Morning comes early. Polly is awakened by a knock on the back door. "Wake up, Legare. I think Tot needs to come in and prepare breakfast. Did you lock the door last night?"

"Yes, I wanted us to sleep as late as possible. I'll let Tot in." Legare and Polly quickly put on their robes. Polly gathers the quilts and pillows, taking them to the bedroom as Legare goes to the kitchen to open the door for Tot. "Good morning Tot!"

"Mornin' Mistuh LeGree. 'E time fuh yuh brekwas. You haffuh leed d'recly fuh de foht." ["It time for your breakfast. You must leave shortly for the Fort."]

"Polly and I'll have eggs and oatmeal this morning. So long as I leave here by 8:30, I'll be on time." Legare turns and goes to the bedroom. Polly has freshened up and is putting on her clothes. "Come over here Polly, I didn't give you a good morning kiss."

Polly rushes over. They hug and share a good morning kiss. Polly helps Legare locate his clothes to wear back to Fort Thunderbolt. While Legare is freshening, Polly lays out the new wool socks, wool gloves, and other clothing Legare is taking to Fort Thunderbolt. "Honey, do you want to take the new boots with you?"

"No thanks, my old ones are fine for now. Besides, someone would steal them if I did not have them on my feet! Just pack the new gloves and wool socks."

Tot knocks on the bedroom door. "De mush ready, tell me when you want me fuh pit on de egg." ["The oatmeal is ready; tell me when you want me to put on the eggs."]

"Thanks, Tot. I'll let you know in a few minutes," replies Polly.

When Polly and Legare come out for breakfast, Tot looks around and asks, "Weh de baby?"

"Little Joshua spent the night with his grandparents at Uncle Richard's and Aunt Charlotte's. I'm going to meet them at the train station in about an hour and bring him home." In no time, Polly and Legare have finished breakfast and Jesse has the carriage in front of the house.

Jesse asks Legare, "Weh yoh bag deh Massuh LeGree?"["Where are your bags Master Legare?"]

"In the bedroom. I think everything is packed. Go ahead and put it on the carriage." Polly and Legare slowly walk outside. The sky is blue and the morning sun's rays are beginning to take the frost from the ground.

Standing next to the carriage, Legare says sadly, "You know I can't get leave for New Year's because I had Christmas leave, but I'll see you a week or so after New Year's." Legare pulls her close and in a longing embrace. "I love you, Polly."

"I love you, Legare."

Legare climbs onto the carriage and Polly releases his hand. "Let's go, Jesse. Don't want to be late."

Jesse snaps the whip and the mare moves forward. Legare turns and blows Polly a kiss. She kisses her fingers and sails the kiss off to Legare. Soon the carriage turns, and Polly can no longer see his face.

JANUARY 1864

During study hall Paul asks, "What do you think General Sherman's going to do Norman?"

Norman lays down his pencil, closes his math book and leans back in his chair. "Well if he enters Georgia he has only one route to take. That's along the railroad line from Ringgold to Atlanta. Our state has been lucky so far. All we had to deal with is the blockade along the coast."

Paul goes over to his bed and adjusts his pillow. "GMI is a militia unit so I suppose if General Sherman enters Georgia, our battalion of cadets will turn to service as soldiers of the Confederate army."

"It's going to be hard to predict since Governor Brown's son, Julius is now enrolled as a cadet. The governor didn't enroll him just for an education."

Paul continues, "You read the same newspaper I did yesterday. The headlines label GMI as 'a haven for avoiding conscription.' Even this afternoon after the parade some of the locals uttered ugly remarks about us drilling instead of fighting."

"Maj. Capers is trying to procure several hundred Austrian rifles on his trip to Milledgeville."

"I sure hope he can get them for us. If we're going to fight, give us the weapons."

The next day Norman asks Paul, "Why are we getting out of class early to go to the quartermaster?"

"Something is up. It's got to do with the war if we are going to the quartermaster. I heard one of the cadets say the new weapons, accouterments, knapsacks, haversacks and canteens have arrived."

Norman and Paul take their place in the Company B formation. One of the first cadets to leave the quartermaster building is Thomas Alexander. Full of excitement and holding his haversack above his head he shouts,

"Look Norman, hardtack and bacon. You know what that means. We are going to war!"

"Right on," shouts Norman. The hardtack[167] and bacon discovery raises the morale of the cadets at the speculation of military action. "Surely Maj. Capers will announce that we will be moving to the front lines during the parade this afternoon."

Norman seriously replies, "Maybe that will shut up some of the locals who have been making those taunting remarks about the corps not fighting."

The cadet battalion form and march with extra pride and skill in the afternoon parade. Paul and Norman are anticipating the announcement from Maj. Capers that the corps will be heading to the front lines soon. However, to their disappointment, there is no announcement at the dress parade. Norman and Paul's company B march to supper attempting to figure out what the future holds.

Even though no announcements are made during the parade, Norman's and Paul's spirit and enthusiasm is now at its height. Norman speculates, "Paul, most all of the fighting is going on above Resaca. Turn us loose on those Yankees and this corps will show them what fighting is all about." Norman looks around the table. "One thing for sure. Show us the enemy and we'll do the rest."

"That's right," shouts Thomas Hamilton. "We'll cut them all down. Just give us the chance."

Norman continues, "Hopefully we'll go north, but there's that rumor floating around that the corps may be going to Milledgeville."

Leaning across the table, Hamilton responds, "Yeah and others say they may be going to the front. Personally I like the going to the front rumor the best." Norman looks directly at Thomas Hamilton, "I think we all prefer the front, Thomas."

FEBRUARY 22, 1864

In Savannah the weather is hazy with a light breeze. Polly and Tot are feeding Joshua when suddenly the house trembles and they hear the thunderous discharge of a cannon coming from the direction of Whitemarsh Island. Polly's eyes widen as she asks Tot, "Did that cannon fire sound like it was coming from Whitemarsh?"

"Yaas Ma'am hit do," replies Tot as they both look nervously toward the island.

Polly leaves the table and hurries to the cupola. As she climbs the stairs, she hears another report from the cannon confirming her suspicion. Standing against the railing, she looks toward Whitemarsh and Fort Thunderbolt. Again, she hears another angry outburst from a cannon.

Now on her tiptoes, she strains her eyes even more, but is still unable to penetrate the thick haze of the day to confirm the origin of the cannon fire. She shouts down to Tot, "Have Jesse bring the carriage around. I want to go to Thunderbolt right away!"

"Yaas, ma'am Polly!"

Polly rushes down the stairs and gets one of the pistols from the bedroom. She releases the cylinder and places one round in each of the chambers. Grabbing her wool throw, scarf, gloves and earmuffs, Polly tells Tot, "Look after Joshua. I'm going to Thunderbolt to find out what is going on." Polly kisses her son and meets Jesse just as the carriage arrives. "Head straight for Thunderbolt. I need to find out what's going on."

Jesse snaps the reins and sets the horse into a steady gallop. As they approach Fort Thunderbolt, she detects that the cannon fire is coming from the direction of Oatland Island. Polly taps Jesse on the shoulder. "Stop here for a minute." Jesse slows the horse and carriage as Polly stands, looking toward the island. The continuous resonance of the cannons is coming from the far side of Oatland Island. Pausing for a few minutes, Polly takes a deep breath and surveys the horizon. "Well, looks like Fort Thunderbolt is safe, and I assume Legare is safe as well. There's nothing we can do so head back to the house."

Around 11:00 the haze is lifting as Polly returns to the cupola. Whitemarsh Island is now visible in the distance. First, Polly can see the final cannon smoke and hear their final report. As the battle subsides, Polly descends from the cupola. "Looks like the battle is over, Tot. I see some steamers pulling away from Whitemarsh. Jesse, ride to Fort Thunderbolt and find out what has happened. I need to know that Legare is all right."

"Yaas' Ma'am." Jesse takes the buggy and departs for Fort Thunderbolt. Polly waits patiently. In about an hour Polly sees Jesse bring the horse and carriage to a stop in front of the house. She rushes out to the side of the carriage.

"What did you find out Jesse?"

"Mistuh Legare en de Fort iz safe, Ma'am Polly."

APRIL 23, 1864

Around 8:30 AM, there's a knock on Polly's door. Tot responds and opens the door. "Good morning, Mistuh Rooster."

"Good morning, Tot. Is Polly available?"

"Yaas' suh. Muhself git Ma'am Polly." Tot walks through the house and out the back door. Polly is in the backyard with Al starting the fires for preparing herbs for the hospital. "Mistuh Rooster iz har."

Polly gets a worried look on her face. "Tot, watch Joshua." Rooster is still standing on the landing with a serious expression on his face. Polly immediately asks, "Is Legare okay?"

"He's sick with some kind of stomach problem. Been that way for a couple of days. He asked me to get some of your blackberry cordial. He thinks that will clear him up."

"Come on in, Rooster. I've got several bottles ready for the hospital. Let me fetch two and I'll follow you back to Thunderbolt."

"Polly, Legare said for you not to come for two reasons: he's not that sick, and he does not want to give you or Joshua what he has. If he gets any worse, I'll come back. He just has a real bad case of dysentery right now."

"Sounds like something he'd say! I really prefer to see him, but I'll do as he wishes. I want to hear from you tomorrow by noon or I'll show up at Thunderbolt. While I have you here, I understand that there's a shortage of blankets for the soldiers and that people are donating carpets to use as replacements. We had these seven rugs washed and rolled up to send down with Legare the next time he comes home, but you can go ahead and take them with you. Several of the larger rugs can be cut up into pieces."

Rooster walks over and examines the rugs. "These are expensive oriental rugs, Polly."

"Legare and I know what they are and we discussed it when he was home in March for Easter. If the 63rd goes to North Georgia this time of year, you will need the blankets. We can buy new carpets after this war is over."

"Well, I know the guys in Company A will appreciate it. We still aren't certain if and when we are going to Dalton. Everything is up in the air with the army in North Georgia right now. The army is low on food and ammo. By the way, those winter greens you have been sending us are really great. Some of the guys tried to plant a small garden at Thunderbolt, but people keep taking the greens before they are ready."

Over the course of the week, Legare improves from Polly's blackberry Cordial wine and sends a note by Rooster:

April 28

My love,

I am much improved, but lost weight and am still weak from the dysentery. Maj. Allen tells us the 63rd will be going to Dalton around the 10th or 12th. Maj. Allen also said I can come home until our departure to get as much rest, strength, and nourishment as possible. Please send Al for me tomorrow around ten o'clock. I will improve greatly when I see your beautiful smile and our wonderful child.

Love, L.

Polly and Tot wake early the next morning to prepare a large pot of chicken soup. When the soup is ready, Polly has Tot fill a glass jar. Then Polly wraps the jar in several towels to keep it hot until she arrives at Fort Thunderbolt. "Tot, keep the house hot. Fill the tub with water and light the heater on it. A good hot bath will relax Legare when we get him home." At 9:30 AM, Polly has Al convey her to the fort's front gate. Upon arriving, Polly asks the duty officer, "Please notify my husband, Legare Hill, that I am waiting for him."

"I'll be glad to send for him, Mrs. Hill. He's really had a time with his stomach. Lost some weight from it all. Just wait in the carriage where you'll be comfortable."

In a few short minutes, Polly sees someone that resembles Legare leaving the barracks. Rooster and John are carrying a haversack, knapsack, weapon, and other personal items. Assuming it is Legare who Rooster and John are accompanying, Polly leaps from the carriage and rushes over to the group. As Polly approaches, she becomes distressed at Legare's appearance. He is bearded, almost skin and bones and looks weak. Polly and Legare have a short embrace.

"How is the love of my life?" asks Legare.

She holds back tears of worry. "The love of your life has some hot chicken soup for you in the carriage and some winter greens for your friends of Company A."

Placing her arm under his, she leans over and gives him a sweet kiss to the cheek. The group continues to walk to the carriage. John and Rooster assist Legare into the carriage.

She unrolls the towels from around the hot jar of chicken soup and takes the lid off. "Start eating and drinking. I need to fatten you up!"

Legare takes the hot bottle of chicken soup in both hands. Slowly, Polly helps him lift the jar to his lips so he can take a good mouth full. Polly turns to Rooster. "Take the greens out of the back of the carriage, Rooster, so we can be on our way." Rooster and John remove the several bundles of greens.

John walks around to the side of the carriage. "Thanks, Polly. You should get better real fast now, Legare. You have the best nurse anywhere looking after you."

"Thanks for helping bring my gear out to the carriage. Polly is going to stuff me full of food so I should have my strength back in a couple of days."

Al snaps the reins, the carriage jerks, and the couple are heading home. Polly pulls Legare's Christmas overcoat tightly around his chest as he takes another mouth full of the hot chicken soup. She removes the scarf from around her neck and places it over his head and around his chin. Sitting as close as possible to him, she assists him in eating and drinking as much as possible.

The day is clear and warmer than usual, yet the morning air is still damp. "This soup is warming my body pretty good."

Polly sits close to her love and places a blanket across his legs and feet to keep him as warm as possible. "Tot, should have the tub ready for you when we arrive home. Full of hot water. You can crawl in and relax. I think she might also have a surprise waiting for you when you finish your bath."

"What kind of surprise?" asks Legare.

"If I let on, it won't be a surprise, will it?"

"No, I guess not, but I'm sure what ever it is, I'll like it. Is it something to eat or is it made out of material?"

"I'm not giving out clues. You can guess all you want to, but I'll never give you a clue, even if you come close."

"How is our precious son?"

"Just like his pa. A perfect young man!"

Legare takes Polly hand. "I miss you and little Joshua every minute I am not with you. I wish we didn't have this war. Life would be perfect for us."

Al halts the horse and carriage in the circle drive in front of the house. Polly and Al assist Legare from the carriage. He stands for a moment, looking around the yard and at the house. "Your flowers are mighty beautiful, Polly. Looks as if they might be smiling the way the sun is hitting them."

Polly replies as she supports Legare, "Everything smiles when you're home. Let's get inside and put you in the hot tub." Al and Polly take Legare up the stairs and into the house. "Tot, we're home!" Tot comes from the kitchen and meets the group. "I told Legare you have a special surprise for him when he got home. He kept trying to get me to divulge what it is. Where's the baby?"

"Him sleab."

"Is the tub ready for Legare?"

"Yaas Ma'am."

"Al, get his belongings from the carriage. You and Tot check to see if they need washing while I get him in the tub." Polly strolls with Legare to the bedroom where Joshua is sound asleep in the cradle next to their bed.

Legare walks over and admires his son. "He just keeps growing and growing. Look at those rosy cheeks."

"Time for you to get in the tub and soak, Pvt. Hill!" The bathroom is warm from the tub heater. Polly tests the water with her hand. "Perfect."

"Hot and good. I feel better just looking at the tub."

Polly helps him take off his overcoat. Then he sits in a chair while Polly removes his shoes and socks.

"Stand up so I can take off your pants! This time, it's for medicinal purposes only!"

And she and Legare laugh and kiss. When he's standing naked in front of her, Polly sees how much weight he has really lost. She helps him into the tub. "I'll wage you've lost fifteen pounds."

Legare eases down into the water and closes his eyes. "I really need this!"

"Soak for a while. When I come back, I'll shave you and trim your hair if you feel like it."

Legare blinks, yawns and closes his eyes. In an instant, he is sound asleep. Polly goes to the kitchen and finds the shoofly pie Tot has prepared. She removes a piece and samples it with her finger. "Mighty good, Tot. This will make Legare feel lots better I'm sure. Get Jesse to kill another chicken tonight. Legare will probably eat one whole chicken himself. He looks half-starved."

Polly goes back in the bathtub room to check on the water temperature and tub furnace. After about an hour of rest, little Joshua's movements in his cradle awaken Legare. Polly comes in to check on Legare and finds both he and their son are awake. She picks up Joshua and whispers, "Your pa is home. Let's go see him. He's taking a bath and has a beard." Polly brings little Joshua in the bathtub room.

Holding out his arms, Legare says, "There's my little man. Come see?" Polly brings Joshua to the tub. Not recognizing his father with a beard, the baby is a little shy at first. Legare reassures him. "It's Papa. Come see Papa."

Joshua recognizes his father's voice. Joshua slurs together "Pa-pa" as he leans over to hug and kiss his father.

"Good medicine," says Legare.

"Do you feel like being shaved, honey?"

"I do now, but I'm glad you didn't ask that an hour ago."

"Let me fetch Tot to take care of Joshua while I get you shaved. Kiss Papa bye." Polly summons Tot with the servant bell and she comes to the bedroom door.

"Yaas' ma'am, Miss Polly."

Polly hands Joshua to Tot. "Take care of Joshua while I shave Legare. You'll see your Papa after he gets out of the tub."

Joshua tugs his father's beard before kissing and hugging him bye. Polly hands Joshua to Tot and then gathers up the razor, shaving brush and soap. Legare has washed his face and hair and looks more refreshed and rested than when he arrived. Polly places a stool next to the tub. She caresses his beard. "Let's see how long it's going to take me to find that good looking face underneath this hair."

"Now don't be in any rush with that razor. I probably can shave myself."

"I know you can, but I want to shave you. Just sit back and don't jump. I don't want to stain the water red!"

"Real funny, honey!" replies Legare, as they pass a kiss.

Polly lathers his beard with the shaving brush. She tilts his head back and begins shaving underneath his chin. Once she has finished shaving and trimming Legare's hair, Polly asks, "Now, how does that feel, honey?" No answer. He has fallen asleep again. Polly leans over and places one hand on each clean-shaven cheek. She gently kisses him on the lips.

Without opening his eyes, Legare gently says, "I know your kiss in my dreams, Polly."

"How do you feel now that you're shaven and your hair is trimmed?"

Legare rubs his face and runs his hands through his shortened hair. "Perfectly wonderful."

Polly reaches to assist him as he stands up in the tub. Using her free hand, she takes a towel and begins drying his lean body. "Tot has your surprise waiting for you. Get your robe on and come to the dining room."

In a weak and low breath, Legare speaks softly, "Polly I'm still weak, but not nearly as dizzy. The chicken soup must be working already."

"That's good news." Polly takes Legare's robe and holds it open so he can place each arm in the sleeve. She ties the belt around his waist and they walk to the dining room. "I think Joshua is waiting for you at the table."

They take a seat on each side of Joshua. "How is my pal? Do you recognize me now?" Legare asks his boy. Joshua looks at his father and feels his face. He smiles and bounces at his father in affirmation. Legare gives little Joshua a kiss on the top of his head.

"Close your eyes, Legare, and get ready for your surprise." Legare closes his eyes and Polly calls out, "All right Tot, bring in the surprise." Tot walks in with the large shoo-fly pie and places the sweet and tasty delight in front of Legare. "Now open your eyes."

Legare opens his weary eyes slowly and upon seeing the shoo-fly pie, opens them more widely. "Shoo-fly pie! Just what my doctor Polly ordered." Taking the knife and fork by his plate, Legare cuts himself a large slice and plunks it on his dish. He grabs his fork and begins stuffing himself. Polly and Tot watch happily yet silently as he takes a drink of black tea to wash down the pie and continues the routine of eating and drinking until practically the entire pie is devoured.

"I'm glad you like that pie, honey. Tonight we'll have baked chicken with beets, greens, rice and plenty of parsley. And for tomorrow, we'll have fresh baked fish. "

"Tot, that pie was the best. Thank you so much! Keep feeding me like this and I'll be back to my normal weight in no time at all."

Polly suggests to Legare, "How about we go in the parlor? You and little Joshua can play by the fire. I need to check with Jesse and Al on the herbs. The pot's boiling with fresh barks and the water's probably ready to be filtered."

Legare goes to the parlor, and Polly brings Joshua. "Tot will stay with you two while I go out back."

Over the course of the next week, Polly slowly nourishes Legare back to strength. Tot is cooking constantly, Polly is feeding constantly and Legare is eating constantly, helping him gain about a half- pound per day. Polly directs Al and Jesse to place a table on the dock so she and Legare can enjoy the warm, spring sun while they dine. She even puts a cot on the deck so Legare can nap outside during warm and sunny days. In the evenings, before supper, they climb up to the cupola to watch the setting sun. The trees and flowers bursting forth with new growth, and the honeysuckles smell sweet once again. Birds are building their nests energetically while whistling their songs.

"Look there, Polly! I think that's the owl that was hooting the night little Joshua was born. He's roosting in the same tree!"

"I think you're right. Papa told me that owls stay in the same area forever ... however long that is!"

THE NOBLE AND THE VALIANT

Early Friday morning on May 6, there's a knock on the front door. Legare opens the door to find his friend. "Good morning, Rooster. Come on in." The two shake hands and Rooster enters. Legare calls out, "Polly! Rooster is here! What brings you out so early?"

"I've come to advise you about our new orders." Rooster places his hand on Legare's shoulder. "You sure are looking better. Still a little under weight, but looking good."

"Thanks, Rooster. Feeling better, too."

Polly and Joshua enter the foyer. She smiles. "Good morning, Rooster. It's good to see you. I just about have Legare back to full weight and strength."

"You have done a great job."

"What's the news from the Fort?"

"Well I came by to let Legare know that our unit is leaving for Dalton on the morning of the ninth. Maj. Allen said he could just meet us at the depot around 9:30."

Looking dismayed Polly responds, "Well, I'm not exactly happy about that news. Come on in and have breakfast with us. I want to give you a couple of smoked hams to divide up among the company."

The two men watch Polly head toward the back of the house and then go to the parlor. Rooster relates the latest news. "Looks like General Sherman is coming on into Georgia. He needs to be stopped."

"If any General can stop Sherman, it's gotta be Gen. Joseph Johnston. From what I have heard and read, the troops admire him and are glad he replaced Gen. Bragg. He does not take risk with their lives like so many of the general's do. But none-the-less I feel that our 63rd is going to North Georgia sooner or later. The Confederate army is not as large as the Union army," responds Legare. He takes a breath and looking Rooster in the eye.

"Personally, I don't think the South has any more of a chance to win this war now than we did when it started."

Polly goes to the kitchen. "Tot, Rooster is going to join us for breakfast. Make him a good one. The 63rd is going to Dalton in a couple of days. Also, have Jesse bring in two of the largest smoked hams we have in the smoke house. I think there are four left."

Polly joins Rooster and Legare in the parlor and listens to the latest update on the war and Thunderbolt. "Legare told me what went on February 22nd when I heard all that cannon fire around Whitemarsh and Oatland, but he never finished telling me about the problem Capt. Tucker had when some of his men cut and ran under enemy fire."

Rooster begins the story. "Well Polly, let me start from the beginning. It was about 8:00 that morning with the high tide, eleven Yankee surfboats transporting about twenty Yankees each made a surprise landing on Whitemarsh."

"Yes, that's about the time I heard some of the cannon fire."

"We later found out they were from the Yankee 85th Pennsylvania Volunteers and two Negroes who knew every creek, hide-a-way and marsh on the Islands were their pilots."

"Did you ever find out who the Negroes belonged to?"

"Never did. The other force of Yankees was from the 67th Ohio Volunteers and some from the 85th Pennsylvania were landing near the Fleetwood outpost on Wilmington Island. Their objective was to capture the Oatland Bridge.[168] Our pickets only saw the Yankees when they were about one hundred yards away."

"The cannon fire you probably heard was from Lt. Richardson's artillery section at the Oatland Bridge and cannon fire from the Union Steamers."

"Could very well have been."

"Lt. Richardson was alerted by our retreating pickets and it was his artillery which stopped the Yankees from taking the bridge. The artillery fire was so heavy the Yankees had to retreat. Word came to Fort Thunderbolt, and all five companies of the 63rd were called out. We formed up and took wagons to Fort Bartow to get further orders. All total we had only about 175 men in all five companies."

"What happened when you got to Fort Bartow?"

"We were ordered to form a skirmish line and proceed to the Gibson house as re-enforcements for Capt. Tucker's weak force who were defending that position. This is where the confusion comes in and his men scattered. You see, Capt. Tucker's unit thought the retreating Yankees were the 63rd and his unit ended up in a cross fire."

"My gosh. That's awful."

"Many of his soldiers stood and fought while a number of them threw down their weapons and ran into the marsh. Before we arrived the Yankees got word of our unit coming as re-enforcements and retreated to their off shore Steamers."

Legare stands and leans on the chair back and takes over the story. "The best part is in their hasty retreat the Yankees left three excellent surf boats, numerous haversacks, canteens, blankets, Springfield muskets and clothing. Some of the equipment was saturated with blood from their wounded. I found some butter-crackers and meat in one of the haversacks."

"And I found ground coffee in another, and that's about all there was to the skirmish,"[169] says Rooster.

"I'm just thankful all of you are safe."

Shortly, the smell of fresh bacon alerts Polly that something good awaits them in the dinning room. "I see Tot has breakfast ready so let's head to the table."

"This looks and smells wonderful, Polly. John and the McCurdy boy will be jealous. But they'll get over it when I show them the hams." After finishing breakfast Rooster shakes Legare's hand and bids Polly good-bye. "I'll see you on the ninth at the depot."

On May 8th, Legare begins packing his knapsack and haversack. Polly hands him a blanket for his bedroll and another eight pair of wool socks. She puts several bars of soap and a couple of washcloths and towels in his knapsack. Last she places paper and pencil so he can write home. "Here's a new toothbrush for you." She picks up the Savannah Republic newspaper. "Come sit next to me on the bed. I want to read this funny article to you about toothbrushes in Charleston."

Legare comes over and sits next to Polly. He looks at the newspaper as she reads,

"A Chance to Get Tooth Brushes

Everybody knows how impossible it has become, now-a-days, to get a good English tooth brush. At the recent sale of imported European goods, the lot of toothbrushes, in consequence of their very great scarcity, excited much competition. There were many eager bidders from several

*States of the Confederacy; but as the people of Charleston and its neigh-
borhood needed the article as much as our more distant friends, Messrs.
Stevenson & Co., were determined that the brushes should remain here,
and purchased the lot at the very extravagant price of $18.50 per dozen.
The purchase was made with a view to accommodate our people and
to supply a universal want. The brushes will be sold at retail by Messrs.
Kenifick & Skrine at a slight advance on the above cost price."*[170]

"I'm putting you some primitive black gum in your haversack to use
with hickory bark in case you loose your toothbrush . . . or sell it!"

"So my choice is pearly white teeth or gold in my pocket. I'll figure
away to have both. How 'bout that?" They laugh and Legare continues,
"Pretty interesting article though. Wonder what a good toothbrush brings
on the front lines?"

Though Polly knows Legare's heart is as heavy as hers, she puts on
a strong and happy face for both of them. "Whatever the market will
bear, honey."

After supper, Tot finishes cleaning the kitchen, and Polly pokes her
head in the door. "Be sure we are up at sunrise, Tot. We need to have a
good breakfast for Legare, before he goes to the depot." She and Legare
take turns playing with little Joshua while he bathes. They lie down together with him on their bed. Polly fabricates a bedtime story about a
happy soldier going to war for little Joshua. "The soldier has a little boy
and the little boy's Mama at home, whom he is going miss dearly. The
little boy and the little boy's Mama are going to miss Papa as much as Papa
is going to miss them. But everybody knows one day the happy soldier
will return home. When the happy soldier returns home, he and the little
boy can fish and hunt together. Mama will be happy also. She and the
little boy's pa can help the little boy grow up to be a strong and good man.
The little boy's mama wants the little boy to grow up to be just like his father, a strong and very loving person who will always look after his family."

Little Joshua falls asleep lying between his mother and father. Legare
picks him up gently and places him in his cradle. Legare takes Polly's
hand and they go to the parlor and sit close together on the sofa in front
of the warm and fragrant fire. Holding hands and looking at each other,
Legare pulls Polly closer, "This is our last night together for a while, Polly.
I hope only for a short while. There are a few items we need to talk about
before I leave."

"Yes I know," she says as a huge lump develops in her throat. "We must talk about the most dreaded scenario of this war, the dreadful possibilities." Holding his hand, she listens and he emotionally proceeds.

"Father went ahead and gave us my share of the stock and bonds in the Georgia Railroad which I would eventually inherit. You know we are getting a good return on that stock and those bonds right now. All of the money goes into our account with Mr. Lilly's bank. I suggest you take some of the money out in gold and hide it here somewhere."

"I know we must discuss these matters, yet no matter how hard I try to understand, this whole thing is like a dream to me ... your leaving, this war, our child, our home. It can never be the same without you here."

The thoughts are too hard to consider, but he knows the rising sun will change everything. "I'll write you every day that I can, however you may not get any letters for a while. People say the mail is extremely unreliable. If you don't hear from me, please know that I have written. If something awful should happen to me, my father and mother have told me and you that you're a daughter to them. They will endeavor to always fill your every need. I know them well."

Tears stream down Polly's soft cheeks. She inhales deeply, trying vainly to stop her tears. She doesn't want Legare to remember her this way. She offers a warm smile and grasps Legare's hands tightly.

Legare smiles back at her, realizing she's not far from completely breaking down. "In the morning, when I depart for the depot, I want you and little Joshua to follow my carriage to the road and stay there until I am out of sight. This is the image I want to remember, knowing that when I return home, you and our child will be standing there waiting for me. It's going to be hard. I know you want to come to the depot, but I only want this for my selfishness."

In a trembling voice, she whispers, "You will return home to me and our child. I'll go outside everyday and stand by the carriage hitch and wait for you to appear in the distance. Then little Joshua and I'll run to meet you before you can reach the house!"

Polly and Legare cry and their tears mix as they embrace. Polly wipes her tears away with her hand. "My love, let's not talk of sad things anymore. We know what we both must do. God has taught us how to perform our duty." She thinks frantically for a moment, trying to find a normal activity to relieve the sadness of this night. "Let's walk out on the dock and look at the stars for a while. Maybe they can disclose something about the future for us."

Legare, still unable to speak clearly, nods his head. They go outside and walk to the end of the pier. Upon reaching the end of the dock, they sit down and hang their feet over the edge. Sitting quietly for a while, they listen to the mullet jumping nearby. Then they hear the friendly owl hooting to claim his territory.

"Yep, that's the same owl all right. I would know his voice anywhere!"

Polly looks up into the clear night sky. "What are all of those lights in the heavens? There's the big dipper and the little dipper you showed me. That one next to the new quarter moon is the morning and evening star, right?"

"You never forget, do you? I can tell you something, and you always remember."

Polly turns to Legare and holding his dear face between her two hands. "I love you, Legare Hill, and don't you ever forget that." She kisses him deeply, and he almost crushes her in his embrace.

"If only words could describe my love for you. Such a word would cover the entire universe." Legare helps Polly to lie back on the dock. He begins to laugh as they talk about how he felt about her before they ran away together in the dark of the night. Legare and Polly talk about how happy they are about their families finally accepting and realizing their love and devotion for one another.

"My mere existence here with you and our child is a constant joy. Today the sunshine was brighter, and tonight the moonlight is softer. The sky is fairer and the earth more seductive. I notice some of the flowers and trees are blooming and budding at odd times with unwonted richness and profusion. Maybe this is a sign to re-enforce our feeling about the strong common bonds that now unite our families."

Polly becomes quieter as her thoughts turn to the war and how Governor Brown could end this struggle with the stroke of a pen. Feeling a chilling breeze, Polly shivers. "Legare, do you want to go inside? It's getting a little cool out here."

"Yes, and let's sleep in our favorite spot in front of the fireplace tonight." Legare gives Polly his hand and assists her up from the dock. Together, they walk with their arms around each other to the house. Inside, Legare locks the back door. Polly kisses her husband and begins undressing him. Legare reciprocates. The fever of their passion for each other begins to rise as the two lovers gather the pillows and blankets and carry them to the parlor. Polly goes to the kitchen and takes a bottle of blackberry cordial and two glasses from the shelf. She brings the glasses and the cordial to the parlor where Legare is lying on the blankets and pillows.

Pouring two large glasses of the cordial, Polly toasts, "This is what got you well, and this is what is going to keep you well. To my dear husband, my lover, and the father of our child. The best there is and ever will be."

They raise their drinks and take a large sip from each other's glass. They sink to the blankets. Sitting adjacent to each other, they watch the fire and slowly finish the cordial. Legare turns and draws Polly nearer. They shut their eyes and enjoy the luxury of lying in each other's arms. At long last they fall asleep.

At sunrise, there's a subtle knock on the door. Polly disentangles herself from Legare's arms and slips from the room to unlock the back door for Tot. "Good morning, Tot."

She and Tot prepare a feast for Legare's breakfast: ho'cakes, eggs, country ham, fresh biscuits, grits and muscadine jelly. By the time they put the food on the table Legare is in uniform and marches into the dining room with Joshua on his hip. Polly smiles and kisses her two favorite people as they prepare to sit at the table. Polly seats herself, and Tot begins to serve. Polly had Tot to prepare places at the table for Al, Jesse and herself. She wants everyone to have this special breakfast together.

The cheerful mood seems forced as Legare says the blessing. "Bless this family and protect them in thy name." Legare can say no more as tears flow from his eyes.

Polly continues, "Protect and guard over this father and husband. Let him return to us as he leaves us. Amen."

After breakfast, everyone gathers outside next to the carriage. Jesse is driving Legare to the depot. Legare and Polly's expressions speak volumes of love. He hugs Tot, shakes and squeezes Al's hands before turning to Polly and little Joshua. Almost in tears, Legare and Polly press heart to heart and share a loving kiss. Polly clings to him, almost unwilling to relinquish him to the war effort.

"I love you, Polly. I love you little, man."

"We love you, Legare."

Legare turns and boards the carriage. His uniform buttons suddenly glisten brightly in the morning sun. He is wearing one the new shirts that has his initials and name "H. L. Hill" embroidered on the sleeve. Tot and

Al are now crying along with Polly. Jesse snaps the reins as he has for many years, and with the usual jerk, the carriage moves from the circle onto the dirt road that leads to the depot. Legare turns and looks at Polly. Crying, Polly and little Joshua follow the carriage to the road never taking their eyes off of Legare. Slowly the image of the carriage becomes smaller and smaller.

The carriage turns and disappears. Polly stands there praying, "Through some miracle, let me wake from this nightmare and find Legare and Joshua sleeping next to me."

DALTON TO RESACA AND A CHANCE MEETING

HEADQUARTERS MILITARY DIVISION OF THE MISSISSIPPI IN THE FIELD, TUNNEL HILL, GEORGIA
May 11, 1864-Evening
Major-General McPHERSON, Commanding Army of the Tennessee, Sugar Valley, Georgia

GENERAL:

The indications are that Johnston is evacuating Dalton. In that event, Howard's corps and the cavalry will pursue; all the rest will follow your route. I will be down early in the morning.[171] Try to strike him if possible about the forks of the road. Hooker must be with you now, and you may send General Garrard by Summerville to threaten Rome and that flank. It will cause all the lines to be felt at once.

W. T. SHERMAN,

Major general, Commanding

❧

Around noon, May 12, the Georgia 63rd arrives at the Dalton depot. Legare peers out the window. "Well, Rooster, here we are. Ready to defend Dalton."

Rooster nods. "It's too late in the day to start shooting Yankees!"

Legare stares at the flurry of activity surrounding the station. "Let's hope tomorrow is lucky for us and unlucky for them."

Col. George Gordon, the 63rd commanding officer, disembarks and orders the troops to formation. He addresses the regiment, "Men of the 63rd, we are here for only a short break. Gather your equipment and chow down on your rations while I get our orders. Your company commander, Maj. Allen, will direct you in unloading the supplies from the Augusta arsenal."

Maj. Allen continues with the instructions, "Maurice Thompson, report to me upon dismissal. Company A, stack your equipment and reassemble at the boxcars in fifteen minutes. Dismissed!"

In the beautiful spring afternoon Legare, John, Alonzo and Rooster gather their belongings. The trees are just about in full leaf and the aroma of budding flowers fills the cool spring air with a feeling of calm. Finding a nice tree, Legare and Rooster take comfort in its shade. Soon, Maurice Thompson, another member of the 63rd joins them. "Well Legare and Rooster, looks like I'm going to be a scout since I know these mountains from one end to the other.[172] They are assigning me to Gen. Wheeler. I'm sure we will see one-another again."

The three exchange hand shakes and Legare says, "Good luck, Maurice, and stay clear of the Yankees!"

Maurice turns away with a wave of his hand is shortly out of sight. Legare and Rooster lay their belongings by the trunk of the large oak tree and stretch out. John Dent and Alonzo McCurdy find a comfortable spot nearby. All four men know they are soon going to have to march somewhere. The bugle sounds assembly for chow. Beef, early greens and bread are supper for the men.

After supper Company A assembles, and Maj. Allen updates the men on the war effort. "Last month on April 24th,[173] Union scouts made attempts to determine our strength South of Ringgold to LaFayette. On Wednesday the 27th,[174] General John McPherson sent reconnaissance forces to determine our strength at Tunnel Hill which resulted in a skirmish with our troops.

"About a week later on May 1st, there was a skirmish at the old Stone Church East of Ringgold, and the next day there were skirmishers at Lee's Crossroads near Tunnel Hill as well as near Ringgold Gap. Last week on Wednesday the 4th, General George Thomas moved East along the Western and Atlantic Railroad from Ringgold. This movement was to secure the Union supply lines from the North. We also had a skirmish at Varnell where Prather's Mill is located.

"This past Friday the 6th Union Generals Schofield and McPherson maneuvered into position for an attack on Tunnel Hill. General Sherman had General McPherson to use Taylor Ridge South of Lee and Gordon's Mill as cover to successfully move south. On the 7th[175] General Thomas attacked in force against Tunnel Hill and was successful in driving off a small picket-guard of our army. There was no damage done to the tunnel or the Railroad.

"At Dalton, General Sherman found Gen. Johnston was entrenched along a high ridge well fortified to attack. He decided to assault and turn our left flank. He sent General McPherson's cavalry in front and toward Snake Creek Gap. Then General Sherman deployed General Thomas against Gen. Johnston's main position, Rocky Face Ridge and also Tunnel Hill.

"This past Sunday the 8th, there was still fighting at Mill Creek and Dug Gap, which is along Rocky Face Ridge, west of Dalton. On Monday the 9th, the war was getting serious. General McPherson encountered strong resistance from our forces as he moved towards the Western and Atlantic Railroad Bridge near Resaca, forcing his army to dig in. Tuesday Gen. Johnston received information concerning General McPherson's maneuver to turn our left flank, he withdrew. It appears that General Sherman ordered General McPherson to swing his entire army of The Tennessee by the right flank through Snake Creek Gap. The head column entered and passed through an undefended Snake Creek Gap,[176] completely surprised a weak cavalry force of Gen. Wheeler[177] and flanked our army. Not knowing the full strength of Gen. Wheeler's force, General McPherson[178] withdrew three miles and set up a defense at the mouth of Snake Creek Gap.

"Now we are here, and expect Gen. Polk's corps from Mississippi to give us reinforcements, enabling us to turn the war north. Any questions? If not, take a short break before distributing the ammunition from the train. DISMISSED!"

Maj. Allen continues to walk and talk with the men, giving more details of recent events. Somewhat bewildered, Legare asks, "Rooster, do you sense panic in the air?"

Rooster looks around at the other men. "When you're out numbered three to one, you have two options: first option is to be smarter than the other guy. If that doesn't work, you better run like hell! I'm betting that Gen. Johnston is smarter than General Sherman."

Legare says quietly," Well, it doesn't look like anybody is running!"

The supply wagons from the various Confederate units are waiting in line for their share of the ammunition. The soldiers form an assembly line and begin sorting and loading each wagon as it draws near. Legare and Alonzo are assigned to a separate wagon from Rooster and John. One officer checks the loading manifests to ascertain that the correct type of cartridge is issued for that specific unit. As the wagons are being loaded, one of the soldiers taps Rooster on his shoulder. "We're really glad to see this ammunition. This load may keep us going for a few more days. Our artillery batteries are so low on shot and shell that some of the batteries only fire in self defense."[179]

Around nightfall, all of the freight rail cars are unloaded and the train begins its journey south. Watching the departure, Legare ponders the sound and sight of the train slowly disappearing into the fading light. It escapes into the forest and around a bend in the track until not even a puff of smoke can be seen. Legare silently thinks, "That train is what brought me here and someday, it will take me back home, back to Polly and Joshua."

Soon, darkness surrounds the camp. Legare, John, Alonzo, and Rooster sit around a small campfire with some of their buddies and begin a game of cards. As the game progresses, the clamor of troops, wagons, horses and artillery become more apparent.

"It's our Gen. Cleburne's troops!" shouts one of the nearby soldiers as Gen. Cleburne's troops continue to pass by Company A and set their camp to the south of the 63rd near another unit of the 63rd, Col. Charles Olmstead's former 1st Georgia.[180] A short while later, the men begin to tire from the day's events. Each soldier takes his shelter half from his bed roll. Legare buttons his half to Rooster's, forming a complete tent. Retiring to their modest accommodations in the cool mountain air, Legare and Rooster drift to sleep as if in unison with the fading light of their campfire.

⚬

May 12, 1864
To Gen. Joseph Johnston
Commander of the Army of Tennessee

The Governor desires me to say that if the Corps of Cadets of the Georgia Military Institute at Marietta can be of any use in resisting raids or in other light duty on temporary service during the present emergency that they are at your orders. Maj. Frances W. Capers, Chief Engineer of the State is the Superintendent and commander of the Corps, and should you deem the services of these young men at any time, necessary, address your instructions to Maj. Capers at Marietta. The Corps numbers 185, of which perhaps 150 could be counted on for active service. By the law of the State Constituting the Engineer Corps. Maj. Capers will be directed to report to you in entering aid to give details as to the capabilities of his command.

Very Respectfully,

Your Obedient Servant,
Henry C. Wayne
Adjutant and Inspector Gen.[181]

Paul, Norman and the rest of the Cadet Corps can smell fighting in the air. They are ready to go to the battle front.

Around 3:00 AM on the 13th, Legare is startled by someone gently nudging him with their foot. Legare sits up, almost blinded by a bright lantern shining in his face. "Time to get up soldier. Just got orders. We are moving out to Resaca in ten minutes. No fires. Eat your ration on the trail or when you arrive at Resaca."

Legare eases from his covers but keeps his blanket around him. The mountain air is chilly and cold dew covers the ground. He pulls his boots from under his blanket, and slips his warm, wool sock, covered feet into the boots.

Rooster rises as well. Soon the entire camp is in motion and their sergeant shouts, "Company A, fall in!"

The men form in line and take their muskets from the stack. They gather their bedrolls, cartridge cases and canteens, before assuming their positions in the ranks. Against the background of distant cannon fire, Company A and the rest of the 63rd begin the march to Resaca.

Legare taps Rooster on the shoulder. "Look! There's Gen. Johnston on his Bay horse. He's wearing the hat with the feather we hear talk about."

"What a way to start out Friday the 13th, passing by Gen. Johnston as if in a review. It's good for our morale to see our commander."

"The rest of the men probably feel the same way."

The troops join in on a "Huzzah! Huzzah!" to show their spirits are high as they pass their beloved commander. Gen. Johnston acknowledges their kindness and respect with a modest smile and a tip of his hat.

Later that day, Gen. Johnston positions his forces along a ridge that lies between the Oostanaula and Connasauga Rivers, just north of Resaca.

This defensive line is meant to protect his supply line to Atlanta, the Western & Atlantic Railroad. Gen. Polk's two cavalry divisions will defend the extreme left flank, paralleling the railroad behind Camp Creek to where it flows into the Oostanaula. Gen. Hood's corps will defend the right side westward and across the railroad extending to the right of the Connasauga River. Gen. William Hardee's corps which Company A of the 63rd is an attachment and will defend the center between Gen. Polk and Gen. Hood.[182]

Gen. Wheeler returns from a scouting mission and reports to Gen. Johnston. "General Sherman's entire army is heading out of Snake Creek Gap. They should be through the Gap by tomorrow. We do not have any time to waste in preparing defenses."

Legare, Rooster and the other members of Gen. Hardee's corps are rapidly cutting trees, digging trenches, preparing breastworks and parapets. Maj. Allen orders out a squad with Pvt. David C. Blount to reconnoiter the terrain for advancing Yankee patrols.

On the afternoon of the 13th, Major General John Logan's XV Corps arrives west of Resaca to discover that Gen. Johnston has reinforced his army with Gen. Leonidas Polk's Army of Mississippi, known as the third Corps of the Army of Tennessee. Gen. Hardee's corps, consisting of four divisions, holds the center line in front of Resaca.

Just before dawn on Saturday, May 14th, a lone rider on horseback approaches the Georgia Military Institute campus. The cadet sentinel, orders him to stop and identify himself. The rider explains that "he has a message from Gen. Henry Wayne for Maj. Capers." The guards remove the weapons from the rider and escort him to Maj. Caper's quarters. Upon entering the house, Maj. Capers recognizes the messenger and has the guards return his weapons before returning to their post.

Opening the orders close to the lantern, he reads, "The Cadets Corps is to report to Gen. Johnston at Resaca and to hold the corps of Cadets in readiness, to obey his orders during the present emergency, whereupon you will receive further orders. The cadets who are of age are to board the first available train to the front. Dated May 12th."[183]

Maj. Capers orders Cornelius to play the "long roll" of the drums. Slowly, the cadets awake by the continuous roll of the drum.[184]

Norman and Paul, along with the rest of the cadet corps, spring from their beds. "It's still dark outside. Something important must be happening with the war," Paul says as he peers out the window

Norman lights the candles. In full dress with their weapons and gear, the cadets seem to assemble quicker than on most other cool spring mornings. Roll call and the familiar "here and present for duty" response is continuous. Finally "in place rest" the cadets are given five rounds of ammunition each.

Following the issue of the ammunition, the cadet commander shouts, "Attention!" Maj. Capers steps forward and reads the order. "The cadets of the Georgia Military Institute who are of proper age are to march to the depot in Marietta and proceed to the front in and around Resaca. The Corps is to report to Gen. Joseph Johnston's headquarters for further orders."[185]

"Hooray! Hooray!" shout the cadets.

"We'll show those Yankees a real fight!" yell other cadets. The feeling of invincibility is strong with the cadets at this moment as they swell with pride and readiness.

The 150 or so cadets march down Powder Springs Road and pass the cemetery on their way to the depot. The sick and underage cadets are given orders to stay on campus.[186] Upon arriving at the depot, the cadets relax and eat some of their rations of bacon and hardtack. Some of the soldiers from Camp McDonald are also at the depot and hear the news that the corps is moving to the front. They mingle with the cadets. "Give 'em hell boys," shouts a departing recruit. "You've been training us so we know you can teach those Yankees a lesson or two!"

Norman is awake early. He is sitting outside his tent as the sun begins to rise and the morning dew reflects the rays. A whistle is heard. He turns his attention toward the depot as the train approaches and comes to a stop. Suddenly Norman sees the camp come to life as the cadet corps rises apparently full of excitement.

Paul comes out of the tent and sees the steam coming from the engine boiler. "Norman look at that engine. For some reason that engine reminds me of a tied up hound knowing he is about to be released for a big hunt."

Norman laughs and replies, "It does look fired up all right."

Norman and Paul are among the first cadets to board the train. Cadet Marsh and Hazelhurst seek and receive permission to ride on top of the coaches with several of their fellow cadets. The train pulls away from the depot.

Norman confides in Paul, "Looks like we finally have a chance to fight for Georgia and the Confederacy."

"Yep. Let's hope we all make it back."

Later on, the train stops at Big Shanty and the soldiers in the camp see the cadets on top of the coaches. A civilian shouts, "Where are y'all going?"

Marsh shouts back, "Heading to Resaca. We're going to beat you there!"

As the train pulls away from the station, the soldiers at Camp McDonald fire their weapons in the air as a salute to the parting cadet corps. Enthusiastically, Marsh, Hazelhurst and the other cadets on the top of the coaches stand and raise their weapons, showing their determination. Norman and the cadets inside the coaches wave their hats out of the windows with vigor and excitement, as if they have already conquered the Yankees.

Around noon, the cadets arrive at Resaca. There's a fury of activity around the depot. Resaca serves as a staging area for troops which are heading north along the railroad to the battlefields in Tennessee and Virginia. After assembly Norman asks Marsh, "How did the country side look from the top of the coach?"

"This whole area is rough and hilly, Norman. All I could see from the top of the train was thick woods and thick underbrush."

Their conversation ends quickly as they hear the thunder of cannon fire in the near distance. Norman feels a chill over his entire body and becomes more conscious that this is not a game. Norman solemnly turns to his friends, "This is the real thing." The bugle sounds assembly and the cadet corps takes formation.

The two companies march to the headquarters of Gen. Johnston. Maj. Capers enters Gen. Johnston's headquarters where he meets BG. William Mackall (sic), the Chief of Staff for Gen. Johnston. Maj. Capers reports to him, "Sir the cadet corps has arrived and is awaiting your orders."

Gen. Mackall speedily briefs Maj. Capers, "Gen. Johnston is in conference and disturbing him at this time is not in order.[187] Gen. Johnston has an order for the cadet battalion to be placed under MG. William Walker's division.[188] Gen. Walker's division has orders to prevent a crossing of the Oostanaula River at a location near Resaca. The Cadet Battalion is to form up and march with Gen. Walker's Division to the Oostanaula River near Resaca. Any questions Major?"

"None, Gen. Mackall. We will report immediately to Gen. Walker's headquarters."

The morning of the 14th, General Sherman orders an attack at Gen. Johnston's center with a division of General John Palmer's XIV Corps. General Palmer's Corps attack across Camp Creek Valley towards the crest held by Gen. Hardee's Corps. There, General Sherman's army confronts devastating infantry and artillery fire. The picture of the first battle for Legare and Rooster is powerfully dramatic. The battle brings to life the reality of war.

Rooster turns to Legare. "They want to kill you as badly as you want to kill them. Capture never enters their mind."

Legare nods. War becomes a game of survival. Grape and canister fly into the ranks. Bombshells burst overhead and the fragments fly on all sides of Legare. A dozen or so of his comrades lay nearby, wounded and screaming or dead. A strange, involuntary shrinking nearly overpowers Legare. He can neither advance nor retreat, but is frozen by his emotions, by his humanity. His cheeks blanch, his lip quivers, and he hesitates to look upon the human carnage.

This has nothing to do with the boastful bravado, the boisterous talk the men shared as they spoke longingly of fighting for the Confederacy. Legare thinks of Polly and Joshua. He wonders briefly if he'll ever see them again, of how they'll manage without him. He recalls his last night with her, her tender kisses. Suddenly he straightens and glances around. He must survive for his wife and son … he must. He swallows hard and inhales the odors of gunpowder, and blood. Legare faces the field with new resolve.

Successive volleys of artillery strike the ground and tree limbs upon which the soldiers lie. The Yankees mass their troops eight deep and advance under a heavy fire of double charges of grape and canister. Soon, the Yankees come within range, and the 63rd renders an incessant volley of musketry. Legare picks out a moving blue target and opens fire against the Yankees in a visible and audible defense. His aim is true and his target falls, as does the soldier Rooster fires on. With his first shot, Legare transforms from a man to a soldier. Fear no longer exists.

No longer mindful of themselves or their orders, the Yankees spring forward in full assault, swarming into the open. Legare, Rooster and the soldiers of Company A receive the advancing Yankees with broad sheets of musket balls, striking the charging and unprotected Yankees with a deadly effect. The artillery resounding on both sides joins the battle, complimenting the rattle and roar with deep, earth-shaking explosions. The air continues to swirl with storms of screaming grape. The trees splinter, splattered with blood on both sides. Hesitation gives way to an uncontrollable desire to rush into the thick of the battle. The dead and the dying comrades serve only to stimulate Legare's revenge. He grows cool and deliberate as the cannon balls pass by him and rake murderous channels though his friends.

No mortal man can stand the Confederate fire. Then, over the battle-field, a bugle call is heard, ordering a retreat for the beaten Yankees. Only the sound of scattering musket shots and the moaning of the distant wounded lying upon the battlefield remain. The noisy voices of the cannons are now still, and the dusky pall of sulphurous smoke rises above the fields. Legare slowly stands. Unnerved and silent he looks on the form of a fellow soldier, who only a few minutes ago, stood in the full flesh of life and happiness. Human brains splashed around, bodies without limbs, limbs with out bodies, disfigured faces, a headless corpse.

The ground is ploughed up and stained with blood. Now come the bloody litter bearers with their woeful burdens. Wounds of every conceivable and unimaginable character. Right arms torn off, not cut off, like a bird's wing with all the muscle and organs closely connected with it. A deadening sensation, thank God. The skull over the cerebellum blown completely away and yet the poor man still lives. There are few groans, except from men unconscious, or from men injured by concussion.[189] Legare begins to comprehend the horrors of war. Quietly he whispers a silent prayer for his fallen comrades.

❧

During the noon briefing Gen. Mackall updates the field commanders on the military engagements. "The only Federal success of the day comes when several brigades of General Logan's XV Corps manages to push back Gen. Polk's troops on the Confederate left." Pointing to a large map on the tent wall Gen. Mackall continues, "Here, the Federals dug in on the recently acquired high ground as Gen. Polk's troops withdraw to a position closer to town." It is apparent that General Sherman has ordered General Sweeny's Division of the XVI Corps, "To move several miles south to Lay's Ferry. I am waiting to receive a reconnaissance report from Gen. Wheeler. Any questions? If not, dismissed."

Later on the same day, General Sweeny assaults a small compliment of Gen. Wheeler's Calvary on patrol with a small scouting party from Company A of the 63rd. General Sweeny orders two regiments to Cross the Oostanaula in pontoon boats to the southern shore.[190]

Gen. Wheeler's scouting party from Company A of the 63rd is in the area and comes under fire. Col. Gordon, the 63rd Regiment Commander sends an order to Maj. Allen for the remainder Company A of the 63rd to set down heavy musket fire against General Sweeny's advancing federal troops of hastening to form a skirmish line on the south side of the river, Company A rushes down the wagon trail. Nearing the river, Company A takes to the woods and forms the line. The discovered scouting party, including Harden, from Company A of the 63rd is in a running gun battle with the pursuing Federals. As company A arrives, General Sweeny's federal troops are also positioning the pontoon boats for the river crossing. There's scattered rifle fire along the riverbank as the scouting party of Company A is in sight. Company A begins to set down the heavy musket fire to prevent the completion of the pontoon bridge.

Legare and John are on the right wing of the skirmish line. "Look. Those are our guys coming this way. It's our scouting party," shouts John.

Legare turns to investigate as the retreating scouting party rushes along the south river bank toward the skirmish line of the 63rd. Legare rushes over to Rooster. "Our scouting party is in trouble. Over there!"

Rooster issues orders to two of the squads. "Set down heavy musket fire against those Federals. Protect our guys!"

The two squads rush over to John's position and open fire. Several Yankees fall to the ground while others jump for cover or take to the river in an attempt to escape. Out of breath and thankful to be alive, the scouting party reaches the safety of Company A. With little hesitation, the party joins the skirmish line and commences firing on the Yankees. Concurrently, the other members of the 63rd and Company A begin to assault the Federals who are still attempting to secure the pontoon boats for the river crossing by General Sweeny's troops.

A member of General Sweeny's scouting party alerts him, Gen. Walker's Division is in route to support the 63rd and is rapidly approaching. Trapped in the water and incurring injuries from an unknown size Confederate force, the federal troops panic and immediately retreat leaving the unfinished pontoon bridge.

Nearly as fast as the skirmish began, the musketry begins to subside. Once Maj. Allen is certain the Yankees are not going to counterattack, he checks for injuries among Company A. Only Pvt. David Blount, who was with the patrol, was taken prisoner by the Federals.[191] The other men are shaken but unharmed.

When Gen. Walker arrives, Col. Gordon reports, "The Yankees have withdrawn back across the Oostanaula River and out of sight."

John and Legare ease over to the edge of the woods near the wagon trail. From the trail, they see a dust cloud over the trees as more of Gen. Walker's troops draw near to their position. Gen. Walker, assuming that General Sweeny will not attempt another river crossing, returns to headquarters and leaves the ferry unguarded.[192]

The various Confederate units are directed to areas of encampment for supper and picket duty. Gradually in the distance, Legare and John see what appears to be a different type of men in uniform. There are shiny buttons glistening in the near noon-time sun, a different style cap, and the unit seems to be well organized in their march.

"I've never seen a unit like that before, Legare."

"Me either," replies Legare. "Who could they be?" After a moment Legare excitedly turns to John. "I think they might be the Cadets from Georgia Military Institute! I need to find out! If they are, Norman is here, I'm sure!" Legare turns to Rooster, "Is it all right if I find out if that unit is from GMI? If they are, my brother-in-law might be with them!"

Rooster replies, "Go ahead, but make it quick. We will be moving out in about an hour."

Legare rushes the hundred yards down the wagon trail to where the Cadet corps has halted to eat their rations. Approaching the bivouac, Legare asks, "You're the GMI cadets, right?"

"Yes sir, we are," replies one of the cadets.

"My brother-in-law is Norman Jernigan." Legare's heart begins to race. "Is he with you?"

What seems like an eternity transpires in a few seconds when the cadet answers and points. "Yes, he should be over there, about twenty five yards or so on the left side of the trail."

"Thanks! "Legare turns, stirring up dust he rapidly strides toward the area where Norman is taking rations. Stopping at the area of the trail where Norman should be, Legare begins to scans the cadets. Most of the cadets have found newly leaved shade trees, just settling down and taking rations from their haversacks. Others are already eating and chatting. Legare spots someone who bears a resemblance to Norman, tall, lanky, yet more mature and masculine than he had remembered. "He has to be Norman!"

Legare's heart is still racing with excitement and his mouth even begins to dry as he quietly approaches Norman. Legare smiles and kneels in front of the man. "Hello, Norman!"

The cadet looks up. "Wrong person, Norman is over there!" He points to another cadet several yards away.

Legare is somewhat embarrassed. "I'm sorry I haven't seen Norman in several years and thought you were him."

"Don't worry about it." The cadet shouts, "Hey, Norman, there's a fellow over here looking for you!" Legare stands, turns, and recognizes Norman at about the same time as Norman recognizes him.

"I cannot believe this is happening!" Norman tells Legare as the two meet at the halfway point. They shake hands and then tentatively embrace. "Ma and Pa wrote me about their surprise visit over Thanksgiving and Christmas. They told me all about little Joshua and Savannah. Then I got the letter from Polly. She told me how happy the two of you are. I couldn't have asked for a better brother-in-law."

"Thanks, Norman. I can still call you Norman?"

"Sure, all my friends at GMI call me that."

"You know I have loved your sister since I first saw her."

"She has loved you as well, Legare. I knew it, but the folks had their mind set on Buster. The power of true love cannot be conquered. You and Polly proved that! Come and sit down. I want you to meet my roommate, Paul Goldsmith." Norman and Legare walk together to where Paul is sitting and eating his hardtack. Paul, having been observing Legare and Norman, stands as they approach. "Paul, this is my brother-in-law, Legare Hill. Legare, this is Paul Goldsmith." Each extends his hand and they shake. "Paul's cousin is James Goldsmith in Stone Mountain."

"I know Mr. Goldsmith. He's the railroad agent at the depot."

Paul motions to Legare. "Have a seat and let's have supper together. Looks like you could use a little food."

"I've lost a little weight over the past couple of weeks. Got some bad meat at Thunderbolt, but I am doing much better now."

The three find comfortable spots in the May sunshine. Legare opens his haversack and retrieves his rations for the day. While eating, their conversations run from the rescue of Norman's cousin George to Legare's experiences in Savannah. Norman and Paul listen to Legare's stories intensely and express their delight in coming to Resaca to fight the Yankees along with their discontent about not being involved in more military operations.

The hour passes by fast and the buglers sound assembly. Legare stands and takes his scarf from his neck. "Your sister embroidered this for me for Christmas. See here, she embroidered this heart, Little Joshua, Polly, and Legare. I want you to have the scarf to wear from the three of us." He hands the scarf to Norman.

Not knowing what to say, Norman holds the scarf in his hands and gently touches the material. "I really can't take this, Legare. Polly made it for you."

"Polly will be glad for me to share our symbol of family with her brother, for we are one family. I must go now. My unit is waiting for me." Shaking hands farewell, Legare bids goodbye to Norman and Paul. "God's speed to both of you." Then Legare turns away, waves and double times back to his unit.

Taking ranks with his company, Legare is asked by John, "Were you able to find Norman?"

"Yes and all is well. I gave him the scarf Polly made for me."

Later in the day, the Cadet Corps moves north of the Oostanaula to reinforce Gen. John Hood's corps. Upon arriving at their new post, Maj. Capers receives orders to place the Cadet Corps behind a split rail fence beyond a copse of woods, joining battle tough veterans. The Cadets quickly take their places behind the fence with the soldiers already there. With a nod to the nearest private, Norman hurries into a spot and motions for Paul to join him.

Lieutenant James Oaks of the 9th Illinois Mounted Infantry takes note of the cadets in uniform coming out of the woods from the direction of Resaca as they line up behind the rail fence.[193]

Paul is practicing aiming his musket. He stares down the sights, catching view of several opposing forces located not too far away. "The Belgian Muskets will work great in this nice weather Norman."

Keeping his eyes toward the enemy, Norman shifts his position slightly and flashes a grin at his friend. "Surely will and my powder is dry and ready."

Maj. Capers is in front of the cadets giving orders to Capt. Austin and Capt. Victor Manget for the proper placement of each company.

Not taking the cadets seriously, the 9th Illinois charge the cadets. On command the cadets give a loud yell. "Come on, you dirty Yankees!" With determination and courage that belies their young age, they launch a volley of fire killing several of the charging Union soldiers on horseback.[194]

After recovering from the surprise, the 9th Illinois launches a full Union mounted regiment up the slope toward the cadets. Against heavy odds, the cadets keep firing as several more of the 9th fall from their saddles. The 9th again retreats to the dense woods for cover and safety. As the battle ebbs, and the whiz of the bullets fade away, the cadets take count. Not a single cadet has received a wound. Continuing to retire deeper into the woods, the cadets are soon withdrawn from the line of battle for some unknown reason.[195]

The cadets are jubilant. Maj. Capers praises them for the exceptional valor while under fire for the first time. "You all knew the elements of the tactical routine. All of you followed orders without hesitation. This shows GMI will graduate the future military leaders of our country. Congratulations! You exhibited the quality of the corps well in one of the first battles of Resaca."

25

DEFIANT GENERALS

Paul and Norman prepare to board a southbound train back to the institute on the morning of the 15th.[196] However, the train includes several hospital cars. Before boarding, Paul and Norman are assigned to assist the wounded soldiers on board. "Be careful with this soldier, Paul. Both legs have bandages and the stretcher doesn't look too sturdy."

Kneeling beside the soldier, Paul says, "Hello fellow. We are going to put you on the train and get you to a hospital in Marietta."

The distraught soldier painfully looks at Paul. "Just be careful, please. They gave me some pain medicine and it is helping a little. Just be careful."

Norman calls two other cadets over to assist in lifting the stretcher. "Here we go soldier. We will be gentle." The four cadets carefully pick up the stretcher with the soldier and place him in the medical car. Soldiers with minor wounds sit with the cadets in the passenger cars. Although excited about their involvement in the battle, Norman and Paul talk with the wounded and listen to their stories. The train stops at Calhoun, Adairsville, Kingston and Cartersville, just long enough to drop off and pick up mail. At any given chance, the cadets inform the people at the station and in no uncertain terms, that there are a few less Yankees around Resaca.

The train finally arrives in Marietta, mid-afternoon on May 15th. Now Norman and Paul truly realize why Marietta is such a busy place, with the battle front just beyond the mountains. Passing trains heading north with supplies and soldiers while trains, like the one they are on, arrive from the north with the wounded and dying. In addition, there are refugees on the trains. Norman and Paul see the trails busy with wagons loads of furniture and families heading south. Upon arriving in Marietta, Paul and Norman dutifully and solemnly assist with the removal of the wounded soldiers from the hospital cars. They assist by gently placing them in the hay wagons which take them along dusty clay roads to the hospitals.

Paul, Norman and the rest of the Corps did not have long to gloat. They now must serve provost duty to protect government and private property for about one week.[197] Their new issue of gray jean uniforms along with knapsacks, canteens and cartridge boxes is an exciting change. Paul looks at Norman. "You look like the real thing now.

We best finish packing our other clothing and personal items and place them in storage as ordered."

The new Belgian muzzle-loading guns of .69 caliber are in the hands of the cadets, but are not exactly what the young men are looking for. With the expectation of arduous duty ahead, they all file complaints about these obsolete and inefficient weapons to Maj. Capers.[198]

❧

The same day as the GMI cadets arrive in Marietta, Gen. Johnston, more than satisfied with Gen. Hood's previous attack, informs his staff Gen. Hood will renew his attack with reinforcements from Gen. Hardee. This will allow Gen. Hood to defeat the left wing of the Federal army.

Also on the 15th, General Sherman's army is advancing through Snake Creek Gap while General Hooker's XX corps is engaging Gens. Stevenson's and Stewart's divisions of Gen. Hood's corps north of Resaca. General Sherman orders General Sweeny to build pontoon bridges and cross his entire division at Lay's Ferry on the Oostanaula River which is about five miles westward from Resaca near Calhoun. General Sweeny's action forces Gen. Polk's cavalry to withdraw closer to Resaca. Polk's withdrawal allows General Sweeny to gain a foothold and threaten the Army of Tennessee's supply line.[199]

Gen. Johnston attempts to call off the attack when he learns that General Sweeny is crossing again at Lay's Ferry. Gen. Stewart receives orders to attack General Sweeny but is already experiencing heavy fighting and is unable to attack. Gen. Stewart loses over a thousand men returning to his emplacements. In addition cannons of Capt. Max Van den Corpit's Cherokee Ga. Battery are captured.[200]

Disappointed, Gen. Johnston dispatches his aid, Lt. Thomas Mackall, with a message to Gen. Hood to cancel all orders for the attack.[201] All during the day of the 15th, without a full assault, the Yankees harass the Confederate line at all points.[202]

A courier from Gen. Polk notifies Gen. Johnston, "Just before dark Federal troops are occupying high ground east of Camp Creek and are constructing artillery emplacements. Gen. Polk did counterattack several times but he was not successful and withdrew to new line closer to Resaca."

Gen. Johnston issues orders to his engineers. "Build a pontoon bridge across the Oostanaula River out of the range of the Union Artillery." Toward evening, General McPherson advances his entire line of battle forward until he gains a ridge overlooking Resaca. From this vantage point, his field artillery is able to shell the railroad bridge across the Oostanaula River. Gen. Johnston's army attempts several times to force a retreat on the Yankees but is unsuccessful.

Gen. Hood and General Hooker's XX corps advance on each other and both sustain the majority of the heavy fighting north of Resaca. This heavy combat continues all afternoon and into the early night on the left, where the Dalton wagon trails enter the entrenchments, and Gen. Hood's troops are driven back. General Howard's corps, which has shadowed Gen. Johnston from Dalton, is in line with General Stoneman's division of cavalry. Together, they flank Gen. Hood on his extreme left beyond the Oostanaula River.

Below Dalton, Gen. Joseph Johnston becomes outflanked by superior numbers of Union troops and has the back of his army against the Oostanaula River. General Sherman's army is at Gen. Johnston's front and rear Saturday and Sunday. Gen. Johnston orders a pull back south out of Resaca across the Oostanaula River on the pontoon bridge toward Calhoun and Adairsville.[203] The weather is on Gen. Johnston's side. It is a cloudy night with limited visibility. Gen. Hardee's and Gen. Polk's corps withdraws over the railroad bridge. The railroad bridge is put to blaze as the last Confederate troops of Gen. Hood's corps crosses by way of the pontoon bridge.

Acting as rear guard, Gen. Hardee's soldiers disassemble the pontoon bridge and load the parts onto wagons. While loading the wagon, Legare asks, "Well Rooster, did we win or lose?"

Rooster answers, "If we won, I think we would be heading north!"

Confederate pickets protect the withdrawal with a steady fire across to the Yankee lines. Around midnight the withdrawal is complete, and the Battle of Resaca is over.[204]

Gen. Johnston briefs his staff. "Our defense at Resaca is not a victory. We met General Sherman's flanking tactics only to be flanked again. The Army of Tennessee sustained 500 killed, 3,200 wounded and 1,400 missing. However, I am confident that we have inflicted far heavier casualties on General Sherman in front of Dalton. The army of Tennessee must turn on the Union forces soon and inflict a mortal gash."[205]

⚡

General Sherman's army engineers have the Railroad Bridge and Wagon Bridge in good repair by early afternoon. General Sherman orders General Howard's IV corps, "to be in close pursuit of the Army of Tennessee." General Sherman splits his strong Union army into three wings. General George Thomas and the main body are to move directly after Gen. Johnston toward Calhoun. General James McPherson is to march his troops to the west while General Joseph Hooker's corps is to circle to the east.[206]

General Sherman advises his commanders at a staff meeting. "Rumors that Gen. Johnston has deliberately designed a plan to give up such strong positions as Dalton and Resaca, for the purpose of drawing us farther south, are simply absurd. Had Gen. Johnston remained in Dalton another hour, it would have been his total defeat. Gen. Johnston only evacuated Resaca because his safety demanded a retreat. Our movement through Snake-Creek Gap was a total surprise to him. My army is about double Gen. Johnston's in size, but Gen. Johnston had all the advantages of natural positions, of artificial fort and trails and of concentrated action. Our Federal army was compelled to grope our way through forest, across mountains, with a large army, necessarily more or less dispersed. Of course, I was disappointed not to have crippled his army more at that particular stage of the game. But as it resulted, these rapid successes gave us the initiative, and the usual impulse of a conquering army."[207]

It is late in the evening of Monday, May 16, when Gen. Johnston and his staff reach Calhoun and set up headquarters in the Curtis house. Gen. Walker's Division rejoins Gen. Johnston at Calhoun later that evening. Gen. Hardee's corps serves as the rear guard defending against the Yankee pursuit.

Legare, John, Alonzo McCurdy and Rooster, along with their company engage in delaying tactics with Gen. Hardee's corps against the advancing Union forces. Gen. Hood's corps takes bivouac and defends the wagon trail south of Calhoun to Adairsville. Gen. Polk's Corps takes bivouac and defends the wagon trail to Rome. Gen. Johnston inspects the area around Calhoun with his mapping engineers and fails to find favorable terrain to trap General Sherman's army. After the inspection, Gen. Johnston notifies his commanders to move south to Adairsville. During a conference with his engineers and commanders, they come to a decision. Gen. Johnston surmises, "The valley north of Adairsville is narrow enough for an attack and the hills high enough to prevent a flanking movement by General Sherman."

Late that night, Gen. Johnston's orderly informs him, "Sir one of your spies has arrived."

"Show him in right away." Gen. Johnston rushes outside of his tent to meet his spy. The spy arrives and salutes Gen. Johnston. "What kind of information do you have for me?"

"Sir, there is a large Union force on their way to cut you off from the railroad supply line. General Thomas's Army of the Cumberland is at your front and Generals Schofield's and McPherson's armies are on your flanks."

Just as Legare, John, Rooster, and Alonzo settle in for a rest, Gen. Johnston issues new orders. "Depart Calhoun late tonight and march to Adairsville."

Gen. Johnston considers making a stand against General Sherman in Adairsville. However, after reviewing the terrain in Adairsville, Gen. Johnston determines that the terrain also is not favorable for a defense. The valley is too wide and hills are not of any great advantage due to their low profile.[208]

Sherman's army is in very close proximity to Adairsville on the 17th. Gen. Wheeler reports to Gen. Johnston. "The enemy is pressing hard!"

Gen. Johnston orders Gen. Polk's cavalry, under the command of BG William H. Jackson along with Gen. Hardee's Corps, "to prepare temporary breastworks against advancing General Howard's IV Corps advance guard."

Heavy skirmishes continue throughout the day and into the early evening with Gen. Benjamin Cheatham's division receiving the brunt of the federal probe. Gen. William J. Hardee and Gen. Jackson are able to retard the advance of General Howard's IV corps.[209] Gen. Johnston orders a withdrawal further south toward Cassville. He orders Gen. Cheatham's division "to remain behind and fight a delaying action in the entrenchments" against the Yankee 44th Illinois and the 24th Wisconsin under the command of Major Arthur McArthur.[210]

Early in the evening, Gen. Johnston meets with his corps commanders at his headquarters. He has information that General Sherman has divided his army, part of which is currently seizing Rome. The bombardment cannon fire against Rome is heard in the distance from Gen. Johnston's headquarters. Gen. Hardee approves the idea of doing battle at Adairsville, but Gen. Hood feels safer behind the Etowah River about fifteen miles away. Gen. Johnston and his four general officers study the map to Cassville.[211] Reviewing the maps in detail, Gen. Johnston consults with his staff topographer and map maker, Lt. S. H.. Buchanan, concerning the terrain around Cassville.[212]

Finally, Gen. Johnston draws a battle plan. "Gen. Hardee is to proceed due south to Kingston with all of the army wagons. This particular segment of wagon trail is parallel with the Western-Atlantic railroad. I hope General Sherman will conclude since Gen. Hardee has been acting a rear guard since Resaca, that our entire army has taken the same route. Upon reaching Kingston, Gen. Hardee is to turn east and block the road between Kingston and Cassville. Next Gen. Hood and Gen. Polk will take the eastern road directly to Cassville."

Gen. Johnston looks at his men to ascertain that they have no questions and continues, "General Sherman will probably dispatch part of his army directly towards Cassville. This road diverges at around a thirty-five-degree angle from the railroad. Since the terrain is thickly wooded and hostile, the Yankee forces will be unable to reinforce each other. From Cassville the forces of Gen. Hood and Gen. Polk will ambush the unsuspecting Yankee forces on the Cassville Road."

Final orders by Gen. Johnston are prepared and issued to all pertinent officers. The Army of Tennessee once again marches at night to their new tactical positions.[213]

After the meeting, Gen. Polk approaches Gen. Johnston. "I have a letter to read concerning you from your wife. I would like to read it with your permission."

Somewhat puzzled, Gen. Johnston agrees. "Of course, please do, though I am at a loss as to why she would write to you. It doesn't seem like her."

"Perhaps, you will understand more when I read the letter to you." Gen. Polk, a former Episcopal bishop removes a letter from Gen. Johnston's wife Lydia, which he had received several days earlier. "Dear Gen. Polk, I would like to ask a personal favor of you. My husband Gen. Joseph Johnston has never been baptized.[214] If it is at all possible and within your power it is the dearest wish in my heart that he should be and that you should perform the ceremony."

Gen. Polk continues, "Would you mind General, if I fulfill your wife's wish?"[215]

"I would be happy for you to baptize me, Gen. Polk," replies Gen. Johnston. Shortly, Gen. Polk returns with the necessary religious text and adornment. Gen. Johnston kneels before Bishop Polk. He administers the sacrament of baptism. Member of Gen. Johnston's staff observes the Holy scene with quiet reverence.

Toward evening, the head of General George Thomas's column, a part of General Newton's division, encounters Gen. Hardee's corps acting as rear guard North of Adairsville. General Sherman is with the head column of General Thomas's unit attempting to get a view of the position of Gen. Johnston's forces. General Sherman is on a rise in an open field. An officer with a Confederate artillery battery is looking through his field glasses and observes General Sherman's command group.

Excitedly, he orders, "Look there, I believe that is General Sherman. Set your cannon and fire immediately." Without hesitation, the battery sets the elevation and loads and fires the cannon. Again, observing through his field glasses, the Confederate officer witnesses the shell passing through the group of General Sherman and his staff officers, exploding just beyond General Sherman's position. Before a second round is fired a shaken, but unharmed General Sherman and his staff turn about and rapidly evacuate their position.[216]

Gen. Johnston departs Adairsville around 4:00 Wednesday morning, May 18, and by 7:30 AM he is setting up his headquarters in Cassville. The Army of Tennessee begins to arrive in Cassville during the morning and go into bivouac in their respective areas as stated in the recent orders. At this time, General McPherson's leading column is about four miles to the west of Kingston at a country place by the name of "Woodlawn." General Schofield and General Hooker are on the direct wagon trail leading from Newton to Cassville, diagonal to the route taken by General George Thomas.

Returning from a scouting mission, Gen. Wheeler reports to Gen. Johnston, "Sir, General George Thomas's Army of the Cumberland is following Gen. Hardee's corps along the Western and Atlantic Railroad. General Schofield's XXIII corps and General Hooker's XX corps are on the east wagon trail to Cassville."

Gen. Johnston is excited with this news and notifies Gen. Wheeler and his staff, "Looks like General Sherman has taken the bait. Now we can destroy a large portion of his army and send him reeling back to the mountains."

∂⊶

During the evening of the 18th, behind breastworks and under the light of the nearly full moon, Legare and Rooster's conversation is overheard. Capt. Buster Phillips has recognized the familiar voice of Legare Hill. Buster positions himself to see the two and hear their conversation without becoming suspect. To him, Legare appears a trifle more slender and more mature than when he vanished from Stone Mountain three years ago with Polly. Otherwise, Legare has little changed in personal appearance. His face, bronzed by exposure to the elements, wears what appears to be a thoughtful look as Buster eases closer to hear better. With hatred in his heart Buster considers a plan to kill Legare and involuntary draws his pistol. With his eyes focused on Legare, his Sergeant taps him on the shoulder. "Sir, the battalion commander wishes to see you right away."

Coming to his senses, Buster returns his pistol to the holster and departs with his Sergeant.

Rooster continues carrying on the conversation. "You're in my neck of the woods now, Legare! Did you know that at one time, Cassville was the largest city between Savannah and Nashville? It's still is the largest city in North Georgia. The citizens of Cassville have changed the name of the city to 'Manassas' and the county from 'Cass County' to 'Bartow County.'"

Legare responds, "I heard about the name changes, but not about the population. Is this the railroad station where Andrews stopped to get water, wood and a train schedule during the Locomotive Chase?"

"Yep, this also is the county seat and where Mr. Akin argued the first case before the Georgia Supreme Court in 1846. Cassville, or the new 'Manassas,' is the cultural and educational center for these parts."

"This is where I want to go to college. My Pa gives high marks to the Colleges here."

"We have two colleges, one male and one female and they are excellent. There are four hotels, a newspaper and wooden sidewalks, which by the way will take you to the first post-office in the state. There's a cotton warehouse, a gristmill and several churches along with plenty of beautiful homes. From what I understand, some of those homes are hospitals now."

"Soon as this war is over, Polly and I will move here so I can get some of my law requirements completed."

Soon Legare and his comrade drift into retrospection. There are strong ties between these two young friends of the same age. Together they have survived the mysteries of why a comrade nearby is killed rather than either of them. Now, they have to brave despair, homesickness and battle fatigue.

Lying on his back, Legare looks at the stars and thinks of Polly and little Joshua. He confides in Rooster, "In all these years the people of Stone Mountain have not drifted out of my milieu."

The moon is brighter and her rays are just lighting the mountains. Rooster answers, "Look at those mountains. There are Yankees somewhere out there, probably behind earthworks just like us. Their possessions and our possessions will become a bitter dispute tomorrow. Over yonder lay our father's people. For though you're true to the land of your birth, you're but half Southerner by blood. I sometimes wonder how a Southern grandfather could have given his fairest daughter in marriage to a cold-blooded, New Englander Yankee. I don't doubt that our noble ancestors have turned in their graves many times since the outbreak of this war."

Legare replies, "A little more common sense would greatly help the blood of the South. It is too hot, and it needs cooling."

"You're right. It's too rash, and needs tempering. We should rely upon the Yankee background of shrewd common sense, patience, judgment and endurance."

"The Yankees have not shown any of those qualities as far as I am concerned when it comes to state's rights." Rooster continues, "Still, if we would graft the qualities of heart and mind of the North and the South, we would have a combination the world would envy. Right now we stand to loose everything."

"The best Southerners do not yield to anyone in their devotion to the South."

"And the Northern instinct provides me with a clearer insight into the tendencies and inevitable conclusion of this fratricidal clash of minds and material," Legare answers back.

"I have never doubted for one moment that the South will meet defeat, but I don't exactly freely give my life to the cause. If only the Lord would bid this carnage to cease and let the banner of peace be again unfurled." Legare's tone becomes very melancholic.

Rooster looks at him sharply. "It's unlike you to be so despondent."

Exhausted and weak Legare responds, "My thoughts come from no lack of courage, but I feel I might not survive tomorrow's fight."

"Turn in and sleep off this nonsense. Your mind is as tired as your body!" Rooster wraps himself in his section of carpet, and bidding Legare a courteous good night, stretches his form upon the gathered hay, which softens the ground beneath, and is soon in a dreamful sleep.

He cannot refrain from thoughts of his Polly and little Joshua. They weigh heavily on his heart and mind. He closes his eyes and can feel Polly and Little Joshua's presence as she walks among the gardens and parks of Savannah. Legare knows Polly patiently awaits his return to be united with her and their son. He smiles within as he sees his Polly easily adapt to the exotics of the Savannah social atmosphere.

These reflections come to Legare as he sees his wife and realizes that what should be an episode in both of their lives, could be fermenting to become a tragedy. His thoughts stray doggedly to Buster Phillips and attempts to formulate what Polly's life could have been if she had loved and married Buster instead of him. Legare struggles not to imagine that he may, on the battlefield, leave his wife and child to the dependency of their relatives. Frightened by these sad images, he takes paper and pencil and by candlelight writes a letter to her.

His heart feels lighter once his thoughts and feelings are penned. He folds and places the letter in his pocket next to his heart. Exhausted by these conflicting emotions, he lies upon the hay and slips into a heavy slumber under his over coat.

MAY 18, 1864

Norman writes around one o'clock, Wednesday morning,

> *Dear Folks,*
>
> *You would never guess who I met in Resaca! Legare! His unit was down the trail from ours. They had just finished a skirmish and were resting. He saw our cadet uniforms and came to find me. Looks like he lost a little weight, but said he had been sick, and Polly got him back to health. He gave me a scarf that she embroidered with her hair for him. He insisted I take it. He could not stay long as his unit was about to depart. Today we slung our knapsacks, blankets and were issued our weapons in*

Marietta. Our spirits were high, thinking we were headed for the front, but instead the Corps intercepted a raiding party of about 8000. They came as far as Cartersville which is the commissary depot. However nothing happened and we returned to campus where we are now resting and awaiting further orders.

Love,

Norman

By the time tattoo sounds, the cadets on sentinel duty maintain their stations. The cadets in the barracks have been on standby all day. They roll out their bedding, turn out the lamps and try to go to sleep. However, the tension is so high that the discussions continue among roommates of what the next day might bring.

※

At dawn, May 19, there's no time for Legare to consign his letter to the safe keeping of Rooster. The sharp jangle of the muskets and the drummers calls him to duty. Slowly Rooster and Legare gather their equipment and prepare to take their positions on the emplacements. Gen. Johnston's aspirations are as elevated as if he is perched high on his horse. He expects a decisive victory by the Army of Tennessee from Gen. Polk and Hood's ambush against General Sherman's army. Gen. Johnston issues an order to be read to his army, "Soldiers of the Army of Tennessee, you have displayed the highest quality of the soldier: Firmness in combat and patience under toil. By your courage and skill you have repulsed every assault of the enemy. By marches you have defeated every attempt upon your communications. Your communications are secured."

Gen. Johnston continues, "You will now turn and march to meet his advancing columns. Fully confiding in the conduct of the officers and the courage of my brave soldiers, I lead you to battle. We may confidently trust that the Almighty Father will still reward the patriot's toil and bless the patriot's banners. Cheered by the success of your brothers in Virginia and beyond the Mississippi, our efforts will equal theirs. Strengthened by His support those efforts will be crowned with the like glories."[217]

Afterwards, Gen. Johnston and his staff make an inspection of the troop positions in relation to the terrain and then he returns to his headquarters. Around 9:30 AM, Gen. Hardee sends a courier with a message to Gen. Johnston. "General Sherman's army is approaching his position and the skirmishing has begun. We are defending between Kingston and Cassville as you ordered."

Unbeknownst to anyone, General Dan Butterfield's brigade becomes lost while searching for General McPherson in Kingston.[218] General Butterfield is traveling south on the Canton wagon trail, which is to the east of Gen. Hood's corps. Gen. Johnston dispatches Capt. Mackall with a message to Gen. Hood, "To advance and make quick work of the Federals. At 10:20 AM, Gen. Johnston hears the musketry from the direction of Gen. Hood corps.

Just as Gen. Johnston's optimism is at its zenith, a courier delivers a message from Capt. Mackall, "Upon arriving Gen. Hood had begun his movements forward around 10:00 AM. Some of his soldiers are already lying low in the woods waiting for the Federals to pass so the assault can begin. After advancing less than two miles, Gen. Hood received a report that a secondary column of Federal troops of unknown strength is off to his right. General Butterfield's forces on the Canton wagon trail are now unknowingly behind and on the right flank of Gen. Hood's forces. Instead of attacking, Gen. Hood and Gen. Polk are withdrawing south of the Etowah River into defensive lines at Cassville and the Etowah valley."[219]

"It can't be! This cannot be happening! This is the very best position that I have occupied during this war!" exclaims Gen. Johnston while retrieving a map. "Even if this report is true or false, the opportunity for the ambush is lost. Gen. Hood should not have cancelled the attack without first investigating the report. He should have continued this critical attack. I must now cancel the entire operation." Angrily, disappointed Gen. Johnston orders a withdrawal to his secondary tactical defensive position in the town of Cassville. "Hopefully General Sherman will launch an attack against us in this new and very strong defensive position."

Positioned in the front, observing the Federal cavalry is the 3rd Texas Cavalry Rangers of Gen. Wheeler's corps. The 3rd Texas Cavalry is dismounted, lying on the ground holding their horses. "Look," shouts one the soldiers. The soldiers jump to their feet and observe not more than two hundred yards away, a Confederate cavalry unit engaged in an impetuous and disorderly fight. The Federal Cavalry is hammering another cavalry regiment with sabers drawn. "To mount! To mount!" commands Gen. Polk and the bugle sounds, "charge."

Suddenly, the 3rd Texas Ranger Cavalry surprises the Federal cavalry of Kentucky. The 3rd and the Federals meet in a hand-to-hand contest of blood and guts. The six-shooter of the 3rd Texas Rangers defeats the saber as well as the six-shooter of the Kentuckians. The sudden surprise attack causes the Union Kentucky troops to quickly yield to the greater, yet inferior force. The Federal cavalry retreats in panic and disorder charging toward their own line endangering their own infantry in their route. Almost instantly, a Federal battery opens fire upon the 3rd Texas Rangers, but the shells overshoot as the 3rd rapidly removes to a location out of range and out of view.[220]

Around noon, General Sherman receives a message from General Thomas. "I have found Gen. Hardee drawn up in a line of battle, on some extensive open ground, about half-way between Kingston and Cassville. Their appearances indicate a willingness and preparation for battle."

General Sherman, full of excitement, notifies his staff, "Now we know where Gen. Johnston is!" General Sherman hurriedly dispatches orders to General McPherson, "To resume the march, to hasten forward by wagon trails leading to the south of Kingston. Leave for General Thomas's troops and supply wagon trains the use of the main wagon trail and come up on his right."[221]

The 63rd Georgia Regiment on the front line of Gen. Hardee's rear guard becomes actively engaged in a light skirmish with General Thomas's division. Pvt. T. F. Burbank is lying adjacent to Legare behind the breast works. A musket ball penetrates the earthworks and shatters Burbank's shoulder.[222] Screaming, Burbank reels over toward Legare. Legare lays down his weapon and moves to assist Burbank. He lifts Burbank from the ground and moves toward the rear line.

Suddenly, Gen. Hardee withdraws to his secondary position to the new location of Cass Station on an eminence southwest of town and across the wagon trail. Gen. Johnston assigns a position to Gen. Polk in the center and to Gen. Hood as the right wing on the south side of the Etowah River. Gen. Wheeler and Gen. Jackson's cavalry are on the flanks of Gen. Hood and Gen. Polk.

General Sherman and his staff ride forward rapidly over rough gravel hills. About six miles below Kingston, General Sherman finds General Thomas with his troops deployed. General Thomas reports to General Sherman, "I only had a short skirmish with Gen. Hardee before he retreated in echelon of divisions, steadily and in superb order, into Cassville."

General Sherman is familiar with the wagon trails by which General Hooker and General Schofield are approaching. These trails will lead them to the seminary near Cassville. It is all-important to secure these wagon trails with the main wagon trail along which General Sherman troops are marching. General Sherman orders General Thomas, "To push forward your deployed lines as rapidly as possible."[223]

Capt. Buster Phillips, Georgia 52nd, Company "I" of the 25th Alabama regiment and a company of the 22nd Alabama regiment occupy the area through the cemetery along the graves and tombstones. Orders are given, "To throw up earthworks as rapidly as possible for protection and if necessary remove any monuments or tombstone which might hinder the construction of the earthworks." The 63rd is also forming a line inside the cemetery. One grave, which has been walled in with brick about two feet high, has a large marble slab covering the grave. The smell of bacon is apparent. When John Dent and Alonzo McCurdy of the 63rd remove the slab, they find a lot of flour and bacon beneath the slab. John and Alonzo leave the contraband food, replace the marble slab and continue to throw up earthworks around the grave.[224] The Union forces post their batteries west of town on a hill and begin an unrelenting fire. The town of Cassville is now directly between the contending armies.

CASSVILLE AND KINGSTON

Capt. Phillips' unit joins Company "I" of the 25th Alabama Regiment and a Company of the 22nd Alabama Regiment. They are given orders to move forward as a skirmish line to check the advancing line of the Yankees. Capt. Phillips' unit is providing covering musket fire as the two Alabama Regiments advance down toward the east side of town only to find that the Yankees have already entered Cassville from the west side. Artillery batteries are in a constant duel directly over the town. Uncertain for whom the cannon balls are intended, both Yankee and Confederate dive for cover as the shells pass overhead. House to house, skirmishes ensue. The Yankees capture the right wing of the Alabama picket line. Lt. Frisby of the 22nd Alabama who commands a portion of the right wing of the line is captured with a number of his men.

Shortly, Lt. Frisby comes running out from the enemy's line bare headed and crying out, "Help! Help! I am mortally shot!" Although a heavy fire is kept up by the Yankees, Capt. Phillips and some of the Alabama Regiment advance to the relief of the young gallant Alabama

officer. When the Alabamians reach Lt. Frisby, he falls in their arms utter-
ing. "I am killed!" Lt. Frisby can still walk. Capt. Phillip's unit continues
to provide covering fire as Lt. Frisby is carried through the skirmish line.
The Lt. is transported to the rear where he soon succumbs.[225]

The 63rd and the 52nd Georgia Regiments become actively engaged in
the fight on the front lines. The 63rd and 52nd assault the Union lines and
victoriously force the assaulting Yankees to retreat to their fortifications.

The town of Cassville was now directly between the contending
armies. A detail under Capt. Phillips consisting of Company "I" of the
25th Regiment and another Company of the 22nd Regiment are ordered
forward as a skirmish line to check the advancing Yankees. As Capt.
Phillip's unit is advancing down toward the east side of town, he finds
the Yankees have already entered the west side of Cassville. The Yankees
capture the right wing of his picket line. To avoid capture, he retreats from
the field and falls back into the cemetery earthworks.

Upon darkness, the firing ceases. Buster receives battle orders and to the
delight of the troops, Gen. Johnston intends to engage General Sherman
at Cassville. Capt. Phillips knows that if this occurs and the Yankees did
advance the next morning in battle line, that all of their lives would be in
jeopardy. If the battle did not occur, Cassville would be remembered only
as a cavalry fight, a couple of artillery duels and a few skirmishes.

During the late afternoon, Gen. Johnston and his Chief of Staff Gen.
Mackall complete an inspection of the defensive fortifications of the lines
of the Army of Tennessee. The two return to Gen. Johnston's headquarters,
which are in the McKelvey log cabin house.[226] Gen. Johnston has already
sent couriers to Gens. Hardee, Hood and Polk to report to headquarters
to discuss the final plans for the battle of Cassville. Around 7:30 PM, Gen.
Polk and Gen. Hood report to Gen. Johnston's headquarters.

Gen. Hardee sends a message, "I will do my utmost to be at the
meeting on time. The delay is due to the defensive concerns we discussed
this afternoon."

Gen. Johnston has his tactical maps on a large table and is going over
the defensive position when Gen. Hood interrupts. "Gen. Polk and I are
in agreement that our lines cannot be held for more than one hour if we
come under attack. We urge that either the Army of Tennessee withdraw
… or from this commanding position, move against the Federals."

Gen. Johnston obliviously is not expecting a confrontation with his
subordinate commanders. "You have failed to follow orders here, once
by retreating without authority from me. One of us is in charge here and

that is me! By retreating under the threat of a small Federal force, you have prevented the possible destruction of General Sherman's Army. We have one more chance to do battle with him here and be successful. Your acts and conduct for failing to follow orders is bordering treason!" Gen. Johnston continues to insist on staying and fighting, but Gen. Hood is just as insistent on withdrawing or attacking immediately..

Shortly before 10:00 PM, Gen. Hardee arrives at the McKelvey log cabin. The McKelvey family is still outside, keeping warm by a campfire since they cannot enter their cabin. Mr. McKelvey sees Gen. Hardee when he arrives. "Evening General, some mighty strong talking going on in there. Best you be ready to argue!"

"Hope it is good for the country," replies Gen. Hardee as he heads toward the log cabin. Once inside Gen. Johnston invites Gen. Hardee to the table where the war conference is taking place.

"Gen. Polk and Gen. Hood are under the impression that they cannot hold their lines against an attack by General Sherman. They insist on attacking General Sherman or withdrawing to the south side of the Etowah River."

Frowning, Gen. Hardee responds, "Gen. Hood, ever since the beginning of this campaign you have wanted to get to the south side of the Etowah River! I am on the extreme left and have no weak defenses in my line. My men's morale is high and they are ready to fight when the command is given. They expect to stand where we are. I have had couriers running back and forth, artillery position fortified and men digging in and preparing earthworks. We are ready to defend or attack. My corps is prepared to follow whatever Gen. Johnston orders of us."

For two more hours, the argument rages until finally Gen. Johnston realizes with the poor attitude of Gen. Hood and Gen. Polk, a strong defense is not possible. Gen. Johnston believes the fears of the corps commanders will communicate to their men and thus weaken the army's will to fight. Gen. Johnston yields to these demands, even though he knows the position to be defensible. However, his confidence in Gen. Hood and Gen. Polk to follow orders is greatly eroded. They have directly disobeyed his battle orders at least twice in the last several days. Gen. Johnston is unwilling to risk an offensive battle with General Sherman and decides to fall back across the Etowah.[227] Gen. Johnston turns to Gen. Mackall, directing him to issue the following orders: "All units of the Army of Tennessee are to withdraw across the Etowah River immediately. We will prepare to dig in and conduct a battle at Allatoona Pass. Gen. Wheeler will dismantle the pontoon bridges and torch the Wagon Bridge and Western and Atlantic Railroad Bridge."[228]

Around 2:30 AM May 20, an officer moves silently along the line and in a whisper, gives the order to withdraw as quietly as possible across the Etowah. The soldiers gather their meager belongings and fall into formation. The night is clear and, dry and unlike the other withdrawals, there's a great deal of confusion. "What has happened to the great call to battle that Gen. Johnston delivered yesterday morning? We stand ready to fight and instead we withdraw in the middle of the night!"

Capt. Phillips responds, "The Gen. must have a better plan to execute later!"

The soldier asks, "Where are we going now?"

"It is my understanding that we are heading for New Hope Church."

During the night, the Army of Tennessee withdraws across the Etowah. As the Army of Tennessee falls back, the feelings of the Confederates are mixed and chaotic as is the movement of the Army of Tennessee's supply wagons. Capt. Phillips sadly informs his men, "We have lost a very strong position at Dalton, and have fallen back from Resaca, Calhoun, and Adairsville. Now we are withdrawing again under cover of darkness. This morning, as we prepared for battle, our spirits were high. Now our disappointment is bitter."

IN PURSUIT OF VICTORY IN WAR AND POLITICS

With daybreak, May 20, the Army of Tennessee has departed. General Sherman dispatches his cavalry in pursuit and reconnaissance. The cavalry scouts report, "Gen. Johnston and his army are south of the Etowah River and have placed the Etowah River and the Allatoona range between us." Now General Sherman controls the Western and Atlantic Railroad gaining the ability to re-supply the Union army. Rather than pursuing Gen. Johnston, General Sherman orders, "The cavalry will hold the ground at Cassville Depot, Cartersville, and the Etowah Bridge. General Thomas will hold his ground near Cassville. General McPherson will hold the ground near Kingston." General Sherman notes, "The officer entrusted with the repair of the railroad is Colonel W. Wright, a railroad engineer. Colonel Wright, with about two thousand men, is so industrious and skillful that the bridge at Resaca was rebuilt in three days."

Union railroad cars full of supplies arrive in Kingston on the 24th. The telegraph also brings the news of the bloody and desperate battle of the Wilderness, in Virginia, and that General Grant is pushing his operations against Gen. Lee with terrific energy. General Sherman drags on his cigar declares to his staff, "I am therefore resolved to give the Confederates no rest! I will also at a later day burn this town for the insult to the Union for re-naming Cassville to Manassas after the Confederate victory, which occurred there."[229]

General Sherman and his staff perform an inspection tour of Cassville. He finds nearly all of the people of the country must have fled with Gen. Johnston. From one of the remaining families, General Sherman procures a copy of an order, which Gen. Johnston had issued at Adairsville. The order recited that Gen. Johnston, "had retreated as far as strategy required, and that his army must be prepared for battle at Cassville."[230]

Several newspapers from the South are found and all are loud in, "Denunciation of Gen. Johnston's falling back before General Sherman without a serious battle. The simple resisting by Gen. Johnston's skirmishing-lines and by Gen. Johnston's rear-guard is not acceptable. "But according to the newspapers, Gen. Johnston's friends proclaim, "It is all strategic and Gen. Johnston is deliberately drawing the Yankees farther and farther into the meshes, farther and farther away from the base of supplies. That in due season Gen. Johnston will not only halt for battle, but assume the bold offensive."[231]

General Sherman returns to his headquarters and informs his staff and commanders, "I have seen some of Gen. Johnston's orders and here are newspaper articles. Read them for yourself. Of course, it is to my interest to bring the Army of Tennessee to battle as soon as possible, especially when our numerical superiority is at the greatest. Gen. Johnston was picking up his detachments as he fell back, whereas I was compelled to make similar and stronger detachments to repair and guard the railroad as we advanced. I found here at Cassville many evidences of preparations for a grand battle. Among them a long line of fresh entrenchments on the hill beyond the town, extend nearly three miles to the south, embracing the Western and Atlantic Railroad crossing. I am also convinced that Gen. Johnston had in hand three full corps, viz., Gens. Hood's, Polk's and Hardee's, numbering about sixty thousand men. I cannot imagine why he declined battle."[232]

TUESDAY, MAY 23, 1864

Paul's parents stop by the Institute. They are red from the dry dust which is covering them, their belongings and their horses. The Goldsmiths have four wagon loads of their personal belongings and most of their home furniture. "Paul, we are going to go to Atlanta and stay with Aunt Bess," explains his father. "The fighting is moving rapidly towards Marietta. The army is transferring the sick and wounded soldiers to the Atlanta hospitals. That is where I am needed."

Paul nods in agreement. "All of the cadets have been ordered to pack their non-essential clothing and either they'll be in storage or the cadets can ship them to their homes. Let me get mine for you. Will you help me, Norman?" asks Paul.

"Sure will," replies Norman.

"I'll take yours, too, Norman," says Dr. Goldsmith.

"Thanks, but mine is already at the depot and ready for the train to Stone Mountain." They gather up Paul's trunk and place it upon the last of the wagons. Paul tells his mother and father, "We think we are going to Milledgeville in a day or two. Maj. Capers has permission for the Corps to stay at Oglethorpe College near Milledgeville. Write me there and give me your address in Atlanta." With sad embraces and "God's Speed," the family departs along the busy dusty clay road toward Atlanta. Paul and Norman stand until there's nothing left to see but the red dust from the dry clay road.

➣

Washington dated June 8, 1864 (referring to events of May 23, 1864): General Sherman dictates a report to General Hazen, "I knew the strength of Allatoona Pass, having ridden through it twenty years ago, and knew Allatoona Pass will reduce our strength by forcing us to operate by the head of a single column. I determined not to attempt this route. I find it advantageous to pass the range by other more devious and difficult natural roads. These roads will permit more equal terms with the enemy should he attempt, to meet us."[233]

General Sherman orders Colonel Phillips on June 6, 1864, "to begin establishing Allatoona Pass as a supply base and defensive position." When the supply base is complete, General Sherman examines Allatoona Pass, and finds the area admirably adapted to use as his secondary base. He then gives the necessary orders to Colonel Poe, "prepare for its defense and garrison. It will be our supply base as soon as the railroad bridge is finished across the Etowah. Then our stores can come forward to our camp by rail."[234]

General Sherman informs his Chief of Staff, Major Joseph Audenried, "I am very familiar with this land. The army will move instead from Kingston to Marietta via Dallas."

"If you would, General, please tell me how you come to know this part of the country especially Allatoona Pass."

"In 1844, I was a lieutenant in the Third Artillery, and I had returned to my post in Charleston, South Carolina. On the 21st of January 1844, I received from Lieutenant Richard Hammond, at Marietta, Georgia, that which was an intimation from Colonel Churchill, Inspector-General of the Army."

"What brought that about sir?"

"Colonel Churchill had applied for me to assist him in taking depositions in upper Georgia and Alabama. This affair concerned certain losses by Georgia volunteers in Florida of horses and equipment."

"How did those losses occur?"

"The results of our investigation were the losses were by reason of the failure of the United States to provide sufficient forage. Then Congress had made an appropriation."

"What did that have to do with Allatoona Pass, General?"

"On the 4th of February the order came from the Adjutant-General in Washington for me to proceed to Marietta, Georgia, and report to Inspector-General Churchill.234[235] After closing our business at Marietta, Colonel Churchill ordered our detachment to transfer our operations to Bellefonte, Alabama. Colonel Hammond lent me his riding-horse. I rode the distance on horseback and had noted well the topography of the country, especially that about, Kennesaw, Allatoona and the Etowah River. On that occasion, I had stopped some days with a Colonel Lewis Tumlin to see some remarkable Indian mounds on the Etowah River called the Hightower mounds. Remarkable they were and I hope to visit the mounds again while I am here."[236]

"Now I know the story. One never knows what past experiences; no matter how small, or large, will benefit you in the future. Thank you for sharing it, sir."

"You're welcome."

MAY 24, 1864

As General Sherman crosses the Etowah River on May 24, he sees a beautiful, Greek revival white house on a hill, about to fall victim to his troops. At the gate stands an old, black man who stayed behind while the resident family, the Shelmans, fled to safety. Riding up to the gate, General Sherman studies the home. Six Doric columns overlook the Etowah River atop a bluff. Sherman and a fellow officer are met by the elderly slave who is lamenting their arrival, "I sho'ly 'uz glad Miss Cecelia hain't yer tu seed hit wid 'er eyes." Shaking his head, the slave utters the same sentence several more times.

General Sherman echoes, "Miss Cecelia Stovall?"

Nervously, the darkie answers, "Yas sah, but now she uz Ms. Shelman. Married Capt. Shelman in '48."

"General, sir," interrupts a fellow officer, "I believe that there's a Capt. Shelman in the Confederate Army."

General Sherman asks the darkie, "Where is Mrs. Shelman now? Is she home?"

"No sah, she uz away hidin'."

"What is your name, darkie?" asks General Sherman.

"Joe 'uz me."

General Sherman continues to question the aged servant and finds that he is the only one left to take care of Cecelia's home. General Sherman writes a note to Cecelia. "See that she gets this. 'You once said that I would crush an enemy and you pitied my foe. Do you recall my reply? Although many years have passed, my answer is the same. I would ever shield and protect you. That I have done. Forgive all else. I am only a soldier. Wm. T. Sherman.'"[237]

General Sherman disappointed, turns and rides away. He wished to visit with Cecelia. He directs his Aide-de-Camp, Captain Lewis M. Dayton issue an order to make sure that everything that had been taken is replaced and for guards to stay and stand watch until the entire army passes through. General Sherman instructs Joe, Cecelia's faithful servant, "Say to your mistress that she might have remained in her home in safety; that she and her property would have been protected."

"General, how do you know this lady?" asks Major Audenried.

"She is the sister of my old roommate at West Point in 1836. His name is Marcellus Stovall and their father is a wealthy cotton plantation owner in Augusta."

"So you met her in Augusta?"

"No. Marcellus invited her to the Academy to attend some of the dances."

"Oh, you met her at a dance."

"Yes, and who should fall hardest for the dark-eyed Southern beauty? None other than me, William Tecumseh Sherman. I can see her now as she entered the Commencement Ball at West Point on a spring evening in 1836. She was a perfect, innocent Southern belle."

"How did she feel about you, General?"

"Believe it or not, Cecelia and I fell instantly in love, and we embarked on a fiery, secret rendezvous despite our broad cultural differences, and that's all I've got to say about it."

THURSDAY, MAY 26, 1864

The faculty members and their families, the sick cadets, disabled and younger cadets, board a train for Oglethorpe College.[238] At midnight, the remaining cadets of combat age receive a special field order from Gen. Johnston to report to Atlanta. The cadet Corps again gathers their equipment, horses and cannons, and marches to the depot. At the depot, the military activity is electric. The cadets begin loading their pride and joy: two brass cannon with the caisson, battery wagon, limbers, and forge wagon. The cadets also load the saddle horses and draft horses into the livestock cars.

Sherman's army is within gunshot of the Institute as Norman writes home from the depot:

> *I have my small bag of salt in my knapsack. We are leaving the campus and many happy memories. I am a soldier now, and the Corps has orders to go to West Point. All of the disqualified cadets are at Oglethorpe near Milledgeville. Dr. Goldsmith and his wife are moving to Atlanta. I'll write you from West Point. I saw Legare on the field near Resaca. Any word from Polly?*
>
> *Love, Norman*

Upon arriving in Atlanta, Gen. Wayne places the cadet corps in the militia and forwards them to West Point. Upon their arrival at West Point, they join a Confederate garrison. After unloading the cannons and gear, the Corps takes formation and receives new disappointing orders. Looking for martial glory and a fight, they receive orders to guard a wooden bridge in the valley east of the Chattachoochee River instead. It appears that General Sherman is attempting to destroy the railroad bridge which supplies Gen. Johnston's army. This bridge is the main rail line that connects Virginia and Georgia.[239]

JUNE 4, 1864

Buck is leaving the hospital after delivering some fresh vegetables to Betty Gail for the patients when he sees Thomas Dean, and J. M. Hambrick, at the depot. Thomas waves and motions for Buck to stop. Acknowledging their request, Buck pulls his horse over and ties the reins to the nearby hitching post.

Thomas Dean updates Buck, "Looks like two more of our Mason Brothers have enlisted. 'Honest John' Tuggle enlisted last month. He's going to be a guard at the Augusta Arsenal. Ransom Thompson joined on April 24 in the 2nd Regiment Georgia Reserves. Ransom said he is going to be a prison guard at Andersonville. They're the only two that went in last month. Any word from your boy or Legare, Buck?"

Buck shakes his head. "Let's go over to the hotel and sit a spell. Maybe we can get caught up on the upcoming re-election of Mr. Lincoln and the where-abouts of Sherman."

The three friends cross the dusty dirt street and enter the hotel. Jesse Lanford is inside, reading a newspaper with several other patrons.

"Hello, Buck, Thomas, J. M. Got a recent paper to read. Lots in here about General Frémont and that Radical Democracy Party. Come on over and take in on the conversation."

"How is Ol' Abe holding us with the continual onslaught of criticism toward his leadership, if I can use the word leadership," asks Buck.

"Well it looks like the Northern voters are still dissatisfied with the Emancipation Proclamation, the war effort and restrictions on certain of their civil liberties," responds Jesse.

Thomas Dean reacts angrily. "You can bet they're not talking about our civil liberties!"

"Keep reading, Jesse."

"On May 31, one week before the Republican Convention, now renamed the National Union Party, the unhappy Republicans unite in Cleveland. Most of the members of this 'new' party are German-Americans from Missouri. A minority of members is abolitionists from New England. This group of Republicans adopted the name 'Radical Democracy Party.'"[240]

Interrupting, Mr. Hambrick asks, "You mean the Republican Party has changed their name to National what party?"

"The National Union Party according to this article. The new splinter group calls itself the 'Radical Democracy Party.'" Jesse continues, "The Radical Democracy Party nominated General John C. Frémont as their presidential candidate and former Congressman John Cochrane of New York as the Vice Presidential candidate. At the Convention, the delegates ratified their platform ... a continuation of the war without comprise, authorizing federal protection of equal rights and an amendment banning slavery, protection of the rights of free speech, free press, and the writ of habeas corpus, confiscation of Confederate property, enforcement of the Monroe Doctrine, a one-term presidency, and last, integrity and economy in government. Upon accepting the nomination, and anticipating the uniting with the War Democrats, General Frémont resigned his commission in order to campaign against President Lincoln."

"General Frémont won't stand a chance. What he's gonna do is split the Republican vote and then maybe we can get a Copperhead[241] for president," responds Jesse hastily.

Thomas Dean adds, "You're right. The Copperheads would let us live in peace and mind our own business ... free and independent!"

Jesse places the paper on the table for a moment and continues, "Well fellows, I like General Frémont, except he is against slavery. Frémont's a Georgia boy. He was born in Savannah, but he has always been a strong opponent of slavery. He is the founder of the Republican Party and was nominated as the party's first presidential candidate. Lost to James Buchanan though. Next to Lewis and Clark, John Frémont is one of the most famous explorers of the American West. Why, General Frémont is the second rank of explorers to follow Lewis and Clark into the American frontier. And remember in 1850? General Frémont became one of the state's first two senators."[242]

"I remember when Lincoln was elected in '60, Frémont was hoping for an appointment to his cabinet. Instead, Lincoln appointed him minister to France. It said in the paper that Secretary of State William Seward protested because John Frémont was from Georgia and couldn't be trusted if a conflict arose with the South," inserts William Barnett who is with Jesse. He continues, "At the outbreak of the Civil War, President Lincoln appointed John Frémont to Major General in the Union Army. But in, I think late August of '61, while in Missouri; General Frémont proclaimed that all slaves owned by Confederates in Missouri were free. President Lincoln became infuriated by General Frémont's unauthorized action ... and rightfully so. Lincoln feared the Border States would join the Confederate forces and asked Frémont to modify his order. General Frémont refused."

"It was rumored that Postmaster General Montgomery Blair persuaded President Lincoln to relieve General Frémont of command of the Western Department. That's why Frémont is against Lincoln and dislikes Blair!"[243]

Thomas Dean leans back in his chair, placing his right finger on his temple. "I think I have a copy of our local paper where The New York Tribune editor Horace Greeley, wrote an open letter to President Lincoln defending General Frémont. Horace Greeley was critical of the president for neglecting to have slavery the most prevailing issue of the war and for relieving General Frémont. He also accused the president of compromising moral principle for political motives. President Lincoln sternly answered Horace Greeley's open letter by saying, 'My paramount object in this struggle is to save the Union, and is not either to save or destroy slavery. If I could save the Union without freeing any slave, I would do it, and if I could save the Union by freeing all the slaves, I would do it.'"[244]

Changing the subject, Buck asks Jesse, "What about Sherman and Gen. Johnston?"

"Well, it appears on Thursday, according to the latest telegrams and papers, Sherman has Allatoona Pass under his control. He marched his three army corps northeast from New Hope Church toward Allatoona and the Western and Atlantic Railroad. Yesterday, Sherman entered Acworth and Raccoon Bottom. Gen. Johnston got out flanked and could not hold onto New Hope Church. So he withdrew again. We'll see what today brings. Surely to God Johnston can stop Sherman before he gets to Atlanta."[245]

JUNE 9, 1864

After Buck unloads the early summer crops to the hospitals, he and Betty Gail walk over to the depot to purchase the Atlanta Examiner newspaper, but none are left. Anxious to find out the latest on the war and get an update on the National Union Party's convention, Buck asks James Goldsmith, "No more papers?"

"Due to the paper shortage, I am lucky to get five or six copies. Jesse Lanford is here first thing every morning. I think he's over at the hotel with a group of neighbors going over the latest news about the Republican convention."

"Thanks, William. Betty Gail and I'll head over to the hotel." Entering the lobby, Buck and Betty Gail observe about fifteen or so citizens gathered around and talking about the latest news. As they greet everyone, Betty Gail and Buck are asked by several neighbors if they have heard from Norman or Legare. "Not a word. Worried to death about those two youngsters."

Thomas Browning, the postmaster, shakes Buck's and Betty Gail's hands. "We're praying for them all, Buck."

It's apparent that the Jernigans do not want to discuss the topic of the children. Talk returns to the current political events. They join the conversation on Lincoln's nomination by the National Union Party.

Jesse Lanford and William Sheppard are discussing other possible presidential candidates. "General Butler is well respected by the War Democrats. Vice President Hannibal Hamlin is strong among the Radical Republicans."

William Sheppard tells the crowd, "I heard that General Grant received a newspaper endorsement and Treasury Secretary Salmon Chase has strong support among the extreme abolitionists and some Radical Republicans."

Jesse replies, "This article states, 'During the month of February, Secretary Chase attempted a clandestine campaign against President Lincoln, but was exposed. Then, after being exposed, Secretary Chase, on March 10th, announced he is not a candidate for the presidential nomination.'"

"The old backstabbing of politics is always there," snaps Buck as everyone laughs.

Jesse continuing to read, "All of these candidates express no interest in running against Lincoln on the National Union Party ticket."

"Can't beat a President in office when there's a war," retorts Buck again.

"You're right Buck," replies another listener.

"This newspaper gives a great summary of the whole mess at the conventions. 'On June 7, 1864, the National Union Party opened their nominating convention in Baltimore. The opening day was devoted to the usual preliminaries of the platform formation. The vote of the delegates was set for the next day. The widespread criticism of Lincoln's handling of the war and the outrage of the conservative forces of the North due to the Emancipation Proclamation made President Lincoln's re-election appear dim.'"

"I know the man is going to be re-elected! If he could win the first time he is going to win this time. He's too strong," Buck says with conviction.

"Listen to what the article says," interjects Jesse. "A few War Democrats joined the National Union Party convention hopefully to form a new alliance. President Lincoln supporters thwarted various insurgencies and secured control of the convention proceedings.'"

"See there. I told you he was smart," replies Buck.

Jesse continues reading, "Although of no great strength, the challenge by General Frémont, for the Presidency caused President Lincoln some distress. The National Union Party platform called for the pursuit of the war until the Confederacy surrenders unconditionally, a constitutional amendment for the abolition of slavery, aid to disabled Union veterans, continued European neutrality, enforcement of the Monroe Doctrine, encouragement of immigration, and construction of a transcontinental railroad."

"They don't want much, do they? Killed our youth, trying to set our slaves free. Take away our State Rights. They'll be down here digging our graves before this war's over," shouts someone from the crowd.

"This paragraph says the convention gave the President high praise for the use of Negro troops and his management of the war. On the first ballot on June 8, President Lincoln receives all of the delegate votes except Missouri's 22, which were cast for General Grant. Immediately after the initial vote, Missouri re-cast their votes to President Lincoln, giving President Lincoln unanimous approval by the delegates."[246]

Jesse continues, "Missouri was suppose to be with us, but the Yankees took over their state. Now this is interesting. Vice President Hannibal Hamlin has always been a loyal supporter of President Lincoln and desired the re-nomination as Vice President. President Lincoln remains neutral as far as the Vice Presidential choice, leaving it to the convention to select. The convention delegates, symbolically and strategically, feel the Vice President should be a War Democrat. After much debate over a Vice Presidential candidate, the convention delegates nominate Andrew Johnson, the Union military governor of Tennessee."

Scratching his head, Buck says to the crowd, "Why Andrew Johnson is both a Southern Unionist and a War Democrat. He'll be real tough on us if anything happens to Lincoln."

"Well, Buck," Jesse says, "Andrew Johnson won the nomination on the first ballot. Secretary of Treasury Chase tendered his resignation to President Lincoln, and the President accepted it."[247]

Maintaining the conversation, William Guess looks at his friend Buck while shaking his head. "So it looks like the Yankees are gonna have to choose between Frémont and Lincoln. At least until the real Democrats hold their convention in August."

Buck seizes the moment and says, "President Lincoln realizes the Union servicemen are an important segment of his base of support. I see where President Lincoln advised his generals to allow the soldiers to return home to vote."

THURSDAY, JUNE 9, 1864

The Convention president, William Dennison, personally notified President Lincoln of his nomination for president. Responding to the delegates of the convention who had gathered at the White House, Lincoln said, "Thank you for your vote of confidence. Our next order of business is to call for a constitutional amendment prohibiting slavery. This amendment of the Constitution, now proposed, is a fitting and necessary conclusion to the final success of the Union cause. I must remind the South; you have been given the opportunity to desist in secession without the overthrow of your institution, but have failed to respond."

James Goldsmith gets the news of the election over the telegraph. "Lincoln wins the nomination!" Taking the message to the hotel across the street, he announces the news. Samuel Alexander, the hotelkeeper, Buck, and William Sheppard were having some fresh cotton bean coffee. "Well, I don't know much good any of this is going to do us," remarks Samuel to the news.

"If McClellan had won," Buck said, "we'd still be in the same fix. I'd rather drink coffee this morning than talk about useless Union politics. Nothing we can do about who's elected president. No matter what the politicians and reporters say, this war is going to be fought in our front yards—and real soon."

Part II
the war rages on

During the course of the Civil War there are no less than 549 different theatres of battle in Georgia. No State in the South suffers so severely as Georgia. She places in the field more than a hundred and twenty thousand soldiers which is twenty thousand more than the voting population at the beginning of the war and looses ten percent of her population. The most common diseases are diarrhea and dysentery, "Camp fever" which included typhoid, typhus, pneumonia, measles, consumption and smallpox.

The taxable wealth of the State in 1867 is more than four hundred and eight–one million dollars less than it was in 1861 representing a loss of more than three-fourths of the State's wealth. After the reconstruction period, all the State has to show, in return for the treasure that has been squandered by carpetbag politicians, is a few poorly equipped railroads that had been built on the State's credit.

The seizures of horses and mules far exceeded the amount needed by General Sherman. Those that are brought in are sorted and the best replaces the weaker, broken-down animals in the wagon trains. The culling of horseflesh goes on constantly so that at the end of the march to the sea, the Union army had better animals that it did when it left Atlanta. According to General Sherman, he had no doubt the State of Georgia had lost by the Union operations 15,000 first-rate mules. Based on the Official Records of the War of the Rebellion, when General Sherman started his march to Savannah, the Union army had about 5,000 head of cattle and arrives with over 10,000. The Union army consumes mostly turkeys, chickens, sheep, hogs, and the cattle of the country. Upon General Sherman's arrival in Savannah the Union army had one beef cow for every six men. This gives an indication of just how rich the area of Georgia had been which he passed through.

THE MESSENGERS

JUNE 15, 1864

Congressman Joshua Hill and Emily are at their home in Madison when there's a knock on the front door. Upon answering the door, the butler finds a wounded Confederate soldier supported with a homemade crutch. Accompanying the soldier is a man and a woman. All of whom are strangers. "Kin I'se help ye?" asks the butler.

The older strange man asks, "Is this the home of Congressman Hill?"

"Ya'as sah. Dis 'uz ez hones'." [Yes, sir. It is his home.]

"We have some information we must share with Congressman and Mrs. Hill regarding their son Legare, if they are available."

"Yo name sir?"

"I'm Rooster."

"We are Mrs. Polly Hill's parents."

"I'se git 'im. Wait 'lease." [I will get him. Wait please.] Shortly the butler returns, "Pleas' cum in."

As they enter, Congressman and Mrs. Hill are rushing to the foyer to meet their in-laws and Rooster. Congressman Hill and Emily immediately observe the heartbroken human forms entering their foyer. Buck and Betty Gail with a disconsolate demeanor look at their friends Joshua and Emily. Emily places her hands over her cheeks and mouth and begins to sob. "Please don't tell me my baby is dead! Please tell me Legare is alive."

Joshua draws Emily close and is unable to speak. Betty Gail walks to Emily and Buck extends his hand to Joshua and clasps his hand in his own. Then in a soft reverent voice, Buck breaks the sad news to Joshua and Emily, "I wish for all of us that I could turn the clock back. Legare is gone."

Emily begins to tremble, nearly falling to the floor. "My boy. My baby boy is gone! Dead. Killed by the Yankees!"

Joshua and Betty Gail assist her to the couch in the parlor with Rooster and Buck following close behind. The butler, also in tears, retires to the kitchen and returns immediately with water. Emily takes several sips and begins to somewhat compose herself.

"When did this all happen, Buck?" Joshua sounds as if he's nearly overcome with grief. Joshua closes his eyes briefly before turning back to his friends.

"Rooster came by early this morning and told us the terrible news. We immediately went to the depot and boarded the train for Madison."

"Please, Buck, you and Rooster have a seat. Rooster please tell us ... tell us everything, where Legare was killed and what happened."

Holding tightly to his crutch, Rooster clears his throat as best he can, lowers his head for a moment, and then looks at his friend's parents. The words momentarily stick in his throat as he fights to control his own emotions. "Well sir, Legare died like a true patriot at the hands of our enemy. He was killed instantly and suffered no pain. It happened above Cass Station on May 19." He pauses for a few seconds to regain his composure. "He was a true friend and a true patriot. I'll sorely miss him, just as you will."

Joshua holds Emily closer. "Thank you, Rooster. We appreciate the effort it must have taken for you to get here with this news." Stricken with sorrow, Emily erupts into wails of anguish.

With tears on his cheeks, Rooster remorsefully says, "Congressman and Mrs. Hill, I'm deeply sorry."

Rooster reaches in his shirt pocket and hands Joshua a sheet of paper and three small envelopes. "I removed these buttons from the uniform you made for Legare. His wedding band is in the other envelope along with several locks of his hair. This last one is a letter he wrote to Polly the night before he was killed. It was ready to be placed in the mail. I thought about bringing a handkerchief Polly made for him, but I know he would want to be buried with the handkerchief next to his heart. That is where I placed the handkerchief ... right next to his heart." Rooster struggles to maintain his composure. "Legare had given the beautiful scarf Polly made for him to Norman Jernigan. They accidentally met in Resaca at the Oostanaula River. Shortly after that Legare was killed ... the only person killed near Cass Station that day. It was when our unit was in retreat to Cassville on May 19th. We did not have time to properly bury Legare in the cemetery due our orders to immediately withdraw to a new position."

"On that sheet of paper I have written down where McCurdy and some other soldiers and I placed his body. John Dent and Alonzo send their deepest sympathy as well."

"Congressman Hill, if there's anything I can do for you or your family please let me know. My address is on the paper showing you where we placed Legare's body." After pausing several seconds, he says, "I must go now."

Betty Gail stands and walks over to Rooster. "Our home is your home, Rooster. Your thoughtfulness for our breaking hearts will never be forgotten." She kisses him on the cheek. Buck shakes his hand tightly and squeezes his shoulder with the other hand. Joshua stands, with pain in his eyes and unable to speak, likewise takes Rooster's hand and places it between both of his and nods.

Rooster walks over to Mrs. Hill and takes her hand, "God bless you all, Mrs. Hill. My heart and sympathy is with you."

The butler escorts Rooster to the front door and hands him a sack containing several biscuits and ham.

"Good day, sah, bless ye en be safe," says the butler as he opens the door.

"Thank you." Rooster makes his way down the stairs with his homemade crutch, biscuits with ham and limps away.

"Buck, if you don't mind, come with me to my study. I suggest we depart on the first train in the morning for Savannah."

"By all means. I checked the schedule and the earliest one leaves at 8:35 in the morning."

"If you will bear with me a few minutes, I may need your help. I must write to James R. Crews, the Superintendent of the West Point Railroad." In a broken voice, "He can assist me in locating my son's remains. We want him buried in our family plot in the cemetery near our home."

Taking a pen and paper Congressman Hill writes, "You have doubtless heard of the cruel affliction this abominable war is bringing to my hearthstone. I can't help thinking this is more than I merit. My poor boy met his death on Thursday morning, the 19th of May, as I am informed, about 2 miles above Cass Station." He pauses and glances up at Buck. "Buck read me the note from Rooster and I will write the specifics in the letter."

Buck takes Rooster's note and reads, "He was killed beyond Ben Johnson's house on the road leading from Cassville to Kingston, about one half mile from the road."

Changing the wording slightly Congressman Hill continues, "He is said to have been brought by some of his comrades nearer the Railroad."[248]

Then Congressman Hill continues with the directions as Buck reads, "His body is left by the side of the public road, somewhere about or near a deserted cabin or perhaps nearer still to a small frame house near the Railroad. No one else was killed."

In closing Joshua writes, "His name is Hugh Legare Hill, age eighteen years with a fair complexion. His hair is light brown and thick and inclined to curl a little but was thin. He is about 5 feet 8 1/2 inches in height, trim, erect figure eyelashes long and dark. He had been sick and was rather thin in flesh, clothing all marked with his initials & name, thus 'H. L. Hill,' pants dark gray, Jeans-new (nearly) & lighter gray jacket, plaid domestic shirt-name on the front. His death wound was received in a retreat and entered at the back of his head."As he writes tears drop from his eyes and stain the letter. He takes his handkerchief to soak the moisture from the paper. "I write these particulars in the hope that, with the shifting scenes through which we are passing, you may see some chance to ascertain the fate of the my son's body, whether it was interred by some kind human or was left to waste away by the action of the elements. My object is to recover his remains-as perfectly as may be. Should any opportunity offer for you to obtain for me this covert information, I know you will take pleasure in receiving it for me. Respectfully, Joshua Hill."[249]

Joshua leans back in his chair. His eyes and nose are red and damp. Then he learns over and adds a postscript,

"I forgot to state that my son had a beautiful set of regular and white teeth."[250] He seals the letter in an envelope and hands it to Buck. "Please have the butler take this to the post office right away."

⚬

Buck, Betty Gail, Joshua and Emily arrive at the Savannah depot around two o'clock in the afternoon. Buck arranges to retrieve their baggage and procure a carriage. When all the bags are loaded, he gives the driver directions to Polly's house. Emotionally exhausted Emily and Betty Gail are clutching handkerchiefs in one hand and holding tight to their husband's arms with the other.

"Our biggest concern is whether or not Polly will be home when we arrive," Buck says. "If she is, poor Polly will know why we are here." Buck stares at the passing scenery a moment.

Joshua nods distractedly. "I hope she is home too and like you said she's bound to know why we're here."

For the first time in his life, Buck dreads seeing his daughter. Being the bearer of the bad news of Legare's death would be one of the hardest tasks he'd ever done. The news will break her heart.

The carriage ride proceeds toward Polly's for what seems like an eternity. As the driver maneuvers the last turn in the road, Polly's house comes into view.

Approaching the turn-about, Emily and Betty Gail begin to feel the emotional strain of their grim duty. Tears flow from their swollen eyes when they see Al in the front yard working in the small flower garden. As the carriage enters the turn-about, Al stands to see who might be approaching. He finally recognizes it is the Hills and the Jernigans and rushes to the carriage. "Mornin' Mistuh Hill Ma'am Emily. Mornin' Mr. Jernigan, Ma'am Betty Gail. Miss Polly no says uh comin.'"

"She isn't expecting us." Buck jumps down from the wagon, his hat in his hand. "Is she, home Al?"

"No, suh, Jess, Miss Polly en baby at de hospital. I tink be bac' soon."

"Where might Tot be?"

"Tot in bac' workin' herbs."

"Take the luggage inside please and fetch Tot."

Buck and the family follow Al as he takes the luggage inside. Then he goes to the back to get Tot. Al expresses his concerns to Tot. This visit has to do with a major crisis, and he suspects it has to do with "Mistuh LeGree." Hastily Al and Tot enter the parlor, and Tot, looking somewhat puzzled, says. "Mornin'. Wehkum. Eb'rt'ing al' right?" [Good morning. Welcome. Everything all right?]

Attempting to hold back their emotions, Emily and Betty Gail walk over to Al and Tot and Betty Gail explains, "We have sad news for Polly and you, but we will wait and tell you the news when Polly comes home."

Nervously Tot answers, "Yaas' ma'am. Uh want tea or coffee suh, ma'am."[Yes ma'am. Would you like some tea or coffee sir, ma'am?]

"Thank you, Tot. We will have some sassafras tea," replies Betty Gail.

Buck looks at everyone. "I believe I will go outside and wait for Polly. It will be better for her to see me when she arrives rather than when she opens the door and finds all of us inside. When she arrives and I speak to her a few minutes, then y'all come outside." Not waiting for a reply, Buck departs and nervously sits on the stairs and begins his painful wait.

He watches a bright redbird scratching the leaves in the fresh flower garden looking for a quick meal. Suddenly he sees a familiar carriage heading in his direction. He recognizes the carriage. It's Polly, little Joshua and Jesse. Buck's eyes begin to tear as Jesse points toward him and looks at Polly. Polly stands in the carriage as Al rushes the carriage to a stop in front of the house. Buck walks slowly down the stairs and stands next to the carriage as Polly leaps to the ground.

Buck grabs Polly and hugs her with all his might! "I'm sorry honey. I'm so sorry honey." They both begin to weep.

"I know why you are here, Pa. I see it in your eyes. Legare is gone! I haven't heard from him in weeks. My letters go unanswered. I hate Joe Brown! I hate Joe Brown! He ordered my dear husband to his death! He killed my husband!" Polly begins to sob even more deeply. Betty Gail, Congressman Hill and Emily emerge from the house and come to Polly's side.

Emily and Betty Gail embrace Polly. Betty Gail whispers, "I love you." Betty Gail, then unable to speak, whispers, "All of our hearts are broken."

With tears on his cheeks, Joshua embraces Polly. "We've both lost a dear person, Polly. Our hearts have been ripped from our chests. We must remember he died as a true patriot, a soldier and a very loving husband and father. Your memory of our son and your husband will always be one of youth. He will never grow old in our memory or yours."

Jesse is holding little Joshua who is becoming very upset. He breaks away from Jesse and rushes to his mother. Tugging at her dress, he looks up to his weeping mother, "Mama. Mama, why you crying?"

Polly picks up little Joshua and squeezes him tightly. In a choking voice, Polly whispers in little Joshua's ear, "Daddy is gone to heaven. Your sweet daddy has gone to heaven."

Al and Tot are watching from the front door. Tot takes her apron, wipes her eyes, takes Al's arm, and says to Al, "Oh no, Mistuh LeGree dead. Oh LeGree dead! Oh poor Miss Polly. Her man is dead." Tot and Al go to Polly. Tot also embraces Polly, "Muhself don' kno' wah fuh to say, Miss Polly. Muhself sad wid you. Muhself en Al h'aa't' bauk'up fuh." [I don't know what to say, Miss Polly. I am as sad as you are. My and Al's hearts are broken too!]

Joshua turns to Jesse, "Go and tell Richard and Charlotte that we are here. Avoid telling them our cause. Just say we must see them."

Jesse wipes his eyes. "Yaas' shur Mistuh. Hill."

Polly looks around at the beautiful day. "The birds are singing, the bees are busy with the flowers, the air is calm … I feel like the angel of death is no longer waiting to deliver me a message. Let's go inside."

Emily offers to take little Joshua from Polly, but he reacts to the disturbing emotional event, turns away from Emily and clings to his mother.

❦

Several days later Buck, Emily and Joshua are on the train returning to their homes. Betty Gail is staying with Polly and little Joshua for the time being. Buck reminds Joshua, "When you hear from Mr. Crews, remember I'll be honored to assist you in any way to recover Legare's remains."

"I will call on you, Buck. Thank you."

Soon the Hills are standing alone on the train platform in Madison. Buck sees the attendant summon a carriage for them as he watches from the passenger car. The train slowly pulls away and heads toward Stone Mountain. Buck hopes tomorrow does not bring him similar news of Norman since he hasn't heard from him for some time.

❦

On the beautiful summer Tuesday, June 21, 1864, Maj. Capers assembles the Cadet Corps to present a Confederate battle flag, fabricated by the ladies of Marietta. Maj. Capers informs the cadets, "Miss Mary E. Jones of Burke County, Georgia proposed to make a battle flag for GMI.[251] However, before she made the trip to Marietta for a formal presentation, our cadet corps moved to West Point, so she mailed the flag to me for presentation. I will read you her stirring note.

"Cadets: A few weeks ago I might have had the pleasure of making this presentation in person, but the present hour finds you marshaled for the conflict with the invaders of our country. Our Cause is not that of *conquest* or *power* but of *rights* sacred to freemen and to which we were born heirs. The flag which we once loved, and which was honored and respected by every nation is no longer the flag of the 'noble and the free.' But I present you with the banner of the Starry Cross. And as you unfurl this new flag to the face of the foe, let its significant motto nerve every arm, and fire every bosom to the contest, until every hostile foot shall be driven from our soil, or until every mountain top in our land shall become an altar of sacrifice."[252]

The Cadets Corps Adjutant Jack Crutchfield orders "Present Arms." Maj. Capers presents the flag to Cadet Color Sergeant George Coleman, who in turn "staffs" the flag.

"Order arms" shouts Cadet Crutchfield and gives his acceptance response. "Sir, I have no words adequate to express our admiration of this beautiful banner, the battle-flag of our beloved country … It is additionally dear to us, presented, through the hands our worthy and honored leader, to the Georgia Cadets, by one of the fairest and noblest daughters of the 'Empire State."[253] Return to her, Sir, our grateful salute, and tell her that by this patriotic gift, the handiwork of her skill, and by the noble sentiments with which it is presented, she has entwined around our hearts a sweet remembrance of herself, to be cherished forever, and, as the forest oak protects the entwining vines, so by us will the memory of her favor be held in perpetual honor.

"In the day of battle, in that hour when dastards quail and tremble and the proud exultantly hurrah; in that hour when Southern blood is poured on Southern soil, a free libation on the altar of our country's honor, then as comrades in line with the embattled hosts of Southern chivalry, the proud colors of the star-decked cross. Unfurled to the foeman's gaze, shall at once remind us of our homes and our altars, and of her, fair queen of our ranks, whose banner bids us breast the shock and quit ourselves like men."[254]

※

Buck's first stop on his rounds in town is at the Post Office. Thomas Browning, the Postmaster,[255] sees him coming and retrieves a letter. "Looks like a letter from your son."

Buck rushes forward as Thomas gladly hands him the letter. "Thanks, Betty Gail is back home from Savannah as is anxious to hear from Norman." He opens it and begins to read.

> *The hot and humid days of June are somewhat less bothersome than normal since we are camping on the river. We have plenty to do at West Point, Georgia. We still train the soldiers in the camps, instructing them the same as at Camp McDonald. The entire Corps is taking good care of the horses since there are no stable hands with us at West Point. The horses are as important as our weapons. We walk and exercise them every day, and the artillery units are drilling every day. Once the soldiers in the Confederate camp learn the basic drilling and manual of arms, the best ones begin training in the use of the artillery.*
>
> *My friend, Cadet Tom Bussey, is always cleaning his musket just like he did on campus. He no doubt has the cleanest and brightest musket*

in the entire Confederacy! Our new cadet friends, Luckier, Williams, Gordon, Adams, and Lamar are new enrollees to GMI this month. So we are drilling them as well. One good piece of news is they are from West Point and their parents have been bringing the Corps goodies from home. The locals are very nice to us. They allow us to sleep in the sheds if it is raining. Most of the cadets are able to ask their families to send or bring a waiter. However, there's now the chance they'll escape to the Yankees. None have left yet, but if the Yankees get too near, I think they'll escape to the Yankee side. Tomorrow, I think I'll be able to do a little fishing in the river. Any word from Polly? Love, Norman

"How is he?" asks Thomas.

"Everything is good," replies Buck as he tips his hat and smiles. He folds the letter, rushes to his wagon, takes the reins of the horse and heads home so Betty Gail can read that their son is doing well.

❧

Norman is suddenly awakened for assembly Sunday morning, July 3rd by the "Long Roll" of the drum. He and Paul quickly dress and take to formation immediately. Maj. Capers is waiting when the corps is formed. He begins reading the orders from the Adjutant General.

"The Cadet Corps of GMI is to report to Gen. Gustavus Smith, commander of the Georgia Militia at Turner's Ferry on the Chattahoochee near Mableton."

Norman looks at Paul. "Looks like we're headed out again."

Maj. Capers then orders the cadet corps to strike camp immediately and prepare to report to Gen. Smith. Upon dismissal, Norman and his friends give a great shout and toss their caps into the air displaying their elevated morale.

Rushing back to their quarters, Norman sits at his desk and looks across at Paul. "We'll show those Yankees just like we did in Resaca."

"I can't wait," replies Paul.

Early the next morning, Norman and the Corps break camp, secure their weapons, horses and cannons and march to the depot at West Point. Monday morning, the cadet Corps reaches the Atlanta depot. Norman and Paul are put in charge of unloading the horses while other cadets unload cannons, caissons and limbers. Norman places the horses in the shade as the July heat bears down. They begin the nearly eight mile march to Turner's Ferry, close to the front lines. Although Norman is in excellent physical condition, the dry summer and July heat begins to wear him down. The Georgia clay dust from the roads turns their perspiration red. Norman talks as little as possible so the dust will not make nostrils and throat even more dry. He sees that most all of corps equipment and clothing have turned red from the dust. The poor horses, also red, are not much better off, sweating and snorting just as the cadets.

Norman notices that the closer the cadet corps gets to Turner's Ferry, the louder the rumble of the cannon fire becomes. He looks over to Paul. "This cannonading reminds me a little of Resaca."

"Yes it does. It just keeps getting closer and louder."

Finally, just before dark, the corps arrives at Turner's Ferry and camps in the woods near a creek. Norman goes to the creek, undresses, throws his clothes into the creek and then wades in. He lies down in the creek and splashes the cool water on his head. After relaxing a while he sits up and cups his hand filling them with water. Then he inhales the water through his nose and the blows it out attempting to remove more of the red dust from his body. After bathing and hanging his uniform to dry, he removes a clean change of clothing from his knapsack and reports for guard duty.

Norman is on duty until one o'clock in the morning, and all is quiet for the entire night. Even though the cadet corps is about four miles from enemy lines, he keeps a vigilant watch while on duty.[256]

Early Wednesday morning, Norman has a hasty breakfast of bacon and hardtack. Afterwards, he and Paul, with their company, gather at the edge of the woods.

They are told to leave the horses and cannons behind. Immediately upon forming with their company, they are given the order to "double-quick" down the dirt road to the river. Placing his weapon in both hands Norman follows Cadet Commander Baker and Maj. Capers as they lead the corps to the river. Arriving at a pontoon bridge Norman is one of the first to begin crossing the river.

All of the sudden, cannon fire whizzes over the heads of the cadets from the federal artillery. As Paul and Norman are crossing the pontoons, shells begin hitting in the river, soaking the cadets and their equipment with water. It appears that the movement of the cadets has stirred up a dust cloud, alerting the Yankee's to their position.[257] Holding onto their equipment and encouraging each other, Norman and Paul begin a cover fire to protect the other cadets who are uniformly crossing the pontoon. Miraculously everyone makes it to across the river safely.

Almost out of breath they take cover in a ditch. Paul turns toward Norman. "You didn't flinch at all from that artillery fire Norman."

"Didn't have time to flinch. I was too busy running."

"Oh," replies Paul.

Once over the river and a quarter mile across an open field, Norman spots friendly troops. "Paul, there's the Confederate unit we're suppose to hook up with waving for us."

The impression of the cadets' vigor, style and precision causes a round of applause and rebel yells from the Confederate soldiers as the cadets join them in the trench line.

One of the Confederate soldiers slaps Norman on his back." Good show there, son. Didn't let those Yanks scare you at all."

Norman smiles. "Thanks. We were just lucky none of us got hit."

Settling in along the line of ditches, cadets Anderson, Luckie, Good, and Edmund Jordan are again in line with the fellow company cadets Paul and Norman. Shortly, the cadet corps Commander Baker comes by see that everyone is all right and that their powder is dry. "Let's show them Resaca ten times over!" exclaims Cadet Baker.

"How about fifty times over, sir," retorts Luckie.

"You got it!" replies Cadet Baker as he departs to finish his troop inspection.[258]

Norman looks toward the sky. "No clouds again and there's not even a slight breeze. It's gonna be another hot one."

"I think you are right, Norman, and there's no shade," replies Paul. A shot is heard as a bit of dirt scatters near Paul's head.

"Better keep low, Paul, those Yankee sharpshooters will be taking a shot at us whenever they can." As the day grows hotter, Norman detects a subtle odor in the air, emerging from the ditches. "Is that what I think it is, Paul?"

"It smells like stale urine." Peering down the line, "Look Norman, these guys are urinating and defecating in the trenches right where they are. All that fellow is doing is taking a handful of dirt and covering it up."

Norman lies back against the wall of the ditch and with a disgusting look reminds Paul, "Stay away from those soldiers and that area unless you want to get sick. Remember the sanitation classes at GMI? That is not what we want to do."

The random fire by the Yankee sharpshooters is a constant threat. Every now and then, Paul or Norman peers through the logs and are able to get a shot off. With high anticipation throughout the day for an assault, the cadets utilize their time cleaning their muskets and assuring all implements are in order for rapid reloading. All during the day and night on Wednesday and Thursday, there's steady fire from the Yankee's with very little to shoot at for the Confederates and Cadets. Finally, on the night of the 8th, after receiving a report that the Yankees are crossing at Isham's Ford, the cadet Corps moves approximately two miles on the east side of the river to be in support of the Carswell's Militia Brigade with Schley's Militia close by.

"I have never been this dirty in my life," says Paul. "I wish I could have a waiter like some of these other cadets to keep me a clean set of uniforms handy. A waiter would give me more time to shoot a Yankee from these ditches."

"It would be nice, I guess," replies Norman. "My family is not wealthy enough to provide me a waiter." Later that evening as the Union cannons continue to fire, Norman tells Paul, "Think about it. This cannonading is awesome at night. Watching the fiery tail of the shells from here is almost like celebrating the 4th of July ... not exactly what I expected on the 4th however!"[259]

"It is a beautiful sight, but it is also a deadly one to watch and wonder who will die from it," muses Paul.

⁂

HDQRS. MILITARY DIVISION OF THE MISSISSIPPI
In the Field near Chattahoochee
July 8, 1864
General SCHOFIELD, Ruff's Station:

It is all-important I should know as soon as possible the general topography on the other side of the river, as to the practicability of the roads in every direction, especially toward Stone Mountain and Decatur. If you can catch a few people who ought to know all about it, send them to me. I will go to the extreme right today. General Rousseau will start from Decatur for Opelika to-morrow, and General Stoneman may feign down as far as Campbellton. I think the railroad bridge was burned last night. No other news.

W. T. SHERMAN,
Major General, Commanding.[260]

General McPherson notifies General Sherman, "We notice a good deal of flutter in the enemy's camps to-day, troops and wagons moving rapidly east and north. Gen. Johnston sees I threaten Decatur and Stone Mountain."[261]

General Sherman grows concerned about a report that five hundred men, a Confederate Texas Regiment near Acworth, is threatening the railroad. He is depending on this northern railroad as his main supply line, "a slender road of life." Around 9:30 in the cool evening on Saturday July 9, he sends a dispatch to General Kenner Garrard.

"Increase your forces at McAfee's Bridge. You are to prevent the Confederate Texas raiders from using the bridge to re-cross the Chattahoochee River and destroy the railroad."[262]

General Sherman sends a message to General McPherson. "At the right time I will leave Generals Stoneman and McCook to cover the front, and cross all the balance of the army and advance it's right on or near Peach tree (sic) Creek, and the left (you) swing toward Stone Mountain Gen. Johnston will be found to occupy his redoubts about Atlanta, Stone Mountain and Decatur."[263]

BRAGG'S DECEIT

Dr. George Washington Maddox is in charge of Dr. Hamilton's hospital in Stone Mountain, next to the railroad depot. More sick and wounded soldiers arrive daily for treatment. Dr. Maddox is also using his home as a hospital. It is located a couple of blocks away from the Georgia railroad. Betty Gail and the ladies of the churches are getting busier since soldiers are retreating from General Sherman's army.

Fresh vegetables are delivered to the depot by the women from their farms and divided into baskets of fresh vegetables, berries, peaches, apples, sweet potatoes. Then they depart for one of the three churches in Stone Mountain: the Baptist, the Methodist and Presbyterian and the hospitals.

The doctors direct the ladies to treat most of the illnesses with one of the sovereign panaceas, either whiskey, quinine or turpentine. As each patient finishes his meal, an orderly changes the stained and ill-smelling dressings. Even with their best attempts, wounds continue to sour; growing more painful and the moans become louder. Betty Gail and the young house maidens are the only blissful respite to these miserable conditions. Only those who are unable to awaken cannot consume the nourishment and comforting smiles from the young maidens. With tenderness, they cleanse the wounds of the ailing and dying.

A dying young soldier takes Betty Gail's hand, "Please ma'am, I know I'm dying. My pa is dead from the war. I don't want my ma to be lost and not know where I am. Please write her for me and let her know where I'm buried so she will not be lost as well."

"I'll fetch a pencil and paper and you can write her and I'll mail it for you."

"I can't write and ma can't read or write. Just put her name on the envelope and mail it to Dalton. She'll get it and have someone read it to her."

Betty writes as the dying soldier speaks his last loving words to his loving mother. She lays the pencil and letter aside. Then she holds his hand until she can no longer feel his pulse and the dying young man slowly drifts into a peaceful and eternal silence.

In the rear of Dr. Maddox's hospital is the whiskey-still for the three hospitals. The slaves are distilling whiskey by the barrel. The fires are ablaze day and night, producing a good barrel daily of either peach brandy or corn whiskey.

The shrill whistle of the train signals that passengers, freight, wounded, dying and dead are arriving at the depot. As the train stops, the hospital staff is somber, afraid that loved ones or neighbors may be among the casualties. Most of the wounds involve the head and the upper limbs. Climbing on board to assist the wounded, Betty Gail fortunately finds no dead among this transport. As the aids unload the hospital car she looks out and sees a wagon approaching the hospital carrying several more wounded soldiers. She hurries to meet the wagon as the horses are tied down. Soldiers with bloody bandages fabricated from their torn clothing cover the gashing wounds. Several slaves come out to transport the sick and wounded into the hospital.

Betty Gail holds the door open as four slaves carry the poor dead soldier to an adjoining wagon for transport to the local cemetery. The soldier still has the horrible smelling bandage with dried blood covering his wound. Betty Gail nods a "Thank you" to the local preachers[264] and a burial group which accompanies him to the cemetery then she walks over to the post office to mail his letter as she had promised.

"Good morning, Mr. Goldsmith."

"Good morning, Hiram and Martha. I see you are on time as usual to sort out the vegetables and meat for the hospitals."

"Yes sir," replies Hiram. "Folks around here have been very support-ive of the hospitals. Fortunately, the crops are plentiful and the livestock healthy." Hiram and Martha Tweedle are in charge of separating the food which is delivered to the depot. The community trusts them to allocate the supply to the churches and hospitals for the staff and the patients.

❧

After breakfast Buck and Betty Gail are sitting in front of the fireplace. "Buck the news from Norman is not coming as often as it use to. I worry about him getting involved in this war as a cadet with the state militia."

"I worry with you and without you. Paper is in short supply, and I know he's going to get involved in more than training soldiers, especially since they had that skirmish in Resaca. And Polly is in Savannah alone and does not want to come back home right now. Sometimes I think maybe we should move there with her, but I know she won't stand for it." Betty Gail puts down her mending, pulls her chair closer to Buck and places his hand in hers.

"Buck, she's always been independent minded. Her last letter said she is doing fine. It seems Richard is taking good care of her. Tot, Al and Jesse are loyal to her as well. Fortunately Legare left her means of support, and she has a good house to raise our grandchild in. We just have to pray for both of them. I've grown older quicker since Legare got killed." Betty Gail begins to cry and takes her apron to wipe her tears away.

Buck squeezes her hand tightly and he turns to hug and comfort her. "My mind is spinning with the same thoughts. We just have to hope and pray that there are no further tragedies in our family."

Betty Gail regains her composure and begins to stare at the edge of the fireplace, "Buck there's a gap forming between the edge of the fireplace and the fake wall." Buck gets up from his chair and walks over to the area Betty Gail points to. She follows close behind. They inspect the gap closely. "If someone else notices that gap it may give them a clue that something's not right," she says.

"Yep, the wood has dried from the heat of the fire and shrunk back. I've got some more of the same wood in the barn. "Running his hand along the wall Buck makes a decision, "I'll make molding to cover the gap from the floor to the ceiling on both sides then go over the mantle and down the other side and tie it all together. I'm glad you saw that. It could have gotten worse with time. Also, I know you won't forget, but remember if something happens to me, I buried our gold at the bottom of the fourth fence post to the left of the back gate. Just the two of us know about where it is buried. I know our valuables and canned goods will be safe behind these two fake walls. I'll find Isaac and get started on repairing the gap."

"Well, we are at war and the war is gonna get closer to us."

"Yep, I'm already worried about killing and burning. Governor Brown needs to come to his senses and make peace. There's no way to hide the livestock."

Betty Gail nods in agreement and starts to go back to her mending. Suddenly, she looks up at him. "Probably the best approach is to turn them loose in the woods. Our county voted against secession, so maybe the Yankees will appreciate us even more since we are flying the Union flag. Sally and I are canning more of our vegetables and fruits today and tomorrow."

"Isaac and I'll try and find another good hiding place for the extra. Don't offer any extras to the church or neighbors. As far as the meat goes, there's plenty of wild game, squirrel, rabbit, deer, and a few bear. Meat's no problem. In the fall we'll have plenty of pecans and chestnuts and wintertime, we can grow greens."

Later in the morning, Isaac and Betty Gail are in town purchasing canning supplies while Sally is at the farm preparing the food for canning. "Best git mo' powder des in case bandits cum 'round. Des a worsen den de Yankees."

Betty Gail replies, "We are going to do our best to survive this terrible war. If it takes hiding food and killing bandits, that's what we will do. They best not come around our place!" Isaac loads the wagon with several large bags of flour, corn meal, canning supplies and grits, and they head home.

FRIDAY, JULY 8, 1864

General Sherman informs General Schofield that "it is all important that he should know as soon as possible the general topography on the other side of the Chattahoochee River, as to the practicability of the roads in every direction, especially toward Stone Mountain and Decatur. If you can catch a few people who ought to know all about it, send them to me. I will go to the extreme right to-day…."[265]

Major Thomas Taylor, Commander of the 47th Ohio Infantry Volunteers skirmishes with Confederates until the morning of the 11th when the Confederates retreated beyond the river.[266]

SATURDAY, JULY 9, 1864

From his headquarters General Sherman sends a message to General McPherson, "We now have a good lodgment on the other bank of the Chattahoochee River….

We noticed a good deal of flutter in the enemy's camps to-day, troops and wagons moving rapidly east and north. Johnston sees I threaten Decatur and Stone Mountain, and now is a good time for Stoneman to strike south. I want him if possible to secure a point at Campbellton or below, and strike the West Point road. I do believe he can do it, for Johnston will spread his force so much that it will be weak at all points.

General Sherman also sends a courier to General Schofield, "General Garrard is across at Roswell, and General Dodge is moving to that point with orders to fortify a tete-de-pont and to build a good trestle bridge. I want from you a minute description of your position and all information as to roads from it to the east of the Stone Mountain. I propose to operate some to the south, to accumulate stores, and then ahead."[267]

SUNDAY, JULY 10, 1864

In the field near the Chattahoochee General Sherman notifies General McPherson; "I have pretty much made up my mind as to the next move, but would be glad to hear any suggestion from you. I propose that General Stoneman shall attempt to break the road below Atlanta, to accumulate stores at Marietta and increase our guards to the rear, then suddenly to shift you to Roswell, General Dodge in the mean time to get you a good tete-de-pont and bridge. General Schofield is already at Phillips' Ferry, across and fortified. He too will make a good trestle bridge. General Thomas will group his [command] at Powers' and Pace's Ferries. But for the next three days, while these preparations are being made, I want you to demonstrate as though intending to cross at Turner's or below, and General Thomas the same at the railroad bridge. When General Stoneman is back, I will give you the word to shift rapidly to Roswell and cross, and in anticipation you can get your wagons back to Marietta, except such as you need. General Thomas will need yours and his pontoons to cross at Powers' and Pace's.

At the right time I will leave Generals Stoneman and McCook to cover the front, and cross all the balance of the army and advance its right on or near Peach Tree Creek, and the left (you) swing toward Stone Mountain. Johnston will be found to occupy his redoubts about Atlanta and also Stone Mountain and Decatur. We can maneuver so as to compel him to weaken his center or one of his flanks, when we can act. If he neglects his right or center we get on his Augusta road. if he neglects Atlanta, we take it. If he assumed the offensive, we cover our roads and base and can make as good use of Peach Tree Creek as he.

Captain Ben North, commander of the 83rd Regiment Indiana Volunteers reported that Confederates crossed the Chattahoochee on the morning of the 10th.[268]

MONDAY, JULY 11, 1864

As General Garrard awakens on Monday morning of the 11th, he receives a dispatch from General Sherman. "Certainly, by all means, save the bridge above Roswell and get me information on the lay of the country from it toward Stone Mountain."[269]

General Dodge from his Headquarters of the left wing of the 16h Corps in Roswell, notifies General Sherman that "All quiet this morning. I had no fear about being able to build the bridge, but thought you might expect it finished sooner than possible, as it was twice as long as I expected to find it, and twice as long as the river is wide down at Sandtown ..."[270]

General Sherman replies to General Dodge from his field headquarters near the Chattahoochee River: "Your dispatch is received. Send me any Atlanta papers you get. I have no doubt you will have the bridge done in time. As soon as you can spare General Newton he should be relieved to join his corps where his camp equipage is. I rode along the river-bank to-day, and the force of the enemy seemed to be merely sharpshooters in small numbers in their forts. All well with us."[271]

He also sends General Garrard a telegram "Certainly, by all means save the bridge above Roswell, and get me information of the lay of the country from it toward Stone Mountain."[272]

At 11:30 that night Lieutenant Colonel Van Duzer informs Major Eckert that he is crossing the river to rebuild the line and add another wire between Chattanooga and Atlanta. "The line is not working south in consequence of storm, though it has worked well all day. Last night the Confederates withdrew entirely from the west bank of the Chattahoochee, and burned the bridge. Information says that Johnston is moving toward Stone Mountain, and will not oppose advance on Atlanta. General's Garrard and Schofield crossed the Chattahoochee, and are intrenched (sic) to protect the crossing of rest of army, which will cross on the 12th or 13th."[273]

TUESDAY, JULY 12, 1864

Still at his field headquarters near the Chattahoochee General Sherman wires General Grant who is near Petersburg, Virginia.

Dear General,

My railroad and telegraph are now up and we are rapidly accumulating stores in Marietta and Allatoona that will make us less timid about the roads to our rear.

We have been wonderfully supplied in provisions and ammunition; not a day has a regiment been without bread and essentials. Forage has been the hardest, and we have cleaned the country in a breadth of thirty miles of grain and grass. Now the corn is getting a size which make a good fodder, and the railroad has brought us grain to the extent of four pounds per animal per day.

I have now fulfilled the first part of the grand plan. Our lines are up to the Chattahoochee, and the enemy is beyond ... At this moment I have General Stoneman down the Chattahoochee, with orders, if possible, to cross and strike the West Point road. General Rousseau left Decatur the 8th Instant, with about 3,000 cavalry and no wagons, with orders to make a bold push for the railroad between Montgomery and West Point and break it good; ... The moment I got Gen. Johnston to the Chattahoochee I sent General Schofield to a ford above, and he effected a crossing without the loss of a man, and has two pontoon bridges. About the same time, General Garrard's cavalry crossed, still above, at Roswell Factory, and has been relieved by General Dodge's corps so that I now cover the Chattahoochee and have two good crossings well secured; by ton-night I will have a third.

As soon as I hear from General Stoneman I will shift all of General McPherson to Roswell and cross General Thomas about three miles above the railroad bridge and move against Atlanta, my left well to the east, to get possession of the Augusta road about Decatur or Stone Mountain. I think all will be ready in three days. I will have nearly 100,000 men.

I feel certain we have killed and crippled for Gen. Johnston as many as we have sent to the rear. Have sent back about 6,000 or 7,000 prisoners, taken 11 guns of Johnston, and about 10 in Rome. Have destroyed immense iron, cotton, and wool mills, and have possession of all the niter country. My operations have been rather cautions than bold, but on

the whole I trust are satisfactory to you. All of Gen. Polk's, corps is still
here and also Hardee's and Hood's, and the Georgia militia, under Gen.
G. W. Smith.

Let us persevere and trust to the fortunes of war, leaving statesmen to
work out the solution."

As ever, your friend,

W. T. SHERMAN[274]

At daylight on the morning of Wednesday, July 13, the IV, XVI and the XXIII Federal Corps began crossing to the south side of the Chattahoochee. By 9:00 AM the crossing is complete and the 93,000 man Union army camp is on the south side of the Chattahoochee River.

✛

President Jefferson Davis states during his Cabinet meeting, "I cannot understand the obvious hesitation of Gen. Johnston to confront General Sherman more aggressively. This apparent delay is producing a profound and negative impact on the military and political events in Georgia. Gen. Bragg, I want you to go to Atlanta and find out exactly what Gen. Johnston's tactics for the future of this war are. He must stop Sherman or I will replace him with another commander."

"Yes sir, Mr. President. I will depart immediately."

President Davis turns to his Secretary of War, James Seddon. "Notify Gen. Johnston that Gen. Bragg will arrive in Atlanta to visit with him July 13th.

Upon his arrival Gen. Bragg sends a telegraph to President Davis. "Have just arrived without detention. Our army all south of the Chattahoochee, and indications seem to favor an entire evacuation of this place. Shall see Gen. Johnston immediately."[275] Gen. Bragg proceeds to Gen. Johnston's headquarters at Dexter Niles' House on Marietta Road.[276] Gen. Johnston greets Gen. Bragg and they go to the dining room for their conference. Immediately Gen. Bragg informs Gen. Johnston, "My mission is to learn and report upon the condition of military affairs to President Davis." After several hours into the conference Gen. Johnston suggests to Gen. Bragg, "I will send for the lieutenant-generals, that you might obtain from them such other minute information as you desire."

"I will be delighted to have a conference with these officers as friends, but only in that manner, as my visit is unofficial."[277]

"Of course." In his mind Gen. Johnston knows better. He considers Gen. Bragg a spy for President Davis, whom he also greatly loathes.

⚶

Early in the morning on the 14th, Gen. Bragg returns to Gen. Johnston's headquarters to confer with Johnston's Corps commanders. Gen. Johnston greets him in the conference room. "Good morning, sir. In anticipation of your arrival I have summoned LGs Hardee, Wheeler, Stewart and Hood, and MG Gustavus Smith. I also invited BG Robert A. Toombs of the Georgia Militia to join this meeting. Gen. Cleburne and Gen. Cheatham are not present because of their distant locations."

Gen. Bragg is not anxious to talk with or listen to Gen. Hardee, who is present, or Gen. Cleburne, or Gen. Cheatham who are not present. In Tennessee, Gen. Bragg engaged in a series of disputes with his subordinates, especially Gen. Leonidas Polk, Gen. James Longstreet, and Gen. William J. Hardee. The departure of these leaders severely injured the effectiveness of the Army of Tennessee. Several top officers left the army for other fields. Gen. Longstreet, on detachment duty from Gen. Lee's Army of Northern Virginia, was sent north to Virginia and Simon B. Buckner was dispatched into East Tennessee. With the army thus weakened, Gen. Bragg was routed at Chattanooga and was shortly removed from command with Gen. Johnston replacing him. These Gens. are Bragg's enemies from his chaotic period as a commander.

Gen. Bragg informs Gen. Johnston, "I only need to talk with Gen. Hood and Gen. Wheeler in a private meeting and the other Generals can return to their commands."

"I will so inform the Generals present of your wishes." Gen. Johnston knows that these two are Gen. Bragg's cronies. Gen. Bragg begins his private meeting with Gen. Hood and Gen. Wheeler.

"First, I want to thank you two men for the confidential correspondences. These correspondences, although critical of Gen. Johnson and his military tactics during the entire campaign in Georgia, are vital to understanding his conduct of the war."

Gen. Hood responds, "We only have the success of the Confederacy in mind sir with these reports."

Gen. Bragg continues, "The most recent correspondence from you, Gen. Hood, stated, and I will read it, I regard the lack of battle as a great misfortune to our country. Gen. Johnston has failed to give battle to the enemy many miles north of our present position. Please say to the President that I shall continue to do my duty cheerfully and faithfully and strive to do what I think is best for our country, as my constant prayer is for our success.[278] I have shared your information with President Davis and your views express his concerns."

Gen. Hood, with Gen. Wheeler's endorsement, refers to his letters to Gen. Bragg during the spring and summer, when he had repeatedly encouraged Gen. Johnston to attack General Sherman's army. "Yet Gen. Johnston would not take advice and simply withdrew to a new location. In our opinion, Johnston should have forced Sherman to fight. In our minds, failing to do so should be regarded as reckless by the officers high in rank in the Army of Tennessee."

Following the meeting, Gen. Bragg returns to his hotel. In solitude he sits at his desk by a window and carefully composes a letter full of misrepresentations to President Davis concerning Gen. Johnston and his military capabilities. Bragg wants Johnston removed as commander. He also promotes Gen. Hood as a possible new commanding officer for the Army of Tennessee:

> *ATLANTA, July 15, 1864*
> *His Excellency, JEFFERSON DAVIS,*
> *President of Confederate States, Richmond:*
>
> *SIR: Unable to convey to you by telegraph all that you ought to learn from this quarter, and knowing the irregularity of the mail, I have determined to send a special messenger.*
>
> *I arrived here early on the 13th, and immediately waited on Gen. Johnston, who received me kindly and courteously. Most of the day was spent with him in ascertaining the position of his army, its condition and strength, and in obtaining from him such information as he could give in regard to the enemy. The recent operations were explained to me more in detail, but in substance there was little but what you have learned by telegraph. Our forces occupy the southeast and the enemy the northwest bank of the Chattahoochee, on both sides of the railroad. The river is not fordable until you get twenty-five miles above here. Within*

the past two days three corps of infantry have crossed to this side, and are entrenched from nine to fifteen miles northeast of here and near the river. The number is about 25,000. A brigade of cavalry in addition accompanies them. On the 13th, this brigade of the enemy's cavalry crossed the river at a point opposite Newnan, and made a demonstration on the West Point Railroad, but were met and driven back, and the bridge was burned by us. As far as I can learn we do not propose any offensive operations, but shall await the enemy's approach and be governed, as heretofore, by the development in our front. All valuable stores and machinery have been removed, and most of the citizens able to go have left with their effects. Much disappointment and dissatisfaction prevails, but there is no open or imprudent expression.

You will readily see the advantage the enemy has gained, and that it may not be his policy to strike us on this side of the river unless he sees his success insured. Alabama and Mississippi will be devastated and our army will melt away. Our railroad communication with Montgomery is now at the mercy of the enemy, and a mere raid may destroy Montgomery, and we would not even know it had moved. This is no fancy sketch, Mr. President, and, however painful, it is my duty to expose it to your view. There is but one remedy-offensive action. This would now be assumed under many disadvantages. Position, numbers, and morale are now with the enemy, but not to an extent to make me despair of success. We should drive the enemy from this side of the river, follow him down by an attack in flank, and force him to battle, at the same time throwing our cavalry on his communications.

Gens. Hood and Wheeler agree in this opinion and look for success. But the emergency is so pressing and the danger so great I think troops should be at once drawn from the Trans-Mississippi to hold the Trans-Chattahoochee Department. On these points I enclose you a copy of a note by Gen. Hood. The suggestion to Gen. Smith I fear will not answer. It is impossible for him to appreciate the vital position here, and delay for explanations may be fatal. I shall proceed to-night or to-morrow to confer with Gen. S. D. Lee-aid him, if possible, in any arrangements to defend his department. At the same time I will endeavor to open communications with Gen. E. K. Smith. The partial returns I have received so far indicate a loss by us from Dalton of more than 20,000 of our effective force. The present effective of all arms and kinds may reach 52,000.

The morale, though damaged of course, is still good, and the army would hail with delight an order of battle. The enemy's morale has no doubt improved as ours has declined, but his losses have been heavy, and he operates with great caution.

His force has always been overestimated. It is now about 60,000 infantry, 5,000 artillery, and 10,000 cavalry, the latter defeated by us in every conflict during the campaign. During the whole campaign, from and including our position in front of Dalton, Gen. Hood has been in favor of giving battle, and mentions to me numerous instances of opportunities lost. He assures me that LG Polk, after leaving Dalton, invariably sustained the same views. On the contrary, Gen. Hardee generally favored the retiring policy, though he was frequently non- committal. LG Stewart, since his promotion, has firmly and uniformly sustained the aggressive policy. The commanding general, from the best information I can gain, has ever been opposed to seeking battle, though willing to receive it on his own terms in his chosen position.

You will see at once that the removal of the commander, should such a measure be considered, would produce no change of policy, and it would be attended with some serious evils. A general denunciation by the disorganization, civil and military, would follow. I do not believe the second in rank has the confidence of the army to the extent of the chief. If any change is made LG Hood, would give unlimited satisfaction, and my estimate of him, always high, has been raised by his conduct in this campaign. Do not understand me as proposing him as a man of genius, or a great general, but as far better in the present emergency than any one we have available.

It affords me great pleasure to report to you the entire and perfect satisfaction which has been given by your recent appointments in the army. I have not heard of a complaint, and in Gen. Stewart's case the feeling is most gratifying.

I would like to refer to some other matters, but must close to get my messenger off by the train.

I am, sir, most respectfully your obedient servant,

BRAXTON BRAGG[279]

As Gen. Johnston has not sought my advice, nor ever afforded me a fair opportunity of giving my opinion, I have obtruded neither upon him. Such will continue to be my course. B.B.

❧

Early in the morning Buck, Betty Gail and Isaac load the wagon with fresh vegetables and fruits for the hospital. On the way to town they pass some cavalry of Col. Dibrell who are their way to Yellow River. Buck and Betty Gail pull over to the side of the road so the cavalry can pass. One of the officers sees the wagon load of food and brings his mount to a stop next to the wagon.

"Have any extra you can spare for us?" asks the officer.

"This wagon load is for the patients in the hospital, but take a bushel of apples and a couple bushels of corn. I can get more in a day or so from my farm." The officer signals for a supply wagon to come over and load the corn and apples. "What's the latest on the approaching Yankees?" asks Buck.

"They are all around McAfee's Bridge. The Yanks are taking over Cross Keys to Pinckneyville, Lebanon Church and all the way to Warsaw. We have run them off from Yellow River. Those Yankees have been trying to destroy the railroad from here to Augusta while we have been trying to cut the railroad north of McAfee to keep them from getting supplies. You best be prepared in case they break through here. We don't have enough cavalry to do both operations. Stone Mountain is right on the railroad to Augusta." Buck steps from the wagon and begins checking what food has been taken.

"Take several more of the watermelons. More will be ripening in a couple of days."

"Thank you Mr. … what's your name?"

"Jernigan. Buck Jernigan. This is my wife Betty Gail."

The officer tips his hat with his fingers. "Thank you Buck and Mrs. Jernigan."

The officer shouts, "Move out!" and the wagon and troops soon disappear towards Yellow River.

Buck leaves Betty Gail and the wagon at the hospital. "While you have the wagon unloaded, I'm going to the depot and get the latest report on our men."

Betty Gail goes inside, finding two orderlies, "There's food on the wagon. How about taking it to the cook house for me."

"Yes ma'am."

Buck walks up to a small group of his friends who are looking at the roster.

"Good morning Jesse. Good morning William." Jesse Lanford and William Nash return a good morning to Buck.

"Looks like George got wounded. Read here Buck."

"George Riley Wells wounded in the wrist on May 15, at the battle of Spotsylvania Courthouse and sent to a Richmond hospital. Isaac Pope, slightly wounded on June 7, at Cold Harbor."

"Well, I'm glad it's no worse. Who's been added to the enlistment roll?"

Jesse shows him the roll and points. "See, John Pickney Tuggle enlisted April 15 in the Augusta Arsenal Guard. Ransom Martin Thompson enlisted April 26 in the 2nd Regiment Ga. Reserves of the Dekalb Militia."

"Poor Ransom lost his older brother Richard not too long ago. Looks like the Yankees are getting close to Stone Mountain. Talked with an officer with Dibrell's cavalry this morning. Said the Yankees are all around trying to destroy bridges and the railroad. Best start hiding your food and goods."

Jesse continues, "We're hiding everything we can. Looks like Ransom is going to be a prison guard at Camp Sumter near Andersonville,"

Buck then cautiously moves over to the "Deceased" Roster. "The only new addition is Pressley Lanier. Buck reads, "Killed at the battle of Spotsylvania Courthouse."

Pointing to Pressley's name, William Nash says, "Preston was in the same unit as George Riley Wells and look here on the captured list. John McClelland was captured on May 10, at the battle of Spotsylvania Courthouse. I almost hate to ask you Buck, but how is Polly doing in Savannah and how about Norman?"

"Polly wants to stay in Savannah in her and Legare's house. Her slaves are still with her, and Legare's Uncle Richard checks on her daily. It's just a terrible thing. Poor Legare was against the war and the war took him anyhow. He truly loved my daughter. Congressman Hill is trying to get through the lines to recover Legare's body." Solemnly his two friends listen. "A cannon ball through our hearts could not do more damage than that sad news from Rooster. Norman is probably going to wind up fighting with GMI as a State Militia. I just pray we don't lose another."

THURSDAY, 14 JULY 1864

From his field headquarters near the Chattahoochee River General Sherman advises General McPherson in Roswell that "The bridge over

Yellow River is too well guarded by men and redoubts to be carried by our cavalry. However General Garrard might dash at the road east of the Stone Mountain. See him, and tell him that it is useless to attempt anything unless he be willing. Not until our infantry is out as far as the railroad he may encounter most of Gen. Wheeler's cavalry, but I have no doubt most of Gen. Johnston's cavalry is gone to the south toward West Point, drawn there by Generals Stoneman and Rousseau. A dash at the road (railroad) would develop the truth, but to be certain, the infantry should be out as far as the head of Nancy's Creek. I hope to hear of General Stoneman to-night.[280]

General Sherman states that "a week's work after crossing the Chattahoochee should determine the first object aimed at, viz, the possession of the Atlanta and Augusta road east of Decatur towards Stone Mountain, or of Atlanta itself," and he issues his Special Field Orders No. 35 from his headquarters near the Chattahoochee River.

> *Preliminary steps having already begun, the following general plan will be observed and adhered to:*
>
> *I. Major-General Thomas will prepare to cross his army at Powers' and Pace's Ferries, and take position out from the Chattahoochee River, until he controls the country from Island Creek to Kyle's Bridge, over Nancy's Creek, ...*
>
> *II. As soon as General Stoneman returns he will dispose his cavalry to watch the Chattahoochee and Turner's Ferry and about the mouth of Nickajack, connecting by patrols with General McCook. . . .*
>
> *III. Major-General Schofield, after having well secured his crossing-place at Phillips', will move out toward Cross Keys until he controls the ridge between Island and Nancy's Creeks and the road represented as leading from Roswell to Buck Head.*
>
> *IV. Major-General Blair will immediately, on the return of Major-General Stoneman, move rapidly to Roswell and join his army. Major-General McPherson will then move his command out, either by the Cross Keys road or the old Hightower trail, until he is abreast of Major-General Schofield, and General Garrard, with his cavalry, will scout from McAfee's Bridge toward Pinckneyville, and if no enemy is there in force will picket McAfee's Bridge and take post on General McPherson's left, about Buchannan's.*

V. The whole army will thus form a concave line behind Nancy's Creek, extending from Kyle's Bridge to Buchannan's, but no attempt will be made to form a line of battle....

VI. Major-General Thomas will study well the country toward Decatur via Buck Head, Major-General Schofield to a point of the railroad four miles northeast of Decatur, and Major-General McPherson and General Garrard that toward Stone Mountain. Each army should leave behind the Chattahoochee river, at its bridge or at Marietta, all wagons or encumbrances not absolutely needed for battle.[281]

By order of Major General W. T. Sherman: L. M. DAYTON, Aide-de-Camp.

FRIDAY, JULY 15, 1864

General Sherman from his headquarters near the Chattahoochee River telegraphs General McPherson in Roswell. "I have heard from General Stoneman. He did not break the lower railroad, but burned a bridge over the Chattahoochee near Newnan. He will be in to-night, and I have ordered General Blair to move for Roswell to-morrow. You may, therefore, make all preparations to move out toward the Stone Mountain the day after tomorrow. Notify General Garrard to move in connection with you, sending his train to yours. The Augusta road must be destroyed and occupied between Decatur and Stone Mountain by you and General Garrard.

General Sherman also asks General McPherson, "What sort of a road do you find the Hightower trail? Do you find a road leading directly to Stone Mountain or to Decatur?"[282]

SATURDAY, JULY 16TH

General Sherman notifies General Halleck that on the 17th "I have yours and General Grant's dispatches. I had anticipated all possible chances and am accumulating all the stores possible at Chattanooga and Allatoona, but I do not fear Johnston with re-enforcements of 20,000 if he will take the offensive; but I recognize the danger arising from my long line and the superiority of the enemy's cavalry in numbers and audacity. I will move my army from the Chattahoochee toward Decatur and Stone Mountain."[283]

The same time, Gen. Johnston receives a telegraph from President Davis regarding Atlanta. "Gen. Johnston, you will forward to me your plans of operations so specifically as will enable me to anticipate events."[284]

General Johnston replies, "As the enemy has double our number, we must be on the defensive. My plan of operation must, therefore, depend upon that of the enemy. It is mainly to watch for an opportunity to fight to advantage. We are trying to put Atlanta in condition to be held a day or two by the Georgia militia, so that army movements may be freer and wider."[285]

3

From his headquarters on Sunday July 17th, General Sherman issues Special Field Orders No. 36:

> *The operations of the army for tomorrow, Monday the 18th of July will be as follows:*
>
> *I. Major-General Thomas will move forward, occupy Buck Head and the ridge between Nancy's Creek and Peach-Tree, also all the roads toward Atlanta, as far as Peach-Tree Creek.*
>
> *II. Major-General Schofield will pass through Cross Keys and occupy the Peach-Tree Road where intersected by the road from Cross Keys to Decatur.*
>
> *III. Major-General McPherson will move toward Stone Mountain to secure strong ground within four miles of General Schofield's position, and push Brigadier-General Garrard's cavalry to the railroad and destroy some section of the road (railroad), and then resume position to the front and left of General McPherson.*
>
> *IV. All armies will communicate with the neighbors. The general-in-chief will be near General Thomas' left, or near General Schofield.*
>
> *By order of Major General W. T. Sherman*[286]

In the afternoon General Sherman in order to clarify his intentions issues a "Memoranda to his Special Field Orders No. 36."

> *The map composed of two parts of the official compilation made at Marietta July 5 and 11, 1864, is the best and will be the standard issued from these headquarters. As a general rule, old roads will be found to*

lead to Decatur, but new roads to Atlanta. The general country is very hilly and stony, but improves south and east as we approach the head of the Ocmulgee. Peach Tree Creek is considerable of a stream, but fordable at all points east of the main road from Buck Head to Atlanta. The first real lines to be found will be on the old Peach Tree Road, which starts at Turner's Ferry, keeps near the Chattahoochee, crosses Peach Tree[287] Creek at Moore's Mill and on a main ridge by Buck Head, Buchanan's and Pinckneyville, in Gwinnett County. Our first line must be in front of this road, leaving it clear for communication, General Thomas, the right, General Schofield, the center, and General McPherson, the left. General Thomas will move substantially on Atlanta, General Schofield on Decatur, and General McPherson, with General Garrard's cavalry, is charged with the destruction of the Georgia railroad between Decatur and Stone Mountain. As soon as the road is broken, all the armies will close on General Thomas, occupying the main roads east of Atlanta, or in other words, the line swung across the railroad near Decatur. General Thomas will press close on Atlanta, but not assault real works, but not be deterred by cavalry or light defenses. General Schofield will threaten the neighborhood of Decatur, but Generals McPherson and Garrard will risk much and break the railroad during the 18th or 19th.

W. T. Sherman
Major General, Commanding[288]

General Garrard sends a dispatch to General John Logan. "I am camping about a mile on the left of your line. I left Colonel Long with two of his regiments to guard the bridge and to picket Stone Mountain and Pinckneyville Roads. Colonel Minty's left rests near Buchanan's and the Peach Tree Road, and all roads leading from the Peach Tree Road toward the river on the left are picketed. Patrols have been out well to the front, and find but few rebels, and most of their tracks lead toward Atlanta or Buck Head. I learned since being here that there are two Cross Keys. The one on the maps is the old one, where there was a post-office some years since, but the name and the post-office was transferred to the present position, some four miles to the east. This will account for the fact that both you and I are so near Cross Keys. We are some four or five miles east of the point laid down on the map as Cross Keys, and about where we were ordered. Buchanan's is only one house. Please send this to General McPherson."[289]

General Logan, Commander of the XV Army Corps issues his Special Field Order No. 55 from his headquarters near Cross Keys:

I. The Fifteenth Army Corps will move forward at 5 AM to-morrow on the Decatur road to Widow Rainey's thence on the Stone Mountain road by Blake's Mill to Bowman's [Browning's] Court-House, at the intersection of the Stone Mountain and Lawrenceville and Decatur roads, where it will be held in readiness to assist General Garrard, if he requires it, in his effort to make a break on the railroad....[290]

General Blair orders General Gresham's 4th Division of the XVII Corps Division to advance to-morrow, the 18th and will move his command promptly at 6 AM on the Decatur road to Widow Rainey's. From there on to the Stone Mountain road to Peach Tree Creek at Blake's Mill, following the Fifteenth Army Corps.[291]

General Dodge is reading the Atlanta newspaper and begins to chuckle while he reads an editorial. The editorial speculates that General Sherman's "probable movements on Stone Mountain is to force the evacuation of Atlanta."[292] He lowers the newspaper, hands it to his adjutant and laughs, "What wild speculation that is. The folks in Atlanta will just have to keep guessing."

SPECIAL FIELD ORDERS,
HDQRS. MIL. DIV. OF THE MISS., Numbers 36
In the Field, Chattahoochee, July 17, 1864

The night of the 17th at Gen. Johnston's headquarters is a typical July evening. Calm, sticky and moonlit. Around 10:00 PM, Gen. Johnston is conferring over a cup of coffee with his chief Engineer Col. Presstman. A knock on the door, and enters Maj. Charles W. Hubner, Gen. Johnston's chief of telegraph. "Yes Charles, what's going on?"

"Sir, I just received this telegram from Gen. Cooper."

Gen. Johnston sees the long, tight face of Maj. Hubner, and perceives trouble. Gen. Johnston stands, extends his hand. "Hand it over Charles." Maj. Hubner hands Gen. Johnston the telegram. Gen. Johnston takes the telegram and begins reading to himself. Col. Presstman raises his eyes and looks over to Maj. Hubner. Maj. Hubner shakes his head and tightens his lips as he gazes toward Col. Presstman.

"Come and join us in a cup of coffee, Major."

"Thank you, sir." Maj. Hubner quietly takes a seat at the table with Col. Presstman and pours a cup of coffee.

Gen. Johnston sighs. "Let me read this to you, gentlemen."

Richmond, July 17, 1864

LG John B. Hood has been commissioned to the temporary rank of Gen. under the late law of Congress. I am directed by the Secretary of War to inform you that as you have failed to arrest the advance of the enemy to the vicinity of Atlanta, far in the interior of Georgia, and express no confidence that you can defeat or repel him, you are hereby relieved from the command of the Army and Department of Tennessee, which you will immediately turn over to Gen. Hood.

S. Cooper
Adjutant and Inspector Gen."[293]

Gen. Johnston lowers the telegram and exhales slowly and deliberately. He takes a seat at the table with Col. Presstman and Maj. Hubner. As he lays the telegram on the table he looks at his two faithful staff members. "No surprise gentlemen. This is what Gen. Bragg's visit was about." Taking a sip of his coffee he continues, "I have been relieved of command." Still maintaining a dignified demeanor, he stands, and walks over to Maj. Hubner, "Send this general order to my commanding officers." He chuckles. "I mean, my former commanding officers, per President Davis!" Maj. Hubner takes down the following message and Gen. Johnston dictates the contents of his general order.

General Orders No. 4
Headquarters Army of Tennessee
Atlanta, Georgia

"I have been ordered by President Davis to immediately transfer my command to Gen. Hood. I cannot leave this noble army without expressing my admiration of the high military qualities it has displayed. A long and arduous campaign has made conspicuous every soldierly virtue, endurance of toil, obedience to orders, brilliant courage. The enemy has never attacked but to be repulsed and severely punished. You soldiers have never argued but from your courage, and never counted your foes. No longer your leader, I will watch your careers, and will rejoice in your victories."[294]

Your obedient Servant,

Joseph Johnston

It is 11:00 in the evening, and Gen. Hood has just retired to his quarters when he has a knock on his door. Sitting on the side of his bed and taking off his boots, he hesitates.

"Sir, you have a telegram from Secretary of War, James A. Seddon. I know the contents will please you."

Gen. Hood still has one boot on as he jumps up and rushes over to take the telegram. He reads it out loud. "You are charged with a great trust. You will, I know, test to the utmost your capacities to discharge it. Be wary, no less than bold. It may yet be practicable to cut the communication of the enemy or find or make an opportunity of equal encounter, whether he moves east or west. God be with you."

"Yes!" Gen. Hood shouts and he raises his hand and then shakes hands with his telegraph officer. "Now we can get on with this war. This war is mine now. Summon my commanders immediately."

> *ATLANTA, July 18, 1864*
> *Gen. S. COOPER:*
>
> *GENERAL: I have the honor to acknowledge the receipt of my appointment as general of the Army of Tennessee. There is now heavy skirmishing and indications of a general advance. I deem it dangerous to change the commanders of this army at this particular time, and to be to the interest of the service that no change should be made until the fate of Atlanta is decided.*
>
> *Respectfully,*
>
> *J. B. HOOD,*
> *GEN.*

> *RICHMOND, JULY 18, 1864*
>
> *GEN. HOOD:*
>
> *Your telegram of this date received. A change of commanders, under existing circumstances, was regarded as so objectionable that I only accepted it as the alternative of continuing in a policy which had proved so disastrous. Reluctance to make the change induced me to send a telegram of inquiry to the commanding general on the 16th instant. His reply but confirmed previous apprehensions. There can be but one*

question which you and I can entertain-that is, what will best promote the public good; and to each of you I confidently look for the sacrifice of every personal consideration in conflict with that object. The order has been executed, and I cannot suspend it without making the case worse than it was before the order was issued.

JEFFERSON DAVIS

NEAR ATLANTA, JULY 18, 1864

GEN. S. COOPER,
Richmond:

Your dispatch of yesterday received and obeyed. Command of the Army and Department of Tennessee has been transferred to General Hood. As to the alleged cause of my removal, I assert that Sherman's army is much stronger compared with that of Tennessee than Grant's compared with that of Northern Virginia. Yet the enemy has been compelled to advance much more slowly to the vicinity of Atlanta than to that of Richmond and Petersburg, and has penetrated much deeper into Virginia than into Georgia. Confident language by a military commander is not usually regarded as evidence of competency.

J. E. JOHNSTON

ATLANTA, JULY 18, 1864

GEN. SAMUEL COOPER,
Adjutant and Inspector General:

I have assumed command of the Army and Department of Tennessee.

J. B. HOOD

JULY 18, 1864-1 AM

GEN. J. E. JOHNSTON:

GENERAL: Much to my surprise I received the appointment you refer to. I accept your congratulations and without its concomitant it would have been more agreeable. I desire to have a conversation with you, and for that purpose will be over early in the morning.

Respectfully,

J. B. HOOD

HEADQUARTERS ARMY OF TENNESSEE, In the Field, July 18, 1864.

SOLDIERS: In obedience to orders from the War Department I assume command of this army and department. I feel the weight of the responsibility so suddenly and unexpectedly devolved upon me by this position, and shall bend all my energies and employ all my skill to meet its requirements. I look with confidence to your patriotism to stand by me, and rely upon your prowess to wrest your country from the grasp of the invader, entitling yourselves to the proud distinction of being called the deliverers of an oppressed people.

Respectfully,

J. B. HOOD,
GEN.

HEADQUARTERS STEVENS' BRIGADE, In the Field, July 18, 1864.

GEN. J. E. JOHNSTON, C. S. Army:

General: Your order turning over the command of this army to General Hood has been read to the troops of this brigade. The announcement that you are no longer to be our leader was received by officers and men in silence and deep sorrow. I have the fullest assurance that I express the undivided sentiment of this brigade when I say that the abiding and unlimted confidence which we have left in the wisdom of your judgment and leadership, has sustained us in the many trying hours of our very arduous campaign. We have ever left that the best was being done that could be, and have looked confidently forward to the day of triumph, when with you as our leader we should surely march to a glorious victory. This confidence and implicit trust has been in no way impaired, and we are to-day ready, as were ever have been to obey your orders, whether they be to retire before a largely outnumbering foe, or to spend our last drops of blood in the fiercest conflict. We feel that in parting with you as our commanding general our loss is irreparable, and that this army and our country loses one of its ables, most zealous, and patriotic defenders. Our most sincere well wishers will accompany you in your future career, and you carry with you the love, respect, esteem,

and confidence of the officers and men of this brigade. We would hail
with joy your return to command us.

I have the honor to be, very respectfully, your obedient servant,

C. H. STEVENS
BG, Provisional Army, C. S.[295]

The news of Johnston's dismissal sent a shock wave through the army. Some were saddened, others angered; nearly all were worried. It was necessary to call together the brigade commanders and through them take steps to soothe and quiet the men, whose devotion to 'Old Joe,' made the danger of mutiny imminent.[296]

❧

Governor Brown realizes that the affairs in Georgia are not good, and asks the Honorable Benjamin H. Hill to confer with Gen. Johnston. Mr. Benjamin Hill reports back to Governor Brown that Gen. Johnston had hoped to find a chance to fight a fair field; that his Confederate cavalry is superior to Sherman's but is necessary to the safety of his own army, and so cannot operate on General Sherman's communications; that he can see no way of resisting Sherman's advance except by Gen. Forrest falling on Sherman's communications.[297]

General Sherman, during his staff briefing informs his commanders, "I respect Gen. Johnston as a fine strategist who knows the art of entrapment. I realize that this command change brings a very dangerous adversary. Notify every part of the Federal army of this fact."

Continuing in a more relaxed, yet serious manner, Sherman tells is staff, "Gen. Hood was severely wounded on July 2, 1863 at Gettysburg, forever losing use of his left arm. During the battle of Chickamauga, Gen. Hood's division broke the Federal line at the Brotherton Cabin, which led to the rout of General William Rosecrans' army. Only the heroic rear guard actions of Gen. Hood's former West Point instructor General Thomas saved the Union Army from destruction. During the battle, Gen. Hood received his second serious wound of the war, resulting in the amputation of his right leg. Gen. Hood was transported to the Clisby-Austin house in nearby Tunnel Hill for recuperation. It is said that Gen. Hood was so severely wounded that his amputated leg was sent with him so that his leg could be buried with him if he did not survive. I must warn you sir, he'll hit you like hell and before you know it."[298]

From his headquarters on Peach Tree Road General Sherman notifies General McPherson,

I am at Sam. House's, a brick house well known, and near Old Cross Keys. A sick Negro, the only human being left on the premises, says we are eleven miles from Atlanta, five from Buck Head, and a sign board says ten miles to McAfee's Bridge and eleven to Roswell Factory. At this place the main Buck Head and Atlanta road is strongly marked and forks, the right-hand looking north going to McAfee's, and the left to Roswell Factory. This left-hand road forks one miles from here, at Old Cross Keys, the main road going to Roswell and left-hand to Johnson's Ferry. The latter is the road traveled by us. I suppose all of Thomas' troops are at Buck Head, with advance guard down to Peach Tree Creek. I think I will move Schofield one mile and half toward Buck Head, where the Negro represents a road to Decatur and forward on that road a mile or so. I think Sam. House's is not far from the northwest corner of lot 273, and if I move him as contemplated he will be to-night about 202, 203. On our map a road comes from the direction of McAfee's toward Decatur, and if you can find position about 192, 191 it would best fulfill my purpose, but be careful to order Garrard to break the road to-day or to-night and report results.

I will stay here or down at the forks of the road to-night. Schofield encountered nothing but cavalry, about 500, according to the Negro's report, and all retreated toward Atlanta. Tell Garrard that it will be much easier to break the telegraph and road to-day and night than if he waits longer. This Negro says there is a road leading to Stone Mountain from a Mr. Lively's, on the Decatur road, on which I suppose you to be. At any rate I will be here till evening and would like to hear from you.[299]

Yours,

W. T. SHERMAN
Major-General

SPECIAL FIELD ORDERS, ON PEACH TREE, GA., Numbers 71. July 18, 1864

III. In accordance with instructions from Military Division of the Mississippi, the following movements will be made to-morrow:

1. Major-General Logan, commanding Fifteenth Army Corps, will, at 5 o'clock, move his command toward Decatur, striking the railroad at the nearest point on his route, tearing up track, burning the ties, making the destruction complete and effectual.

2. Major-General Blair, commanding Seventeenth Army Corps, will, at 5 o'clock, move toward Decatur, following the command of General Loan, via Henderson's Mill, or by an intermediate route between the positions of General Logan and General Dodge, if a practicable road can be found. Should General Blair discover a road intermediate, leading to the railroad, his men will also be employed in tearing up tracks, burning ties, twisting rails.

3. Major-General Dodge, commanding Left Wing, Sixteenth Army Corps, will, at 5 o'clock, move forward across the creek toward Decatur, striking the railroad east of that place, and employing his troops in the effectual destruction of the road.

4. Brigadier-General, commanding cavalry division, will, at 5 o'clock, move eastward along the line of the railroad, in the vicinity of Stone Mountain, continuing its destruction as far as possible

5. The several corps of this command will pursue the line of march toward Decatur, keeping up communication with each other as far as practicable, converging at that point and continuing their work until night, when the lines will be closed on General Schofield about Pea Vine and Decatur.

6. Should indications of a heavy battle be heard, each corps will move to the right and close in on General Schofield, but not otherwise.

7. Corps commanders will see that sufficient wagons are brought forward from their trains to supply their troops with three days' rations. Empty wagons will be sent back for supplies and all trains will move under proper guards.

By order of Major General James B. McPherson[300]

At 5 AM General McPherson and the XV Corps reaches the Atlanta and Augusta railroad at a point seven miles east of Decatur and four miles from Stone Mountain. General Garrard's cavalry dismount and stacks arms and set to work to destroy the railroad. Accompanying him are Colonel Abe Miller's Lightening Brigade and Colonel Robert Minty's 1st Brigade with a section of the Board of Trade Battery. Soon General Morgan Smith's division of infantry arrives and joins with General Garrard's troops. Col. Dibrell's cavalry launches an attack on the Union forces.[301]

General John Logan moves his command at 5 o'clock from Nancy's Creek, near Cross Keys, to the intersection of the Stone Mountain and Lawrenceville roads for the purpose of assisting Brigadier-General Garrard to break the railroad, if he should need assistance. When the head of General Logan's column reached the road leading from McAfee's Bridge to Browning's Court-House, General Garrard arrives, moving in the direction of the railroad, some four miles distant. After his column passes, at the suggestion of the general commanding, he will move down within two miles of the railroad; then send one brigade of infantry, commanded by Brigadier-General Lightburn, to the railroad.

He later reports that he effectually destroyed some two miles of rail and ties of the road to within a short distance of Stone Mountain, burning water-tank, wood, and several culverts. During the time that General Garrard and General Lightburn were destroying the road in an easterly direction, Major Hotaling in charge of fifty mounted men, made up of the Eighth Indiana and the escort company, moved on the main Decatur road to within three miles of Decatur, destroying two culverts and some small portion of the railroad track. In the march to and from the railroad to my present position no resistance is met anywhere. One prisoner is captured and is quite unwell. Quite a number would have been captured if found, and all been in the same condition as this one. The loss in the whole command, so far, is one horse with pains in his belly from eating green corn.[302]

HEADQUARTERS LEFT WING, SIXTEENTH ARMY CORPS,
In the Field, near Peach Tree Creek, Ga., July 18, 1864.
Major General J. B. McPherson,
Commanding Department and Army of the Tennessee, in Field, Ga.:

GENERAL: Scout in from Atlanta. He left there this morning. Says the enemy were moving troops all night last night there; all the wagon trains were started off on the Augusta road; that Bate's division moved up on Peach Tree road and is entrenched on south side of that creek near Howell's Bridge; that the bridge is ready to be burned. He also reports one brigade of dismounted cavalry at Buck Head, prepared to contest our advance. This morning Bate's division was the extreme right of Gen. Johnston's infantry, and Gen. Kelly's division of cavalry on north side of Little Peach Tree between me and Buck Head. This agrees with report of rebel lieutenant captured by me this morning. This scout says it is the general talk that if Atlanta falls Polk's corps will go west toward West Point, while the remainder of Johnston's army will go toward Augusta or Macon. On yesterday Hood had the left, Polk [Stewart] the center, and Hardee the right, the militia on the left. Johnston has received no re-enforcements up to to-day. The enemy are at work on their forts and entrenchments around Atlanta.[303]

I am, general, very respectfully, your obedient servant,

G. M. DODGE
Major-General

Colonel W. S. Jones, Commander of the 2nd Brigade of the 2nd Div of the 15th Corps departs his camp on the south side of the Chattahoochee River and marches seven miles toward Decatur in the direction of Stone Mountain, supporting General Garrard's cavalry. His command reaches the Atlanta and Augusta Railroad, near Stone Mountain, about 3 PM, being the only infantry that reaches the road. He command destroys about three miles of railroad and returns to corps, which was about three miles west from the road. From there the 2nd Brigade March on the Decatur road, and bivouacked at 9 PM.[304]

Lieutenant Samuel Edge, with the Signal Detachment of the 16th Ohio Infantry of the XV army Corps. moved to the railroad one mile from the mountain. He and three companies of General Garrard's division of cavalry proceed to the Stone Mountain Station (Wood), but are driven back by Col. Dibrell's or Gen. Kelly's cavalry.[305]

General Lightburn commander of the 2nd Division of the XV Corps marches from Cross Keys at 5 AM to the Stone Mountain railroad and assisted in destroying one mile and a half of the railroad. Afterwards marched to Peach Tree Creek to camp for the night.[306]

Lieutenant Colonel George Hildt, commander of the 13th Ohio Veteran Volunteer Infantry around 5:00 AM marched about eight miles from their camp near Stony Creek to the Stone Mountain Railroad. They advanced near the station and demolished a large portion of the track from the station westward. They returned and camped about five miles from the railroad, much jaded.[307]

Colonel James Martin, commander of the 111th Regiment Illinois Vol. Infantry broke camp at 6:00 AM on a creek on the Decatur Road. Then the 111th march in the direction of Stone Mountain in support of the cavalry force cutting the railroad. The 111th march three miles to the right and camped for the night.[308]

Lieutenant Colonel Fulton, commanding the 53rd Regiment Ohio Vet. Vol. Infantry departs his camp on the south side of the Chattahoochee River and march to the railroad near Stone Mountain to assist in the destruction of the tracks.[309]

Lt. Colonel Owen Stuart, commander of the 19th Regiment Illinois Infantry Volunteers, starts marching at 7:00 AM and halts for a short time about four miles north of Stone Mountain. The march resumes in an easterly direction until midnight when the 19th sets up camp.[310]

Captain Chauncey Reese, the Chief Engineer with the Corps of Engineers is sent from Browning's Court-House, where the Fifteenth Corps is supporting Garrard, who is breaking the railroad near Stone Mountain, to Henderson's Mill, to examine the country at that point, with a view to moving the Fifteenth Corps there, to be near the other corps of the army, the Seventeenth Corps being at this time at Blake's Mill and the Sixteenth on the West Decatur road, some three miles south of Widow Rainey's.[311]

Major I. T. Moore, commander of the 54th Regiment Ohio Vet. Vol Infantry arrives in the evening of the 18th aiding in completely destroying the railroad near Stone Mountain. Moving in the direction of Decatur at 10:00 PM and camped.[312]

Lt Colonel S.R. Mott, Commander of the 57th Ohio Volunteers march via Stone Mountain to get to Decatur to assist in destroying the Augusta railroad.[313]

Colonel Delos Van Deusen, commander of the 6th Missouri Infantry assists in destroying the Western and Atlantic railroad near Stone Mountain.[314]

HDQRS. MILITARY DIVISION OF THE MISSISSIPPI,
In the Field at Sam's House, Peach Tree Road, Five miles northeast of
Buck Head, Ga., July 18, 1864

A courier delivers a message to Gen. Wheeler from Col. Dibrell stating that the Yankees are at Buchanan's and heading for the railroad and the Stone Mountain Depot. Gen. Wheeler gets word to Gen. John Kelly to send a regiment to the depot for protection.

Around one PM, about six miles beyond Buchanan's, the Federal advance guard reaches Browning's courthouse in Tucker. They are ready to turn onto Fellow Ship road at Browning's Courthouse[315] and proceed to the City of Stone Mountain.

Approximately fifty Confederate cavalry surprises the advance guard of the Union Army. General Garrard has information from a Confederate deserter that in fact it is Gen. John Kelly's[316] cavalry.

The sun is slightly past noon on Tuesday as General Garrard's troops reach the end of Fellowship Road and approach the railroad about three mile west of the Stone Mountain Depot. The other troops dismount and once the rope corral is secure they tie their horses along the circular length of rope. Next, the men go to the supply wagon and obtain the tools and fuel to begin the destruction of the railroad ties and tracks. Captain Dartt discusses the task at hand with the men, and instructs them where to begin and work and head directly toward the Stone Mountain Depot. The men take off their shirts and line up along the tracks. Soon the first section of track is separated. Soldiers drag the ties and place them in a pile. Another soldier pours fuel on the ties and with a "swoosh" from the ignition the ties begin to burn sending a rising stream of smoke into the July sky.

When the large force of troops arrive at the railroad, Colonel Miller and Colonel Minty finds Captain Dartt's troops are already hot, sweaty and stinking from the July heat and humidity and are taking a short break. They confer with Captain Dartt and he informs the two Colonels about the rumors of a large Rebel force in the area. "We have a strong advance guard to protect us from a surprise attack. So we are moving with great speed, no matter how hot and humid the day."

"Thank you, Captain Dartt, for the briefing."

"No problem sir." Captain Dartt salutes Colonel Minty and departs.

Colonel Abe Miller's Indiana troops lack experience in the mechanics and art of rail and tie removal. General Garrard arrives and orders the

Hoosiers to tear down nearby fences and builds large fires at the end of each rail section. As the fires grow hotter, the Hoosiers begin to observe the expanding rails to twist and release the spikes from the cross ties. The Hoosiers quickly adopt their own technique. They begin cutting poles for levers. Then, they turn over railroad track sections thirty to one hundred feet in length. Rallying at their success with the outcome of the method of destruction, they frantically gather more wood rails and toss them on the blazing fires.

Lt. Colonel George Hildt's Thirtieth Ohio Veteran Volunteer Infantry advance near the station and demolish a large portion of the track from the Stone Mountain Station westward.[317]

In the meantime, Colonel Minty's 1st stack their Spencer carbines and take ranks elbow to elbow along one side of the tracks. "Heave!" orders the officer and the soldiers bend over, grasping the rail with two hands. With all of their strength, they lift and flip the rails and cross ties. The loosened cross ties are piled with the other wood. Then the metal rails are placed on top, and the fire lit, causing the rails to warp.

It is around 3:30 PM and Brigadier General Joseph A. Lightburn of the XV Corps arrives. He orders his foot soldiers to begin the destruction of the track away from Stone Mountain toward Decatur.

James Milliken, a local farmer, wonders where all of the slaves are and notices several heading in the same direction away from his place. He mounts his horse and follows a good distance back. Appearing slightly over a ridge, to his astonishment, is a large group of slaves talking with the Union Army! There are thousands of troops. He turns, and in a full gallop notifies as many neighbors as possible. A Union guard notices James Milliken's sprint and chases for about one mile before stopping and returning to his unit. James continues to head to Stone Mountain to warn the citizens about the large Union force heading in their direction. Riding into Stone Mountain and stopping at city hall, he relays to the clerk what he has seen.

The clerk immediately rings the bell at City Hall, which beacons to the locals to gather for an important announcement. The little town of Stone Mountain[318] becomes a beehive of activity as the city clerk announces the news of the approaching Union forces. The stores close, and people head for their homes, hoping no foragers arrive at their doors. The hospital makes plans for more wounded and dying to arrive. Very few of the populace have ever been in direct contact with a Yankee military force.

Yet, the seriousness of the situation overtakes any concept of panic at the hospital. Yankees are known to take over Confederate hospitals and even burn them down. The staff hopes that its work with Union patients, as well as their own, might spare the hospitals. "We must continue our work in an orderly fashion if the Yankees make an appearance at the hospitals," says Dr. Maddox.

Buck and Isaac are tending the fields as Jesse Lanford and Mark Beauchamp arrive at his farm simultaneously. It is one of those July days when the air is still, the bugs are plentiful and the dust is thick. Even in the shade, there is no comfort from the searing sun. Mark dismounts and walks to the farm bell in front of the house. He grasps the long rope and begins to toll the bell. Buck is on the far corner of his farm as the bell sounds. All of the slaves and Buck mount their wagons and horses immediately and head for the house at full gallop.

Arriving in a matter of minutes, Buck sees Mark and Jesse standing by the farm bell. Jesse and Buck rushes to meet each other. "What's the matter Jesse?" asks Buck.

"The Yankees are at the end of Fellowship and are tearing up track on the railroad. There must be 5,000 Yankees, some heading to Decatur and some to Stone Mountain."

"How about the ladies at the hospital?" asks Buck.

"None wants to leave. They say their duty is there, and ours is to get the crops hid before the Yankees steals-um!" retorts Jesse.

Mark, somewhat unsure, says, "Buck, the Yankees are not known to bother women and children, except for taking their food. Y'all best get and hide your stock."

Buck removes his hat and wipes the sweat from his brow. "I'm grateful to both of you for the warning."

Buck sends Buster Phillips' slaves back to their farm and directs them to secure all belongings and to hide food. Once they are out of sight, Buck and Uncle Isaac enter the house. Sally stays outside with Old Charlie to watch for any signs of humans, friend or foe. Fake walls have been built on each side of the massive fireplace inside the parlor. Shelving is within the walls from floor to ceiling. The walls match the old decor of the house perfectly and are undetectable. Each wall is divided into three horizontal sections that are easy to remove.

The Jernigan's table and storeroom have fifty or sixty jars of freshly canned vegetables. Removing one layer of the horizontal fake wall, Buck and Uncle Isaac begin placing the jars on the shelves. The upper most shelves contain the family heirlooms, extra clothing, bedding and cooking utensils, along with ammunition and weapons. They complete their task in a timely manner and set the wall in place without any sign of disturbance. Several canning jars of vegetables remain on the tables in case Sherman's bummers show up demanding food.

Sally hurries inside." Mars Buck, I seed dust yonder and don't know who hit be!"

"Stay calm, Sally, it's too early for the Yankees. They gotta get to the depot first before they head out here," replies Buck.

A wagon comes to a halt in the yard. William Sheppard jumps out. "Have you heard about the Yankees?"

"Sure have! How about town and the hospitals?" asks Buck.

"The stores and hotels are closing, but all is well at the hospitals. There's no worry for their safety. Mrs. Jernigan said to let you know she is gonna stay the night either at the hospital or the church. She sends me here to bring in some fresh corn. They need more corn silk for stomach broth and corn to feed the patients."

⸎

The people of Stone Mountain are exceedingly nervous. What few women are left feel helpless with most all of the men gone to war. The shocked women try to find hiding places for their few, yet precious heirlooms. Some use the chimneys as a secret storage space. The horses and livestock are turned loose in the woods, and the chickens are set free from their enclosures. The women gather the children in their homes and lock the doors. Betty Gail has all of the food brought into the hospital. She instructs her assistants, "Do not leave any food outside. Take the horses and hide them over the hill. Nobody knows how long these Yankees will be here. There are some commissary supplies at the depot." She informs one of the assistants, "I'll take two or three slaves and get whatever I can from the commissary car at the depot and bring them here for safe keeping." A few have an old musket. With such a small population and with most of the men in the army, the only defense the city can depend on is Gen. Joe Wheeler's forces.

Hastily, Gen. Wheeler orders Col. Dibrell's cavalry force to the Stone Mountain depot. They arrive and wait for the Union advance into the city of Stone Mountain. Col. Dibrell orders his men to take cover in the buildings and surrounding woods. Col. Dibrell arrives at the depot and sees Betty Gail unloading the commissary car. "Ma'am, I suggest you get back to where you came from for now. The Yankees are coming into town."

She points to the hospital. "Col. Dibrell, I am in charge of the hospital over there. Just trying to save as much of these supplies as we can for the army."

"It's just too dangerous right now. You don't need to get shot."

"We'll take what we have and get on back to the hospital," Betty Gail says.

Col. Dibrell has already directed his commanders to their positions for a surprise attack on the Yankees and has his aide rush to alert the bugler of the plan, "When the last Yankees passes our position at the edge of town, man, sound charge and our forces will open fire at once." Col. Dibrell takes his place in the woods with his staff and observes the Union force. Leaving their horses behind so as not to be detected, they become alarmed at the size of the Union force. Col. Dibrell begins to wait for the last of the Pennsylvania, and Ohio troops to pass. Soon he realizes that the lead column is probably already at the depot while the end of the Pennsylvania and Ohio are not even in sight. His bugler points in the direction of the depot. "Look sir, something is burning near the depot."

"It must be the depot and water tank." Realizing what is happening, Col. Dibrell orders his bugler to sound "charge." The firing commences and surprises the Yankees. Dibrell's forces have the advantage and charge the Yankees. Numerous Pennsylvania and Ohio soldiers fall wounded or dead from their mounts. Some of the wounded remain in their saddles, slumping and trying to find their way to the rear. Several Yankees had dismounted in the back and front of the outside of the hospital when the attack begins. Unable to get organized against Dibrell's cavalry, the Yankees, thoroughly disorganized and unsure of the number in Col. Dibrell's cavalry, hastily mount and escape from town. The battle is over in less than five minutes, and Col. Dibrell's cavalry suffers no losses.

Betty Gail opens the front door to the hospital and observes the water tank as two of it's support legs are roped to six cavalry horses. With a smack from the Union riders the horse tear away the legs and the water tank falls to the ground splashing it's contents along the tracks. She observes another group of Yankees throw fiery torches onto the roof of the depot. Slowly the flames begin to grow larger and spread across the roof.

Twisting her apron in her hands she sternly tells her assistant, "Nothing we can do about the depot fire. Just have to let it burn itself out. It's mostly granite except for the roof. We need to gather the wounded and bring them here. Send for the horses so we can hitch them up."

Her assistant rushes out and disappears over the hill. She returns inside and begins checking on the patients. Many are aware of the skirmish, yet many are so sick they are unaware of their surroundings. She and the nurses attempt to calm the wounded and sick, reassuring them that the Yankees will not harm soldiers in hospitals.

Betty Gail sees the slaves hitching the horses and mules to the wagons. She goes outside with several of her nurses. "Go with the wagons and bring back the wounded. Bring back both the Yankees and Confederate wounded and dead."

Without discussion, the nurses climb onto the wagons and begin the search along the dirt road running along the railroad tracks.

❧

The three Pennsylvania Companies and the Signal Detachment of the Sixteenth Ohio Volunteer Infantry, under the command of First lieutenant Samuel Edge which General Garrard sent to Stone Mountain, are hastily returning from the vicinity of the Stone Mountain Depot.[319] The commander reports to Colonel Minty that they ran into Rebel cavalry around 3:30 PM. As 5:00 PM approaches, General Garrard is unsure of the enemy strength to his left. Captain Levi T. Griffin is given orders to take his Company I of the 4th Michigan Cavalry on a reconnaissance mission. This time, Col. Dibrell's bugler sounds charge as the front guard of Captain Griffin's Company enters the center of the town of Stone Mountain. Surprisingly, Captain Griffin immediately orders his bugler to sound retreat. The remainder of his regiment gathers their arms and is also heading for the depot.

Near the city limits, they meet Captain Griffin's Company retreating. Lieutenant Edge reports to Captain Griffin. "There is a pretty strongly posted compliment of Rebel cavalry in town that caught us by surprise. I ordered my company to withdraw. Fortunately, it has not suffered any casualties." Colonel Minty forwards this information to General Garrard who in turn orders a withdrawal of all troops before dark. The 4th Michigan is given orders to cover the retreat.[320]

The sun is beginning to set as General Lightburn's troops are heading for Browning's Courthouse. He and Captain Lofland are returning together. He asks Captain Lofland, "How did your Second Brigade do today?"

"We destroyed one and a half miles of the railroad. May have been able to do more if it had not been for the rebels."

Behind General Lightburn are General Garrard's men on foot. The foot soldiers turn west at Browning's Courthouse and at Henderson Mill hook-up with the Major General John Logan's XV Corps. General Garrard issues an order for Colonel Bob Minty's Michigan 4th to cover the retreat to Browning's Courthouse.

The foot soldiers of General Lightburn retire from their exhausting July day near Stone Mountain. Dusty, sunburned and dehydrated, they turn left at the courthouse and head to Henderson Mill to hook-up with the XV Corps.

"This may have been the passenger train that reached the broken tracks at Stone Mountain and turned back," replies Captain Lofland.

A train on its way to Atlanta stops at the Stone Mountain Depot. James Goldsmith runs out to speak with the engineer. "Yankees tore up the tracks about a mile from here."

The engineer asks, "Why didn't you telegraph us?"

"There are no working telegraph lines along this stretch of the Georgia Railroad," remarks the nervous station agent, James Goldsmith. In the meantime, he places the station clock on the wall, which he had escaped with as the Yankees came into town on the previous day. The townspeople and Confederate military alert the engineer that the tracks were destroyed during the day by Union General Garrard's troops. The agent directs the engineer which side track to park the freight cars with the cargo. Moving the freight cars to the sidetrack, the train begins a long backward journey to Lithonia where there's a turn-around and heads back south.

SAVING THE HOSPITALS

General Garrard drafts his report to be forwarded to General McPherson headquarters at Blake's Mill on Peachtree Creek. "In obedience to orders, I left my camp at 5:00 AM this morning to break the railroad between Stone Mountain and Decatur. At Browning's Courthouse I struck the rebel pickets, and skirmished for three miles to the railroad, which I effectually destroyed for more than two miles, including several culverts, a wood yard and the water tank at Stone Mountain depot. I sent a force into Stone Mountain, and found the Rebels there about 5:00 PM, but not in force. The depot was not burned."[321]

General McPherson finishes reading General Garrard's report. He combines his daily report with General Garrard's and has his courier deliver the reports to General Sherman. It is another warm and muggy July night as the courier arrives at the Samuel House at the intersection of Old Cross Keys and Peachtree Roads, General Sherman's headquarters.

"General Thomas, I have reports from General McPherson to 2 PM. He has reached the railroad at a point two miles from Stone Mountain and seven miles from Decatur. He has broken the telegraphs and road. By 5 PM tomorrow, he will have four or five miles broken."[322]

JULY 18, 1864

SPECIAL FIELD ORDERS, HDQRS. MIL. DIV. OF THE MISS.,
Numbers 37. In the Field, near Cross Keys, Ga.,
The movement of the army to-morrow, July 19, will be as follows:

I. Major-General Thomas will press down from the north on Atlanta,
holding in strength the line of Peach Tree, but crossing and threatening

the enemy at all accessible points to hold him there, and also taking advantage of any ground gained, especially on the extreme right.

II. Major-General Schofield will move direct on Decatur and gain a footing on the railroad, holding it, and breaking the railroad and telegraph wire.

III. Major-General McPherson will move along the railroad toward Decatur and break the telegraph wires and the railroad. In case of the sounds of serious battle he will close in on General Schofield, but otherwise will keep every man of his command at work in destroying the railroad by tearing up track, burning the ties and iron, and twisting the bars when hot. Officers should be instructed that bars simply bent may be used again, but if when red hot if they are twisted, they cannot be used again. Pile the ties into shape for a bonfire, put the rails across, and when red hot in the middle, let a man at each end twist the bar so that its surface become spiral. General McPherson will dispatch General Garrard's cavalry eastward along the line of the railroad to continue the destruction as far as deemed prudent.

IV. All the troops should be in motion at 5 AM, and should not lose a moment's time until night, when the lines should be closed on General Schofield about Pea Vine and Decatur.

By order of Major General W. T. Sherman[323]

General Garrard decides to send Colonel Abe Miller's command and Lieutenant George Robinson's 2nd section of the Board of Trade Battery on the road to Stone Mountain around noon. Captain Adam Pinkerton's 72nd Indiana Company is the advance guard.

Col. George Dibrell's Tennessee Mounted Infantry are lying in wait for the 72nd Indiana as they approach the picket line at Browning's Courthouse. Col. Dibrell's forces launch a surprise infantry attack from the woods. Captain Pinkerton's Unit dismounts and forms a skirmish line.[324] There's now a thin Line of Gray and Blue, soldier against soldier, Yankee Spenser rifles against Rebel muskets.

Both Union and Confederate are equal in courage and self-reliance. Moreover, they are zealous in their cause. A Confederate officer instructs his men from the skirmish line, "Just sight the location of one of the Yankees from a puff of smoke from his weapon. That's how to locate him."

Each side firing, the Gray advances and then the Blue advances. Both sides gain and lose a few yards. A Confederate soldier dodges from tree to tree to protect himself. Out of breath, he drops his belly upon the ground. He peers cautiously just to find a rise or an advantage ditch, so he can take aim upon a Yankee. His eyes are always to the front. He strains his eyes as he scans the battle for the slightest motion, hopeful to deliver his gift of death to a Yankee. The confederate soldier never exposes himself. He loads his weapon, as if it is an unconscious act. He bites his salty paper cartridge and drives the charge home with his ramrod, primes his weapon with a percussion cap. Seeking and finding his target, he fires at the enemy, three shots per minute.

The Yankee cavalry has a great advantage. The Yankee soldier simply loads his metal case single round into the rifle chamber and fires. His weapon carries a bullet further and faster than that of the musket. The bullets whiz by the Confederate as commands are shouted. He hears his wounded comrade moan, and sees his dead friend lay silent. The Confederate raises his hat as another comrade looks for a Blue to take the bait. The Yankee does. The Confederate aims and fires a shot and watches the enemy fall as his crimson blood flows from his mortal wound. The two Confederate soldiers congratulate each other and continue to tease and seek out another Yankee.

Captain Pickerton cannot hold his line and anxiously requests reinforcements from Colonel Miller. Colonel Miller orders the 17th Indiana, the 123rd Illinois and Lieutenant Robinson with his two Parrott cannons to reinforce Captain Pinkerton's precarious unit. Lieutenant Robinson fields the Parrott Battery and opens fire. The Confederates witness a sudden rattle, a whoosh of air passes overhead and the shells begin to explode. The solid shot sings as it passes through the trees. The Confederate soldiers hug the ground as huge branches are torn away and without mercy descend upon them. "Aim lower. Aim at the earthworks," shouts Lieutenant Robinson. Suddenly the Parrott Battery fires and destroys the earthworks.

Bits and pieces of mutilated Confederates fly from the path of the cannon balls. The noise of the cannon fire is that of an exploding volcano. The Confederate soldier is deafened and cannot hear the orders from Col. Dibrell. He turns to look for his leader and disappears from another blast of the Yankee cannon. The Confederate advantage is quickly reduced. Col. Dibrell's unit hastily withdraws through the tall timber. The Confederates are able to get to the railroad where the 4th Michigan's destruction of the railroad ended the day before. Gen. Wheeler's Confederate Cavalry, under the command of BG. John H. Kelly, covers their withdrawal.

Gen. Kelly orders snipers to take refuge in and around the houses along the railroad track at the city limits of Stone Mountain. With the provident eye of the majestic granite mountain in the background, the sharpshooters take their position. With his telescopic rifle, each Confederate sharpshooter sights along with the infantry and commences firing from the upstairs windows.

Parrott cannons[325] of Lieutenant Robinson artillerymen arrive and open fire against the Confederate sharpshooters.

The initial cannon ball rips through the second floor of the house. Crashing into the front room, several inches above the floor, the cannon ball knocks the chair out from under the owner. Terrified, the owner hastily exits through the hole produced by the cannon ball in the far wall. The shock of the cannon fire again disrupts the Confederates and the sharpshooters rapidly abandon the house. Colonel Miller's men charge. As the Parrott guns continue to fire, Gen. Kelly's Cavalry are in full retreat with Colonel Miller's in hot pursuit through the woods surrounding Stone Mountain.

The roar of the nearing cannons signals the citizens that the war is coming to Stone Mountain. Then the rifle and musket fire draw closer, louder and sustain longer. Betty Gail locates a large white sheet she and Bennett Jeffares had stored.[326] On the sheet in large print is the word 'HOSPITAL.' She and Bennett go outside and tie the sheet across the front of the hospital. Betty Gail checks the tie-downs to be sure the sheet can withstand any strong winds. "I hope the sheet will send a message to the Yankees that this is a hospital and should not be disturbed," she says. "Maybe they will leave the patients alone."

"It just depends on which Yankee shows up from what I understand. Some good and some bad. I've heard that some of the Yankees come in and steal from the patients," replies Bennett.

The hospital staff, standing in front of Dr. Hamilton's hospital, located across the railroad track from the depot turns their attention to the distant sound of horses' hoofs and clouds of dust, which appear over the tree line. Betty Gail fears the Yankees are close by, but she is surprised when the retreating Confederate cavalry rush and scatter through town. Soldiers on foot follow behind. Some stopping, taking cover, loading the clumsy musket, firing and retreating. Betty Gail and the nurse dash inside and observe from a window. In horror, Betty Gail sees one soldier fall. Then another falls. Then four more poor soldiers surrender their lives.

An orderly taps Betty Gail on the shoulder. "Miss Betty Gail, some of the patients are trying to scramble out of here." She leaves the horrific view from her window and begins to visit and reassure the patients that they are safe but panic breaks regardless. Even the most critical vainly attempt to escape.

"The Yankees will not harm you!" exclaims Betty Gail over and over as she attempts to comfort the patients. She sits beside a critical soldier and holds his hand and tries to reassure him that the Yankees are not going to harm him. At that instant a stray bullet breaks a window and some of the shattered glass falls on the suffering soldier. Startled, with his eyes wide open, he tries to raise his head and speak. Betty Gail can feel his rapid pulse and suddenly she feels no pulse and hears a long shallow relaxing exhaling of his last breath. She releases the soldier's hand and quietly says a prayer for him. Then she gently pulls his sheet over his sleeping face. Bennett Jeffares is standing nearby and witnesses the soldier's demise.

"I'll take him to the cemetery when the town settles down, Mrs. Jernigan."

"Thank you, Bennett."

Betty Gail hears the front door open and is concerned that someone is trying to leave. She hurries to the front and finds James Goldsmith, the station agent holding a large wall clock under his arm. "Hello Betty Gail. Sorry to disturb you, but the Yankees are nearby, and I only had time to get the wall clock out of the station and run over here."

"That's fine James. You can help us comfort some of the nervous patients."

"I'll be glad to help. Gen. Kelly told me he has instructions for his cavalry to burn the provisions at the depot if they are unable to beat the Yankees back."

"Just put the depot clock under the sofa," said Betty Gail. "And go to one of the rooms and sit with some of the patients."

He places the large clock underneath the sofa in the front room and goes to one of the patient wards. Betty Gail smells smoke through an open window and hurries to see where it's coming from. Dr. Maddox opens the front door, and Betty Gail and he sees smoke surrounding the depot across from the hospital. "Not looking good Dr. Maddox. Looks like Gen. Kelly is burning the provisions at the depot." She shakes her head sadly, understanding the implications. "Not a good sign, I'm afraid."

"I suppose we best prepare for a Yankee visit," replies Dr. Maddox. "And hope that they're compassionate."

Col. Dibrell's Confederate forces set fire to two hundred bales of cotton, thirty-five hundred bushels of corn and three freight cars of commissary goods before continuing the retreat.

⚬

The Yankees arrive close behind the retreating Confederates.

Now they have orders not to pursue the Rebels beyond the depot. The woods are too dense and it's getting late. Yankees begin to forage against the flames and set fire to the depot containing quartermaster commissary supplies.[327]

Colonel Abe Miller, accompanied by his staff and guards, enters the hospital. He glances at the assembled hospital workers. "Who is the Doctor in charge here?" shouts Colonel Miller.

"I am," replies Dr. Maddox, as he approaches Colonel Miller.

Betty Gail inhales deeply and steps forward. She looks directly into the eyes of Colonel Miller. "We have critically wounded and sick soldiers here, from both the north and the south, sir. A kinder and mellower voice would be appreciated." The nurses and orderlies are quiet and continue the routine of caring for the patients.

Hesitating for a moment, the Colonel replies, "Show me the Union soldiers, Ma'am."

"This way please," says Betty Gail as she motions with her head. "We treat whoever needs treating, without regard to their loyalties."

"May I return to my patients?" asks Dr. Maddox.

"You may. Go with him Lieutenant," retorts the Colonel as he follows Betty Gail upstairs.

As they enter room number two at the head of the stairs, Betty Gail informs the Colonel, "Here they are. Four of your Union men along with twenty-four Confederates. One private is recovering from a scalp wound. Another private has severe chest wounds with complications of high fever and delirium. The third, an amputated foot."

They move among the patients as she points them out to Colonel Miller. He hesitates a moment at each bed and looks at the patients. At the bed of the amputee, he looks more closely at the bandages. Betty Gail waits until he catches up to her.

"And, the fourth is this Sergeant who is recovering from malaria," says Betty Gail, pointing to the Sergeant.

"I see you're caring for these soldiers as if they are your own kin." Removing himself from the room, he asks, "What is your name, lady?"

"Mrs. Betty Gail Jernigan."

Colonel Miller moves toward his adjutant. "Bring all Confederate and Union wounded to this hospital immediately." The Adjutant salutes, removes himself to execute the Colonel's orders. "Mrs. Jernigan, generally we take over hospitals, especially those on the railroad or else we burn them to the ground. I am aware that DeKalb County voted against secession. This is but a small hospital and since you have obviously shown compassion for federal troops, I am placing an order on the door that this hospital is to be spared by all federal troops passing through."

"Thank you, Colonel, but there's an even smaller hospital two blocks from here and a Wayside 'round the Mountain. Could you render the same courtesy to those as well? And allow us to keep one horse and one mule at each hospital?"

"I see no problem with your request, after I examine the other hospitals. Show my Sergeant where the hospitals are and, if it is as you say, I'll direct my clerk to draw up the two other orders," states Colonel Miller.

"Thank you, sir. Now, may I go to attend the wounded?"

"In a few minutes. Where is the calaboose?"

"There, by the depot and all of the doors are open. Nearby where your men are fighting the fire to get the commissary goods from the freight cars," replies Betty Gail.

"You may return to your patients now." Colonel Miller begins talking to Dr. Maddox while waiting for the Sergeant to return with his report.

"Sir, I checked the hospital across the way, and I'm certain it would meet with your approval. The other one the lady mentioned is far around the mountain. I hesitate to go there with the thick woods, sir, unless you feel it is that important."

"Thank you, Sergeant. If the other hospital you inspected is as this one, I feel comfortable in signing an order for all three. Send my clerk in here, Sergeant."

"Yes sir?" Colonel Miller directs his clerk to draw up the orders to spare the hospitals and the Wayside and grant the right to keep one horse and one mule at each location. He signs the documents, gives them to Dr. Maddox and Betty Gail and then departs.

The Yankee ambulance Corps moves into town and begins to recover the mortal casualties. The Union's wounded refuse to enter Dr. George Washington Maddox hospital for initial treatment and are taken to the Union field hospital instead. The conscious Union soldiers thank Betty Gail and the other ladies for their kindness as they board their ambulance and head to the federal field hospital.

❧

Colonel Miller reports to General Garrard. During the course of Col. Dibrell's withdrawal, Colonel Miller's men recovered a battle flag belonging to Col. Dibrell's unit.[328] General Garrard is content to continue the railroad track destruction up to the depot and orders the complete destruction of the remaining supplies at and around the depot.

As the sun is beginning to set on this hot, humid and indelible day in Stone Mountain, an urgent report is given to General Garrard. The report contains intelligence information that Gen. Wheeler is ordering reinforcements for the retreating Confederates. Due to the time of day, General Garrard orders his army to fall back to Browning's Courthouse.

The two academies, one common school, three churches, saw mill and cotton gin are intact as the Yankees depart, but eighty Confederate soldiers, mostly unknown, lay dead. The local Baptist Pastor, Fielding Maddox, and the local Methodist Pastor, Mr. Davies, pray for their souls as Bennett and his helpers bury the dead.

At sunset, Buck peers up the narrow dirt road in search of Betty Gail. Concerned for her safety he heads out to determine what has delayed his wife. Isaac watches as Buck departs and then continues to feed the chickens, ducks and hogs. His last chore before dark is to secure the horses in the barn.

MONDAY, JULY 19, 1864

Captain Cyrus Browne, commander of the 55th Illinois Infantry, departs Nancy Creek and marches five miles toward Stone Mountain and destroys the track on the Augusta railroad before marching to Decatur.[329]

The 13th Ohio Veteran Vol. Infantry departs its campsite near Stony Creek and marches to Decatur. There they strike the railroad again in Stone Mountain and continued to destroy the track as usual.[330]

The 111th break camp at 5:00 AM and march on the Decatur Road which is the left main road and strikes the railroad east of Atlanta. The task was cheerfully performed and upon completion the 11th marches at 12 midnight for Decatur and camps there for the night.[331]

Colonel Fulton, with the 53rd Regimental Ohio departs camp and marches six miles. After driving away the Confederate pickets of either Col. Dibrell or Gen. Kelly the 53rd was able to destroy about one mile of railroad before marching to Decatur. The 53rd had 19 killed, 201 wounded, and 16 missing during this period.[332]

JULY 19, 1864-10 PM

HEADQUARTERS CAVALRY DIVISION, General Garrard files his report to General McPherson.

> *GENERAL: I have to report that, owing to the appearance of the enemy in this vicinity last evening, I sent a regiment to the Peach Tree road, one to McAfee's Bridge, and ordered Colonel Long, with his two regiments, up; also, that trains, stragglers, &c., constantly passing along this road, I did not feel justified in moving forward until all was secure. This delayed me till 12 m., when I sent the Third Brigade, Colonel Miller commanding, toward Stone Mountain. They met strong opposition just outside of my pickets, and had heavy skirmishing to within a mile of the depot. I then moved up Long, and we went into the town. We fought two brigades, but the country being so unfavorable for cavalry, I was unable to reap the fruits of the victory gained by my dismounted men. We captured no prisoners, but captured one set of colors, which they dropped in their hasty retreat. The depot, containing large amount of quartermaster and commissary stores, was burned, also about 200 bales of cotton, also the railroad as fast as we advanced. The delay caused by skirmishing prevented me advancing beyond the mountain, and I have just reached my camp of last night. These two brigades came in last night, and I have no doubt that it was in view of saving the Government property in the depot. The rebels set it on fire after we reached the edge of the town. We had to use artillery to drive them out of the houses. I could only spare five regiments for this duty, and if I am to guard such an extended flank it will be impossible for me to do anything else. I*

would suggest the destruction of McAfee's Bridge, and that my line be contracted. I then can be of assistance to you and guard the left.

Very respectfully, your obedient servant,

K. GARRARD
Brigadier-General, Commanding Division[333]

On Wednesday, July 20, 1864 General Garrard receives permission from General Sherman to burn McAfee's Bridge and to give further attention to the road between Lithonia and Covington and, if possible, to burn the Yellow River Bridge west of Covington.[334]

General Sherman reviews earlier telegram information from General Grant concerning certain possible troop deployment by Gen. Lee. General Grant's Intelligence Officer reports that Gen. Lee is probably going to deploy an entire Corps from his Army of Northern Virginia to Georgia. The troops will arrive by railroad to reinforce the Confederate troops in the defense of Atlanta. General Sherman's resolve to disrupt Gen. Lee's battle-hardened troops and their movement is matter-of-fact. Locating these Confederate troops within ten miles of his rear and flank could lead to disaster for the Union forces.

At 1:00 in the morning on Thursday, July 21, General Sherman completes his orders for General Garrard and sends his courier to deliver them. He arrives in Decatur around 1:30 AM.

HDQRS. MILITARY DIVISION OF THE MISSISSIPPI, In the Field, near Atlanta, July 20, 1864-midnight
General GARRARD, Commanding Cavalry Division:

GENERAL: After destroying the bridge at McAfee's, which I suppose is already done, you will send to General McPherson's guard at the bridge at Roswell your wagons, led horses, and baggage, and proceed rapidly to Covington, on the main wagon and rail road east, distance about thirty miles from Decatur. Take the road by Latimar's touching the railroad at or beyond Lithonia, and thence substantially along the railroad, destroying it effectually all the way, especially the Yellow River bridge this side of Covington, as well as the road bridge over Yellow River, after you have passed. From Covington send detachments to destroy the rail and road bridges east of Covington over the Ulcofauhachee. Try and capture and destroy some locomotives and cars, and the depots and stores at Covington, but of private property only take what is necessary for your own use, except horses and mules, of which you will take all that are fit for service, exercising, of course, some judgment as to the animals belonging to the poor and needy. On your return select your own route, but I would suggest that by way of Sheffield, Rock Bridge, and Stone Mountain, or even farther north if you prefer. I want you to put your whole strength at this, and to do it quick and well. I know it can be done. By passing Yellow River by the road bridge, and then pushing for the railroad bridges right and left, the guard will run or even burn their own bridges. You ought to catch some trains about Covington, as there is no telegraph to give them timely warning. I believe that the cavalry is mostly withdrawn from that flank of the enemy, and that you can ride roughshod over any force there; at all events, it is a matter of vital importance and must be attempted with great vigor. The importance of it will justify the loss of quarter of your command. Be prepared with axes, hatches, and bars to tear up sections of track and make bonfires. When the rails are red hot they must be twisted. Burning will do for bridges and culverts, but no for ordinary track. Let the work be well done. The whole thing should be done in two days, including to-morrow. I will notify General McPherson that he may look out for his rear and trains.

I am, with respects, yours, truly,

W. T. SHERMAN
Major-General, Commanding

If the McAfee Bridge is not already burned you can send messenger to the guard already there to do it and move to Roswell. This need not delay your departure for Covington at once.[335]

After reading General Sherman's order, General Garrard immediate dispatches couriers to recall his units, some of which are in distant locations.

HEADQUARTERS CAVALRY DIVISION
Decatur, July 21, 1864.
Major-General SHERMAN, Commanding Army:

GENERAL: I have the honor to acknowledge the receipt of your orders last night at 1.30 AM. At that time one brigade (three regiments) was at Cross Keys, ten miles from here, with pickets in every direction from there to four miles; one regiment was at McAfee's Bridge and one at Roswell, leaving me only five regiments, which were all on duty here guarding the roads. I at once took the necessary steps to carry out your instructions, and will leave here during the day, and by traveling to-night make up for the time lost in concentration. My pickets on the road to the south and east are constantly exchanging shots with rebel cavalry pickets, and this morning one of my patrols down the Covington road captured 2 prisoners belonging to a brigade camped, when they left it, at Latimar's. As your object is to destroy the bridges and six or eight miles of road east of Stone Mountain, and as my chance of success is better by varying some from the route indicated, I deem it best to do so. I desire to succeed, as you place so much importance in having it done, and I will endeavor to do it. I would have started with my five regiments here, but my force would have been too weak to tear up railroad. If no misfortune happens I will burn the bridge east of Covington by 12 m. to-morrow, and by doing this first I will catch all west of that point. I then propose breaking up everything between the two rivers. Trusting my views may meet your approval.

I remain, very respectfully, your obedient servant,

K. GARRARD
Brigadier-General, Commanding Division[336]

THE BATTLE FOR DECATUR

JULY 21 1864

The front door to Mary Gay's house flies open. "Yank, Yank," yells Telitha, Mary's slave.

Mary and her mother try to slow Telitha as she runs through the house to the parlor. "What's wrong Telitha?" asks Mary nervously.

Telitha picks up a blue pillow and shakes it while pointing outside. She shouts, "Yanks, Yanks."

Mary rushes to the front door behind Telitha. Mary's mother follows close behind. Mary puts her hand over her chest and takes a deep breath, "Oh my. The Yankees have arrived." It is the first notion that the enemy has come to Decatur.[337] In a matter of minutes her two acres are covered with Union troops. Afraid to the challenge the intruders, she and her mother hold each other around the waist at the wonderment of such a large Union force taking over their property. Mary sees several soldiers looking in their direction so she and her mother silently go back into the house.

The Yankee soldiers run and jump on the porch of the house and push the door open before Mary and Telitha are able to close and secure the lock. Mary and Telitha nearly fall to the floor as the Yankees force their way in.

"Get out of my house," Mary shouts and pushes on the chest of one of the soldiers. He takes her by the wrist and shoves her to the sofa.

"You sit here." He turns to her mother and Telitha. "You two join her and stay on the sofa until we leave." Mary rubs her wrist and tries to comfort her nervous mother at the same time.

The soldiers ransack the house and are laughing as they walk outside. Their arms are filled with furnishings including silverware and bedding material and even bureau drawers. As the last Yankee departs the front door, he turns back with a broad sinister smile," You can get up now and clean up your house."

Mary jumps up and slams the front door shut. Her shaking mother and Telitha join her at a window. Mary pulls back a curtain and watches as the Yankees show off their prizes. The bureau drawers are given to privates for feeding troughs. Mary watches as they pour oats into them for the hungry livestock. Shocking sounds are heard from the barn area. A pig squeals, a shot is fired. Then silence.[338]

Around noon on the 21st, Colonel Ed Kitchell's 98th Illinois arrives in Decatur. Colonel Bob Minty's 1st departs Cross Keys around midmorning, marches south, reaching Decatur later in the afternoon.

General Garrard departs for Browning's Courthouse without Colonel Minty who arrived later. Around 5 o'clock Colonel Eli Long's 3rd and 4th Ohio, Colonel Abe Miller's mounted Infantry and the center section of the Board of Trade Battery depart Decatur.

JULY 22, 1864

After sleeping late, the Board of Trade Battery troops allow their horses to feed on the local lawns. Most of the Battery's foragers are with the two cannons accompanying General Garrard to Browning's Courthouse. Gen. Wheeler's cavalry is leading Gen. Hardee's corps on a forced fifteen-mile night march to Decatur approaching Decatur from the southwest. Gen. Wheeler is acquainted with the roads and general area around Decatur. While the Board of Trade Battery soldiers smell the sweet aroma of the noon meal several soldiers enter camp. Lieutenant Griffin notices several familiar soldiers walking hastily toward him. "Sir, there are Confederate troops scouting our picket lines. Looks like cavalry."

"Gen. Wheeler's cavalry and Gen. Hardee's corps have been reported in this area," replies the Lieutenant. "Any idea how many there are, soldier?"

"I think a goodly number sir."

The Confederates continue northeast along the ridge, which has a dense forest to provide cover along the rough wagon trail, which leads to Stone Mountain. The Confederates' cavalry dismounts, and using the dense woods and underbrush, place themselves behind the Federal entrenchments. Gen. Wheeler's scouts report back to Gen. Wheeler. "Sir, General Schofield's 23rd corps is entrenched along the south and east of

Decatur. Pretty strong force there." Gen. Wheeler quietly summons his field commanders and sets a battle plan. "Immediately dismount and begin a surprise attack all along the federal line. Attack on the sound of three successive shots."

Alarmed by the report of his soldiers, Lieutenant Griffin observes the Michigan battery and the Infantry forming a line of battle not too far from his command. He meets Colonel Sprague from General Schofield's 23rd Corps. "Sir, I just received a report from some of my men that there are Confederate scouts in the area." Colonel Sprague gazes at Lieutenant Griffin for a moment, "Doesn't appear to be much going on here. I haven't received any such report from my men." Colonel Sprague shrugs his shoulders.

"Lieutenant it's probably only a few Rebel cavalry trying to cause a problem, but I can handle it." Lieutenant Griffin is still not convinced there will be an attack on his unit. As he is returning to his battery, he plainly hears occasional rifle fire raising his suspect of an imminent attack. He is very apprehensive when he returns to his battery and instructs his men, "Prepare the horses and guns quickly for deployment on my command. We may be coming under attack from the enemy soon."

The men rush to their posts and hitch the horses to the guns and caissons. Just as the slack is drawn from the trace chains, several Confederate artillery shells explode dangerously near in the road to their left. Some of the men take cover while others hold the reins of the horses attempting to pull away.

Another long, loud and shrilling signal from a Confederate cannon awakens the remaining drowsy Yankees. "To Arms! To Arms!" shout commanders and the surprised Yankees rush from their tents, grab their weapons and scatter for cover. Taking positions, they wait for the Confederates to appear. Lieutenant Griffin and his Sergeants shout, "Hitch horses and mules to the wagons and move out as quickly as possible."

The Confederates come out of the woods in large numbers. The Yankee infantry begin laying small arms fire but are unable to slow down Gen. Wheeler's troops. The Yankees begin to retreat, but Gen. Hardee's foot soldiers are unable to maintain the pace of Gen. Wheeler's men. Gen. Wheeler looks back for Gen. Hardee's 6000 troops and sees they are exhausted from their all night march in the heat and dust. Gen. Wheeler reels his horse back. Raising his hand he signals his commander to halt his cavalry where they are. Then orders the bugler to sound 'To the Colors.'

signaling his cavalry to regroup and wait for Gen. Hardee's troops to catch up.

Shot and shell fly every direction, but Mary manages to stand her ground for a few moments longer. As calmly as possible she enters the house and again takes a spot by the window to observe the growing tumult outside. Leaves, limbs and tree bark hail down outside her vantage point, and she can hardly see the road at times.

The roar of cannons and the barrage of musketry complete the grand cacophony. Amid the absorbing scene, she exits the house, ready to rush into the conflict as if she is a soldier.

One of her guests, an old woman descended from George Washington, wanders out. Mary restrains the woman as best she can, "Are you trying to be like your great ancestor?"

"This is my war. My folks fought for this country, and I'm ready to fight too!"

"Why you're so old, you can't even make it to the front door." Mary takes the determined old lady by the arm and leads her back inside. "Just stay with me and let this pass. You are bordering on four score years and ten, and I'm not letting go of you. Besides you might go in the opposite direction and join the ranks of the Yankees."[339]

Colonel Sprague no longer needs convincing that a Confederate force is in the area. Keeping his head low he orders Lieutenant Griffin. "Deploy the cannons forward in support of the Infantry."

"Yes sir, Colonel." Lieutenant Griffin's battery begins changing it position and is able to move only a couple hundred yards. Gen. Wheeler's cavalry begins to gain on the battery and kills several of the battery soldiers. Colonel Sprague is observing the action and orders Lieutenant Griffin, "Retreat to your original position at the Decatur jail."

"Look! That Yankee Colonel's troops are in full retreat," Mary Gay says waving her handkerchief. "Go get'um Gen. Wheeler."

From her vantage point on her front porch, she is able to see Lieutenant Griffin wheel his two Parrotts next to Lieutenant Henry Bennett's first section. Mary prays to herself. "Please let Gen. Wheeler get there before those Yankees start firing." Suddenly, the four breech-banded Parrotts commence firing canister[340] into Gen. Wheeler's assaulting Confederate ranks. Mary jumps from fright and places her hands over her ears as screams come from her frightened mother in the house.

Lieutenant Griffin turns to Colonel Sprague, "Looks like we stopped them for now Colonel." The Parrott cannons temporarily neutralize Gen. Wheeler's dismounted Cavalry, consisting of eight Regiments of approximately 6,000 men.

In disbelief Mary shouts, "Don't stop now, Gen. Wheeler. You got'um on the run."

Colonel Sprague seizes the opportunity to organize his three Regiments around the Decatur Courthouse. At the new position, through his field glasses, he observes Gen. Wheeler's massive troop line teeming over the railroad berm. Mary yells inside to her anxious mother, "Look over there. Here our guys come again."

The Confederate forces assault Colonel Sprague's line diagonally, engaging in hand-to-hand combat. Bright bayonets become stained red, pistols fire. The dying drop their arms and fall motionless to the ground. Lieutenant Griffin's men fire the Parrotts and hail the Confederates with canister. Mary becomes distressed at the carnage and retreats inside with her head down and her hands over her ears. Telitha is doing her best to comfort Mary's mother. Colonel Sprague's battery troops have not been able to get fully organized and are running out of ammunition. As the battery is overrun by the Confederates, Colonel Sprague has the bugler sound 'Retreat'.

Lieutenant Griffin shouts another order, "Remove the Parrotts from the Courthouse Square to redeploy the four guns to the rear." Two companies of the 63rd Ohio fix bayonets and charge rushing to protect the two Parrotts against the advancing Confederates as the Parrotts retreat successfully.

Mary goes back on her porch observing Gen. Wheeler's artillery target Lieutenant Bennett's unit south of the square. With her hands over her ears she shouts toward Gen. Wheeler's artillery, "That's the way to teach those Yankee's a lesson."

However her excitement is short lived. To Mary's dismay, Lieutenant Bennett quickly silences the Confederate artillery just as the dismounted Confederate troops attack him from both flanks.

Lieutenant Bennett orders, "Turn one gun away from the railroad and fire canisters into the advancing Confederate troops."

Swab, load, ram, and fire! The Confederate soldiers begin to fall, some screaming, some lying still, and some able to retreat with their wounds. Through the smoke and smell of sulfur, Mary stands proudly as the bulk of Gen. Wheeler's force is triumphant and capture Lieutenant Bennett's position.

Lieutenant Griffin, running out of ammunition and also unable to defeat the overwhelming Confederate force, shouts, "Both Parrott Battery sections retreat immediately." His Battery, now short of men, mounts the lead horses and retreat in the direction of Shallow Ford Road. Three companies of the 9th Illinois Mounted Infantry, escorting a supply train down Shallow Ford Road, are keenly aware of the skirmish and rush to give assistance to Colonel Sprague's and Lieutenant Griffin's troops and block the Confederate advance.

Soon the smoke clears although there is gunfire in the distance, and the battle of Decatur draws to an agonizing close. Mary yells through the door, "The coast is clear. Everyone can come outside now." Soon Telitha bracing Mary's frail mother, peers cautiously through the door passage. Mary smiles and takes her mother's arms and the hugs her. Proudly she boasts, "Mine is, no doubt, the only feminine eye that witnessed the complete rout of the Federals on this occasion. I am happy! Oh, so happy I saw the splendid Federal army of General Schofield's Division ignominiously flee from a little band of lean, lank, hungry, poorly-clad Confederate soldiers. I doubt not an over-ruling Providence will lead us to final victory."[341]

Late in the afternoon Gen. Wheeler talks of the battle with his adjutant while they inspect his cavalry, "We captured 225 Yankees and a large number of small arms. One twelve-pounder gun, caisson and six wagons and teams."

As they approach the prisoners his adjutant says, "Sir, there is Captain Bennett. He commanded the battery which we captured. Stopping near Captain Bennett, Gen. Wheeler's adjutant smiles, "Welcome Captain, I see you and your men have involuntarily come to the Confederate side." With no comment, Captain Bennett returns the adjutant's comment with a grim stare.

❧

General Sherman receives information from General Schofield. "Gen. Hood has abandoned Atlanta." Sherman hurries to the two-story Howard House at the center of the Union line to direct a Union pursuit of Gen. Hood. Peering across the terrain, he confides in Major Audenried, "It appears the Confederate Infantry are cutting and preparing small trees and setting abatis. Gen. Hood is not ready to abandon Atlanta. Look for yourself Major."

Major Audenried places his field glasses upon his eyes and peers toward the Confederate lines. "You're right, sir. He still wants to fight some more. Hood has simply fallen back to contract his lines. This way he can form a new ring of works a couple of miles from the center of Atlanta."

"Not going to do him any good at all. If it's another fight he wants, I'll give it to him."

Shortly after noon, Gen. Hood orders Gen. Hardee, "Prepare your entire Corps to launch a surprise attack at the rear of the Federal Forces."

However, as Gen. Hardee's Corps emerges from the woods in deep lines of three and four columns, they come head to head with General Dodge's XVI Corps. General McPherson hears the percussion of the battle and rides into the open to observe the situation. Realizing there's a large gap between the Union forces, he sends his staff officers for reinforcements. General McPherson is not more than one hundred yards from the front line when Gen. Hardee's soldiers from Gen. Cleburne's Texas Brigade under the command of BG James A. Smith begin yelling, "Shoot that man on the horse!" On his black horse, General McPherson and his orderly dash into the woods. They suddenly confront Gen. Hardee's Texas Brigade's soldiers. General McPherson wheels too late and falls from his saddle. He dies instantly from the result of a fatal shot through the heart.[342]

General Sherman is awaiting anxiously the outcome of the battle when General McPherson's adjutant Lieutenant Colonel William T. Clark, gallops up and declares that "General McPherson is either "killed or a prisoner."[343] Shortly, another aid rides in and confirms General McPherson's death.

"McPherson's dead! Can it be?" General Sherman is stunned by the news.

Now, the Confederates attacking with vigor break through General Dodge's right flank and strike General Frank Blair's XVII Corps from the front, from the flank, as well as from the rear. Gen. Hood orders three fresh divisions into the fight at 3:30 PM and successfully breaches General Blair's right flank.

General Sherman is unaware of the successful attacks of the Confederates as General McPherson's staff arrives with the honorable General's body. Carrying the stretcher inside, and ripping a door from its hinges, they make a primitive bier by placing it across two chairs. General

Schofield and a few others somberly and quietly stand by. General Sherman weeps over the lifeless features of his friend and subordinate. "The whole Confederacy," he says. "Cannot atone for the sacrifice of one such life." Tenderly, General Sherman draws the flag over General McPherson and directs two aids to escort the body to Marietta. "Better start at once and drive carefully," he says in a voice choking with emotion.[344]

General Sherman follows General McPherson's body onto the porch as General Charles R. Woods, Commander of the First Division of the XV Corps hastily approaches and bounds from his horse. A guard rushes over and takes the reins. General Sherman sees General Woods sprinting toward him." Yes, General Woods. What is it?"

"Sir, the Confederates are breaching strongly on my left."

General Sherman cannot believe this is occurring. "General Woods, go immediately and confirm the strength of the Confederates at the breach."In General Woods's absence General Sherman retrieves a bottle of whiskey from his saddlebag. He opens the bottle in front of his men and takes a stiff drink to help him contain his emotions over the loss of his close friend. Then he lights a cigar and returns inside to his headquarters with General Schofield.

Shortly, General Woods returns to report to General Sherman, "Gen. Hood's soldiers have the 2nd Division of the XV Corps in full retreat, and the Confederates have captured two batteries."

General Sherman holds his cigar in his hand and studies his maps on the table, taking a few moments to note the most recent changes. "Your recommendations, General Woods?"

General Woods observes, "Rotate your Division left and flank the Confederate column. General Schofield, you are to bring up all of the batteries you can find and place them on the high ground in front of the this house. General Howard, you stay here until I determine where your IV Corps can be of assistance."[345] Generals Schofield and Woods know the gravity of the situation and with their staffs depart hastily to carry out General Sherman's orders.

Soon, the gunners are firing shells and spherical case shot from the Howard house. General Sherman sits on his horse in front of the Howard House observing the battle.

General Howard taps his adjutant on the shoulder. "Look at General Sherman over there. I've never seen him with such a look on his face."

"Yes sir. His eyes even appear to be flashing."

General Sherman does not speak to anyone and no one interrupts him. He only watches the front. General Howard gives another stern look at General Sherman. "Check the expression on General Sherman's face. Look at his whole pose."

The adjutant studies General Sherman for a moment. "His concentration seems to show his fierceness as if he is in the battle himself."

When General Sherman witnesses General Logan lead the charge that seals the breach in the Union line and retakes most of the captured guns his expression relaxes, and he lights another cigar. General Sherman takes his cigar in his hand and proudly states to General Howard, "This day witnesses some of the most intense and violent combat of the war."

As a result of cannons, cavalry, and hand-to-hand combat, at the day's end, the grass has turned from green to crimson red. Three thousand, seven hundred Federals and five thousand Confederates are dead, suffering from wounds or have been taken prisoner. Gen. Hood has failed to save Atlanta. General Sherman turns about at sundown, as his Army of The Tennessee wins its greatest battle, yet he suffers a great personal loss.[346]

Lieutenant Griffin and his battery join General Garrard's Division. General Garrard order the mules hitched to the wagons and progresses up Shallow Ford Road as fast as possible. He remarks to his adjutant, "It was wonderful to see men drive and they can thank their stars the road was wide and all the fences down. They drove at a tearing gallop three or four abreast, nonstop for any obstruction."

The silhouette of the majestic granite mountain looms before General Garrard's Federals. As the brooding skies and the slick red Georgia clay enter darkness, General Garrard's columns turn sharply to the southeast at Choice's store.[347] The Yankees occasionally rouse farmers out of bed to demand the keys to barns, stables, and smokehouses. Colonel Eli Long's Advance Guard is not encountering any Confederate resistance and is able to travel twenty-one miles to cross the rock bridge over the Yellow River shortly after midnight.[348]

Thomas and Elizabeth Maguire are returning from the north field of their 956 acre Promised Land plantation, near Lithonia just below Rockbridge. Thomas sees a horse and buggy approaching in front of a dust cloud. "That looks like your cousin William Davis coming this way." Thomas stops his wagon and stands up and gazes to be certain. "Yep, that's William all right. Wonder what he doing here this time of week. He's got crops to tend too."

William draws his buggy to a stop next to Thomas and Elizabeth and says, "Afternoon."

"Afternoon, William," reply Thomas and Elizabeth. Thomas asks, "What brings you this way?"

"Don't know if you heard, but we are cut off from Gen. Wheeler's forces." Thomas and Elizabeth look at each other in surprise.

"You mean we are now within the Yankee lines."

"That's right. You best hide what you can and watch your slaves. Some of ours have already begun running away. I just wanted to let you know what I found out. I gotta git now."

"Thanks for coming by, William. I'll secure everything the best I can and set the cattle and horses loose in the woods."

By ten o'clock Thomas and his slaves have secured his home from the unwelcome visitors. Nervously Thomas and Elizabeth take turns observing from their porch for any sign of approaching Yankees.

Around midnight, Friday, July 21, Elizabeth calls, "Thomas I hear the clanging of wagons and the sound of horses. It must be the Yankees."

Thomas rushes outside and watches as the forces of General Garrard occupy his plantation. He hears the commands of General Garrard. "Halt, the men are to keep the saddles on their horses and no fires. Gen. Wheeler may be in the area, and we do not want our position discovered."

General Garrard does not set up a headquarters tent and sleeps on a wagon. While he is sleeping, his men silently begin raiding the Promised Land outbuildings. Thomas and Elizabeth rush inside, locking their doors only to be greeted by pounding upon the front door, which frightens and wakens the rest of the family. Thomas opens the door and the Yankees push him aside. Quickly the house is bright from the lanterns and full with thieving Yankees.

"Don't you have any respect for our heirlooms, utensils or privacy?" shouts Thomas. Several Yankees push him to the floor. Elizabeth and their children scream.

"Shut up mister. Shut up all of you or I'll burn you down." The Yankees cleared the house of nearly all valuables they could carry off in a very short time. As the last Yankee departs, he put his lantern in Thomas's face, "If you come outside, I'll shoot you dead."

Thomas watches silently and cautiously as the last Yankee leaves the house. Feeling safe, he and his family find their lanterns and begin to survey the damage.

Crying, Mrs. Maguire says, "Look they broke open all our trunks. They threw our drawers on the floor. There are no keys to the out buildings."

"They must have them," replies Thomas. He turns off his lantern and peers out of the window. "See they are in the barns and out buildings. Nothing we can do." Distraught he says, "These Yankees must have practiced roguery from their childhood up, so well they appear to know the art."[349] Looking in his desk drawer, "I see they stole my gold watch and pocketbook."

The next morning the Yankees leave the plantation on their way to Covington. Thomas and his family walk over the plantation and send the slaves out to gather up the roaming livestock. "Looks like the thieves took everything not nailed down, including two of our bee gums."[350]

Colonel Bob Minty's First reaches Rockbridge after a total of thirty-two miles march. Suffering from extreme fatigue, his unit removes the saddles and lies down to sleep. Not an hour passes before they are awakened. "Mount and hastily break camp."

General Garrard orders, "Have a small rear guard burn Rockbridge." The rear guard, obeying the order to make haste, does not wait to make sure the fire destroys the bridge. Thomas Maguire and some of his slaves are observing the action from the nearby woods. They are able to save enough of the bridge for a footpath.

A locomotive with one passenger car and twelve freight cars chugs up to the Conyers depot around midmorning. Two companies of Yankees charge into the town and gunfire ensues from the train. The startled conductor and engineer balk and run as the Yankees dismount and surround the train.

The commander of the 98th Illinois Mounted Infantry shouts, "All of you in the passenger car listen. My men are coming on board. Anyone who shows signs of resistance will be shot. You Confederate soldiers in there throw out any weapons you have, butt first, and then put both arms out of the windows."

The Confederate soldiers follow the instructions. Then the Yankees rapidly board the train, and sixteen Confederate soldiers are taken prisoner. The several frightened civilians and Confederates are taken inside the depot for questioning. The only useful information obtained from the shaken civilians is that a passenger train and a construction train are stranded between Stone Mountain and Yellow River. The commander of the 98th directs a detail to, "Burn the locomotive, passenger car and freight cars." As the blaze lights and smokes the sky, the Yankees depart toward Covington.[351]

Following the railroad eastward, the 98th Illinois Mounted Infantry arrives shortly at their objective, the 555 foot trestle spanning Yellow River. Several old men and boys guard the wooden span as well as a wagon bridge several yards downstream. Their weapons consist of ancient muzzle-loaders and shotguns. One of the young boys, acting as a picket, sprints toward the bridge and shouts, "There's a bunch of Yankees heading this way."

"Take cover boys and get ready."

Everyone deploys to an advantageous location against the approaching Yankees. The picket arrives quickly and finds a spot among his friends. When the Yankees appear, a man anxiously fires the first shot at a distant Yankee and misses. The surprised 98th returns the volley with their Spencer rifles. The man is shot and killed. Realizing they are about to suffer the same fate, the others run for their lives and disappear in the woods.

The Yankees approach the east bank of the bridge. One of the soldiers confirms that the old man is dead, "Shot right through the chest." The commander of the 98th has a detachment set fire to the Wagon Bridge and trestle. A short distance downstream, there's a large flour mill containing 8000 bushels of corn, a large quantity of flour and the house of the miller. Unmercifully, the Yankee torch the mill.

The rest of General Garrard's Division of 3,500 men travels another road to the north. Some of the Regiments begin lagging behind because troops are continually departing the ranks from exhaustion or sore feet.

General Garrard orders a halt around 11:00 AM and has a meeting with his commanders at his command wagon. "Colonel Long, in a half hour, take your men and travel eastward and burn the railroad trestle over the Alcovy River. Colonel Minty, take a battalion directly into Covington from here.

"The remainder of the Division will follow Colonel Abe Miller's mounted infantry to Oxford." General Garrard, eager to get to the railroad, departs Oxford with a detachment of Colonel Abe Miller's to guard his right flank.

IN DEFENSE OF. . .

The citizens of Covington begin to panic when they see the pillars of smoke rising high from the burning bridges over the Yellow River. One of the defenders of the bridge has told them about the capture of the west-bound train at Conyers and the capture of the on board Confederates. When the Yankees enter Covington. Citizens in a frenzy are driving wagons, buggies, and livestock from town. Convalescents at the hospitals are fleeing and begging for rides from the passing wagons.

Captain Hathaway receives a report from a cavalry scout. A Rebel wagon train is parking somewhere on the outskirts of town. Capt. Hathaway forms his battalion and they head off in search of the train. Colonel Abe Miller meets the two companies of the 98th Illinois outside of Conyers. Under the protection of Colonel Minty's troops, Colonel Miller's men begin pulling down fences along the right-of-way and pre-pare roaring fires at the joints in the track.

Repeating the techniques from Stone Mountain they continue to work steadily in an eastward direction until they finally reach the depot on the north side of Covington around 2:00 PM. The depot, full of furni-ture belonging to many local families, is set afire. In addition, the Yankees set fire to a nearby water tank and a large warehouse full of cotton and Confederate commissary supplies. The large new hospital built to ac-commodate 10,000 patients, composed of thirty buildings, is set ablaze producing flames nearly one hundred feet high.[352]

Colonel Biggs's men wreak devastation, breaking into stores and loot-ing them. With about a dozen army and confiscated civilian wagons, they begin loading the wagons with sacks of tobacco, sugar, meat, salt, coffee, flour, corn, syrup, candles, soap, nails, shoes, and clothing and any other items of food, cooking utensils or clothing they can steal. Colonel Eli Long's 3rd and 4th Ohio are at the east of Covington and capture the undefended 250-foot covered railroad bridge and adjacent wagon bridge over the Alcovy River.

Colonel Long's advance guard crosses the wagon bridge and charges toward a train. The engineer sees the Yankees approach and with a full head of steam escapes. In the haste of the escape, the engineer abandons the baggage cars and passengers. This time, the Yankees instruct the passengers to remove their possessions before setting fire to the bridges and cars. Hurriedly the grim passengers obey the order. Colonel Long's men destroy three miles of track and trestle over Cornish Creek. Colonel Long's troops, hot and exhausted, finally reach the outer edge of Covington before sunset.

Around 5:00 PM, General Garrard receives an intelligence report from another cavalry scout. "Gen. Wheeler's Cavalry, with strength of about 1,500, is about five miles away and rapidly closing." General Garrard calls a staff meeting at his headquarters. He and his staff and commanders review the area maps and he decides to send three Brigades back to Oxford to act as an additional rear guard.

Passing through Oxford, Colonel Miller's men plunder warehouses and homes, setting fire to each. The resulting massive fires in Oxford send orange and red flames upon the dark sky. The flames and accompanying full moon light the path for the advancing Yankees. General Garrard orders a halt at Sardis Church at 10:00 PM, and the two hundred Confederate prisoners are placed under guard there for the night.

At 6:00 AM, General Garrard starts his columns northward and two miles north of Sardis Church they come to Walnut Grove. From Walnut Grove on to Social Circle and then to Loganville continuing with the consistent destruction and pillaging of property. The rear guard burns three to four hundred bales of cotton and confiscates mules and horses from local citizens.

At 1:00 PM, General Garrard orders Colonel Minty's First north to Lawrenceville. He leads the 2nd and 3rd Brigades southwest on the Stone Mountain Road. Colonel Minty encounters about fifty Confederate soldiers as he approaches Lawrenceville near Tilford McConnell's farm. The Confederates open fire and after a brief skirmish, he captures the Confederates whose total represent about fourteen different Confederate units.

A recent fire had destroyed the only cotton mill in town. With nothing to plunder, Colonel Minty leaves Lawrenceville and camps on the banks on the Yellow River, three miles from town. Slaves, barely clothed, who are runaways, cautiously and silently observe the Yankees from the nearby woods. They are hungry and anxiously await the departure of the Yankees so they can search the camp for scraps of food. General Garrard's columns cross Yellow River at Holt's Mill around 3:00 PM. After burning the bridge at Holt's Mill, General Garrard follows the road from Choice's Store to Rockbridge and heads west. The columns reach Trickum Crossroads and camp on a branch of Stone Mountain Creek on the 23rd.[353]

⚓

Gen. Joe Wheeler's scouts return to headquarters with alarming news. "A large Yankee force has taken over Monroe." Gen. Wheeler sends for Gen., Kelly and when he arrives they discuss the situation. Gen. Wheeler makes a decision. "Move your division eastward on a twenty-five mile march through Lithonia and Conyers on the Covington Road."

Gen. Kelly moves his division as directed and finally reaches Yellow River around midnight. Upon arriving he discovers that the wagon bridge and railroad trestle had been burned. Gen. Wheeler is unaware that the Yankees are in camp a few miles upstream and orders his troops to make camp near the river.[354]

At 6:00 AM on the July 24, General Garrard has completed his circle of destruction and leads his columns toward Decatur. As the advance guard approaches the outskirts of Decatur around noon, they come under attack by Confederate Cavalry. General Garrard sends a messenger to Colonel Abe Miller, "Have your troops dismount and advance on foot. There's evidence of a ferocious struggle in every direction from my location." Colonel Miller reaches the square in Decatur without incident and halts his advance. All is quiet.

That evening General Garrard begins to dictate his report to his aide detailing the events of the past three days. "Write exactly what I dictate to you in the report. First, I destroyed three wagon road bridges and one railroad bridge 555 feet in length over the Yellow River. Then the 250 foot Railroad Bridge over the Ulcofauhachee River was burnt. Next, my Cavalry Division in Army of the Cumberland destroyed six miles of track between the two rivers. In Covington, the depot and considerable quantity of quartermaster and commissary stores were burned. Are you with me?"

"Yes sir."

"Next, I burned a locomotive and train in Conyers, then one train platform was burnt at Covington, a small baggage train at station near Ulcofauhachee was captured and burnt. The engine to the last train was detached across the river. I questioned some citizens at the depot and they report a passenger train and a construction train, both with engines were cut off between Stone Mountain and Yellow River."

"I'm caught up, sir."

"Put in the report that we burned over 2000 bales of cotton. The biggest fire was a large new hospital under construction at Covington. When completed it would have accommodations for 10,000 patients from this army and the Army of Virginia. The hospital was composed of over 30 buildings besides the offices, which were just finished. They were burned as well. A very large lot of fine carpenters' tool, several large tents, and thirty unfinished hospital buildings completed these tasks against the Confederates. Make a new entry here."

"Yes sir."

"In the town of Oxford, two miles north of Covington, and in Covington Hill hospital there were over 1,000 sick and wounded in buildings used for hospitals. The convalescents who were able to walk scattered through the woods while our operation was going on in town. I did not have time to hunt them up before dark. Those in the hospital, together with their surgeons, were not disturbed.

"The Confederate forces no longer can rely upon the railroad for direct access for munitions and reinforcements from the Carolinas and Virginia." End this report with 'Very respectfully yours, K. Garrard, Brigadier-General.'"[355]

"Yes Sir."

JULY 25, 1864

During the afternoon, William Sheppard rides around the mountain, seeking his pal, Buck. Appearing very distraught, he dismounts and hurries over to the porch where Buck is securing food to be hidden from the bummers of Sherman's Army. "What's wrong, William?" Buck asks anxiously. "Is your family okay?"

Yes, they're fine and all went to Athens two weeks ago. Have you heard about our friends Presley Jones and George Daniel? Both have been shot and killed!"

Buck is stoic. "Have a seat William. Have some sassafras tea with me." Buck pour a cup of tea, hands it to William as he settles into a chair next to Buck. He leans back and takes a sip. Buck continues, "I heard of the awful clubbing and shooting of Presley after the Yankees captured him for shooting two of their comrades."

Williams leans forward, "Yes, but even more awful is after all that the Yankees shot him in the head in front of his daughters and began to made fun of his daughters tears!"

Buck shakes his head in a attempt not to visualize such a scene. "Did the Yankees do any further harm to his daughters?"

"Just walked away laughing at his distraught daughters while pointing at Presley."

Buck grunts in disgust and exhales deeply. "Bless him, to old to be a soldier but not to old to fight. What about our friend George? How was he involved in this matter?"

"George chanced to be home on furlough for several days from his Confederate quartermaster unit. He happened to take his gun with him to meet his daughter at the depot who was retuning from a visit in Conyers. When the Yankees saw him armed, they were still upset from their comrades deaths so they arrest him."

Buck drops his hand and pats Charlie on his head. "What happened next."

"You want believe it, but the Yankees had what is known as a drumhead court martial. They charged him as a 'suspect of resistance' and in a matter of minutes sentenced him to be shot."

Buck stands up quickly, looks straight at William and shouts, "Shot!"

William drops his head, "Yep, and took poor George to the grove north of Col. W. W. Clark's home and shot him."[356]

Unable to believe what he has just heard Buck paces for a moment. Turning to Williams he raises his first, Another victim to the humane influence of Northern civilization. The Yankee officers have no control over their men.

"Many more are gonna die cause this war was lost before it started!" Changing the subject to clear his mind Buck asks, "How were you able to keep your buggy and horse?"

"I had them hid deep in the woods. Around midnight, I was able to sneak out on the trail by the creek. There were no Yankees camping there."

"You see the bluebellies came through here, tearing up the railroad and burning the depot and got everybody scared in town. Did you stop by our friend Thomas Maguire's place and see how he is doing?"

"Sure did. He said the Yankees hit his place around midnight on the 21st. They came in force and held his family at gun point. Soon his house was filled with the thieving Yankees. They robbed them of everything they could carry off. He and Mrs. Maguire said they busted open the trunks and threw all of the dresser drawers on the floor. Finally, the Yankees left around 8:00 in the morning on their way to Covington and Social Circle with some of his runaway slaves. From what he could find out the Yankees circled back to Lawrenceville and Monroe. Some others went by Durand's Mill and set Rockbridge on fire. He's pretty shaken up."

"Stay for dinner William. We'll eat early and then you can get on the road."

"Thanks, but I need to git." William is somewhat rested but still visibly upset. "Thanks, Buck, for the invitation, but I got a few more stops before I get home."

"Just be careful. There's still some Yankees in the area. Last I heard the folks in Gwinnett caught some lone bummers and strung 'um up."

"Serves 'um right," replies William as he waves good-bye to his friend Buck."[357]

❧

The cadets expect West Point, Georgia to be their permanent station for the remainder of the war. They engage in training the Militia Brigades in warfare tactics. Unfortunately, Maj. Capers receives orders on the Monday, July 25, to join Gen. Smith's Georgia Militia again, but this time in the trenches in Atlanta. Paper is in short supply, so Norman uses a piece of cardboard as a postal card.

> *I am not too far from home now. We are in our positions in the trenches in Atlanta. We got here Wednesday around six o'clock in the evening. Don't have much space to write on, food is scarce, but we know how to manage. Any word from Polly?*
>
> *Love Norman*

One week later the corps is taking a break from being under heavy fire every day. There is no breeze in the trenches. Norman sniffs the air and turns his nose up, "Paul, I don't know about you, but these trenches stink, and I'm beginning to get sick from everybody using them as out-houses."

Paul, feeling nauseous himself, replies, "It's not the cadets, it's the stupid, dirty soldiers from those other units."

Norman continues, "I know that, but with the flies, the rats and the stink, I'm afraid we are coming down with diseases of filth. The flies are everywhere! Smell of stench everywhere!" Norman turns his head away from a pile of human waste.

"I try not to look at the flies feeding on the urine and feces and then landing on our food. Capers expects us to eat the food!" Paul gazes at Norman and then back at the flies.

"That's why you and I only eat the food we prepare." Paul appears worried and is quiet for a moment. Norman, our commander Willie Baker, Edmund Jordan and our friend John McLeord in Company A have come down with a rose-color rash, really bad stomach aches with fever and diarrhea. They have been sent to the hospital."

"Look! More rats," shouts Norman. He stands up, grabs his musket and chases after the rat. He traps the rat as it tries to climbs the steep dirt trench and stabs the rodent with his bayonet. He sticks his bayonet into the ground to clean off the blood. "There are rats everywhere, just like the flies. I've seen the rats lick and eat the dried blood from the wounds of sleeping soldiers. I get sick in my stomach from watching."

"Good job on that rat." Still staring at the rat, Paul continues, "Norman, I think those lice are bad business too, I am always removing them from my body. I guess they come with the rats. The rats aren't afraid of anybody. They come right up to us day and night. We must have stabbed a hundred or more with our bayonets and stomped on them."

Getting somewhat gloomy Norman lowers his head. "Paul, I don't know which is worse, contending with the pestilence, or the constant roaring of cannons." Then he raises his head, "At least our artillery battery follows orders and maintains a constant fire upon the Yankee entrenchments that are close to ours."

"You're right about that. The Yanks see us, and we see them and we exchange shots. We've been lucky so far that no cadets have been wounded or killed, but that could change."[358]

Under heavy fire on the Sunday, the 7th of August, Goode screams out "I'm hit! I'm hit!" Norman and Paul rush over to render aid to Goode.

He has an awful frightful expression on his face. "Help me, Paul. Help me, Norman." His shirt is turning red from a wound in the arm.[359] Goode is bleeding heavily. Paul rips away part of Goode's shirt and ties it around his arm. Norman grabs a stick to tighten the tourniquet. Goode grabs Norman's arm. "Thank you. Thank you both."

Norman holds to the stick and tries not to register the shock he feels to his core. "Hold on and stay still or the bleeding will increase. The medics will get you to the field hospital. It looks like just a flesh wound. The bleeding has stopped. Just lay still until the medics come and the firing settles down."

As darkness approaches, Goode is in severe pain as he gets an escort to the field hospital. "If you wind up in Stone Mountain, let my folks know that I'm all right," Norman asks of Goode as he departs. As the days go, Norman tells Paul, "We've been lucky, Paul. Several of our fellow cadets have received wounds but our good friend, Allen Luckie, gets a non-fatal shot in the eye."

Paul remarks, "What will tomorrow bring to us?"

AUGUST, 1864

Still in Atlanta area on Friday, August 12, the Confederate forces and the Cadet Corps are under heavy fire on the trench line as well as from cannons. Feeling that he was in a safe location behind the breastworks, Archibald Alexander of Company A begins preparing a meager supper of rice and bacon. Archibald, needing some water, picks up his canteen and takes a few steps toward a nearby spring. Suddenly, a loud series of booms from a Yankee cannon occurs with a sweeping type of fire power. Norman watches as one cannon ball strikes the cadet's trench from the flank and sees Archibald turns in response to the noise. At that instant Norman sees another cannon ball bounce and pass directly through Archibald's body, throwing him several feet into the air. Cadet William Breese is just a yard or two away and rushes to Archibald. Blood gushes from his massive wound as Breese grasps him until his life ebbs.

Norman jumps to his feet and he and other cadets rush over and pull Breese, soaked in blood, from their fallen comrade. Breese stares at his bloody hands. "The cannon ball passed entirely though his body, from right side to left, amid his ribs, and it rolled away about fifty feet."

Norman knows the good and noble heart from which the cannon ball so rudely has taken life. Archibald was dead in an instant. During the night his body is placed in an ambulance and carried over towards East Point to the train. Cadet Dews, who is his roommate, is asked to escort Archibald's body to his home and family in Forsyth.

Somewhat despondent, Paul confides in Norman, "I hate it, but it looks like Archibald Alexander is the first cadet from Georgia Military Institute to receive a mortal wound during this Civil War. Which one of us will be next?"[360]

By the time the Cadet Corps receive orders from the Governor on Sunday, August 14, to garrison in Milledgeville, their ranks are reduced by nearly thirty percent. The reduction is due primarily to diseases acquired in the trenches and at least three deaths resulting from mortal wounds on the battle field.[361]

Although Julius Brown does not ask for, nor receive, any special attention, the Corps stills feels that the governor is looking more after his son than the cause. Gen. Wayne sends additional orders expressing that the "Governor desires that all troops of the Garrison including the home guard perform a parade daily at the capitol square. In addition, a proper system of scouts and system of scouting should be established to foretell of any enemy activity encroachment."

Arriving in Milledgeville, the cadets find an abundance of citizens fleeing from Atlanta, as well as from the coast. All of the housing accommodations are full. Initially, the returning cadets are using box cars for temporary quarters. Then tents are set up on the Capitol Square. The setting in Milledgeville is relaxing, and the cadets are able to return to an abbreviation of their classroom schedule, drills, parades and guard duty. The facilities at Oglethorpe College are a welcoming site after having been through the trenches of Atlanta and Resaca.

Full of war stories, the returning cadets have the ears of the younger students. Their friend Edmund Jordon, still mortally sick from the disease he acquired in the trenches, is given furlough home. Norman and Paul bid him farewell. Edmund is so weak that Norman and Paul lift him into the wagon and lay him upon the hay bed. They know Edmund is dying, so they ride on the back of the wagon a short distance encouraging him to fight as he has always fought. Soon the wagon stops, and they jump off and grasp Edmund's hand. With deep agonizing emotion in his voice, Norman, bids his friend good-bye. "So long good soldier and good friend. God speed!"

Norman and Paul, sad with heavy hearts and broken voices stand silently until the wagon is out of sight. "Let's sing "The Dying Soldier" for

Edmund Paul suggests Norman. As the two friends walk side by side, they begin to somberly sing,

> Gather round him where he's lying, Hush your footsteps, whisper low,
>   For a soldier here is dying, In the sunset's radiant glow.
> Beating, beating, slowly beating, Runs the life-blood through his frame;
>   Swift the soldier's breath is fleeting, And he calls his mother's name.
> "Mother, mother, come and kiss me, Ere my spirit fades away,
>   For I know you oft will miss me, When you watch the sinking day.
> "Brother, sister, nearer, nearer! Place, oh place your hands in mine,
>   You whose love than life was dearer, Let your arms around me twine.
> "Father, see the sun is fading From the hill-tops of the west,
>   And the valley night is shading—Farewell, loved ones, I'm at rest"
> Dying, dying! Yes, he's dying! Close the eyelids, let him rest;
>   No more sorrow, no more sighing, E'er again shall heave his breast.
> Sleeping, sleeping, calmly sleeping, In the church-yard cold and drear,
>   And the wintry winds are heaping O'er him leaflets brown and sear.
> And he's resting, where forever clang of trumpet, roll of drum,
>   Roar of cannon, never, never, Never more to him shall come.

The cadets dedicate a parade and fly the Garrison flag at half mast in honor of the students who became sick, were wounded or died. Maj. Capers writes to Gen. Wayne concerning the cadet Corps service in the trenches of Atlanta. "There was fatigue and blood and death in their ranks but no white feathers."

The governor appoints Maj. Capers as commandant of the military garrison at Milledgeville with Adjutant Gen. of Georgia Gen. Wayne as the commanding officer. The Garrison consists of the cadet Corps, a Georgia State Line Cavalry Company of mounted scouts under the command of Capt. Matthew H. Talbot, Capt. William H. Prudden's Artillery Battery, Williams Militia Company of Infantry and former officials of the penitentiary.

AUGUST 29-30, 1864—BEGINNING OF THE DEMOCRATIC CONVENTION

Buck and a few friends are meeting at the depot to study the war roster of the citizens of Stone Mountain. "James, I dread coming here more and more every day."

"It's not pleasant at all, Buck," responds James Goldsmith. "All of us are really suffering emotionally. I got this old newspaper from the North from a soldier who passed through last night. Listen to this news, fellows. Those Copperheads may save us yet!"Buck, along with, William Jones, William Camp, Benjamin Woodsen, and John Fowler, sit on the steps of the loading platform and begin to listen.[362]

"This old Northern newspaper states the Copperheads of the Democratic Party held their convention in Chicago, August 29-30.[363] Former Congressman Clement Vallandigham, a vehement opponent of President Lincoln, operated behind the scenes and influenced the adoption of the Copperhead platform. The Convention was full of criticism of President Lincoln, especially for issuing the Emancipation Proclamation, the military draft, the use of black troops and his violation of civil liberties."[364]

Buck and his friends chuckle, and Buck says, "Keep on reading, James!"

"Roddy goes on to say 'he blames the abolitionists for prolonging the war and denounces the government as increasingly despotic.'"Continuing, James reads, "Listen to what this Ohio editor has to say. 'He can see no reason why anyone should be shot for the benefit of niggers and Abolitionists!' Marcus Pomeroy of the Wisconsin newspaper calls Lincoln "fungus from the corrupt womb of bigotry and fanaticism, and a worse tyrant and more inhuman butcher than has existed since the day of Nero the ruler."

"Here's a new word for us—'miscegenation.'"

"What the devil does that mean?" asks Buck.

"Here the article says 'miscegenation' means a marriage between two different races and this is what President Lincoln and the Republicans want."

"Don't believe a word of it myself!" retorts John Fowler.

"So, what is the Copperhead platform?" asks Benjamin Woodsen.

Reading silently for a moment, James Goldsmith finally says, "Their proposals for a cease-fire and negotiated settlement with the Confederacy were ratified by the delegates and incorporated into the official party platform."

Buck shakes his head and tightens his jaws. "Sounds like there could be two separate countries yet!"

"Well, who did the Copperheads nominate to save the South?" asks William Camp.

"The delegates elected General George B. McClellan, a War Democrat, and gave him an anti-war platform. When General McClellan accepted the nomination, he rejected the peace plank, guaranteeing in its place to bring the war to a conclusion with more skill and energy than President Lincoln."

"Who's the Vice President for the Copperhead Democrats?" asks Buck.

"It says here a Peace Democrat, Ohio Congressman George Pendleton, was elected as the Vice President Nominee."

Buck stands up and stretches. "Never work! One for war and one for peace. They are already fighting each other! We're no better off! Time for me to get."

THE FORTUNE OF WAR

SEPTEMBER 1864

Late that afternoon Buck returns to the depot to catch the latest news as the telegraph begins to click. James sits down by the keypad and happily says, "Looks like we are hooked up again, at least for a while." James begins writing with Buck watching. "Mayor Calhoun may soon have to surrender Atlanta. Stop."

Buck and James look at each other in wonderment. "I don't find that to be a big surprise. Do you, James?"

"Surely don't. What's next for us? We got nobody in town."

Buck responds while shaking his head, "We're at the mercy of the thieving Yankees. I best git on home. The Yankees 'bout cleaned us out, and I'm sure they'll be back for more."

⁑

General Sherman tells his staff, "The Confederate forces suffers severe defeats and high casualties at Peachtree Creek, The Battle of Atlanta, The Battle of Ezra Church and The Battle of Jonesboro. All these battles were fought over possession of the railroads. With their lifeline of supplies now cut off the Confederate forces are beginning to withdraw from Atlanta to escape being captured.[366]

THURSDAY, SEPTEMBER L, 1864

Atlanta is almost in a state of anarchy. Many of the citizens are under the impression that the fight at Jonesboro is a Confederate victory, but their sanguine hopes are destroyed by a few deserters who arrived during the day seeking hiding places in the houses of their friends. They tell a different story.

"Throughout the day troops are moving in every direction and unusual bustle and activity prevails. The citizens notice that they are no longer halted and made to show their papers on the streets. Crowds of strange Negroes also made their appearance, but they are acting with great caution, and spent most of their time in cellars and houses abandoned by their owners. The citizens can not believe that the city was to be given up. Yet that is what is happening.

"By 5 PM Gen. Hood's evacuation is under way. Commissary stores which can not be moved are distributed among the citizens of Atlanta. Gen. Hardee and Gen. Cleburne have retreated from Jonesboro to Lovejoy. Gen. Lee's Corps, is ordered to retrace much of his march, this time going to Lovejoy's Station where he will join Hardee's corps.

"Gen. Hood, with his staff, depart the city for Lovejoy's via the McDonough Road, followed by the state militia under Gen. Gustavus W. Smith and, finally, by Gen. Stewart's corps. Whenever the departing soldiers passed a garden, several men would rush through it, stripping it in a minute of every stalk of corn, and every green legume that could be eaten by man or beast. No one objects. All now know that their brave defenders are leaving, to return no more in the role of a Confederate soldier.

"By midnight most of the troops have left the city. But a few cavalrymen linger. They have a special assignment. Gen. Hood is not leaving behind, in usable condition, ammunition and military stores for the use of General Sherman's army.

"Shortly after midnight the citizens who remain in the city are startled by a series of violent explosions down the Georgia Railroad toward Stone Mountain and the rolling mill.

"Hood's ammunition trains, consisting of seven locomotives and 81 loaded cars are set afire to deny them to the Federals. As the flames reached each car, it explodes with a terrific din. Five hours are occupied in this work of demolition, which also includes the rolling mill. Flames shot to a tremendous height and the exploding missiles scattering their red-hot fragments right and left. The earth shakes as if from an earthquake. Nearby houses rock like cradles, while on every ear is heard the shattering of window glass and the fall of plastering and loose bricks. Hundreds of people flock to high places and watch with breathless excitement the volcanic scene on the Georgia Railroad."

Fortunately all the citizens in the vicinity of the explosions had been ordered to leave their houses before the work of blowing up the ammunition trains commenced. Every building, for a quarter of a mile around was either torn to pieces or perforated with hundreds of holes by shell fragments.

A new day was dawning when the last car let loose, and the last Confederate cavalrymen gallops out McDonough Road (Capitol Avenue) to rejoin Hood's retreating army."

Then, for the people of Atlanta, came the awful hours of waitin— waiting for the unknown. Men with wives and daughters stayed home, weapons at hand, ready for any emergency. The center of the city began to fill with the flotsam and jetsam of war-riffraff, stragglers and deserters. The Negroes are delirious and confused over their strange sense of free- dom. Lean and haggard men and women of the lowest class plundering stores and vacant dwellings.

FRIDAY SEPTEMBER 2, 1864

Such was the state of affairs in the morning when General Slocum's XX Corps moves into Atlanta. General Sherman informs General Slocum, "The recent explosions in Atlanta lead me to believe that Gen. Hood has abandoned the city with Gen. Stewart and the Georgia Militia. Send out a reconnaissance to investigate."

Atlanta, worn out and shattered by the storm of war, lay stranded be- tween two flags, under the protection of neither, abandoned by one, and with little hope of mercy from the other. As the early morning hours slip by with no sign of the enemy's approach, Mayor James M. Calhoun de- cided upon a course of action. The city had not been formally surrendered by Hood. Therefore, the mayor will take care of this detail himself. He held a conference with several members of council and other prominent men. All the conferees mount horses and include, besides Mayor Calhoun, Thomas G. W. Crusselle, William Markham, Thomas Kile, Julius A. Hayden. All knew a dangerous trip lies ahead, and although none knew exactly where General Sherman is located, it is assumed he is camped a few miles out on the Marietta Road. Instead he is at or near Lovejoy's, but General Slocum, with the 20th corps, is at the river guarding the Western & Atlantic R. R. bridge and other crossings of the Chattahoochee.

General Sherman had heard the explosions and seen the glare of the fires in Atlanta at 2 AM, although he attributed the explosions to heavy firing and so wired General Thomas at 4 AM, Friday. At 8 PM he was still uncertain as to what had happened in the city, for he then telegraphed Thomas as follows: "Until we hear from Atlanta the exact truth, I do not care about your pushing your men against breastworks. Destroy the railroad well up to your lines; keep skirmishers well up, and hold our troops in hand for anything that may turn up. As soon as I know positively that our troops are in Atlanta I will determine what to do...."

General Slocum, is at the river and considerably closer than the twenty-six miles that separated Sherman from the city, had also heard the explosions and seen the fire. He guesses correctly that Gen. Hood is evacuating Atlanta, and by daybreak dispatches units of the 20th corps en route to town via the Mayson and Turner Ferry Road.[367]

The mayor's group, after a lively discussion as to the propriety of carrying firearms, in addition to the white flag of surrender, and which was finally settled in the negative, set forth out Marietta Street. This route leads the party through that section of the city which has suffered the most damage from the recent bombardment. Nearly every residence has been abandoned, and many of the houses were piles of splintered timbers. The street is badly torn up, and the riders, even in broad daylight often found it difficult to thread their way through the scattered debris. A few homes near the city limits are more or less intact including the shot-riddled Ponder home. Soon the dismantled Confederate breastworks are reached at Fort Hood. With the exception a few spiked cannons, they are entirely deserted.

Finally at a point beyond Fort Hood, Mayor Calhoun and his contingent met a small body of Federal 20th Corps troops commanded by Captain H. M. Scott, of the 70th Indiana Volunteer Infantry. Introducing himself and fellow citizens to the captain, the mayor inquires as to the whereabouts of General Sherman. Scott replied, "General Sherman is twenty miles from here, sir; down about Jonesboro. If you want to reach the commanding officer of this department, you will have to see General Slocum, at the bridge. He will shortly be in command in Atlanta."

At this juncture a larger body of Federal soldiers advance along the same road, and Captain Scott reports to the Colonel Coburn, "The mayor of Atlanta is present sir and would like to talk with you." Colonel Coburn arrives and dismounts. He shakes Mayor Calhoun's hand, "I am Colonel John Coburn, commanding the Second Brigade of Ward's Division. I understand you are the Mayor of Atlanta and wish to surrender the City. Is that correct?"

"Yes I am Mayor Calhoun and am here to surrender Atlanta. The fortune of war has placed Atlanta in your hands. As mayor of the city, I ask protection of non-combatants and private property."[368]

"Sir, write a formal note embodying your desire to surrender the city and address it to Brigadier-General William T. Ward, the nearest general officer." Mayor Calhoun takes a memorandum book from his pocket and tears out a blank page and writes thereon the following message:

> Atlanta, Ga., September 2, 1864
> Brigadier-General Ward,
> Comdg. Third Division, Twentieth Corps:
>
> Sir: The fortune of war has placed Atlanta in your hands. As mayor of
> the city I ask protection to non-combatants and private property.
>
> JAMES M. CALHOUN
> Mayor of Atlanta

By noon the whole line of Marietta Street is blue with Union soldiers, and the citizens of Atlanta are hailing the conqueror with mixed emotions. Some, tired of the war, or now feeling free to express long concealed Union sentiments, greeted the Federals with a show of enthusiastic welcome; others took little pains to conceal the fact that they regard the Northern host as "vandal invaders." Even the small boys of staunch Confederate families whistle "Dixie" and "The Bonnie Blue Flag," for the benefit of, but not to the amusement of Sherman's boys, who retort, via brass bands, with loud renditions of "Yankee Doodle" and "The Battle Hymn of the Republic.

That evening General Slocum sends a telegram from Atlanta to Edwin M. Stanton, Secretary of War. "Mr. Secretary: General Sherman has taken Atlanta. The Twentieth Corps occupies the city. The main army is on the Macon road, near East Point. A battle was fought near that point, in which General Sherman was successful."

On September 3rd Sherman, near Lovejoy's Station, telegraphs General Slocum, commander of the 20th Corps in Atlanta. "Move all the stores forward from Allatoona and Marietta to Atlanta. Take possession of all good buildings for Government purposes, and see they are not used as quarters. Advise the people to quit now. There can be no trade or commerce until the war is over. Let Union families go to the North with their effects. All cotton is tainted with treason, and no title in it will be respected. It must all go to Nashville as United States property, and pretended claimants may collect testimony for the pursuit of the proceeds of sale after they reach the U.S. Treasury in money."

SUNDAY, SEPTEMBER 4, 1864

Sherman decides not to pursue Hood south of Atlanta, and issues Special Field Orders No. 64, providing for the distribution of his troops. They read:

> *The army having accomplished its undertaking in the complete reduction and occupation of Atlanta, will occupy the place and the country near it until a new campaign is planned in concert with the other grand armies of the United States.*

A second order reads:

> *HDQRS. CHIEF OF CAVALRY, DEPT. OF THE CUMBERLAND*
> *Camp near Lovejoy's*
> *September 4, 1864*
> *Brigadier General K. GARRARD,*
> *Commanding Second Division Cavalry:*

> *The general commanding directs that you have your command in readiness to march to-morrow, although the precise hour cannot be stated, and that you cover the rear and right flank of General Schofield's corps in its march to Decatur, Ga. You will ascertain from General Schofield when his command will move, allowing it to pass to the north of you. On the arrival of General Schofield's corps at Decatur you will with your command, take post, headquarters at Cross Keys, picketing from Stone Mountain to the crossing of the Chattahoochee on the road from Pinckneyville to Warsaw. It is designed to established a signal station on Stone Mountain, if, in connection with General Schofield's cavalry, it can be made secure. You will keep yourself informed of any movements of the enemy toward Lawrenceville. On your arrival at Cross Keys establish a courier line, in charge of a non-commissioned officer, to these headquarters at or near Atlanta.*

> *I am, general, very respectfully, your obedient servant,*

DAVID F. HOW
Lieutenant and Acting Assistant Adjutant-General[369]

✦

Buck and Isaac are checking the fences when they spot about a dozen Yankees rapidly approaching. Stopping the inspection, they watch the Yankees as they pull up next to the split rail fence.

"Hey Mister," shouts the Lieutenant who is leading the scouting party for General Garrard, "What the best way to get up this mountain?"

Buck spits his tobacco over the rail and looks at the Lieutenant. "Walking."

"We need to take our horses up."

Buck looks sternly at the Lieutenant, "They can walk with you. The mountain is solid rock. Lots of good places for a horse to break a leg."

Getting somewhat irritated, the Lieutenant remarks, "You best tell me which way is the easiest route if you want to keep your fences."

Buck points. "Yonder way is the most gentle slope."

"Hey, darkie, you know you are free. Do you want to go with us?"

"No, sah."

The Lieutenant jerks his horse's reins and directs the members of the scouting party to follow him.

Buck takes his handkerchief and wipes his forehead and looks at Isaac, "I bet you those Yankees are looking to establish a signal post on top."

THURSDAY SEPTEMBER 15, 1864

During his staff meeting General Sherman proudly states, "Atlanta is fully under the control of our Union force. This city has surrendered and Gen. Hood has withdrawn." He takes a long drag on his cigar then slowly exhales. "Smart move on his part. He just spared the inhabitants of the city from further suffering. Colonel Poe, what is the status of the telegraph and railroads?"

Standing, Colonel Poe responds, "General, the telegraph and railroads are repaired, and we have uninterrupted communication to the rear. The trains arrive with regularity and dispatch, and deliver ample supplies."

"Good News. Thank you Colonel. The latest on Gen. Wheeler is his cavalry has been driven out of Middle Tennessee. He escaped south across the Tennessee River at Bainbridge. Gentlemen as far as military matters go, looks as though we are to have a period of repose."[370]

SEPTEMBER 16, 1864

Betty Gail arrives at the post office to get the mail and notices a stack of pamphlets by the door. She picks up one and begins to read. To her surprise it is from Mayor Calhoun to the citizens of Atlanta. Standing outside she's frightened by the contents and rushes home to share the news with Buck. When she arrives she spots Buck in the field and waves to him. He takes off his hat and returns her wave and leans against his potato spade until she pulls along his side and stops.

"Buck, read this pamphlet from Mayor Calhoun. Matters are getting serious in Atlanta. I'm afraid a real storm is brewing over this." Buck takes the pamphlet and begins reading out loud.

"Major-General Sherman instructs me to say to the citizens of Atlanta that you must leave Atlanta. That as many of you as want to go north can do so, and that as many of you as want to go south can do so. All of the citizens can take with them their movable property and servants if the servants desire to go. It must be understood that the citizens cannot use force upon anyone to accompany them. General Sherman will furnish transportation for persons and property as far as Rough and Ready. From Rough and Ready, Gen. Hood will assist in carrying on the evacuation. Like transportation will be furnished for people and property going north. General Sherman is requiring that all events contemplated by this notice will be carried into the execution of his instructions as soon as possible.

"All persons are requested to leave their names and number in their families with the undersigned as early as possible." Buck looks at his wife. What is going on here? Why does he want everyone to leave Atlanta?" Let's go back to town and find out what exactly is going on." He climbs onto the wagon and takes the reins from Betty Gail. "Isaac take those potatoes to the house when you finish digging."

Buck snaps the reins and heads toward town. They arrive at the depot and spot their friend, William Sheppard among a crowd gathering at the depot. They tie off the horse at the hitching post and climb down. William walks towards them, "Have you heard about General Sherman demanding the citizens of Atlanta evacuate as soon as possible?"

"Yes, Betty Gail brought me a copy of Mayor Calhoun's pamphlet."

"We got a couple of newspapers and they tell the whole story. Been a might big argument between Sherman, Hood and Mayor Calhoun. Let's go over to Liberty Hall where we can have a drink and you can read the newspaper."

Buck takes the newspaper from William and asks, "What does this sound like to you William?"

"Don't rightly know. But it doesn't sound good. The newspaper gives a good summary of the events. Seems like it all started last Wednesday the 7th of September."

Buck begins to read, "General Sherman sends Gen. Hood a letter stating that he has deemed it to the interest of the United States that the citizens now residing in Atlanta should remove, those who prefer it to go south to Rough and Ready and the rest north by way of train." Buck lowers the newspaper. "I just don't understand. The rest of this part deals with what Mayor Calhoun has in the flier."

"Read on Buck. It gets better or worse depending on your outlook," remarks William.

Betty Gail is listening intently as Buck begins to read some parts out loud.

"Gen. Hood wrote back to General Sherman on the ninth. He seems somewhat mellow in his agreeing to go by what Sherman has more or less ordered him to do. Listen to this, 'I do not consider that I have any alternative in this matter. I therefore accept your proposition to declare a truce of two days, or such time as may be necessary to accomplish the purpose mentioned, and shall render all assistance in my power to expedite the transportation of citizens in this direction.' but he goes on to leash out at General Sherman. Listen to this Betty Gail. 'And now, sir, permit me to say that the unprecedented measure you propose transcends, in studied and ingenious cruelty, all acts ever before brought to my attention in the dark history of war. In the name of God and humanity I protest, believing that you will find that you are expelling from their homes and firesides the wives and children of a brave people.' Pretty strong language from a General who just got defeated in battle."

"Buck turns to the next page of the tattered newspaper. He folds it back and begins to read. I see Sherman does not like what Hood had to say. Listen to his reply to Gen. Hood. 'I have the honor to acknowledge the receipt of your letter of this date [9th], at the hands of Messrs. Ball and Crew, consenting to the arrangements I had proposed to facilitate the removal south of the people of Atlanta who prefer to go in that direction.

I enclose you a copy of my orders, which will, I am satisfied, accomplish my purpose perfectly."

Buck laughs and looks over to Betty Gail. "General Sherman must have gotten really upset with Gen. Hood's remarks. Listen to what Sherman had to say, 'You style the measure proposed 'unprecedented,' and appeal to the dark history of war for a parallel as an act of "studied and ingenious cruelty. If we must be enemies, let us be men and fight it out, as we propose to do, and not deal in such hypocritical appeals to God and humanity. God will judge us in due time, and He will pronounce whether it be more humane to fight with a town full of women, and the families of 'a brave people' at our back, or to remove them in time to places of safety among their own friends and people."

"Well, Buck, General Sherman is right in what he said. But why is he evacuating Atlanta?"

"Nobody can figure that out, Betty Gail," says William as he leans back in his chair.

Betty Gail touches Buck's arm. "What happened next Buck?"

Buck reads silently for a moment and then says, "Looks like Mayor Calhoun and the council got involved on the 11th, and sends a letter to General Sherman stating, 'We, the undersigned, mayor and two of the council for the city of Atlanta, for the time being the only legal organ of the people of the said city to express their wants and wishes, ask leave most earnestly, but respectfully, to petition you to reconsider the order requiring them to leave Atlanta. Many poor women are in advanced state of pregnancy; others now having young children, and whose husbands, for the greater part, are either in the army, prisoners, or dead.'"

"I wonder what else the Mayor had to say since these are just excerpts from the letters?" remarks Betty Gail.

"Well here's how General Sherman responded to the Mayor's request the next day. 'I have your letter of the 11th, in the nature of a petition to revoke my orders removing all the inhabitants from Atlanta. I have read it carefully, and give full credit to your statements of the distress that will be occasioned by it, and yet shall not revoke my orders, simply because my orders are not designed to meet the humanities of the case, but to prepare for the future struggles in which millions of good people outside of Atlanta have a deep interest. We must have peace, not only at Atlanta but in all America.'"

Buck lays down the newspaper after reading the last passage. He looks at his friend William and his wife. "Finally it looks like last Thursday the Fourteenth, General Sherman told Gen. Hood there will be no more discussion on the matter and to continue to carry out his order to evacuate Atlanta."

Betty Gail picks up the newspaper and glances over the article and shakes her head. "What will become of this Buck?"

"Lord only knows." He leans across the table. "Thanks William for sharing the newspaper. Betty Gail and I best head back to the farm in case those bummers show up again. The two friends shake hands and Buck and Betty Gail depart.[371]

COLLEAGUES FOR THE UNION

The butler delivers the daily mail to Congressman Hill. Joshua looks through the mail and hurries to find Emily. Holding the letter in his hand, "I have a reply from our friend James Crews."

She eagerly rushes to Joshua's side and looks at the envelope. "Open it and find out if he has any news about our son." Joshua takes his fingers and separates the seal then he begins to read. "Dear Joshua and Emily, I have been fortunate to locate the body of your late son...."

Emily begins to cry and holds Joshua closely and whispers, "We can bring him home now."

"Yes, we can, I must telegraph our dear friend, Congressman Nathaniel Foster. He can help me get through the Union lines." Joshua summons his driver and carriage and goes to the depot. At the depot, he instructs the railroad agent. "Send the following message to Congressman Nathaniel Foster."

"Yes sir, Mr. Hill." The agent takes a seat at the telegraph desk and Joshua begins to dictate the message. "Nathaniel, I received word from James Crews that he has located my dear son's remains. I would appreciate you going to assist me in arranging a meeting with General Sherman."

※

Together Joshua and Nathaniel Foster approach the picket line of General Sherman at Decatur. They identify themselves to the picket. Joshua glances around briefly. "We are former members of Congress, and particular friends of General Sherman's brother, John Sherman. We are requesting to speak with General Sherman if he is available."

The guard has the two former Congressmen escorted to the Duty Office. Upon arriving, the picket introduces Congressman Hill and Congressman Foster to the Duty Officer.

He shakes their hands. "Have a seat Gentlemen, and I will have General Sherman informed of your wishes."

Joshua quietly confides in Nathaniel, "I hope General Sherman will extend us a visit."

"I feel that he will, especially since we are Union supporters. Besides, he's probably very curious to know why we are requesting to meet with him."

The Duty Office returns. "General Sherman has approved your request. Please follow me."

Joshua and Nathaniel breathe a sigh of relief, smile at each other, and the Guards escort the pair to General Sherman's headquarters.

As Joshua and Nathaniel enter, General Sherman comes forward, extending his hand in greeting. "Welcome to my headquarters Mr. Hill, Mr. Foster. I have heard my brother speak fondly of both of you and I know both of you were against secession. I suspect you have something of importance to discuss with me is why you requested this visit."[372]

Joshua shakes Sherman's hand. "Thank you for honoring our request, General."

"Please have a seat around the conference table gentlemen. Captain Dayton, my Aid-de-Camp will join us." General Sherman opens a box of cigars, "Would either of you care for a fresh cigar."

"Thank you General, if I may," replies Nathaniel as he removes an aromatic cigar from the box and passes it beneath his nose.

Joshua hands the box to Captain Dayton who returns it to General Sherman. "No thank you, General. I'm not a smoker."

General Sherman removes a cigar for himself, and he and Nathaniel light up. General Sherman places his cigar in the ash tray and leans back in his chair. "To what do I owe the honor of your visit today, gentlemen?"

Joshua clears his throat. "My main purpose for our visit today is to seek your permission to recover the body of my son, Legare."

General Sherman blinks surprisingly and again extending his hand, nods slightly. "You have my deepest respects, Mr. Hill. Where was your son killed?"

"Legare was killed as Gen. Hardee's army fell back somewhere near Cassville. My friend, James Crews, with the railroad located his burial site. I am simply asking your permission to go through your lines."[373]

"Again Mr. Hill, you and Mrs. Hill have my regrets for the loss of your son. I will gladly grant you permission to go by rail to the rear. Captain Dayton, have the clerk write a directive to the commanding officer, General John E. Smith, at Cartersville. Instruct him that he is required to furnish Congressman Hill and Congressman Foster an escort and an ambulance for the purpose of recovering his dear son's remains."[374]

Joshua stands. "Thank you General. Thank you not only for me, but for my wife, daughter-in-law and from all our family members."

"You are quite welcome sir."

Captain Dayton proceeds to the clerk with his instructions.

"Gentlemen, please accept my invitation for dinner at the officers' mess."

"Thank you kindly General. We will be glad to accept," replies Joshua.

He can't help but notice General Sherman's careless dress, which affirms the rumors he has heard. Sherman is physically spare and of good height. His hair is not unpleasantly red, his forehead is very fine, and his eyes clear and restless. Sherman impresses Joshua as a man with an active temper with a somewhat dyspeptic facial expression and views him as an ordinarily kind-hearted individual. However, he has heard that when the General becomes aroused, he is severe and utterly unrelenting. His manner is very frank and outspoken. Joshua has been told General Sherman possesses extraordinary mental power and is blessed with an abundance of nervous energy.

During dinner General Sherman tries to make conversation easy for his guests. "Atlanta was the industrial center for the Confederacy. The factories produced large quantities of mortar shells, pistols, saddles, brass buttons, clothing, and torpedo fuses. Thousands of tons of steel have been forged as armor plate for ironclad ships in Atlanta. You have seen a part of the country over which the Union army has passed. I can easily apply the same measure of desolation to the remainder of the State if necessity should compel us to go ahead to Augusta."[375]

Nathaniel asks, "General Sherman what is it you would request us to do? Vice President Stephens is our best hope for peace."

"Governor Brown should fully realize the dangers and that further resistance on the part of the South is madness."

"We agree with you whole-heartedly on this subject, General," replies Joshua.

"I hope your governor will so proclaim that fruitless efforts on his part will lead to the destruction of the entire state. The governor can withdraw his people from the rebellion, in pursuance of what was known as the policy of 'separate State action.'"[376]

Joshua replies, "I only see Governor Brown burying his head in the sand."

"If you see Governor Brown, please describe to him fully what you have seen. Please attempt to enlighten the Governor that if he remains inert, that I will be compelled to go ahead and devastate the State in its whole length and breadth."

"We will be glad to be your emissaries to the Governor, General."

"Also relate to the Governor, there's no adequate force to stop us. Ask him to issue a proclamation withdrawing his State troops from the armies of the Confederacy. If he does this I will spare the State, and in the passage across Georgia, the Union troops would be confined to the main roads."

"We will talk with the Governor and give him your message," replies Joshua.

"Also assure the Governor, the Union army would moreover pay for all the corn and food it needed. Then invite Governor Brown, in my name, to visit Atlanta. I will give him safeguard if the Governor wants to make a speech; I will guarantee him as full and respectable an audience as any he has ever spoken to."

Joshua looks into Sherman's eyes and with a stern, yet disheartened look. "Your offer to discuss the fate of our state is very amiable, but frankly I don't believe the governor will accept your invitation or offer. However, you can count of us to do our very best for the sake of the people of our state and for the Union."

"I have also sent similar messages by Judge Wright of Rome, and by Mr. King, of Marietta to Governor Brown hoping for a response through them."[377]

At the conclusion of the dinner, Joshua rises to take his leave. "Thank you again General for your consideration of my request. My family will always remember your gracious act of compassion. Nathaniel and I will do our utmost to convince Governor Brown to consider your offer to visit with you."

As they depart the general's headquarters, Joshua remembers his conversation with Buck. "Nathaniel I must telegraph Buck as soon as we arrive home. He offered to accompany me to recover Legare's remains."

EXECUTIVE DEPARTMENT MILLEDGEVILLE, GEORGIA,
September 10, 1864
General J. B. HOOD, Commanding Army of Tennessee

*GENERAL: As the militia of the State were called out for the defense
of Atlanta during the campaign against it, which has terminated by
the fall of the city into the hands of the enemy, and as many of these left
their homes without preparation (expecting to be gone but a few weeks),
who have remained in service over three months (most of the time in the
trenches), justice requires that they be permitted, while the enemy are
preparing for the winter campaign, to return to their homes, and look
for a time after important interests, and prepare themselves for such
service as may be required when another campaign commences against
other important points in the State. I therefore hereby withdraw said
organization from your command.*

JOSEPH C. BROWN
Governor

❧

*HEADQUARTERS MILITARY DIVISION OF THE MISSISSIPPI IN
THE FIELD, ATLANTA, GEORGIA,*
September 17, 1864
President LINCOLN, *Washington, D. C.:*

*I will keep the department fully advised of all developments connected
with the subject in which you feel interested.*

*Mr. Wright, former member of Congress from Rome, Georgia, and Mr.
King, of Marietta, are now going between Governor Brown and myself.
I have said to them that some of the people of Georgia are engaged in
rebellion, began in error and perpetuated in pride, but that Georgia can
now save herself from the devastations of war preparing for her, only
by withdrawing her quota out of the Confederate Army, and aiding me
to expel Hood from the borders of the State; in which event, instead of
desolating the land as we progress, I will keep our men to the high-roads
and commons, and pay for the corn and meat we need and take. Mr. Hill
and Mr. Foster, under separate circumstances, also are contacting the
Governor on these matters.*

*I am fully conscious of the delicate nature of such assertions, but it
would be a magnificent stroke of policy if we could, without surrendering principle or a foot of ground, arouse the latent enmity of Georgia
against Davis.*

The people do not hesitate to say that Mr. Stephens was and is a Union man at heart; and they say that Davis will not trust him or let him have a share in his Government.

W. T. SHERMAN, Major General[378]

⋙●

General Sherman telegraphs General Halleck. "I have not the least doubt that Governor Brown, at that time, seriously entertained the proposition; but he hardly felt ready to act, and simply gave a furlough to the militia, and called a special session of the Legislature, to meet at Milledgeville, to take into consideration the critical condition of affairs in the State. I also have information that Jeff Davis was with Gen. Hood at Palmetto Station on September 22. One of our spies was there at the time, which came in the next night, and reported to me the substance of President Davis's speech to the soldiers. It was a repetition of those the President had made at Columbia, South Carolina, and Macon, Georgia, on his way out, which I had seen in the newspapers. Davis seemed to be perfectly upset by the fall of Atlanta, and to have lost all sense and reason. He denounces Gen. Johnston and Governor Brown as little better than traitors; attributed to them personally the many misfortunes, which had befallen their cause. Davis informed the soldiers that now the tables were to be turned. He also informs the soldiers that Gen. Forrest was already on our roads in Middle Tennessee; and that Hood's army would soon be there. He asserts that the Yankee army would have to retreat or starve, and that the retreat would prove more disastrous than was that of Napoleon from Moscow. He promises his Tennessee and Kentucky soldiers that their feet should soon tread their "native soil," etc., etc. He made no concealment of these vainglorious boasts, and thus gave us the full key to his future designs. To be forewarned was to be forearmed, and I think we took full advantage of the occasion."[379]

HDQRS. MILITARY DIVISION OF THE MISSISSIPPI, Atlanta, Ga.,
September 20, 1864
Major General H. W. HALLECK, Chief of Staff, Washington, D.C.:

GENERAL: I have the honor herewith to submit copies of a correspondence between Gen. Hood, of the Confederate army, the mayor of Atlanta, and myself touching the removal of the inhabitants of Atlanta.

In explanation of the tone which marks some of these letters, I will only call your attention to the fact that after I had announced my determination, Gen. Hood took upon himself to question my motive. I could not tamely submit to such impertinence....

I am, with respect, your obedient servant,

W. T. SHERMAN
Major-General, Commanding[380]

SEPTEMBER 20, 1864

The preacher concludes, "For Thine is the Kingdom, the Power and the Glory, forever and ever, Amen."

Buck, Betty Gail, Uncle Isaac and Aunt Sally stand along with Polly, Little Joshua, Congressman Hill, Emily and their children. Uncle Richard, Aunt Charlotte, Tot, Al, and Jesse stand on the opposite side of Legare's casket as it is slowly lowered into the ground.

Motionless, Polly clutches the gold necklace Legare gave her at Christmas. On the necklace is a button from his overcoat and a locket containing a strand of his hair.

Joshua turns to his daughter-in-law. "My dear Polly, Emily and I love you as a daughter and will always think of you as such. We have a sealed letter for you from Legare, given to us by Rooster. I thought maybe you would want to read it at his grave side alone." Lips quivering, Joshua reaches into his pocket, removes the sealed letter and presses his hands to Polly's with the letter.

She acknowledges Joshua's gesture with tight lips, a simple smile. Tears stream down her soft cheeks. Little Joshua is standing by his mother's side and holding tightly to her black dress.

Buck slides his arm around his daughter. "I love you Polly. Will you be all right?"

Betty Gail wipes the tears from her own eyes and then Polly's. "I love you, Polly, God rest his soul." She kisses Polly and little Joshua.

Polly resolutely nods.

Emily moves closer to Polly and little Joshua. In tears, she kisses Polly then kneels to the ground to bid her son farewell. Polly holds her hand and they give each other comfort in their grief.

Joshua helps Emily stand. "We will go to our carriages and wait for you, Polly. Please be in no hurry to depart."

Polly, all alone except for Little Joshua, sits on the soft grass next to Legare's open grave. The gentle breeze and beautiful fall foliage divulges nature's own story of the cycle of life. Polly tenderly pulls Little Joshua into her lap and draws him near. Almost as if afraid, she opens the last letter she'll ever receive from her husband.

> *My Dear Polly,*
>
> *I sleep with you and our child at my side every night, and we walk together every day. I feel your breath and smell your sweetness even when you are not with me as I sleep. You are a true jewel of our Southland, a Cherokee rose in full bloom. You have the inherent beauty of mind, of soul, and of character. These three qualities lift you as an icon to a higher power and give you exquisite charm.*
>
> *You possess the Spartan traits of the South ... endurance, fortitude, courage, and superiority of mind. These compel respect, even from Aunt Charlotte, and these traits will inspire in our child, loyalty in our slaves, and good will of our neighbors.*
>
> *My dear Polly, my love, you possess the strength which is born of prayer, the tranquil calm which comes from faith, and the serene smile whose divine source is love. Whether in a pillared mansion, in our home, or your parents' home, whatever you say or do, bears the hallowed hallmark of the old nobility which reveals the gentle molds of the ancestry from which you sprang.*
>
> *My dear precious one, you furnish the golden urn in which my heart is enshrined. You hover over me as I sleep in this bivouac as if you are making the sentinel rounds of my tent. You have made medicine for and have bent over the wounded and dying in the hospital. I only hope God continues to make me worthy of your gentle love and sweet loyalty.*
>
> *My reverence will forever linger at your altar. Kiss our son each day that I am away.*
>
> *With an abundance of love I can only describe as infinity plus one,*
>
> *Legare*[381]
>
> SEPTEMBER 22, 1864

On their way back from Savannah, Buck confides in Betty Gail, "I wish Polly had stayed with us in Stone Mountain for a while longer. I truly worry about that girl and grandson of ours."

"She's independent just like you, Buck. She's got her mind set on working at the hospital. She feels she owes it to Legare. Besides, it keeps her busy and helps clear up her mind from this awful tragedy."

"Here we are at the Madison Station. I see Joshua got my telegram. His driver is waiting for us." After supper Joshua and Buck retire to the parlor. Joshua informs Buck, "I have just written a letter to my friend, James Crews, in West Point. I would like you to read it and give me your opinion."

"Sure."

"I saw a great deal of Atlanta-houses and people. There has been no wanton destruction of property to any extent beyond fencing and outbuildings, which in some parts of the city has suffered. If I could see you I could tell you much more than I can undertake to write. I can say of a truth that General Sherman was right in his arbitrary order to evacuate Atlanta. Those who remain are generally in a pitiable condition with small available means and with no market, they are faring badly … I was treated with marked kindness wherever I went. I spent a week nearly about Cartersville and Kingston and several days at Rome. From Kingston to Atlanta, the country as far as the eye can reach is one prolonged scene of desolation. The silence that reigns is only broken by the sound of movement … men, teams of wagons, squadrons of cavalry and occasionally a railway train. I wish it could be seen by every war man in Georgia. But I doubt if it would do any good, so visionary and fanatical have our leaders grown."[382]

"I think you define the situation very accurately," says Buck. "Is this also a draft for the Governor?"

"I'm not sure what I can do about the Governor, especially since I ran against him. But for Georgia and our good family and citizens I will do my best. I have a meeting scheduled with General Sherman on the 28th."

Joshua Hill and Nathaniel Foster, along with Judge Wright, arrive at the appointed time at General Sherman's headquarters.

Hugh Legare Hill's headstone, Madison, GA city cemetery.

"Gentlemen, I want you to understand that President Lincoln appreciates any effort you can afford to bring this conflict to a close. You have his full support, and I will provide any assistance you request to this end. "During the course of the meeting military statistics, army strengths, munitions, and the general morale of both sides are compared. At the close of the meeting, General Sherman says, "Gentlemen, please do your very best to persuade Governor Brown to abandon his crazy vision and save the lives of an untold number of young and energetic men. Thank you for your support of the Constitution and the Union. Go in peace."

Immediately following the meeting General Sherman has Captain Dayton telegraph President Lincoln:

HEADQUARTERS MILITARY DIVISION OF THE MISSISSIPPI IN THE FIELD, ATLANTA, GEORGIA,
September 28, 1864.
President LINCOLN, Washington, D. C.:

I have positive knowledge that Mr. Davis made a speech at Macon, on September 22, which I mailed to General Halleck yesterday. It was bitter against Gen. Jos. Johnston and Governor Brown. The militia is on furlough. Brown is at Milledgeville, trying to get a Legislature to meet next month, but he is afraid to act unless in concert with other Governors. Judge Wright, of Rome, has been here, and Messrs. Hill and Foster, former members of Congress, are here now, and will go to meet Wright at Rome, and then go back to Madison and Milledgeville.

Great efforts are being made to re-enforce Hood's army, and to break up my railroads, and I should have at once a good reserve force at Nashville. It would have a bad effect, if I were forced to send back any considerable part of my army to guard roads, so as to weaken me to an extent that I could not act offensively if the occasion calls for it.

W. T. SHERMAN
Major General

On the same day General Sherman receives a telegram from General Halleck regarding the evacuation of Atlanta.

WASHINGTON, SEPTEMBER 28, 1864
Major-General SHERMAN, Atlanta, Ga.

GENERAL, Your communications of the 20th in regard to the removal of families from Atlanta and the exchange of prisoners, and also the official report of your campaign, are just received. Not only are you justified by the laws and usages of war in these matters … I do not approve of General Hunter's course in burning private houses, or uselessly destroying private property. That is barbarous; but I approve of taking or destroying whatever may serve as supplies to us or to the enemy's armies.

Very respectfully, your obedient servant,

H. W. HALLECK
Major-General and Chief of Staff[383]

A FRIEND'S TALE OF WOE

Betty Gail is at the hospital preparing to go home when a waiter from the Johnson Hotel across the street enters, "There's a lady looking for you at the hotel Miz Betty Gail. Says her name is Mary Gay."

"Mary Gay? My word what is she doing here?" Betty Gail leaves with the waiter, dashes across the railroad track to the hotel and finds Mary sitting at a table sipping sassafras tea. When she sees Betty Gail, she jumps from her seat and they meet with a huge embrace. "I'm so glad to see a familiar face in these parts Betty Gail."

"What brings you to Stone Mountain, Mary?" She stands back from Mary and takes a good look. "You look exhausted. Where have you been?"

"In a big circle," replies Mary. She clasps Betty Gail's hand, and they sit at the table in the hotel kitchen. "How did you get to Stone Mountain, Mary?"

"It's a long story which started with the arrival of the Yankees at my place earlier this month."

"I hear they were ruthless to everybody."

"Yes, and I believe they are the sons of the devil. The advance guards of the Yankees came into Decatur and our home, surprising everyone. They dispatched from their horses and entered our house without invitation. Why, one idiot got on his knees and hands, pawed the ground, and roared like an infuriated bull. Another Yankee, accompanying this 'king's fool' laughed, and ask me if I had expected to see the Yankees with hoofs and horns."[384]

"What did you say to the Yankees?"

"My simple reply was, 'I expected to see some gentlemen among you Yankees, and I am very sorry that I have not seen any.'"

"My gosh, did that bring them to their senses?"

"No, I think it made matters worse. They laughed, and that horde of thieving Yankees stole and carried off everything of value in the house, while the other Yankees outside descended upon the live stock killing one cow, two calves and twelve hogs. They left me only one sitting chicken."

"What did you do?"

"Couldn't do a thing. Poor Mama was shaking so bad, I thought she was dying." The waiter brings Betty Gail a cup of tea and re-fills Mary's cup.

"Was that the end of the ordeal?"

"No, several hours later in the evening, there was a loud knock on my door. By the light of the brilliant moon I could see a half dozen Yankees on my piazza. I asked, 'Who's there?'"

"And what did they say?"

"'Gentlemen,' was his laconic reply. Then I told the gentlemen, 'If so, you will not persist in your effort to come into the house. There's only a widow and one of her daughters, and two faithful servants here.'"

"What happened then?"

"The Yankee shouted, 'We have orders from our headquarters to interview Miss Gay. Is she the daughter of whom you speak?'"

"She is, and I am she,' was my reply.

"My word. Why did they want to interview you? You must have been terrified." Betty Gail could only imagine how her friend must have felt.

"I was terrified. The Yankee was Major Campbell from General Schofield's staff. So I opened the door, and the Major told me he had information that I was some kind of threat to the Yankees.

"He went on and told me that I boast that I'm a rebel, and that I'm ever on duty to aid and abet in every possible way the would-be destroyers of the United States government. If this be so, they cannot permit me to remain within their lines. Until Atlanta surrenders, Decatur will be his headquarters, and every consideration of interest to their cause requires that no one inimical is to remain within the boundaries established by the Union forces."

"Oh, Mary! How could he be so cruel? How did you respond to his charges?"

"I told him, that without question, I was true to the South and to the men of the South. He just stood there while I told him that the Yankee abolitionist and Yankee haters of the South caused this war, and since the North would not secede, we decided to secede. You come down here stealing everything in my house and on my farm and have the nerve to say I'm the threat."

Betty Gail takes a sip of her tea and watches Mary pick up her cup with both hands and take a long drink. "Those Yankees are a cruel bunch all right," said Betty Gail. "So the Major left you alone after that?"

"Pretty much so. He had a little meeting in the yard with some other Yankee and then told me that we could stay in our home."

"But how did you get here?" asks Betty Gail.

"Well I needed to visit my sick sister in Augusta. I knew our friend, Mr. Frederick Williams, had influence with General Schofield. So I asked his assistance in getting me permission to go out and return during the armistice."

"So I guess Mr. Williams was successful."

"Yes, he was." Mary takes her purse and removes a letter and hands it to Betty Gail. "Here's a letter of introduction he wrote to a Yankee Colonel by the name of Parkhurst."

Betty Gail takes the letter and reads.

HEADQUARTERS, ARMY OF OHIO
DECATUR GA,
SEPT. 14, 1864

MY DEAR COLONEL—I have the honor to introduce Miss Mary A. H. Gay, of this village, and I recommend her case to your favorable consideration. I do not know exactly what orders are now in force, but if you think you can grant her desires without detriment to the public service, I am confident the indulgence will not be abused.

Very respectfully your obedient servant,

J. W. Campbell

"That's great. What happened next?"

"I was able to get a few croaker sacks from the Yankees for packing the supplies to take with me."

Betty Gail pours more tea for Mary. "What kind of supplies?"

Mary looks at Betty Gail with a tricky smile. "Confederate winter clothes from Gen. Johnston's army when he was in Dalton. They were left behind by my brother, and some of his comrades plan on delivering them to him."

"Were you able to get the uniforms through the line?"

"Yes, with the help of Posey Maddox. He had secured the use of an entire freight car for his family for the evacuation and gladly let me ride with them to Jonesboro."

"That was gracious of Mr. Maddox. What happened at Jonesboro?"

"When I got off the train, I informed the Confederate officer in charge that I had some clothing for General Granbury's men and needed a ride to his headquarters."

"Did he get one for you?"

"After a while he returned with a wagon and driver. But during the interim, I peered around and began to observe how horrible this situation really was at Rough and Ready. The entire Southern population of Atlanta, with all but an occasional exception, were dumped out upon the cold ground without shelter and without any of the comforts of home. The autumn mist and drizzle, slowly but steadily, saturated every article of clothing upon them. Surely pulmonary diseases in all stages await them from the danger of this exposure. Aged grandmothers, tottering upon the verge of the grave, and tender house maidens in the first bloom of young womanhood and little babes not three days old, in the arms of sick mothers, driven from their homes, were all out upon the cold charity of the world."[385]

"So, I hope you found your brother, Thomie."

"I did. Gave him the beautiful knitted scarf from his wife in Texas. His eyes lit up. He grasped the scarf and rubbed his face trying to smell the scent of his lovely wife."

Betty Gail thinks of Polly and Legare exchanging gifts at Christmas. She blinks her eyes to keep away the tears. She gazes and partly smiles at Mary. "How sweet."

"Then we gave the warm clothing to the troops. The next day I reached Augusta, saw my sister was well, stayed the night and headed for home the next morning."

"Excuse me a few minutes, Mary. I need to get some fresh air. Your story has so many truths."

"I need some as well, Betty Gail. I'll walk outside with you." The two friends stand together outside in the fresh cool air of a spring evening.

Betty Gail is solemn and crying, yet does not disclose Legare's death to Mary wishing not to dampen Mary's spirits after visiting with her family. She pulls Mary close and hugs her. "I understand and feel your thoughts, Mary." Betty Gail is crying deeper on the inside than Mary realizes. "Let's go back inside and have some food. You must be starving." Inside the hotel, the waiter cuts some fresh ham and serves a sweet potato to fill their small plates. "Eat and rest a bit Mary."

"Thank you for the food and beverage." Mary takes a few minutes to eat. When Betty Gail sees that Mary has finished eating, she asks, "Please let me hear the rest of your story." Warming her hands with the sassafras teacup, Mary looks at Betty Gail and ponders for a moment before continuing.

"Lovejoy is the same as Jonesboro. The face of the earth is literally covered with crude tents and side-tracked-cars. The cars were occupied by exiles, defenseless women and children, and an occasional old man tottering on the verge of the grave."

"Poor things."

"The next morning I boarded the train for Social Circle. From Social Circle I took an ox cart to Covington since the tracks are torn up from there. Several other ladies joined me and we shared the ride to Stone Mountain.

"The long tramp coming here to Stone Mountain was very lonely," Mary says sadly. "Not a living thing overtook or passed us. We soon crossed over the line and entered a war-stricken section of the country. There were only chimneys standing where previously were pretty homes and prosperity. No wonder they are called 'Sherman's sentinels,' as they seem to be keeping guard over these scenes of desolation. The very birds of the air and beasts of the field have fled to other sections. By constant and unflagging locomotion, we reached Stone Mountain sometime after dark. When I asked the clerk of your whereabouts and told her my name, she smiled, knowing of my family in Decatur and your whereabouts as well. She sent her stable boy for you at the hospital and put me in this kitchen."

Betty Gail suggests, "Mary let me take you 'round the Mountain to our house. Buck, Sally and Uncle Isaac will be delighted to see you and have you stay there."

Mary softly answers, "Thank you, but I must sleep here since it is closer to Decatur."

Betty Gail knows it is a lost cause to argue with Mary. When her mind is made up it is made up. Betty Gail and Mary embrace. She escorts Mary to a comfortable area of the hotel in the manager's office.

"Tomorrow, I will walk to Judge Bryce's and then home."

Betty Gail interrupts, "I can get the ambulance driver to take you there in the morning Mary. We have only one mule left for the hospital and must be careful that it is not taken from us. I have a letter giving us protection at the hospital, but I do not know if it will mean anything to the run-of-the-mill bummers when I am away from the hospital … but to Judge Bryce, I think is safe."

"Don't worry yourself. We will discuss that more in the morning. It is a mere six miles to Decatur and much shorter to the home of Judge Bryce," replies Mary.

Then Betty Gail rushes to the hospital and secures some blankets. She returns to prepare Mary a comfortable bed on the floor in the hotelkeepers office. Mary takes the final sip of tea and almost instantly falls to the blankets and is fast asleep.

Early the next morning, just before the sky lightens, Mary slips from the hotelkeepers office. Footsore and without breakfast, she starts all alone walking toward Judge Bryce's home and Decatur.

In a time shorter that she realizes, Mary arrives at Judge Bryce's once beautiful, but now dilapidated, home. Judge Bryce and his wife give Mary an affectionate greeting and breakfast to calm her growling stomach. "I beg you, Judge Bryce, please go with me part of the way to Decatur."[386]

Betty Gail awakens and rushes over to the hotel to find out how Mary slept during the night. She peeks into the hotelkeepers office and find the blankets folded neatly with a note attached. She takes the note, which is written on a small scrap of paper and reads the contents. "Betty Gail, Thank you, your friend, Mary."

Betty Gail rushes to the hospital. The mule and wagon are already hitched and await her. Betty Gail boards the wagon, snaps the reins, and heads the mules in the direction of Judge Bryce's. Approaching his poor dwelling, she halts and jumps from the wagon. Judge Bryce sees her through the window and meets her outside.

"Have you seen Mary Gay this morning?" She asks Judge Bryce.

"Yes, she departed here about an hour ago and should be close to Decatur by now. She had breakfast before leaving."

"She stayed in town last night, and I told her I could bring her as far as your place this morning, but she did not wait."

"In spirit, she is a true Southern soldier," confides Judge Bryce.

"Yes, she is. I must get back to the hospital now. Thanks for seeing her and feeding her this morning." Betty Gail mounts the wagon and heads back to the hospital in Stone Mountain, praying that she'll see Mary and her family again.

SEPTEMBER-OCTOBER 1864

Shortly after arriving in Milledgeville, Norman is sitting on his bunk across from Paul discussing their current situation. "Peace and quiet for a while Paul. Maybe we can get some studying done as well as our military responsibilities of the garrison."

"Looks like a flock of new guys are enrolling as cadets. I guess we will have to teach them the rules of the game," says Paul.

Norman agrees with him and laughingly replies, "I hope the corps will really get to fight somewhere to foil the triumphant invader of our native soil."[387]

HDQRS. THIRD DIVISION, TWENTIETH ARMY CORPS

Atlanta, Ga., October 24, 1864

COLONEL: I have the honor to report that the late foraging expedition under my charge moved from Atlanta as per order at 6 AM on the 21st October instant. The troops consisting of the following: First Brigade, First Division under Colonel Selfridge, 1,000; First Brigade, Second Division under Colonel Flynn, 1,000 men; Third Brigade, Third Division, under Lieutenant-Colonel Buckingham, 888 men; Cavalry under General Garrard, 400 men. Total, 3,228 men; Also two batteries of artillery, Captain Winegar.

The command moves to Decatur, where the train stands by for more complete organization. From Decatur, expedition takes the road to Latimar's with cavalry in advance. Detachments of cavalry are also on the road to the right to Flat Shoals, and to the left toward Stone Mountain, all converging at Latimar's, where the expedition encamped for the first night.

On the 22nd, some 450 wagons are loaded in season to move back t wo miles and a half toward Decatur to Snapfinger Creek where the expedition encamped for the second night. By noon of the 23rd, all the wagons are loaded. At 1 PM, the head of the column moves out on the return march with the intention of parking at Decatur for the third night. Just at this time, Colonel Carman, with his brigade, reports with communication from corps headquarters. Coming up in our rear, he moves his brigade to the head of the column, which occasions some delay in the march.

The last of the trains park at Decatur at 1:30 at night. The command moves from Decatur for Atlanta at 7 AM on the 24th. No enemy is seen, except a few straggling cavalrymen, one of whom is taken prisoner. Only one or two acts of unwarrantable pillaging are reported.

Four hundred wagons can be loaded with corn in the vicinity of Latimar's. A considerable quantity is reported two or three miles north of Lithonia. The rapid manner in which the wagons are loaded and the quick return of the expedition is to be ascribed, in a great measure, to the efficiency of the brigade commanders, and to the prompt and energetic personal attention which they gave to the work assigned to their commands. The wagon train is a most unwieldy thing, and under so many untoward circumstances the quartermaster of the expedition, Capt. Summers, deserves great credit for his untiring industry in the execution of his arduous duties and for tritons. Lieutenant-Colonel Hurst, Seventy-Third Ohio Volunteer Infantry, deserves much commendation for the efficient and diligent performance of his difficult duties as general field officer during the entire expedition.

I respectfully suggest that hereafter these expeditions should not be encumbered with more than 400 wagons, and that measures be taken to prevent an increase of this number by a thorough organization of the train on the day before starting.

Respectfully submitted,

DANIEL DUSTIN
Colonel, Commanding THIRD DIVISION, Twentieth Army Corps.[388]

TUESDAY OCTOBER 25, 1864

Thomas Maguire is at his Promised Land Plantation near Lithonia when his neighbor, Wesley, stops by to share with him the latest news. "Got word that the Yankees were driven back."

"That is good news. Hopefully they won't come back to my place. It's hard to hear the truth even from the other side of the river, Wesley. I just hope if it's true that the Yankees have been driven back that we will have sufficient force to keep them back."

"Yes, we all hope for that, Thomas."

"Thanks for coming by. I guess you finished moving your belongings yesterday?"

"Pretty much so. I got to run for now. Hope to see you again soon." Wesley touches his hat with his fingers, and departs. Thomas rushes inside and informs his wife of the good news.[389]

WEDNESDAY, OCTOBER 26, 1864

Lt. Cooper, eight men and fourteen horses arrive at the Promised Land Plantation to spend the night. Thomas sits with the Confederates stirring the campfire and listens as Lt. Cooper fills him in on the whereabouts of the Yankees. "Mr. Maguire, the Yankees are at Indian Creek, and there are no troops coming from Athens. Don't worry, there's still hope for help."

Thomas informs the Lieutenant, "There were fourteen scouts here last night, and they left here at half past nine fearing the Yankees would come and catch them. I hope these are not the soldiers you expect to help us. Poor fellows. They may make soldiers, but it will take some time first. They were badly scared and left as soon as they finished eating."[390]

꩜

General Geary receives instructions from Major-General Slocum to conduct a foraging expedition to and around Stone Mountain.[391] At six o'clock on the morning of October 26, the following troops and wagons report to General Geary on the Decatur road: Third Brigade, First Division, numbering 1,200 men, under command of Colonel Robinson; Third Brigade, Second Division, numbering 945 men, under command of Lieutenant-Colonel Van Voorhis; Second Brigade, Third Division, numbering 642 men, under command of Major Brant; Two batteries of artillery, under command of Captain Bainbridge, 450 cavalry of the Army of the Ohio, under Colonel Garrard. Wagons as follows: Headquarters Twentieth Corps, 42; First Division Twentieth Corps, 83; Second Division, Twentieth Corps, 100; Third Division, Twentieth Corps, 87; Fourteenth Army Corps, 130.

Captain Hade, post quartermaster, 21; Ordnance train, Department of the Cumberland, 54; Medical supply train, 20; Batteries and outside detachments, 115; making the total number of wagons 652, which, with the addition of 20 smaller wagons, made the entire train consist of 672 wagons.

At seven o'clock, General Geary moves toward Decatur, without incidents of note, and arrives three hours later. In Decatur, General Geary talks to some wandering Negroes and determines that there's a force of the Confederates ranging in number from 2,000 to 4,000, between Stone Mountain and Lawrenceville. One of General Geary's scouting parties reports that detachments from this Confederate force had been in Decatur on the previous day. Colonel Garrard's cavalry scouts confirm the same information. Concerned about Col. Dibrell's cavalry induces General Geary to ask General Slocum for reinforcements of artillery and infantry to guard against any attack on the foraging train from the right and toward Stone Mountain.

General Geary detaches the main force of cavalry, seven hundred infantry under Lieutenant-Colonel Van Voorhis, and a section of artillery, the whole under command of Colonel Garrard, to move directly to Stone Mountain and secure and hold all the roads and passes there. With the remainder of his command and the wagon train, Geary moves from Decatur on the Lawrenceville Road for about six miles, passing to the right over a wood road. At the mountain, General Geary joins Colonel Garrard's command. Geary leaves a strong cavalry guard to hold the village, moves on Stone Mountain and Lawrenceville road to Trickum's Crossroads, parking the wagon train and forming camp for the troops on the farm of Mr. Bracewell.[392]

About nine o'clock in the evening, an aide reports that the Second Brigade of the Second Division under Colonel Mindil and one section of artillery are four miles beyond Stone Mountain. General Geary orders Colonel Mindil to push as near the mountain as possible during the night and to join him on the following morning. Further reports of Confederate forces from the slaves in the vicinity of the camp confirm those already received at Decatur.

During Thursday morning, the 27th, several attacks are made upon the pickets and outposts, by Col. Dibrell's cavalry. One Union soldier is killed and another severely wounded. General Geary remains in camp during the day, sending out detachments of the wagon train under strong guards.[393]

The inclement weather has given Colonel Robinson an extra degree of surprise. Buck is unaware of the Yankees' presence. Buck and Isaac are up early making the rounds to the fields, checking the Irish and sweet potatoes on his farm and at Buster Phillips' place. Charlie barks loudly as a large force of Yankees on wagons appears suddenly on his property.

Buck and Isaac rush to the house and prepare to meet the riders. Betty Gail is standing on the porch wiping her hands on her apron. The Yankee units consist of ten wagons and at least one hundred soldiers. He begins to wonder if these are the dreadful bummer troops coming to steal their belongings.

Buck has his Union flag flying outside while the Confederate flag is flying at Buster Phillips' place. Soon, the wagons appear at his front and he realizes his fears are turning into reality. Betty Gail steps from the porch and clutches Buck's arm. Now standing face to face, the bummer rides up asks, "Do you own this place?"

"It's mine all right," replies Buck.

"I see you're flying the Union Flag. That means a lot to us. But never-the-less, we need food for our troops. We are part of Colonel Robinson's unit and have orders to take whatever food we need. Just don't interfere and you'll be okay. Sergeant, take two wagons and begin loading what you can find from those two barns. Corporal, take another wagon and pick and load the potatoes from that field." The wagon drivers snap their reins and hastily move to the barns and the fields. "Lieutenant, post guards along the trails to this place. We have already had enough encounters with the Confederates."

Peering into the bummers wagons, Buck sees a rocking chair, a baby carriage, and several large trunks stacked together with stolen rations from other farms. The bummer then orders two Yankees inside to take whatever they can find. He orders the other to gather the chickens, turkeys, ducks, and hogs. Buck turns and starts into the house behind the invading Yankees.

"You just stay where you are, mister and everything will be okay. Lady, you take a seat in that rocking chair on the porch."

"I'd just as soon stand here with my husband, if you don't mind, Lieutenant!"

"I'm going to ask you one more time nicely, to kindly take a seat in that rocking chair on the porch."

Buck pushes her along toward the porch. "Best do as he says, Betty Gail." With a determined frown Buck continues, "As for your supplies, since I don't have a choice, I suggest you help yourself. Your friends at the signal station on top of the mountain come by here regularly and help themselves just like you."

Soon, the bummer comes out the house wearing Buck's old tri-cornered hat and carrying Buck's Masonic plaque. "Not much in this place, already been cleaned out. Just a few eggs and some greens as far as food and this here squirrel rifle. Don't have any use for it." He throws Norman's rifle to the ground.

"You best leave the Masonic plaque," retorts the commander. "Several of the generals are Masons, and they will take serious offense if you have it in your possession." The Bluebelly throws the Masonic plaque onto the porch.

"Check the cook house and smoke house and bring back all the meat you find. Hey darkie, where's all the food?"

Isaac replies, "Dun all gone! Yankees on da 'ountain gots it de other day." Soon the Yankees bring out the horses from Buck's and Buster's barns.

The other cavalrymen are rounding up the cattle from the pastures and driving them to the road. The lieutenant shouts to one of his men, "Get that mule lying on the ground over there."

Isaac steps forward, "Jus' gots one ole mule, it gots bads tail en jonts. Layin' yonder 'n da pastur 'bout to die."

The lieutenant looks at Jack and sees his gray whiskers. "We'll leave the half dead mule, one cow and one hog since you're a Mason and flying the Union Flag. I see you have chickens."

Buck looks at the Lieutenant. "I appreciate you leaving the ole mule sir. He's just a pet." The officer pays little attention to his thanks and hastens his men to claim the chickens and kill and dress the hogs. Shots ring out, and the hogs fall one by one to the ground.

"Hang those hogs by their hind feet. Then slice their throats and let the blood run or the meat will sour. If it's a boar, cut his testicles out to save the meat from spoiling." The Yankee shooter takes his knife and runs in under the dead hogs' chins. He backs away and watches the blood ooze slowly from the still animal. "Round up the rest of those cows. We'll bring them with us. Burn his cotton gin and sorghum press!" He turns his attention to Isaac. "You know, darkie, you're a free man now. You can leave this place."

"I'se knows!"

"Who lives there?" He points to Buster Philips' place.

"Mars Buster, he's gone!"

"He has the enemy flag flying. Where is he now?"

"Off a-fighting, but my peoples livin' dat house"

"Have all of the darkies move back into their places. Sergeant, take a couple of men and get that house cleaned out and set it to blaze." The Yankees go into Buster's house and carry off all the household supplies. Soon, smoke and flames begin churning from the windows.

In the meantime, the Lieutenant orders some of Buster Phillips' Negroes to begin cleaning and dressing out the hogs. The bummers chase the cackling chickens down one by one. They tie the chicken's legs together and toss them in the wagons. The cattle are herded together.

Two hours pass, and the bummer orders all of the Negroes to gather 'round his horse. "If you tell me where the rest of the food is hidden, I'll give you a nice reward and allow you to come along with us. If you know and don't tell me, I'll burn your house down! So, where is the food buried or hidden on that mountain?"

Standing quietly, some simply shake their head. "Ain't no more food. Blues gots it all."

Suddenly, one of the bummers turns the corner of Buck's house shouting, "I've found the cellar, but nothing there—no apples, peaches or pears!"

"Mister, you're lucky you're flying the Union flag or I would burn your house to the ground just like your neighbor's!" shouts the lieutenant.

Buck doesn't respond.

General Sherman's bummer on a foraging expedition.

"Who lives down that road?"

"Just the Wayside. When Colonel Abe Miller was here in July, he left orders not to disturb the Wayside. Otherwise, nobody else now. All the men are in the war!"

"Why aren't you fighting?"

"Too old and got a bad hand." Raising his hand, he continues, "Lost these fingers in the war with Mexico."

The Yankee commander of the bummer ignores Buck and orders the darkies to place the dressed hogs in the already overloaded wagons. Then the Yankee orders, "Burn all of the buildings on that enemy farm, except where the Darkies are living. Leave them some food, but get all the potatoes." Offering a few indignities to the slaves, the foraging party begins driving the livestock away from Buck's farm.

Loaded down with the day's bounty of poultry, meal, meats, sweet potatoes, honey, and sorghum and without having room for any more provisions, the Bummers organize the wagon train and watch the flames for a while, then head back toward Colonel Robinson's main unit.

Betty Gail leaps from the porch as Buck, with a steaming temperament, turns and picks up Norman's squirrel rifle. Betty Gail picks up the Masonic plaque and simply hangs it on a nail on the porch wall. "Those bummers are nothing but a band of marauders," Buck mumbles to himself. "There's no need to fight the fires at Buster's place, Isaac. The buildings are already too far gone. Just let them burn out. Those Yankees are mad because this particular farm is not the land of milk and honey they are accustomed to!"

Buck and Isaac enter the house and find the place has been ransacked. Broken furniture, cut-up bedding, turned over tables and upset vanities litter the floors. "Isaac, it appears bummers feel free to take what they can carry away and what they cannot carry, they spoil and destroy. Just mind your tongue, and we will survive this ordeal, the Lord willing and the Creeks don't rise. The pecans will be coming in soon. It'll be a good source of food for all of us. We've got rabbit boxes, deer and squirrels, too."

Looking over at Buster Phillips's place, Buck notices that the wood shed, gin house and silo are burning. The barn's doors are smoking but the fire did not take to the structure for some reason. Some of Buster's slaves are already throwing water on the doors as he and Isaac rush over to assist them. Reaching for the sledge hammer, Buck knocks the hinges loose and the two sizzling barn doors fall to the ground. The slaves lash the doors and drag them into the dirt away from the barn. Buck thanks the darkies for being alert. "Lucky day, these doors are fresh green wood. Probably why they didn't catch."

Betty Gail is still standing on the porch when Buck returns. Looking at the ruins of Buster's place, she tears up and leans against him. "There's nothing left for Buster now. His heart, soul and property … all gone." Taking her apron, she wipes her tears away and sits in the rocking chair and begins weeping out loud as Buck comforts her.

PREPARATION

Colonel Robinson returns to camp at 6:30 PM with the 101st Illinois and 82nd Ohio Veteran Volunteers and brags to his officers, "We have succeeded in loading 196 wagons, in spite of the very inclement weather and prowling detachments of Col. Dibrell's cavalry. It appears this foraging expedition succeeded in loading about three hundred wagons across Yellow River towards Lawrenceville."[394]

Later in the afternoon, Lieutenant-Colonel Way, commanding a regiment of cavalry, reports to General Geary, "I met approximately four hundred of Col. Dibrell's Cavalry and possibly Col. Anderson's Infantry near Yellow River but did not engage them. The slaves in the area state that a force of possibly 4,000 is in Lawrenceville."

General Geary is told by his scouts that Col. Dibrell's troops have retreated across the river and destroyed the bridge. General Geary directs Colonel Way, "You are to follow, and push toward Lawrenceville to ascertain, if possible, the whereabouts of Dibrell's Confederate force."

"Yes sir." He directs his troops toward Lawrenceville in pursuit. Upon reaching Lawrenceville, he orders, "Charge!"

His cavalry charges furiously upon the town, surprising and driving Col. Dibrell's and Col. Anderson's forces through Lawrenceville in great disorder. The Confederates scatter in all directions and fire very few shots. General Geary mulls over the report and informs his officers, "With the bridge out, it is going to be impossible to load the remainder of our wagon train west of the river. From my reconnaissance there is an abundance of forage to be procured east of the river, so proceed there."[395]

At 10:30 AM Yankees ride up to Thomas Maguire's property. They take Phillip's wagon and two horses, all of Thomas's meat and flour, one keg of syrup and several articles from the house and the last bushel of grain. Lastly, they take his brother's saddlebags and a large tin cup. Later in the afternoon, the foraging wagons are in the fields.

At the end of the day, Thomas is troubled and discusses the situation with his family, "This is a very troublesome life to lead. Tomorrow, I suppose will bring our fate and probably our destruction with it."[396]

Accordingly, on Friday morning October 28, General Geary meets with Colonel Robinson. "Take 250 wagons with a guard of fifteen hundred infantry, a regiment of cavalry, and a section of artillery, and cross the Yellow River. The fields just beyond are very productive. Load the wagons there. The remaining empty wagons go with a guard of four hundred infantry and a section of artillery and are to report to Colonel Garrard who is encamped on the Rock Bridge Road. He is about three miles from the main camp and east of the mountain."

Colonel Robinson's brigade has no difficulty loading the entire wagon train toward Berkshire at 3 PM. He crosses Yellow River upon a bridge, which, though partly burned by the enemy the previous day, is nevertheless easily rendered passable for the train after a few minor repairs.

At three o'clock, General Geary's couriers report in from Colonel Robinson and Colonel Garrard that their wagons have been loaded and are ready for the returning march. Robinson's column reaches Berkshire at sundown and pushes forward, following the remainder of the expedition, which has already preceded them on its return march.

General Geary, desiring to move as rapidly as possible toward Atlanta, sends orders to Colonel Garrard. "Move with your trains on the road leading south of the mountain and to the village at its base."

General Geary knows Colonel Robinson's command will reach the camp easily before all the wagons there have moved out. Geary starts at four o'clock with the Second Brigades, of the Second and Third Divisions as advance guard. "Position pickets at every road and other important points along the line of March. They are to remain until the rear of the entire train has passed Stone Mountain."

Around seven o'clock, the wagon trains begin parking for the night on the farm of Thomas Johnson[397] on the Decatur Road. The wagons, laden by Colonel Garrard, commence arriving about 11:30 PM. Colonel Garrard joins General Geary about one AM on the 29th. All of General Geary's troops and wagons have reached camp at that time.

General Geary orders his command, "To commence moving toward Atlanta at seven o'clock on Saturday morning, October 29." He divides the wagon train into sections and interposes a strong guard of infantry between each wagon train. Colonel Robinson's brigade will form the vanguard of the expedition.

Colonel Robinson's brigade returns without incident to its encampment at Atlanta. He reports to General Geary, "Sir, we secured about 6,000 bushels of corn, besides the usual amount of provisions and other miscellaneous articles."

General Geary moves with the advance guard, posting as on the previous night a picket at every road and commanding position, to remain until the entire wagon train passes. Geary's advance guard reaches Decatur at 11:30 AM. In Decatur, he finds the First Brigade of the First Division, which had been sent out to meet, and, if necessary, assist him. After halting for some time at Decatur to close up the wagon train, General Geary resumes the march ordering, "The First Brigade of the First Division will act as the rear guard." They reach Atlanta without incident at 3 PM. From here the troops and wagon train are ordered to rejoin their respective commands.

General Geary reviews his quartermaster's report; The amount of corn procured to be 9,300 bushels, five loads of wheat, four bales of cotton, 100 head of cattle, all of which were distributed among the several commands.

He then proudly dictates a letter to Major General Slocum.

> *I take great pleasure in commending the officers and men under*
> *my command for the hearty cooperation yielded me during the labors*
> *of the expedition. My thanks are eminently due to Colonel Garrard,*
> *his officers and men, for the activity and zeal manifested, and for*
> *information obtained. I regret to exempt from my commendation*
> *the officers and men in command of the exterior picket who was cap-*
> *tured on the 27th. Armed with Spencer rifles, captured in broad*
> *daylight, without firing a shot, by a force scarce more than its equal,*
> *this picket was undoubtedly guilty of gross neglect. No words of reproach*
> *can be too strong for an officer, who, allowing care for personal ease to*
> *exceed his zeal for duty, permits himself and command to be ignomini-*
> *ously captured.*

Subjoined is a list of prisoners captured from the enemy.

I am, sir, very respectfully, your obedient servant,

JNO W. GEARY
Brigadier-General, U. S. Volunteers[398]

NOVEMBER 3, 1864

Governor Brown addresses the General Assembly in Milledgeville, and among other items, reflects on the Georgia Military Institute.

"Upon the advance of the enemy, in the direction of Marietta, I directed the superintendent, professors, commanding officers, and cadets of the Georgia Military Institute, to report to the Military commanders for orders, and to aid in the defense of Atlanta, or other such points as they might be assigned to. The order was obeyed with promptness and cheerfulness and they were, for a time, placed at the bridge at West Point, then at a position on the river in front of Atlanta, and finally in the trenches. In every position, they acted with coolness and courage and won the respect and confidence of their commanders. Finally, when it became necessary to place troops at Milledgeville, for the defence (sic) of the Capitol, against the raids of the enemy, I ordered them to this place, where they are covered with tents, engaged in study part of each day, and the balance of the time attending to their duties as a battalion of troops. I have ordered them supplied with provisions by the Commissary, while engaged in this service, and it will be necessary to pay the professors out of the Military fund, or to make a special appropriation for that purpose."[399]

A smallpox outbreak in Milledgeville in late October puts everyone on edge. Nearly all of the cadets have had the smallpox vaccination. Norman writes a letter home:

There's considerable excitement in Milledgeville and in our Battalion created by smallpox. Three of the Negroes in our Battalion have contracted the loathsome disease, and I look for nothing else than for it to be spread throughout the entire command. There are several cases in the city, and every day we hear of a new case or two. The Negroes have been removed to a fish house down on the river, but I do not think the necessary precautions have been taken with them by the community. Last night, one of the Negroes, being delirious with fever, left the fish house and came to our camp. Fortunately, I was not there or I would have been subjected to the disease as all who were in camp were. The Negro who was guarding the fish house went to sleep and let him get away. Our surgeon would not vaccinate me for he said it was not necessary when he saw my bright scar from my earlier vaccination.[400] *I think about Polly every day. Oh, how I wish I could see her and my nephew. I shall never get over Legare's death. He truly loved my sister. I tried to get a pass to visit her in Savannah, but Maj. Capers will not allow any of us to leave. I think he is afraid we might desert.*

After a briefing at headquarters on Election Day, Tuesday, November 8, General Sherman is dining with his commander. "The last week in October and several days in the first of November have been inspiring for the Union army," he says, "The completion of repairs for the railroad between Atlanta and Chattanooga shall allow the re-supply of our army. The trains heading north carry loads of wounded and sick troops along with surplus artillery and camp supplies. The returning trains bring the provisions that will carry the army to Savannah and the sea. The hard tack, pork, coffee, sugar and ammunition all will be plentiful. Here are the figures my Chief Quartermaster officer has given me concerning the total provision for the march. We have 2,500 supply wagons with six mules pulling each wagon. Our army has 600 ambulances with either two mules or horses in tow. Our foraging parties have gathered 10,000 head of cattle and 25,000 combined horses and mules. Last, we have sixty-five cannons and each cannon and caisson has eight horses in tow." General Sherman pauses, lights a cigar and takes a couple of drags, "The reorganization of the army is now complete. The news of President Lincoln's hopeful re-election is good news for the Union. In my opinion the fall of Atlanta should propel President Lincoln's popularity and help lead him to victory. So now we must plan to evacuate Atlanta and begin our march to Savannah and terminate this war."

General Sherman begins his campaign in Kingston, Georgia. Major Audenried, General Sherman's Chief of Staff, hands out the orders to the commanders. "Tomorrow I will issue another set of orders at our meeting." Each General begins reading:

Special Field Orders, No. 119
November 8, 1864

The general commanding deems it proper at this time to inform the officers and men of the Fourteenth, Fifteenth, Seventeenth, and the Twentieth Corps, that he has organized them into an army for a special purpose, well known to the War Department and to General Grant. It is sufficient for you to know that it involves a departure from our present base, and a long and difficult march to a new one. All the chances of war have been considered and provided for, as far as human sagacity can. All he asks of you is to maintain that discipline patience and courage, which have characterized you in the past; and he hopes, through you, to strike a blow at our enemy that will have a material effect in producing what we all so much desire, his complete overthrow. Of all things, the most important is that the men, during marches and in camp, keep their places and do not scatter about as stragglers or foragers, to be picked up by a hostile people in detail. It is also of the utmost importance that our wagons should not be loaded with anything but provisions and ammunition. All surplus servants, non-combatants, and refugees, should now go to the rear, and none should be encouraged to encumber us on the march. At some future time we will be able to provide for the poor whites and blacks who seek to escape the bondage under which they are now suffering. With these few simple cautions, he hopes to lead you to achievements equal in importance to those of the past.

By order of Major-General W. T. Sherman
L. M. Dayton, Aide-de-Camp."[401]

On Tuesday, November 9, from Kingston, Georgia, General Sherman is meeting with his commanders. "The election is over, whether for good or evil to the South."[402]

Some of the state counts are delayed due to severe storms, but the results become clear that President Lincoln is re-elected with 55% of the vote. Electoral vote for President Lincoln 212, for General McClellan 21." All of the commanders and personnel present stand and give cheer and applause. It appears the National Union Party also gains seats in Congress to retain unassailable control, 149 to 42 in the House. The National Union Party now controls the Senate, 42 to 10. The Party also takes back several state legislatures; and lost only the governorship of General McClellan's home state of New Jersey."[403]

Again the commanders and other personnel stand and applaud. "After this meeting is complete, I have some very fine wine for us to offer a toast to the President, but first let us finish the campaign."

Special Field Orders No. 120
November 9, 1864

1. For the purpose of military operations, this army is divided into two wings, viz: The right wing, Major-General Oliver O. Howard commanding, composed of the Fifteenth and Seventeenth Corps; the left wing, Major-General H. W. Slocum commanding, composed of the Fourteenth and Twentieth Corps.

2. The habitual order of march will be, wherever practicable, by four roads, as nearly parallel as possible, and converging at points hereafter to be indicated in orders. The cavalry, Brigadier-General Kilpatrick commanding, will receive special orders from the commander in chief.

3. There will be no general train of supplies, but each Corps will have its ammunition train and provision train, distributed habitually as follows: Behind each regiment should follow one wagon and one ambulance; behind each brigade should follow a due proportion of ammunition wagons, provision wagons, and ambulances. In case of danger, each Corps commander should change this order of march, by having his advance and rear unencumbered by wheels. The separate columns will start habitually at 7:00 AM and make about fifteen miles per day, unless otherwise fixed in orders.

4. The army will forage liberally on the country during the march. To this end, each brigade commander will organize a good and sufficient foraging party, under the command of one of the more discreet officers, who will gather, near the route of travel, corn or forage of any kind, meat of any kind, vegetables, cornmeal, or whatever is needed by the command, aiming at all times to keep in the wagons at least ten days' provisions for his command, and three days' forage. Soldiers must not enter the dwellings of the inhabitants, or commit trespass; but, during a half or camp, they may be permitted to gather turnips, potatoes, and other vegetables, and to drive in stock in site of their camp. To regular foraging-parties must be entrusted the gathering of provisions and forage, at any distance from the road traveled.

5. To Corps commanders alone is entrusted the power to destroy mills, houses, cotton gins, etc.; and for them this general principle is laid down: in districts and neighborhoods where the army is unmolested, no destruction of such property should be permitted;but should guerrillas or bushwhackers molest our march, or should the inhabitants burn bridges, obstruct roads, or otherwise manifest local hostility, then army commanders should order and enforce devastation more or less relentless, according to the measure of such hostility.

As for horses, mules, wagons, etc, belonging to the inhabitants, the cavalry and artillery may appropriate freely and without limit; discriminating however, between the rich, who are usually hostile, and the poor and industrious, usually neutral or friendly. Foraging parties may also take mules, or horses, to replace the jaded animals of their trains, or to serve as pack mules. In all foraging, of whatever kind, the parties engaged will refrain from abusive or threatening language, and may, where the officer in command thinks proper, give written certificates of the facts but no receipts; and they will endeavor to leave with each family a reasonable portion for their maintenance.

7. Negroes who are able bodied and can be of service to the several columns may be taken along;but each army commander will bear in mind that the question of supplies is a very important one, and that his first duty is to see to those who bear arms.

8. The organization, at once, of a good pioneer battalion for each army Corps, composed if possible of Negroes, should be attended to. This battalion should follow the advance guard, repair roads and double them if possible, so that the columns will not be delayed after reaching bad places. Also, army commanders should practice the habit of giving the artillery and wagons the road, marching their troops to one side, and instruct their troops to assist wagons at steep hills or bad crossings of streams.

9. Capt. O. M. Poe, Chief engineer, will assign to each wing of the army a pontoon train, fully equipped and organized; and the commanders thereof will see to their being properly protected at all times.

By order of Major-General W. T. Sherman
L. M. Dayton, Aid-de-Camp"[404]

❧

Buck, Jesse, Betty Gail and William Sheppard visit with James Goldsmith at the Depot to get the latest news. James asks, "Have you heard the latest? Looks like Lincoln and Johnson are in."

"Not much we can do about it one way or the other. We got no say-so in the matter," replies William.

"You're right, no say-so at all. The South is on the edge of a steep cliff. I just hope we can back off before we fall or get pushed over," interjects Jesse.

"There were some more people coming through Saturday night from Atlanta. They said the last train for the north leaves the morning of the 13th, which is tomorrow. They hear rumors that Union soldiers are scattered along the railroad a hundred miles north, and as soon as that train passes, the work of destruction will commence. The railroad will be completely destroyed and every bridge burned."

"The refugees think General Sherman is getting ready for some kind of a march because the Union armies are assembling in Atlanta They hear rumors that after destroying the city, the Union army will commence to march." Buck angrily says, "They are gonna steal and destroy everything in their path. I fear their track will be one of desolation no matter where they go."

James continues, "One fellow said he had been to the railroad depot for the past three days several times and had a conversation with General Slocum. The General told him that he had witnessed many sad and some ludicrous scenes."[405]

"Such as?" asks William.

"General Slocum went on to say that all citizens, white and Negroes are beginning to apprehend that something is about to happen. The few white people remaining after their families were sent away are alarmed. This is the reason he and many are leaving the city, giving up horses, lands, furniture, Negroes and all. He said the Negroes want to go north, and the Train Car House is surrounded by them."[406]

"Let'um go and live with the abolitionists," retorts Jesse.

"Shaking his head in agreement with General Slocum as General Slocum told him that hundreds of cars are literally packed with Negroes and their dirty bundles, inside and outside. He said the sight is pitiful, old toothless hags, little pickaninnies, fat wenches of all shades from light brown to jet black, are piled up together with their old bags, bundles, broken chairs, and whatever else they could carry. Some of 'um gnawing old bones, some of 'um squatted by cars making hoecakes, some of 'um crying for food which the Union cannot supply."[407]

William says, "Why I read that Sherman said he would feed those who wanted to go north. Just another Yankee lie."

"What else did the man say, James?" asks Buck.

"General Slocum points at the rail cars and tells the old fellow, "Many of the white people are as anxious to get north as the darks. They even gladly accept a place in a rail car reeking with the odor peculiar to the 'American of African descent.' It is a sad sight, and I anticipate seeing many such before spring."[408]

Buck asks, "So want was the final outcome of his conversation with General Slocum?"[409]

The General pats the old fellow on the shoulder and tells him, "I wish for humanity's sake that this sad war could be brought to a close. I must go and write my wife about what I have seen. While laboring to make it successful I shall do all in my power to mitigate it horrors," and departs.

Buck shakes his head. "He not the only one. Let's git Betty Gail. I'll drop you off at the hospital and then check the mail to see if there's a letter from Polly or Norman."

That evening General Slocum begin his letter to his wife:

> The last train for the north leaves here tomorrow morning. Our soldiers are scattered along the railroad a hundred miles north, and as soon as that train passes, the work of destruction will commence. The railroad will be completely destroyed and every bridge burned. Then the armies of the Tennessee and Georgia will assemble here, and after destroying the city will commence to march. I fear their track will be one of desolation....[410]

⁑⸎

"Upon awakening Saturday, November 12, General Sherman peers out of his bedroom window at the Neal House. Today hopefully is the beginning of the end. I will do or die in the course of the next month or so. Brushing aside his thought he prepares to meet with his commanders the last time before his army begins movements toward Savannah. His final meeting begins at 10 o'clock in the morning. As he enters the conference room his commanders and their staffs stand.

"Please be seated gentlemen. We have a lot to discuss today but first I want to congratulate all of you."

The commanders acknowledge General Sherman's unexpected remark with a smile. "Thank you Sir."

"When our Union troops moved into Georgia from Chattanooga, our engineers located the Georgia land lot maps in courthouses across North Georgia. The Land Lot numbers became handy reference points and General McPherson, used the land lot numbers as references for his location throughout the North Georgia Mountains.

"My Commissary Officer Colonel Beckwith was aware of Governor Brown's restrictions on cotton production. These restrictions increased the Georgia farm production of crops of wheat, corn, rice, sugar, lumber and livestock. Thanks to Colonel Beckwith's analysis, my decision to march to Savannah and the sea is largely due to the fact that the heartland of the Confederacy is a land overflowing with milk and honey; along with the undeterred will of the Southern people to prosecute the war."[411]

"Colonel Beckwith will now explain the agriculture findings the engineers compiled. Colonel Beckwith." Colonel Beckwith approaches several large maps on the wall.

"Thank you, General Sherman. Gentlemen," says the Colonel pointing to several locations on a map of Georgia. "Our engineers compiled the census data on the agriculture and livestock producing areas. Now that they we are at war, it is wise for us to look at where the most productive farm land is located." The commanders are very attentive and study the map as Colonel Beckwith discusses the data. "That is where the Confederate bread basket will be found. With the issue of garden foods and livestock, it becomes apparent which route our great army must take to Savannah and the sea."[412] His presentation last for about ten minutes.

General Sherman stands and approaches Colonel Beckwith. "Thank you Colonel. A great job. Next, we must destroy as much of the railroad that runs along the Ogeechee River as possible." General Sherman stands and points to a map of the state. "This railroad is a major artery between central Georgia and the rail systems that run from Augusta and Savannah northward. Gen. Robert E. Lee, who is under siege at Petersburg, Virginia, is dependent upon these railroads for supplies and munitions. The junction at Millen is especially critical.

"General Slocum will now detail the method of destroying the railroad. General Slocum."

General Slocum stands at the podium. General Sherman sits, lights a cigar and listens.

"Thank you General Sherman. Gentlemen, knowledge of the art of building railroads is certainly of more value to a country than that of the best means of destroying them. However, at this particular time the destruction seems necessary in order to preserve the Union. To organize the mission, a detail of men to perform the destruction should be made on the evening before operations are to commence. The number in the detail will of course depend upon the amount of destruction. I estimate that one thousand men can destroy about five miles of track per day, and do it thoroughly. Before going out in the morning, supply the men with breakfast, for soldiers are more efficient at this work, as well as on the battlefield, when their stomachs are full than when they are empty.

"Divide your detail into three sections of about equal numbers. I will suppose the detail to consist of three thousand men. The first task is to reverse the relative positions of the cross-ties and the iron rails, placing the cross-ties up and the rails under them."

"Sir, you mean simply to turn the entire track upside down?" Asks Colonel Hobart.

"Yes, that's correct. Here how the task should be completed. Section No. 1 consisting of one thousand men, is distributed along one side of the track, one man at the end of each tie. At a given signal each man seizes a tie, lifts the tie until it assumes a vertical position. Then at another signal pushes it forward so that when it falls the cross-ties will be over the rails. Then each man loosens this tie from the rail. This done, Section No. 1 moves forward to another portion of the road. Now Section No. 2 advances and is distributed along the portion of the road recently occupied by Section No. 1. Everybody with me so far?

"The duty of the second section is to collect the cross-ties and place them in piles of about thirty cross-ties each. Then place the rails on the top of these piles, the center of each rail being over the center of the pile, and then set fire to the cross-ties. Section No. 2 then follows No. 1.

"As soon as the rails are sufficiently heated, Section No. 3 takes the place of No. 2. Section No. 3's responsibility is the most important duty, the effectual destruction of the rail.

"Section No. 3 should be in command of an efficient officer who will see that the work is not slighted. Unless watching closely, soldiers will content themselves with simply bending the rails around trees. This should never be permitted. A rail which is simply bent can easily be restored to its original shape. Do not regard any rail as properly treated until it has assumed the shape of a doughnut; it must not only be bent but twisted as well. To do the twisting Colonel Poe's railroad hooks are necessary. With this railroad hook, the soldiers will not use their bare-hands to seize the hot iron. This, however, is the only task which I ever knew a man in General Sherman's army to decline. Therefore a stern officer must be in charge. With Colonel Poe's hooks a double twist can be given a rail, which precludes all hope of restoring it to its former shape except by re-rolling.[413] Just to remind you, after you start the march, the XX Corps orders contain additional instructions to strike the Georgia Railroad at Social Circle and destroy the railroad from there to Madison. The other Corps of General Slocum's, the XIV Corps, will depart on the 16th with me. The XIV Corps is to destroy the railroad from Lithonia to Yellow River and on to Covington and then to Eatonton. Both the Left and the Right wing have seven days to reach the State Capital in Milledgeville, a distance of about one hundred miles.[414] Once the XX Corps reaches Fellow Ship Road, each of the three divisions of the XX Corps can send out foraging parties to the surrounding countryside.

"Any questions?" asks General Slocum. "Thank you gentlemen for your indulgence."

General Sherman takes the podium. "Your orders are in your hands. Follow them well and stay in contact, for I will not be in touch with General Grant and President Lincoln until we reach Savannah." Peering toward his commanders he asks, "Any questions?" Pausing for a brief moment he continues to look at his commanders. "If none, return to your respective units."

The commanders and their staffs stand and salute General Sherman and depart.

Monday, November 14, General Sherman's 56,204 marching troops, 5,063 cavalry and 1812 men with 65 artillery pieces, 2,500 wagons, and 600 ambulances arrive at or near Atlanta. Each infantryman carries 40 rounds of ammunition. The wagon train holds another 200 rounds per man.[415]

From his headquarters at the Neal House, General Sherman orders, "Remove all of the sick, lame, non-combatants, and those that may falter from your commands. This action is imperative in order for this army to maintain momentum and mobility. The composition of the army must be men whose bodies will endure hardship and disease without consequences."

Chief Commissary Officer Colonel Beckwith submits his final report to General Sherman. "Sir, there's a 20 day supply of rations which is approximately 1.2 million rations in the possession of the troop. We have a good supply of beef cattle on the hoof which will accompany the two wings. Additional rations are plentiful along the route of the march for both wings."

Under a full moon on that November 14th night, Colonel Poe pays a visit to General Sherman at the Neal House. "Have a seat and a cup of coffee, Colonel."

"Thank you sir. Just wanted to report that my staff of engineers have been busy all day preparing the material for the complete destruction of the list of properties which you have listed. You will be able to watch the fireworks from your headquarters later this evening sir. Sit back and enjoy the show. I just wanted to double check the list to be certain you did not want to add any other building."

"I believe the list is complete, Colonel, so proceed with your orders."

"Yes, sir, on my way."

Colonel Poe's large force begins its destructive mission. First, there are scattered levels of a red glow as the great depot, the roundhouse, and the machine shops of the Georgia Railroad are reduced with explosives and then set ablaze. One of these machine shops is used by the rebels as an arsenal, and in it are piles of undetected shot and shell, some of which proved to be loaded. General Sherman is watching the growing flames of the night when a hideous bursting of shell fragments come uncomfortably near. General Sherman dashes inside, "That was a close one. I almost didn't get to leave Atlanta for Savannah."

He takes another cigar from his humidor and lights up. Returning outside, he and his staff take chairs and scan the skyline as the flames reach the block of stores near the depot, then more to the heart of the city where two thirds of the trees, the theaters, jail, slave markets and fire stations begin to turn to ashes.

General Sherman is going over orders again with Major Audenried. General Sherman's eyes become strained. He lays his pencil down and looks out of the window, "Colonel Poe has orders to leave the courthouse and the great mass of dwelling houses.[416] Maybe Governor Brown can see the flames in Milledgeville or at least smell the smoke tomorrow. His entire state is going to look like this if he doesn't come to his senses."

11

EYE WITNESS

Betty Gail and Buck are home, sitting by a small fire after dinner, reading the Bible when Isaac rushes in, pointing to the sky exclaiming "It's on fire!"

"What's on fire?" Buck asks as they rush outside behind Uncle Isaac.

Looking southwest from Stone Mountain, the Jernigans view the full moon against an eerie red sky. Becoming anxious Buck remarks, "My gosh I think Sherman is burning Atlanta!"

Betty Gail takes Buck's arm. "How could he do such a thing?"

"Don't rightly know, but let's climb the mountain to get a better view. Isaac, stay at the house and keep all the lanterns lit and wait for us to come back home." Just as Buck and Betty Gail begin their climb, they hear the sound of horses rapidly approaching. Buck places his lantern on the ground. He and Betty Gail back away so they can see who the riders are as they come closer. Buck recognizes the riders as they approach under the full moon. "It's Jesse Lanford and James Goldsmith."

"I guess you see the flames from Atlanta," asks James, dismounting.

"Surely do! We're going to the top to get a better view. Want to come along?" asks Buck.

Jesse shakes his head. "Better not. I hear there are some bandits in the area."

"I'll climb with you. My wife is staying with my cousins," says James.

"Here's a lantern for you." Buck passes the hissing lantern to James.

With his musket in hand, Buck leads the group up the moonlit gray sentinel.

Steadily they climb, making their way over the familiar bulging boulders. The night is cool from the mid-November breeze. Quietly, they pass the abandoned and disintegrating saloon the Dents built.

At the last steep barrier, negotiating the remains of the stone wall, Buck stops as Betty Gail takes a moment to catch her breath. As Buck looks toward Atlanta he turns, gasps and points. Without saying a word, he is stone-faced and silent for a moment. Then he shouts, "Look there! Atlanta is burning!" Betty Gail jumps to her feet.

She places one hand over her mouth and takes Buck's arm with her other hand. "Oh my God."

Buck stands in awe, viewing a sight none have ever seen before and one he hope never to witness again. The heavens seem to burst with huge, dark clouds of smoke. Roaring flames follow with finger-like projections pointing to the moon. Thundering sounds of the distant explosions boom in the air, followed by more dense, black smoke and fireballs. Blown by the wind, huge walls and massive balls of fire race from the south of Atlanta to the north.

Buck looks up at the moon as it pales from the smoke, and their path becomes darker. "Let's get on to the top for a better view." He takes Betty Gail's hand as they climb to the highest point of the mountain where they witness the flames becoming more aggressive and intense. Although they cannot feel the heat, Buck feels the flames charring deeper into his heart. He begins to sneeze as the night breeze brings the remaining ashes of Atlanta to his eyes and nostrils. Finally, before daybreak, Buck is sitting next to Betty Gail, and they silently observe the raging inferno that sinks from the sky. The blazes are no longer aggressive and the angry, startling waves of flames no longer roll as high. The color grows paler and slowly fades with the sunrise.

Buck looks over his shoulder as the morning sun peers over the horizon, and the sky regains its natural blue color. The stillness of the morning air is eerie. An umbrella of dense black smoke isolates the circle of annihilation and the whispering remains of smoldering ruins. The smell of smoke is strong on top of the mountain. Buck takes Betty Gail's hand, nods somberly to his friend and the three of them proceed slowly down the mountain.[417]

⅏

Standing on the porch of the Neal House on a chilly Tuesday morning of November 15th, General Sherman confides in Major Dayton, "Today we march and the march from Atlanta to the sea begins. Generals Oliver Howard's XV and XVII Corps, is the right wing. By now he should be departing down the McDonough Road to follow the Macon and Western Railroad southeast to Jonesboro.

"The last report indicates that he has already begun his movement. The XX Corps, part of General Slocum's left wing, has also departed down Decatur Street on the Georgia Railroad through Decatur to Stone Mountain.

"I suppose General Slocum will camp around Stone Mountain tonight … give him time to check his supply trains. Then his orders read for him to head towards Madison and proceed to Social Circle. We'll catch up with him in a day or two. Send for Colonel Poe."

"Yes Sir," replies Major Dayton.

Shortly, Colonel Poe arrives. "I want to inspect the destruction of the buildings to determine if any remain which could be of use to the Confederates we'll need to see the supply wagon trains," remarks General Sherman. The two men with General Sherman's guards and Major Audenried take to their mounts and begin the inspection. "You almost got me with that huge explosion from the machine shop," jokes Sherman.

"That was a big surprise to all of us, sir," replies Colonel Poe.

"Good job, Colonel, even though it almost got all of us."

"Evidently there were some hidden explosives in the building."[418]

"No doubt."

Riding up and down past the supply wagons, General Sherman observes they are in order and all of the supplies are secured. After nearly three hours, General Sherman returns to his headquarters for dinner where he speaks with his staff. "Well gentlemen, it appears we're ready to depart Atlanta tomorrow. All of you are to be commended for the splendid execution of my orders. I salute you with a toast of fine wine."

The men stand and raise their glasses. "Here, here." They salute General Sherman and with a nod, he accepts their return of his toast.[419]

❧

On her way to the hospital, Betty Gail senses a loneliness in her little hamlet. It is now practically a ghost town. She is exhausted from her previous night on the mountain, watching the destruction by fire of Atlanta.

She waves at a neighbor as she rides through town where most of the buildings are still standing. She prays General Sherman does not burn the town as he did Atlanta, especially since it is maintained by the women and small children. Betty Gail stops at City Hall. Buck had asked her to deliver some chestnuts to Mayor Browning.

Around nine o'clock AM, Clarissa McCurdy, wife of the late Robert McCurdy, and her daughter, Agnes, are heading out of town in their buggy when they witness the clouds of dust brought on by the approaching Yankees. They stand up in the carriage to confirm their sighting.

"Those are Yankees, Agnes! Sit down and hold tight. We've got to warn the folks in town." Clarissa hastily turns the horse and buggy and rushes back into town. All is quiet until they thunder in as the Paul Reveres of the South. "The Bluebellies are coming!" She stops in front of City Hall and shouts, Mayor Browning, Bluebellies are coming!" Mayor Browning and Betty Gail rush out of City Hall. "What did you say Clarissa?" asks Betty Gail.

Clarissa points toward Fellow Ship Road, "Hundreds and hundreds of them! Yankees heading our way. Coming from Fellow Ship Road. I got to go and warn my folks." She snaps the reins and speeds off toward south. Betty Gail and Mayor Browning look around and see the few men in town run out of their stores.[420] Clarissa is very clear in her vivid detail of the Yankee column, as she spreads the word of the approaching Yankees. Panic sets in as the store owners attempt to load wagons and flee with their belongings before the Yankees arrive.

Mayor Browning mounts his horse. Betty Gail shouts to Mayor Browning, "Wait, I'll ride with you. Less chance of you getting hurt with a woman along."

"You best stay at the hospital Betty Gail. I am going to introduce myself as the Mayor of the town to the Yankees." He heads toward Fellow Ship Road to confirm the sighting of the approaching Yankees. Mrs. McCurdy's last stop is at the hospital and she hurries to inform one of the attendants of the approaching Yankees. The she continues her escape to the south of town. The nervous attendant rushes inside and informs the staff what is happening.

In a short time Betty Gail arrives, and as she enters the front door, the excited attendant runs to her, "Miss Betty Gail ... Miss Betty Gail ... em 'ankees a comin!"em 'ankees a comin!"

"I already know that. We have a duty to care for our patients, regardless of the chaos outside."

Confirming his worst nightmare, Mayor Browning stares at the approaching advance guard of Colonel James Selfridge and waits. Well in front is a small detachment of six mounted infantry. They hold their reins in one hand while resting their carbines across the pommel of the saddle. They usually move at a faster pace than the main army to investigate any suspicious activity or circumstances.

The detachment of the advance guard sees the lone rider and approach as they point their weapons toward the Mayor. "What is your mission, mister?" asks the squad leader with a snappy voice.

"I am, Thompson A. Browning, the Mayor of Stone Mountain. I would like to speak to your commanding officer."

"Do you have any weapons?"

"Not on me or with me at the present time, sergeant."

"Anybody else with you or hiding to bushwhack us?"

"As far as I know, I am alone. One of our lady citizens was riding this way and saw your column. She returned to alert us that you were heading in our direction."

"If you're lying you'll be shot! Wait here. Corporal, stay with the rest of the squad and guard Mr. Mayor while I talk with Colonel Selfridge." The sergeant reins his horse, kicks up dust and heads back to meet the column of Yankees.

The sergeant salutes Colonel James Selfridge as he comes closer. "What did you find out, sergeant?" asks the Colonel.

"The man says he is the Mayor of Stone Mountain and his name is Browning. He would like to speak to you, sir. The squad has him under guard."

The colonel and sergeant return to the location of the advance guard where Mayor Browning waits. "I am Colonel James Selfridge. I understand you're the Mayor of Stone Mountain. What can I do for you?"

"Yes, I am Mayor Thompson Browning. There are no Confederate forces in our town. We only have forty male citizens remaining. Ten are youth ages sixteen and seventeen years old and thirty are men in their forties and fifties. We have three hospitals in town and one Wayside 'round the mountain. We have nothing with which to defend ourselves against you and only ask that you pass through and leave us be."

"If your people do not brother us, Mayor, my soldiers will not bother them. You may go back to town and relay my message."

Mayor Browning aims his mount toward town and gallops away. As he comes close to the cemetery, the grave diggers are preparing to bury another unknown casualty of the war. Halting at the cemetery, Mayor Browning passes on to the diggers part of his conversation with Colonel Selfridge. "I have just spoken with the commander and he told me if we bring the Yankees no harm, they'll bring us no harm."

Appearing more at ease, one of them comments, "After what they did to Atlanta last night, Mayor, I don't trust them!"

"We really don't have a choice right now, just pray all goes well for the next couple of days. I need to get on into town."

Around ten o'clock, the Union advance guard draws near to the cemetery. The grave diggers appear uneasy as the advance guard approaches. "Hold up there, you digging that grave. We want to check that coffin!" shouts a lieutenant in the advance guard. The two white and two Negro diggers stop and lean on their shovels or spades. The lieutenant rides closer with his sergeant and several other troops.

"Sergeant, open the coffin and any others which are recently buried." The Sergeant and two men dismount. They direct the diggers to get crow-bars from the wagon. Doing so, they hand the crow-bars to the sergeant and his men. They commence to pry open the coffin.

"Nothing in here sir except a dead rebel!"

The Yankee sergeant points his pistol at the grave diggers, "Uncover those four graves with the fresh dirt." Soon four more coffins are unearthed and the sergeant and his men take the crow-bars. Exposing just the top of the next three coffins, the sergeant jumps in the hole along side, prying the top off of each one of the coffins.

"More dead Rebels, sir!"

Then he observes the fourth coffin. As the sergeant and his men approach it, the diggers back away toward the wagon. Noting their behavior, the sergeant looks at the diggers and says, "So this is the one with the bounty, huh?" The lieutenant draws near on his horse and the sergeant and his men take the crow-bars and hastily rip its top off. The lieutenant is thrown from his horse, the sergeant and his men turn and retch uncontrollably at the extremely nauseating odor and site. Inside, there are at least a dozen decaying amputated limbs. Covering the blood stained rotting flesh are maggots and oozing sour fluids. Pale and struggling to catch their breath, the soldiers leap from the hole and fetch canteens from their mounts.

Once the lieutenant regains his composure, he says, "Okay, diggers, rebury your dead. You darkies are freemen now and can go wherever you like. Sergeant, bring the wagon and let's get on up the hill to meet Colonel Selfridge at the depot."

Taking the mule straps, the sergeant mounts his horse, tugs at the mule and points the team up the hill. Once over the hill, he views the town. All the sergeant encounters is plenty of dust from the other members of the advance guard, but not any obvious panic or disruption by the civilians. The town appears ghostly. The other members of the advance guard are scouting the surrounding area and buildings to ascertain if any Confederate sharpshooters are in position or in hiding.

Unable to locate any Confederate troops' presence, the Yankees go to the depot to remove what supplies would benefit their army or their personal needs. Colonel Selfridge arrives to investigate the hospitals and the jail for wounded or imprisoned Yankees. Mayor Thompson is at the hospital with Betty Gail, standing in front. Betty Gail is clutching the orders of Colonel Abe Miller. Colonel Selfridge approaches her with several of his troops. "Step aside, Ma'am, we are here to remove any Union wounded and to take the able Confederates as prisoners."

"Before you make any hasty decision, Colonel, I suggest you read this order from your Colonel Abe Miller." She deliberately unfolds and presents the document to Colonel Selfridge. The Colonel appears somewhat surprised by the document. As he finishes reading the orders he says, "Do you have any Union soldiers in either of the hospitals?"

"No, we do not. I don't know if you have been in a hospital before but I'll be glad to take you on a tour if your stomach can bear the sights and smells, Colonel!"

"Please do. What is your name, Ma'am?"

"Mrs. Betty Gail Jernigan"

"May I ask where your husband is?"

Betty Gail inhales deeply, never taking her eyes off the colonel. What should she say? She chooses honesty, feeling that, perhaps, this Yankee will not be like so many who have come before. Sternly staring the colonel, she responds, "Working on the farm 'round the mountain. I'm sure your foragers will pay him a visit before the day ends!"

The colonel motions for two of his troops to follow him inside and the others are to stand guard outside. As they enter, a sense of nervousness appears on the faces of the soldiers. Although it is November, there has not been a real cold snap and flies are everywhere. Placing a handkerchief over his nose, the colonel passes several soldiers who are gasping, their eyes heavy-lidded. The lady members of the churches sing quiet songs, while others read from the bible to comfort the patients in their remaining hours of life.

"Colonel, these soldiers are preparing to meet their maker. Some of them have names, but many do not. These poor souls will never hear again the cry of 'Charge' or the smell of the sulfurous air from the discharge of gun powder. Look at their pale lips as they struggle hopelessly against their mortal pain."

Without acknowledging her comments, the colonel begins climbing the stairs to the second floor. The moderate November weather makes the stench even stronger. In room number two,[421] the colonel finds twenty six wounded soldiers, each with crimson stained bandages, crowding in the twelve by twelve room. He sees no flag, no bayonet, no plume, no lance and no gun. Just fading human shadows, conveying more than tongues can speak. None of the soldiers is moaning—just quiet human forms with empty expressions on their war torn faces.

"I've seen enough, Mrs. Jernigan. I certainly will respect Colonel Miller's order and leave the hospitals as is. Please direct me to the other hospitals so that I may inspect them."

"Over yonder." She points in the direction of the second hospital. "They'll direct you to the third hospital from there. We also have a Wayside 'round the mountain. They also are protected by this order."

Colonel Selfridge turns and departs. Thus terminates Betty Gail's first encounter with Bluebellies who are coming within reach of little City of Stone Mountain.

Soon, the sergeant locates Colonel Selfridge. "Colonel, we just took this wagon from the grave diggers, what do you want us to do with it?"

"Return it to the grave diggers. There are orders not to disturb the hospital, the Wayside, its patients and its contents or supplies. Post a guard as well to insure the orders are obeyed."

Appearing puzzled, the sergeant replies, "Yes sir." He snakes the team about and heads back to the cemetery. Once there, the Yankee sergeant pulls up and shouts, "Here's your wagon and mule boys! You're lucky to keep them. But keep digging 'cause there will be plenty more Rebels for you to bury!" He details a private to stand guard to inform the passing troops to leave the wagon and mule alone. He slaps his horse and gallops back towards town.

Shortly the Pioneer Battalion appears. They begin passing by the depot and hospital. Betty Gail observes some of the wagons are full of Negroes. Others are full of rope, chains, block and tackle, saws, shovels, picks and spades. Betty Gail turns to the Union guard, "What do the Negroes do for your army?"

"Their job is to keep the roads clear of fallen trees, remove traps set by the Rebels, and fill gaping holes on the roads. In other words, to keep the army moving."

"They look like slaves."

"No Ma'am, they are former slaves, freedmen we have hired."

"I see. And where is your army going?"

"No one really knows, but we all suspect we are on the march to Savannah, ma'am."

"Savannah!"

"Yes Ma'am, Savannah!"

Betty Gail turns and walks away in shock. Her heart suddenly beats faster, and she feels a lump in her throat as she becomes emotional. She takes her handkerchief from her cuff and wipes tears as she walks to the back of the hospital to regain her composure. She knows Polly is safe for now, but what about Norman. "Where is my boy? We haven't heard from him lately. I can only pray he is safe."

Around one o'clock the dust cloud begins to build. The thunder of hooves and foot soldiers shake the ground as the Bluebellies pour through town. Suddenly a Yankee commander shouts, "Halt," and the troops slowly come to a stop. "Take a dinner break."

The men begin moving to the sides of the road, finding places in the shade whenever possible. Betty Gail watches many of the soldiers retrieving hard tack and pork from the knapsacks. Then without warning many of the Bluebellies embark on the besieging of houses and businesses. She observes soldiers emerge from doorways and backyards, bearing quilts, plates, poultry and pigs, attacking beehives, honey in the hands and besmearing the faces of the boys. Several of the soldiers come near the hospital while swarms of others poke hundreds of bayonets in the corners of yards and gardens, after concealed treasure.

"Why is this happening?" She wonders and wipes her tears on her apron. Standing on the front porch, she sees a Bluebelly running across the railroad track proudly raising his shining silver candle holder prize.

She witnesses the shouting and scrambling, and how the Yankees exchange their spoils for another with their comrades. Betty Gail silently prays, but her quiet beseeching prayers go unheard.[422]

As she and the hospital staff look helplessly on from across the road, the Yankees amuse themselves in their folly of robbery and destruction. She watches as the town and its surroundings become victims of the Yankees foraging parties, who break into the stores and buildings. In about thirty minutes, any item of value is on the Yankee wagons or on their person.

⚬

Buck is making his rounds in the fields, checking the cabbage and lettuce crops on his and Buster Phillips' place when Charlie begins barking. Buck and Isaac hurry to the house and prepare to meet a rider who is thundering down the road. Malcolm Hamby, a local wagon maker, rushes to Buck's place. "Yankees heading your way!"

Buck hollers, "Is Betty Gail all right?"

"Was when I left." He departs hastily at the same break-neck pace as he arrived.

Malcolm is no sooner out of sight, than Buck can see the Union column heading in his direction, the Union Flag is being held by a soldier on the head mount. From his vantage point, he can't determine how many soldiers are in the detail. But one Union soldier is too many in his opinion.

Buck slaps his hat against his leg. "Isaac, looks as if the bummers are here again!" The Union flag still flies in front of his house, so he feels less uneasy than he might otherwise. The Captain in charge of the expedition canters up to Buck. "I assume this is your place, mister?"

"That's right, I own the place … or what's left of it."

"Why are you flying the Union flag?"

"That's becoming a good question after what we've been through with you Yankees, but I still believe in the Union my forefathers fought for, those who believed in Thomas Jefferson. Take what you can find. Another expedition was through here on the 27th of last month … cleaned us out and burned my neighbor's buildings, except for his barn and slave quarters."

"Where is your neighbor now?"

"Off fighting for the Confederacy." Buck glances over to the wagon train. "Looks like you have had a good day so far. Your wagons are nearly full of Georgia grown and Georgia raised."

The captain replies sarcastically, "We've got a large army to feed and we appreciate you folks raising the food for us! Take that barking hound and sit over there by the fence."

Buck takes Charlie and he and Isaac find a comfortable spot by the fence. Realistically, there was nothing he could do except watch. He was thankful the captain wasn't a more violent man. The captain gestured toward the out buildings. "Check the house, barns, and cellars. Bring all the cows here. Kill and dress any hogs. Check the barns. Load all the corn, hay and syrup on the wagons."

The troops snap the reins and the wagons move toward the barns. Other soldiers follow the now familiar routine of checking for buried goods while others invade the house. Sally stands silently on the porch as the Bluebellies rush by her. The captain looks toward her and the Masonic Plaque catches his eye. He rides over to Buck. "I see you're a Mason."

"That's right. I am a Third Degree Mason." The captain sees Jack lying in the pasture. "Is that mule dead?"

Buck knows Jack has a mind of his own when it comes to strangers. Hoping for the best, he answers the captain, "Almost. Got stuck by lightning and has bad joints. Lays down most of the time and can hardly walk."

"Sergeant, see that mule over there? See if you can get him up." The sergeant climbs the wooden fence and goes over to Jack, who lies still as the sergeant begins to examine him. Jack lifts his head and neighs heavily as if saying to leave him alone.

"Looks pretty bad, sir. Even his tail is messed up! Do you want me to shoot him?"

Buck looks alarmed and begins to stand up, but the captain waves him off. "Save your bullet for a Rebel!"

Buck resumes his position as if he is getting more comfortable. Two Yankees bring the only cow left on the place and tie her to the back of one of the wagons. A pig squeals, and a shot rings out. Then silence.

The captain orders the sergeant, "Gather all the darkies and bring them here."

The sergeant takes several other soldiers with him as the captain dismounts and climbs the steps to the porch as the slaves gather around. "Listen to me." All of you are free now. You can go anywhere you want to go. However, for the time-being, General Sherman recommends that you stay on the farms and draw wages for your work. There really is no other place for you to go right now." He looks directly at each individual. "I'll give you a reward if you show me where any food is hidden."

One of Buster's darkies steps forward, holding his hat in both hands, "New greens growing now. Blues gots it's all utter day."

"Okay. Sergeant, I see all of the wagons are back. Set that rebel barn on fire and burn this man's gin and smoke house. I know he is hiding food somewhere!" In a few minutes, Buster's barn is ablaze. Buck's smoke house and gin are set to flames. The captain watches as the smoke begins to climb, then orders his foraging expedition to depart.

Buck and Isaac go to the house and enter with Sally. "Looks like the Bluebellies tore everything up again. You and Sally get it together, and I'll see what I can do about keeping the fires from spreading with the other hands." Buck goes outside. He and the other hands extinguish any grass that begins to burn around the smoke house and the cotton gin.

There's no rifle or cannon fire this time in town, only troops and more troops. Approximately 15,000 Yankees, 625 supply wagons and 150 ambulances on this day alone pass through the once prosperous tourist town. The Yankees peer at the burnt-out granite hull of buildings. They pass the lonely hospital, sitting next to what used to be the main depot and a main Confederate railroad supply line for troops, munitions and commissary provision.

The first unit, after the advance guard and the pioneer battalion, to enter the Village of Stone Mountain is Major General Henry W. Slocum Commander of the XX Corps. Flying the Union flag and the colors of the XX Corps, he is well under the protection of his staff and troops on mounts. All of his headquarters' units have the Spencer repeating rifles. His provision wagons are close behind. Dust begins to cover the town, already dingy from the movements of previous columns of soldiers.

Shortly, the First Division of the XX Corps under the command of Brigadier General Alpheus Williams begins its parade through the little village, flying the Union flag and the Division Colors. Behind General Williams are his some 5500 troops; the First Brigade with six, the Second Brigade with five and the Third Brigade with six. Some of the troops are mounted infantry and some are foot infantry. At the rear of each regiment, there's one ambulance wagon and one provision wagon. At the rear of the division, there are three hundred provision wagons containing ammunition and food plus fifty additional ambulances. Some of the more able bodied patients at the hospital come out and sit near the railroad track. From here, they watch the parade of fat and happy Bluebellies march past totally unaware of their presence.

With each passing hour, more marching Yankees, more mounted Yankees, and more wagons pass. Betty Gail sits with some of the wounded. "I cannot imagine this many soldiers anywhere. Where are our troops?"

The Second Division of the XX Corps passes with Union Brigadier John Geary with his colors and staff, three and seventeen regiments. At the end of the Second Division is the Artillery. The most pervasive integrating part of artillery equipment is not the cannon or caisson, but the great horse. Each lumbering horse must pull roughly 700 pounds. The average cannon and caisson weighs around 1,700 pounds. The Artillery Unit of the XX Corps is under the command of Major John Williams. His artillery unit has fourteen 3 inch Ordinance Rifle cannons made out of wrought iron. The eight 12 pounder Napoleons are made out of bronze. Each limber which tows the artillery piece is drawn by six horses or mules. Another six mules or six horses struggle to pull another limber which tows the caisson. Even on a good day with smooth, well drained dirt roads exhaustion occurs rapidly from towing nearly 20 miles in 10 hours. Exhaustion encourages disease and death. The last insult to this great majestic horse is its large size, making it a ready target for the enemy. The life expectancy of the artillery horse is around only eight months.

Finally, the Colors of the Third Division appear under the command of Union General William T. Ward. His command consists of three brigades with twelve regiments and one squadron, the same amount of ambulances and supply wagons. Each of these brigades, regiments and companies has its own color and Guidon Bearer. The officers are sitting high upon their horses with their shiny sabers flashing in the bright sun. The cavalry chooses the best horses while the artillery gets the second choice of the remaining horses. All of the animals are healthy, strong and well fed.

General Ward points out several locations to his Adjutant, which Colonel Miller had told him about during his skirmishes in Stone Mountain in July. As General Ward approaches the partially burned depot, he notices it is pretty much still functional. He looks toward the hospital. "See the hospital there?" I think that's where the Union soldier was being cared for." General Ward instructs his second in command, "Stay with the troops while I visit the hospital." He and his Adjutant rein up to the front of the hospital, the guard snaps to attention and salutes. General Ward returns the salute and the guard opens the door for him. "I am General Ward. Is there still a lady in charge of the hospital?"

"Yes, sir. I believe the lady I have been talking with is in charge."

"What is her name?"

"I heard her say Mrs. Jernigan, sir."

"Where is she now?"

"She said she was going to the cook house out back to begin preparing the supper meal, sir."

"Thank you," replies General Ward. Then the General and his adjutant enter the hospital. He passes through the ward and the smell of rotting flesh to the rear of the buildings. Standing in the door he asks, "Are you Mrs. Jernigan?"

Betty Gail, not recognizing the General's voice, turns with a mighty surprised look. "Yes, General, I am."

"Colonel Miller spoke highly of you and asks that I stop in for a visit to insure that his orders not to disturb this place are still being carried out."

"So far, General Ward, there have not been any problems. A Colonel Selfridge came by earlier, and I told him we have no Union soldiers here this time. I showed him Colonel Miller's order and he informed me that he would have it verified."

"I'll remind Colonel Selfridge that I am familiar with Colonel Miller's order and I will also endorse the order today. You'll be fine, Mrs. Jernigan. Your thoughtfulness in treating any soldier is a blessing to all of these poor dying and sick soldiers."

"To you sir, I will offer a cup of tea and some corn bread." Betty Gail pours a cup of tea for the General and his adjutant. She places them on a saucer along with a small piece of corn bread on the side. She walks over and hands the tea and cornbread to the two soldiers.

"Thank you kindly, Mrs. Jernigan. I do hope your family is well. I know this war is devastating to both sides. Maybe by the first of the year, this dreadful conflict will end." He raises his cup and takes a sip. "What kind of tea?"

"Sassafras. Made from the root of the sassafras tree. You can identify which trees are sassafras because their leaves are the first to change color, sometimes as early as late July. It's a popular tea in Georgia. I hope you enjoy it." Then she pours a cup for herself.

"Again, Mrs. Jernigan, don't worry. I'll inform Colonel Selfridge not to disturb these hospitals and Wayside around the mountain. I just wanted to stop by and say hello and thank you again for caring for the wounded Union soldiers. I must get back to my command. Maybe when the war is over, maybe our families can become friends. Just for your information, tomorrow the soldiers are going to destroy the rails on the road. One of those unfortunate events of the war." They set their cups down. "Thanks for the tea and corn bread."

"Yes, thank you, ma'am," says the adjutant.

General Ward takes her hand in both of his. "God speed, Mrs. Jernigan."

"Thank you, General, for your kindness to these soldiers." Betty Gail watches them leave and returns to her duties in the outside kitchen. She ponders what will become of him before the war ends.

The General and his adjutant turn and depart. Outside, the General instructs the guard to inform Colonel Selfridge that he has been here and Colonel Miller's orders stand.

"Yes, sir" replies the guard. He retrieves the General and the Adjutant's horses. They mount and gallop away to return to the head of their column.

Betty Gail continues caring for the wounded and dying throughout the day although she is exhausted from the previous night on the mountain. The guards at the hospitals change about every hour. Every so often, a band comes by. Some bands play marching music while other bands carry their instruments. There is always the sound of beating drums and occasionally the sound of a fife. Sometimes, she peers out of the window to view the never ending column of Bluebellies. Having seen enough of the Yankees, she continues to assist with preparing supper for the patients: corn bread, pork and pumpkin pie.

Now the bummers appear up the road from town to the area of the cemetery. The grave diggers are placing their shovels, picks, and spades in the wagons preparing to go back to the hospital. The officer in charge of the bummers stops and asks the diggers, "What's in the coffins?"

"Here we go again!" mutters one of the grave diggers, and he sternly replies, "The dead!"

"Dig them up and take his wagon and mule Sergeant!"

At this point, the Yankee guard approaches the commander of the bummers, salutes and says, "Sir, we have orders from General Ward and Colonel Miller not to disturb any property, any food, or any animals with the hospitals in this area. Also, sir, these coffins have been dug up and all is clear there, sir. The orders are at the hospital by the depot, sir."

The lieutenant, with a look of disgust, "General Ward and Colonel Miller must have relatives here to give them all of this protection!"

Suddenly, a herd of about two hundred mooing and belching cattle begin passing the cemetery. All anyone can do is wait. Cows running through the cemetery, cows spooking the mules, cow plots all along the way and more dust.

As the last of the cattle and drivers pass, the bummers fall in behind the herdsman. The grave diggers sit on the wagon and wait until the bummers are over the hill and out of sight. Then, they snap the reins and direct their mule and wagon to the hospital. "I sure would like to dig just one grave and put a thousand dead or alive Yankees in it."

"Make it one hole and two thousand!" replies another of the diggers.

Even the Yankee invaders wear red cloths over their faces. Although she knows they are wearing kerchiefs over their mouths and noses, Betty Gail ponders how the men in the column can handle all of the dust accumulating on their clothes, skin and in their lungs. By the end of the day, the red dust is so thick that the patients watching the parade near the railroad track have covered their faces to filter the air and keep from turning red from the dry dust. Even the hospital has a red hue on the walls. Never has so much dust been stirred up in one day in this once prosperous village.

"I figure if all of the provision wagons and ambulances alone were lined up, they would stretch from Stone Mountain, up Fellow Ship Road and almost to Brown's Court House." Betty Gail sighs and starts to return to her work, but another sound catches her attention. She places her finger to her mouth motioning to be quiet. "Do you hear cows?"

"Me's do." replies the kitchen assistant, and they rush to the front of the hospital. Several stray cows rush past the depot from the herd. One of the drivers chases and turns them back to join the herd.

Betty Gail turns to the guard. "Wonder who you stole those from?" The herd rumbles through town and eventually ends up in the bellies of the Yankees. As the herd passes through, she sees the bummers with their wagons full from their ritual of marauding excursions. "I wonder if they went by our place?" she murmurs, fighting the urge to go home and check on Buck.

Soon, all is quiet as the last of the cattle mosey through town. Shortly, supper is ready, and the attendants file in to eat early. Then they begin feeding the soldiers. Tables are set for the few who are able to walk while the others are having the staff encourage them to slowly sip and eat as much as possible. Betty Gail is about to fall asleep on her feet, in the kitchen, but she sees the inviting chair near the fireplace. She wearily drops into the comfortable seat. Taking her shawl from the chair, she wraps it around her shoulders and falls into a deep sleep almost instantly.

12

WITHOUT RESISTANCE

Reaching Rockbridge Road, General Jackson's First Division sets up camp on the Southwest side of the road going to Lithonia and Rockbridge Road.

This allows his division to cover the road to Lithonia. General Geary's Second Division camps on the northeast side of Rockbridge and the Lithonia Road to protect and cover the roads to Stone Mountain and Rockbridge. The 29th Ohio Infantry, last unit of his command arrives around 11.[423] General Ward's Third Division camps three miles to the rear near Snapfinger Creek.[424] General Kilpatrick's Fourth Division is to guard the supply wagons.

Throughout the night, Yankee horsemen are on patrol. Occasional citizens hear the sound of glass shattering as Yankee thieves burglarize a home or building. Some women and children escape on foot, fearing for their safety as their homes are set on fire. The perpetrators are hopping and howling at the site of the growing blaze. Satisfied with their success, they proceed to torch the next structure.

Around 7 o'clock AM on Wednesday, November 16, General Sherman mounts his horse, Sam, and departs Atlanta by the Decatur Road. He passes through two hundred acres of ashy desolation. He shakes the dust from his hat and looks at his staff. "I have made arrangements with General Grant[425] and President Lincoln to cut all lines of communication with my superiors. Colonel Poe has completed that task." This independence energizes General Sherman as he knows now he is on his own.

Accompanying General Sherman is his personal staff, and a company of 1st Alabama cavalry under the command of Lieutenant Snelling.[426] A company of 9th Illinois Mounted Infantry under the command of

Lieutenant McCroy guards the General's small supply train forming the rear guard of the XIV Corps. The marching men and wagons of the Fourteenth Corps are under the command of Major General Jefferson C. Davis.

As their sleep has just begun for the Union soldiers of the XX Corps, the bugler sounds reveille as the day begins to break. The sleeping army begins to stir as the men unwillingly stumble out for roll-call in the cool November morning. Throwing more wood on the near dead embers from the previous night's camp-fire, the men gather to prepare their breakfast. Some fetch water, some fetch more wood and others begin the meal. Each soldier has his supply of coffee beans which he smashes and boils in water. The commissary delivers potatoes to the soldiers from the bummers previous day's hunting and stealing. The aroma of sizzling bacon fills the air.

About an hour after reveille, assembly sounds. Each regiment, brigade and division forms under their commands. At General Slocum's headquarters the previous night, the orders for the task of tearing up the railroad were given to each division commander. The destruction of the railroad from the Stone Mountain Depot to Lithonia is to be complete by mid-afternoon. Colonel William Cogswell's Second Massachusetts Volunteer Regiment of the First Brigade of the First Division will remain and destroy all public buildings before uniting with the main body at the Yellow River and Rockbridge Road. The bummers are out and about, gleefully robbing and burning for the good of General Sherman's fat and happy army.

The Third Brigade of the First Division of the XX Corps takes their respective position along the railroad. Beginning at the Stone Mountain Depot, the 82nd Ohio Regiment is in place at the three mile mark and the other five regiments assemble up to the five mile mark. This gives each division around two miles of track to destroy before eventually reaching Lithonia. One of Colonel Robinson's Regiments remains in the city to destroy several hundred yards of the spur track to the quarry works before beginning their mission of destruction of the main road with the other units of the Third Brigade. Slowly, the ransacked City of Stone Mountain is awakening to the Yankees' movements as they prepare to destroy the railroad.[427]

An orderly shakes Betty Gail gently. "Wake up Miz Betty Gail. Them Bluebellies 'uz back. Lookin' dey ready ter destroy de road."

Betty Gail opens her eyes. "My goodness, it's daylight! I don't even remember getting in this rocker, much less falling asleep. Did I hear you say the Bluebellies are about to destroy the railroad?"

"Yes-um, looks yonder. Seed dems all in line"

Betty Gail stands and goes to the window. "Look at those Bluebellies. Lining up toward Rockbridge Road as far as you can see. We just about had the road repaired and now they're tearing it up again. I don't understand why that Yankee General Sherman doesn't use the road to move his troops about. Just does not make any sense … but again, I'm not a general." Trying not to dwell on this disturbing subject, she continues, "It looks like the oatmeal and grits are ready for the patients. I'm sorry that I didn't wake in time to help you with breakfast."

"No worry, ye tired fum yistiddy!"

⁂

A detail of about three thousand men is divided into three sections. The soldiers in section one line up on the west side of the track. Each man takes a position in front of a railroad tie. The cross-ties are about twenty-four inches center to center or fifteen inches apart. The end man of the section unbolts the bracket that holds the rails together. One thousand men cover about two thousand feet of road. Facing the Yankees from the center of the line is a colonel. Every one hundred feet to his left and to his right are captains, lieutenants and sergeants.

When the soldiers are in position they send a verbal to the colonel. "We are all ready, sir." The commander then shouts the command, "Grasp cross-ties!"

Each of his subordinates repeats the order. Every soldier in section one bends over grasping the tie in front of him. Once the colonel hears, "All are ready" he shouts "HEEEEAVE HOOOOO!"Each Yankee soldier repeats the "HEEEEEAVE HOOOOO" and lifts the cross-ties and track to the vertical position. At the command, "Push Over," the track and cross-ties are thrown into the upside-down position. Using the Poe Railroad Hook, the men of section one separate the rail from the cross-tie.

As each soldier in turn finishes his task, he moves to the west side of the track. Once the entire section is in line, they march toward Lithonia to begin another section.

Now the section two commanders move into the positions previously occupied by the section one commander. The one thousand soldiers of section two remove the cross-ties from the road grade and begin piling them into stacks. Each stack has approximately thirty cross-ties. They place the center of the rails on top of the piles and set the wood on fire.

Once the fire begins and all of the soldiers are on the west side of the road, they march to the new location and fall in line behind the section one soldiers. The commanders of section two also fall in behind the commanders of section one who are preparing to repeat the process.

The section three commanders take the place of the section two commanders and the one thousand destructive Yankee soldiers wait for the rails to become red hot. Then, one of the captains, lieutenants, or sergeants will supervise the bending and, most important, the twisting of the rails. The Bluebellies bend and twist the rails around trees and posts. They call them "Sherman's neckties." Particular attention is also given to the glass insulators on the telegraph poles which are broken by the section two soldiers. The entire operation of rip and burn is a festive occasion for the Bluebellies, especially since there is no threat from the Confederate Army.

Other Yankees follow each of the three sections. Some are on horseback tugging on a line of horses that the laboring Yankees rode into town. Others slip away and break into homes or stores. One smiling thief comes out, holding his bounty of sterling silver in the air. "Look what I got. They had it hid in the chimney!" He laughs and brags as he places the stash in the saddle bags.

A few others have live rabbits from pens and traps. "Gonna make a good supper!" Tying the back legs of the squirming rabbits, the Yankee places them on the commissary wagon. Other men are trotting all over the streets in town, peeking, looking and exhibiting greed as if their mission is on the order of Holiness.

Around 9:00 AM, General Sherman approaches the hill near the Howard House, close to the intersection of Moreland and Dekalb Avenues, the Confederate defense line of July 22. He pauses and turns to reflect upon the scenes of the past battles. "Major Dayton, we are standing upon the very ground whereon the bloody battle of July 22 was fought. I think there is the copse of wood where McPherson fell. He was a much better General than I." Major Dayton quietly listens. "Behind us lies Atlanta, smoldering and in ruins. The black smoke is still rising high in air. It hangs like a pall over the ruined city."[428]

"Yes, sir, it does General."

Off in the distance on the McDonough Road, is the rear of General Howard's column, the gun-barrels are glistening in the sun. The white-topped wagons stretch to the south. The Fourteenth Corps is immediately behind him. The troops are marching steadily and rapidly, with a cheery look and swinging pace. It seems to make light of the thousand miles that lay between the Union army and Richmond.[429]

General Sherman turns his horse's head to the east. Atlanta is soon lost behind a screen of trees. It becomes a thing of the past. In his mind, that city clings to many a thought of desperate battles, of hope and fear that now seems like a memory of an almost forgotten dream. The day is extremely beautiful, clear sunlight, with bracing air. An unusual feeling of exhilaration and things to come, vague and undefined, still full of adventure and intense interest, seems to pervade all minds. The general sentiment is that the Union armies are marching for Richmond. There, the war should end. The marching soldiers do not seem to care about their destination or the progress of the war. They neither measure the distance nor count the loss of life. They do not bother their minds about the great rivers to cross or the food for man and beast which must be gathered on the way. There's a "devil-may-care" feeling pervading the officers and men that made General Sherman feel the full load of responsibility, for success would be expected as a matter of course, whereas, should he fail, this march would be adjudged.[430]

As General Sherman reflects upon these scenes, a XIV Corps band strikes up the stirring music of the "Battle Hymn of the Republic" to which the lyric of "John Brown's Ballad" is written. The marching men catch the strain and the Decatur Road begins to vibrate with it.[431]

> *John Brown's body lies a mould'ring in the grave*
> *John Brown's body lies a mould'ring in the grave*
> *John Brown's body lies a mould'ring in the grave*
> *His soul is marching on.*
> *He has gone to be a soldier in the army of the Lord,*
> *He has gone to be a soldier in the army of the Lord,*
> *'Mid the thunder of the cannon and the roll of the drums.*
> *His soul is marching on.*
> *Glory, glory hallelujah!*
> *Glory, glory hallelujah!*
> *Glory, glory hallelujah!*
> *His soul is marching on.[432]*

For each division of the XX Corps to cover their two miles on the road, about six separate applications of rip and burn will be required. The commissary wagons follow each section, furnishing fresh water as needed. For dinner, they'll provide potatoes and beef, along with hard tack that is always presented.

By two PM, the destruction of the road to Lithonia is complete. The men return to camp and move out down Rockbridge Road to Yellow River. The XX crosses Yellow River and sets up camp for the night on Thomas Maguire's Promise Land Plantation. Here, the XX Corps wait for the supply trains to close up on the main body.

✤

Buck and Isaac try to replant some greens for the winter from his store of seeds. They are returning to the house when Buck notices a cloud of dust coming from Tower Road. Again, straining his eyes, he is able to distinguish it is the same bummers who paid him a visit yesterday. He goes calmly to the gate with Isaac to meet the foragers. When the Lieutenant reaches the gate, only the wagon and the Lieutenant stop while the other soldiers scatter across his place. "We thought we would pay you a surprise visit today to determine if you were lying yesterday. For your sake, I surely hope everything is the same. What did you have for dinner, mister?"

"I had a hare from the rabbit box yonder' and the gin house is just as you left it!" Buck forces himself to remain calm and spits his chew toward the Lieutenant's horse. Yet he realizes these men are very serious, but he isn't willing to compromise his dignity to preserve the ego of this arrogant officer.

Peering over at Buster Phillips barn, the Lieutenant is surprised to find it is still standing. "We set that barn on fire before we left. I see it did not burn so we will give it a better start today!"

Behind Buck, one of the horsemen rounds his house and dismounts. Throwing the door open he enters saying, "Everything is the same as yesterday, Lieutenant!"

"Go look in the cellar you found yesterday," orders the lieutenant. The bummer dashes to the back of the house and finds the door ajar, just as yesterday. He checks the cook house and the crib. They are also as they were the previous day. He reports back to the lieutenant. "Everything's the same, sir."

"Corporal, we did not do a complete job on the barn yesterday. Seems like it did not want to burn. Get those darkies to gather up plenty of wood and straw and set the Confederate barn to a good blaze this time."

"Yes sir." The corporal mounts his horse and rides to the other side of Buster Phillips' house where the darkies are. They had not seen the bummers arrive at Buck's and become anxious as the corporal approaches. He reins his mount to a halt. "You darkies get all the wood you can carry and head to the barn. We got some cooking to do!" says the corporal with a smirk.

"Cookin'?"

"That right … cookin'," replies the corporal.

The darkies deliver the kindling to the barns nervously. In the meantime, another Yankee adds several piles of straw in the inside corners of the barns, as well as in the loft. "Set that wood on top of the straw in the corners inside, and you," pointing to a younger darkie, "get a big pile in the loft on top of the straw. Get a move on it! We are in a hurry to see this place burn!" exclaims the corporal.

"Burns dat barn?" asks one of Buster's slaves.

The Corporal replies angrily, "That's what I said. Set it on fire now."

The darkies look at each other more nervous wondering exactly what the Yankee meant about cookin'.

One of Buster's darkies eyes grow wide and whispers to another darkie, "He's ain't gonna be cookin' me's," throws down the kindling and make a dash for the woods. They are out of sight before the Yankees realize what has happened.

"Let 'em go. Just stack the wood and torch this place. We need to get back to camp with our haul," orders the corporal. By the time he and his squad return to the lieutenant, the barn is smoking with flames emerging from the hay door.

"See you around mister!" shouts the Lieutenant as he snaps the reins on the wagon teams and heads toward camp.

∞

General Sherman surveys the surrounding terrain from his horse. "Major Audenried, that must be Stone Mountain looming in the distance. Send my headquarters staff to the XIV Corps camp site. I want to see this monolith up close. On my maps, sometimes it's called New Gibraltar and sometimes Stone Mountain. We will take the wagon trail along the railroad to get there. This way I can inspect the road destruction first hand."

Before reaching the roads, tall columns of black smoke climb into the sky and eventually drift back together, forming a long stream of darkness.

"The results of the cross-tie burning and rail twisting, I hope," says the General. Upon reaching the road, he brings his horse to a stop. Looking in both directions he studies the destruction of the road. There are only a few mounted infantry patrolling this stretch of devastation.

He views the piles of cross-ties, some smoldering, some still in full blaze. The rails are now around trees twisted and shaped into his namesake. The General smiles. "Perfect, not a straight rail in sight. I expect no less from General Slocum!"

Approaching the town, Colonel Spencer, the Commander of the 1st Alabama Cavalry sends a scouting party to town. They are to determine the best direction to the mountain. The advance party stops and asks Colonel William Cogswell of the Second Massachusetts Volunteer Regiment for directions. "General Sherman is on his way to view the mountain, sir. Which is the best way to the mountain, clear of any rebels?"

"The only Rebels here are in the cemetery, the hospitals and the Wayside. They've all lost their will to resist. Most of them are just waiting to die. The General will be safe here. Just turn right at the end of this block. The wagon trail name is Tower Street and it will take you to the mountain.[433] We are to destroy all public buildings and other structures that might benefit the Confederates this afternoon. We will wait until the General returns from the mountain, just in case we run into any hidden explosives," explains Colonel Cogswell.

Soon the 1st Alabama, General Sherman and his headquarters guard, the 7th Ohio Sharpshooters, enter town. Colonel Cogswell greets him at the depot. "All is clear here, sir. For your safety, I'll wait until you return from the mountain before we set fire to the depot and a couple of other buildings."

"That will be fine, Colonel," replies General Sherman. Sherman and his guard pass several double log-houses in the midst of large oak groves with autumn leaves on their branches. The cabins rest upon the gentle hill sides of Tower Street toward the Wayside.

The advance platoon observes the bummers approaching and, with weapons drawn, orders them to halt. The lieutenant in charge of the bummers approaches cautiously and explains who they are. They proceed to the Wayside together. The Lieutenant halts his unit and approaches Colonel Spence of the 1st Alabama. Saluting, he informs the colonel they are heading back to the main column, but were preparing to investigate the Wayside area. Colonel Spence tells the lieutenant to continue to the main column. The lieutenant salutes, turns and directs his bummers forward.

General Sherman observes many Confederate soldiers at the Wayside from a distance. "Major Dayton, Instruct Colonel Spence to investigate that location."

Rushing inside and seeking to find Mary Hamilton, Joe the attendant shouts, "Miz Hamilton! Miz Hamilton! Yankees! Coming down da road." Mary Hamilton places her hands on Joe's shoulders and takes a deep breath. "Calm down. It won't do us any good to panic. Let me think."

"Yez'um," he says, gulping for air.

"You go through the wards and quietly and calmly tell everyone what's going on." Joe hesitates and glances down the road at the approaching dust cloud. "Go ahead Joe and urge the patients' to remain calm no matter what because I have a copy of orders from Colonel Miller to leave us alone. We should be fine."

"I'se not sure. Dem last Yankees didn't wanter leave us be."

"We're not looking for trouble Joe." She turns toward the door and prepares to face the coming confrontation.

Many of the patients become extremely nervous. A few who are able leave by the back door run to hide in the woods. Mary retrieves Colonel Miller's order and dashes outside. She is waiting as Colonel Spence appears with his horsemen. By now, most of the wounded Confederates have withdrawn to the interior of the Wayside and are peering out of the windows and around the front while others peep from behind trees and bushes at the rear of the Wayside.

"Madam, is this a Confederate hospital or what?" inquires Colonel Spence.

"This is a hotel built by my father, Andrew Johnson, but now is a Wayside for the wounded and sick soldiers who are returning to their homes. I have a copy of orders from Colonel Miller. When he was here in July he issued orders not disturb this place and these orders have recently been endorsed by General Ward." She hands him the copy of the order. With a surprised look, Colonel Spence takes and reads it.

"Are there any Union soldiers here, madam?"

"None at all, Colonel."

"I still must inspect this facility, madam." He summons a Captain and explains the order from Colonel Miller. "Give this place the once over, but do not disturb or remove anything. If you find any of our men, bring them with you. Do not take any prisoners unless there's a confrontation."

"Yes sir, Colonel." The captain explains the orders to a lieutenant who, in turn, takes his platoon to inspect the site as quickly as possible. "Stay with me, madam," directs Colonel Spence.

The lieutenant sends two squads on horseback to check the woods and two squads to inspect the interior of the building. Going from room to room, the Yankees find nothing unusual. One Yankee goes through the kitchen and grabs a hand full of fresh cornbread. "Sure is fresh and hot! I bet that good looking lady who takes care of you could be just as fresh and hot as this here cornbread!" He laughs, grabs another hand-full of cornbread and departs by the back door.

In about ten minutes, the platoon is back together. The lieutenant reports to the captain and colonel. "There are no Union soldiers in the Wayside but we did find several wounded Confederates in the woods. Evidently, they were frightened and were hiding."

Colonel Spence orders the men back to the column. He acknowledges Mrs. Hamilton and dismisses her at the same time.

By now, General Sherman is taking a squad about a hundred yards up the mountain. Colonel Spence rides his horse and reports to General Sherman that the hotel is a wayside for wounded Confederates returning home. He informs the general that in July, Colonel Miller wrote an order not to disturb the Wayside or hospitals in the town. The order has also been recently endorsed by General Ward. It said he had found Union soldiers at the hospital and they were being treated as well as the Confederate soldiers.

"Fine, let's travel on and see if we can ride all of the way around this large pebble," General Sherman advises Colonel Spence. They rejoin the column and head East on Tower Street.

TÊTE-À-TÊTE

General Sherman and part of his guard proceed to the steep side of the mountain. Once they come to a clearing, they see the smoke from Buster Phillips' farm and Buck's place. General Sherman directs Colonel Spence to send a platoon forward to reconnoiter the area. As they wait for the results of the scouting mission, the other troops spread out to insure General Sherman's safety. Betty Gail Jernigan approaches the column. As she rounds a bend in the road, she is taken by surprise by several of the Yankee soldiers.

One has his Spencer rifle pointing directly at her. "Get off of your horse!" shouts a sergeant. "Where are you heading?"

"I live just a stone's throw from here and my husband is expecting me."

The sergeant walks up and grabs the reins from her. "Mighty fine mount. Might just keep it for myself. You best follow me."

"You best check with General Ward before you make that decision, mister! I have an order from him stating I can keep this horse. Where are you taking me?"

"You'll see," as he leads her and her horse toward the area where General Sherman is waiting for the return of the scouts.

Colonel Spence sees the two approaching and meets him part of the way. "Sir, this lady was riding through and we stopped her. Says she lives not far from here."

Betty Gail sees the smoke coming from the area of their farm. Lunging forward in a panic, she shouts, "That smoke is coming from our place! What have you done to my husband and home?"

The sergeant and a corporal restrain her and she renders a good kick to groin of the corporal. He grabs his crotch and falls to the ground. The sergeant yanks a hand-full of her hair, pulling her to the ground face first. As Betty Gail falls to the ground, the sergeant takes his foot and places it firmly on the length of hair and near her skull so she is unable to move. Betty Gail screams from the pain as the hair is pulling from her head. Attempting to scratch the sergeant's legs, she reaches but cannot get to an area above his high boots.

"Calm down, lady. We've done nothing to your place, and I have sent some scouts there to find out what's causing the smoke." The corporal, still rolling and moaning, slowly rises to his feet and moves away to sit in the shade of a nearby a tree. "I'll tell the sergeant to let you up, but another scene we'll have you in ropes. Do you understand?"

Silent for a moment, she responds with a definitive "Yes. Let me up and let me go to my husband and my place."

"Just hold her there a few more minutes, sergeant and then let her up. If she gives you any more trouble, bind her."

"Yes, sir."

In about fifteen minutes, the scouting party returns to report to Colonel Spence who is at the side of General Sherman. "A barn and slave house are burning and some small out buildings have been burned. There's a Union flag flying on the porch next to the burning house!"

Colonel Spence orders the Lieutenant, "Go to the rear and bring me that woman whom the sergeant is restraining." The lieutenant departs as the colonel describes the incident about the woman to General Sherman. The lieutenant reaches the sergeant and gives him the orders from Colonel Spence. By now Betty Gail is sitting up. "On your feet woman, we are going to see Colonel Spence and General Sherman." Betty Gail is still so mad she does not comprehend what the sergeant has said. She stands up, and they walk the fifty or so yards to General Sherman.

"Ma'am, I'm General Sherman and would like to know who lives in the house with the Union Flag out front."

Still upset and now taken back by who has just spoken to her she says, "That is our place and it seems as if some of your abominable Bluebellies have lived up to their reputation. I would love to give you the same compliment that I just gave to your corporal!"

Ignoring her statement, General Sherman asks, "Who lives there with you?"

"My husband and some darkies!" she replies in a stern voice while looking directly into the General's eyes.

"Colonel, send in several platoon and secure the entire area. I want to go in and talk with Mr. . . . What is your husband's name, lady?"

"Buck Jernigan, General!"

Buck, Isaac and Sally are cleaning up the ashes and cinders from the gin fire when Isaac sees the approaching Yankees. "Here's day com' agin," shouts Isaac.

Buck wheels around as the column approaches and begins to spread out in both directions as they are surrounding his place. Buck says angrily, "Another two hours in hell is coming our way again!"

The lead horses approach, and the Yankees dismount. "We are here to inspect your house and out buildings, mister. You're about to have an important visitor. Anybody in your house?"

"No, look for yourself," Buck looks surprised and expresses his feeling to the lieutenant, "I don't need any important guests around here. I just need you Yankees to leave us be."

Soon, the lieutenant returns and details a couple of privates to stay with Mr. Jernigan. He rides to Colonel Spence and informs him of the all clear. Colonel Spence turns to Betty Gail and says, "Come along, Mrs. Jernigan." The sergeant releases the horses' reins to her, and they gallop up to Buck's unbelieving eyes. The two privates salute Colonel Spence. "Mr. Jernigan, I believe," says the colonel.

"That's me all right!" replies Buck as he races to Betty Gail, who leaps from her mount and runs to him. They embrace momentarily, and Betty Gail moves to his side. Turning slightly sideways, she places one arm under his arm and the other hand on his shoulder.

"They stopped me on the way home, but I'm all right now."

"What's going on here?" Buck asks the Colonel.

"We are the rear guard of the XIV Corps, and General Sherman is with us. He is curious about the Union Flag flying from your porch and would like to talk with you."

"If it's truly General Sherman, bring him in, there are a few things I would like to say to him as well. I'll be waiting on the porch, but don't expect any tea from us!"

Colonel Spence rides to get General Sherman. Buck and Betty Gail go to the porch where she relates her harrowing experience with the Bluebelly sergeant.

Isaac is on the porch the entire time, pressing his straw hat close to his chest with both hands. "What them Bluebelly want Mars Jernigan?"

"Don't reckon I know yet, Isaac, but we'll find out soon enough. Bring a couple more chairs over here."

Isaac brings two more chairs from the other side of the porch and puts them near where Betty Gail and Buck are sitting. The sound of horses approaching becomes more distinct as General Sherman, Colonel Spence and six other Yankees approach the porch. As soon as the group brings their mounts to a halt, a Sergeant jumps from his horse to take the reins from the General as he dismounts.

General Sherman looks around a moment and admires the Union flag. He climbs the several stairs leading up to the porch where Buck, Betty Gail and Isaac are waiting. "I'm General Sherman, and I am curious why you're flying the Union flag."

Buck stands. "I'm Buck Jernigan. This is my wife, Betty Gail, and my farm hand, Isaac. Have a seat, General." Observing the manner of dress of General Sherman, Buck snaps, "You dress as shabby as everyone says! Don't your troops call you Uncle Billy?"[435]

Suppressing a smile, General Sherman replies, "Yes. That's one of the better ones. My manner of dress has followed me all my life. At West Point, I had the grades but I did not get above the rank of private because of it." While taking his seat, he repeats, "I'm curious about the flag."

"Simple, we are Union people and did not endorse the secession as did most folks around here. My neighbor signed up for the Confederacy. Our son is somewhere with the Georgia Military Institute—Lord knows where. My family fought to form the Union and I fought in the war with Mexico. Your foraging party was here yesterday and again this morning. For no reason other than my neighbor being in the Confederate Army, they set fire to his barn and out buildings, just like you burned Atlanta." Buck turns and points to the top of the mountain. "If you wanted to see hell, you could've seen it from the top of the mountain as Atlanta was burning Monday night." He points to the Masonic plaque hanging on the porch wall. "One of the bummers brought out my Masonic plaque and showed it to the lieutenant. According to him, that saved my house from his match. I obeyed every request, gave no resistance and still lost nearly everything."

"We are at war and I must feed my army," responds General Sherman. "The foragers are under strict orders to leave food for the citizens. If Governor Brown had accepted my invitation to discuss peace, then the burning of Atlanta would not have occurred.

Buck vigorously responds, "The Constitution is the Constitution. The Constitution, Independence and State Rights, is what our forefathers fought for. Do you think there would've been a war if the North seceded?"

"Probably not. But States Rights and constitutionality is not a good reason for slavery," responds General Sherman.

"Remember 'Uncle Billy,' the antislavery movement began in the South although slavery was just as common in the North. Thomas Jefferson led the emancipation effort. When Oglethorpe settled Georgia, the Charter of 1732 said, that all and every person who resides within Georgia shall be free. Georgia was the only colony of the thirteen which did not allow slavery."

General Sherman leans back. "I did not know this about Georgia. So how did Georgia become a slave state?"

"Reverend George Whitefield, by 1748, had Negro slaves caring for his Orphan House at Bethesda, near Savannah," Buck began. He and the Honorable James Habersham had a great influence with the trustees of the Charter. Mr. Habersham asserted that the Colony was unable to prosper without slave labor. Reverend Whitefield based his support for slavery on philanthropy. He boldly declared it would be of great advantage to the African to be brought from his barbarous surroundings and be among those that are civilized and Christian."[436]

"So when did slavery become legal?" asks Sherman.

"In 1749 the trustees in London came to the conclusion that it would be better to permit slavery. Then the colonists of Georgia were able by law to own and use slaves and the article prohibiting slavery was repealed."

"Seven Northern states abolished slavery because it was not profitable," retorts Sherman.

"Yes and they sold the slaves to the Southerners. There were plenty of white men, women and children slaves in those days. And there are a great number of free Negroes in Georgia today. I just read that Virginia has about sixty thousand free Negroes. Alfred Cuthbert, a former Representative and United States Senator who also was a prominent planter, emancipated his slaves and paid their passage to Liberia."

"What do you think makes slavery so profitable, Mr. Jernigan?"

"See the pile of ashes over there?" Pointing to the remains of his cotton gin and sorghum press. "In the South, cotton is king. The invention of the cotton gin in Savannah, by Eli Whitney, is how the South makes slavery profitable. Cotton cannot be profitable without the cotton gin and slaves are not profitable without cotton. They more or less hold hands. All other crops are secondary. The cotton gin machine can clean more seeds from cotton in one day than one hundred hands can clean in several months. From what I have read, cotton exports went from around 400 bales in 1800 to 82,000 bales in 1810."

"So where did the farmers come from, and why to Georgia to grow the cotton?"

"General I think you are giving me a history quiz."

"Maybe so, Mr. Jernigan. The last question might just be a bonus question."

"Georgia population began to increase with families moving from Virginia and North Carolina. What caused this migration, General, is that neither the soil nor climate in Virginia and North Carolina are suitable to grow cotton. Slavery came to Georgia as the families from Virginia and North Carolina brought their slaves with them to work the cotton fields. Crops are more profitable and the surplus cash is used to buy more Negroes."

"Just good simple economics, Mr. Jernigan. With the increase in the population, cotton cropland became more valuable. Now the cotton gin had not only increased the demand for Negroes but also the demand for land."

"Right, General. The cotton gin was one of the most important inventions ever made. It gave and still gives to the commerce of the world a staple commodity which is in universal demand, and it gave to the people of the South our most valuable and important crop … cotton. The gin has proven to be practicable, except when you see it smoldering in ashes like that over there," he said, rolling his head again in the direction of the gin house. "So, General, would you feel it safe to say that the cotton gin is the root cause of this Civil War?"

Raising his eyebrows and tightening his chin, General Sherman ponders over the last statement. "Not so much the cotton gin. It's just the catalyst for the greed and profit that enslaves humans. I am not an abolitionist and I certainly do not believe in Negro equality."[437]

"Impressive statement, General. Then why are you here?"

"I am a soldier fighting to preserve the Union!"

Buck continues, "Lord Macaulay said Eli Whitney did more to make the United Sates powerful than Peter the Great did to make the Russian Empire dominant."

"Very true," replies the General. "I hate to see it fall apart in the South."

"Well, General, you and your bummers come through here and steal our livestock, our vegetables, our poultry, our cotton, our tobacco, and our family valuables, then burn what's left. But just think, when all of the food is eaten, either by you or us, it's gone. Won't have a new crop for one year. Guess what, General? You cannot beat us economically in Stone Mountain."

"Why do you say that, Mr. Jernigan?"

"Because we have the granite. You cannot burn it, eat it or take it away. We can harvest granite twelve months each year. The granite is not a seasonal commodity. It does not depend on the weather or the plow. Anyone who wants a job in the quarries has a job. It's the big plantation owners who are going to suffer from the economic impact of the Emancipation Proclamation, including your bummers. Our granite quarries will rebuild the South!"

"Do you have children, Mr. Jernigan?"

"We have twins, a boy and a girl. Least ways, we still hope we have two. Like I said, my son is a cadet at GMI, and Lord knows where he is now. I read where you had the honor to burn the GMI campus as well. Our daughter eloped with Joshua Hill's son Legare. You Yankees killed him. None-the-less," Buck said, fighting to contain his emotion. "I must thank you for allowing Congressman Hill to recover Legare's body.

Taken aback by this statement, General Sherman cuts his eyes to the colonel and then to Mrs. Jernigan. "Your family certainly has my condolences, as do all of the families on both sides of this conflict who have lost love ones. I am a soldier as are your generals. We have a duty to do. Mine is to restore the Union." He stands and surveys what's left of the Jernigan farm.

"I know about war. I lost these fingers in the Mexican War. Joshua Hill is a great man for our state. He should be the governor, not the secessionist Joseph Brown. If Joshua was Governor, you probably would not be on my front porch today!"

General Sherman nods in agreement. "Mr. Hill is one of the men I met with and asked to deliver a message to Governor Brown. I offered to meet the Governor, and hopefully sway him from entering the war, and avoiding the ultimate destruction of your beautiful State. From current events, you're aware, he turned my invitation down.[438] You have noble men fighting for the Union, the likes of Alexander Stephens and Robert Toombs. Combining Robert Toombs' powerful and sometimes reckless character with his articulate English makes him a natural leader in truth. There's also Herschel V. Johnson and Benjamin H. Hill. All good men who favor the Union."

Betty Gail shakes her head. "The newspapers attempted to portray Toombs as pro-secession, but he came home, and quickly let it be known that was not the case. He stated that a call for the state convention to consider secession had brought dishonor to the state. He urged everyone to stand by the constitution. The convention met and The Georgia Platform was adopted. The Platform says Georgia holds the American Union secondary in importance to the rights and principles of Georgia. That Georgia will resist any act prohibiting slavery in the Territories or a refusal to admit a slave State into the Union."

"That's right," says Buck. "Then there are the crazy abolitionists. The pitiful old man John Brown, who worked himself into a frenzy and attacked the federal arsenal at Harper's Ferry in Virginia.[439] He was going to use the weapons to start a war and to free slaves.

One of his sons and twelve men were killed plus several darkies. Your people of the North think he gave his life for a just cause and is some kind of a martyr. Under normal social conditions, his act would probably have gone mostly unnoticed. He deserved to be hung. He is regarded as a murderer by us. You sing his praise: 'John Brown's body lies a-mouldering in the grave, his soul goes marching on!' We sing to the same tune, but different words, 'We'll hang John Brown on a rotten apple tree, as we go marching on.'"

"When President Lincoln issued the Emancipation Proclamation, the Italian General Giuseppe Garibaldi hailed President Lincoln as 'the heir of the aspirations of John Brown,'" remarks General Sherman. "Personally, I regard slavery as being an indispensable part of the Southern economy, and it does me no good to judge slavery's morality. I strongly believe in the Union. So what was your reaction to the Proclamation?"

Buck pauses for a moment. "First, the freedom the Proclamation promises depends upon a Union military victory, and this gives the war two goals: keeping the Union united and freeing the slaves. The North has more than just territory in mind to than saving the union."

"What might that be Mr. Jernigan?" asks General Sherman.

"Why the loss of the Southern States means loss of ninety percent of the tax revenues from the tariff, like the Morrill Tariff, which burdens the southern economy."

"You must admit, realistically, it appears the Union shall prevail."

"Most probably," retorts Buck looking directly at General Sherman.

General Sherman leans forward and looks earnestly at Buck. "Since the Proclamation was issued on January 1, 1863 the Negro enlistments have approached 200,000 men. However, the Proclamation impact on the military has had some units near mutiny and desertion, while inspiring other units to focus not only on reuniting the Union but to fight for Liberty as well. It is apparent as the slaves become free your Confederate war engine slows, cracks and begins to fall apart. No longer are slaves producing and preparing food, serving in hospitals, making uniforms, working on farms, building fortifications and rebuilding railroads. Freedom has taken its toll on the South."

"What do you think will happen to the freed slaves?" Buck leans over and spits a stream of tobacco over the porch rail. "I support Governor Brown on one item concerning the freeing of slaves. First, most of the former slaves will remain in the South since some of the Northern States have laws prohibiting former slaves from settling in their states. Second, the wealthy land owners instead of buying slaves will buy land for cultivation. Now, the poor whites and the poor freed slaves will become tenant farmers. With no land and no money, they compete as day laborers of the land owners. And finally with a large paid labor force, the wages of the poor whites will equal the lower wages of the poor free slaves. Discontent by the poor whites with this intrusion will lead to more conflict."

General Sherman takes a drag of his cigar. "If your true conservative disposition had prevailed under the flag you're flying, I think you could have had the support of that large and influential body of Northern men who were and still are sincere to have the elements of the Constitution fulfilled. So how did Georgia end up with Joseph Brown?"

"By hook and crook! The people of the mountains are extremely independent and overwhelming in favor of the Union. Joe Brown is the exception. The mountain folk have few slaves. The battles in Congress supporting the protection of slavery in the Territories are of no interest to them. Lucky for the mountain folk Joe Brown is Governor or there would be serious trouble between this Union part of the State and the State government. The State militia would hang us all for flying the Union flag if had not been for Joe Brown."

"What about his character?"

Buck gestures as to describe the physical being of Joe Brown. "Joe Brown is angular, awkward, and cold, determined and pale looking. He has a simple and homely style and applies common sense to problems.

This trait is common among the Puritans who live in the mountains of East Tennessee and North Georgia. This makes, Joe Brown whose nickname is 'Old Judgment' irresistible to the people of Georgia."

Still draging on his cigar, General Sherman nods. "My army has had some experience with the mountain population and recognizes their feelings. We saw a great many Union flags in the mountains. I would like to know more about your governor."

"The year of his second nomination in 1859, John Brown made that preposterous raid. Joseph Brown supported the indignation created by John Brown's raid. People remember the horrors of the San Domingo slave rebellion spread fear that the Northern abolitionists were going to send agents to Georgia and the South to organize a Negro insurrection. Sectional feeling began running high over the incident."

"Exactly how does the South describe an abolitionist?"

"In the South an abolitionist is one who favors emancipation and is an infidel, a murderer, a thief, a ravisher, an incendiary plus all of hell's accumulated horrors which are not otherwise appropriated. This led to the emotionally active movement which led to secession and to you sitting on my porch." Leaning forward, Buck looks very serious. "Uncle Billy."

"I look around this area and see only women and children and only a few men older than you. Where are all of the men of the state?"

"You know where they are. Out there staining the ground red. By the time the war was going good, Georgia had given one hundred twenty thousand soldiers to the Confederate armies."

Betty Gail interrupts, "That is twenty thousand more than the voting population of the state. Harrison Riley[440] is from Lumpkin County and was going to seize the mint in Dahlonega and hold it for the United States. The delegate from Pickens County refused to sign the ordinance of secession. To show their discontent when secession was final the citizens raised the Union flag in Jasper, the county seat in Pickens. The mountain people are hardy and independent, ignoring all pleas to send troops to North Georgia. The Governor was able to contain the irritated secessionists and let the North Georgians do as they may."

"Yes, but what I see and hear, Joseph Brown's Home Guard turns out to be nothing more than official murderers and horse thieves. From my officers understanding from the mountain people, the Home Guard has the authority to obtain draft animals and supplies and to deal with draft evaders and deserters. Their tactics include executions without trial, and torture in retaliation against friends and families of confederate resisters."

"Kinda reminds me of similar traits of some of your Union soldiers, General."

Colonel Spence intercedes, "Watch your tongue, Mr. Jernigan."

"Let him speak, Colonel."

"Yes, sir." replies the red face colonel.

General Sherman continues, "I sent Union troops to Pickens County and several others places to rescue families and to suppress your Home Guards. In return for the protection by the Union, many of these mountain folks gave me their assistance as spies against the pro-Confederate families.[441] What is your feeling about the Conscription Act,[442] Mr. Jernigan?"

"The Conscription Act is the most demoralizing piece of legislation every contrived and passed by the Confederate Government. It is still a dim-witted piece of legislation and its passage has cut into the zeal of the people at home as well as those in the army. This law is a slap in the face on the patriotism of the entire Southern population. Just like the one Lincoln had passed. I read it caused riots in New York."

"Didn't Joshua Hill run for Governor in '63?" asks General Sherman.

"Surely did and got beat. The majority did not want a Union supporter in office. Although he tried to act as if he supported the Confederacy, he did not convince the voters. Joseph Brown got more than fifty percent and beat Joshua Hill and Timothy Furlow. Timothy Furlow is a passionate supporter of secession."

The General stands and turns toward the late afternoon sun. "Colonel Spence, have my clerk write an order over my signature for the protection of Mr. Jernigan's place as well as a script for one thousand dollars to replace his property."

"It has been an interesting conversation with both of you Mr. and Mrs. Jernigan. I hope this war can come to a sensible conclusion soon and all of us return to normal for the good of the United States." General Sherman walks over to the remains of the cotton gin. In his mind he visualizes the entire destruction of the Southern economy as nothing more than a larger pile of ashes after the war.

"Why are you studying my burned down ginny, General? Your troops have burned houses, barns, and feed bins for the pure pleasure of seeing smoke and flame."

General Sherman lights another cigar. "Care for a cigar Mr. Jernigan."

"Don't smoke. Just chew." Buck turns and spits on the ground.

"Mr. Jernigan, I admit a lot of mischief goes on during a war. However, my orders are to destroy structure and machinery which is of value to the Confederate war effort. I decided to base this decision on my experience when I was the military administrator of Memphis on July 21, '62. I found the place dead. No one doing business, the stores closed, churches, schools, and everything shut down. The people were all more or less in sympathy with our enemies, and there was a strong prospect that the whole civil population would become a dead weight on our hands. Inasmuch as the Mississippi River was then in our possession northward, and steamboats were freely plying with passengers and freight, I caused all the stores to be opened. Churches, schools, theatres, and places of amusement, to be reestablished, and very soon Memphis resumed its appearance of an active, busy, prosperous place. I also restored the mayor, whose name was Parks, and the city government to the performance of their public functions, and required them to maintain a good civil police.[443]

"Soon I began to receive reports that citizens were giving secret support to the Confederacy. So when a party of guerrillas in the town of Randolph, north of Memphis, fired on an unarmed Union steamboat carrying civilian passengers, I ordered Randolph burned, stipulating that a single house be left standing to mark the place."[444]

Buck listens anxiously. He and Betty Gail are appalled. Neither had heard the story. General Sherman walks back to the porch and takes his seat. Major Dayton offers him a cup of water. As the general finishes his last swallow, Buck can tell that General Sherman is still upset by the events of Memphis. After lighting a cigar and taking a few drags, he leans forward in the rocking chair, "Mr. Jernigan, when one nation is at war with another nation, all the people of the one are enemies of the other. Then the rules are plain and easy to understand."

"That's pretty much true General."

"Most unfortunately, the war in which we are now engaged has been complicated with the belief all of the Southerners are not enemies. It would have been better if, at the outset, this mistake had not been made."

"So the acts of the citizens of Memphis set your mind to the destruction of property?"

"It would have been wrong to continue to be misled by compassion of my Southern countrymen. I had to proceed on the basis that all in the South are enemies of all in the North. Not only are they unfriendly, but also all who could procure arms now bear them as organized regiments, or as guerrillas. There was not a Union garrison in Tennessee where a man could go beyond the sight of the flag-staff without being shot or captured."[445]

"In all due respect General, you would react the same way if your city was occupied by Confederates."

"Probably so. But it so happened that the people had cotton, and whenever they saw our large armies move, they destroyed the cotton in the belief that we would seize it, and convert it to our use. They did not and could not dream that we would pay money for the cotton. It had been condemned to destruction by their own acknowledged Confederate government. The cotton was therefore lost to the Southern people. It could have been, without injustice, taken by us. We could send it away, either as absolute prize of war, or for future compensation."

"But the citizens turned to the commercial enterprise of the Jews. The Jews soon discovered that ten cents would buy a pound of cotton behind our army. That four cents would take it to Boston, where they could receive thirty cents in gold."[446]

"I think the citizens of Memphis had rather sell it cheap on the black market to whoever wanted to buy rather than surrender it to the Union," replies Buck.

"But at that time the Union was willing to pay for the goods. Nevertheless the bait was too tempting, and it spread like fire. When the Jews discovered that salt, bacon, powder, fire-arms, percussion-caps, etc., etc., were worth as much as gold, they sold these goods as well for a huge profit; and, strange to say, this traffic was not only permitted, but encouraged. Before we in the interior could know it, thousands of barrels of salt and millions of dollars had been disbursed. I have no doubt that Bragg's army at Tupelo, and Van Dorn's at Vicksburg, received enough salt to make bacon. No other way could Bragg and Van Dorn have moved their armies en mass. When from ten to twenty thousand fresh arms, and a due supply of cartridges were also obtained, I knew what was happening. As soon as I got to Memphis, having seen the effect in the interior, I ordered my own command that gold, silver, and Treasury notes, were contraband of war, and should not go into the interior, where all were hostile."

"I guess you could call the Jews 'War Brokers,' but I know there were Union sympathizers in Memphis," says Buck.

"So, what was the 'gold' rule all about?" asks Betty Gail.

"Every gold dollar that was spent for cotton was sent to the seaboard, to be exchanged for bank-notes and Confederate scrip, which would buy goods in Memphis, and was taken in ordinary transactions. I therefore required cotton to be paid for in such notes, by an obligation to pay at the end of the war, or by a deposit of the price in the hands of a trustee, viz., the United States Quartermaster. Under these rules, cotton was being obtained about as fast as by any other process, and yet the enemy receives no 'aid or comfort.' Under the 'gold' rule, the country people who concealed their cotton from the burners, and who openly scorned our greenbacks, were willing enough to take Tennessee money, which bought their groceries. Then that trade was encouraged, and gold paid out. I admit that cotton was sent in by our open enemies, who can make better use of gold than they can of their hidden bales of cotton.[447]

"I wrote my brother and told him that the entire South, man, woman, and child is against us and that the South's fighting spirit has to be extinguished. Civilians as well as soldiers have to be regarded as enemies, thus making the war terrible even against some who are personal friends."[448]

General Sherman's clerk interrupts. "Sir, here is the order you requested."

Buck clears his throat and moves close to Betty Gail. Looking at Betty Gail, he simply raises and lowers his eye brows. He isn't certain what to expect from the General.

General Sherman continues to drag on his cigar as he reads the contents, signs the order and the script, stands and hands them to Buck. Buck accepts the documents.

"I very much enjoyed our conversation, and if I should see Joshua Hill, I'll give him your regards, General. Again I thank you for allowing us to recover Legare's remains."

There's no offer of either's hand in this departure. The sergeant brings General Sherman's horse to his side and the general readily mounts. Betty Gail whispers to Buck, "That's the sergeant who threw me to the ground and held me there with his foot on my hair."

Buck walks over to the sergeant. "Excuse me, Sergeant."

"Yes?"

"Just one thing, Sergeant. If we ever meet again on equal terms, I would suggest that you have your head shaved." Buck then spits a wad of tobacco on the Sergeant's boot.

The Sergeant's face turns beet red and gives Buck the "I'm ready now look," takes to his mount, and then snaps his horse around.

Colonel Spence orders the bugler to "sound assembly." He and General Sherman turn-about and the column moves toward town on

Tower Street. Soon, the last of the Union troops are out of the surrounding woods. General Sherman gives his horse the rein, and canters away towards town with that easy, swaying seat, so characteristic of a leisurely well-to-do general.

Colonel Spence, riding adjacent to General Sherman, smiles and says, "That was a slick interrogation General. That farmer had no idea you were extracting information from him."

General Sherman grins. "A very interesting man, that Mr. Jernigan. Knows his history. I wonder what his two children are like. His daughter is the widow of Joshua Hill's son and Jernigan's son is a cadet at Georgia Military Institute."

"Well, Colonel, the Union has won this war. We just need to reach Savannah."

"A very interesting man indeed," answers the colonel.

Buck and Betty Gail observe a piece of history disappear as the afternoon shadows grow longer, and the last Yankee horses round the bend where they appeared earlier. Buck comforts Betty Gail. "Good or bad, failure concerns General Sherman as much as success. He's not afraid to take a chance to succeed. He's a General for sure."

General Sherman instructs Major Dayton, "Let's get on to camp. My staff should have the reports from all of the units for the days march when we arrive at headquarters." As the scouting party of General Sherman rounds the corner in town, Colonel Cogswell of the Second Massachusetts Volunteer Regiment is given the alert that the General is not far behind. Colonel Cogswell orders his troops to stand at attention next to their mounts as General Sherman passes. Colonel Spence summons Colonel Cogswell for General Sherman.

"Yes sir, General, you summon?" asks Colonel Cogswell.

"Where does this spur track go?"

"Sir, it goes around the mountain to the quarries. My men tore it up to the mountain."

"Go ahead and destroy this depot and any other building you feel are a threat to the Union or are of a military advantage to the Confederates."

"Yes, sir." He salutes and returns to his Company commanders with the order from the General. As soon as General Sherman is out of site, the Second Massachusetts Volunteer Regiment begins burning the depot. While General Sherman was touring the mountain preparations for the destruction and burning of the depot and other structures was taking place. Straw from the fields and fence rails have been taken inside the depot. Several homes and buildings which the colonel found to have been a place to hide munitions are also a target for the torch.

The order is given and each company of the regiment mounts and goes to the buildings and homes that are to be set ablaze. Again the sky is darkened with plumes of black and white smoke and the accompanying red flames. Several adjoining structures catch on fire because of their proximity. The gleeful Union regiment gathers in clusters to observe their superiority against the Confederacy and the people of Stone Mountain.

Sitting high upon his horse, Colonel Cogswell ascertains the orders have been carried out completely. "Great job men. You can return to camp now for supper." The soldiers form up their company columns and parade out of town next to the still smoldering cross-ties and twisted rails of the road.

The few remaining citizens flee to the churches or to one of the hospitals. The hospital attendants, patients and citizens stare nervously as the flames jump from dwelling to dwelling and cover the town in smoke and soot again. The rising and falling cinders land in open, dry fields setting numerous rapidly moving brush fires which engulf the surrounding landscape.

General Sherman reaches his headquarters with the XIV Corps camp by the roadside near Lithonia. Stone Mountain is still in plain view, cut out in clear outline against the blue sky. The whole horizon is lurid with the bonfires of railroad ties and groups of men of the XIV are still carrying the destruction of the railroad. General Sherman inspects the progress and comments to Major Dayton, "It seems that Colonel Poe's tool for ripping up the rails and twisting them when hot works well, but the best and easiest way is by heating the middle of the iron-rails on bonfires made of the cross-ties, and then winding them around a telegraph-pole or the trunk of some convenient sapling." General Sherman attaches a great deal of importance to the destruction of the railroad and gives his personal attention and reiterates his orders to his staff on the subject.[449]

⚬

Thomas Maguire is standing on the porch on his Promised Land Plantation explaining to his neighbor. "I spent the night pacing and remained awake nearly till morning worrying about those Yankees coming by here again."

They look up and see a rider coming around the corner and up to the porch. The rider, unknown to both men, hesitates only long enough to say, "The Yankees are coming this way after burning Atlanta, Decatur and some houses at Stone Mountain."

Thomas and his neighbor rush to begin hiding boxes of tools, a horse, a buggy and other goods throughout the woods. When they finish, Thomas waits for the worst to come, still hoping the Yankees won't come their way.

A little after ten o'clock his wife shouts, "They're here. They're here again Thomas."

Thomas rushes in from the back of the house and observes the Yankees arriving in force.

Slocum's Corps camps all round the house. At every side hogs and sheep are being shot down and skinned to satisfy the Yankee palates.

Thomas manages to slip out so he and his neighbor sleep in the woods all night again, trying to keep the horses and cattle out of sight and sound of the Yankees. Although his wife is safe, he still worries, "It's not very pleasant for either body or mind not knowing what is going on at home."[450]

On Wednesday, November 17, Thomas is still in the woods and unable to sleep. He scurries about in the woods trying to see the Yankees from his hiding place. Finally, the Yankees leave about 11:00 PM. He arrives home at two in the morning, tired and sleepy, glad to find that the home folks are safe, although there's great deal of destruction of the property. The gin house and screw are still burning and the stables and barn are in ashes. His carriage and big wagon are gone, along with the corn, potatoes, sheep, chickens and geese. Upon further inspection, Thomas finds the damaged syrup boilers and one smoldering barrel of syrup. The saddles and bridles are in the same fix.

Now Thomas engages in gathering up the fragments of the spoils. He knows it is useless to try to record the destruction of property. His only hope is that his family has enough food to survive. He thinks they have plenty of corn, wheat and syrup hidden. There are ashes of some twenty bushels of wheat in the gin house, some of which some belongs to Mr. Minor. Fortunately, Thomas is able to save the corn cribs. The gin house is still burning, as are the straw piles along with three bales of cotton. The others were cut open to make beds for the Yankees. All of the cotton belongs to another neighbor, Ed Turner. The gin thrasher, fan, the castings lying next to the cog wheel and other parts of the machinery are in ruins. The destruction on the Promise Land Plantation is the destruction of Jerusalem on a small scale.[451]

Although not very strong in numbers the bushwhackers in and around Lithonia are producing casualties among the Yankee forces. The Yankee forces are destroying the railroad to and through the center of town.

Infuriated by the bushwhackers, the Yankee commander issues a special vengeance order against the Lithonia residents' bushwhacking activities. "Burn everything in town. Place guards at the Masonic Hall and allow no damage to be done there!" When the day becomes night, "Sherman's Neckties" extend from Stone Mountain to Lithonia. Columns of smoke rise above the few homes and businesses constituting the sleepy little town of Lithonia.

As night approaches, General Sherman is at his camp by the road-side near Lithonia. Stone Mountain is still in view. Major James A. Connolly, standing next to General Sherman, says," Stone Mountain has to be one of the great natural curiosities of this continent."

"Yes, it is," replies General Sherman, "and so are its citizens."

The whole horizon is lurid with the bonfires of rail-ties as the groups of Yankees continue to carry the hot rails to the nearest trees, bending them around the trunks. General Sherman is proud of his accomplishments. Standing outside his headquarters tent chewing on a cigar, he seems almost poetic. "The glowing fires from the camps which are piercing the darkness, remind me of a political torch light parade,[452] he says to his chief of staff.

✺

It begins to rain on Thursday. Thomas is still roving around trying to save whatever he can from the grasp of the droves of his plundering neighbors. However his family is still cheerful and hopeful that the worst is over and the Yankees are gone forever. The Yankees took the opportunity to kill several horses and mules for no apparent reason. Thomas has one horse left which he hid in the nearby woods. However the animal must have had an accident because one of the poor horses' hoofs is nearly off. He is hopeful he can doctor him up.

Wandering strangers prowl around Thomas's place as well as the abandoned Yankee camp throughout the day. The people take any and everything they can find no matter who the owner may be.[453]

As the rain subsides, the Left Wing passes through the handsome town of Conyers and into Covington. General Slocum directs his commanders, "Have the soldiers close up their ranks. Have the color-bearers unfurling their flags, then have the bands strike up patriotic music. Let them know the proud Union army has arrived, and that General Sherman is marching through their town."As the Union troops begin marching through Covington in parade formation, the nervous white people slowly begin coming out of their houses to behold the sight in spite of their deep hatred of the invaders. However as the Union army passes they see the Negroes are smiling, waving their straw hats and frantic with joy.

"General Sherman is coming," shout several Union soldiers. Soon a group of Negroes see a distant group of horsemen being lead by color-bearers. They seem to surround what appears to be an important soldier. A white woman standing next to a Union guard inquires, "Who is that coming down the street?"

"Why that's General Sherman." The Negroes hear the guard's answer and they scream with joy and rush to cluster about his horse. The Negroes throw their arms into the air as they shout and pray in their peculiar style, which has a natural eloquence that can move a stone. General Sherman studying the scene sees a poor girl, in the very ecstasy of the Methodist 'shout,' hugging the banner of one of the color-bearers and jumping up to the "feet of Jesus."[454]

General Sherman detours around a street in Covington to avoid the crowd that is following the marching column. As General Sherman passes through the main part of town, his clerk approaches. "Sir, a lady asked for this message to be delivered to you. He opens the envelope and reads, "General, I am the sister of Sam Anderson who was a classmate of yours at West Point. I would be honored to have you as a guest for dinner at my home."

"Send my regrets to the lady." General Sherman rides on to camp, at the crossing of the Ulcofauhatchee River, about four miles to the east of the town.

He and Major Henry Hitchcock walk up to a plantation house. Close by there's a gathering of Negroes at one of the small wooden slave dwellings. The generals walk up to the gray-haired old Negro man who is sitting on the steps of the small one room wooded dwelling. The Negro man has no reason not to recognize General Sherman. General Sherman looks at the Negro man and says, "Mister I have a question for you."

The Negro man simply raises his eyes toward the general.

"Do you understand about the war and its progress?"

The other Negroes gather round quietly as the old Negro man replies sharply, "I'se do and I'se been alookin' fer de 'angel of de Lord' since I wuz knee-high. I'se know'd you to be fightin' fer de Union. I'se suppose dat slavery is de cause."

Surprised at the old Negro's answer, General Sherman nods. "Our success in preserving the Union will grant your freedom. I hope all the Negroes understand this."

"I'se do and so do de others."

General Sherman, concerned that the Negroes may attempt to follow his army, explains, "I want you to, in no uncertain terms, let the Negroes know they are to remain where they are, and not load us down with useless mouths. The extra people would eat up the food we need for our fighting men. Our success is your freedom. I can enlist a few of the young hearty men as pioneers. However, if your people follow us in swarms of old and young, feeble and helpless, it will simply load us down and cripple us in our great task."

"I'se understand, sir, en I'se spread de message to de slaves. "I'se kinnot promise da will not follow you."[455] When General Sherman departs, the old Negro asks one of the remaining soldiers, "Who dat man?"

"Why that's was General Sherman."

The old Negro's eyes grow large and he raises his hands toward the sky and screams, "Da angel of de Lord wus here!"

From Covington, the Fourteenth Corps (Davis's) turns to the right for Milledgeville, by-way-of Shady Dale. As General Sherman's army passes through Shady Dale and Newborn, they burn the cotton warehouse and cotton mills. They do not disturb the school house between Sandtown and Shady Dale or the single church between Shady Dale and Newborn. In Newborn, General Sherman's bummers raid the plantation of John Howard Walton. He is off serving in the Confederate army and also is a descendant of George Walton, one of the signers of the Declaration of Independence.

His wife, Mary, recently had a baby and is living alone with a young slave girl whose name is Sara. Sara is there to help her care for the new baby, Lulu Belle. Sara and Mary get word the Yankees are coming and carefully hide all of the silver and other valuables. They see the bummers coming and run outside with the newborn baby.

The bummers arrive in typical fashion rounding up livestock and other eatables. Never saying a word, several horsemen ride up the stairs to the front door and crash inside with their horses. They ride through the hallways, then dismount and search every drawer in every room. Suffering through one hour of torment, Mary tries to comfort her crying baby as she and Sara stand by each other as the bummers remove their food and furnishing. Returning to the outside with their horses and their plunder, the lieutenant mounts his horse, and laughs at Mary and Sara, "Since you have that new baby, we'll let you keep the house, but everything else is ours." He snaps his reins and then he and his foragers begin driving the cattle away from the plantation.

General Slocum is ahead of Sherman at Madison after destroying the railroad with the Twentieth Corps. General Geary's division is on its way to the Oconee, to burn the bridges across the river. At the daily staff meeting, Sherman proudly informs his commanders, "The agriculture maps are accurate. The land of corn, molasses, meal, bacon, and sweet-potatoes lay in wait for our army. The herds of cows and oxen, as well as large numbers of mules on the large plantations easily replace our exhausted animals. All in all, this area is quite rich in food and treasures. The recent crop is excellent and is in storage for the winter, making the pickings easier for our foraging expeditions."[456]

⊰●

Major Capers looks down the rows of the GMI cadets. "I have sad news this morning. On Sunday, November 13 and 14, General Sherman was in Marietta reviewing General Kilpatrick's Cavalry Division. According to the news, Marietta, along with the Georgia Military Institute, was burned. Gaunt chimneys and the superintendent's quarters are the only reminders of the proud school."[457]

Sadly, Norman asks Paul, "Do you think we will ever rebuild?"

Rubbing his forehead, Paul looks despondent to Norman. "Only if we win this war."

On Saturday, November 19, Gen. Wayne receives a report from Gen. Johnston, "General Sherman's army is heading for either Macon or Augusta." Gen. Wayne issues an order to move six hundred troops, the cadet corps and Robert Guards, consisting of 150 convicts on parole, who promise to fight, to Gordon.

Although Norman and Paul are still recovering emotionally from the news of the destruction of the GMI campus, they and the cadets are eager for battle. Norman and Paul are greasing the wheels on the caissons and cannons. Norman sits on the cannon brace. "I guess we are preparing our last two brass cannons for the movement to Gordon. That major railroad center seventeen miles from here needs a good brass cannon to protect it from the Yankees."

"Looks that way Norman."

Upon arriving in Gordon, the cadets build breast works and set up the artillery before dark and the garrison is able to light some camp fires.

Sitting by the campfire, Norman says, "Feel the moisture in the air Paul? Looks like the weather is about to change to bitter cold with rain or snow. Best bundle up good tonight."

The next morning, Sunday November 20, 1864, Gen. Wayne and Maj. Capers are attempting to telegraph Macon. Gen. Wayne briefs Maj. Capers, "The lines have been cut by the advancing Yankees. I'll send a scout to determine the location of the Federal forces." Maj. Capers replies, "There's a soldier named James Rufus Kelly who is home after losing one leg. I know him and he was a great scout."

"Fetch him for me."

James Kelly is located and reports to Gen. Wayne. "I understand you're looking for me, Gen."

Gen. Wayne studies Kelly standing there with one leg missing, and being supported by a forked branch for a crutch. He is slender in frame, but mighty gritty looking and appears to be full of spunk. "I need a scout to find the Yankees. Can you help?"

"Glad too, Gen. I need to work on my score sheet." So Kelly volunteers and is on horseback to spy on the advancing Yankees for Gen. Wayne.

"Maj. Capers, attach five passenger cars and three flatbed cars to the best locomotive out of the nine at the Gordon depot. Pick the best of the one hundred and fifty railroad cars as well. We must reposition to the east as soon as possible."

James Kelly returns from his scouting mission and reports to Gen. Wayne, "The Union forces are heading directly for Milledgeville."

"I've been trying for eight hours, and I am still unable to reestablish communications." Gen. Wayne studies his maps for a moment. "We will abandon Gordon. It's a non-essential military position. Order our command to withdraw to the important Oconee Central Railroad Bridge. We can better defend the bridge against the Yankees rather than defend Milledgeville. Stronger units can defend the Capital."[458]

❧

On the same day, several citizens rush to Congressman Hill's home in Madison. The butler answers the loud and repeated knocks. As he opens the door and before he can speak, one nervous man conveys to the butler, "I am the Mayor. Fetch Congressman Hill." He points to the outskirts of town, "Inform him that the Yankees are approaching our town and we need his help."

Joshua and Mrs. Hill rush to the front entrance and see the Mayor and several other familiar citizens on the porch. "Morning Mayor, what's this about the Yankees?"

"They are on the outskirts of town. Hopefully, you can exert your influence so that they will not destroy our town and our homes."

"Emily, I'll be back shortly. See what I can do to help the Mayor. Let's go before it's too late."

Joshua hurriedly boards his carriage as Emily shouts, "Be careful Joshua. Be careful."

On the edge of town, Joshua and the group of citizens wave a white flag as they meet General Slocum's advance guard. A Union officer with several soldiers on horseback approaches.

"What is the purpose of the white flag?" asks the officer.

"I am Congressman Hill, and I would like to speak to your commanding officer."

"Escort Congressman Hill to General Slocum. The rest of you wait here."

General Slocum meets Joshua and knows from General Sherman that he is pro-Union.

"I would like to request that you spare Madison from destruction. We have no Confederate troops in Madison and support the Union."

After some conversation, General Slocum honors Congressman Hill's request. "I'll issue orders to my commanders not to disturb any residences, churches and in general to leave the town spared.

However, facilities such as the depot, cloth factories, cotton gins, cotton and any other facilities or supplies which will aid the Confederacy will be destroyed."

"Thank you, General. We appreciate your consideration." Joshua heads back home with the Mayor under Union escort.

※

The following morning, Friday, November 22, Gen. Wayne's and Gen. Caper's small command begin the series of loading the cannons, horses, and troops. The cadets direct the men of Roberts Guard in loading their cannon, caisson and limbers. Cannons will be able to fire from the flatbed cars when necessary.

In a low voice, Norman says, "Paul, Clayton keep a close eye on these guys, they don't even look like their mothers can trust them."

"You are right about that," replies Clayton. "Several of them tried to slip out of camp last night. When the guards challenged them, their reply was 'we just want to pee.' Some others said they wanted to help the guard on duty. No matter what, they were ordered back to camp."

By four o'clock PM, all of the provisions and troops are on board the train when Rufus Kelly returns on horseback from Macon. He reports that a large Union force is just outside of Gordon. Gen. Wayne informs Kelly, "We are going to defend the Oconee River Bridge."

Kelly, visibly upset, becomes incredulous and curses the general, "You're a white-livered cur with not a drop of red blood in your veins... well, you damned band of tucktails, if you have no manhood left in you, I'll defend the women and children of Gordon!"[459]

The entering Union forces fire shots at the train as it pulls away from the station. The cadets prepare for a fight, but the train roars out of range quickly. Kelly and one other townsman by the name of Bragg begin firing on the Yankees with their new Henry repeating rifles. One Yankee bites the dust and the others scatter. For nearly one hour, the two men keep the Yankees at bay.

Kelly says, "The whole world it turning to Yankees."

Kelly retreats to the Solomon Hotel. Inside, Mrs. Solomon is very aware of the skirmishing on the street. She sees Kelly high-tailing towards her hotel in his attempt to elude the Yankees. All he has is his pistol and crutch. As he rushes into the hotel, Mrs. Solomon yells at him, "Rufus, throw your crutch toward the back and get over here quick."

Kelly hurls his crutch toward the back door and heads for Mrs. Solomon. "Get under here quick and be very still" she directs Kelly as she lifts the bell of her hoop skirt. Kelly, somewhat hesitant and with an astonishing look asks, "No offense, Mrs. Solomon, but did I hear you right … did you say get under your hoop?"

"If you want to live, that is what you best do, and do it now!" whispers Mrs. Solomon.

Kelly, too nervous to be embarrassed, ducks under the bell of her hoop skirt. The Yankees burst into the hotel lobby with guns and swords ready. Mrs. Solomon is standing and waiting for their grand entrance into her hotel.

"Where's that rebel that came in here?" demands a lieutenant after jerking open the door of the lobby.

Placing her hand upon her bosom and the other on her forehead, Mrs. Solomon says "Yonder through the back door-a … he nearly caused my death!"

By now, other Yankees are arriving. The lieutenant directs some of them to search the entire hotel. He and several others rush out of the back door in search of the elusive Kelly. In the meantime, the other rebel, Bragg, is able to escape into the thick woods.

Shortly Mrs. Solomon sees that the area is clear and informs Kelly, "All of the Yankees are out of sight," and she lifts her bell again and he emerges timidly.

"I truly wanna thank you, Mrs. Solomon. You saved my life."

"Now get and go kill them Yankees, Rufus!" directs Mrs. Solomon.

Kelly slips around from the back of the hotel to the woods near the area where the Yankees entered town. There, he finds one rifle on the ground near where he shot a Union horseman earlier. He launches a surprise one man assault on the Yankees. This time, after killing and wounding several more Federals, he runs out of ammunition. The Federals surround and capture him without any further resistance.

The Yankees force Kelly to witness the burning of the depot, railcars, and locomotives, as well as the destruction of the railroad tracks. The lieutenant does not order the burning of the Solomon hotel. He remembers seeing a Masonic plaque in its lobby. Being a Mason, he questions Mrs. Solomon concerning the plaque. She proudly lets the lieutenant know that her late husband was a Mason.

That evening, a court martial finds Kelly guilty of murder. He receives a sentence of death and is to die the following day.[460]

⁂

The twenty mile, two hour train ride to the Oconee River Bridge, south of Milledgeville, concludes without any military action. There is an extremely chilling November wind. Gen. Wayne and Gen. Capers immediately order the unloading of the troops and supplies, but leave several cannons on the flat railroad cars. The Confederate Fourth Kentucky Mounted Infantry troops of the Orphan Brigade sent early by Gen. Wheeler establishes a stockade two miles west of the bridge. The Kentucky Brigade includes other small reinforcements from Savannah, the Ashley Dragoons, a cavalry company from South Carolina, Maxwell's Light Artillery Battery with two twelve pounder Napoleons, one hundred infantrymen from the 27th Georgia Battalion and a brigade of Gen. Wheeler's cavalry. These units add another 1,200 troops under Wayne's and Capers's command.

"Defending this important bridge of the Central of Georgia Railroad should not be too difficult. The Yankees will have to cross the swamp to get to us. When they try, we will have a nice surprise for them." Gen. Wayne looks from officer to officer for questions as he closes the briefing.

TUESDAY, NOVEMBER 22

The roads are muddy and dilapidated from the rain and snow. Gen. Wayne meets with Gen. Capers. "We do not have enough troops to hold back the approaching Union's XVIIth and XVth Corps with 30,000 men." He orders Capers, "Have the cadets and the Fourth Kentucky to form a line of works on the left side of the bridge on the west bank. Have the convicts to do the same on the right side of the bridge on the west bank of the river."

Gen. Capers calls for Norman, Clayton, Marsh and Paul. "Gentlemen, instruct the convicts on breastwork construction."

They gather the convicts and while keeping a suspicious eye on them, Paul draws pictures in the sand and uses small twigs to demonstrate the manner of construction of the breastwork.

Norman watches and then stands by a small sapling. "See this sapling. This is the size to be cut. Old fence rails are good. Stones and rocks make great revetment. When complete, the relief is two by five and the width no less than eight feet. If you do not construct the breastworks correctly, the likelihood of the Yankees killing you goes up markedly. So do a job suitable for saving your life."

Paul looks over at the convicts. They appear to be of hard but calm character. They follow instructions willingly."

Gen. Wayne decides to use the train cars for protection against the elements. All day he has the prisoners gathering additional wood for the stoves of each passenger car. As night falls, so does the temperature. The cadets begin changing guards every hour. Each company is assigned a passenger car. The guards are posted near the bridge and at each train car.

"About one hour of guard duty is all I can stand," Norman tells Paul as they climb aboard the train car platform after being challenged by the guard. The thermometer reads fifteen degrees and it has been snowing heavy. They rest their cold muskets against the side of the car and shake off the frozen snow. Grasping the cold iron barrel of the musket and with chattering teeth, they enter the warmth of the car happily.

The only light source aboard the car is the glow from the stove. Attempting not to disturb any of the sleeping cadets they rush to the stove. As they place their feet as close as possible, Cadet Sergeant Scott Todd, from the previous guard detail, pours Paul and Norman a cup of plain hot water. Still trembling, they hold their cups with both hands to prevent spilling the warm water that will revive them. The aroma of fresh pork and sweet potatoes cooking is welcoming. Removing the now cool rocks from their pockets, they place them on the top of the stove to heat them for use on another sentry duty.

Cadet Sergeant Todd explains, "I have been here for over an hour and am just now thawing out! When you're ready to take over, let me know. Help yourself to the food."

"Go ahead and take your nap. It's our turn to man the stove," Paul says.

"Thanks." Cadet Todd takes his blanket from near the stove and finds an empty seat on the train in which to snooze. Throwing the blanket over his head, he falls rapidly into deep sleep.

"Paul, the Yankees are just as cold as we are. Campfires are not the answer to this cold and snow," says Norman. "I also hope they don't have a house or barn to get in."

Warming up a bit, they remove the wet blankets and place them near the stove. As with the blankets, the two begin to dry. Steam comes from the heating of the moisture in their clothes and blankets. They finally settle even more and remove their boots which are also steaming from the release of moisture. Huddling near the stove, they dish up their meal. Now warmer, they are able to eat and drink without shaking. After they finish their meals, they make sure the hot water kettle is full and replenish the pork for the next cadets coming in from guard duty.

The thermometer on the train platform reads ten degrees above zero on the morning of Wednesday, Nov 23, 1864. The Confederate Fourth Kentucky Mounted Infantry is under the command of Capt. John Weller. Their outpost is two miles west of the Oconee River Bridge. At midmorning, the outpost is under attack by General Giles Smith's Brigade. After skirmishing for several hours and resisting against overwhelming odds the Confederate troops are driven back toward the bridge.[461] At noon, Gen. Wayne orders Maj. Hartridge with Heyward's Ashley Dragoons,

Huger's section of artillery, Talbot's Militia Company and around eighty troops from the 27th Georgia Battalion to picket Buffalo Creek Ball's Ferry where Union troops are expecting to cross the river.

The Cadet Corps at the Oconee Bridge hears the sound of gun fire. The cadets and the convicts take their positions behind their breastworks in the swamps on the west side of the river. Cadet Lt. Hill is the Ordnance Officer in charge of the Georgia Military Institute artillery. Peering over the breastworks, the Fourth Kentucky Infantry troops keep firing as they retreat. Several fall with wounds or fatal shots. Rapidly, the Fourth Kentucky joins with the Cadets behind the breastworks.

❧

The Union cavalry is forced to dismount due to the swamp land. They launch an offensive. Capt. William Pruden has several of his light Artillery Battery cannons on the flatbed rail cars ready and waiting. As soon as the Yankees attempt to hit the swamp at the edge of the river, Capt. Pruden's artillery begins firing.

The cadets on the west side, still recovering from the freezing night, bring the muskets into action. The Fourth Kentucky and the cadets begin laying blistering firepower to the Federal forces.

As the skirmish rages, bullets whiz over head and the Federals are caught by surprise in the swamp. The advance of the Federal skirmish line is slow and deadly. Gen. Capers issues the command, "Charge!"

The cadets give the "rebel yell," in return.

Along with the 4th Kentucky by their side, they mount an assault to drive the Yankees back from the area surrounding the bridge.[462] As the charge begins, Norman and Paul roll over the breastworks and form in the line for the assault. Clayton climbs upon the breastworks and a Yankee Minnie ball smashes and tears into his right groin.[463] He falls to the ground in such a way that his twisted legs slow the bleeding almost to a stop.

Norman is about halfway down to the river's edge when, what appears to be the last volley from the Yankees, a Minnie ball ploughs along the right side of his face, carrying away part of the upper lobe of his ear. Holding his musket in his left hand, he feels his ear. "Warm and slippery, not good." He looks at his blood-covered fingers and begins to wonder exactly how severe his injury is. Fortunately, the Yankees are in full retreat.

Paul turns to Norman and sees his bloody hand. Rushing over to him along with some of his fellow cadets, Paul examines the wound. "Just nicked your ear." Taking a rag from his haversack, Norman squeezes it on his ear and they head back to the breastworks. "Have you seen Clayton, Norman?" asks Paul.

"He was behind us when we came over the works, but I don't see him now," says Norman. Looking around the area between them and the breastworks causes them to wonder where Clayton is. Unaware of their classmate's wounds, the company heads back to the breastworks.[464]

At the works, Gen. Wayne informs the cadets of the injuries of their fellow classmates. He also notifies the cadets that cadet Mac Hazelhurst is escorting Todd and Marsh, who have the most severe wounds, to the field hospital. Containing their emotions, they embrace each other. In one sense, they are glad they did not see their classmates in a grave condition, but they need to be with them for support. Shortly, Cadet Myrick appears with a bandage around his head. He sees Norman and asks, "Did you get grazed too?"

"Not a graze, just took off part of my ear. Did you see Todd or Marsh or Clayton before they left?" replies Norman.

"Yes, I was with them for a while. Todd is probably going to lose his arm, and I don't want to say what I feel about Marsh and Clayton," responds Myrick.

Norman pulls the small sack of salt from his haversack. He wets his bandage and pours some salt on the wet bandage. "What are you doing with the salt?" asks Paul.

"Pa said if salt will cure meat, it will help cure a wound," replies Norman. He soaks and squeezes his ear as he attempts to ignore the burning from the salt.

Gen. Capers assembles the Cadets, the Fourth Kentucky and the convicts for a quick briefing and to issue orders, "The Federals will surely return and look for us to still be on the west bank of the river so set up breastworks on the east bank. We'll defend both sides of the bridge. The Fourth Kentucky is to prepare to defend the center of the bridge. One of Capt. William Pruden's Battery guns is still mounted on the platform car for support. Gen. Wayne sends out a scout team to forewarn of any Union troops approaching. A member of the scout team is to report to him every hour. The small force rushes to establish new breastworks with trees, logs, trestle posts and rocks on the other side.

❧

Around three o'clock in the afternoon, the Yankees regimental band is playing the "Death March" in preparation of Rufus Kelly's hanging. Fortunately for Rufus, General Sherman enters the city of Gordon and the execution comes to a standstill. The general questions the lieutenant about the charges against Rufus. The lieutenant explains that a court martial was held yesterday and Rufus was found guilty of murder. General Sherman inquires as to whom he murdered. "Soldiers in my unit, sir" is the Lieutenant's reply. "He is a confederate soldier but is home on leave to recover from his wounds. Therefore, I consider him a civilian and not a soldier, sir."

"A soldier is a soldier, Lieutenant, whether on leave or on the field of battle. This man is a prisoner of war and his treatment is to be that of a prisoner. Bring him to my headquarters for questioning," orders General Sherman angrily.

The execution squad removes the nervous and shaking Rufus from his bindings and escorts him to General Sherman. The general questions Kelly in detail about supply depots between Gordon and Savannah. Rufus informs him that he has only been home for a week and therefore, can only pass to him about the military activity around Gordon. Upon dismissal, the General orders Rufus under guard.[465]

It becomes apparent as the sun begins to set that the Federals will attempt another assault on the Oconee Bridge before daybreak.[466] Another cold night in the trenches awaits Norman, Paul and their fellow cadets. Double sentries are posted along the trenches in case the enemy launches a surprise attack. Fortunately, no attack comes during the night.

15

PROUD AND STRONG

NOVEMBER 24, 1864

President Lincoln declares the day to be one of thanksgiving and praise. The same day, the cadets are thankful to see the rising sun and the warmth it will bring. The frost on the ground is as thick as a fresh snow.

As the cadets finish their dinner around 1:30 PM, long range artillery shells begin falling near the bridge. The light artillery barrage continues for most of the day, confining the cadets and prison soldiers in the trenches. Before dark, the Yankees become more earnest in their attempt to destroy the bridge.

"Look yonder, Norman!" shouts Paul. "The Yankees are placing cannons near the bridge."

Suddenly, a loud roar shatters through tree branches. In shock, the convicts retreat but the cadets stand fast. Under the cover of their own fire and darkness, the Yankees are able to set fire to the west end of the trestle leading to the bridge. The cannon fire stops.

"Are the Yankees still there?" asks Norman.

"Don't know. Maybe they are satisfied now that the bridge is on fire and are moving on. Just have to wait and see," replies Cadet Montgomery.

No sooner than that is said, another round of artillery comes whizzing overhead. The Yankees are approaching the bridge on foot, taking positions and begin a sweeping fire from along their line. The cadets return the fire with their muskets and, along with the railroad mounted cannon, hold the Yankees at bay for the entire day.

All through the night, Gen. Wayne's cadets can see fire and soldiers from the east side of the river. Little can be done to prevent it from spreading closer to the bridge.[467]

NOV 25, FRIDAY

The federal artillery continues to cover the burning trestle of the bridge with their infantry and light artillery. When all appears to be quiet, Cadet Hamilton moves through the trench to get some bacon and hard-tack. As he crosses an opening between two trenches, a Yankee sniper places Hamilton in his sights and fires. "Smack" sounds the sniper's round as it finds its mark. Hamilton rotates from the impact to his shoulder.[468]

Dropping his musket, he screams "I'm hit! I'm hit!" and at the same time, grabs his shoulder as he falls into the adjoining trench.

Cadets Brumby and Hazelhurst quickly attend his wound. Removing his jacket and shirt, they slow the bleeding with a pressure dressing hastily made from a torn part of his shirt.

Studying the extent of the wound Brumby relaxes. "You're lucky, Thomas. Looks like a flesh wound. No broken bones. Lie here and rest. We need to get you to the train and the hospital. You're going to be all right. The bleeding is stopping."

Finally, late in the afternoon, they see the Yankees removing their light artillery from the area. Gen. Capers sends out scouts and an advance guard to be sure that the Yankees are indeed gone. The scouts return and inform him that the Yankees are attempting a crossing above and below his position at the bridge. As dark approaches, Gen. Capers dispatches the cadets to extinguish the flames which by now, are beginning to burn several feet of the bridge proper.[469]

Cadet Marsh arrives at the Guyton Confederate Hospital,[470] unconscious and suffering with a high fever from a wound to the groin. Jennifer, who is now a nurse at Guyton, assists the stretcher bearers as they bring Cadet Marsh into the operating room. She recognizes Marsh as a cadet of GMI from the emblem on his uniform and remembers the discussion she and Polly had about how proud Polly was of her twin brother being a cadet at the institute. With Cadet Marsh being at her hospital, she realizes that the cadet corps must be somewhere close by.

Dr. William Lawton enters the operating room and examines Marsh. Probing with his fingers, he determines that his wound extends through the bladder and into the intestines. "There's nothing we can do for this poor lad. He is eaten away with infection. He'll not last another day. God be with him. Keep him as comfortable as possible." He leaves the room and heads to examine another wounded soldier.

Jennifer grasps the hot hand of Cadet Marsh with one of hers and feels his feverish head with her other. She thinks about Polly and Norman. She feels she must stay with Cadet Marsh, hoping he'll regain consciousness and let her know where he was wounded. Throughout the night, Jennifer sits and comforts his motionless body. At sunrise the next morning, his breathing becomes very shallow and is accompanied by a gurgling sound. Jennifer places her cheek next to his. He takes one last breath. His body turns gray and his lips darken as his soul departs his body. Tears seep from her eyes as she says a final prayer and gently places the sheet over his silent body.

Jennifer has the stableman gather her horse and buggy. They drive swiftly to Bartow Hospital. Upon arriving, she jumps from the buggy and rushes inside. Running to the front desk, she asks, "Is Polly Hill here today?"

"Yes, she's in the back preparing herbs. At the end of the hall. Last door on the right."

Jennifer rushes to find Polly who is preparing to leave with some herbs as Jennifer opens the door. "Hello, Jennifer. What a pleasant surprise," says Polly.

"Polly, I need to talk with you a minute. Can we sit down?" Polly detects some apprehension in Jennifer's voice and points to the two chairs nearby.

"Let's sit over here. What's going on?"

"Well, late yesterday, an ambulance brought in a wounded soldier. He was unconscious, suffering with high fever and had sustained a mortal wound to his groin, bladder and intestines. I stayed with him all night hoping he would regain consciousness. He never did and passed this morning with me at his side."

Polly, listening intensely, begins to understand that Jennifer's visit has to do with a loved one. Her eyes become wide as she asks, "Who was this soldier?"

Jennifer takes Polly's hands, "His name is Marsh and he is a GMI cadet." Polly stands and rushes to the window. Staring off into the distance, she utters, "That means the Cadet Corps and my brother are nearby!"

"But where? Poor Marsh had been transferred several times before arriving at Guyton and no one knew during which battle he was wounded. What army we have left is constantly moving, trying to get the best of Sherman, but his army outnumbers ours almost ten to one."

"I'll go to the Confederate headquarters and find out where the cadets are. I want to see that my brother is all right."

"My buggy is outside. I'll take you there," says Jennifer. They rush past the orderly and Polly informs him she is going to the Confederate Headquarters and that she may not return for the rest of the day. Outside, Jennifer unties the reins from the hitching post and they climb aboard the buggy. With a snap of the whip, the horse gallops toward the headquarters which is about one mile away. Once there, the two young women approach the guards.

"My name is Polly Hill and I would like to talk with your commander, please."

"Step inside and the orderly will assist you, Ma'am," replies the guard.

Inside, the sergeant asks, "What may I help you with?"

"I have a brother in the GMI cadet corps and understand they may be in this area. I would like to know their where-abouts if possible."

"Wait here. I'll ask the colonel if he has time to talk with you." The corridor in which they are waiting is extremely busy as soldiers pass in every direction, carrying stacks of papers and maps. They enter and leave the several different rooms on the second floor, as well as the ground floor. In a few minutes, the sergeant escorts a colonel from an office and introduces him to Polly and Jennifer.

"I understand you have a brother in the GMI corps and want to know their current location. I'm very sorry, but we cannot divulge troop locations. Gen. Hardee is currently in the field issuing new orders. However, the last report I received had the corps guarding the Oconee River Bridge, but they are no longer there. I wish I could give you more information and hope you understand. If you would like to write a letter to your brother, I'll be glad to place it in the army mail service."

"Thank you. I'll write it now, if you would be so kind to give me paper and pen."

"Certainly." The Colonel turns to his left, "Sergeant, allow this lady to sit at your desk to write to her brother."

"Yes, sir." He directs Polly to his desk and chair. He opens his top drawer and removes one small piece of stationery. "We are short on supplies, Ma'am. I hope this will do. Just fold the stationery and write your brother's name and unit on the outside. I'll seal your letter and place it in the mail." The sergeant and Jennifer move to one side and begin a conversation as Polly begins to write.

Thirty minutes later, Polly finishes her letter, signs it, and re-reads it. She hesitates a moment, satisfied with what she's written, and signs it.

Wiping a tear from her cheek, she gently kisses the letter, folds it in half and addresses the letter. After sitting for a moment, she summons the sergeant to let him know that the letter is ready. "Thank you, Sergeant, for allowing me to use your desk."

"You're welcome, Ma'am. I'll seal your letter." He reaches into another drawer and removes a wax stamp. He heats some sealing wax with the candle. Folding the letter a little more, he places the sealing wax upon its seam. Polly and Jennifer depart.

"I must get back to Guyton, but if you need me to stay with you, let me know," Jennifer says.

"I truly cannot thank you enough for coming by, Jennifer. Let's stay in touch." Polly watches until Jennifer is out of sight then goes back to the herbal medicine preparation. She remains very quiet for the remainder of the day. Her thoughts are with her brother. "First Legare and now Norman...." Polly shakes her head in an attempt to remove any desperate thoughts she has for her brother's well-being.

※

Gen. Hardee orders Gen. Wayne's command to load the trains and assemble in Tennille. The fatigued cadets, along with the remaining Confederate forces, depart the Oconee River Bridge a little after midnight. Awakening to the squeaking brakes and jerking motion of a slowing engine, the cadets arrive at Tennille around 5:30 on the morning on the 26th.[471] Gen. Capers gives word to the cadets that there's no enemy in the area, and they can continue to rest on the train. Huger's artillery is given orders to transfer to Gen. Wheeler's command.

Gen. Wayne finds out that his forces had held up an entire Yankee Division. He compliments them for holding the enemy in check for three days at the Oconee Bridge. Around 9:00 AM, Gen. Wayne receives orders to take his troops and the cadets to the Ogeechee Railroad Bridge.

"At least we are going by train this time!" exclaims Norman.

"Yep. Nice, dry, and warm," replies Paul. Wayne's command force now consists of 375 troops: the cadets, the Washington County Militia, the Milledgeville Infantry and Pruden's battery.

From November 29 until December 2, Gen. Wayne's command travels along the Central Road between Oliver's Station and the Ogeechee Station, strictly to observe the enemy. They maintain communications with Gen. Wheeler, informing his headquarters of Yankee troop movements and military activity. Gen. Wayne's troops are given orders not to fight since he does not have sufficient force.

On December 3, Gen. Wayne's force receives additional support from Baker's Brigade from North Carolina, the State Line, and the First Brigade of the state militia from Gen. G. W. Smith's Georgia Division, along with three cannons from Pruden's Battery. These forces are under the command of Gen. Robert Toombs with Gen. Capers serving as Chief of Staff. Orders are given to the new Confederate force of nearly 4,000 troops to form a line of battle on the east side of the little Ogeechee River.[472] On Sunday morning, Dec 4th, all is serene in the cadet's camp. Although the camp fires are burning briskly, the cadets are slow to rise. The shortage of rations and clothing is becoming somewhat bothersome. There's just enough to fill a grumbling stomach on this cold, crisp morning. Fortunately, there's an ample supply of ammunition. Norman puts on his warm boots and heads to a spring to fetch water. Again today, there's a great covering of frost on the ground. Startling a rabbit, both he and the animal jump with surprise. "You're all right, little fellow. I need to save my ammo or you'd be breakfast!"

Placing his pail in the clear water, Norman fills it nearly to the brim. Returning to the camp, he pours some water in a small kettle and sets it on the fire to boil. He and Paul warm by the fire along with their fellow cadets. Tightening his chin Norman confides in Paul, I'm really worried about Marsh. I pray he will be okay."

"So do I. We all hear the horror stories about going to a hospital. Maybe the ones in Savannah are better." Looking skyward, Paul says, "Hey the sun's coming out. Maybe that's a good sign that God heard our prayer."

The sun continues to climb in the sky, warming the clothes and souls of Norman and Paul. The water in the kettle finally begins to boil, and Norman takes a cloth and removes the kettle. Pouring some water into a bowl of grits, he refills the kettle and replaces it for use by someone else.

He takes a huge helping and savors it. "I never knew grits could taste so good." After their meager breakfast, the cadets gather round and begin cleaning their muskets.

Norman hears one of the cadets say, "These ol' muskets have served us well. No telling how many Yanks they've killed."

"Not near enough, though," replies another.

Norman shouts back, "Gotta get more to even the score for Marsh."

Paul is still warming his hands by the fire when he reflects his thoughts to Norman, "You think about this war Norman and we really haven't made an advance against those Yanks. We just sorta stay in front of them. No doubt we will be in Savannah before them."

Cadet Lt. Hill and some other cadets begin cleaning GMI's last two cannons and greasing the wheel axles. "Looks like our school is gone, Paul continues, and I sorta feel like we are polishing the cannons for their funeral. I just don't have a good feeling about our pitiful efforts."

"Well, Paul, just maybe these cannons can send a few hundred Yankees to their graves before they reach theirs. The other cannons have been abandoned because the cavalry needed the horses. Where will these two wind up? Our corps has been very fortunate. We've stuck together. We have had no desertions, very few injuries and only a few unfortunate deaths. We are probably the best the Confederacy has, yet we are more or less helpless," says Norman.

Paul folds his arms, "Yep Norman. That's no doubt probably true, but we are at the mercy of Joe Brown on one side and our commanders on the other side. But I know the Yankees are going to have the final say-so."

The others make rounds and hand out ammunition. As the sun rises to the noon hour, the sky is clear, and the young men are feeling much better. Some locals have brought sweet potatoes and cured ham by for them to eat for lunch. "Good food sure makes a difference," sighs Paul.

"Gets us in a mood for a good fight," replies Norman.

Around 1:30 PM, a scout hurries into camp, leaps from his lathered mount and reports to Gen. Wayne. "Sir, part of the advance guard of the Union XVII Corps is about three miles away and approaching on the left front of the cadets." Immediately, Gen. Wayne rushes from his headquarters tent and has his Aid-de-camp inform Gen. Capers, "Have the cadets march about a half mile and take position on the east side of the Ogeechee Creek. Put three artillery pieces of Prudden's mounted artillery in place along the river."

The giant pines rise straight toward the sky for nearly one hundred feet. Their crowns are a brilliant green. The trees are not thick and have very few if any lower branches to keep the ground free from undergrowth.[473]

Gen. Capers, orders Cadet Sgt. Coleman, a vedette, Cadet Rogers, Cadet Frank Patillo, and a squad to picket less than a mile from the camp. Rushing to their respective positions on the road, the cadets begin preparing their cover just as two of General Kilpatrick's cavalrymen come riding inattentively along the road.

Cadet Sgt. Coleman spots them first. "Look! Yankee's! Take cover."

When the Yankees are about fifteen feet from the cadet's outpost Coleman and Rogers jump from cover and, raise their muskets toward the heads of the Yankees. The other cadets are ordered to stay under cover in case more Yankees approach.

Coleman spots a Yankee. "Halt, dismount and surrender."

Caught by surprise, the Yankees rein their mounts to a halt. Instead of following the orders of Cadet Coleman to surrender, one of the Yankees demands, "I advise you, and the rest of those cadets or whatever you are, to surrender yourself."

As the Yankee is issuing his command, he attempts to draw his pistol. Without hesitation, Cadet Coleman, with his gun to his shoulder, aims and fires. The bullet goes straight to its mark, crashing through the head of the cavalryman. As the smoke of Cadet Coleman's rifle rises, the Yankee falls from his saddle, a dead man. The other horseman turns quickly and gallops away. The other horse, without its rider, runs behind him.

Taking a parting shot at the retreating scout, Coleman and his fellow pickets approach the dead Yankee. "This one is for Marsh." Coleman retrieves the dead Yankee's splendid pistol and new shoes.

"These should fit me." Coleman sits and removes his old, worn out ones and puts on the newly acquired Yankees boots. The other cadets search the body and remove gold and jewelry.

Admiring a gold watch, Rogers says, "Probably taken from the homes of a fellow Georgian." The pickets hurry to bury the dead Yankee. They are about to place him in a grave near where he was shot, when they hear horse hoof beats. "Look, Yankee cavalry! A bunch heading our way," shouts one of the cadets picketing down the road. The cadets throw down the shovels immediately and make a bee-line for the Confederate lines as the Yankee cavalrymen begin shooting at them the entire time.

Norman, Paul and the cadets hear the rifle fire. "Take your positions behind the breastworks," shouts the cadet company commander.

Norman and Paul rush to their positions behind the breastworks and are ready and waiting for the Yankees to approach. As Coleman and the other cadets begin crossing the stream, Norman and the cadets on the bank pour a volley of fire into the approaching cavalrymen, wounding and killing several of the attackers. The Yankees retreat. Breathing heavily and sweating profusely, Coleman and his fellow pickets take up arms next to the other cadets in the line. By now, the sun is high in the sky. Its warm rays and the flow of adrenalin prime the cadets for more action. Shouting orders all around, the cadets take their positions, load their muskets, attach their bayonets and look for the dust cloud that will accompany approaching horses.

Soon, the Yankees are back. Norman peers over the breastworks. "Back for more punishment. Helps even the score for Marsh and Hamilton."

The swamp, with all of its echoes, reverberates with the howling of musket fire. Loading and firing with sweat pouring from their brows, Norman, Paul and the cadets are unrelenting and merciless. They are acutely accurate in their mark on each Yankee who comes into their musket sight. The cannons cut through the trees and level a large number of the Union cavalry. Beaten, the Yankees retreat again and again and return only to receive the same punishment from the cadets.[474] "Looks like the Yankee ambulances are moving in. Guess they got all of us they wanted."

"Looks that way, Paul. I like war when we can get eye-to-eye with the enemy."

"Yes, Norman, but we had the river between us and them this time. Otherwise they would have overrun our position by their sheer numbers."

"I don't think so. Our cannon fire compensates for our lack of numbers. Anyhow we won the day."

Late in the afternoon, Gen. Lafayette McLaws arrives from Savannah to take command of Gen. Wayne's forces. McLaws knows that the Yankee forces out-number his and orders the troops to prepare to march back to Savannah the next day, December 5. Wayne is given orders to return to his desk in Milledgeville. The cadets and convicts are to remain on duty throughout the cold December night and are to rotate in and out of the train cars as has become the custom.

The cadets arrive at their new post on the 6th of December. Around mid-afternoon, they take position about three miles from Savannah and set up camp. The convicts serve as cooks, orderlies and waiters for the cadets. They are fed a good, hot meal of fresh rabbit, which had been caught by snares, and collards. The warm camp fires and good food compensates for the clear and cold December night. The Cadets are anxious to hear Cadet Coleman's story about killing the Yankee.

"Got a good pair of shoes, and we got some fine jewelry from the Yank. The jewelry probably was not his to start with. He probably stole it from around here! Best thing was his shoes." He lifts his feet to show the quality pair he now wears.[475]

Soon, the aroma of the stew is gone. Everyone turns in early, hoping to get a restful sleep. The convicts are given orders to rotate turns and keep the campfires going. All is quiet except for the crackling of new wood as it is thrown on the fire.

The GMI group is now under the command of Confederate Gen. Gustavus W. Smith's Militia Division.[476] Smith is under the command of Gen. Hardee who had charged him with defending a line approximately two and one half miles long with a scant 2000 troops. As the cadets approach the line early on the morning of December 7, they find that the terrain is very similar to that of the Oconee Bridge territory. The cadets and the convicts immediately began the construction of fortifications and trenches on the high ground overlooking the swamp. They complete the job, along with excellent emplacement positions for the cannons. Unlike Atlanta, these trenches have good drainage and are relatively quiet. The convicts have time to dig crude latrines and establish respectable kitchens. During the next ten days, with the help of the cadets, the Confederates are able to hold the line against the unaggressive forces of General Sherman.

There are no snipers, so the cadets are able to leave the trenches without fear of being shot. Some of the cadet corps receives orders to go to Fort Hardeman while others are sent to picket in advance of the front line beyond the rice fields.[477]

In the Federal earthworks facing the cadets are troops of the Third Division of the XX Corps. The two lines are far apart, and neither the Confederates nor Yankees are necessarily aggressive.[478] The roar of shells is heard only occasionally. The cadets get the news from Gen. Smith that no reinforcements are forth coming to aid in the defense of Savannah. He also discloses to the cadets that Sherman has sealed off all approaches to Savannah except for one road which leads from the eastern bank of the Savannah River into South Carolina.

AGAINST ALL ODDS

SATURDAY DECEMBER 10, 1864

SAVANNAH, GA.,
Friday December 9, 1864
Lieutenant General W. J. HARDEE, Commanding:

*GENERAL: It is my desire, after the consultation that has taken place, that
you should hold this city so long as in your judgment it may be advisable to
do so, bearing in mind that should you have to decide between a sacrifice of
the garrison or city, you will preserve the garrison for operations elsewhere.*

Very respectfully yours,

G. T. BEAUREGARD[479]

General Sherman changes his plans and concentrates on opening the
Union lines of communication for food and ammunition. The capture
of the railway bridge linking Savannah with Charleston prevents Gen.
Hardee's army from escaping the city.

General Sherman informs his staff, "All of our columns are pursuing
leisurely their march toward Savannah. Although corn and forage are becoming more and more scarce the rice-fields which are beginning to occur
along the Savannah and Ogeechee Rivers, will provide a good substitute,
both as food and forage." Looking skyward Colonel Dayton replies,

"The weather is fine, the roads good, and every thing seems to favor us.
Never do I recall a more agreeable sensation than the sight of our camps
by night, lit up by the fires of fragrant pine-knots."

General Sherman then tells Colonel Dayton, "It appears that Gen.
Hardee demonstrates that Savannah is well fortified and with a good

garrison. My first step is to open communication with the Union fleet, which is suppose to be waiting for us with supplies and clothing in Ossabaw Sound."[480]

The only major obstacle preventing General Sherman from reaching the Union navy at Tybee is Fort McAllister on the Great Ogeechee River. The fort's primary construction is to defend naval assaults. However, with the coming of General Sherman, the Fort becomes vulnerable by land.

⬥

Maj. Anderson comes ashore at Whitemarsh early and has his Regiment to take ranks. "Stand at ease, gentlemen. I have some new orders and news for some of you today. General Sherman is marching toward Savannah. I am going to assign two companies of this regiment as reinforcements for Fort McAllister. The fort is twenty-five miles from Savannah on the Ogeechee River and six miles below the railroad bridge. All of the men, who are not on outpost or guard duty on Whitemarsh, prepare for the battle at Fort McAllister.[481] Gather your equipment and we will depart immediately. Dismissed."

Samuel Moore begins to gather his equipment with his brother Spencer. "From what I have heard neither Gen. Johnston nor Gen. Hood have been able to slow Billy Boy down. It's going to be a tough battle at McAllister. Those Yanks are gonna have to come and get us because we are not going to give the Fort to them. I've got to finish gathering up now, but we will see each other again." Samuel turns and goes to his tent and remaining equipment.

Shortly, his commander orders, "Fall-in."

Soon the two regiments are on the boats heading for Fort McAllister. As Samuel and his brother depart, Samuel gives his remaining comrades on Whitemarsh Island a hearty salute and smile, "See you soon."

When Samuel, his brother and their fellow soldiers arrive and are settled, Maj. George Anderson gathers the two regiments for a briefing on the Fort. "This fort is built on the south side of the river, and east of it is a marsh. The south and west side are protected by a moat ten feet wide and six feet deep. As you can see, we have an unrestricted view of the front. The moat is full of water. Look toward the moat and see the abatis."

Samuel moves closer to the wall of the Fort and visually inspects the area as Maj. Anderson continues, "The pointed edge and leaning of the fresh oak should hold back any enemy that is able to cross the moat. Fifty feet outside the moat are two rows of Chevau-de-frise. Capt. Clinch and his men have just completed this array of barbed wire and the wire is strongly attached to the wooded poles. Lt. Hazzard just completed the last project. The planting of one hundred torpedoes that will explode with five pounds pressure. So do not go down into that area without Capt. Clinch or one of his men."

"Capt. Clinch, take some men and set fire to all officers' quarters which are outside the fort. Leave the milk dairy. Once the officer quarters are burning, finish completely cutting the trees that are within two hundred yards of the fort with the exception of some large pines near the dairy."[482]

"Now, let's take a quick walk around the inside. There's a bomb-proof shelter here in the center of the Fort."

"What's a bomb-proof?" somebody asks Samuel.

Maj. Anderson looks at the soldier and explains, "A bomb-proof is a shelter built of heavy timber and covered with soil. The gun chambers in the fort are constructed in the same manner. The bomb-proofs are almost impossible to penetrate with cannon or mortar fire."[483]

Samuel and several others proceed to gather hay and straw and place huge amounts in the several officers' quarters. At a given signal, each of the quarters is set to blaze. Standing somewhat apart from the quarters, they see smoke first starts from the under the door. Soon the windows explode outward from the heat as the flames begin to show their ugly tongues. Satisfied the fires are sufficient, Samuel is issued a two-man saw. He and another squad member begin the task of removing the remaining marked trees in front of the fort.

One day after the preparations are complete, a hog wanders through the woods and steps on one of the torpedoes and is killed instantly. With the sound of the exploding torpedo, Samuel takes up his arms rushing forward to his post. Expecting to see Yankees advancing on the fort, he's puzzled. There are no further ordinances heard, no shots are fired and there are no advancing Yankees.

Their regiment commander orders, "Take this squad out to inspect of the area of the explosion."

Cautiously, the squad moves about, knowing where all of the mines are buried. As they approach the area in question, to their surprise they find a dead pig.

"Man, oh man, fresh meat is scarce around here. This sure is a welcomed accident. A supply of pork out of the clear sky!"[484] Samuel motions for help. The men are happy to help move the hog to a safer area, hang it head down from a tree, and slit its throat.

For supper, the fresh pork and rice stew is a special treat. Samuel and his fellow soldiers enjoy the feast immensely. While Samuel and his friend Michael Stone are eating, fragments from a shell begin falling all around. Samuel ducks a little and turns his head while looking over his shoulder, "Those fragments are coming from the battle at the railroad bridge. They must be firing at a high angle since the bridge is about six miles away."

Just at that time, a piece of shell falls right between Samuel and Michael, throwing some ash from the campfire into the plates. Samuel falls back from fright, but Michael looks straight up as if expecting another shell and exclaims, "Egad, they like to have got me that time, didn't they? I think the Yanks know we have fresh pork and are jealous."[485]

Samuel stands and shakes the ash from his clothing. "Could have got either one of us."

MONDAY, DECEMBER 12

During his staff meeting, General Sherman turns to General Kilpatrick. "I want you to cross the Great Ogeechee and scout the approaches to Fort McAllister. Several nights previous, I had General Howard send one of his best scouts, Captain Duncan, with two men, in a canoe, to drift past Fort McAllister. They are to convey to the naval fleet knowledge of my approach."[486]

The next day, General Kilpatrick reports to General Sherman, who is meeting with General Slocum and General Howard. "Sir, I have reconnoitered the area around the fort with my scouting party. With a little help from the infantry, my cavalry can capture that little sand fort fairly quickly."[487]

"Okay, General Kilpatrick, thank you for your report. Now I want your cavalry to transfer to the south bank of the Ogeechee. You will open communication with a vessel belonging to our blockading fleet. Begin your operations immediately."

"Yes sir." General Kilpatrick salutes and departs headquarters.

One-armed General Oliver Howard says, "I know General Hazen and his division of infantry. His division is the same old one which I had commanded at Shiloh and Vicksburg. I have a lot of special pride and confidence in this division." General Sherman shakes his head in agreement.

General Sherman reviews the reports with Generals Slocum and Howard and studies the maps of the area. "It appears that Fort McAllister has a strong defense against an approach from the sea, but I believe a land based attack will be successful."

Returning to the conference table General Howard tells General Sherman, "I would like to volunteer Hazen's Division for the assault."

"I see no reason why General Hazen's brigade of the Fifteen Corps could not be successful in an assault on Fort McAllister," replies General Sherman. "General Howard, send a division with all your engineers to Grog's Bridge, fourteen and a half miles southwest from Savannah. They are to rebuild the bridge. General Slocum you are to press the siege on Savannah as soon as possible.[488] Any questions?"

General Howard and General Slocum shake their heads and each answers, "No questions, sir."

"Then proceed."

On the evening of the 12th, General Sherman rides over King's Bridge and spends the night at King's house with General Howard and General Hazen's division of the Fifteenth Corps. His engineers are hard at work on the bridge, completing the repairs the previous night. At sunrise, Hazen's division passes over Grog's Bridge. General Sherman himself gives General Hazen his orders, "March rapidly down the right bank of the Ogeechee. From there and without hesitation, your division is to assault and carry Fort McAllister by storm. I know the fort to be strong in heavy artillery against an approach from the sea but it is open and weak to the rear. On your action, and your action alone, depends the safety of the whole Union army, and the success of the campaign. General Kilpatrick is farther down the coast to Kilkenny Bluff, or St. Catharine's Sound. There he hopes to be successful in establishing communication with a Union vessel of the blockade fleet. Good luck and God's speed, General."[489]

"Thank you sir." General Hazen salutes and departs, realizing his awesome task and he prepares mentally for the assault. General Sherman and General Howard escort General Hazen to his waiting mount and observe his departure.

Although the bridge is about eight miles from Fort McAllister, Samuel and the members of his regiment stand on the battery walls. The garrison at the fort is able to witness the fight for the bridge. General Sherman's troops capture the bridge is less than an hour.

Samuel turns and warns Stone. "There's nothing between us and the bridge but marsh. I think tomorrow will be our time to meet the Yankees."

The troops begin checking to ascertain that the necessary preparations are in order for giving Sherman's men a warm reception. The men check that ammunition is at every point for the sharpshooters and riflemen. The artillery soldiers place extra cannon balls and powder at each battery. The big guns are set to fire directly at the avenues of approach of the advancing Yankees.

⚬❧

Maj. Anderson rises early to witness a beautiful, sunny Tuesday, December 13th, morning. During Assembly, the roll call has 155 men answer present for duty. "Our scouts reports Union forces in our area and they may attempt to take the Fort. Each soldier is to man their station. Take ammo and rations and stay at your post until further notice. Dismissed."

At daybreak on the 13th, General Hazen places his troops into motion and reaches the vicinity of Fort McAllister around 11 AM. About one mile from the fort his scouts capture a Confederate picket who is taken to General Hazen's headquarters. Under severe interrogation the Confederate reveals the whereabouts of a line of torpedoes across the jetty to the fort. Under guard, the prisoner is taken to the area and assist in removing the torpedoes. No loss of life occurs.[490]

Now that the danger of the torpedoes are removed, General Hazen orders eight regiments of the Fifteenth Michigan and the Ninety-ninth Indiana in reserve. He has the Third Brigade form the center division line with the Ninetieth Illinois on the right. From here General Hazen directs the Fort-eight Illinois to the center of the line and the Seventieth Ohio on the left.

When the troops are in position General Hazen raises his sword as the signal and the troops begin moving forward to about 600 yards from the fort.[491]

About ten o'clock in the morning, Maj. Anderson, scanning through his binoculars spots the enemy entering the woods and beginning to form in line of battle.

"Look there, Sergeant," says Maj. Anderson. "The Union infantry is taking cover behind the big trees near that small dairy building." Looking further, he observes other Yankees filling the dairy building to capacity. "Sgt. have our sharpshooters take a crack at every 'Bluecoat' that dares to expose himself."

An artilleryman approaches. "Sir, may I place a cannon ball through the dairy building?"

"Be my guest Lt." The Lt. sets his sights and fires a 30 pound rifled shot through the center of the dairy. "Sgt. alert all of the men. The action is fixin' to pick up."[492]

"Yes sir."

General Hazen's 1500 troops of his 9000 continue to deploy in a skirmish line near the fort to keep Maj. Anderson's gunners from firing their cannons with any effect toward the rear in the barbette. The environment renders the deployment of that part of the line slow and difficult.

⋇

General Sherman and General Howard ride with their staff ten miles down the left bank of the Ogeechee. Here, they reach the rice-plantation of a Mr. Cheevea. General Howard establishes a signal-station to overlook the lower river. They watch for any vessel of the blockade squadron which General Kilpatrick has communicated.[493]

On reaching the rice-mill at Cheevea's, General Sherman finds a guard on post and notes that a couple of twenty-pound Parrott of De Gress's battery are missing. However, other cannons fire an occasional shot toward Fort McAllister which is in plain view over the salt-marsh about three miles distant. Fort McAllister has the rebel flag flying, and occasionally sends a heavy shot back across the marsh to the Cheevea's plantation. General Sherman says, "Everything about the place looks as peaceable and quiet as on the Sabbath except for the cannon fire."[494]

The signal officer builds a platform on the ridge-pole of the rice mill. General Sherman and his staff leave their horses behind the stacks of rice-straw and climb on to the roof of a shed attached to the mill. From here, General Sherman can communicate with the signal officer above and look out toward Ossabaw Sound and across the Ogeechee River at Fort McAllister at the same time.[495]

About two PM, General Sherman gets General Howard's attention and points toward Fort McAllister, "There are some signs of commotion in the fort. Look there. One or two guns firing inland." The two generals take their field glasses and study the Fort and its surrounding woods.

"General Sherman, there's some musket-skirmishing in the woods close to the fort." General Sherman turns his attention in that direction.

❧

Maj. Anderson directs Capt. Clinch's 4th Georgia Artillery Company, "Rain a deadly artillery fire upon the advancing Yankees."

A hail of artillery fire ensues upon the advancing Yankees.

General Hazen raises his sword toward his sharpshooter directing them to keep up a steady fire on the Confederates who are operating the guns. With their powerful scopes and Spencer Rifles, the sharpshooters are able to kill off numerous gunners as they attempt to sight the cannons.

Maj. Anderson rushes to aid the artillerymen, barely avoiding death himself. Each time a Confederate attempts to sight a cannon he is taken down by a Union sharpshooter. Unable to maintain the cannon fire after several hours, the Yankees pass over the Confederate obstacles.

"I can only assume the assault is the approach of Hazen's division toward Fort McAllister." Pacing, General Sherman says, "I am growing impatient with this slow progress. It is growing late." Chewing on his cigar, he returns, "Signal General Hazen to take the fort today."

General Sherman, by now vigorously chewing on his cigar, strains his eyes to witness the attack by General Hazen's forces. The signal officer rushes to General Sherman. "Sir, I have a message from General Hazen."

"Well, what is it? Give it to me."

"I am preparing to assault the fort. Is General Sherman present?"

"I hope you replied before bringing me this message."

"Yes sir, I did. I assured General Hazen of this fact and that you expected the fort to be in Union hands before night."

As the sun moves deeper into the western sky, General Sherman receives by signal the assurance of General Hazen that he is making his preparations and will soon commence the assault. General Sherman becomes dreadfully impatient.

At that very moment, someone discovers a faint cloud of smoke and an object gliding, possibly a union naval vessel, along the horizon above the tops of the sedge toward the sea. Little by little, the image grows. It is the smoke-stack of a Union steamer coming up the river.

"It must be one of our squadron!" shouts General Sherman excitedly. Soon, the flag of the United States is plainly visible. General Sherman and his staff's attention is now divided between the approaching steamer and the expected assault. When the sun is about an hour high above sunset, another signal-message comes from General Hazen that all is ready.

Sherman replies, "Tell the man to hurry and that I am waiting." As the Union steamer is approaching from below, they are able to make out a group of officers on the deck of this vessel, signaling with a flag.

"Who are you?" The answer went back promptly,

"General Sherman."

Then follows the question, "Is Fort McAllister taken?"

"Not yet, but it will be in a minute!" Almost at that instant of time, 4:45 PM, the bugle sounds the forward and General Hazen's troops charge forward in one thin line as possible to avoid being struck until they are in close quarters with Maj. Anderson's garrison.[496] General Sherman throws down his cigar, and then he and General Howard strain their eyes watching every possible move of the battle, "Our men are passing the fallen trees. Some have fallen but are getting back up. Must be the snares."

Elated General Howard tries to direct General Sherman's attention, "Over there General, to your left, a large group of our men are already over three rows of abatis and two rows of chevau-de-frise."

"Yes, another company is across those wide ditches. The men of the second division are performing gallantly. They've crossed every obstruction. I have yet to see anyone wavering nor faltering for an instant."

With adrenaline pumping, General Hazen leads as the Yankees' charge violently up the parapets. As General Hazen's troops come out of the dark fringe of woods that encompasses the fort, General Sherman shouts, "Look, there they are, almost to the fort. The battle lines look like a dress parade. Even the flags are flying and moving forward with a quick, steady pace as if to predict victory."

Fort McAllister is now all alive; Capt. Clinch orders big guns into action. The dense clouds of smoke soon envelopes the union's assaulting lines. "Even if you can't see the Yankees, keep firing." commands Maj. Anderson.

General Sherman lowers his field glasses. "I just saw the Color Bearer of the Seventieth Ohio killed while climbing over the abatis."

Major Howard scans the charging troops for the fallen Colors. "Just got picked up, General."[497]

As the lines advance the fighting becomes desperate and deadly. Just outside the works is a line of torpedoes which explode blowing many

Yankees to atoms. General Hazen's troops continue the assault over, under and through abatis, ditches, palisading, and parapets. Captain Grimes, Fort-eight Illinois Volunteers sharpshooters silence two of the 10 inch guns bearing down on the advancing Union troops.

Then there's a pause, a cessation of fire faintly seen in the white, sulfurous smoke. As the smoke clears away, the parapets are covered by the blue of the charging Union soldiers. The flag of the Seventieth Ohio is the first on the fort. Samuel sees Capt. Clinch, already suffering from wounds, take on a Yankee officer with a blow from his sword, demanding him to surrender. Capt. Clinch assaults the Yankee Captain as several other Yankees cut Capt. Clinch. He grimaces at least six times from the saber and bayonet wounds, and finally, two gunshots bring him down.[498]

Samuel sees Lt. Hazzard lying on the ground with the blood oozing from the side of his mouth. Then he sees Capt. Clinch being surrounded by Yankees, but he is unable to load any faster. He engages a Yankee in hand-to-hand combat with bayonets. Samuel brings the Yankee down as he runs his bayonet through his neck. The screaming and moaning of the wounded and the silence of the dead becomes more apparent as Samuel and his Confederates are driven from one bomb proof shelter to another. The assault ends almost as fast as it began with each Confederate individually, soundly overcome.

Lowering his field glasses, General Sherman glances over at General Howard. "The battle was desperate and deadly." He looks at his watch. "It took Hazen fifteen minutes to capture the fort with our mass of troops."

Samuel Moore surrenders as he watches while the last shot fires from a 12-pound Howitzer. The soldier who was to fire the cannon is holding the lanyard and is ordered to let it go by a Yankee officer before the flag is raised.

The man looks the Yankee sternly in the face, "I am not taking orders from you yet, you Yankee dog."

The Yankee officer, without hesitation, shoots the Confederate soldier with his pistol. The Confederate grabs his chest with one hand, determined from within as he recoils and falls, his other hand never releases the lanyard and his body weight pulls the lanyard firing the cannon. With charging Yankees not three feet from the mouth of the cannon, the ball opens a space through the charging line removing heads and limbs of the unfortunate.[499]

Even with his severe wounds, Capt. Clinch survives the battle. He receives medical treatment and is taken prisoner with the remainder of the garrison. Many of Lt. Hazzard's men of Company B of the Ga 4th, "Glynn Guards" die or become prisoners. The fort never surrenders. It is captured after sixteen Confederates are killed and fifty-four are wounded. Twenty were killed and seventy two wounded on the Union side.[500]

General Sherman calls his signal-officer over. "Signal our navy friends on the approaching gunboat and give them the good news that Fort McAllister is ours." As the Union flag is raised over the parapet, General Sherman turns to General Howard, "In the language of the poor Negro at Cobb's plantation, "This nigger will have no sleep this night!""[501]

Samuel, sitting in the prisoner line, says to one of his comrades, "We killed more Yankees than we had on our side of the battle. It is a mystery to me how those Yankees moved that barricade, crossed the moat, and captured Fort McAllister what seemed like inside of four minutes."

His comrade, Michael Stone answers, "They had 9,000 men!"

⁂

General Sherman says, "I must personally communicate with the Union fleet, Major Audenried."

At the wharf, belonging to Cheeves's Mill, is a small skiff. Later Audenried returns. "General, I have a volunteer crew and several young officers who are good oarsmen to take you to Fort McAllister."

"Do you mind if I accompany you?" asks General Howard.

"You certainly may." The two Generals climb into the skiff and take seats near the stern of the boat. The tide is strong, with small white caps glistening in the moonlight. The crew has a hard pull even though the distance is only three miles as the crow flies. On the way, they pass the wreck of a Union steamer which had been sunk during a naval attack on Fort McAllister some years before. General Sherman views the wreck in silence wondering, how many sailors were lost in this encounter.

The wounded of both sides are taken to the McAllister homestead for medical treatment. Samuel, still ill, though not wounded is on the sick list. His cough is deep and his throat sore. He places his hand on his throat each time he swallows in a vain attempt to ease the pain. The homestead is crowded with Yankees and Confederate wounded.

The smell of blood from the moist bandages reeks in the still air, even with the cold December temperature. The morphine keeps most of the pain under control. Yet as Samuel is assigned to his bunk with a badly wounded Yankee boy, a still unconscious patient appears on a stretcher with only one leg and a bright red bandage covering the stub below his knee. Exhausted, Samuel is concerned about his brother and lies down. He yawns once and sleep overtakes him rapidly.[502]

Later on in the night, Samuel is awakened by the Yankee boy lying next to him. He is hot with fever and mumbling loudly. Samuel sits up and takes the young lad's hand.

The boy grasps Samuel's hand, turns his head toward him and gasps, "Thank you, kind sir." A long dying breath follows.

Samuel releases the lad's hand and then gently closes his open lifeless eyes, and says," God bless you son."

When the nurse comes by, Samuel whispers to her, "The boy is dead."

The nurse pulls the cover from the lad's face. "You're right. I'll take him out directly."

Samuel is too exhausted to stay awake and lies back down next to the dead boy. When he wakes up the next morning, the cold stiff body is still next to him.

Soon the Yankee nurse comes to his bedside and says, "I am sorry that I have not removed the body."

Samuel responds, "Oh, that's all right; he has not disturbed me at all. It has always been my policy to accept conditions over which I have no control without question or complaint. Wouldn't have anything for my throat, would you?"

"Sore throat medicine is only for Union troops."

Night has set in when General Sherman and his crew discover a soldier on the beach. Sherman inquires if he knows the location of General Hazen's headquarters. The soldier replies, "General Hazen is at the Middleton house of the overseer of the McAllister plantation, sir."[503]

"Take us there." After tying the skiff to a drift log, they follow the soldier through bushes to a frame-house which is standing in a grove of live-oaks near a row of Negro quarters.

General Hazen is there with his staff, preparing supper. "Hello and congratulations General Hazen."

Surprised and joyful, General Hazen rushes to General Sherman and salutes, then shakes hands and invites General Sherman and his staff to join them for supper. "We're having fresh pork, greens and cornbread. Found some good wine around here too."

During supper Generals Sherman and Howard toast General Hazen most heartily. "For your brilliant success and you have our praise in its manner of execution."

General Hazen explains to Sherman the exact results in detail. "We found the fort is an enclosed work. Its land-front was in the nature of a bastion and curtains, with good parapet, ditch, fraise, and chevaux-de-frise."

General Sherman replies, "We observed your division crossing over."

"Luckily for us, the rebels had left the larger and unwieldy trunks on the ground, which serve as good cover for the skirmish-line. Our line crept behind these logs. I had my sharpshooters positioned there. A great advantage point for us. They kept the artillerists from loading and firing their guns accurately. Nearly every time an artillerist exposed himself, he was shot."

"Which line did you come from?"

"The assault was made by three parties in line, one from below, one from above the fort, and the third directly in rear, along the capital. All were simultaneous, and had to pass a good abatis and line of torpedoes."

"You mean the Confederates put out those torpedoes again? Need to have the Confederates walk the area themselves blindfolded to clear the area."

"Unfortunately sir, the torpedoes actually killed more of the Yankees than the heavy guns of the fort, which generally overshot the mark. Our entire loss is, killed and wounded, ninety-two."

"So we saw your men coming from the woods."

"Yes, sir, each party reached the parapet and the inside of the garrison about the same time. There were about two hundred and fifty Confederates. We killed or wounded about fifty. The rest were overpowered by our troops."

"Did you capture or kill the commanding officer."

"The commanding officer, Maj. Anderson, became our prisoner. Sir, may I invite Maj. Anderson to have supper with us?"

"Yes, I would like to talk with the Maj. Invite him." After social amenities, General Sherman levels his gaze at the Confederate Major enter into a lively discussion about military tactics and torpedoes.

General Sherman informs General Hazen, "There is a Union gunboat in the river below the fort and out of sight by a point of timber. I must board the gunboat tonight at whatever risk or cost to check on the advance on Savannah."

After supper, General Sherman and his staff walk down to the fort which is nearly a mile from the house. As Sherman approaches the fort, a sentinel cautions him, "Sir, be very careful, as the ground outside the fort is full of torpedoes." No sooner has the sentinel spoken than a torpedo explodes, and General Sherman retreats a few steps. The explosion tears to pieces a poor soldier who is hunting for a dead comrade.[504]

Inside the fort, General Sherman has the guide raise the lantern as he passes the dead, lying where they have fallen. A swamp rat races across General Sherman's boot. Taking the lantern from the guide, the General sees rats around every corpse competing with the flies for the abundant blood. The rats lick the blood from the skin and clothing of the dead. They eat at the open wounds and the flies crawl over the exposed skin picking at the cool flesh. The light breeze does little to keep the odor of the decomposing blood and exposed flesh from the noses of the viewers … General Sherman thinks, "These brave men, whoever they are can hardly be distinguished from their living comrades. They simply appear to be sleeping soundly side by side in the pale moonlight. May their souls rest in peace."

In the river close by the fort, a good yawl is tied to a stake, but the tide is high. The volunteers require some time to get it in to the bank. The commanding officer of the fort mans the boat with a good crew of his men. General Howard and General Sherman board and pull downstream, cautiously aware of the warnings about the torpedoes.

The night is unusually bright. General Sherman expects to find the gunboat within a mile or so. However, after pulling down the river for fully three miles and not seeing the gunboat, he begins to think she has turned and gone back to the sound. Following the bends of the river for about six miles below McAllister, he spots her light, and soon is hailed by the vessel at anchor. Stopping alongside, Sherman announces his presence. When he boards, he is greeted with great warmth and enthusiasm by half a dozen naval officers, among them Captain Williamson, United States Navy. The ship is the *Dandelion*. She is a tender of the regular gunboat *Flag* with her post at the mouth of the Ogeechee.

General Sherman's clerk rushes to him. "Sir, I have a message for you from Captain Duncan." General Sherman takes the message and reads it out loud to General Howard.

"I have safely reached the squadron and communicated the good news of their approach. Admiral Dahlgren commands the South-Atlantic Squadron and is engaging in the blockade of the coast from Charleston's south. He is aboard his flag-ship, the *Harvest Moon*. It is lying in Wassaw Sound. General John Foster is in command of the Department of the South, with his headquarters at Hilton Head. Also there are several ships with stores for the army. They are anchored in Tybee and in Port Royal Sound. All thoughts seem to be on you, sir, in Georgia since all communication is cut with General Grant. Sir, the Rebel newspapers say you've been harassed, defeated and starving and that you're fleeing to the coast, Signed, Captain Duncan."

"Well, we are at the coast. They got that much right!" General Sherman laughs.

He asks for pen and paper. He writes several hasty notes to General Foster, Admiral Dahlgren, General Grant, and the Secretary of War, giving in general terms the actual state of affairs, including the capture Fort McAllister. Most important is General Sherman's request that means must be taken to establish a line of supply from the vessels in port up the Ogeechee to the rear of the his army. As a sample, General Sherman gives one of these notes, addressed to the Secretary of War, and intended for publication to relieve the anxiety of their friends at the North generally, to his staff to be posted.[505]

ON BOARD DANDELION, *OSSABAW SOUND,*
December 13, 1864, 11:50 PM

To Hon. E. M. STANTON, Secretary of War, Washington, D. C.:

Today, at 6 PM, General Hazen's division of the Fifteenth Corps carried Fort McAllister by assault, capturing its entire garrison and stores. This opened to us Ossabaw Sound, and I pushed down to this gunboat to communicate with the fleet. Before opening communication, we had completely destroyed all the railroads leading into Savannah, and invested the city. The left of the army is on the Savannah River three miles above the city, and the right on the Ogeechee, at King's Bridge. The army is in splendid order, and equal to anything. The weather has been fine, and supplies were abundant. Our march was most agreeable, and we were not at all molested by guerrillas.

We reached Savannah three days ago, but, owing to Fort McAllister, could not communicate; but, now that we have McAllister, we can go ahead. We have already captured two boats on the Savannah River.

I estimate the population of Savannah at twenty-five thousand, and the garrison at fifteen thousand. Gen. Hardee commands.

We have not lost a wagon on the trip; but have gathered a large supply of Negroes, mules, horses, etc., and our teams are in far better condition

than when we started. My first duty will be to clear the army of surplus
Negroes, mules, and horses. We have utterly destroyed over two hundred
miles of rails, and consumed stores and provisions that were essential to
Lee's and Hood's armies.

The quick work made with McAllister, the opening of communication
with our fleet, and our consequent independence as to supplies, dissipate
all their boasted threats to head us off and starve the army.

I regard Savannah as already gained.

Yours truly,

W. T. SHERMAN, Major-General[506]

Late that night, the tide is running ebb-strong. General Sherman's appearance is stern. "Captain Williamson, tow me and my staff up as near
Fort McAllister as possible but beware of the torpedoes."

"Yes, fear not about the torpedoes, I dread them as much as you, sir."

The *Dandelion* steams up some three or four miles, till the lights of
Fort McAllister are visible and anchors. General Sherman arrives at the
fort in their own boat. General Sherman and General Howard walk up to
the McAllister House. Inside General Hazen and his officers are asleep on
the floor of one of the rooms. Tired himself, General Sherman lies down
on the floor and soon is fast asleep but is awakened shortly. He could hear
that someone in the room was inquiring for him among the sleepers.

"General Sherman, sir!"

"I am here, soldier. What is it that you need?"

The young officer replies, "Sir, I am told that an officer of General
Foster's staff is here from a steamboat anchored below McAllister. The
courier states the general is extremely anxious to see you on important
business, but that he is lame from an old Mexican-War wound, and cannot
possibly climb to the house."[507]

General Sherman is extremely weary from the incessant labor of
the day and night before, but again walks down the sandy road to Fort
McAllister. There he finds a boat awaiting him and his staff. He and his
staff board the craft and travel three miles down the river, to the steamer
W. W. Coit. On board, General Sherman finds General Foster.

"Greetings General Sherman."

"Greetings to you, General."[508]

"I have just come from Port Royal, expecting to find Admiral Dahlgren in Ossabaw Sound. However hearing the delightful news of the capture of Fort McAllister, I decided to visit with you." General Foster describes the condition of affairs with his own command in South Carolina. "We made several serious efforts to effect a lodgment on the railroad which connects Savannah with Charleston near Pocotaligo. However, we failed in reaching the railroad itself, though I have a full division of troops. They are still strongly entrenched, near Broad River, within cannon-range of the railroad. Moreover, at Port Royal, abundant supplies of bread and provisions, as well as of clothing, designed for your use is in waiting."

General Sherman responds, "We still had in our wagons and in camp abundance of meat, but we need bread, sugar, and coffee. It is all important that a route of supply should at once be opened for which purpose the assistance of the navy is indispensable." Sherman accordingly steams down the Ogeechee River to Ossabaw Sound, in hopes to meet Admiral Dahlgren. Upon arriving, Sherman finds Admiral Dahlgren absent. He continues on by the inland channel to Warsaw Sound, where he finds the *Harvest Moon*, and Admiral Dahlgren.

Admiral Dahlgren gratefully informs General Sherman, "There is nothing in my power, which I would not do to assist you and to make our campaign absolutely successful."

The admiral goes at once to find vessels of light draught to carry supplies from Port Royal to Cheeves's Mill or to Grog's Bridge. From there, they can be taken by wagons to General Sherman's camps. "I'll return to Fort McAllister with you, General Sherman, to superintend the removal of the torpedoes, and to relieve you of all the details of this most difficult work."

"Thank you, Admiral. That is a big help," replies General Sherman.[509]

Later the next morning, Samuel is able to sit on a log and talk to a messmate, exchanging experiences of the day before, when a Yankee soldier comes and sits with them. The Yankee's head is so bandaged that one of his eyes is closed.

"My chum was one of the sharpshooters, and he was pretty sure he got one of the Yankees. Said he shot at him just as he peeped around a tree and saw the bark fly, but did not see the Bluecoat anymore," relates Samuel.

"I guess I was the one." He shows Samuel where the bullet had just grazed his eyebrow, "I thought I would lose my eye." Surprisingly, the Yankee talks about his experience without any apparent animosity.[510]

Samuel lays down his fork, stares across the table at his messmate and the Yankee, "It is hard to understand how two men on opposite sides of a battle, sitting on a log after the smoke has cleared away, calmly and peaceably discuss how they tried to kill each other the day before."

The Yankee doctors are patching up the wounded of both sides. Samuel, though still sick, watches one surgery on a terribly dismembered Yankee. He ponders, "Slight wounds will sometimes prove fatal and another person might recover when terribly mutilated. I am watching a Yankee soldier carved just to my taste. His left arm is unjointed at the shoulder. He has three fingers removed from his right hand; his left leg is amputated below the knee. His right leg amputated above the knee. A liberal slab of his skull is being trepanned and replaced with a silver plate, and the man recovers."[511]

Samuel finds out that his brother Spencer is mortally wounded during the battle and has to beg the authorities everyday to let him visit his brother. Samuel remains persistent and when poor Spencer's condition is critical, the doctor allows Samuel to visit his dying brother. Samuel spends two hours sitting by the bedside and holding the hand of his brother. Spencer can barely speak and his color is pale. His fever is high and his perspiration has a strong odor. Samuel takes a warm damp cloth and gently wipes his brother's brow, face and neck. Spencer whispers to Samuel, "I joined the Presbyterian Church on the island. I know I am going to die, but the hope of a glorious resurrection awaits me." Spencer inhales deeply as his wounds allow. "Be true to the South and your God."[512]

Then Spencer closes his eyes and continues his shallow breathing.

Samuel begins to cry as he kisses his brother on the forehead and on his hands. He whispers in his brother's ear, "May your soul rest in peace."

Spencer dies the following day.[513] By the 16th, many steamboats pass up as high as King's Bridge; among them, one which General Grant dispatches with the mail for the army which has accumulated since General Sherman's departure from Atlanta. This mail is most welcome to all the officers and soldiers of the army, who have been cut off from friends and the world for two months.

17

SURRENDER OR DIE

DECEMBER 18, 1864

General Sherman receives information from General Foster that the Union fleet is in position and near enough to reach the centre of Savannah. He tells his Chief of Staff, "I will demand Gen. Hardee to surrender. If Gen. Hardee is alarmed, or fears starvation, he may surrender, otherwise I will bombard the city." After taking a drag on his cigar he continues. "I will not risk the lives of our men by assaults across those narrow causeways."

General Sherman concludes all of his needful preparations and rides from his headquarters, on the plank-road, over to General Slocum's headquarters, on the Macon road. From General Slocum's headquarters he dispatches (by flag of truce) into Savannah, by the hands of Colonel Ewing, who is General Sherman's brother-in-law and the inspector-general, a demand for the surrender of Gen. Hardee's army.

General Ewing approaches Gen. Hardee's pickets. "I am here to deliver a message to Gen. Hardee from General Sherman. Would you escort me to his headquarters." The pickets escort General Ewing to Gen. Hardee's headquarters. General Ewing enters Gen. Hardee's headquarters are the two soldiers shake hands. General Ewing opens his satchel and removes a letter from General Sherman. "Gen. Hardee, this is addressed to you from General Sherman. He is asking that you surrender your garrison immediately."

Gen. Hardee tells General Ewing, "Please have a seat at the conference table while I read the letter."[514]

HEADQUARTERS MILITARY DIVISION OF THE MISSISSIPPI,
In the Field, near Savannah, GA, December 17, 1864
General WILLIAM J. HARDEE,
Commanding Confederate Forces in Savannah:

GENERAL: You have doubtless observed from your station at Rosedew
that sea-going vessels now come through Ossabaw Sound and up
Ogeechee to the rear of my army, giving me abundant supplies of all
kinds, and more especially heavy ordnance necessary to the reduction
of Savannah. I have already received guns that can cast heavy and
destructive shot as far as the heart of your city; also, I have for some
days held and controlled every avenue by which the people and garrison
of Savannah. I have already received guns that can east heavy and
destructive shot as far as the heart of your city; also, I have for some
days held and controlled every avenue by which the people and garrison
of Savannah can be supplied; and I am therefore justified in demand-
ing the surrender of the city Savannah and its dependent forts, and
shall await a reasonable time your answer before opening with heavy
ordnance. Should you entertain the proposition I am prepared to grant
liberal terms to the inhabitants and garrison; but should I be forced to
resort to assault, and the slower and surer process of starvation, I shall
then feel justified in resorting to the harshest measures, and shall make
little effort to restrain my army-burning to avenge a great national
wrong they attach to Savannah and other large cities which have been
so prominent in dragging our country into civil war. I inclose you a copy
of General Hood's demand for the surrender of the town of Resaca, to be
used by you for what it is worth.

I have the honor to be, your obedient servant,

W. T. SHERMAN, Major-General

Gen. Hardee lays down the letter from General Sherman and opens
the enclosure and reads:

HEADQUARTERS ARMY OF TENNESSEE,
In the Field, October 12, 1864
TO THE OFFICER COMMANDING U. S. FORCES AT RESACA, GA.:

SIR: I demand the immediate and unconditional surrender of the post and garrison under your command, and should this be acceded to, all white officers and soldiers will be paroled in a few days. If the place is carried by assault no prisoners will be taken.

Most respectfully, your obedient servant,

J. B. HOOD, General[515]

Gen. Hardee stands and is red-faced. He looks at General Ewing and says, "Wait a moment General Ewing and I give you my reply to deliver to your brother-in-law." General Ewing nods in agreement as Gen. Hardee goes to his clerks desk and drafts his reply. Shortly he returns and hands General Ewing the reply. "Have a good day General Ewing. My men will escort you back to the lines. The two General's shake hands and General Ewing departs.

General Sherman receives and reads Gen. Hardee's reply:

HDQRS. DEPT. OF S. CAROLINA, GEORGIA, AND FLORIDA,
Savannah, GA., December 17, 1864
Major General W. T. SHERMAN,
Commanding Federal Forces, near Savannah, GA:

GENERAL: I have to acknowledge receipt of a communication from you of this date, in which you demand "the surrender of Savannah and its dependent fort," on the ground that you have "received guns that can cast heavy and destructive shot into the heart of the city…."

Your demand for the surrender of Savannah and its dependent forts is refused. With respect to the threats conveyed in the closing paragraphs of your letter, of what may be expected in case your demand is not complied with, I have to say that I have hitherto conducted the military operations intrusted to my direction in strict accordance with the rules of civilized warfare, and I should deeply regret the adoption of any course by you that may force me to deviate from them in future.

I have the honor to be, very respectfully, your obedient servant,

W. J. HARDEE, Lieutenant-General[516]

General Sherman reads Gen. Hardee's reply. He tell Aid-de-Camp, "More or less what I expected. Send the following orders to General Howard."

HEADQUARTERS MILITARY DIVISION OF THE MISSISSIPPI,
In the Field, near Savannah, GA, December 18, 1864
Major General O. O. HOWARD,
Commanding Army of the Tennessee:

GENERAL: The General-in-chief has just returned from General Slocum's, where he made a demand or the surrender of Savannah, &c., which was denied. He wishes you to make the necessary preparations at once for assaulting the place. He wishes to know if the crossing of the creek is practicable, and if you can make a diversion about Rosedew. General Slocum has received his orders, and General Davis and General Williams are ready, or nearly so.

I am, General, with respect,

L. M. DAYTON, Aide-de-Camp[517]

At his camp by the side of the plank-road, eight miles from Savannah, Sherman studies Gen. Hardee's letter declining to surrender. General Sherman takes a deep breath, then a long drag on his cigar, "Major Audenried, I was hopeful Gen. Hardee would surrender. This leaves me with only one option. Launch a full assault. I will completely surround Savannah on all sides so as further to excite Hardee's fears. If this is successful, I will entirely capture the whole of Hardee's army. We already have troop emplacements on the north, west, and south. Yet on the east, there remains the use of the old dike or plank-road leading into South Carolina."

"Looks like to me Hardee will have to construct a pontoon-bridge across the river in order to escape," replies Major Audenried.

"Hopefully we can block that." During his staff meeting, General Sherman develops a plan for the capture of Savannah. "When I meet with General Foster, I'll have his division commanded by John P. Hatch move from its current position at Broad River by water down to Bluffton. From this location, he can reach the plank-road, fortify and hold it."

General Sherman points to the map. "If Hardee has enough men, which I truly doubt, and can avail himself of his central position, he can attack this detachment with his whole army." He faces his Generals, noting the glowing confidence in his plan. "At this period of the war. I don't want make a mistake like the one at Ball's Bluff,[518] Virginia in 1861. So before I finalize my plans, Major Dayton, Major Audenried and I will ride to Grog's Bridge on the Ogeechee and boat to Admiral Dahlgren in Wassaw Sound. From there we will meet with General Foster to ascertain whether or not we are safe from Hardee's troops." General Sherman directs his attention to Generals Howard and Slocum. "You two are to make all possible preparations for an attack, but not to attack, during my two or three day's absence."

"Yes, sir."

"I will review your plans when I return. I feel the end is near for the Confederates. If there are no questions, have a good day, Gentlemen."

General Sherman, Colonel Dayton and Colonel Audenried arrive at the wharf and take a boat for Wassaw Sound. The December day is pleasant and the river calm. Admiral Dahlgren greets General Sherman. "Sir, I have my personal boat, the *Harvest Moon*, ready and available for your trip to Hilton Head. I know General Foster is expecting you."[519]

"Thank you Admiral. I would like to visit with you, but I must be on my way. The entire success of the war is at hand."

General Foster meets General Sherman upon his arrival and immediately proceeds to headquarters. After an hour of map study and discussion of the proposed tactics, General Foster promptly agrees. "Great strategy. You have my assurance that I will devote my personal attention to this plan."

Early Monday, December 19th, General Sherman transmits orders to the XX Army Corps. "Cross the Savannah River."

Gen. Hardee receives information from his scouts. "Sir, the Union forces are crossing the Savannah." Gen. Hardee instructs his clerk to organize a staff strategy plan meeting immediately. When his commanders are all sitting at the conference table discussing the Union move across the Savannah River, Gen. Hardee concludes, "This action by Sherman will cut our only escape route from Savannah. It is the same tactics Sherman used in the siege of Atlanta; a slow and methodical manner." His commanders listen intensely. "Savannah is my birthplace, and I wish to defend her, but my state militia force cannot withstand a full assault from General Sherman's army. I know our meager ten thousand man force would energetically follow orders to defend Savannah, but the fight would be futile against the Union sixty thousand man army and the end for this command. Send the following dispatch to Pres. Davis immediately."

SAVANNAH, December 15, 1864
(Via Hardeeville 16th)
His Excellency President DAVIS:

Sherman has secured a water base, and Foster, who is already nearly on my communications, can be safely and expeditiously re-enforced. Unless assured that force sufficient to keep open my communications can be sent me, I shall be compelled to evacuate Savannah.

W. J. HARDEE, Lieutenant-General[520]

Leaning over the maps he informs his commanders, "We must devise a plan, a secret plan to allow our withdrawal from Savannah without detection. After all, Savannah is no longer of value to the Confederate High Command." Gen. Hardee addresses his chief engineer, John G. Clark. "You are to construct a mile pontoon bridge across the Savannah River. You have my authority to call upon any unit for soldiers to assist in the construction."

"What of materials, sir?"

"Use your skills to construct this bridge with local materials since there are no military pontoon supplies available. Gather every barge, every skiff, and every rice flat along the Savannah River. Use every man available and work around the clock. You are to begin immediately."

Col. Clark begins his construction. The Confederate soldiers gather every barge, skiff and rice flat they are able to locate. Another detachment brings in train car wheels. As rapidly as they arrive, Col. Clark supervises the methods of securing the boats together with chains and ropes. Once secure, the new pontoon platform is carefully put into position on the river. The train car wheels now become the anchors. Concurrently, other Confederate troops are dismantling the city wharves and several buildings for wood flooring over the pontoon platform.

The soldiers hammer and nail the wooden planks in place to create the flooring. The several hundred loads of rice straw cover the wood floor in order to smother the sound of supply wagons, cannons and troop movement. Col. Clark reports to Gen. Hardee. "Sir, the three sections of the bridge are complete. The first extends from Broad Street to Hutchinson Island, a distance of one thousand yards. The bridge extends from Hutchinson Island to Pennyworth Island and finally, from Pennyworth Island to the South Carolina side."

Gen. Hardee and his staff accompany Col. Clark for the final inspection of the bridge. Walking part of the first section, Gen. Hardee comments, "This will suffice. Everyone must approach and move slowly across this bridge. Panic or driving the horses rapidly will cause the bridge to sway. How much I don't know. So warn everybody as they approach the bridge to proceed slowly." Gen. Hardee shakes Col. Clark's hand. "Job well done, Col."

During the morning of the 20th, Hardee sends a message to the mayor, "Mr. Mayor, the bridge to South Carolina is open. Any citizen who wishes to leave Savannah may do so."

Mayor Richard Arnold immediately dispatches his police to spread the word that the pontoon bridge is ready for passage. Soon families on foot or with their belongings on wagons begin to cross the bridge at Broad Street. Some have been waiting all night to insure their spot in the escape. Polly and Tot are awakened early from the noise of the carriages and wagons passing by on their way to the river.

Jesse knocks loudly. "Miss Polly, 'e might be dane'gus fuh go tuh town teday. People duh hurry 'cross de ribbuh tuh Kahlinuh. Deh plennie uh bad tings gowin on een town."[Miss Polly it may be dangerous to go in town today. People rushing across the river to Carolina. There are a lot of bad things going on in town.]

"Yes I know," replies Polly. "Reverend Blount told me the white scum of the city are out of their dens like nocturnal beasts to the work of pillage. Mainly Men, women and children force open doors like hungry dogs after a bone, each for himself, indifferent to the property or the rights of others. They grab, smash, pull, tear, anything, everything, shoes, meat, clothes, soap, hats, whatever comes to hand. First they take, then run to hide their spoils in some place, only to return and swell the crowd at some other point."[521]

Tot wrenches her hands. "Me's scared fer you ma'am Polly."

"Most citizens are probably leaving today, but I must stay and care for the wounded and sick. If you want to go Tot, you, Jesse and Al certainly are free to do so."

"No ma'am, I's stayin' wid you Ma'am Polly."

"Gather everything we need and put it in the carriage. Load and bring the two pistols as well." She and Tot begin packing bags with cloth and food supplies. When each piece of baggage is full, Jesse puts the baggage in the carriage. Polly sends Tot out to the carriage with little Joshua and returns inside. She opens the secret closet and carefully places some of the valuable items inside. Polly secures the wall and checks to be sure that it is undetectable. She exits the house and does not lock the front door. When she boards the carriage, Tot says, "Ma'am you don' lock de door."

"If the thieves want to come in, the door is open. That way we won't have to replace it. Besides, Al will be here." Tot hands Polly the two pistols and she places them under her lap blanket.

"Les' tek de long road to de town, Ma'am Polly. I tink 'e gwoin saffuh since de murderas deh een de town now." [Let's take the long road to town, Miss Polly. I think it will be safer since the marauders are mostly in town right now!]

"Okay, let's git!"exclaims Polly.

Jesse heads the carriage toward the round-about road to the hospital. The ride is uneventful until they near the first row of houses in town. Just as they approach the homes, two bushwhackers on foot jump from the bushes. One grabs the bridle and pulls the horse's head as low as possible. The other bushwhacker circles the carriage. Polly pulls back the hammers of the two pistols and whispers, "Stay, calm Tot!"

Tot draws Little Joshua closer to her. The green eyes of the white scum are flashing as he approaches. His hair is long and full of tangles. He has an ugly and dirty face with a few black teeth on bottom and bare mouth on top.

He shouts, "You, with the kid, get out now! Pretty lady, you stay put! We's taking this here carriage and I'm gonna take you with me!"He reaches for Polly.

Tot pulls Joshua even closer as Polly jumps up. Her blanket falls to the floor of the carriage. Simultaneously, she takes aim and fires into the chest of the bandit. The force of the bullet sends the bandit to the ground flat on his back. With a single spasm, his body goes limp as blood begins to seep through his filthy clothes.

The horse recoils from the sound of the shot and throws the second marauder to the ground. Nervously, Jesse steadies the horse. Pulling the hammer back, Polly jumps from the carriage, bypassing the dead bandit. She approaches the other marauder as he is getting up from the ground. He has his back to Polly. While on the ground, he gathers a hand full of sand and fully realizes that his pal is probably dead.

"Stay where you are or I'll shoot ya!" Shouts Polly.

Pretending not to hear Polly, he stands and turns toward her. He smiles as if to show off his single, rotten front tooth. As Polly begins to talk about sparing his life, he throws the sand in her face and lunges for her. Polly realizes her peril and quickly forces her eyes open long enough to fire both pistols. He is within one foot of Polly. One bullet strikes him in the groin, and the second bullet strikes him in the left side of his neck. He grunts, and with his eyes wide open, he reels to his left as he falls to the ground. Blood erupts from the artery covering his neck and chest. Holding the reins of the nervous horse, Jesse jumps down to comfort Polly. They walk and stand over the second dead bandit as he takes his last breath. Her pistol is still smoking as his body falls still and silent, blood slowly oozing deep in the sand. Jesse assists Polly back to her seat in the carriage. Little Joshua is still clinging to Tot.

Tot gets water and pours it on Polly's eyes. Softly, Jesse utters, "I een kno' wah fuh say Miss Polly! You look moh cahm 'dan me." "I don't know what to say Miss Polly! You appear calmer than I am."

Although her son is too young to realize what is happening, Polly reaches for Little Joshua and hugs him tightly.

"Wah we do wid de boddie Miss Polly?" asks Jesse.

"Leave them to rot! Let's get on to the hospital." Onward to town, they pass homes and businesses with broken windows, doors open and goods scattered all about. People are running in all directions with arms full of bounty. Another bandit attempts to stop the carriage, but this time Jesse snaps the reins, nearly running him over and speeds past him. Soon, they are in the safety of the hospital. Polly instructs Tot, "Take Little Joshua to Ms. Cazier's office and stay there. I'll file a report about the shooting with Dr. Blair."

DECEMBER 20, 1864

General Sherman, delighted with his conference with Admiral Dahlgren and General John Foster, leans back in his chair. "Well, gentlemen this completes our meeting at Port Royal on a strategy to trap Gen. Hardee. This is a very comprehensive plan and should bring a quick end to this conflict."

Admiral Dahlgren, setting his eyes sternly at General Sherman, "Whenever you are ready, General, the *Harvest Moon* is ready for you to board and head for the Ogeechee River."

"If you have food on board, I'm ready now Admiral."

"Plenty of food on board, sir."

"Let's board. We've got a war to win."

The wind is strong out of the northwest and is bitter cold. Admiral Dahlgren directs the pilot of the *Harvest Moon*, "Take the inside route and run toward Tybee. Use your draftsman to work your way through to Wassaw Sound and to the Ogeechee River by the Romney's Marsh."

"Yes, sir, but the tide will probably be low in that area and the water shallow." Deep inside Romney's Marsh, the *Harvest Moon* is caught by a low tide. The ship runs aground and, with a sudden stop, throws General Sherman and the crew to the deck.

After laboring some time, embarrassed Admiral Dahlgren politely informs General Sherman, "I'm sorry for the delay, General. The tide is too low to move out from here. I have ordered my barge out to pull us through these shallows."

General Sherman and his staff board the barge and are pulled through this intricate and shallow channel. Now General Sherman's oarsmen row for the Ogeechee River on one of the coldest nights ever in Savannah.[522] "I don't need delays at this late time." Sherman declares to himself.

During the day, civilians begin crossing the bridges. Gen. Hardee holds his last staff meeting and issues his final orders in Savannah. "I'm still unsure if Sherman has picked up on my plan to evacuate Savannah. However, here are my final orders. "The Confederate iron-clad *Savannah* is to shell the Union positions close to the river in order to prevent any possible troop concentration. Gen. Wheeler, your three regiments of infantry re-enforcements will arrive around four this afternoon. Place these regiments in plain view of the Union forces. This hopefully will dampen the possibility of a Union attack. Do nothing else. Do you understand my order?"

"Yes, sir, Gen. Hardee, I understand your order." Gen. Hardee's staff quietly looks on.

"Do you have any questions or comments concerning this order, Gen. Wheeler?"

"No sir, I fully understand the order."

"Capt. Anderson."

"Yes, Gen."

"At sun down, take charge of the big guns which the pontoon bridges will not support. These guns are to begin shelling the Union lines. Expel all shot and shell, then spike the cannons and destroy the caisson wheels before departing for Broad Street. This bombardment should keep the Union forces behind their breastworks."

"What should I do with the left over gunpowder, sir?"

"All excess Confederate gun powder and artillery ammunition is to be thrown into the river or the canals."

"Gen. Beauregard, you are in charge of our troop withdrawal."

"Yes, sir."

"The withdrawal begins at dark, and the first across the bridge will be the light artillery, Field Batteries and supply wagons. Gen. Wright your division should begin crossing around 9:00."

"Yes, sir."

"Gen. Lafayette McLaws, your Militia will march behind Gen. Wright's division."

"Yes, sir."

"Around midnight, Gen. Smith,[523] your Militia will follow."

"Remember the pontoon bridge might be somewhat treacherous, so take each movement slowly."

"Col. Clinch."

"Yes, Sir."

"The GMI cadets will act as rear guard.[524] The rear guard of the forces is composed Companies A, B, and K of the Sixth Regiment, Confederate Reserves, commanded respectively, by Lieut. Bilboe, Capts. W. M. Davidson and J. R. Johnson. This battalion is under Maj. Cunningham as provost marshal and is composed of cadets with a few men to fill out the ranks. To these boys was paid the compliment of the post of danger which is the post of honor: to protect the rear of Hardee's corps and guard the city until the last minute, and only to leave when the enemy is in half a mile of their position.[525]

Before the rear guard passes, set fire to the *Isandiga*, the *Firefly* and the new gun boat *Milledgeville* and blow up the floating battery *Georgia* at her moorings. I have discussed these plans with Mayor Arnold and he fully understands my decision to withdraw from Savannah. Any Questions? Dismissed."

The evening turns to a cold, dark and foggy night. There appears to be no rhyme or reason in the chaotic movements of humans or animals. Random Confederates fire their weapons into the air, cursing and chasing after the nymphs of the night in a last call for glory and love.

Obeying orders, the men burn campfires continuously to give the concept of a strong defense. The withdrawal begins once darkness falls completely on the river. Starting with the light artillery, the Field Batteries and supply wagons, the well-ordered withdrawal proceeds slowly, dictated by the instability of the road across the boats and pontoons. Around 9:00 PM Gen. Ambrose Wright's division crosses.

Jack watches in the dim light as the soldiers in front of him amble forward. He occasionally glances behind as if expecting Sherman to appear beside him. Jack isn't afraid of dying. "Say, Ferry, what'll happen to your wife and daughter if you don't make it back home?"

Ferry casts a glance at Jack, as if he'd rather not even think about that possibility. "Well Jane and little Robin are at home with Mama. Pa is somewhere off fightin' the Yanks, too, but Mama and Jane'll probably get along. My Jane is a spunky gal, all right. What about you?"

Jack hesitates, thinking of his own dear wife and two sons. I'm afraid if I git killed, my oldest son'll want to join up. He's fourteen. Old enough by some standards, I reckon." Jack spits into the shallow water of the river. "My youngest ain't near old enough. But, my Linda is a fine woman. She'll manage, but it'll be hard on her."

Fog slides in to provide more cover for the covert withdrawal of the Confederates. Slowly Jack starts across the make-shift bridge, following a brace of cannons being pulled by mules. Progress is slow. The mules are skittish, prancing anxiously as the muffled sound of their hooves thud along the planks.

Suddenly, one of the mules is spooked. He jerks on his leads and, even as his handler tries to calm him, begins to dance uncontrollably. The platform rocks precariously. Jack realizes what's happening and hurries over to help, but he's too late. The mule blunders off the edge. Before anyone can separate the mule from his harness, the cannon plunges into the river. The other mule begins to gambol about in spite of attempts to soothe him. Seconds later, soldier, mule and cannon disappear into the inky ebony depths of the Savannah River.

Jack falls flat onto the planks to keep from tumbling into the river. Ferry teeters desperately before splashing into the cold water. Jack crawls to the edge. "Ferry! Hey, Ferry."

Nothing. Jack searches the onyx surface of the water, but never sees Ferry's head. After a moment, he stands up, glances once more at the river, and continues his slow journey toward South Carolina.

At 10:00 PM, cadets Frank Loftin, Goldsmith, Brown and Norman are given an order. "Spike the cannons and join the army in the retreat back." Through foggy Savannah, the cadets prepare to spike the cannons. Cadet Loftin hesitates and places his hand on one of the cannons. With tears in his eyes, he grasps his tattered GMI cap and places it next to his chest. Overcome with feeling, he utters in a broken voice, "To spike these faithful cannons is to place a spike into the soul of the Cadet Corps and the spirits of our faded cadets; Anderson, Alexander, Baker, Jordan, Mabry, McLeod Smith and Marsh."

Norman feels the transfer of Frank's emotions. They remove their worn caps as their eyes also swell and tears begin to flow. All four, silent, quietly back away. The cloudy moon light glistens brightly from the frost on the cannon barrels as if to say "thank you" from their fallen comrades. The cadets regretfully depart, leaving the cannons intact.

They know that the war is nearing the end. They prepare to become the rear guard of the retreating Confederate army. Reuniting with the Cadet Corps, the Cadets march just over three miles back to Savannah and form the Confederate Army's rear-guard between the Louisville Road and the Savannah River.[526]

Company A, under the command of Lt. Bilboe, Company B under the command of Capt. W. M. Davidson and company K, under the command of Capt. J. R. Johnson of the Sixth Regiment, Confederate Reserves and the Cadet Corps compose the rear guard under the command of Maj. Cunningham.[527]

Near midnight, all Confederate shelling ceases. Slowly, the Federal troops begin to emerge from their damp, cold and slimy earth works. Taking over a more dry area, most sleep through the night.

As the cadets enter Savannah in the early morning they set fire to their remaining supplies. Norman and Paul are given an axe by Col. Clinch's engineers. "Hold on to these. We will need assistance in releasing the pontoon bridges." Norman holds the axe in one hand and his musket in the other. Explosions are not only heard, but felt as the ships in the navy yard and Savannah Harbor are also being blown apart.

As the cadets approach the pontoon bridge, the provost guard explains to each company, "As rear guard, you command the post of danger and a post of honor."[528]

"Our orders are to protect the rear of Gen. Hardee's Corps and guard the city until the last minute. We are to leave Savannah only when the enemy is within a half mile." As Norman and the Cadet corps march along they can hear the roar of the robbers and the breaking in of doors, which with the click of their heels on the sidewalks made melancholy music, the only music in that sad hour by which to keep time.

Every arrangement had been made for the removal of the army from Savannah. Those who are familiar with the location of the city know that it is built on the south side of the Savannah river with Hutchinson Island in front. North of that island is also another river which that has to be bridged.[529]

Paul looks around at the dark and weird surroundings, "Norman, I don't think we have to worry too much about the Yankees bothering us tonight."

"I doubt it as well. I just hope Polly is in Stone Mountain. She does not need to be here with the Yankees just around the corner. I have worried about her the whole time we have been here."

"Yes, I know. Surely she has returned to Stone Mountain by now."

"There goes the rockets signal for the completion of the crossing."

"Let's move out," shouts the provost guard. The cadets begin crossing the bridge. Though they are the last to cross of the rear guard, they present a pitiful sight. Their uniforms are shaggy and the temperature is cold and damp.

"Paul, look at us, any person seeing us in this silhouette of the light from the fires at the east of the bridge would consider us an immense funeral procession stealing out of the city in the dead of night."

Looking toward the flames, Paul nods. "Yep. You're probably right. These immense flames no doubt produce a morbid backdrop."

"Take your axes and cut the bridge loose from the docks," shouts Col. Clinch to his engineers. Paul and Norman move to the edge and back of the pontoon bridge. With simple, yet determined strokes, the ropes are cut and that portion of the bridge slowly pulls away from the Savannah side of the river. The flats which form the pontoon bridge are set on fire after the army crosses the river. Some are entirely consumed, others drift and lodge against the bank on Hutchinson Island, some are still linked together and are burning fiercely. Others are floating down the river like huge torches.

Norman stands silently and observes above the Habersham Rice Mill at Krenson and Hawks Shipyard, a number of unfinished gunboats for the Confederate government all on fire below the city. Other gunboats are also in flames at the Willink's Shipyard. Norman point up the river and tells Paul, "Look the only war vessel saved from the flames is the *Savannah*. It's just there gleaming in the light from the flames."

Leaning on their axe handles after cutting the third portion loose and as the last of the rear guard, the Corps of Cadets, reaches the sandy hills of South Carolina.[530]

"What's next, Norman?" asks Paul.

"Where to from here Paul?" asks a weary Norman as their feet touch the South Carolina shore.

In the dim light he taps Paul, "Look, there's Gen. Hardee standing with his staff under the Confederate National Flag. The river breeze has her really flying tight."

"Maybe she's happy that we are all still alive," retorts Paul.

Gen. Hardee tells his clerk, "Send the following dispatch to Pres. Davis:

His Excellency JEFFERSON DAVIS:

On the 19th the enemy forced a landing on the South Carolina side, so near my communication that to save the garrison it became necessary to give up the city. Its evacuation was successfully accomplished last night. All the light artillery and most of the stores, munitions, &c., were brought off. I learn that there is a misapprehension as to the force disposable for the defense of Savannah. it summed up, land side and water side, militia, reserve, dismounted cavalry, local and details, 9,089. I did not burn the cotton for fear of setting the city on fire.

W. J. HARDEE, Lieutenant-General[531]

Mayor Arnold and the city aldermen remain at the Exchange throughout the night, and they finalize plans for the surrender of the city to General Sherman. Arrangements are made for horses and carriages to transport the mayor, and aldermen and some prominent citizens to the front lines under a flag of truce. The city clerk comes into city hall, and the Mayor asks, "Are our hacks[532] ready?"

"Well Mayor, seems that Gen. Wheeler's men took the hacks except one and left all the carriages." He looks at his watch. "It's 4 o'clock, and the sun will be coming up soon. Let's load the one carriage and head out to find General Sherman and surrender the city before we are under assault."

Aldermen John O'Byrne and Robert Lachlison advise the group, "We'll walk, Mayor. You and the rest take the carriage. We'll try to keep up."

Aldermen O'Byrne and Lachlison become separated from the group in the rush and wind up on the Augusta Road. A Union picket surprises the two aldermen. "Halt. What is your business this close to the Union lines?"

"We're aldermen from Savannah and were with Mayor Richard Arnold. We are looking for General Sherman. We want to surrender Savannah to him," explains John. The two aldermen are taken prisoner by a Union picket and marched to General Geary. His division is already marching toward Savannah under orders from General Sherman. John and Robert explain to him who they are and that Gen. Hardee and his division have crossed the Savannah River into Carolina.

"I am aware of the evacuation and will accept your surrender. However, I need to find your Mayor and confirm your actions."

Proceeding down the Augusta Road, General Geary's advance guard spots Mayor Arnold near the intersection of the Charleston railroad and Augusta Road with the white flag of truce. The officer in charge of the advance guard sends a rider back to inform General Geary. "Sir, the Captain thinks that Mayor Arnold is up ahead."

General Geary rides forward and shortly he meets the Mayor, pulls his mount to a stop and leans forward and says, "Mayor Arnold, I presume."

"That is correct. I am Mayor Arnold."

"I am General Geary. I understand you desire to surrender the city of Savannah."

"Yes, Sir. The city of Savannah was evacuated last night by the Confederate military and is now entirely defenseless. As chief magistrate of the city, I respectfully request your protection of the lives and private property of the citizens and our women and children."

General Geary replies, "I accept the Mayor's surrender of the city and grant your request." General Geary turns to his Chief of Staff, "Immediately issue the following orders:

1. Divides the city into eastern and western military districts.... Each regiment will be assigned definite limits to perform guard duty and each commander is held responsible for peace and good order ... All public and private property will be protected ... Officers must apply for occupation of private property ... All persons connected with the Confederate army shall register ... No citizen will be arrest except for misdemeanor ... The fire department will continue to operate under current personnel ... The same applies to the Water works and gas work ... All soldiers found within the city limits without passes will be arrested ... Citizens wishing to leave the city may do so ... Citizens destitute of provisions can make application at the city store ... Tattoo will be beaten throughout the city at 8 PM and Taps, at 9 ... with a curfew to follow...."[333]

Returing his attention to Mayor Arnold he tells him, "Mayor Arnold, lead me to the Exchange Building."

Before the sun can rise at 6:00 AM, General Geary leads a division under the command of Colonel Henry Barnum of the XX Corps into Savannah at early dawn and before the sun first glides the morning clouds the National colors, side by side with the colors General Geary's division are unfurled from the dome of the Exchange and over the U.S.

custom-house. As the Union troops enter the city, the majestic ancient oaks, with their great branches, some as large as the trunks of mature trees with boughs hang flowing with tender drapes of Spanish moss. The gentle ocean breeze produces a caressing flow within the moss in contrast to the night, when the waving moss appears, as the spirits of lost hopes.

All is not quiet, however, Anarchy is the rule of law. Buildings are burning. Slaves and poor whites are fighting over supplies of food. General Geary immediately issues orders. "Guards are to be posted at every building and warehouse immediately. Colonel Barnum, you are take a brigade and begin patrolling the city. Arrest any person who violates your orders to restore peace."

"Yes, sir."

General Geary sets up headquarters, and his Adjutant delivers him a copy of the Republican newspaper, dated December 21. General Geary takes the paper and reads the front page article by James R. Sneed, the Editor.[534] "To the Citizens of Savannah. Under the fortunes of war, we today pass under the authority of the Federal military forces."

Up nearly all night at the hospital, Tot continues to keep the fire glowing in the stoves and watches over little Joshua as he sleeps. The Mayor has heavily armed police surround the hospital during the night to ensure the safety of the staff and patients. Tot hears the sound of slowly moving horsemen and awakens Polly. Tot hurries to the window, moves the curtain back. She turns to Polly with her hand on her chest and says, "Oh, Ma'am Polly yar come de Yankees. Dem thick iz bees."

Polly jumps up and feels the shaking from the tramping of the horses. "Looks like the city is safe from attack. The mayor kept his word and surrendered."

By noon, the Union forces have restored law and order and are in total control of the town. Polly meets with Dr. Blair. "Could you please summon a policeman so I can file the report of the shooting?"

"Sure. I'll get the officer in charge of the hospital guard to come in and take your statement." Polly meets the policeman in Dr. Blair's office, and he interviews Polly, Tot and Jesse.

His last question is, "What did you do with the bodies, Ms. Hill?" asks the officer.

"Let them lay where I shot 'em. If the rats and buzzards haven't eaten them, they're still there!" Dr. Blair snickers to himself.

The policeman, somewhat red-faced with her blunt answer, clears his throat. "That will be all. If I need any more information, I'll contact you." He departs.

The hospital is operating normally, and Polly is anxious to return to her house on the river. "Dr. Blair, do you think you can contact the police chief and ask him to give us an escort home and maybe post a guard for a day or so?"

"Don't mind at all, Polly." In the meantime, Polly gathers her belongings, and they load the carriage. In the course of making final rounds, Polly see Jennifer enter the ward and rushes over to her.

"Polly!" she shouts. They meet and embrace. "I have missed seeing you. I've been by here a couple of times since I told you about Cadet Marsh dying at our hospital. I hope you were able to find out where the GMI cadets were so you could find your brother."

"Never could. Nobody really seems to know where any of the troops are since the war is moving so fast. I don't even know if they came to Savannah and made it to Carolina with Gen. Hardee. Just have to pray all is well with him and my family in Stone Mountain. What are you doing here today?" asks Polly.

"I've come with armed guards to get some supplies. Most everybody abandoned the hospital when they heard General Sherman's troops were approaching. Even Dr. Lawton left. Just the sick and some nurses are left behind.

There are still patients in the Guyton Methodist Church who need help. We have our hands full just like over here. I need to get back; your commissary manager put all he could spare in my carriage." They embrace and Jennifer hurries to her carriage.

Dr. Blair returns. "Polly, wait and talk with one of General Geary's staff." The police are busy keeping the city buildings safe, and the chief cannot spare a single person right now. As you probably know, Mayor Arnold surrendered the city early this morning. General Geary gave assurances that no harm will come to the city or the citizens."

"Without warning, the city has become the Mecca for the thousands of Negroes who are following General Sherman's army. They are stampeding and overrunning the city and adding greatly to the confusion. They have joined in the ruthless foraging for food and valuables," remarks Dr. Blair.

"I still have my pistols with me. If anybody enters this hospital in a threatening manner, they will meet their match. Do you want to carry one on you, Dr. Blair?"

"Wouldn't mind at all Polly. Never thought you would ask. Mine are at home."

"The other one is in my bag." Polly reaches under her coat and retrieves one of her pistols. She holds the pistol around the cylinder and hands it to Dr. Blair. "Take this one. I get the other one. But when I'm ready to leave I would like to have this 'un back."

"General Geary is sending patrols through the streets to break up the lawlessness, Dr. Blair continues. "I was by the Masonic Hall this morning where guards are posted and they were hauling off the thieves trying to steal the valuable mementoes of the lodge."

They walk outside. Black smoke rises into the sky from several directions. Mounted Union soldiers are with Union foot soldiers guarding groups of the lawless poor whites and Negroes who are caught pillaging and setting fire to property.[535] "I suggest you wait until later or even tomorrow to go to City Hall to talk with Mayor Arnold about a guard," Dr. Blair said.

"That's probably the best idea. I'll dispense medicine in the meanwhile. I'll be in the herbal medicine room if you need me," replies Polly.

"I think your house is far enough out of town to be safe."

"Hope so." She turns her attention to Tot, who is standing nearby, "Remove the baggage from the carriage and return to Madam Cazier's office. We're staying here a while longer."

⋈

Toward evening of December 21st, General Sherman views an approaching tug the *Red Legs*. Sherman knows the tug belongs to the Quartermaster's Department. The tug pulls next to General Sherman's barge and a staff-officer on board delivers letters from Colonel Dayton to General Sherman and the Admiral. Opening the letter, Sherman is speechless, somewhat disappointed, yet he smiles. The letter reports, "The city of Savannah was found evacuated on the morning of December 21st and is now in Union hands. Mayor Arnold met me on the outskirts of town and surrendered the city."

General Sherman boards the tug and orders, "Get to Savannah at full speed."

"Yes, sir, General" replies the captain as the tug turns sharply and heads toward Savannah.

Early the next morning of December 22nd, General Sherman, from his bivouac on the road to Kings Bridge, rides into the city with a small staff and a few orderlies. The city is quiet and peaceful, and he rides down Bull Street. He points out many of the houses and squares to his staff which he is familiar with from his stay in 1846. Soon, he reaches the River Bank below the Pulaski Hotel. The general sees a guard on top of a public building and has his orderly take the reins of Sam. General Sherman dismounts and climbs to the top of the building. Once there, he surveys the smoldering remains of the Confederate Navy Yard, the unfinished *Ram* burnt and the wreck of the floating bridge by which the Confederates withdrew to South Carolina. Shaking his head and tightening his chin, "Well, General Howard, so Hardee did just as I thought. He knows me well." Descending from the building he mounts, Sam. He and his staff ride back to the Pulaski Hotel.[536]

The Landlord is an acquaintance of General Sherman from New Orleans. The General and his staff plan on making arrangements for his headquarters and stabling at the Pulaski Hotel for at least a month's stay.[537]

One of General Sherman's guards sees an approaching man, "Halt!" shouts the guard. "What is your business here?"

"My name is Charles Green. I would like to talk to General Sherman concerning his quarters already selected by General Howard." Checking Mr. Green for any weapons, the guard escorts Mr. Green to General Sherman who is standing by his horse.

"Sir, this man, Charles Green, has some information for you from General Howard." General Sherman peers at Mr. Green whose clothes are neat, and appears to be a gentleman of refinement and culture.

"What type of information do you have for me, Mr. Green?"

"General Howard has already selected your headquarters, sir."

General Sherman curiously inquires, "Where might that be, Mr. Green?"

"My house, close by, is one of the best, if not the very best, in the city. It is large, commodious, full of fine furniture, has a large stabling and a vacant lot for wagons and spare horses."

Appearing somewhat distant, General Sherman replies, "I do not like to occupy a private house, because no sooner do we depart, than we are charged with stealing, pilfering and all sorts of false nothings."

"General, I am incapable of such meanness. My family is away and all I need is the use of two rooms above the dining-room for me and for my man-servant. I prefer you, Sir, not some other general."

"I'll be with you in a moment, Mr. Green." General Sherman mounts Sam and continues a conversation about his stables while he waits for the return of his staff, who is seeking livery stables close to the Pulaski Hotel. His staff returns one-by-one, each unsuccessful in their search for nearby stables. General Sherman tells Mr. Green, "I am going to ride the interior lines and will inspect your place on my way back." He round-about, his mount and departs.

Mr. Green walks back to his house. Returning from his tour, General Sherman sees General Howard, General Slocum and Mr. Green waiting at Mr. Green's house on Bull Street Square. Both generals stand and salute as General Sherman dismounts and walks to the front of the mansion. "At rest, gentlemen. General Howard, Mr. Green said you have chosen this mansion as my headquarters." General Sherman slowly looks around and admires the beautiful exterior Gothic style.

"Yes sir," replies General Howard. "I feel you'll be very comfortable at Mr. Green's. His place has all of the amenities that you and your staff will require." General Sherman has General Montgomery Meigs, his Quartermaster, to check out the Stables and stable yard.

"Now, give me a tour, Mr. Green" asks General Sherman.

"This way, General" answers Mr. Green as he leads General Sherman toward the front door. Entering, General Sherman sees the finely carved tables, chairs and chandelier appointments which furnish the eloquent drawing room, sitting rooms and dining room. Sherman studies the pictures from Europe. He passes and admires the beautiful Italian statuary which graces the halls. The water closets have the luxury of fresh cold running water. Nearly every window has stained glass. Soon, General Meigs returns and informs General Sherman that the stables and stable yard are ample for their needs.

"A gratifying and sumptuous home," General Sherman says to himself. "These accommodations will be satisfactory, Mr. Green. Thank you for offering your home for my headquarters and that of my staff." Sherman and his staff establish quarters therein.[538]

Within an hour General Sherman has taken up quarters in Mr. Green's house, when a Mr. Albert G. Browne[539] of Salem, Massachusetts, the United States Treasury agent for the Department of the South, asks to meet with him. "Come in Mr. Browne. What can I do for the Treasury Department?"

"I know you are very busy General, and I will get right to the point of my visit."

"What point, Mr. Browne?"

"I am here to claim possession in the name of the Treasury Department of all captured cotton, rice, buildings, and commissaries forth-right."

General Sherman takes his cigar from his mouth and walks from behind his desk and stands directly in front of Mr. Browne. "Forth-right you say." Raising his voice and points his cigar toward Mr. Browne. "How dare you come into my office ordering me around? I take my orders from the President, the Secretary of War and General Grant, not from some underling of the Treasury. My army has use for these articles and this army has fairly earned the use of them. In no uncertain terms neither I nor any of my staff will surrender the quartermaster's possessions unless so ordered by my superiors."[540]

Mr. Brown is not aware of the confidential message to General Sherman from Secretary Stanton stating, "…I hope you will give immediate instructions to seize and hold the cotton. All sorts of schemes will be got up to hold it under sham titles of British and other private claimants; they should all be disregarded; and it ought not to be turned over to any Treasury agent, but held by military authority until a special order of the Department is given for the transfer."

Frightened by General Sherman's attitude, Mr. Browne says, "My mistake, General Sherman. I am following my orders from the Treasury Department and hope to be of assistance to your army."

"You, sit down. I'll tell you what I'll do and what you can do." Mr. Browne nervously takes a seat and General Sherman returns to his desk lights a cigar and takes a drag. He blows smoke rings and watches them disappear. Then he learns over his desk, "After the proper inventories are completed, if there remains any provision for which the army has no special use, I'll turn them over to the Treasury." Colonel Dayton is standing nearby. "Colonel Dayton, get me the latest inventories on the captured commissary supplies." Sitting and waiting for Colonel Dayton to return, General Sherman continues to indulge in the silent pleasure of his cigar, while Mr. Browne devises a shrewd and clever plan to better himself with General Sherman.

Colonel Dayton returns and hands General Sherman the report. He studies the report and advises Mr. Browne, "The preliminary inventory so far shows that in the warehouses there are at least twenty-five thousand bales of cotton. Also, in the forts, there are at least one hundred and fifty large, heavy sea-coast guns. This belongs to my army until further notice."

"Very well, General," pausing and standing, Mr. Browne approaches General Sherman, "General, there's a vessel that is preparing to sail for

Old Point Comfort. If she has good weather off Cape Hatteras, she'll reach Fortress Monroe by Christmas Day."

Then appealing to General Sherman's ego, "If I may, I would like to make a suggestion, General,"

"Go ahead. I hope it is better than your last one."

Clearing his throat, he states, "General, I would like to suggest that you send a telegram to President Lincoln, giving the President Savannah as a Christmas gift."

General Sherman thinks, "No doubt something like this is what this little weasel Treasury guy had in mind for himself."

Mr. Browne continues, "The President would especially enjoy such a pleasantry."

General Sherman immediately answers back. "Good suggestion and a great idea. Have a good day yourself, Mr. Browne." Colonel Dayton escorts him from General Sherman's office.

Taking to his desk General Sherman sits down and writes on a slip of paper to be left at the telegraph office at Fortress Monroe for transmission, the following:

> *SAVANNAH GEORGIA,*
> *December 22, 1864*
> *To His Excellency President Lincoln,*
> *Washington, D.C.*
>
> *I beg to present you as a Christmas-gift the city of Savannah, with one hundred and fifty heavy guns and plenty of ammunition, also about twenty five thousand bales of cotton.*
>
> *W. T. SHERMAN, Major-General*[541]

REFLECTIONS

FRIDAY DECEMBER 23, 1864

Polly is up early with the security of her house on the river foremost in her mind. She tells Tot and Dr. Blair that she is going to visit Mayor Arnold to seek protection of her home. Polly feels somewhat safe as Savannah is much quieter and guards are visible in all directions. Putting on a heavy coat, she departs for the mayor's office. She walks by several Yankee soldiers who acknowledge her passing with a bob of their heads. A slight breeze stirs the fog as she reaches Mayor Arnold's office. When she enters City Hall, Polly finds Mayor Arnold's staff busy talking to the Yankees about the locations of the food, cotton and military supplies. Mayor Arnold is standing in the conference room as Polly pokes her head around the corner.

"Hello Polly. What brings you here this morning?"

"Dr. Blair said since I am working at the hospital that I could ask you to send a policeman to my house to keep it secure."

"General Sherman and General Geary have already established security around town and at private homes as well. You'll need to talk to either General Sherman or General Geary about placing a guard at your home."

"Congressman Hill gave me a letter of introduction to General Sherman. He said I might need it someday. He is a good friend of General Sherman's brother. He met General Sherman in Decatur when Legare was killed in Cassville," replies Polly.

"That's great!" Pausing and turning red, Mayor Arnold continues, "Excuse me, Polly, I mean it's great that you have the letter."

"No bother, I know what you meant."

The mayor continues, "General Sherman is meeting with citizens and city officials, so let's go over to Mr. Green's house while I have time." Once outside the office, the mayor suggests that they walk since Mr. Green's house is not far away. "You know, the war is basically over. What are your plans?"

I'll stay in Savannah in memory of my husband until the war ends, and the patients at the hospital no longer need me to make medicine. Then I'll return to my family in Stone Mountain at least for a while." Polly wiped at a tear that streaked down her check. The wound to her heart from Legare's death still hurts. "Jennifer told me about a GMI cadet dying at Guyton Hospital. My brother is a cadet at the Georgia Military Institute. Evidently, the cadets were conscripted into the Georgia Militia by Governor Brown. Jennifer also told me the GMI Corps was not too far from Savannah when the cadet came to the hospital. He never regained consciousness and died within a day of his arrival. I just pray that Norman is okay. I went to the Confederate garrison and wrote him a letter. The sergeant said he would send it through the Confederate mail right away. I know if Pa or Ma told him I was in Savannah, he would try to find me."

"You and the women of Savannah have kept this city alive during these dark days. Although Savannah is the same externally, she is bleeding internally. All of you ladies set the example of loyalty to the cause. You rose to the demand of the moment with such a noble spirit, as if inspired directly by God. Of course, some say that if the women had not encouraged the war, it is possible it could have never come about!"

"I don't think I exactly fit in that mold, but the poem that is signed by the Lady of Savannah probably demonstrates that militant spirit." Polly hesitates a moment and then recites the poem that has come to mean a great deal to her.

> Oh! I wish my blue eyed
> Were but twenty summers old!
> I would speed him to the battle—
> I would arm him for the fight;
> I would give him to his country,
> For his country's wrong and right.

She attempts a smile, but it never reaches her eyes.

"Strong words from a mother, but we'll never know, will we, Mr. Arnold!"

Approaching Mr. Green's house, she sees a long line forming. As the mayor passes, many of the citizens standing in line acknowledge his surrender with gratitude. The mayor and Polly approach the guard at Mr. Green's front door.

"I am Mayor Arnold, and this is Mrs. Polly Hill. Mrs. Hill would like to speak with General Sherman if he is available."

"One moment, sir." The guard enters the house and returns shortly. "Step inside and the orderly will escort Mrs. Hill to General Sherman's office."

"Follow me, Mrs. Hill."

Polly precedes the mayor into the house, and an orderly comes out of one of the rooms. "General Sherman can see you now, but only for a few minutes."

The orderly knocks on General Sherman's office door and from the other side a voice says, "You may enter." The orderly opens the door, and Polly enters looking directly at General Sherman as he stares back at her. "What is it I can do for you, young lady?"

"General, my name is Polly Hill. I believe you know my father-in-law, Congressman Joshua Hill."

General Sherman pushes his chair from behind his desk and stands. "Please take a chair, Mrs. Hill. Yes, I do know your father-in-law. He is a strong Union man and after meeting your mother and father, I find them to be strong Union people as well."

Polly's eyes widen and her heart races. "You know my Ma and Pa!"

"Yes, I do. I had the pleasure of accidentally visiting your family farm while viewing that big pebble you call Stone Mountain." He laughs. "Your family is doing fine. I left them a letter of protection before departing. Your father, mother and I had a long discussion about this unfortunate war and this great union.

Polly clasps her hands together. She never realized she would hear this from General Sherman. "Thank you kindly for that, sir."

"You Southern women are the toughest I have ever known. You've thrown yourselves body and soul into this war. I believe the men would have given up long ago but for the women. You'd keep the war going for thirty years, if you had the power."[542]

"Yes, General, most of the Southern women have the virtues of hero-ines. They are more firm, courageous and patriotic than I even thought I could be. Yes, I'm a Union supporter like my family, but I must stand by the South." Polly continues, "Mr. Hill told me of your kindness concern-ing my late husband. I can only say thank you." Polly's voice begins to tremble a little as she composes herself.

General Sherman understands her feelings, and he attempts to mask his. She unknowingly reflects the same emotions as General Sherman. As if in a trance and day dreaming, General Sherman recalls after the fall of Vicksburg, when his wife, Ellen brought Willy and his other children to visit him at their camp on the Big Black. The family spent six weeks together at the camp during the respite in the battles. The day the family left, Willy contracted camp fever and became extremely ill. Six days later, poor nine year old Willy died. His youngest son, Charley, died only eighteen days ago, on the fourth of December 1864.[543] Charley was only ten months of age. He never saw or held Charley.[544]

After a moment of reflective thought, General Sherman returns his thoughts to the present. "If there was a way to turn back the history of this war and have a peaceful nation, I would be the first to reverse this painful conflict. I am sorry for the loss of your husband, Mrs. Hill. This war is a huge cost to every family of this country, North and South. Our nation is going to lose fully two percent of her population."

Regaining her demeanor, Polly softly replies, "Thank you for your kind thought and kindness toward my family, General Sherman. I have but one request."

"What is it, Mrs. Hill?"

"Could you please post a guard at my home on the river? I work at the hospital formulating herbals for the patients. Usually, I leave Tot there with my son, but with the marauders and bandits about, I'm afraid they may damage the house and harm Tot and Little Joshua."

"I can certainly take care of that matter for you. Do you plan to return to Stone Mountain?"

"As soon as the war is over and the patients' crisis is over, I'll take Little Joshua and Tot and go back home at least for a while. Our child was born here, and I last laid eyes on my husband here. So my heart is in Savannah, and I can never remove Savannah from my soul."

"I will have an order written for your protection as long as you remain in Savannah. Also, the order will have a provision for an escort for you back to Stone Mountain, no matter how you travel. Is there anything else, Mrs. Hill?"

Polly rises and extends her hand in gratitude, while crying on the inside. General Sherman softly takes her hand as if to comfort not only her soul but his as well. While holding her hand, he escorts her to the door of his office. He instructs his orderly to obtain Mrs. Hill's address.

"Thank you again, General Sherman." Polly gives the orderly directions to her house and then meets Mayor Arnold in Mr. Green's library. The mayor and Mr. Green are engaging in a general conversation as she walks into the library. "Hello, Mr. Green. It has been a while since I last saw you."

"Good morning, Polly. It has been a while. I hope General Sherman was able to comply with your request."

"Yes. He said he'll post a guard at my house as long as I am in Savannah."

Mayor Arnold conveys to Mr. Green and Polly, "We must get along now. I think it smart of you to have General Sherman as your guest. Like you say Charles, extending such a courteous gesture will hopefully preserve your estate."

"Just as good a move as yours, Mayor. Saving Savannah from the torch and more human suffering takes a great statesman. I hope you and General Sherman have a constructive meeting this afternoon. You and Polly have a good day."

They bid each other farewell and depart. Once again on the way down the path from Mr. Green's house, some of the citizens recognize the mayor and greet him, while others reach to shake his hand. The early morning sun is climbing in the sky and the moist winter air hints of heat as the mayor and Polly head toward the hospital and City Hall.

"Look! Isn't that Mrs. Nellie Gordon?"[545] Polly says as she points toward an approaching lady.

"Yes, I believe it is," replies Mayor Arnold. As Mrs. Gordon gets closer, they recognize her for certain. "Good morning, Mrs. Gordon" says Mayor Arnold and Polly.

"Why, good morning to you two. I am going over to a dear friend's and have been passing the city squares. It looks like they've become quarters for Union soldiers. They are so built up that if we did not have street signs, I would have a difficult time distinguishing some of the streets."

"Yes, it is horrible. They are even digging outhouses in the middle of the squares," remarks the mayor. Polly glances and sees a pistol in Mrs. Gordon's belt. "Nice looking pistol you got there! Don't be afraid to use it if you have to!"

"Not a problem for me, Polly. I want the Yankees to see that I am carrying it, so they'll think twice before getting flirtatious!"

"I'm sure that will make any Yankee think twice." says Mayor Arnold with a broad smile.

"Well, I need to get along now. See you soon." They bid good-bye to each other.

Later that afternoon, Mayor Arnold returns to Mr. Green's mansion to meet with General Sherman. Once again, he approaches the guard.

"I'm Mayor Arnold and have an appointment with General Sherman this afternoon. Could you please notify the General that I am here?"

"Wait here and I'll inform General Sherman's adjutant." One guard enters while the other remains outside. Shortly, the door opens and the guard introduces Mayor Arnold to Major McCoy, General Sherman's adjutant.

"Follow me, please, Mayor Arnold. General Sherman is expecting you." As Mayor Arnold approaches General Sherman's office, he notices the door is open. The adjutant stops in front of the opening and announces, "General, Sir, Mayor Arnold is here."

"Bring him in," replies General Sherman. As Mayor Arnold enters the room, General Sherman, looking very stern, comes from behind his desk and extends his hand. Mayor Arnold extends his in return. "Major, you stay and take notes. Mayor, have a seat." General Sherman takes his cigar box from his desk. "Have one if you would like, Mayor."

"Thank you, General Sherman." Choosing a cigar, Mayor Arnold inhales as he passes the cigar by his nose. "I love the aroma. May I have one for later?"

"Most certainly." Mayor Arnold takes another cigar and runs it past his nose. "Mighty fine. Thank you." General Sherman returns to his desk. "I am glad to see that, as mayor, you were able to see the uselessness of standing against my army. The white people here are the most whipped and subjugated I ever saw."[546]

"Reality is real, General." Mayor Arnold pauses briefly. "It is criminal to form resistance when the situation is hopeless. I could not allow Savannah to become the second Griswoldville, and one Ebenezer Creek is one too many. Allow me to give my thanks to General Geary for bringing peace and order to Savannah and for having most of his troops camp outside the city. The city police force is meager since most of the men of age are serving in the military, or are wounded or buried. We only have women and children, old men and darkies." General Sherman drags on his cigar and continues to listen. "All are somewhat hungry, but not starving, thanks to the sea and rice fields. I would like to extend my hand with yours, and restore order and feed the people of Savannah. They are, in a measure, destitute, and will have to be supported, to a certain extent, until such time as the ordinary course of labor and supplies is resumed in the city."[547]

General Sherman leans back in his chair. "So Savannah realizes that the Union prevails?"

Mayor Arnold replies, "The citizens of Savannah do not need the suffering and destruction of an invading army. Resistance would only strengthen the destructive consequences of Northern punishment over Savannah. Most of the citizens want the war to end and feel that the war was lost some time ago. Savannah wants to be at peace with the Union!"

General Sherman walks to the large stained glass window and ponders for a moment. "Savannah is unique and I have many fond memories of this city. My first thought was to let the citizens fend for themselves, since Gen. Wheeler seems to care less about their plight. However, I respect your character and strong convictions. I'll publish an order giving you the authority, as Mayor, to issue rations from all subsistence stores to destitute citizens."

Mayor Arnold immediately stands. "There's another important and dire matter I would like you to address, General."

"What is it?"

"The Colonial Cemetery General. Reverend Blount toured the cemetery and there's a great deal of emotional anguish due to the ravishing of the historic Cemetery for family silver rumored to be hidden there. Bones from the unearthed graves and ransacked vaults lay strewn about by greedy ghouls who stripped jewelry from the dead and pried gold from dental work. Please put a stop to this degradation of the dead, sir."[548]

"Most certainly, I'll have that taken care of immediately." Mayor Arnold walks to General Sherman and extends his hand. They shake and Sherman says, "Major McCoy, have the orderly escort Mayor Arnold to meet Colonel Beckwith. Colonel Beckwith is in charge of all quartermaster and subsistence stores."[549]

"Thank you, General Sherman. I am sure we will be in touch again."

"Follow me, please, Mayor," says the orderly. They depart.

General Sherman turns to Major Audenried, "I don't feel that I can appoint anyone from my army better suited to act as mayor. I'll retain Arnold as Mayor of Savannah. Not only does he have his citizens to feed, he has the 20,000 free slaves which are following us to feed as well. If only Governor Brown had as much sense!"General Sherman continues, "There doesn't seem to be much of a rebel spirit in Savannah compared with Atlanta or Memphis."

General Sherman's friend from Chicago, Colonel John Kinzie, has a daughter living in Savannah. Colonel Kinzie is one of the founding fathers of Chicago. His daughter's name is Eleanor "Nellie" Kinzie Gordon. Earlier in the day, General Sherman sends one of his orderly's to find her home and seek permission to for him to visit. Soon the orderly finds the Regency style architectural house on the corner of Bull and South

Broad Streets. He dismounts and ties his horse to the hitching post. As he approaches the front door, a voice from behind asks, "Can I help you?" Caught by surprise the orderly observes Nellie with her hand on a gun tucked neatly behind her belt.

"Yes ma'am , but there is no need for alarm. I am General Sherman's orderly and he asked me to locate your home. He would like to come and visit with you."

"Why I will be glad to have General Sherman visit. In fact he has an invitation for supper. Tell the General I will expect him tomorrow night at seven o'clock. If that is not satisfactory please let me know. He and my father have been friends for many years."

"Yes ma'am, I will give him your message. You have a nice day." The orderly tips his cap and departs. Nellie removes her hand from her pistol.

Around four o'clock, there is a knock on her door. She peers out of the window adjoining the door and recognizes the orderly from earlier in the day. She opens the door with the butler by her side.

"Mrs. Gordon, General Sherman sends his acceptance to supper tomorrow evening. He will be here at seven o'clock with two of his staff members. He will also post some guards around your house. He asks if there is anything he can bring?"

"Tell General Sherman fortunately we still have food but he will have to eat as the rest of the citizens in Savannah, sorta lean."

FRIDAY DECEMBER 24, 1864

Early in the morning, General Sherman's order for provisions to the citizens of Savannah reads, "Citizens destitute of provisions can make application at the city store, where they'll be supplied upon the order of Mayor Arnold, Mayor of the city."[550] The mayor and aldermen are permitted to continue their civil functions. Acting in concert with the military, they are to see that the water works is operational, the fire companies maintained, the streets cleaned and lighted and a good understanding between citizens and soldiers is established.

Once Mayor Arnold receives his copy of the provisions order, he immediately sends word to Dr. Blair at the hospital. Dr. Blair is to dispatch his staff to the main Confederate commissary warehouse to obtain food for the hospital. Dr. Blair rapidly forms a group of five wagons and fifteen staff members under the direction of Ms. Cazier and Polly to secure the rations for the hospital. Dr. Blair also secures a Union escort from the commander of the guard at the hospital for the transfer of the food. Mayor Arnold also has his staff post notices around town. The notices state the locations where provisions and commissary items will be available for citizens beginning that afternoon. The word spreads fast and lines begin to form at all of the locations.

Fights begin to break out over positions in the various lines. Soon more federal guards are summoned to keep order and after numerous arrests, a resentful calm returns.

At seven o'clock, General Sherman knocks on the door of Nellie's home. Nellie has the butler open the door. "I am General Sherman and we are here to dine with Miss Nellie."

"Yes, she is expecting you, sir. Follow me. please." General Sherman and his two staff members enter the house. The interior is sophisticated, but comfortable and makes a very warm impression. The butler takes them to the sitting room where Nellie and her children are anxiously in attendance.

"Hello, Nellie. I am William Sherman. It is kind of you to allow me to visit your home. Your father and I have been friends for many years."

She offers her hand to General Sherman, "Welcome to our home, General Sherman. These are our children. This is Eleanor our oldest. This is Juliette, our second child. We sometimes call her Daisy." Holding her third child, "and this is the latest addition born last year. Her name is Sara Alice." General Sherman kneels down, "Good evening ladies. You are all so pretty." The Eleanor and Juliette put their little hands together and giggle, "Thank you sir." "Would you like to sit with me? I have young children I would like for you to meet someday. I know you would be good friends." General Sherman takes their hands and walks to the sofa and the two little girls follow along. The Butler and house servant begin passing wine and hot hor doures.

"I have some letters for you from your in-laws." He takes them from his Aid and presents them to Nellie. "I know your husband is off fighting with Gen. Wheeler. I hope he is doing well and no harm comes to him in this conflict."

"Yes, William is doing well. He is a Capt. now and hopefully this war will end soon." Changing the subject, she tells General Sherman "that this house was built for Savannah Mayor James Moore Wayne who later became a Supreme Court Justice. Let me give you a tour. As you can see, the house is full of stylish Egyptian Revival furniture and classical furniture from the early 19th century. Most of it came with the house when we purchased it."

After the tour and supper, General Sherman feels comfortable around Nellie and her children. Missing his own family, he begins playing and "keeping them in shouts of laughter long past their bedtime."

Finally, the events of the evening draw to a close around midnight and General Sherman graciously thanks Nellie for her hospitality.[551]

CHRISTMAS—1864

During his daily staff briefing, General Sherman addresses his staff. "The mayor was completely subjugated and, after consulting with him, I authorized him to assemble his City Council to take charge generally of the interests of the people; but warned all who remained must be strictly subordinate to the military law, and to the interests of the General Government."

General Sherman keeps his word to Mayor Arnold and liberalizes his food distribution plan. "Citizens destitute of Provision can make application at the city store, where they'll be supplied upon the order of Dr. Arnold, Mayor of the city."[552]

❧

Polly and Little Joshua awaken on Christmas morning to the warm aroma of Tot's breakfast. Polly hears Joshua squirming in his crib next to her bed. She gets up and sees his sweet smile. He catches his mother's eyes and begins kicking his feet and hands joyfully. She gently picks up the little boy and gives him a big hug and kiss. "Merry Christmas, my little angel. This kiss is from me." She kisses him again and begins to cry. "This one is from your father. I know he is looking at you right now and wishing you a merry Christmas." She lies on the bed clutching Little Joshua and begins to sob heavily. She thinks about her wonderful Christmas the previous year and wonders about her family. How are Ma and Pa, Isaac and Sally? Where is my brother? Is he still alive? How I miss them and dream of my home and my family in Stone Mountain. Hopefully, there will be peace soon and the poor soldiers will suffer no more wounds or die.

There is a knock on the door. She hears Tot's voice, "Miss Polly, I had Massuh Little Joshshuh bottle ready."

"Come on in, Tot."

Tot enters and sees Polly on the bed holding Joshua. Looking somewhat puzzled, "You 'n Massuh all right Ma'am Polly?"

"It's just Christmas Day away from home and my loved ones. It would not be so bad if I could find out about my brother. Not knowing about him. That is the hard part." Tot hands Polly the baby bottle and she sits up in bed. Little Joshua kicks his feet and grasp the bottle, trying to put it in his mouth. "Don't fret. You'll be able to handle it just fine one day soon." Polly holds Joshua close to her bosom, rocks slightly and whispers a song.

"Muhself cook good Chris'mus brekwas fur you and mistuh Joshua."

"Sure does smell good, Tot." Soon Little Joshua finishes the bottle, and Polly takes him and goes to the table. "What a great Christmas breakfast! Fresh eggs, rice grits and ham! When we finish, you need to have Jesse to fetch the carriage so we can go to the hospital. I'm sure you made some breakfast for him as well."

"Yass um, membuh you tell me las' night fuh mek 'nuff so 'e kin hab some to. 'E got um 'n 'e happy. 'E kno' you prob'ly want fuh go to de hosbiddle, so 'e 'hab de carriage ready fuh you." ["Yes ma'am, remember you told me last night to make enough so he could have some as well. He already got his and is happy. He knows you probably want to go to the hospital, so he will have the carriage ready for you."]

"Let the guards outside know we will be going soon, so one can follow us. You can give them a respectable meal. After all, it is Christmas."

As they go through town on the way to the hospital, most all of the women are wearing black as they walk to and from their homes and church. Passing by the Union camps on the various squares in town, Polly cannot help but see the small trees sticking up in front of the Union tents. They have hardtack, and pork dangling from the branches instead of the traditional cakes, oranges, and candy.[553]

For the most part, it is a very somber day. When Polly, Tot and Little Joshua reach the hospital, Polly turns to the Union escort. "I'll be ready to head home just before dark. Please have someone here to escort us."

"Yes, Mrs. Hill, and thanks once again for the piece of Christmas ham."

Tot takes Little Joshua and goes to Mrs. Cazier's guest quarters. Tot is to keep Little Joshua away from the patients for fear of contagious diseases. Polly goes to the herbal medicine supply room and checks on the supply. She finds a sufficient amount on the shelves. There appear to be fewer sick or wounded soldiers arriving. She decides to visit with patients. Comforting the dying on Christmas Day is very difficult. Polly meets Mrs. Cazier in the ward. They hug and wish each other a merry Christmas.

Polly watches the near empty hallway a moment, "Today, life's blood curdles in my heart. The awful shadow of this fiend war is all around us."

Mrs. Cazier replies, "Yes, my blood curdles as well, Polly. These poor soldiers hear our voices with tears and reply with a grateful smile. Yet their lives are like a giant pine tree shattered by a lightning strike." The two continue going from bed to bed, comforting and feeding some to recovery, some to the hereafter.

❦

General Sherman and Henry Hitchcock attend services at Saint John's Episcopal Church, across the street from Charles Green's mansion. After church, General Sherman returns to his temporary home and writes to his wife Ellen. "I am at this moment in an elegant chamber of the house of a gentleman named Green. The house is splendidly furnished with pictures and statuary. My bedroom has a bath and dressing room attached, which look out of proportion to my poor baggage and other personal items.

"There are many fine families in the city, but when I ask for old and familiar names, it marks the sad havoc of war and destruction. They are all gone or in poverty, and yet the girls remain, bright and haughty and proud as ever. The aroma of the fine baked turkeys and trimmings for our Christmas dinner party filled the air and places my heart with my family. Mr. Green has his finest china in place on the large mahogany dining room table. Generals Slocum and John M. Corse and several other ranking staff members joined me for the Christmas dinner. With Union flags decorating the lavish dining room, General Slocum offered me a toast for my 'continuing success and good health.' I, in turn, offered a toast to Mr. Green for his hospitality. Mr. Green responds with an 'as happy a little after-dinner speech' as one of the guests ever heard."[554]

❦

Buck and Betty Gail are not fairing quite as well as General Sherman. Christmas Day is gloomy and cold. The smoke from the chimney rises straight into the sky. Entering the house, Buck gives a few vegetables to Betty Gail. "This is about all the greens Isaac and I can find this morning. We did find a fat rabbit in the box. I think he's probably full of greens."

Standing over the stove with Sally, Betty Gail replies, "Well, a fresh pecan pie along with two chickens and some fresh greens will do us for Christmas dinner. We are lucky to have this much left between the Yankees and those State Militia coming through here stealing whatever they want."

Betty Gail begins to cry and goes to Buck. He takes her hand and walks with her over to the warm fireplace, fresh and glowing in the crisp winter air. "Our souls and spirits are empty. We haven't heard from Norman or Polly. Governor Brown putting those Cadets in the Militia to fight is not right. Although his son is still with the cadets, I suppose. I pray every night for their safe return. I check their rooms every morning, hoping to see our sweet children and grandchild sleeping in their beds, hoping the war is just a bad dream."

"Lord knows where the cadets are. I don't think the military really knows where all of our soldiers are located," replies Buck.

Taking her apron, Betty Gail wipes tears from her eyes. "For fear I might hear the worst."

Buck bends over, picks up a log and throws the wood upon the hot cinders. He places his arms around her and pulls her close. "I know how Polly is and when she gets ready to come home, she will. I miss them more than even you can imagine." Buck's eyes swell with tears. "She's always been an independent gal and knows how to care for herself. Norman has good sense and thinks things through. Now that Sherman has Savannah, the war is over for Georgia. Brown just needs to wake up. Enough is enough." Suddenly Ole Charlie begins barking. They rush to the door to see what excites him so much. "It's Mr. Hamby. He must be coming to get some of his chickens or livestock. Got his goat pulling a cart. Good morning, Mr. Hamby."

"Good morning to the two of you. I hope you're having a fair Christmas Day. I know it's hard on all of us not knowing where our loved ones are," says Mr. Hamby as he ties the goat to the fence. "Looks like we got a break from all the rain and sleet. Worst winter ever, I believe."

"Very true, cold weather and cold hearts. No word from Norman or Polly. Sure would make our Christmas brighter if we only knew that they were safe," replies Betty Gail.

"Just trust that God's watching after them, Betty Gail. Well, I've come over to get a couple of guinea hens or a couple of the Plymouth Rock chickens for supper."

Buck replies, "Several of the neighbors came by yesterday and got some turkeys and chickens. The whole flock has done well since the neighbors brought in one or two each. They're breeding and laying good. Everybody around here should have a decent supper for Christmas with the Yankee bummers gone! I'll give you a hand catching those guineas. They're pretty fast."

"Thanks, Buck." Buck climbs down from the porch and they head to the chicken pen. "Have you heard from Buster?"

"Last word from him, he was okay. Don't have any paper to write on so I haven't told him about his slaves running off with Sherman. I hope he's home by spring time. The place is too big for me and Isaac to keep up. Some of Governor Brown's Militia came through the other night looking for conscripts and deserters. They talked to me and Betty Gail for a while, checked the house out. Wanted to know why we had so much livestock and poultry. I just told them that all the neighbors got together thinking the more we put together the better the breeding. I didn't say nothing about Sherman's orders. They shot one small pig and took the eggs. They ate the pig for supper. They searched our barn looking for evaders, and then decided to stay on Buster's place for the night. Mean looking bunch. They came back the next morning and took more eggs and some chickens and turkeys before leaving."

"Who were they looking for?"

"Never did say. Just asked questions about who's been coming and going. Wanted to know where Norman was and I told them. No need to try and catch the guineas running loose in the yard." Buck opens the gate to the chicken pen. He and Mr. Hamby chase a couple into the laying boxes. Reaching in, they pull the squawking guineas with their wings flapping out of the laying box and tie their legs.

Mr. Hamby asks Buck, "Have you heard from Miz Gay?"

"Not a word. Have no idea where she might be."

Laying the chickens in the cart, he unties the goat. "Let me get on to the house. Thanks for everything and I hope you and your family have a blessed day." Buck climbs onto the porch. He and Betty Gail go inside and are greeted by the smell of the warm pecan pie. The crackling fresh logs send a warm glow throughout the room.

Betty Gail looks around. "Feels like the fire is talking to us. Letting us know the kids are all right. Do you feel their warmth coming from the fire, Buck?"

Buck again holds Betty Gail tight. "There's something special about the fire today and that must be what it is. We need to keep it burning as long as possible, especially today."

The back kitchen door opens suddenly. Isaac and Sally come in from the cook house. The aroma of the two chickens sizzling and ready for the table overpowers that of the pecan pies. Sally places the chickens on the table, while Buck and Betty Gail gather up the greens from the hearth and place them on the table. "Well, let's all sit. Isaac, you and Sally join us like you always have for the holidays." Sally and Isaac render their usual smile and set a place at the table.

"Today, instead of prayer we will listen to the spirit of Christmas coming from the glowing fire in the fireplace," says Betty Gail as her voice trembles.

"The chil'ens gonna be all right Miss Betty ... I knows it," says Sally as she touches Betty Gail's hand. The crackling fire and its warmth embody the thoughts of Betty Gail and Buck during their quiet dinner. Buck, Betty Gail, Sally and Isaac take their seats at the small dining room table. There are four other plates set, and Buck looks to those four empty seats and offers his Christmas prayer. "God guide and protect our children and grandchild." His voice somewhat cracking, Betty Gail reaches and takes his hand and squeezes it gently. "Let your eternal love bring peace to this land. Amen."

Decatur is still a vast waste and Mary Gay, her mother and Telitha are extremely hungry. There is absolutely nothing left to eat in the city. She sees a lonely crow flying over and never comes down to pick a morsel. Mary Gay learned several weeks before Christmas that a Confederate commissary is exchanging lead for food. With her basket in hand she proceeds to the place where General Hood blew up his ordinance train. There in the extreme wind and cold she takes an old and dull case-knife and plunges it into the frozen ground. She and Telitha begin harvesting former missiles of death to exchange for food to keep from starving. Slowly she and Telitha extracts bullets while their hands and feet freeze. Their hands begin to bleed from abrasions. While on her kneed Mary Gay begins crying long and loud almost like a baby. Yet she continues to stab the frozen ground and ply lead so she and her family can eat.[555]

At length her basket is full. There are no streets to follow and no labyrinths to tread yet she is able to find the commissary. A courteous yet wounded gentleman in a faded gray uniform approaches and ask, "What can I do for you?"[556]

"I hear that you give provisions for lead and I have brought some to exchange." After a moment of scrutiny by the gentleman he asks, "What would you like in exchange?" Urgently Mary replies, "If you have sugar, and coffee, and meal, a little of each if you please. I have nothing to eat at home." The gentleman takes the baskets of lead and weighs them. Returning shortly he has a two full baskets containing sugar, coffee, flour, meal, lard, and the nicest meat she has seen in a long time.

Full of elation, Mary says, "O, sir, I did not expect this much!"

"You are due more and here is a certificate for your use at a later date." No joy or thrill comes upon Mary only satisfaction as she is homeward bound with the two baskets to feed her mother and Telitha.[557]

❧

Standing in front of their fireplace in the parlor with three of their slaves, Dick, Francis and Phillis, poor Mr. Thomas Maguire takes his wife's hand and shares his thought with his wife Elizabeth, "No need for celebration this year."

Looking at the mantle with a simple Christmas Manger scene accented with fresh cedar branches, Elizabeth agrees. "Yes, my dear, I had to force myself to do these little preparations for Christmas. Even our children are not making much fuss about the Holy Day."

"Nothing like it used to be in years past. Elizabeth, hand me another warm, wet cloth. This wound on Francis is looking pretty good, and it's only been one week since I whipped the three of them for stealing."[558]

❧

Union soldiers who are Masons begin to gather at the Solomon Lodge number 1 of Ancient, Free and Accepted Masons in Savannah. The Lodge has become the center of fraternizing between Union Masonic soldiers and the Savannah Masons pray together. Union soldiers bring rations for a dinner with their brother Masons. They mingle and enjoy Christmas as if no war is going on.

～

The cadets have an exhausting and strenuous march in South Carolina. They pass through Hardeeville, finally reaching the railroad in Bamberg on Christmas Day. Hungry, dirty, unshaven and a long way from home, they are unrecognizable, demoralized from the recent events as they gather around the stove in the depot.[559] Some of the cadets' feet are in a terrible state as a result of blisters from the long march from Savannah. Paul, Norman, and several other cadets are given permission to go hunting for squirrels and rabbits.

While the group of cadets is away hunting, the Confederate militia mail agent arrives to deliver the mail. "Mail Call!" shouts the clerk. Smiles come upon the faces of the cadets as they rush to the clerk, hopeful their name is on one of the letters. Holding a stack of about ten letters, the clerk calls out, "Coleman!"

"Here!" replies Coleman as the mail passes to him.

The clerk continues as the cadets cheerfully pass letters back to their comrades. "Norman Jernigan!"

"He's out hunting, but I'll hold it for him," signals Julius Brown. Slowly, the cadets return to the stoves and the aroma of the Christmas feast. Each cadet with his letter has several close friends to gather round for the latest news from home. It appears that one letter elevates the morale of twenty cadets as most of the contents are read aloud.

Returning with their kill several hours later, Norman, Paul and the other cadets enter the depot to a huge gathering of local citizens. They lay an abundant feast of delicacies that have not been seen for a month.[560] There's turkey and dressing, fresh ham, corn bread, collards and cabbage. Upon seeing the hunters return, two of the local men offer to clean the squirrels and rabbits. Norman and Paul gladly hand over the still warm bounty.

Julius rushes over to Norman with his hands behind his back. With a broad smile, he says, "Got a surprise for you, Norman!"

Norman is unsure of what the surprise might be and asks, "Should I guess?"

"If you would like to guess, go ahead, but no more than three. But I'll give you a hint; it is a great Christmas present!"

"New shoes is my first guess."

"Nope!" responds Julius with a broader smile.

"You got it behind your back, right?" questions Norman.

"Right!" responds Julius.

"So it's gotta be small. How about a letter from Pa and Ma?"

"Close. I'll give you a clue." Julius snaps the letter to Norman's face and at the same time says, "Even better, a letter from Polly!" Norman is speechless. He slowly lifts his hand and takes the letter from Julius.

Norman carefully studies the handwriting and looks for an isolated corner of the depot. Paul, Julius and several other cadets eagerly accompany him and all sit together. Norman stares at the letter as if he is afraid to open it, thinking that the contents might be more than he can bear.

"Open it, Norman," says Paul. "Let us all share this Christmas Day with you, good or bad. It's a good day for a long awaited letter." Norman opens the folded letter and wipes tears from his eyes before he starts reading it. Paul sees Norman's emotions running deep and suggests "Let me read it to you." He hesitates and then hands Paul the letter. Paul begins to read:

"My Dear Norman, I hope you are well and surviving this conflict."

"If you only knew!" Norman laughs.

"I am still in Savannah."

"Still in Savannah!"shouts Norman along with the other nearby cadets.

Continuing, Paul reads, "I imagine Ma and Pa told you the whole story. But if not, I will fill you in. Legare and I came here after we eloped and were married in Augusta. I also assume you know you now have a wonderful nephew. His name is Joshua, and he looks just like his father."

"Congratulations!" holler the other cadets, shaking his hand while others pat his back.

"We all expect a cigar from you sooner or later, Norman!" says Julius as they all sign on in agreement.

Paul reads ahead while the others are congratulating Norman. He becomes solemn and clears his throat, placing his hand on Norman's arms, "This isn't a good part, Norman. Maybe you should read it to yourself," says Paul with a choking voice. Paul hands Norman the letter and he slowly reads:

"Legare enlisted in Savannah on his birthday. He was killed in Cassville this past May. Our eyes never parted until his carriage was out of sight. He did not want me to go to the depot with him. I know he was right, now. Ma and Pa came to Savannah with Congressman and Mrs. Hill. Pa was sitting on the steps when I came home that day. I knew right away why he was there waiting for me. It was written all over his face. Congressman Hill gave me a lock of Legare's hair and I wear it around my neck in a locket which also contains his only picture. After the funeral, Ma and Pa asked me to go back home with them. I told them, I'll stay here until the end of the war helping to make herbal medicine at Bartow Hospital in memory of Legare." Paul's chin is already shaking as he vainly whispers to the other cadets the sad news. They all become somber and quiet. Norman passes the letter back to Paul.

Within a few minutes, Paul has his composure back and continues to read, "The Hills have a very nice home on the river and ours is close by. Legare's Uncle Richard gave me a slave by the name of Tot to stay with us. Have you heard from Pa and Ma? I miss them so. They and the Hills came for a surprise visit on Legare's birthday. We became a united family before Legare enlisted. You would have loved Legare as a brother-in-law.

"I do not know where you are. One of your schoolmates, Marsh, passed away this morning at Guyton Hospital. His wounds were severe and he was unconscious when he arrived at the hospital yesterday. A friend of mine came and told me this morning of his death."

Norman pauses again as the cadets quickly pass the word that Marsh passed away in Savannah. He continues, "If you come to Savannah, I am on the south end of town on the river. Just ask where the Hill House is or come by the Bartow Hospital and ask for me. I love you, Norman and miss you more than you know. God be with you. Love, Polly."

Norman stares for a long moment at the letter before he looks up at his friend. Norman shakes Paul's hand. "Thanks, Paul. You're a true friend."

The two locals skin and clean the kill quickly and set them to roasting. Other residents sing Christmas carols. They sit and talk to the cadets, curious about their service in the Confederacy. Some even take notes for an article in the newspaper. After the meal, the cadets join in singing. Finally, a little after dark, the cadets grow tired. They graciously thank the citizens for sharing Christmas and food with them. Slowly, the citizens depart, and the cadets are left with only three of the cadets' parents: Calhoun's, Breese's, and Hill's.

Cadets Calhoun and Breese are from South Carolina and decide to join their state units. Cadet Lt. Hill is being transferred to Gen. R. W.

Carswell's staff. He has been assigned as Assistant Inspector Gen. for the First Brigade of the Georgia Militia. "Farewells do not come easy," Norman explains to his comrades, as they gather for one last song:

We Conquer or Die
The Briton boasts his coat of red,
With lace and spangles decked;
In garb of green the French are seen,
With gaudy colors flecked;
The Yankees strut in dingy blue,
And epaulets display;
Our Southern girls more proudly view
The uniform of gray.

That dress is worn by gallant hearts
Whoever for defy,
Who stalwart stand, with battle-brand,
To conquer or to die!
They fight for freedom, hope and home,
And honor's voice obey
And proudly wear where'er they roam
The uniform of gray.

What though 'tis stained with crimson hues,
And dim with dust and smoke,
By bullets torn, and rent and shorn
By many a hostile stroke;
Go forth in the pathway our forefathers trod;
We, too, fight for freedom—our Captain is God;
Their blood in our veins, with their honor we vie,
Theirs, too, was the watchword,
"We conquer or die!"
We strike for the South-Mountain, Valley and Plain—
For the South we will conquer again and again;
Her day of salvation and triumph is nigh,
Ours, then, be the watchword,
"We conquer or Die!"

Taking his turn in line, Paul whispers, "This is the last time all of us shall be together," as he embraces his three departing comrades. They quietly leave the depot and board the carriages with their families. The Corps stands outside, and waves until the light falling snow muffles the sound and sight of the departing coaches. Returning inside the depot, each cadet finds a spot and falls into one of the deepest and safest sleeps they have experienced in a long time. Norman wraps the scarf which Legare had given him around his chilled neck, re-reads his letter alone and drifts off to sleep, still clutching it tightly in his hand.

QUESTIONS AND ANSWERS

"Norman, time to Get up."Opening his eyes, he puts his hand on his stiff neck and looks up.

"Morning already, Paul?"

"Yep. We gotta head to the depot."

"Where are we going?"

"Augusta. We'll eat on the train."

Paul extends his hand to Norman and helps him from his torn blanket. Norman slides on his worn out shoes and puts on his rotten gloves. Stepping outside he wraps, what's left of his blanket, around him. "Brrr." Norman shakes to fight off the sudden cold. The December temperature is bitter as they disembark for the depot.

When the cadets arrive in Augusta they go into marching formation. A Confederate officer greets them. "Your winter quarters are about three miles outside of town.[561] You are now a part of Gen. Gustavus Smith's State Militia."

Norman looks around. "Pretty nice place Paul. Wonder where the church is where Polly and Legare were married?"

"Maybe we can ask around. Did she say what denomination?"

"No, but we always went to the Stone Mountain Baptist Church, so I assume they were married in a Baptist church."

"Halt!" shouts the officer from Gen. Smith's headquarters. This is the building you will be quartered in. Settle down and you will receive additional orders this afternoon. Dismissed."Although the sun has warmed the air, the cadets shiver as they enter the cold building.

"Oh my God," shouts Paul as he enters the building ahead of Norman.

"What is it Paul?"

"The convicts on parole are also assigned to our unit." The morale of the Cadet Corps universally sank even deeper.

Cadet Montgomery conveys his thoughts to Norman. "Looks like we are as low as the convicts when it comes to the service of the Confederacy. The more prisoners the governor releases, the more they desert. We must keep our eyes on them at all times. Even when we get our half rations, they try to steal as much as they can. I think we should shoot any prisoner caught stealing!"

At that moment, Maj. Capers enters the quarters. The cadets come to attention as usual when an officer enters. "Stand at Ease!"

The cadets look at each other, noticing that the major's speech is slurred and that he is somewhat off balance. Holding onto a chair, the Maj. tries to welcome the cadets and praises the Corps for the standard they have set in their tour of duty. During his speech, his voice is slow and full of burps. He finally is able to brief the cadets. They'll be on guard duty for several weeks and, the Corps will be getting new clothes and boots in a day or two. After the tour in Augusta, the Corps most likely will return to Milledgeville. As he departs, he directs one of the convicts to assist him to his quarters.

After seeing Maj. Capers drunk, the mood of the cadets sinks even deeper. Norman bows his head and whispers to Paul. "Not only is our commander a drunk, but he feels better having a convict assist him to his quarters!" exclaims Montgomery.[562]

"I can't disagree with you," says Norman. "Those convicts are our waiters. They must keep the fires going and do the cooking. Just keep your musket by your side at all times."

Paul joins the conversation. "Let's get the water boiling so at least we can bathe and shave. Maybe we can turn this poor beef ration into some kind of decent stew." Slowly, the quarters warm up, and the smell of the half ration of beef aroma begins to fill the air.

"I would like to take leave, and go to Savannah and visit my sister and nephew." Norman says, "But I know it's not possible at this time. The Yankees are still there. Maybe I can take leave later."

Paul nods. "At the rate the war is going, we will all be home before summer gets here. I know you're anxious to see Polly and Little Joshua, but be patient."

On December 26, General Sherman receives a dispatch from President Lincoln:

EXECUTIVE MANSION,
Washington, December 26, 1864.

MY DEAR GENERAL SHERMAN: Many, many thanks for your
Christmas gift, the capture of Savannah. When you were about leaving
Atlanta for the Atlantic for the Atlantic coast, I was anxious, if not fear-
ful; but feeling that you were the better judge, and remembering that
"nothing risked, nothing gained," I did not interfere. Now, the undertak-
ing being a success, the honor is all yours; ....

Yours, very truly,

A. LINCOLN

DECEMBER 28, 1864

Dr. Blair informs Polly, "I would like for you and Mrs. Cazier to accompany me to a citizens meeting with Mayor Arnold at the Masonic Lodge at noon. I understand that about seventy-five of the citizens, by petition, have asked to meet with him. In response to the petition, the mayor is going to discuss the results of his conversation with General Sherman and the future welfare of the city. Mrs. Cazier has already accepted and told me to invite you."

"I would surely like to hear what Mayor Arnold and the General have been discussing."

Dr. Blair, Mrs. Cazier and Polly reach the Masonic Lodge a little before noon. They find at least one hundred people are in attendance. The mayor is already there and takes note of the citizens' concerns. Polly listens to the general conversations. Most Savannah citizens believe the Confederacy is beaten. The citizens are sick of the war, and the presence of the Union Army of occupation crystallizes this latent peace sentiment in the city. The citizens complain about the food shortage, the fuel shortage, and the destruction of some of the businesses by the looters.

At noon, Mayor Arnold goes to the front of the assembly hall and stands before the podium. The hall slowly becomes silent.

"I want to thank all of you who have asked me to come here today to discuss the future of Savannah. I have weighed our options anxiously and have arrived at a positive conclusion."

Polly notices the general attitude of several groups. She leans close to Mrs. Cazier.

"The citizens appear somewhat cold and aloof from these proceedings. They need to give Mayor Arnold a chance to explain himself. After all, he did save Savannah from destruction."

"They are hungry and scared, Polly. Hopefully, Mayor Arnold can settle their anxiety."

"As Mayor, and with the permission of General Sherman, your governing body has adopted the following resolutions. These resolutions will lead the way for Savannah's recovery. I will now read you these resolutions.

"That we accept the position, and in the language of the President of the United States, seek to have peace by laying down our arms and submitting to the national authority under the constitution, leaving all questions which remain to be adjusted by the peaceful means of legislation.

"That we do not put ourselves in the position of a conquered city asking terms of the conqueror, but we claim the immunities and privileges contained in the Proclamation and message of the President of the United States and in all the legislation of Congress in reference to a people situated as we are, and while we owe on our part a strict obedience to the laws of the United States, we ask the protection over our persons, lives, and property recognized by these laws.

"That laying aside all differences and burying bygones in the grave of the past, we will use our best endeavors once more to bring back the prosperity and commerce we once enjoyed.

"That we respectfully request his Excellency, the Governor, to call a convention of the people of Georgia by a constitutional means in his power, to give them an opportunity of voting upon the question whether they wish the war between the two sections of the country to continue."

Polly looks around and begins to see many of the citizens nodding their heads in agreement.

"That Major-General Sherman having placed as military commander of this post Brigadier-General Geary, who has, by his urbanity as a gentleman and his uniform kindness to our citizens done all in is power to protect them and their property from insult and injury, it is the unanimous desire of all present that he be allowed to remain in his present position and that for the reasons above the thanks of the citizens are hereby tendered to him and the officers under his command."[563]

"These resolutions, we feel, are in our best interest," says Mayor Arnold. "I would like to see by a show of hands those that are in agreement with these resolutions."

A tall citizen stands and remarks, "The sooner we get back to normal, the better off we'll all be. I recommend we, as citizens, accept these resolutions."

The citizens all stand and let their voices be heard that they are in agreement. Mayor Arnold responds, "Then by your vote, I will submit Savannah to the National authority under the Constitution in accordance with Lincoln's amnesty proclamation."

Polly puts her hands together and turns to Mrs. Cazier and Dr. Blair. "At least Savannah is at peace with the United States of America."[564]

❧

Colonel Julian Allen has been in Savannah since Tuesday, December 27, after arriving from New York. He is a Polish-American and is interested in assisting Savannah because of Casimir Pulaski.[565] He immediately meets with General Sherman who quickly takes note of him. On Saturday, General Sherman and Mayor Arnold review Colonel Allen's impressive record. Colonel Allen offers to advance twenty thousand dollars to the food relief effort.[566] They are impressed with his characteristics and qualifications as a soldier, salesman and especially as a crusader. Jointly, Colonel Allen is selected by General Sherman and Mayor Arnold as the committee" and "Special Agent" to sail to the North. His mission is to sell the $265,000 worth of rice and raise funds for the relief of Savannah.[567]

DECEMBER 30, 1864

General Sherman receives a confidential message from his close friend, General H. W. Halleck. It appears that the abolitionists and Radical Republicans are furious that Union forces have not given freedom to more slaves during the march from Atlanta to Savannah:

> *HEADQUARTER OF THE ARMY*
> *WASHINGTON, D.C., December 30, 1864*
> *Major-General W. T. Sherman, Savannah*
>
> *My Dear General: I take the liberty of calling your attention, in this private and friendly way, to a matter which may possibly hereafter be of more importance to you than either of us may now anticipate.*

While almost everyone is praising your great march through Georgia, and the capture of Savannah, there is a certain class having now great influence with the President, and very probably anticipating still more on a change of cabinet, who are decidedly disposed to make a point against you. I mean in regard to "inevitable Sambo." They say that you have manifested an almost criminal dislike to the negro, (sic) and that you are not willing to carry out the wishes of the Government in regard to him, but repulse him with contempt! They say you might have brought with you to Savannah more than fifty thousand, thus stripping Georgia of that number of laborers, and opening a road by which as many more could have escaped from their masters; but that, instead of this, you drove them from your ranks, prevented their following you by cutting the bridges in your rear, and thus caused the massacre of large numbers by Wheeler's cavalry.

To those who know you as I do, such accusation will pass as the idle winds, for we presume that you discouraged the negroes (sic) from following you because you had not the means of supporting them, and feared they might seriously embarrass your march. But there are others, and among them some in high authority, who think or pretend to think otherwise, and they are decidedly disposed to make a point against you.

I do not write this to induce you to conciliate this class of men by doing anything which you do not deem right and proper, and for the interest of the Government and the country; but simply to call your attention to certain things which are viewed here somewhat differently than from your stand-point. I will explain as briefly as possible;

Some here think that, in view of the scarcity of labor in the South, and the probability that a part, at least, of the able-bodied slaves will be called into the military service of the rebels, it is of the greatest importance to open outlets by which these slaves can escape into our lines, and they say that the route you have passed over should be made the route of escape, and Savannah the great place of refuge. These, I know, are the views of some of the leading men in the Administration, and they now express dissatisfaction that you did not carry them out in your great raid.

Now that you are in possession of Savannah, and there can be no further fears about supplies, would it not be possible for you to reopen these avenues of escape for the negroe (sic), without interfering with you military operations? Could not such escaped slaves find at least a partial supply of food in the rice-fields about Savannah, and cotton plantations on the coast?

I merely throw out these suggestions. I know that such a course would be approved by the Government, and I believe that a manifestation on your part of a desire to bring the slaves within our lines will do much to silence your opponents. You will appreciate my motives in writing this private letter.

Yours truly,

H. W. Halleck[568]

JANUARY 10, 1864
THE GREYHOUND *SAILS FROM BOSTON TO SAVANNAH*

The next day the revenue-cutter arrives in Savannah unannounced. On board are Simeon Draper, Esq., of New York City, the Hon. E. M. Stanton, Secretary of War, Quartermaster-General Meigs, Adjutant-General Townsend, and a retinue of civilians who have come down from the North to regulate the civil affairs of Savannah.[569]

Secretary Stanton dispatches a messenger from the cutter to General Sherman's headquarters to notify the general of Mr. Stanton's arrival. The dispatch is given to Colonel Dayton aide-de-camp who in turn delivers it to General Sherman. Sherman opens the dispatch. "I have just arrived at the wharf on a revenue cutter and wish to visit with you as soon as possible. E. M. Stanton, Secretary of War."

General Sherman directs Colonel Dayton and other members of his staff to welcome Secretary Stanton on his arrival at the wharf. Dayton departs immediately and seeks to meet with Mr. Stanton. "Welcome to Savannah from General Sherman."

Mr. Stanton replies, "Thank you Captain! You're a welcome sight. Where, may I ask, is General Sherman?"

"General Sherman should be at his headquarters at the Green Mansion when you arrive there, Mr. Secretary. I have several carriages waiting to take you there." The entourage walks a short distance and boards the waiting carriages. Upon arriving at headquarters, Secretary Stanton and his staff proceed to General Sherman's upstairs office. Only Mr. Stanton, his aide, General Sherman, his clerk and chief of staff are present for the initial meeting.

General Sherman meets Mr. Stanton at his office door. "Welcome to Savannah, Mr. Secretary. What brings you here?"

"Primarily rest and relaxation, but there are a few matters I need to discuss with you while I am here." Looking around, Stanton continues, "Very nice accommodations you have here, General Sherman."

"Yes, they are, Mr. Green was kind enough to offer his residence for my headquarters. He is an excellent host."

Secretary Stanton wastes little time. "Who is in charge of the city government?"

"A Dr. Arnold is the Mayor. He and his Aldermen are in charge in conjunction with my military. Dr. Arnold is extremely capable, a Union supporter, and I place my full confidence in his ability to care for Savannah."

Secretary of War Stanton continues, "The first order of business is for you to transfer to Mr. Draper the custom house, post-office, and such other public buildings as these civilians need in the execution of their office to regulate the civic affairs of Savannah. Also, you're to deliver into their custody the captured cotton."[570]

General Sherman turns to Colonel Dayton, his Aide-de-Camp. "Draw an order immediately for my signature addressing the matters which Secretary Stanton and I have been discussing.

"Secretary Stanton, I have, up to this time, had the cotton carefully under guard. General Euston has my orders to ship it by the return-vessels to New York for the adjudication of the nearest prize-court. Accompanying the cargo are invoices and all evidence of title to ownership. Marks, numbers, and other figures, are carefully preserved on the bales so that the court might know the history of each bale. This should help you with the inventory."

To his surprise, Mr. Stanton, who surely is an able lawyer, replies, "General Sherman, order the obliteration of all the marks; so that no man, friend or foe, can trace his identical cotton."[571]

General Sherman finds this extremely strange and attempts to enlighten Mr. Stanton. "Mr. Stanton, for sure claims, real and fictitious, will be filed against this identical cotton of three times the quantity actually captured. The reclamations on the Treasury will be for more than the actual quantity captured, maybe as high as thirty-one thousand bales."[572]

Secretary Stanton, apparently irritated by Sherman's remarks says simply, "Do as I say, General."

〰

*Special Field Orders, No. 10. HEADQUARTERS MILITARY
DIVISION OF THE MISSISSIPPI, IN THE FIELD, NEAR
SAVANNAH, GEORGIA
January 12, 1865*

*1. Brevet Brigadier-General Euston, chief-quartermaster, will turn over
to Simeon Draper, Esq., agent of the United States Treasury Department,
all cotton now in the city of Savannah, prize of war, taking his receipt for
the same in gross, and returning for it to the quartermaster-general.
He will also afford Mr. Draper all the facilities in his power in the way
of transportation, labor, etc., to enable him to handle the cotton
with expedition.*

*2. General Euston will also turn over to Mr. Draper the custom-house
and such other buildings in the city of Savannah as he may need in the
execution of his office.*

*By order of Major General W. T. Sherman
L. M. DAYTON, Aide-de-Camp*[573]

Once the order is drawn, General Sherman asks, "Mr. Secretary, would
you like to tour the city at this time?"

"Yes, I would like that very much."

Sherman stands and escorts Secretary Stanton outside. The day is
clear, with a slight breeze and moderate temperature. General Sherman
suggests, "Let's take a walking tour through town and you can inspect the
bivouac areas of the various commands on the squares. However, most of
my troops are camping outside the city. I'll have the carriage follow along
behind us." They leave Sherman's headquarters and begin their tour.

As they walk, Mr. Stanton again discloses to General Sherman, "As I
said, my primary reason for coming to Savannah is for the sole purpose of
rest and recreation in Savannah. I have been having a good deal of internal
pain, and I sometimes feel that the pain may be life threatening. If the
pain continues, it may compel me to resign from public office."[574]

General Sherman knows why Mr. Stanton is in Savannah from the confidential communication he received from his friend, General Halleck.[575]
"You look robust and strong to me, Mr. Secretary."

Mr. Stanton continues the pretense of 'rest and recreation.' "There's so much bickering and jealousies at the national capital that it keeps me awake at night wondering what will be the topic of discontent the next day. State Governors quarrel with each other and assault me and the president about their quotas for the military. Yet the governors want to preserve the Union and do away with slavery."

General Sherman simply shakes his head. "That's definitely a political problem which I feel confident that President Lincoln will be able to resolve. He's carried the nation this far in this conflict and he will see a positive conclusion for the Union." General Sherman continues to listen while they walk toward the bivouac areas.

"If you think Confederate money is useless, why, you would not believe that the price of everything has so risen in comparison with the depreciation of the money. There's a danger of national bankruptcy which may threaten the very existence of the government!"

"No time for alarm, Mr. Secretary. Our nation had a lottery to fund the American Revolution. We have fought too long and hard, not only with this conflict, but others as well. In my opinion, the treasury will regain when the war ends. Europe wants our raw materials badly and is willing to pay high prices for them. Here we are, Mr. Stanton. This is one of several bivouac areas. I don't know if you have been in Savannah before, but there are twenty-four such squares in town. Very nice, central locations for my troops. They have good sanitation with deep latrines and plenty of running water. Rations are better now that Fort McAllister is taken and supplies can travel up the river. Although Savannah citizens are suffering somewhat from food shortage, they have plenty of rice and of course food from the ocean and river. I also turned over the abandoned Confederate provisions to the mayor for distribution to the citizens. If there's a problem, it is not having enough fodder for the animals, so daily excursions are made to the country side to collect it."

"Are your troops ready to move on to South Carolina?" asks Mr. Stanton.

"Yes, as soon as my resupply is complete in a couple of weeks. My troops are anxious to finish this conflict, as am I. We all see the end near at hand."

Their stroll takes them down to River Street where General Sherman points out the remains of several Confederate ships and the general condition of the city buildings and dwellings. As darkness approaches, Sherman says, "You're invited to supper tonight at my headquarters where you can meet Mayor Arnold and the Aldermen. Mr. Green's staff prepares a great meal."

"Thank you, General. I assume Mr. Draper, General Meigs and General Townsend are included in your invitation?"

"By all means, Mr. Secretary," replies General Sherman.

"I would like to return to the cutter so I can rest and go over some notes. What time will your carriage pick us up this evening?"

"Around 6:30, sir, if that is convenient for you."

"That is perfect. We shall see you then."

❧

Upon the arrival of Secretary of War Stanton's party, General Sherman greets them at the door with three of his senior staff aides with the rank of colonel. The reception line inside the mansion consists of General Geary, General Kilpatrick, General Osterhaus, General Howard, General Hazen, General Blair, General Slocum, General Davis, Mayor Arnold and the Board of Aldermen and finally, Mr. Green. General Sherman escorts Secretary Stanton along the line and introduces each person. Then one of General Sherman's staff aides-de-camp escorts, Mr. Draper, General Meigs and General Townsend in a similar manner.

During supper, Secretary Stanton sits between General Sherman and Mayor Arnold. After grace, Mayor Arnold offers a toast. "The city of Savannah welcomes Secretary of War Stanton and his staff to Savannah. May your visit be purposeful, fruitful and in your eyes see that Savannah is truly for the preservation of the Union." All raise their wine glasses and take a sip.

Secretary Stanton stands and offers a toast as well. "To General Sherman, a true soldier and a patriot, and his army and to their success. May their successes continue. To Savannah, may you continue to prosper from your sound decision not to resist the grand army of the Republic. Let this conflict come to an end and the Republic be united."Again the wine glasses are raised.

During supper, Mr. Stanton and Mayor Arnold discuss the occupation of Savannah and how well the civic leaders and the military are cooperating. "It is for the benefit of the citizens of Savannah and the preservation of our city," concludes Mayor Arnold.

After supper, Secretary Stanton sits privately with General Sherman. They discuss a few general issues, but finally Secretary Stanton narrows the conversation to a specific topic. "General, I want to talk about the Negro issue tomorrow morning around 9:30." Standing and excusing himself, Secretary Stanton looks sternly at General Sherman. "Please have your carriage available to transport me from the cutter."

"The carriages will be at the wharf at 9:30, Mr. Secretary." General Sherman rises in deference to Secretary Stanton and accompanies him to the door.

"The evening has been delightful and I'll see you in the morning," replies Secretary Stanton as he and his staff depart for their quarters on the cutter.[576]

General Sherman knows that the conversation that will occur the following day is the main purpose for Mr. Stanton's visit. Purely political, concerning the Negroes and not related to the success of the army.[577]

General Sherman wakes up the next morning and prepares his office with a round conference table. Secretary Stanton arrives sharply at 9:30, and Colonel Dayton escorts him to Sherman's office. "Good morning, Mr. Secretary. I trust you had a good night's sleep after such a grand meal." They shake hands and sit at the conference table.

"Fell asleep like a baby and slept like one as well."

The waiter places a silver pot containing hot water for tea on the table along with a pot of hot coffee. An assortment of sweets is placed in the middle of the table. "Colonel Dayton will join us, Mr. Secretary, to take down the meeting, if that meets with your approval."

"That is satisfactory, General," replies Secretary Stanton. "I would like to discuss General Jefferson Davis first.[578] I know he is a Democrat, and some say he is hostile to the Negro. What have you observed of General Davis in regards to the Negro?"

"I assure you that General Davis is an excellent soldier, and I do not believe he has any hostility to the Negro."

"Then explain to me, General Sherman. What role does the Negro have in your army?"

General Sherman responds, "In our army, there are no Negro soldiers, and, as a rule, we prefer white soldiers. The white soldier understands orders, weapons and is easier to train for combat. We have supportive positions where we employ a large force of Negroes as servants, teamsters, and members of the pioneers. All Negroes so employed have rendered admirable service to our army."

Secretary Stanton opens his valise, reaches inside and produces a newspaper. He hands the newspaper to General Sherman and points to a specific article, "This is an article detailing an account of General Davis taking up his pontoon-bridge across Ebenezer Creek. It states that he left sleeping Negro men, women, and children, on the other side, in anticipation of them being slaughtered by Wheeler's cavalry. What is your rebuttal to this newspaper account?"

General Sherman reads the article for several minutes. He places the newspaper on the table. "I have heard of such a rumor. However, Mr. Secretary, before becoming prejudiced, please allow me to send for General Davis. He can explain the matter since he is the officer who was at the river."

"Please do so. It will be interesting to hear his account of this accusation."

General Sherman turns to Colonel Dayton. "Dispatch a sentry to summon General Davis to my office immediately."

"Yes sir, General." Dayton leaves the room and issues the order to the Sergeant-Major to summon Davis who happens to have his quarters at the Green mansion as well.

Shortly, General Davis arrives at General Sherman's office. Davis enters and salutes. "Good morning, Mr. Secretary and good morning, General Sherman."

"General Davis, have a seat. Secretary Stanton has some questions he would like for you to address concerning the Ebenezer Creek crossing."

"I'll be glad to answer any questions you may have Mr. Secretary."

Secretary Stanton takes the newspaper which contains the article about Ebenezer River and the abandoned slaves and hands it to General Davis. Again he points out the article. "Would you kindly read this article and explain what exactly happened from your viewpoint?"

After a brief passage of time, General Davis lays the paper on the table and gives a slight snicker. "Well, Mr. Secretary, it is a newspaper article written to keep the fever of the slave issue prominent. The truth is that as my columns approached the seaboard, the freedmen in droves, old and young, followed the columns to reach a place of safety. It just so happens that my route into Savannah followed what is known as the 'River Road.' We had to make constant use of my pontoon-train. There was so much water that the head of my columns would reach some deep impassable creek before the rear of the column was fairly over another. My columns on numerous occasions utilized the pontoons both day and night in order to meet our objective."[579]

"I see." Secretary Stanton glances at the other men. "Continue, General Davis."

"On the occasion referred to, the bridge was taken up from Ebenezer Creek while some of the camp-followers remained asleep on the farther side. Some of the freedmen awoke and, in their fright, were drowned in trying to swim over. The fright was probably caused by the proximity of Gen. Wheeler's cavalry. For some reason, they were afraid of being killed by them.[580] My intentions were not to block the slaves from crossing. We were in need of my pontoons to span another creek. However, you know as well as I do, that Gen. Wheeler is not a person who would deal in genocide. His troops, as far as I know, took freedmen as prisoners and attempted to return them to their owners.[581]

"At crossings operations, the same turn of events might have occurred to General Howard, or to any other of the many most humane commanders. That is my analysis and summary of the course of events at Ebenezer Creek, Mr. Secretary."

Secretary Stanton and General Sherman sit silent for a moment before Secretary Stanton asks, "Do you have any questions of General Davis, General Sherman?"

"I do not, Mr. Stanton."

WHAT DO YOU THINK?

Secretary Stanton gazes over his glasses. "Then you may go, General Davis. Thank you for your time."

Davis stands and salutes. Sherman nods his head in return and Davis departs. "With all due respect Mr. Secretary, I must tell you that General Jeff Davis is strictly a soldier, and doubtless hated to have his wagons and columns encumbered by these poor Negroes. We all feel sympathy, but sympathy of a different sort from you, which is not of pure humanity, but of politics."[582]

Secretary Stanton cuts his eyes at General Sherman in a somewhat irritated fashion. "Enough about Ebenezer Creek for now, General Sherman. You know the political eventualities of the day are that freedmen will become voters, and the complexion of the ballot box is going to change."

General Sherman replies, "I do not believe the right to vote will happen but do know that slavery, as such, is dead forever. I do not suppose that the former slaves will be suddenly, without preparation, manufactured into voters, equal to all others, politically and socially."[583]

"It is definitely an eventuality, General Sherman. Next, I want to interview the leaders of the slave society. Arrange an interview for me in a couple of days here in your office. I expect you to invite the most intelligent of the Negroes."[584]

"I'll have them assemble here in a couple of days, Secretary Stanton."

"Let's call it a day, General Sherman. I'll assume the Negroes will be here in two days at 8:00 PM."

"They'll be here, Mr. Secretary." They shake hands and Colonel Dayton escorts the Secretary to his carriage.

General Sherman invites Dr. Pollard, a Negro veterinarian to his office and informs him, "Dr. Pollard, Secretary of War Stanton is currently

visiting Savannah. He would like to interview as many of the leading Negroes of Chatham County and the surrounding area. Secretary
Stanton would like for them to hear the reading of the Emancipation
Proclamation. He request that these individuals be here on the evening
of the 17th at 8 PM."

"I'll invite as many as possible. Some may show up and some may not."
Accordingly Dr. Pollard invites the most intelligent of the Negroes, mostly
Baptist and Methodist preachers, to come to the Green Mansion to meet
the Secretary of War. Twenty Negroes respond. They all arrive by 8:00 PM
and are treated as guests in Sherman's quarters.

Secretary Stanton and Adjutant-General Townsend also arrive at 8:00
PM, and Colonel Dayton escorts them to General Sherman's quarters.
Adjutant-General Townsend takes down the conversation in the form
of questions and answers.[585] There are twenty comfortable chairs facing
the rectangular conference table. At the conference table are seats for Mr.
Stanton, General Sherman, Adjutant-General Townsend, Colonel Dayton and a seat for their interpreter and spokesman, Mr. Garrison Frazier.

After a brief period of socializing and introductions, all parties take
their respective seats. Mr. Stanton says, "Now if each of you gentlemen
will give your name and partial history for our records." Each of the
twenty states his name and gives a brief history of his vocation.[586]

Minutes of an interview between the colored ministers and church of-
ficers at Savannah with the Secretary of War and Major-General Sherman:
HEADQUARTERS OF MAJ.-GENERAL SHERMAN, CITY OF
SAVANNAH, GA:

Jan., 12, 1865—8 PM

On the evening of Thursday, the 12th day of January, 1865, the following persons of African descent met by appointment to hold an interview
with Edwin M. Stanton, Secretary of War, and Major-General Sherman,
to have a conference upon matters relating to the freedmen of the State
of Georgia, to-wit:

William J. Campbell, John Cox, Ulysses L. Houston, William Bentley,
Charles William Gaines, James Hill, Glasgon Taylor, Garrison Frazier,
James Mills, Abraham Burke, Arthur Wardell, Alexander Harris, Andrew
Neal, James Porter, Adolphus Delmotte, Jacob Godfrey, John Johnson,
Robert N. Taylor, and James Lynch. Afterwards, they select Garrison
Frazier as their spokesman.

Garrison Frazier, being chosen by the persons present to express their common sentiments upon the matters of inquiry, makes answers to inquiries as follows:

First Question: State what your understanding is in regard to the acts of Congress and President Lincoln's [Emancipation] proclamation, touching the condition of the colored people in the Rebel States.

Answer in Gullah: Well, when I steady (study) muh head 'bout dem tings, 'n wha' de President Lincoln hab fuh say, dat eff deh pit down dem gun 'n heed tuh de law ob de nunineted state b'fo' janeery fus,' ateteen sixty shree, all gwoi' be well; but eff deh don't, den all de slab dem een de souden state had fuh be free, henc'fort' 'n forebbuh. Dat wah I steady my head on.

Answer translated: So far as I understand President Lincoln's proclamation to the Rebellious States, it is, that if they would lay down their arms and submit to the laws of the United States before the first of January, 1863, all should be well; but if they did not, then all the slaves in the Rebel States should be free henceforth and forever. That is what I understood.

Second Question: State what you understand by Slavery and the freedom that was to be given by the President's proclamation.

Answer in Gullah: Slabbery is recebbin' by de gret power de wuk ob unettah man, 'n not by him 'greemint. De freedum, de way 'e come een my head, promis' by de procamation, is tekin' we from unduh de yok' of bondidge 'n pittin' we weh we kin reep de fewu't ob we own labuh.

Answer translated: Slavery is, receiving by irresistible power the work of another man, and not by his consent. The freedom, as I understand it, promised by the proclamation, is taking us from under the yoke of bondage, and placing us where we could reap the fruit of our own labor, take care of ourselves and assist the Government in maintaining our freedom.

Third Question: State in what manner you think you can take care of yourselves, and how can you best assist the Government in maintaining your freedom.

Answer in Gullah: De bes' way we kin tek kah ob we self is fuh had we own lan', 'n turn um 'n till um we self- dat is, by de wuk ob de ummon 'n chillun 'n ol' man; 'n soon we kin tek kah ob we self and hab suppin' left obbuh. 'N fuh help de gubmint, de young men dem shu'd jyin up fuh de serbis ob de gubmint, 'n ser'b een uh way dat want em fuh ser'b. We want fuh be put on lan' 'til we able fuh buy 'n mek um we own.

Answer Translated: The way we can best take care of ourselves is to have land, and turn it and till it by our own labor—that is, by the labor of the women and children and old men; and we can soon maintain ourselves and have something to spare. And to assist the Government, the young men should enlist in the service of the Government, and serve in such manner as they may be wanted. (The Rebels told us that they piled them up and made batteries of them, and sold them to Cuba; but we don't believe that.) We want to be placed on land until we are able to buy it and make it our own.

Fourth Question: State in what manner you would rather live—whether scattered among the whites or in colonies by yourselves.

Answer in Gullah: I radduh lib to by we self, 'cause dere is uh prejudice 'ghenst we een de sout' dat gwoin' tek yeahs fo' git obbuh. I cahnt' talk fuh my bredduh.

Answer Translated: I would prefer to live by ourselves, for there is a prejudice against us in the South that will take years to get over; but I do not know that I can answer for my brethren. Mr. Lynch says he thinks they should not be separated, but live together. All the other persons present, being questioned one by one, answer that they agree with Brother Frazier.

Fifth Question: Do you think that there is intelligence enough among the slaves of the South to maintain themselves under the Government of the United States and the equal protection of its laws, and maintain good and peaceable relations among yourselves and with your neighbors?

Answer in Gullah: We hab good sense. We know how fuh mek it.

Answer Translated: I think there is sufficient intelligence among us to do so.

Sixth Question: State what is the feeling of the black population of the South toward the Government of the United States; what is the understanding in respect to the present war—its causes and object, and their disposition to aid either side. State fully your views.

Answer in Gullah: I tink you'll find dat we had plenny who be glad fuh mek sakuhfice fuh help de Gubmint of de Nunited State, 'n deh duh plenny who ready fuh fight wid de gun. I don' tink you goin' fin' uh dozen men who 'pose de Gugmint. I unnuhstan', 'bout de war, dat de sout' is de bad people. President Lincoln bin 'lected President by de mos' ob the Nunited State wah gahntee him de right fuh hol' de office 'n do de right ting fuh de all de Nunites State. De sout', widdout kno' wah 'e goin' do, got bex 'n fight. De war bin staat by de Rebel b'fo' 'e staat een de office. De main ting ob de war was not at fus fuh free de slabe, but de main ting is fuh bring de grumblin' States back een de Knewnyon 'n fuh bem fuh be loyal to de Nunited State. Aftuhwood, knoin' de whalu set on de slabeby de Rebel dem, de President taw't da 'e proclamashun would stir dem up fuh put down de gun,'n had dem fuh be obedient, 'n help bring back de rebel State; 'n dey not doing dat den mek de slabe ting paat ob de war. "E duh my 'pinion datdeh ain' one man een de city dat could be staatfuh help de Rebel one inch, fuh dat would be killing yuh self. Deh bin two black man lef' wid de Rebel 'cause de bin tek up wid de Rebel, 'n taw't suppin' might b'fall dem if dey stay b'hin'; but deh ain' anudduh man. If de pra' dat we sen' up fuh de Knewyon ahmy could be read out, you would not git schru' dem dees two week.

Answer Translated: I think you will find there are thousands that are willing to make any sacrifice to assist the Government of the United States, while there are also many that are not willing to take up arms. I do not suppose there are a dozen men that are opposed to the Government. I understand, as to the war, that the South is the aggressor. President Lincoln was elected President by a majority of the United States, which guaranteed him the right of holding the office and exercising that right over the whole United States. The South, without knowing what he would do, rebelled. The war was commenced by the Rebels before he came into office. The object of the war was not at first to give the slaves their freedom, but the sole object of the war was at first to bring the rebellious States back into the Union and their loyalty to the laws of the United States. Afterward, knowing the value set on the slaves by the Rebels, the President thought that his proclamation would stimulate them to lay down their arms, reduce them to obedience, and help to bring back the Rebel States; and their not doing so has now made the freedom of the slaves a part of the war. It is my opinion that there is not a man in this city that could be started to help the Rebels one inch, for that would be suicide. There were two black men left with the Rebels because they had taken an active part for the Rebels, and thought something might befall them if they stayed behind; but there is not another man. If the prayers that have gone up for the Union army could be read out, you would not get through them these two weeks.

Seventh Question: State whether the sentiments you now express are those only of the colored people in the city; or do they extend to the colored population through the country? And what are your means of knowing the sentiments of those living in the country?

Answer in Gullah: I tink de feelin' is de same 'mong de cullud people ob de State. My'pinion is fix by persunal message een de time ob my ministry, 'n fum de de towsin dat follow de Knewnyon ahmy, lebbin' deh home 'n feelin' sufferin'.I don' tink deh would be so many, de numbuh su'pris' my 'spectashun.

Answer Translated: I think the sentiments are the same among the colored people of the State. My opinion is formed by personal communication in the course of my ministry, and also from the thousands that followed the Union army, leaving their homes and undergoing suffering. I did not think there would be so many; the number surpassed my expectation.

Eighth Question: If the Rebel leaders were to arm the slaves, what would be its effect?

Answer in Gullah: I tink dey would fight as long as dey been b'fo' de "bayonet," 'n jest as soon as dey could git way dey would run way, in my 'pinion.

Answer Translated: I think they would fight as long as they were before the bayonet, and just as soon as soon as they could get away, they would desert, in my opinion.

Ninth Question: What, in your opinion, is the feeling of the colored people about enlisting and serving as soldiers of the United States? What kind of military service do they prefer?

Answer in Gullah: A big numbuh bin gon' as sodjuh to de Poat Raw'l fuh be train 'n put een de serbis; 'n I tink deh duh towsin ob young man dat would jyin up. Dere ris suppin 'bout dem dat prob'ly is wrong. Deh don' suffuh too long fum de Rebel dat dey want fuh showlduh de musket. De res' want fuh go in de Quartermassuh or Commish service.

Answer Translated: A large number have gone as soldiers to Port Royal [S.C.] to be drilled and put in the service; and I think there are thousands of the young men that would enlist. There is something about them that perhaps is wrong. They have suffered so long from the Rebels that they want to shoulder the musket. Others want to go into the Quartermaster's or Commissary's service.

Tenth Question: Do you understand the mode of enlistments of colored persons in the Rebel States by State agents under the Act of Congress? If yea, state what your understanding is.

Answer in Gullah: De way I see dis is dat, de cullud person inlis' by de state agent is list as substute, 'n gib credit to de state 'n not fuh broaden de ahmmy, 'caus' ebby black man wha' 'list by uh state agent leeb uh white man home; 'n also dat lahg bounties duh gib, or promis', by de state agent dahn wah gib by de nunineted state. De ting dey should do is fuh push shru' dis rabellion de shortest way; 'n dere seem fuh be suppin fuh want een de 'listment by de state agent, fuh it ain' scren'n de ahmmy, but tek on way fuh ebby cullud man wah list.

Answer Translated: My understanding is, that colored persons enlisted by State agents are enlisted as substitutes, and give credit to the States, and do not swell the army, because every black man enlisted by a State agent leaves a white man at home; and, also, that larger bounties are given or promised by State agents than are given by the States. The great object should be to push through this Rebellion the shortest way, and there seems to be something wanting in the enlistment by State agents, for it don't strengthen the army, but takes one away for every colored man enlisted.

Eleventh Question: State what, in your opinion, is the best way to enlist colored men for soldiers.

Answer in Gullah: Well, I tink, sir, dat all de deman' oparashun shoul be put to stop. De preachuh dem would tawk to de young men dem, 'n dey would 'lis.' 'E duh my 'pinion dat 'e would be bettuh fuh de state agent fuh stay home 'n de 'listment be mek fuh de nunineted state unduh de 'rechun ob Gen'rul Sherman.

Answer Translated: I think, sir, that all compulsory operations should be put a stop to. The ministers would talk to them, and the young men would enlist. It is my opinion that it would be far better for the State agents to stay at home, and the enlistments to be made for the United States under the direction of General Sherman.

Mr. Stanton turning to General Sherman, "General, I would like to present the last question to the body without your presence." General Sherman somewhat taken aback, simply stands and withdraws from the room.[587] In the absence of General Sherman, the following question was asked:

Twelfth Question: State what is the feeling of the colored people in regard to General Sherman; and how far do they regard his sentiments and actions as friendly to their rights and interests, or otherwise?

Answer in Gullah: We look 'pun Sherman, 'b'fo' him gittin yah, as uh man, een de will ob god, special set apaht fuh finish dis wuk, 'n we feel gratitude to him, lookin 'pon him as uh man who should be honor fuh de fateful way 'e carry out 'e job. Some ob we call 'pun him soon as 'e git yah, 'n prob'ly 'e ain't meet de secuhtery wid mo' curts'y dan 'e did we. 'e conduct 'n mannus to we kharecturize him as uh frien' 'n uh gent'mun. We hab confudince een gen'rul sherman, 'n tink wha' 'cern we could not be een bettuh hand. 'Dis duh we 'pinion now, fum de short 'quaintance 'n tugettuhness we had fuh him.

Answer Translated: We looked upon General Sherman prior to his arrival as a man in the Providence of God specially set apart to accomplish this work, and we unanimously feel inexpressible gratitude to him, looking upon him as a man that should be honored for the faithful performance of his duty. Some of us called upon him immediately upon his arrival, and it is probable he would not meet the Secretary with more courtesy than he met us. His conduct and deportment toward us characterized him as a friend and a gentleman. We have confidence in General Sherman and think that what concerns us could not be under better hands. This is our opinion now from the short acquaintance and interest we have had.

Mr. James Lynch states that with his limited acquaintance with General Sherman, he is unwilling to express an opinion. All others present declare their agreement with Mr. Frazier about General Sherman.

Some conversation upon general subjects relating to General Sherman's march then ensued, of which no note was taken.[588]

After the twelfth question is answered, Secretary Stanton instructs Colonel Dayton, "Invite General Sherman to rejoin the meeting." All are standing and in a general conversation when Sherman enters. The guests shake General Sherman's hand, and thank him for arranging the meeting with Secretary Stanton. After they have departed, Secretary Stanton takes a sip of coffee and writes a few notes on his pad as General Sherman stares at him quietly.

Secretary Stanton finishes his notes and looks at General Sherman. "Thank you for assembling such a representative group of negroes (sic) for my interview. I'll meet with you again in the morning around 10:00 AM to further discuss the Negroes' situation and your campaign." At that point, all parties shake hands, and Sherman escorts Mr. Stanton and Adjutant-General Townsend to their carriage.

The next morning, General Sherman meets with Secretary Stanton in his quarters in Mr. Green's mansion. After the customary coffee, tea and breakfast, Mr. Stanton, General Sherman, Adjutant-General Townsend and Colonel Dayton Mr. Stanton starts out with, "Let's talk about your campaign past, present and future, and how I can assist you to end this war."

"My aim then and now is to whip the rebels, to humble their pride, to follow them to their inmost recesses, and make them fear and dread us. Fear of the Lord is the beginning of wisdom.[589] I need fresh supplies of food and fresh horses and mules. I need new shoes and warm clothes for my troops. My Quartermaster has a complete listing of the indispensable items for the prosecution of the next stage of the campaign. I am quite impatient to get on with it.[590] Frankly Mr. Secretary, this city life has become dull and tame. My units are anxious to get into the pine-woods again where they are free from the importunities of rebel women asking for protection and of the civilians from the North who are coming to Savannah for cotton and all sorts of profit."[591]

"Adjutant-General Townsend will get the complete list from your Quartermaster, and I promise you I'll hasten the supplies you're requesting at the first possible moment. It appears that you have an excellent relationship with the Negroes. Explain to me, how did it happen?"

"Very simple, Mr. Secretary. Extending kindness to the race, encouraging the freedmen to have patience and forbearance, procuring them food and clothing. I assert that no army ever did more for the Negro race than the one I commanded in Savannah."

"From my questioning it appears that the Negroes know what they want."

General Sherman replies, "It seems that the Negroes understand their own interests far better than do the men in Washington, who are trying to make political capital out of this Negroe (sic) question.[592] The idea that such men hang around Mr. Lincoln, to torture his life by suspicions of the officers, who were toiling with the single purpose to bring the war to a successful end, to liberate all slaves, is a fair illustration of the influences that can poison a political capital."[593]

Mr. Stanton does not respond but asks, "Now, how about the Negro enlistments?"

"Well sir, in the language of Mr. Frazier, the enlistment of every black man did not strengthen the army, but took away one white man from the ranks, and I feel the same way."[594]

Mr. Stanton responds, "I want you to issue an order to provide fully for the enlistment of colored troops, and I want to review the order in it's entirely before I depart. There are several other provisions to be in the order as well. What about granting the freedmen certain possessory rights to land?"

"Well, Mr. Stanton, the freedmen can have certain possessory rights to land. However, after the war, these rights become matters of judicial inquiry and decision. Of course, when war prevails, the military authorities have a perfect right to grant the possession of any vacant land to which they can extend military protection. Under military law, I cannot under-take to give a fee-simple title. All that the special field order can do is make temporary provisions for the freedmen and their families during the rest of the war or until Congress should take action."[595]

Secretary Stanton responds, "Land rights need to be in the field order. Once the war is over, the courts and Congress can decide on its continu-ation. Draft an order on the subject in accordance with your own views. The order needs to meet the pressing necessities of the case. Complete the order, and together we will review the document before publication."[596]

"It will be ready for your review tomorrow around 10:00 AM, if that is satisfactory," replies General Sherman. The men stand and shake hands. Colonel Dayton escorts Secretary Stanton to his carriage. After Secretary Stanton departs, General Sherman and Colonel Dayton go over an out-line of the order. Soon, the first draft is complete and General Sherman reads it over in detail with Dayton. After noting a few revisions, he sets the second draft as ready for Secretary Stanton to review the next morning.

Secretary Stanton arrives the following day and begins a very careful review of the order. After some discussion and verbal modifications, he gives his approval. He leans back in his chair, placing his thumb under his chin, "You may now publish your Field order No. 15, General Sherman."[597]

General Sherman and Secretary Stanton meet for the last time at the wharf in Savannah. Secretary Stanton promises Sherman that he will go North without delay, so as to hurry back the supplies Sherman has called for, as indispensable for the prosecution of the next stage of the campaign.[598]

General Sherman replies, "Thank you, Mr. Stanton. I hope your visit to Savannah for rest and recreation was successful." Mr. Stanton glares at General Sherman and boards the revenue cutter.

Special Field Orders, No. 15.
HEADQUARTERS MILITARY DIVISION OF THE MISSISSIPPI, IN
THE FIELD, NEAR SAVANNAH, GEORGIA

January 16, 1865

1. The islands from Charleston south, the abandoned rice-fields along the rivers for thirty miles back from the sea, and the country bordering the St. John's River, Florida, are reserved and set apart for the settlement of the Negroes now made free by the acts of war and the proclamation of the President of the United States.

2. At Beaufort, Hilton Head, Savannah, Fernandina, St. Augustine, and Jacksonville, the blacks may remain in their chosen or accustomed vocations; but on the islands, and in the settlements hereafter to be established, no white person whatever, unless military officers and soldiers detailed for duty, will be permitted to reside; and the sole and exclusive management of affairs will be left to the freed people themselves, subject only to the United States military authority, and the acts of Congress. By the laws of war, and orders of the President of the United States, the Negro is free, and must be dealt with as such. He cannot be subjected to conscription, or forced military service, save by the written orders of the highest military authority of the department, under such regulations as the President or Congress may prescribe. Domestic servants, blacksmiths, carpenters, and other mechanics, will be free to select their own work and residence, but the young and able-bodied Negroes must be encouraged to enlist as soldiery in the service of the United States, to con-tribute their share toward maintaining their own freedom, and securing their rights as citizens of the United States.

Negroes so enlisted will be organized into companies, battalions, and regiments, under the orders of the United States military authorities, and will be paid, fed, and clothed; according to law. The bounties paid on enlistment may, with the consent of the recruit, go to assist his family and settlement in procuring agricultural implements, seed, tools, boots, clothing, and other articles necessary for their livelihood.

3. Whenever three respectable Negroes, heads of families, shall desire to settle on land, and shall have selected for that purpose an island or a locality clearly defined within the limits above designated, the Inspector of Settlements and Plantations will himself, or, by such subordinate officer as he may appoint, give them a license to settle such island or district, and afford them such assistance as he can to enable them to establish a peaceable agricultural settlement. The three parties named will subdivide the land, under the supervision of the inspector, among themselves, and such others as may choose to settle near them, so that each family shall have a plot of not more than forty acres of tillable ground, and, when it borders on some water-channel, with not more than eight hundred feet water-front, in the possession of which land the military authorities will afford them protection until such time as they can protect themselves, or until Congress shall regulate their title. The quartermaster may, on the requisition of the Inspector of Settlements and Plantations, place at the disposal of the inspector one or more of the captured steamers to ply between the settlements and one or more of the commercial points heretofore named, in order to afford the settlers the opportunity to supply their necessary wants, and to sell the products of their land and labor.

4. Whenever a Negro has enlisted in the military service of the United States, he may locate his family in any one of the settlements at plea-sure, and acquire a homestead, and all other rights and privileges of a settler, as though present in person. In like manner, Negroes may settle their families and engage on board the gunboats, or in fishing, or in the navigation of the inland waters, without losing any claim to land or other advantages derived from this system. But no one, unless an actual

*settler as above defined, or unless absent on Government service, will
be entitled to claim any right to land or property in any settlement by
virtue of these orders.*

*5. In order to carry out this system of settlement, a general officer will be
detailed as Inspector of Settlements and Plantations, whose duty it shall
be to visit the settlements, to regulate their police and general arrangement, and who will furnish personally to each head of a family, subject
to the approval of the President of the United States, a possessory title
in writing, giving as near as possible the description of boundaries; and
who shall adjust all claims or conflicts that may arise under the same,
subject to the like approval, treating such titles altogether as possessory.
The same general officer will also be charged with the enlistment and
organization of the Negro recruits, and protecting their interests while
absent from their settlements; and will be governed by the rules and
regulations prescribed by the War Department for such purposes.*

*6. Brigadier-General R. Saxton is hereby appointed Inspector of
Settlements and Plantations and will at once enter on the performance
of his duties. No change is intended or desired in the settlement now on
Beaufort Island, nor will any rights to property heretofore acquired be
affected thereby.*

By order of Major-General W. T. Sherman,

L. M. DAYTON, Assistant Adjutant-General[599]

After Secretary Stanton's departure, General Sherman retires to his
headquarters and invites Colonel Audenried to join him. "Have a cigar
with me, Colonel."

"Thank you, sir. Don't mind if I do."

"Pour us a drink as well."

"Yes, sir."

Colonel Audenried opens General Sherman's bar. "White wine sir?"

"Rather have brandy today." Colonel Audenried pours the General
a glass of brandy and places it on the general's desk. General Sherman
picks up the glass of brandy. "Thank you, Colonel." He raises his glass to
Colonel Audenried. "Here's to Mr. Stanton's departure." They take a long
drink. The general puts his glass on the desk and lights his cigar. Leaning
back in his chair, he places his feet on the desk.

"It certainly was a strange fact that the great war secretary should cat-echize Negroes concerning the character of a general who commands a hundred thousand men in battle, has captured cities, conducted sixty-five thousand men successfully across four hundred miles of hostile territory, and has just brought tens of thousands of freedmen to a place of secu-rity; but because I have not loaded down my army by other hundreds of thousands of poor Negroes, I am construed by others as hostile to the black race."[600]

"It's the abolitionists, sir," replies Colonel Audenried.

General Sherman takes another swig from his glass and then another drag from his cigar. "Here I terminated the 'March to the Sea,' and I only add a few letters, selected out of many, to illustrate the general feeling of rejoicing throughout the country at the time. I only regarded the march from Atlanta to Savannah as a 'shift of base,' as the transfer of a strong army, which had no opponent, and had finished its 'then work,' from the interior to a point on the sea-coast, from which it could achieve other im-portant results. I considered this march as a means to an end, and not as an essential act of war. Still, then, as now, the march to the sea is generally re-garded as something extraordinary, something anomalous, something out of the usual order of events; whereas, in fact, I simply moved from Atlanta to Savannah, as one step in the direction of Richmond, a movement that had to be met and defeated, for the war is necessarily at an end."[601]

"Don't sell yourself short, General. You have set a new standard for military operations and tactics."

"Were I to express my measure of the relative importance of the march to the sea, and of that from Savannah northward, I would place the for-mer at one, and the latter at ten, or the maximum."[602] Reaching over and retrieving the quartermaster report of the march from Atlanta, he enlight-ens Colonel Audenried. "I now close this long chapter by giving a tabular statement of the losses during the march, and the number of prisoners captured. The property captured consisted of horses and mules by the thousand, and of quantities of subsistence stores that aggregate very large, but may be measured with sufficient accuracy by assuming that sixty-five thousand men obtained abundant food for about forty days, and thirty-five thousand animals were fed for a like period, so as to reach Savannah in splendid flesh and condition. I am going to draft a few more, important letters to General Grant, and Halleck, which illustrate our opinions at that stage of the war. Look at our small losses Colonel, and explain to me that this wasn't a surprise to all of us. Colonel Audenried takes the report from General Sherman and reads:

"Statement of casualties and prisoners captured, by the army in the field, campaign of Georgia. Our army lost 10 officers and 93 men in action. There were 24 officers wounded along with 404 men. We have one officer and 277 men missing and 77 officers and 1,261 men captured."[603]

"Sir, only Secretary Stanton and the abolitionists could fault you."

SATURDAY MORNING, JANUARY 14, 1864

The *Rebecca Clyde* sails with the New York joint committee as passengers. "As the *Rebecca Clyde* sails into the port of Savannah, gaily dressed in colors, she is greeted with cheers and salutes from all sides."[604] In her cargo hold are 428 barrels of cornmeal, 15 boxes of hams, 150 quarters of beef, 20 boxes of mustard, 970 barrels of flour, 47 boxes of bacon, 5 kegs of bicarbonate of soda, 25 barrels of molasses, 10 barrels of pickles, 10 barrels of vinegar, 100 sacks of salt, 5 cases of lard,5 boxes of shoulders, 50 barrels of beans, 21 barrels of pork, 6 drums of cod fish, 407 bags of potatoes, 10 boxes of onions, 60 boxes of pilot bread, and 100 slaughtered sheep.[605]

January 15: The *Daniel Webster* sets sails to Savannah from New York with 138 the donation of supplies from Boston.

January 16: Bishop Potter announces that a cargo for Savannah was ready as soon as a ship can be located.[606]

January 19: The *Rebecca Clyde* arrives in Savannah and anchors at Four Mile Point near Salters Island. A joint meeting is held at the Cotton Exchange to determine how the food should be distributed.[607]

January 20: The *Daniel Webster* drops anchor near the *Rebecca Clyde*.

January 21: The *Greyhound* arrives with a full cargo similar to the *Daniel Webster*, Colonel Allen and the Boston Committee members on board.[608] A meeting is set up by Mayor Arnold and Colonel Allen at the Cotton Exchange to make provisions to distribute the relief supplies. At City Hall, The Boston Committee members read a letter from Mayor Lincoln to the citizens of Savannah;

"We remember the earlier kindness and liberality of the citizens of Savannah towards the people of Boston in the dark colonial days. We recall the meeting held there on the tenth day of August, 1774, when a committee was appointed "to receive subscriptions for the suffering poor of Boston. The memory of past days of common danger and suffering of a united people struggling to be free stands before us. Your gracious donation of rice helped to relieve the hungry people who were suffering because the British had closed the port. The annals of the South and the North, engraved together upon the tables of memory, still live; and we believe that neither the South nor the North will permit them to die.[609] We hope soon to hail the day when all the people of the United States will, in the language of the President quoted in your resolutions, 'find peace by laying down their arms and submitting to the national authority under the Constitution,' leaving all questions which remain to be adjusted to the peaceful means of legislation, conference and vote.[610]

Meanwhile the cargo is being unloaded and transported for ware-housing at Bay and Barnard Streets. Tickets in hand and, standing in line awaiting their turn, a motley crowd fills the intersection, of both sexes, all ages, sizes, complexions, costumes, gray-haired old men, old uncle Neds … well-dressed women wearing crepe for their husbands and sons … women in linsey-woolsey, demi-white women wearing Negro cloth, Negro women dressed in gunny cloth; men in Confederate uniforms, a ragman's affair. Charity, like a kind angel, has suddenly stepped in to ward off the wolf which is howling at their doors. The half-starved rationers, poles apart in social and economic status, rub kindred elbows.[611]

JANUARY 21, 1865

General Sherman departs for South Carolina. Many fear that his successor will be less Christian and sympathetic. Captain Albert Stearns takes charge. In two months, 568 carcasses of animals, 8,311 cart loads of garbage and 7,219 loads of manure are removed. Repairs are made to the streets. A coating of whitewash is applied to the entire row of warehouses along the bay producing quite a tidy contrast with their moss covered condition. Six thousand two hundred trees are whitewashed to a height of seven feet."[612]

On Colonel Allen's return to Savannah, he is praised by the *Daily Herald*. Christian generosity has never been more "liberal and munificent." The city's Northern benefactors were warmly thanked by a Savannah Committee. "The hand of sympathy so generously extended to us ought to carry conviction to every unprejudiced mind," says a resolution, "that there is but one course to pursue, and that is to aim at a speedy termination of the unfortunate strife which has been devastating the country for nearly four years."

January 25: Mayor Arnold calls a general meeting of the citizens to allow everyone a chance to discuss the goodwill of Boston and New York and the yet to come Philadelphia cargo. A brass band is present to add pomp and circumstance for the event. The mayor asks the guests from Boston and New York and Colonel Allen to speak. "The applause given to the efforts of the respective addresses evinces a full appreciation of the occasion. Taken altogether, it is a brilliant, pleasing and highly interesting record of good feeling and true fellowship."[613]

JANUARY 27, 1865

During the night an extensive conflagration breaks out in Savannah, in the western part of the city. The fire breaks out in a stable, supposedly caused by rebel incendiaries. Owing to the inactivity of the Fire Department, the flames spread rapidly and reach the Arsenal on Granite Hill by midnight. A large quantity of shells was stored in the buildings just as it had been left by the rebels. There are a series of explosions during the next two hours. Exploding shells hurl deadly fragments through the air, piercing a water tower and forcing city fire fighters to abandon their equipment and flee. Several squares are destroyed by the fire, and hundreds of unfortunate women and children were driven from their homes into the streets. Nearly all the 200 houses consumed were private residences. Union soldiers haul wagon loads of shells away from the great fire. After eighteen hours, the raging fire dies out, narrowly missing the arsenal packed with sixty tons of gun powder.

Governor Brown sends a Correspondence to the Senate and House of Representatives from Macon, the interim capital of Georgia, on February 15th 1865.

THE GEORGIA MILITARY INSTITUTE

The number of cadets in this institution has been considerably increased.

Upon the advance of Sherman's army, the battalion of cadets was ordered into active service. At the Oconee Bridge and other places where they met the enemy, they acted with distinguished gallantry. The State has much reason to be proud of this gallant young corps.

*Pruden's Artillery and the other troops of Maj. Caper's Battalion are
also entitled to honorable notice. This whole battalion under its chival-
rous leader, in presence of Adjutant and Inspector-General Wayne, who
accompanied them during the campaign from Gordon to Savannah and
thence to Augusta, discharged their duty energetically and faithfully.
The report of Gen. Wayne will be laid before the Military Committee of
the two Houses upon application.*

Joseph E. Brown

FEBRUARY, 1865

Norman finds some paper and writes a letter home in the middle of
the month.

Dear Ma and Pa,

*I know you're wondering if I am still alive or not. Well I am, but I'll
have to admit that I'm somewhat worn and callous from the ordeals
of this war. The Cadet Corps was the last Confederate unit to cross
the Savannah River. We cut loose the pontoon bridge as we reached
the South Carolina side. The evacuation of Savannah was a terrible
sight, looting, rioting, stealing, burning and mass confusion both by the
military and the citizens. The Cadet Corps has suffered several deaths
from the Yankee enemy and from diseases, mostly typhoid. We had fairly
good rations until around the end of November, but now have a supply
of half rations, some of which are good. One of my good friends, Seaborn
Montgomery, had been getting weaker and weaker and was sent home
on furlough. We now have new shoes and good clothes again. We can
probably thank the Governor for his assistance. We all feel that since
his son is a cadet that we have not been able to meet the enemy head-
on. Now I think 'active duty' is over and, until that Yankee General
Sherman decides his next move, we will be on guard duty in Augusta.
Maj. Capers is back from furlough and informs us that the Corps is going
back to Milledgeville. Our morale is low, but our spirits are high, if such
a paradox can exist! Paul is doing well also and sends his regards.*

Your affectionate son,

Norman

❧

Early in the morning of the 15th of February, Maj. Capers informs the Cadet Corps they'll be leaving for Milledgeville the next day and will be camping on the old bivouac area on the Capitol grounds.

"It's obvious that we have to be provost in Milledgeville," says Paul.

The next morning, the two hundred or so cadets board the train for Milledgeville. There are still a few convicts present. Most of the other convicts have deserted. The entire cadet corps load and remain quiet for the trip to Milledgeville. "It looks as if our dream of Southern independence is fading fast. Even though we are full of devotion to the cause, there's really little hope," Paul says.

Upon their arrival in Milledgeville, the unhappy Cadet Corps returns to the remnants of the once beautiful depot. Soon, they are at the familiar bivouac site on the Capitol grounds. The capitol is almost in ruins with numerous broken windows and missing doors. Norman and the Corps in general, begin to display more unhappiness toward the Governor and his policies toward their military capability. However, to their surprise, after a tour of the Capitol, Norman finds that the only properties destroyed by General Sherman are the magazines, factories, arsenals, penitentiary and a few storehouses.

"Paul, have you heard a rumor that the Corps has orders waiting," asks Norman.

"What kind of orders?"

"Orders for us to perform guard duty at the quartermaster and commissary stores. The railroads are becoming operational again and several of the cadets are already in charge of delivering corn to the starving families of North Georgia."

"Really."

"Yep, and they have orders to stand guard on the trains and to shoot any person who attempts to interfere with the delivery of the corn to the North Georgia authorities."

"I don't see how drilling and attending to the provost duties is going to decrease the resentment towards Governor Brown for not letting us fight."

"That resentment is getting worse now that we are back on the capitol grounds."

"You just watch, as the weather gets warmer so will the temperament of the Cadet Corps," Paul says.

As the spring air warms, Norman picks up some of the rumors that maybe the Corps should show their disappointment toward the Governor for not allowing them into direct combat by hanging an effigy of him. Sure enough, one spring evening, Norman and Paul get the word, "Gather for a 'hanging' at the giant oak tree not far from the governor's office." In the warm late afternoon sun, Norman sees several cadets approach with a bulky blanket in a roll.

Paul leans over and tells Norman, "That's gotta be the effigy of the governor in that blanket." Placing the blanket on the ground next to a hedge row of budding azaleas, a couple cadets unroll it to expose the effigy. Poor Julius Brown stares at the effigy in disgust.

Cadet Lt. Hazlehurst tries to calm Julius. "This has nothing to do with you. We all know that you have stood with the Cadets Corps all of the way and have executed your duties honorably. It's just that the entire Corps feels that we could have done more fighting if the governor's son was not in our Corps."

Julius responds, "Well, there may have been, and maybe still is, some parental protection coming from my father. Remember though that he asked me to leave the Corps and go with my family when Sherman was coming through Milledgeville. I told him I was staying with the Corps."

Norman attempts to enlighten the group, "We are one corps period. Each of us belongs as much as the other." He turns to Julius, "This is just to let your father know that the corps has suffered, and some of the cadets have given their life for the cause of Southern Independence. We wanted to meet the enemy head on and were never given the chance."

Norman struggles a moment, looking for the right words to express the feelings of the cadets. "Plus, we do not like the convicts in our ranks. We are not equal to them and they certainly are not equal to us. This is our way of showing our disappointment in your father's decisions."

A cadet takes a long rope and tosses it over the low limb of the giant oak. Julius turns and walks away. The other cadets stand aside and allow him to pass. Some cadets place the hangman's noose around the effigy's neck. Norman and several other cadets on the other end of the rope pull the effigy from the ground. The Corps shouts. "LET US FIGHT! LET US FIGHT! LET US FIGHT!"

APRIL 9, 1865

Before the day is over, the bugler sounds assembly.

"Why are we assembling this time of day?" Norman asks Paul, and they rush out to the assembly area.

"Maybe the effigy did some good, and we are going to the front."

"Front of what?" asks Norman.

Maj. Capers stands before the assembled Cadet Corps. "Gentlemen, just a few moments ago I received word that Gen. Lee has surrendered at Appomattox. The terms of surrender were: In order for the officers and individuals to receive paroles, they must swear not to take up arms against the government of the United States until properly exchanged, and each company or regimental commander shall sign a like parole for the men of their commands … neither side arms of the officers nor their private horses or baggage are to be surrendered; and, as many privates in the Confederate Army owned horses and mules, all horses and mules claimed by men in the Confederate Army are to be left in their possession. I also have another telegram from Capt. John Bradford, a GMI graduate. He is with Company H of the 1st Regiment Confederate Engineer Department in Gen. Lee's army. Capt. Bradford served from the battle of Gettysburg to Appomattox. Part of his telegram states, 'I believe I saw the last man fall on the other side on the morning of the 9th of April 1865.'"

Maj. Capers continues, "Gentlemen, you are dismissed. Return to your quarters and await further orders."

Norman immediately feels grave disappointment. He looks around at the rest of the cadet corps and recognizes that the same feeling has overcome all of the GMI Garrison. "Paul, I can't help but think of Anderson, Alexander, and Marsh. All killed, and for what? We lost."

"Yep, and poor Baker, Jordan, Mabry, McLeod and Smith all died from disease."

The two friends head back to their quarters. "Yet, we still must perform drills and provost duty at the commissary and quartermaster stores."

Several days later while on his way to guard duty, Norman notices that unsettled crowds are beginning to gather at various locations where the Cadets are on provost duty. Just as they begin to relieve the cadets who have been on guard duty, a mob of citizens and deserters overpower them. With their unloaded muskets and without firepower, Norman and the guards are roughed up and pushed aside by the mob.

Someone in the mob shouts, "You, cadets, go home to your Ma and Pa. We're taking over this place."

Unable to defend the commissary and quartermaster stores, the cadets retreat toward headquarters. Already alerted, by the cadet officer of the day, Maj. Capers has the Corps in formation. Norman, breathing heavy from his run back to the garrison, takes his place in the ranks of the Corps and whispers to Paul, "That mob is wild and will tear down and burn everything to get what they want."

Gen. Wayne addresses the assembled cadets. "We have a riot starting, and we must secure the commissary and quartermaster stores. Double time in formation to the commissary!"

When the cadets arrive at the commissary Gen. Wayne orders, "Fix bayonets and load muskets."

The cadets form a line with bayonets. Norman's company forms behind the bayonet formation. The cadets move forward. Norman's company fires into the air. The mob realizes the cadets mean business and begins to scatter when they hear the warning shots from the muskets.

For nearly two days, Norman's company guards the commissary while the remainder of the garrison protects and secures the quartermaster building. The supplies are for the returning soldiers who now may have to go hungry and seek assistance from other commissaries. Hundreds of soldiers from Gen. Lee's army are coming through Milledgeville on their way to their homes. Thousands of soldiers are unable to depart Milledgeville because the railroad to Macon is still in disrepair. Wearing rags for clothing, many are on crutches, some with empty sleeves, many pale from sickness and wounds. Some are the walking dead. They realize they are not returning to the beautiful country they left and deepens their depression even more. The problem is so overpowering that the Ladies' Aid Society at the Wayside are unable to manage this nightmare of human misery.

SUDDENLY

Saturday, April 15, 1865: J. W. Goldsmith enters the depot and notices his clerk at the telegraph hastily taking down a message. Looking over the shoulder of the clerk, he reads the message: "Last evening, April 14, 1865, Good Friday, while attending a special performance of the comedy, 'Our American Cousin,' President Abraham Lincoln was shot in the back of the head. Accompanying him at Ford's Theater were his wife, Mary Todd Lincoln, Major Henry R. Rathbone, and other dignitaries. As the play was in progress, a figure with a drawn derringer pistol stepped into the presidential box, aimed, and fired. The president slumped forward."

Shock and chills fill J. W.'s body as he reads as fast as the message is put to paper. "The assassin has been identified as John Wilkes Booth. Booth dropped the pistol and waved a dagger. Major Rathbone lunged at Booth and, though slashed in the arm, forced Booth to the railing. Booth leapt from the balcony and caught the spur of his left boot on the flag draped over the rail. Upon landing on the stage, Booth shattered a bone in his leg. Though sustaining an injury, Booth rushed out the back door and disappeared into the night on horseback.

"A doctor in the audience immediately rushed upstairs to the box. The bullet entered through Lincoln's left ear and lodged behind his right eye. President Lincoln was paralyzed and barely breathing before being transported across Tenth Street to a boarding house opposite the theater. All of the doctor's best efforts failed to sustain the President. The President was pronounced dead at 7:22 AM on April 15th. Vice

President Andrew Johnson to be sworn in as President at eleven o'clock today at the Kirkwood Hotel by Chief Justice Salmon P. Chase. End of message."

Grabbing the message, J. W. rushes outside shouting, "LINCOLN KILLED! SHOT!"Rushing to the hotel across the street, J. W. swings open the door and repeats his message to the few early morning patrons. Those on the street follow him inside. Everyone gathers around, anxiously waiting for the telegram to be read.

J. W. hands the telegram to a hotel patron. "You read it, sir. Too much for me right now!"

The patron takes the telegram and reads the contents to the assembly of citizens. When he finishes, some of the citizens take the telegram and read it again in dismay while others flee to spread the word. J. W. takes the telegram back to the depot and makes a copy. He takes the copy and posts it on the depot bulletin board for the citizens. In a short time, the few people remaining in town begin to assemble and read the frightening news.

⁍

Betty and Buck leave the farm for town around noon. Betty Gail has a basket of spring lettuce, cabbage, and spinach. The hospital staff and church members are gathering food for Easter Sunday for the patients.

The town is slowly rebuilding. Saws and hammers sound throughout town as Buck and Betty Gail round the corner of Tower Street and Main. "Looks like we are going to have a beautiful, but cool Easter this year Betty Gail."

"We had a decent crowd at church last night. Lots of crippled and disfigured men were there. Wish you could have come along, Buck. It was a beautiful service."

"Lots of thieving still going on. Can't leave the place at night. Buster's place is nothing but ashes. Gotta get that ground turned since we bought it from him. Gonna miss him as a neighbor, but it's probably for the best since he will never be happy living in Stone Mountain."

Stretching to see the crowd at the depot, Betty Gail peers at the throng. "Wonder what the excitement is at the depot? Lots of people reading the bulletin board."

"Must be some important news for that many folk to be hanging around this time of day." Buck reins the buggy and ties the horse to a hitching post. Walking to the depot, Buck asks a passer-by, "What's all the excitement?"

"Haven't you heard? Lincoln's been killed! Assassinated by a fellow named Booth!"

Taken by surprise, Betty Gail's hand flies to her mouth and she gasps. She and Buck hurry over to read the telegram. They read the second telegram: Vice President Andrew Johnson sworn in as President at 11:00 this day. The new President states, "The course which I have taken in the past, in connection with this rebellion must be regarded as a guarantee for the future."

"This is unreal! Killed the President! Those Radical Republicans and abolitionists are probably going to make life tough on the South. At least President Lincoln opposed that radical meanness. Johnson is gonna be much harder on us, just because he's one of us!"

Ten days later another telegram divulges the sad story, "On April 26, 1864 Gen. Joseph Johnston surrenders." The terms of Gen. Johnston's surrender are analogous to those which Gen. Lee signed at Gettysburg. General Sherman then orders his generals to extend the same conditions of surrender to the Confederates in their area of military operations.

❧

Under a flag of truce, Gen. Wayne sends several hundred men with a request for aid to General John Wilson in Macon. General Wilson is able to feed these refugees from the Union commissary stores and from captured Confederate cattle.[614]

MONDAY MORNING, MAY 1, 1865

Upon awakening the cadets receive new orders. They are to return to Augusta and guard the arsenals and government stores from looting.

Norman reads the Special Order and hands it over to Paul. "I guess we are heading for provost duty again in Augusta. At least it will be warmer than it was in January. I just hope the citizens understand that we are here to keep the peace and to protect their property."

"We have nothing to cheer about except that we're still alive and pray that our families are all well. At least we have warm clothes and boots. We started out protecting our state against Yankee invaders. Now we are protecting our state against our own people," replies Paul.

After a few short hours on the train, the Corps arrives at Augusta City hall. The scene in Augusta is not much better than Milledgeville. Thousands of ragged, skinny, veterans with wounds, with disease and missing limbs pass through the town.

⚬

Governor Brown receives a letter from General Wilson on Tuesday, May 3rd. The letter extends to the governor the same honorable terms of surrender which had been granted to Gen. Lee and Gen. Johnston. General Wilson also states that he'll accept the surrender and that of his officers.[615]

⚬

Governor Brown, Gen. Wayne and other officers of the Confederacy arrive in Macon on the beautiful spring day, of Friday, May 5. In the solemn ceremony of the surrender, Governor Brown surrenders the Georgia State Militia and receives his military parole as the Commander-in-Chief of the State Militia. Each Confederate officer present takes the oath of surrender individually and steps aside.

The war in Georgia is over.

The Cadet Garrison is able to maintain the peace and protect the stores until May 20, two days after the Federal Troops arrival in Augusta.[616]

During the midmorning of the 20th, the Yankee garrison is to relieve the Georgia Military Institute Corps of their provost duty. The cadets return to City Hall and turn in their weapons and tents. In formation, with most of the cadets in GMI uniform, they are waiting command for dismissal. The Yankee commander orders the color bearer to turn over the Georgia Military Institute colors to him. Cadet Coleman, the battalion's color bearer, removes the colors from the flag staff, walks to the Yankee commander and plants the flagstaff at the feet of the Yankee Officer. Cadet Coleman places it under his shirt then buttons his vest. Returning to his post he shouts, "Damn the man who unbuttons this vest!"

The Yankee commander angrily leaves his post and approaches Coleman as if to confront him. The corps of cadets watches this event with a keen eye. Suddenly, as with a single mind the entire Cadet Corps breaks ranks and encircles the Yankee Commander and Coleman.

Realizing the gravity of the situation and not desiring to instigate any confrontation, the Yankee Commander hesitates. Biting his lip and twitching, he taps his finger on his hat brim, "The flag is yours to keep!"

He then sharply turns about as the cadets cheer and make an opening for the Yankee to pass through. Returning to the reviewing stand, he directs Maj. Capers to dismiss the Georgia Military Institute Corps of cadets. "The final fight is yours, honorable cadets. You are dismissed to return to your homes."

Suddenly the war is over.

The boy soldiers of GMI are the last to do duty in the cause of the Confederate States of America east of the Mississippi. It is now time to head home to rebuild an uncertain South.[617]

Norman asks Paul, "Do you realize that on May 14th of last year we were at Resaca? Now we have one mission left and are lucky to be alive to complete it!"

"Yep! For 371 days there was glory in hell!" Paul replies.

"Remember what we discussed the other night about our next mission?"

"I certainly do, Norman."

"Are you still up for it?"

"We've been through too much to separate now. Although I miss my folks as much as you do, this needs to be done. I'm with you because I know you would do the same for me."

Norman and Paul are among those waiting to board a train.[618] They are now a part of the mass of skinny, demoralized soldiers gathered at the depot. They board the train. The whistle blows and with the jerk of the engine, the war is left behind. The train is loaded with passengers, military cargo and Union soldiers. The worn and tattered gray uniforms match the disheartened and torn souls of the defeated Confederate soldiers.

After a two hour ride, the train reaches Norman's and Paul's destination. The platform is busy with loved ones looking for a special person as the solemn rag-draped soldiers disembark from the passenger cars. Many of the soldiers spot their families and rush to each others' embrace. Some soldiers can only stand on crutches and wait with anticipation of the forthcoming welcome. The crutches drop on contact as their emotions carry them into the loving arms of their children, wives, or relatives. Smiles mix with tears, compassion with gladness, but most of all love and brotherhood.

Federal troops begin unloading commissary box cars. Several other passenger cars have Federal soldiers to reinforce the garrison already occupying the town. In a short time, the platform gradually clears. Arm in arm, many of the Confederate soldiers scatter with their families and friends to places unknown to Norman and Paul. A few rag clad Confederate soldiers remain on the platform standing alone, looking about, in hopes of discovering a familiar face. Finally, the realization that there's no one seeking their presence, the disheartened Confederates join together and walk without a purpose toward town.

Once in town, Norman points out. "Look at those freedmen. Don't they look dazed, like they don't know what to do with their newfound liberty? Some of these darkies must have followed Sherman here. They are just wandering aimlessly everywhere."

Paul replies, "One fact for certain, the darkies may be poorer than their late masters, but they are better prepared for poverty. They have been accustomed to want, exposure, and toil. Slavery had been a hard school but the darkies have learned more than one lesson. The lesson we are learning is the darkies will endure the present better than their old masters' families. Also, they never learned to dread the future."[619]

Norman looks around. "From what I remember, we need to head in that direction. It should take us about forty-five minutes or so to get there."

Paul looks at the position of the sun for the time of day. "That has to be in the right direction. Let's start walking."

Slinging their haversacks and knapsacks over their shoulders, the two GMI Confederates begin their mission. The mid-afternoon sun gleams down filtering through the trees and the two comrades proceed along the dusty dirt wagon road. "Seems a little different than when we were here last time."

"Surely not as cold as before. I can still feel that bitter cold whenever I think about how miserable we were," replies Norman.

About thirty minutes into their walk, the pair stops by a local store and asks for directions. The store clerk looks at them suspiciously and questions, "Why do you want to know?" Norman explains who they are.

Upon further questioning, the clerk is satisfied with their answers and steps outside with them. "Go about a mile, then take a turn to the left. It will be the second wagon trail. Then take the first wagon trail to the right. It will be the first on your left. Can't miss it."

"Thank you very much." Norman and Paul shake the clerks hand and proceed to their final destination.

Walking at a quicker pace, they pass the first wagon trail. Gazing ahead on the trail, Norman says, "Look, there's the second trail the clerk was talking about." His heart begins to beat a little faster as the object of his and Paul's mission draws nearer. Rounding the corner of the second trail, the pair strains their eyes to find the next turn. By now, they are in a double-quick step. Nervous, Paul and Norman begin to breathe heavy.

Norman shouts, "Look! There, one hundred yards ahead! The next turn is there! I can see the roof through the woods!"

"I see it! I see it!" shouts Paul.

The two begin running as fast as their weary legs can move. Dashing around the last turn, they spot the building not more than another hundred yards away. Slowing down a bit, Norman draws his canteen from his side. Still walking rapidly, he takes a mouthful of water, and then hastens his pace again. Finally, reaching their destination, they stop in front.

One of the Federal guards notices the two Confederate soldiers, "Halt and stay where you are. Do not move. Put your hands up!" Approaching Norman with his Spencer rifle, the guard demands, "What are you two Rebels doing here?"

Norman, nearly breathless from his dash, explains and asks the guard to please confirm his statement with the owner. "Keep your hands up." Then the Federal guard instructs his partner to notify the occupants that there's someone out here they need to identify. The second guard proceeds to the door. When the door is opened, he gives the butler a message. The butler looks beyond the guard and sees the two Confederates with their hands high in the air. He closes the door and the guard waits for the owner to appear.

"I wonder if she'll know me. It's been nearly four years." Soon the door opens and a radiant young lady steps out. Norman sees his sister and shouts to the top of his crying voice, "Polly, it me! Norman!"

Placing her hand over her mouth, Polly screams, "Oh my God! It's my brother! He's alive! Norman, it's really you!" Polly begins to cry uncontrollably, leaps past the guard, and rushes to her brother. The other guard moves aside. Norman drops his arms and dashes to meet Polly. Meeting near the foot of the steps, Polly and Norman embrace and boldly cry.

Paul witnesses a truly awe-inspiring moment and sits. He places his face in his hands and begins to release all of his emotions. Paul looks toward Polly and Norman, then to the heavens and swallows the lump in his throat. "This war is over! This war has ended for all of us!" Paul begins to stand and the nearby guard offers him his hand in assistance. Paul accepts the help, "Thank you." Picking up his and Norman's belongings, Paul walks to where Polly and Norman are standing. Polly turns to Paul, wipes the tears from his red eyes, and hugs him dearly.

"Hello, Paul. Welcome." Then Polly stands between the two friends and places her arms around their necks. Polly draws their cheeks to hers and together they walk to the house.

Entering the house, Polly introduces Norman and Paul to Al, Tot, and Jesse. "They were slaves of Legare's uncle and aunt. Now they work for me and live in the quarters in back of the house. You two look very tired. I know you would like a hot bath."

"That would be the greatest!" responds Paul.

"Al, you and Jesse get hot water going in the tub downstairs and upstairs. Tot, how about preparing something for Norman and Paul to eat while the water is getting hot."

"Yas Ma'am," replies Al, Tot, and Jesse. Polly, Norman, and Paul take a seat in the parlor. "Why the guards, Polly? Are you under some type of house arrest?" asks Norman.

Sitting next to Norman, Polly laughs, "You won't believe the whole story, but General Sherman met Ma and Pa in Stone Mountain, and General Sherman's brother is a good friend of Congressman Hill. Congressman Hill gave me a letter of introduction in case I ever needed one, so I presented it to General Sherman and asked him for a guard at the house. He ordered the guards posted as long as there is Union presence in Savannah or until I feel I no longer need it."

"Whoa!" responds Norman. "Tell me more!"

"There's plenty of time to talk later. Right now let me show you to your rooms. I still have Legare's clothes here …" Polly is silent for a moment. "I know he would be glad for you and Paul to wear some of them. Oh, I hear your nephew waking up! Let's go get him!" Norman and Paul follow Polly to the bedroom. Little Joshua is standing in the cradle. Polly picks him up and turns to Norman. "Looks just like his handsome pa, wouldn't you say Norman?"

Norman responds, "Exactly! Come see your Uncle Norman!" He reaches for Little Joshua and the tot throws his arms toward him. Norman takes his nephew in his arms and heads to the parlor. Polly's chin begins to quiver, seeing Joshua in the arms of her brother.

They have an early supper and invite the two Federal guards to join them. Tot prepares fresh fish and rice with spring greens and beets. After supper, Polly takes Paul and Norman to the dock. Norman carries Little Joshua on his shoulders until they reach the end of the dock. The four sit down and Norman holds Joshua in his lap.

"If you ever want to relax, this is the place. Right here on the end of the dock. Just lay back, and at night you can see every star in the universe."

Norman sighs and stares at the river for a moment. "Paul and I came to Savannah to check on you, but also to find out if you're ready to come home with us, at least for a while. Ma and Pa would love your visit."

"I know. I'm ready to visit for a while, but this is my home now. Legare and I lived here and Legare still lives in my heart. Our child was born here. I can never leave this place." Polly begins to cry a little. "My heart will always be here."

Norman moves closer to his sister and takes her hand. "This place is beautiful Polly, and I truly understand why it is your home now."

She looks toward the house. "Legare's spirit circulates throughout this dwelling and through me every day. I still climb to the cupola and fish from this dock with him. Legare will never grow old. He will always be young, and debonair." Norman squeezes his sister's hand. "The war's over now. Let's send Ma and Pa a telegram that we are safe and healthy."

"I tried to send one a week ago and the lines were still down then, but let's try again."

"You and Paul rest for a couple of days, then I'll go to Stone Mountain with you. Tot's family is from Decatur, and I promised her that I would take her with me when I visit my family, the Hill's and Legare's grave in Madison. She would like to try and find some of her family."

"I'll go to the telegraph office, Polly."

During the next several days, Norman and Polly talk about their experiences. Norman shares with Polly the details of his brief meeting with Legare. "I have the scarf in my haversack you made for him. He insisted that I take it. I wore it around my neck during the cold spells and always thought of the three of you. I was really proud to have him as a brother-in-law. Are Jesse and Al going to stay and work for you, and watch your house while you're away?"

"Yes, I pay them one dollar a week, plus give them a place to live and food to eat. They both know they're free to leave whenever they want to but they're very old and have no family."

Paul asks, "What tongue do the darkies speak in Savannah?"

"It's Gullah. From what I understand, the Gullah language is a Creole blend of Elizabethan English and African languages. It was born of necessity on Africa's Slave Coast, and developed in the slave communities of the plantations of the Southern coast. It's difficult to understand unless you listen closely. When Tot was given to us by Legare's Uncle Richard, it took me a while to understand her."

It is apparent to Norman that his twin sister's heart and mind have matured even more rapidly than her person.

HOMEWARD BOUND

Early in the morning, several days later, Polly, Little Joshua, Norman, Paul and Tot prepare to board the train for Stone Mountain. Polly looks at her loyal servants. "Jesse, I'll be back around the middle of July. You and Al take care of the place for me. You shouldn't have any problems while I am away. Here is a letter to show anyone who questions you. The guards will still be at the house. See you in a month or so." Jesse takes the letter and tips his hat.

"Polly, I'm going inside to send a telegram to let Pa and Ma know we will be there on the afternoon train. I wrote them from Augusta and told them Paul and I were going to bring you home, so they are expecting us."

The conductor shouts, "All aboard!" Norman is carrying little Joshua in his arms. Tot, Polly and Paul are following behind. The conductor takes Tot by the arm, "To the rear car!"

Norman stands eye to eye with the conductor and levels a stare that rises from the maturity he gained as a soldier. "She is the nanny for our child. She is going to be with us."

Begrudgingly, the conductor says, "The darkie will have to sit with one of you! Get on board!"

The clack-a-de-clack of the train mesmerizes little Joshua to sleep in his uncle's lap. Norman gazes silently as the train nears the Oconee River. All through the countryside the scars of war unfold before his eyes. The forts, earthworks and stockades are still standing, as if waiting for soldiers. Army wagons, ambulances, dead mule and horse skeletons are scattered everywhere. The odor of decaying animals fills the passenger cars as the train flees past the gruesome sights.

Norman sits quietly most of the trip. He is touched by the gloom that covers the face of the land. Reflecting on the scenes at the various depots along the route to Stone Mountain, the returning of the brave brings no joy to the loving hearts that sent them forth. These scenes pierce Norman's thoughts, "Nay, their very presence kept alive the chagrin of defeat. Instead of banners and music and happy greeting, there's only silence and tears to welcome the defeated home. Not only for the dead are these lamentations, but also for the living. If the past is sorrowful, then the future is scarcely less so. A piece of cornbread, with a glass of milk, and a bit of bacon, is perhaps, the richest welcome-feast that family love can devise for the returning hero. Time and the scathing results of the war have wrought ruin in his home state. A part of the reunited country is in light, and the other part in darkness and between the two is a zone of bloody graves."[620]

Lithonia is the last stop before Stone Mountain. "Wonder how Mr. Maguire survived the war, Polly?" Norman asks.

"We'll have to ask Ma and Pa. Hopefully, he didn't lose too much."

Shaking his head, Norman replies, "Wouldn't count on that."

Polly learns over and tells Tot, "You want to get off in Decatur. Either one or two stops after Stone Mountain. The conductor will announce the station. Here's four five-dollar gold pieces. This should take care of you for a while. If you can't find your kin, come back to Stone Mountain and talk to the railroad agent, Mr. Goldsmith. He will get you in touch with me. Also, here is a letter explaining that you work for me, and I gave you the money. Show the letter in case you run into any problems. Good luck on finding your family."

Little Joshua is wide-awake, taking in all of the scenery and talking very well. "Uncle Norman, Uncle Norman, look!" He points to a small lake. "River!"

"That's a lake. You can walk around a lake but you can't walk around a river."

In a short moment the landscape becomes familiar. Norman stands Little Joshua on the floor. "Polly, hold him for a minute. Paul and I want to look ahead."

Getting up from their seats, Paul and Norman go to the rear of the passenger car and look out over the half door. The whistle blows and the train begins to gradually slow down. They see people standing along the wagon trail next to the railroad. Some ladies use their hands to block the afternoon sun as they strain to recognize a loved one who might be on board. A few older men raise their hats and wave as the train slows down.

Young children run along the wagon trail trying to keep pace, but gradually give up their quest to beat the train to the depot. Polly gets up and makes her way to the back of the swaying passenger car. Norman can see the engine passing the depot and listen to the steam being released from the engine boiler in preparation to come to a stop.

At an instant, and to their overwhelming joy, Betty Gail, Buck, Uncle Isaac, Aunt Sally, Turner and Maria Goldsmith, J. W. Goldsmith and his wife Lucretia Johnson Goldsmith come into view. The conductor quickly opens the door panel and descends the steps. Norman leaps to the ground, followed by Paul. They rush to greet their families. The conductor places the ladies step and helps Little Joshua and Polly also to the ground. Tot follows behind closely. Though her heart is still dark and empty, Polly is consumed in tears as she witnesses the joy and happiness of love ones reuniting.

"All aboard!" shouts the conductor. Polly immediately recognizes Chip as one of the conductors on the train when she and Legare eloped.

"You better get on board, Tot, before the train leaves. You have the money and letter. If you need me, you know how to find me." Tot turns to board the train.

Chip stands in front of the door to the passenger car and points to the rear car. "Sorry, darkies ride in the last car."

"Come, Tot, I'll walk there with you," says Polly. "There is no use arguing right now."

Saying nothing, Tot tearfully hugs Polly and Little Joshua, boards the train and the conductor closes the half door. Finding a seat next to a window, Tot waves as the train slowly pulls away. Polly walks along side of the train until she reaches her family. The train picks up speed and disappears around a curve heading toward Decatur.

With emotions beginning to wane, Buck turns his attention to Polly and little Joshua. Polly kneels down next to Little Joshua. "Remember the stories about Granny and Papa, Uncle Isaac and Aunt Sally. This is your Papa who came to visit you last Christmas. Over there is granny, Uncle Isaac and Aunt Sally.

Buck's bends over and lifts Joshua. He pats Buck's face and says, "Papa. I love you." These are the first words to come out of Joshua's mouth as he continues to rub Buck's strained, yet smiling face. Soon, the rest of the group gathers around Polly, talking all at once in their excitement at being re-united.

Facing each other, Norman places his hand on Paul's shoulder. "Well Paul, we made it home despite all odds." The family members become quiet as Paul and Norman say their farewell.

Hesitating, and finally speaking with a broken and emotional voice, Paul grabs and embraces Norman tightly. "Yes, we did Norman! We survived!" The two comrades embrace as their families watch filled with joy, love, admiration and deep respect for their two soldier boys.

Little Joshua and Papa are quickly becoming big buddies. Each day, he and Little Joshua walk around, checking on the hired help. Buck decided to convert Buster's cornfield into a pasture. The hired help is rebuilding the split rail fence around it. "Little Joshua, let's go over to the fence. I'm gonna show you how to inspect a split rail fence." Walking around the fence, Buck looks at the manner in which the split rails are interlocked. "See here," Buck places his hand between two rails and tries to pull the rails apart. "This is what you call 'hog tight!' Stick your hand in between the rail and see if you can lift them."

Little Joshua bends over and finds a little space to put his hand. He pulls and pushes. "Can't, Papa!"

Buck smiles. "I guess it's 'hog tight' then. Now, we have to get the rails high enough. The rails should be 'horse high'. That's about here on me." Buck places his hand across his collarbone. "Now in your case, your collar bone is not tall enough. Stand next to me. See? You're about knee high. Let's fetch that new horse I bought from that farmer in Elberton to measure the fence." Buck and Little Joshua walk over to a hired hand working the cotton. "How about bringing that horse over to the fence? Little Joshua needs to be sure the rails are high enough."

The worker positions the horse close to the fence. Buck picks up little Joshua and moves so the horse is between them and the fence. "Now, look over the horses back." Little Joshua lifts his head and peaks over the big animal. "See how high the fence is? Just about as high as his back. That makes it just right!"

Little Joshua shakes his head in agreement and says, "Big horse and big fence, Papa. Little horse, little fence."

"You are absolutely right! You kinda sound like your Uncle Norman! Let's go over and check on the sorghum press. The help should have some new oak rollers cut today."

❧

Sally is cleaning up after breakfast, when there's a knock on the Jernigan's door. She goes to the door, opens it and immediately recognizes the person. "Mars Hugh!" she shouts. Wiping her hands on her apron, she pulls him inside and gives him a big country hug. "My ye look 'ood! She runs to the back porch and excitedly says. "Miz Betty, Miz Polly, sum'ody yer ta see ye! Come on!"

Betty Gail and Polly stop sewing and jump up. Polly takes Little Joshua's hand while Betty Gail asks, "Who is it, Sally?"

"Ye will seed," is Sally's reply. All three hasten into the parlor.

When Betty Gail sees Hugh, she rushes over and gives him a big hug. "We are so glad to see you and to know that you're all right." She turns. "I'm sure you remember Polly."

"Why, yes I do. Hello, Polly." He hesitates. "I sure am sorry to hear that Legare was killed in the war." Polly drops her head. Hugh looks at Little Joshua and says, "I bet this is Joshua."

"Sure is," responds Polly.

"He looks just like his father. Brother John told me about him. Strong looking young fellow." Hugh approaches Joshua and gives him his hand. "Hi little man, my name is Hugh. What's yours?" Bashfully, Joshua slides around behind Polly's skirts and peeks back at Hugh. Polly takes him by the hand and squats down with him.

"This is a friend of your father's and Uncle Norman's. His name is Mr. Hugh Dent. Show him how you can shake hands." Joshua extends his little hand, and Hugh extends his, and they exchange a greeting.

"Where is Norman?" asks Hugh.

"He went to Atlanta with Paul Goldsmith. They'll be back tomorrow. I know he'll be upset that he missed visiting with you," replies Polly.

"Please give him my regards. Let him know I asked about him."

"Sally, go out to the cotton field and tell Buck that Hugh Dent is here to visit. Buck and Isaac are sweeping the cotton today."[621]

Sally departs to summon Buck.

When Buck arrives, Polly, Betty Gail and Hugh are enjoying a cup of fresh coffee on the porch. "Hello, Hugh, last time I heard about you was when you joined the Newnan Guards. It sure is good to see you safe and sound."

Betty Gail and Polly ask to be excused and depart. Buck pours a cup of coffee and the two friends sit on the porch. "Hugh, do you know you're sitting in the same rocker that General Sherman sat in?" Hugh looks kind of strange. "It's a long story, so begin with your whole experience during the war. I'll fill you in on Sherman later."

Still uncertain about the comment on the chair he is sitting in, Hugh begins his story. "Well, just before graduation, I left the Newnan Seminary at the Alderhoff's Institute in Lookout Mountain in '61. Although I was just sixteen, I was six feet tall so the recruiter thought I was older. My first four years I served with the Newnan Guards. Finally, I volunteered for the sharpshooters."[622]

Buck leans back in his chair and rocks a bit. Then he says, "Fort Stedman was Gen. Lee's final offensive!"[623] Rocking a few times, Buck asks, "Are you going up the mountain today?"

"I think I will. Would you like to walk with me?"

"Think so. But I'll warn you in advance that there's not much left of your father's grand salon."

As the two journey up the familiar mountain path, Hugh continues, "The family is probably going to sell some of the interest on the mountain. My brothers, Joe and John are the executors of Dad's will. I know Lewis Tumlin and Congressman Hill were interested at one time."

Buck interrupts, "Lewis married Lucy Elizabeth Goldsmith.[624] Her brother was Norman's roommate at Georgia Military Institute. They have been together throughout this whole war."

Hugh continues, "My sister, Mary and her husband Sterling Elder are also interested.[625] Our friend, Congressman Hill, with his connections with the Georgia Railroad, has also shown interest. I know he and my father had talked before my father's death about a business venture with the mountain and the granite."

The two approach the site of the hotel and stand in silence. "Things are mighty different!" says Hugh.

Buck in turn replies, "Yep. The tower on top is nothing but a pile of unsightly stones and lumber."[626]

Hugh sadly studies the dilapidated remains. "It's sad to see such visions of my father and others laying here in pieces because of the war."

Buck takes his hat off and fans himself a bit. "I guess, Hugh, you might say all of this is wrecks of the past."[627]

"What's come of Buster? I see you're working his land."

"Got a letter from Buster not more than a month ago. Sent me a power of attorney to his place, and ask me to telegraph him three hundred dollars. He was wounded and found a spread in Tennessee. That's all he had to say. So I dug up some of my money, took it to J. W. at the depot and telegraphed Buster three hundred dollars."

Hugh asks, "Never got over Polly running away with Legare?"

"Never did. It's best he stays gone from here and starts a new life somewhere else. I'm glad he's safe and all, but I don't need him around here crying over spilt milk. Nobody in the world could have been more in love with each other than Polly and Legare. My twins, my wife and my grandson are my concerns now."

Buck and Hugh descend the mountain as they have many other times in the past. Even though a lot has happened since the last time they made this descent, the two men settle back into an easy friendship. Together, they again sit on the front porch and discuss the plans for the future. "Buck, now that the war is over, hopefully we can start over again. It's going to take a lot of granite to rebuild Georgia."

Betty Gail leans out of the door with little Joshua holding her hand. "Polly has a great supper ready, and there are no Yankees to worry about this year!"

Once at the table, Buck asks Little Joshua, "Would you like to say the blessing for us?"

"Yes, Papa." Everyone bows his head. "Dear God, thank you for this day and my family. God, take care of my pa, I love him very much. Amen." Polly leans over and kisses Little Joshua on the forehead. Buck begins passing the chicken.

"We turned all of our chickens loose in the woods so the Yankees couldn't have them. So we're having left over Yankee chicken," says Buck. "This is about the only meat we have to eat right now. Yankees got most everything else. We have plenty of spring vegetables so help yourself to whatever you want."

"Thank you for having me to supper."

Polly looks across the table toward Hugh as she passes a plate of greens to him. "How is John?"

"He is doing just fine and probably will start a newspaper in Newnan. What are your plans, Polly? Are you staying in Stone Mountain?"

"John and Legare were the greatest of friends. Please give him my regards and let him know that he is more than welcome to come by and visit.

I am going to return to Savannah soon, plus I'm thinking about writing a book about this horrid war.

⋙

Buck goes into town the next day to purchase grease for the newly constructed cotton gin and sorghum press. The town is rebuilding slowly. Not many newcomers yet. Noticing Jesse Lanford, Isaac Nash, Mark Beauchamp and some other friends in a crowd in front of the hotel, he decides to stop and chat a bit.

As he approaches the crowd, he can hear there's a hot debate going on about the consequences of the war.

"Afternoon."

"Afternoon, Buck."

"Good afternoon, Isaac. I'm glad to see that your wrist amputation has healed."

"Yes, I'm thankful. After that wound I got in Gettysburg and that ordeal with gangrene in the Hospital in Winchester, Virginia, I'm feeling lucky to be alive."[628]

Buck asks, "Who is this fellow?"

Jesse replies, "It's Joe Livsey[629] stopping for dinner on his way to Rockbridge."

"My goodness, haven't seen you in quite a few years," replies Buck. He listens as Joe becomes very vocal and holds up a Northern newspaper, "This is the Northern idea of the freedman. Here's what they have to say, "The Negroes are free now, and must have a fair chance to make themselves something. What is claimed about their inferiority may be true. It is not likely to be proven, it but true or false, they have a right to equality before the law. That is what the war meant and this must be secured to them. The rest they must get as they can, or do without as they choose."[630]

Buck listens to the conversation.

Joe lays aside the newspaper. "Slavery might be ended as a legal status by proclamation, but as a living fact, it cannot be. The slaves' hands can be unshackled by a constitutional amendment. On the other hand, the heart and brain must have an opportunity to expand, before the freedman can be capable of automatic liberty."[631]

Jesse becomes somewhat upset at the agitating, "Joe, the North has nothing to fear, because we have lost our slaves, our bank stock, everything by the war. We have been beaten and have honestly surrendered. Slavery is gone."

Joe looks towards Jesse, responding, "The slave is now free, but he is not white. We have no ill will towards the colored man as such and in his place, but he is not our equal, cannot be made our equal. We will not be ruled by him or admit him as an equal with the white race in power. We have no objection to his voting, so long as he votes as his old master, or the man for whom he labors, advises him, but when he chooses to vote differently, then the Negro must take the consequences."[632]

Buck decides it's time for him to intercede. "The Northern man feels now that the Negro is a voter, the Southern people will have to treat him well, because we of the South will need his vote. You can count on the Negro to remain true to the government and party which gave him liberty, in order to secure that party's preservation. Enough of our own Southern whites will go with the Negro for the sake of office and power in order to enable them to retain permanent control of those states for an indefinite period."

John Rankin raises his voice to be heard, "The Northerners think the Negroes will go to work, and things will gradually adjust themselves. The Northerners think we would have the Negroes as slaves just to keep the country in constant turmoil for the sake of slavery."

Isaac Nash lifts his handless arm and shouts, "The Northerners blame the South for bringing on the war, and killing a million men. Now the Northerner says we cannot complain if the very weapon, referring to slavery of course, by which the South held power is turned against us. Supposedly this justifies the means of righting the wrongs which the North says we have created."[633]

Again, Joe Livsey retorts, "I think I can speak for most Southerners. I feel the Negro is made a voter simply to degrade and disgrace the white people of the South. The North cares nothing about the Negro as a man, but only enfranchises him in order to humiliate and enfeeble us. Of course, it makes no difference to the people of the North whether he is a voter or not. There are so few colored men there. That means there's no fear of one of them being elected to office, going to the Legislature, or sitting on the bench. The whole purpose of the measure is to insult and degrade. But restored, with the Blue Coats out of the way, we will show them their mistake."[634]

Buck hears enough. He looks at Jesse Lanford and John Rankin. "Listen up, folks." The crowd directs their attention to Buck. "You must remember that neither the nature, habits of thought, nor prejudices of men are changed by war or its results. The institution of slavery is abolished, but the prejudice, intolerance and bitterness that it has fostered and nourished are still alive. These prejudiced feelings will live until those who have been raised beneath the glare of this war have moldered back to dust.[635] Joe, you are making yourself sick. States Rights were defeated on the battlefield. Now the legal structures of the Constitution to resist tyranny and despotism are no longer strong. The executive, judicial and congress who are the ultimate guardians of liberty, the Tenth Amendment and States Rights are now tied up and choked. The war is over. Pick up the pieces and start over. Try living in peace for a while!"

Buck, Jesse Lanford and John Rankin walk away from the small gathering. "Do either one of you need a lift?"

"We're good, Buck. Came together."

Buck gives a goodbye wave and directs the horse and wagon to his farm, leaving the two strangers to spread their venomous message.

IN THE SHADOW OF THE GRANITE SENTINEL

When Joshua wakes the next morning, Polly brings him to the breakfast table where his Papa and Uncle Norman are waiting for him. When he sees his grandparents and uncle, he tears away from Polly and rushes over to the table. "Good morning, Papa. Good morning, Granny. Good morning, Uncle Norman." He gives everyone a big hug and kiss.

Betty Gail displays a grand smile. "Looks like we all got our warm-up kisses for the day!"

"Can't ever get too many from this little fellow. Now Little Joshua, right after breakfast, we have a surprise for you. So let's eat."

"Okay Uncle Norman. What's the surprise?"

"Can't tell you, I have to show it to you. So eat all your breakfast." Polly helps little Joshua into his chair. He quickly finishes his breakfast of child sized portions of eggs, grits and a small hoecake.

Little Joshua looks at Uncle Norman. "All through! All through!" He tries to lift the tray attached to the high chair.

"Mama will help you get down." Polly wipes his face and hands. She lifts the tray over his head and to the back of the high chair. Norman gets up and takes little Joshua's hand. Buck follows right along.

"What's the surprise, Uncle Norman?"

"It's in the yard next to my room."

Betty Gail, Polly, Buck, Norman and little Joshua depart by the front door, go down the porch steps and head around the house to Norman's bedroom window. When they round the corner. "Look little Joshua. See that box? The surprise is inside. Come on over and listen." Little Joshua stares at the box as they walk quietly, so they can hear. Norman gets on his knees and puts his ear to the box. "Put your ear here like mine and listen Joshua." Little Joshua gets down close to his uncle and puts his ear close to the box. "Can you hear that scratching?"

Little Joshua's eyes get big with excitement. "Yes! See?"

"I'll open the box and take the surprise out for you. Sit right here in front of the box."

Polly sits next to little Joshua. The boy anxiously watches as Norman gently lifts the front of the box. Cautiously, he slides his hand under the trap door and takes hold of the occupant. Suddenly, a baby rabbit appears. The child's eyes light up with delight.

"Look! It's a baby rabbit," explains Polly. "Uncle Norman pets the baby rabbit to calm him down."

Norman gets on his knees. "Here Joshua, you pet the baby rabbit while I hold him." Little Joshua cautiously feels the soft fur. Gleefully, he responds in the emerging voice of a three year old child. "Nice rabbit, Uncle Norman. I want to hold him."

"Let's go inside the chicken coop just in case he tries to run away." Uncle Norman and Little Joshua go inside the chicken coop and begin playing with the rabbit.

Buck follows them to the chicken coop, "While you children are play-ing with the rabbit, we are going to pick some fresh vegetables for dinner. I'm going to check out the watermelons. Betty Gail, you and Polly get some greens and carrots and whatever else you want for dinner."

"After Little Joshua and I get a little house for the baby rabbit, we'll be out there to help," says Norman.

Polly and Betty Gail pick up a basket on the way to the back garden. As they walk down the rows of broccoli, Betty Gail notices Polly appears to be holding back tears. Betty Gail waits for Polly to catch up, "What's bothering you? We can talk if you would like."

"Yes, I know, Ma. It's just that … over there at that window in Uncle Isaac and Aunt Sally's cabin is where they wished me and Legare the best when we eloped that night." Polly begins to cry, and Betty Gail puts her arms around her daughter's shoulders. "It seems like it was yesterday. I can see them now. 'Bless you both!' they whispered to us as we disappeared into the moonlit night. Time is such an illusion." Betty Gail rubs Polly's back a few short minutes. "Let's cut greens and pull some carrots, Ma."

Soon, the two women begin the harvest, joined by little Joshua and Norman. Getting on his knees, Norman demonstrates for Joshua the technique for getting the carrot out of the ground. "Watch me. Put your hands around the bottom of the green leaves and pull up real hard … Like this." Norman pulls the carrot out of the ground.

"Let me try, Uncle Norman!" Polly and Betty Gail laugh and watch Norman give Joshua a helping hand in pulling up a carrot on his own. Finally, with a stubborn jerk, the carrot pops out of the hard ground.

"Look, Mama! I got me a carrot!"

Polly kneels down and gives him a hug. "Good work. You're going to make a great farmer."

Betty Gail sees Buck in the nearby watermelon patch, "Let's go find out if Papa found a ripe watermelon. It's July and some of them should be ripe."

The weather is very warm, almost hot in fact. The sun shines bright, so Buck's forecast for a blistering day appears to be coming true. Buck sees his family heading in his direction. "Found the first ripe melon of the season. Come on over here, little Joshua." The family has gathered around Buck. He has one knee on the ground as he takes his handkerchief and wipes the sweat from his brow. He pulls little Joshua close to his side. "There's no wa-termelon better than a good, ripe Fourth of July Georgia watermelon. Why, a ripe Georgia watermelon is sweeter than a hogshead of sorghum syrup." Pulling Joshua closer, Buck points to the brown stem on the watermelon.

"First, my boy, you've got to find a brown stem, just like on this watermelon. The next thing you do is thump the melon. If it thumps like your forehead, it's not ready. But if it thumps like your belly, it's right as rain." Buck thumps little Joshua's belly and watches him jump away and giggle and rubs his belly. Buck and little Joshua take turns thumping the melon, listening for the right sound. "Let's cut it loose. We can take the watermelon and put it in the creek to cool before dinner. What do you say about that?"

"Pull it, Papa!" says Little Joshua jumping up and down.

Buck reaches and pulls the melon from the vine. He grins and stands up with his prize. Everybody chatters about the melon as they start to walk toward the creek. Everyone but Buck. His face takes on a strained appearance. He doesn't move or talk for a few seconds. Suddenly, he drops the watermelon. It bursts and scatters on the ground. Buck slumps over and falls. For a fleeting second, nobody moves.

"Buck! Buck!" screams Betty Gail.

Polly and Norman rush over to him. Falling on their knees, they find their father motionless. He has no color in his lips. His skin color is fading. His eyes are looking upward with the pupils fixed. He is no longer breathing.

"Oh, Pa!" Polly takes his hand and clutches it to her breast. She's seen death too many times not to recognize it. "No...."

Betty Gail falls to her knees, as she tenderly raises Buck's head, holding his face gently in her hands. Her eyes seem to penetrate through his lifeless eyes into his soul. She had visited this place so many times before, but now all she sees is sadness and uncertainty. "Buck! Buck!" she wails. "Don't leave me! Please don't leave me!"

Polly is holding her father's hand against her cheek while sobbing uncontrollably. Little Joshua is frightened and clings to his mother's skirt, hiding his face from the tragic scene which he doesn't understand.

Norman kneels between his sister and mother. He does not want to believe what he sees unfolding before his eyes. He closes his eyes willing the scene before him to dissolve into what he hopes is a nightmare. When his Ma reaches out to him with her trembling hands, he realizes this is no dream. His Pa is dead, and his Ma needs him. Norman places one hand across his mother's back, and with his other, pulls his sister close. His chin begins to quiver as tears flow from his eyes.

Betty Gail hugs Buck around his neck, while quietly assuring him, "I love you Buck. I love you Buck."

Dismayed little Joshua utters, "Pa Pa, Ma Ma!" His mother places her other arm around her son and gazes intently at him through her tears.

"Papa has gone to join Daddy in heaven. We're not ready for him to leave us, but he has just the same." She removes her father's hand from her chest. "Kiss Papa goodbye, little man. He wants to take your kiss with him to your Pa."

Little Joshua's looks at his mother and kisses his Papa's lifeless hand. Then Polly gently caresses little Joshua cheek with his papa's hand. Polly reflects upon Legare's birthday when their family was once again united. How her father had always been her hero. How he loved her mother and her brother and his grandson. What's going to happen to all of us … to Ma, Uncle Isaac, Aunt Sally and our family … now that Pa is gone? Her tears increase as her heart wails in pain. She returns her dear father's hand to her chest.

Norman's mind flashes back to the time his pa bought Jack for him, when his pa gave him his first squirrel gun and the joy of their trips to GMI. He has always loved his pa for the strong foundation he made for their family. He was a large chunk of granite standing in their midst. Now, what would they do?

From a nearby field, Uncle Isaac and Aunt Sally bear witness to the tragedy. Assuming something terrible has befallen Buck, they harness a horse to a wagon and rush over to the sad scene. The family is unaware of their presence as they stop nearby. Betty Gail, Norman and Polly are deaf to the entire world until Isaac and Sally step forward and kneel on the other side of Buck.

Norman looks up from his somber daze. His heart is aching, and he is afraid Ma and Polly can hear it breaking inside his chest. He must be strong for them. As he gulps in a deep breath of air, Norman reaches across his lifeless pa's body and takes Uncle Isaac's hand. "Pa's gone, Uncle Isaac, Aunt Sally, Pa's gone."

Uncle Isaac places his other hand on Buck's arm, "We's so, so sorry Mars Norman. God bless 'im," replies Isaac with a strained voice.

Aunt Sally stands, and in what seems to her as slow motion, walks around to kneel next to Polly. Tears flow from her eyes and roll down her dark cheeks in burning streams. There is no comfort now, only sadness and heart felt pain. Filled with emotion, she is unable to speak. Polly embraces Sally. "Pa loved you and Uncle Isaac. You raised and cared for us as if we were your own children. We love you as much as he did. What are any of us going to do without him?"

Norman places his hand on his ma's shoulder. "We've got to get Pa to the house, Ma." Norman stands up and takes his mother's arm. "Come on, Ma."

Betty Gail slowly releases Buck. She stands and places both hands over her face. She looks again at Buck, praying he would stand up with her. After all four rise, they embrace, and in their dark sadness, they comfort each other.

Norman steps away. "Uncle Isaac, help me put Pa on the wagon." Isaac releases Buck's hand. He walks over to the wagon and takes the reins of the horse. Quietly, he moves the wagon close to where Buck's body rests so unnaturally still. Betty Gail, Polly and Sally wipe their tears away as they watch Norman and Uncle Isaac gently placing Buck's body in the wagon.

Norman helps his grieving mother and sister onto the wagon. Betty Gail eases close to Buck and places his head in her lap. She looks lovingly at him and caresses his face. Polly clasps her pa's hand. Norman holds little Joshua in his lap. Uncle Isaac and Aunt Sally slowly walk with the wagon as Norman drives the team that carries Buck home from his final trip to his watermelon patch.

Uncle Isaac halts the wagon at the front of the house. Norman silently gets out and places little Joshua in Sally's arms. Proceeding to the rear of the wagon, he studies the scene of his mother and sister beside Buck. They both look so lost.

His thoughts reflect, "A love lost forever."

"Ma, let me help you and Polly down. Uncle Isaac and I will take Pa to the bedroom where he and Sally can prepare him." Betty Gail tenderly lifts Buck's head from her lap. She kisses him on the cheek and hesitantly slides away from his still body. Polly kisses his hand again as Norman helps them from the wagon.

Aunt Sally hurries inside and brings a sheet to Norman. He and Uncle Isaac prudently wrap Buck's body in the sheet. In the meantime, Sally is dressing the bed properly with additional sheets in preparation for her and Isaac to bathe and clothe their former owner.

Betty Gail, Polly and little Joshua follow Norman and Isaac to the bedroom where they place Buck's body. Norman gently takes his ma's arm. "Ma, you and Polly come on in the dining room. Aunt Sally will fix you something to drink." Betty Gail and Polly gaze at the white sheet and feel even more grief stricken. Norman sits with his Ma and sister and holds their hands.

"This is terribly hard on all of us, but Ma, I've got to go to town and make some arrangements. I need to find a way to get Pa's grave dug, go by the undertakers, and buy a coffin. Then I'll notify Pastor Maddox[636] about Pa's death. I also got to send a telegram to the Hills." Betty Gail takes a deep breath and nods her head. He kisses his Ma, Polly and little Joshua.

"Little Joshua, you are in charge until I get back. Take care of Granny and your ma while I'm gone." Little Joshua looks at his uncle and sits in his mama's lap, hugging her tightly.

Norman's first stop is at Pastor Fielding Maddox's house. Norman ties off his mount and sees Pastor Maddox returning from his small garden. "Hello Norman, what brings you this way today?" As Pastor Maddox draws closer, he observes the solemn look on Norman face. He extends his hand to Norman. "What has happened?"

Norman lowers his head, fighting to contain his grief. "Pa died a couple of hours ago in the garden. Just fell over and died in an instant, right before our eyes. Took his last breath."

"Norman, my son, he rests with God now. I am so sorry. Come sit down with me and tell me what I can do for you and your family."

"Thank you, Pastor Maddox. We would like to have pa's funeral around four o'clock tomorrow. Would that be a good time for you to perform a grave side service in the City Cemetery?"

"I will be privileged to do just that. Mrs. Maddox and I will inform our members and we'll visit with you this afternoon."

"Thanks Pastor." Norman shakes his hand. "We look forward to having your visit later today." Norman departs to the depot to have James Goldsmith telegraph the Hill's. When he enters the depot, Mr. Goldsmith is completing a telegram and signals that it will be just a minute before he is available. While he is waiting for Mr. Goldsmith to finish, Jesse Lanford comes into the depot. Norman turns to see who it is.

"Hello Norman. I saw you pull up out front. I want to talk to your Pa about some seed. Is he with you?" Immediately, Jesse sees the strong sense of sadness on Norman's face and looks quizzically at him.

"Mr. Lanford, I hate to tell you this, but Pa died a few hours ago in the garden. Just fell over dead right in front of me. I'm here to send a telegram to the Hills."

Appearing dismayed and in shock, Jesse grabs Norman's hand. "Norman, I don't know what to say. Your dad and I have been the best of friends for thirty years or more."

Mr. Goldsmith hears the conversation and rushes over. "Did I hear you say your Pa died this morning, Norman?"

"Yes sir, he did. Died while he was finding a watermelon for little Joshua. I need you to let Congressman and Mrs. Hill in Madison know. Tell them Pa has passed and the funeral is at the cemetery at four o'clock tomorrow."

"I'll send it right now. Don't leave. I want to talk to you more about what happened and what we can do for you and your family." Jesse takes a seat on one of the depot benches near Norman and invites Norman to come and sit beside him.

"Norman, your pa was a proud Mason. If it meets with your approval, I will gather his brothers for a Masonic funeral."

"Yes, Mr. Lanford, please do that. Dr. Goldsmith is a Past Master of the Lodge. I want to please ask him to lead the service."

"I will telegraph Mr. Maguire to come and represent the Lithonia Masonic Lodge. I will go with you to Dr. Goldsmith's house. Then I can gather his fellow Masons and prepare the grave site."

"Thank you so much for your help, Mr. Lanford."

"Norman, I telegraphed the Madison station. They wired me back that Congressman and Mrs. Hill will not be back from Washington for about two more weeks."

Norman looks down, scratching his head, "Thank you Mr. Goldsmith. Ma and Polly are going to be even sadder when they learn the Hills can't be here. Tell the telegraph operator to notify the Hill's of Pa's death and we can visit when they return."

"Be glad to, Norman."

Jesse stands. "Let's go over to Dr. Goldsmith's when you are ready Norman."

Mr. Goldsmith returns to Norman and Jesse. "Everything is taken care of, Norman. Lucretia and I will be at your Pa's place this evening. Please extend our sympathy to your mother and Polly. Your Pa was a cornerstone of this town."

"Thank you, Mr. Goldsmith," Norman says. He pays the fifty cents for the two telegrams and he and Mr. Lanford depart for Dr. Goldsmith's in Jesse's wagon.

Finding Dr. Goldsmith not home, they proceed to the undertaker where Norman selects a coffin. Standing by the wagon at the undertaker's, Jesse leans on the wagon, and says to poor Norman, "I'm sorry neither Dr. or Mrs. Goldsmith were home, but I will see them later today. They must be out making calls on the sick. Don't worry about the grave, the site you showed me will be ready by tomorrow. I'll tell the Mayor, Levi and Dr. Hamilton. They'll all pass the word about your pa to the other folks in town." He places his hand on Norman's shoulder in a gesture of comfort. "I'm glad the undertaker already had a few coffins made. Let's go get your wagon, and I'll help you load the coffin. I know you are exhausted and need to get back to your ma and Polly."

"I can't thank you enough, Mr. Lanford." Norman extends his hand to Jesse. "You have truly been a friend today."

On his lonely ride home, Norman constantly looks over his shoulder to be sure the coffin is there and that he is not dreaming. As he nears their farm, he sees a horseman approaching. He pulls his wagon over and waits for the rider to reach him. It's John Rankin, another one of the family friends. John eases his horse over to the wagon, close enough to see the coffin, dismayed and curious, he asks, "What's happened Norman? Who passed?"

"It's Pa, Mr. Rankin. Died this morning. We're going to have the funeral tomorrow." John dismounts and walks over to Norman. He reaches for Norman's hand for a manly shake.

"This is a shock, Norman. It's like you have pulled a piece of my heart away. Your dad always looked after the folks around here. Everybody cared about him. How are your mother and Polly?

"Heartbroken, just like me. I can't hardly stand it myself. Him just dying all of a sudden like that. Mr. Lanford is setting up the Masonic funeral, and Pastor Maddox is doing the service at four o'clock tomorrow."

"Please give my respects to your Mother and Polly. Eliza and I will visit tonight, and I will most certainly be a part of the funeral rites tomorrow."

"Thank you, Mr. Rankin. I'll tell Ma and Polly. Gotta git now." John Rankin watches the new head of the Jernigan family, homeward bound to fulfill his inherited responsibilities.

Betty Gail and Polly see Norman approaching. They go outside to stand in the yard as he pulls up and stops. He leaps from the wagon and gives his ma and sister big hugs. Tears return to Betty Gail's and Polly's eyes when they see the coffin.

Norman takes their arms and leads them inside.

Betty Gail follows Norman to the dining room. "I know you must be starving. Sally fried a couple of chickens and they are still warm. Sit down and eat and tell us what arrangements you made in town."

Norman takes a seat and pulls off a chicken leg. "I didn't know I was so hungry." In between bites he relates the details of his visit to town. "I talked with Pastor Maddox, and he can preach the funeral tomorrow at four. The Hills are in Washington for a couple more weeks. I couldn't find Dr. Goldsmith."

"Mr. Lanford was a big help," Norman continues. "He's getting the Masons to open the grave. He and I picked out a good grave site for Pa. The Masons are going to perform their Rites at the funeral. Mr. Lanford is notifying the Mayor and the other citizens around town about Pa. Saw John Rankin on the way home. He had just left the quarry. I didn't think he would be working yet, since he just got home late last month from the war. There's still not very many men back from the war. We probably don't have seventy-five young men in Stone Mountain just yet." Norman looks around. "Where's little Joshua?"

"He's taking a nap. He's so confused about what's going on," Polly sadly remarks.

"He's not the only one. Why don't you and Ma go out to the garden while Uncle Isaac and I bring the coffin inside? It's going to be hard enough on me putting him in it. You certainly don't need to watch. Where do you want me to place the coffin, Ma?"

"I've been thinking. Polly and I feel in front of the fireplace would be best. Your Pa always liked sitting in front of the fire to read his newspaper."

Norman nods in agreement. "Where's Uncle Isaac, Ma?"

"Sitting with your pa. You know we can't leave his body alone."

He stands to assist his mother and sister from their chairs. Betty Gail and Polly embrace Norman while he escorts them to the back door. They pass Sally in the kitchen. "Aunt Sally, go and stay with Pa while Uncle Isaac and I bring the coffin inside." Sally stops washing the dishes and dries her hands. "Yuz sah, Mars Norman." She goes to Buck's room and sits next to Uncle Isaac.

Norman stands in the doorway to his Pa's room. Uncle Isaac watches Norman as he gazes at his father. "I've got the coffin in the wagon, Uncle Isaac. I need you to help me with it. Polly and Ma are in the backyard waiting for us to set him by the fireplace."

Norman and Uncle Isaac go the living room, seeking a table or some structure to use as a bier. "Can't use the dining table, Uncle Isaac. People are going to be coming by and bringing food." He scratches his head. "I have an idea. How about using saw horses?"

"That wuks Mars Norman. I goes git'em."

Norman takes a seat in his Pa's rocking chair. In a matter of seconds, he nearly falls asleep only to be startled by Uncle Isaac's return. Norman shakes his head when he hears Uncle Isaac's voice, uncertain of his whereabouts.

"I see you found the two saw horses, Uncle Isaac." Norman takes one and positions it in an appropriate location just in front of the fireplace. Judging the length of the coffin, Norman positions the second saw horse near the other end of the fireplace. "Let's bring the coffin inside to be sure we have the saw horses spaced just right." Norman and Uncle Isaac lift the coffin from the wagon and carry it inside to its bier.

Norman steps back and looks. "Need to bring that one a little closer together, Uncle Isaac." Norman lifts the coffin while Uncle Isaac slides the saw horse closer to each other. Then, Norman lets the coffin rest on the bier and inspects them again. "Looks okay, Uncle Isaac." Norman checks the lining of the coffin to be sure it wasn't displaced while bringing it home. He presses against the cotton batting inside to assure that it is evenly spread underneath the cotton lining. He picks up the veil the undertaker had placed inside the coffin and lays it on his Pa's rocking chair. Norman stands silent for a moment, visualizing his father in the coffin. Taking a deep breath, he heads toward his father's bedroom soberly, "Let's get Pa, Uncle Isaac."

They enter the bedroom just as Sally swats a fly with the swatter. "Em flies gittin' bad, Mars Norman.

"I know, Aunt Sally. I have a veil to place over Pa after we lay him in the coffin. Uncle Isaac, you take his feet. Sally you hold his legs, and I'll take him by the shoulders." Norman reaches down to pick up his pa and feels the cold and stiff body. He releases his grip immediately and steps back to the bedroom door, leaning there for a while. He knows what he has to do, but the reality of this final contact with his loved one is difficult to accept. Uncle Isaac and Sally stand silently, watching their "Wee Bean" gather his strength. Norman remembers his Pa laughing and giving him advice. How he would hold his Pa's warm hand while walking together. Now his Pa is cold and stiff. Without life or laughter. Emotions from deep within are forced to the outside of Norman's being. He breathes deeply for a few moments until he regains his composure. Walking over to his pa's body. "Okay, let's move Pa."

Norman adjusts his father's body in the coffin and places the veil over the open coffin. Buck's hands are folded over his chest. He is clothed in his overalls and brown shirt. "Uncle Isaac, you and Aunt Sally accomplished your difficult task well. I know it was a chore, but one from your hearts. Thank you so much."

Holding hands, Uncle Isaac and Aunt Sally gaze at Norman. "Thank ye, Mars Norman. Yo' Pa belong ter us too."

"Stay here with Pa, Uncle Isaac, while I go and get Ma and Polly. Aunt Sally how 'bout fixing something else for us to drink."

"Yas Suh."

He locates his Ma and Polly sitting in the gazebo. He soon discovers they are holding hands and their heads are resting upon one another.

Norman touches their joined hands. "Ma, Polly, I hate to bother you, but we have Pa by the fireplace. Come see if you are satisfied with the way he is laid out."

Betty Gail and Polly stretch their arms into the air as they awaken. Betty Gail stands and gives her son a hug. "I don't know what I would have done during this dreadful time without you and Polly."

"If there's any reason to be glad Ma, it's the fact that we all were together during Pa's final moment."

Polly takes her Ma's and brother's hands. "Let's go in the front door."

Betty Gail wipes her eyes from tears of affection. They climb the steps onto the porch and enter the front door.

Sitting next to the coffin are Uncle Isaac and Aunt Sally. Both have fly swatters in their hand. They stand next to the family and gather close to the coffin. The severe shock of Buck's sudden demise is waning. Betty Gail pulls the veil back and assesses dear Buck's appearance. "You bathed and dressed our Buck nicely. His body is here now, and although he will be gone forever, his memory will live until the last one of us dies."

Suddenly Polly hears little Joshua stir in her room. "I better get him up. I've got to feed and dress him. Folks are going to be coming to visit soon. Aunt Sally, would you prepare some food for my little man?"

"Yas 'um."

Norman hears Charlie bark and goes to the front window. "Looks as if folks are starting to arrive, Ma."

"Mighty nice of them. He was well respected by most everybody in town."

Norman and Isaac step outside to greet the neighbors. The first to arrive is Preacher Maddox and his wife. Uncle Isaac takes the horse's reins and secures them to the hitching post. Norman helps Mrs. Maddox from the wagon. She takes Norman's hands in each of hers. "You have our deepest sympathy, Norman."

"Thank you, Mrs. Maddox. It is a terrible shock, but all of you visiting tonight will make my family feel much better. Ma and Polly are inside."

"Fielding and I brought some food. Got to feed all these folks coming to pay their respects."

"Thank you again. Everyone has been very thoughtful."

"Fielding, take the basket into the kitchen." Mrs. Maddox turns to Norman, "I'll go inside to be with your mother and sister. I know you have duties outside right now."

"Yes ma'am."

Norman takes the reins of the horse pulling Dr. Goldsmith's wagon. His wife Louisa is with him. As they climb from the wagon, Mrs. Goldsmith hugs Norman. He can hardly contain himself the embrace from her and the handshake from Dr. Goldsmith. No words are spoken, nor need they be. It's all in the eyes. Dr. Goldsmith looks at Norman sadly, "I sent a telegram to Paul in Florida. He sends his condolences and wanted to be with you. He said to tell you the Florida salt water is helping him to recover, and he hopes to be home soon."

Louisa dries her tears. "I know that you and Paul are like brothers. You have been through tough times together. He sincerely wanted to be here for you."

"Thank you both. Paul, no doubt, is my dearest friend."

"Now, go tend to your other neighbors. Turner and I know our way." Norman is tired and is doing his best not to show how despondent he really is. He continues to greet his neighbors as they arrive; John and Eliza Rankin, James and Lucretia Goldsmith, Mr. &. Mrs. Lanford, James and Celia Sheppard, Dr. John and Mary Hamilton, Hiram and Matilda Holley, Phillip and Celia McCurdy, the Nash brothers, John and Mary Tuggle, the Wells, and the Winninghams are but a few of the friends expressing their compassion and showing their kindness.

Later in the evening Norman is with his Ma, Polly and the guests, when Dr. Goldsmith approaches him. "Norman, Pastor Maddox and I would like to talk with you a moment on the porch where it is a little quieter."

"Why certainly, Dr. Goldsmith."

Each one takes a chair onto the porch, and Pastor Maddox begins, "I talked with your mother and Polly and they told me what they wanted to me to say about your Pa. Is there anything special you would like said?"

Norman says, moving his arms to include the people. "Just look around you, Pastor. This is what my Pa was about. This here home, this here farm, his family and look at all his friends who have come by tonight. This scene tells it all. I can't add anymore to that."

"I understand. Your Ma and sister asks me to keep my preaching short and simple, and I will most certainly honor their request."

"Thank you, Pastor Maddox." Norman gazes toward Dr. Goldsmith. "What do you think Dr. Goldsmith?"

"Well, Norman, I have talked with most all of the brothers. We would like to escort your father's body to the cemetery and perform the Masonic funeral service for him, after Pastor Maddox finishes his service. Your mother said to check with you, but that it was okay with her and Polly."

"My Pa lived by the Masonic principles, and I hoped to have him sign my petition." Norman pauses for a moment to regain his composure. Dr. Goldsmith pats him on the leg.

"I understand Norman, and I will be honored to sign your petition whenever you are ready."

"A Masonic funeral will be a high honor for him and for us. Thank you so much for offering such a fine farewell gift."

JULY 3, 1865

Norman looks at the old family clock on the mantel. "It's time to go, Ma."

Betty Gail, Polly and Aunt Sally are dressed in black. Norman is wearing his GMI Kepie and a dark suit. Uncle Isaac walks next to Sally as Norman takes his mother and Polly by the arm and escorts them to the side of Buck's wagon. They stand silently and watch the Stone Mountain Lodge Number 111 Pallbearers place Buck's coffin on his wagon. Then the family boards another wagon behind Buck's. The members of the Lodge on horseback line up behind them. Silently, Dr. Goldsmith leads the entourage toward the Stone Mountain cemetery.

A large assemblage of friends solemnly gathers near Betty Gail, Polly, and Norman while the Pallbearers place Buck's coffin on straps near the end of the prepared grave.

Pastor Maddox, standing next to the Jernigans moves forward to deliver Buck's eulogy. "Dear Friends, I talked with Betty Gail last evening and asked her what she would like for me to tell you about her late husband and to give a short eulogy because everyone present already knew Buck's virtues." Pastor Maddox fixes his eyes toward Betty Gail and her family.

"She told me, if I said nothing else, just be sure and let everyone know what a great person Buck was. And that he was! Today is one day before the Independence Day of America. Buck was against secession and proudly flew the Union Flag during the conflict. His devotion to his God, his country, his family, friends and neighbors in war and peace was always the same. Put them first. Protect and love them. This he did until yesterday.

Pastor Maddox signals Dr. Goldsmith to proceed with the Masonic service and then returns to his place next to the Jernigans.

The Granite Sentinel glistens from the morning rays of sunshine as she peers silently over the solemn gathering on a hillside in the Stone Mountain cemetery. The Masonic Brothers of Stone Mountain Lodge III have gathered to perform a funeral service at the grave site of their departed brethren, Buck Jernigan.

Members of the Lodge attending the funeral are: John Rankin, J. R. Bracewell, Z. Estes, W. W. Veal, John R. Mehaffey, W. T. Ray, J. A. Seay, James W. Goldsmith, John W. McCurdy, Lewis Wiggins, James Learce, George W. Minor, E. Steward, R. A. Ray, E .F. Mosley, Dr. George K. Hamilton, Oliver Winingham, and William Winingham.[637] Thomas Maguire is attending to represent Lithonia Masonic Lodge No. 84. All members are wearing their Masonic aprons and white gloves. The officers of the Lodge take their position around Buck's casket.

Standing at the head of the coffin, which is generally reserved for the Worshipful Master of the Lodge, and leading the Masonic grave side service is Past Master Dr. Turner Goldsmith. He removes his hat in respect for his friend and Masonic brother....

Dr. Goldsmith recites, "From time immemorial, it has been the custom of free and accepted Masons, at the request of a brother, or his family after his death, to accompany his body to the place of interment and there to deposit the remains with the usual formalities.

"In conformity with the custom, we have assembled here today in the character of Masons, to consign the body of Brother Buck Jernigan to the earth whence it came and to offer up the last tribute of our affection, thereby demonstrating the sincerity of our past esteem and our steady attachment of the principles of Masonry."

"Brethren, the imperious mandate of the dread messenger, Death, against whose entrance within our circle the barred doors and Tyler's sword afford no defense, calls upon us to mourn the loss of one of the sons of light. The dead body of our beloved brother Buck Jernigan, lies before us in its narrow house overtaken by the fate which must sooner or later overtake us all; which no power or station, no virtue or bravery, no wealth or honor, no tears of friends or agonies of loved ones can avert; teaching the impressive lesson, continually repeated yet soon forgotten, that each one of us must ere long pass through the valley of the shadow of death."

Dr. Goldsmith removes his gentleman's hat. "Brother Chaplain, lead us in prayer."

John Rankin, the Chaplain prays, "Brethren, the solemn notes that betoken the dissolution of this earthly tabernacle have again alarmed our outer door, and another spirit has been summoned to the land where our fathers have gone before us. Again, we are called upon to assemble among the habitations of the dead to behold the narrow house appointed for all the living. Here around us sleep the unnumbered dead. The gentle breeze fans their earthly covering, but they heed it not. The sunshine and the storms pass over them, but they are not disturbed. Stones and monuments symbolize the affection of the surviving friends, yet no sound proceeds save that silent but thrilling admonition: Seek ye narrow path and the straight gate that lead unto eternal life....

When it shall please the Grand Master of the universe to summon us to His eternal presence, may the trestle-board of our lives pass such inspection that it may be given to each of us to 'Eat of the hidden manna,' and to receive the 'White stone with a new name' that will insure perpetual and unspeakable happiness and God's right hand."

Dr. Goldsmith holds the lambskin apron in front of him and says, "The lambskin, or white leather apron is an emblem of innocence and the badge of a Mason: more ancient than the golden fleece or Roman eagle; more honorable than star and garter, when worthily worn; this emblem I now deposit in the grave of our deceased brother."

Dr. Goldsmith deposits the lambskin apron on the casket. "By it we are reminded that life made pure by the blood of the lamb, so essentially necessary to gaining admission to the celestial lodge above, where the Supreme Architect of the universe presides."

He then deposits the glove on the casket. "What virtue unites death never parts."

Holding up a sprig of a cedar he recites. "The evergreen, which once marked the temporary resting place of one illustrious Masonic history, is an emblem of our faith in the immortality of the soul … We commend his spirit to God who gave it … And we consign his body to the ground."

Dr. Goldsmith continues, "Unto the grave we consign the body of our deceased brother, there to remain until the general resurrection, in favorable expectation that his immortal soul may then partake of the joys which have been prepared for the righteous from the foundation of the world. And may Almighty God, of His infinite goodness, at the grand tribunal of unbiased justice, extend His mercy toward him and all of us, and crown our hopes with everlasting eternity. This we beg for the honor of His name, to Whom be all the glory, now and forever more. Amen!

"For as much as it has pleased Almighty God to take out of this world, the soul of our beloved brother, we therefore commit his body to the grave. Earth to earth, ashes to ashes, and dust to dust … sleep on my brother.

"Would everyone please join us as we pray the model prayer?" Everyone recites The Lord's Prayer. "Amen." All Masons quote together, "So Mote it be!"

Pastor Maddox returns to the head of the grave site. The pallbearers take their respective positions around Buck's coffin, each holding to an end of the strap beneath the coffin. Pastor Maddox opens the Bible and recites, "Ashes to ashes. Dust to dust. We commit thee to Your love." The pallbearers slowly lower Buck to his eternal resting place.

Betty Gail and Polly, with tears in their eyes, tightly grasp Norman's arms as they witness the last sight of their beloved husband and father disappearing forever. Pastor Maddox leads the friends as he expresses his final condolences to Betty Gail, Polly, Norman, Uncle Isaac and Aunt Sally.

JULY 4, 1865

Polly wakes early. After breakfast, and helping clean the dishes, she lays the dish towel on the sink. "I think little Joshua and I'll go to the cemetery this morning and place some flowers on Papa's grave. The Fourth of July was always such a special day for him."

Norman responds, "If you can wait until later in the day, Ma, and I'll go with you. Got a few chores to do around here first."

"Actually, I kinda want to be alone for awhile, but would be happy to go back with you this afternoon."

Norman winks. "That's fine."

Around ten o'clock, Polly has finished helping her mother gather eggs, feed the chickens and harvest a few beans and squash for dinner. Before she and little Joshua depart for the cemetery, they walk through the small flower garden to select some fresh summer flowers. She points to yellow daises. "Joshua, Papa would really like these." They cut a few to place on his grave. When they are ready to leave, Norman has their wagon and only horse ready for Polly and little Joshua. As they board the wagon, Charlie gives out a weak howl indicating he'd love to ride along.

"Come on, Charlie. I'll help you onto the wagon." Norman gently picks up the dog and places him in the back of the wagon, close enough for little Joshua to pet. As they approach the cemetery, all is quiet and serene. She and little Joshua tie off the horse near her father's final resting site.

Charlie lifts his head and gives a happy yap as they approach. Little Joshua pats him on the head which elicits a whine for even more attention. Polly rubs the old dog. "Be back in a minute, then we will head home." She and Little Joshua walk the short distance to her father's grave. They kneel and lay the flowers across the simple plot. "I see Papa smiling at you, little Joshua. He must have delivered your kiss to your Pa."

Polly points to a song bird in a nearby tree. "Hear that bird singing? Your grandpa sent him to tell us that he is in heaven with your Pa and that he appreciates that little kiss you sent." Suddenly, Polly is startled as a shadow appears over her right shoulder. She takes little Joshua's hand and stands. Before her about ten feet away is a man in a suit, holding his coat over his arm. Polly stares and studies the figure. He is aged and slender, yet has a familiar face.

"Hello, Polly. I was passing through on de train. When I went by to see your folks, dey said I could find you here. I am truly sorry 'bout your pa. I jest want ter say hello."

Polly pulls little Joshua close as her eyes widen. She murmurs, "Buster, is that you?"

⅗ THE END ⅖

Rooster Rooster returned to his North Georgia family farm, continued to live there, and maintained a casual contact with Polly. After meeting Polly at Buck's grave, Buster Phillips left Stone Mountain and was never heard from again.

Tot could not find any members of her family in Decatur and returned to work for Polly. Tot, Jesse and Al worked and lived with Polly in Savannah for the remainder of their lives.

Mrs. Katherine Turner and her family moved to Nassau permanently.

Norman stayed in Stone Mountain with his mother working the family farm. He eventually entered Medical School in Atlanta.

Polly and John Dent have been seen on several occasions, strolling hand in hand around Stone Mountain as well as dining at the Pirates' House in Savannah. Little Joshua is growing up quickly, the pride and joy of his mother, grandparents and his uncle. He inherited the best traits of his southern heritage from the Hills and the Jernigans, and promises to be as good a man as his father.

The Confederacy had approximately 1.4 million men for the war while the Union has approximately 3.5 million men available. The Confederacy had approximately 800,000 men under arms while the Union had approximately 2 million men under arms. On the average 1 out of every 43 are killed in action; 1 out of every 39 died from wounds; 1 out of every 6.7 were wounded. The Confederacy had approximately 95,000 killed in battle or mortally wounded plus 165,000 to die from disease. The Union had 110,000 either killed in action or were mortally wounded plus another 225,000 to die from disease.

The Total United States horse population in 1860 was 4,416,000 with 1.7 million horses in the South and approximately 801,000 mules while the North had approximately 329,000 mules. There were approximately 857,000 oxen in the South and approximately 1,384,000 in the North.

Lincoln was buried at Oak Ridge Cemetery in Springfield, Illinois on May 14, 1865. His Administration is known for; The Emancipation Proclamation, Conscription, Issuing of paper currency and the Income Tax law.

Joshua Hill was appointed collector of customs at Savannah in 1866 and registrar in bankruptcy in 1867 but declined both offices. He also began buying parcels of the Mountain in January of 1866. Joshua Hill was elected as a Republican to the United Senate on July 28, 1868 and took the oath of office on February 1, 1871 after Georgia was readmitted for representation in Congress. In 1872 Senator Hill took an active part in discussing the civil rights bill with Charles Sumner. Senator Hill served until March 1873 and was not a candidate for reelection. Joshua Hill returned to Madison and resumed the practice of law and became a member of the State constitutional convention in 1877. Senator Hill died in Madison, Georgia March 6, 1891. Senator Hill had a grandson by the name of Joshua who was the son of his daughter Anna Hill Bowles. Joshua Hill Bowles was willed bonds in the Georgia Railroad and Banking Company, and his grandfather's winding gold watch and chain.

Julius L. Brown, Governor Brown's son, graduated from the University of Georgia during reconstruction and was admitted to the bar in 1869. He went to Harvard in 1870 and graduated from Law School. He developed a very lucrative law practice and served as his father's attorney in dealing with the Western & Atlantic Railroad, the coal mines and the Citizen's Bank. Julius was well known for his very short temper. In 1880, by court order, he was prevented from fighting a duel with a man by the name of Dr. Westmoreland. Hal T. Lewis of Company B becomes a Supreme Court Justice. Samuel Spencer of Company B. becomes president of Southern Railway. Colonel Brumby's slave Crawford Monroe becomes wealthy by investing the earnings he has accumulated at GMI in real estate and manufacturing after emancipation.

Two of the Georgia Military Institute's brass six-pounder howitzer cannons were returned to Marietta. One was mounted as a memorial in the Marietta Conference Center, the site of the Georgia Military Institute. The second cannon was mounted in the Marietta Confederate Cemetery with a plaque stating that the cannon has been returned by the United States Government in 1910. The two twelve pounder howitzer cannons were mounted on the steps of the Georgia State Capitol in Atlanta.

February 25, 1863—The Mountain was purchased by Winston Wood and John Meadow for $22,638, exempting certain quarrying rights.

January 6, 1866—Lewis Tumlin sold his interest in Stone Mountain to Senator Joshua Hill.

February 5, 1867—The Mountain was purchased for $37,000.00 by the Stone Mountain Granite and Railroad Company.

March 1867—Alexander H. Stephens, U.S. Representative, V. P. of the Confederacy, U.S. Senator and Governor of Georgia bought approximately 170 acres in various size plots within and around the city of Stone Mountain. His Company was the Enterprise Company. According to the deeds his company was to work in conjunction with the Hotel Company owned by Thomas Johnson.

November 3, 1868—Paul Turner Goldsmith died at the age of twenty four and was buried in the Stone Mountain City Cemetery. A Georgia

Military Institute alumnus speaking to a veterans group remembered Paul Goldsmith, "as one of the "better-natured boys that I have ever known."

1869—The railroad spur line to the quarry was re-built. The original was built by the Georgia Railroad and was destroyed in 1864 by Union troops. Freedmen become hired laborers begin working in the quarry. Many of the local former slaves congregate together and begin a new neighborhood on the southern section of the city of Stone Mountain. The name of the new community is Sherman town. This event marks the first major effort for the large-scale commercial venture for the production of Stone Mountain granite.

August 24, 1869—Senator Joshua Hill sold his interest in Stone Mountain to the Stone Mountain Granite Company.

July 15, 1870—Georgia was originally readmitted to the union in 1868 but was expelled in 1869 because she refused to ratify the 15th Amendment of the Constitution. This amendment made it illegal to deny the right to vote on the basis of race. Georgia finally ratified the amendment in 1870 and was permanently readmitted to the Union on July 15, 1870. Census for Stone Mountain was around seven hundred.

maps appendix

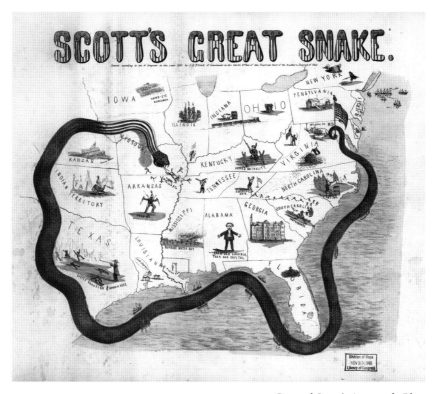

General Scott's Anaconda Plan

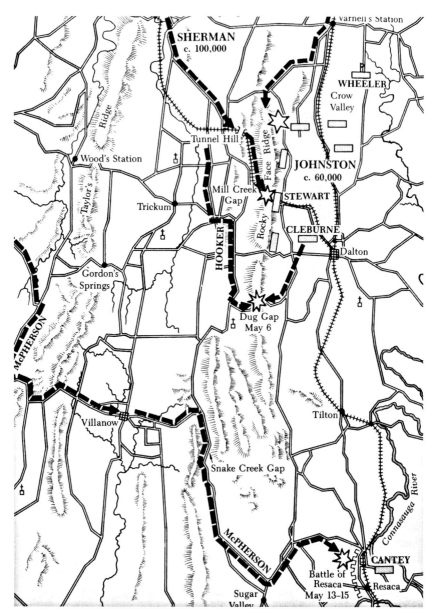

Dalton to Resaca, May 4-16, 1864
Courtesy of Ms. Irma Clipson

Cassville, May 16-20, 1864
Courtesy of Ms. Irma Clipson

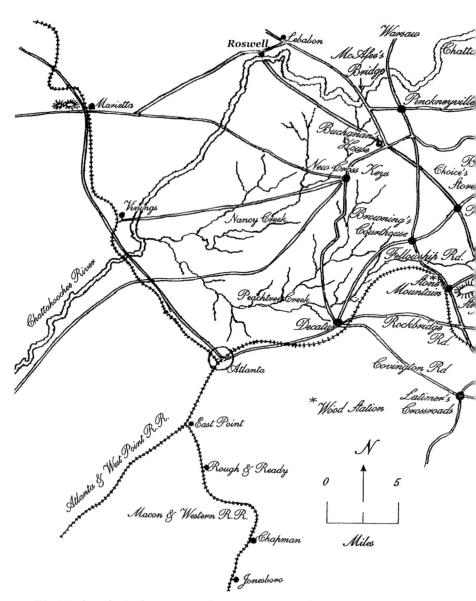

The March to the Sea began November 15, 1864. The Left Wing was initally divided into two separate routes from Decatur, GA. The XX Corps of General Sherman's army marched via Fellowship Road through Stone Mountain. On november 16, 1864, the XIV Corps of General Sheran's army took the Rockbridge Road route

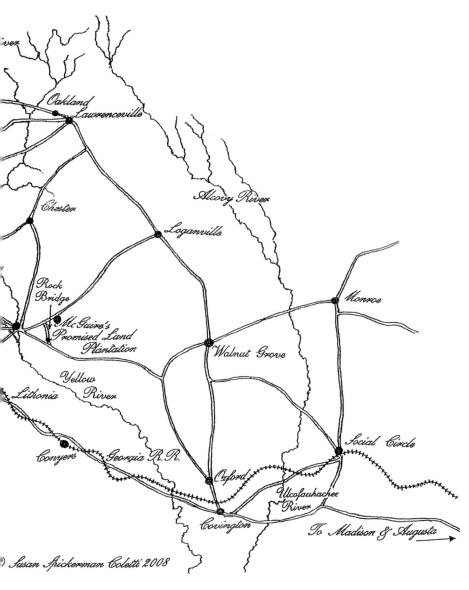

from Decatur and camped at what is now the intersection of Rockbridge Road and Stone Mountain-Lithonia Road. General Sherman accompanied the XIV Corps. Approximately 15,000 Union troops camped in and around Stone Mountain.

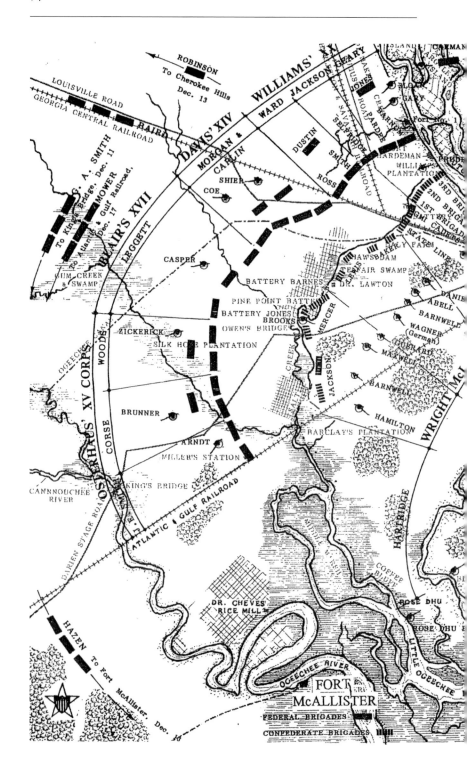

endnotes

1   Francis M. Allen, James Allen, William C. Austin, George P. Bradley, John M. Bradley, E. F. Camp, Eliphaze Andrew Carter, Augustus T. Cochran, William Vardy Cronic, William F. A. Dickerson, James Andrew J. Duren, Robert O. Foard, Rufus P. Furgerson, Solomon Gibson, Paul Turner Goldsmith, John W. Goza, James R. Hadaway, Dr. John L. Hamilton, Thomas W. Hardman, William F. Hardman, Benjamin F. Harris, James C. Harris, William David Harris, James F. Henderson, John T. Hendrix, Milton Andrew Herndon, Samuel J. Hill, James J. Hix, Hiram J. Holley, Nathaniel N. Humphreys, Benjamin Thomas Ivie, Miles Andrew Killian, Charles King, Elihu Paden Lanford, Presley Lanier, William J. Lee, James A. Mackin, Luther Mason, John H. F. Mattax, John Forsyth McClelland, John Wilson McCurdy, Philip Buford McCurdy, William S. Mehaffey, John Glosson Miller, Edward Newton Nash, Francis Marion Nash, Isaac Newton Nash, James Oliver Newsome, Elwin Litchfield Phillips, Isaac B. Pope, John Gray Rankin, Britton Sanders, John L. Sawyer, John W. Scruggs, James M. Shepard, James R. Smith, George L. Summey, Jesse Boland Taliaferro, Thomas Jefferson Thomas, Andrew Jackson Thompson, Ransom Martin Thompson, George Presley Trout, John Pickney Tuggle, George Riley Wells, Thomas P. Wells, Wilburn Ransela Wells, John Thomas Willingham, Michal Winningham, Oliver Winningham, Ebenezer Thomas White.

2   *Stone Mountain Or the Lay of the Gray Minstrel: An Epic Poem in Twenty Four Parts*, Lucian Lamar Knight, 1923 State Historian

Part I
PROLOGUE

3   The Confederate Records of the State of Georgia, Candler, Vol I 1860.

CHAPTER 1: APRIL 16, 1852

4   Act of the General Assembly December 1838 … *And be it further enacted by the authority aforesaid*, That James Diamond, William Meadows, and Thomas Bolton be, and they are hereby appointed Trustees of the Stone Mountain Academy, in the county of DeKalb. Stone Mountain had the reputation of having exceptional education facilities.

5   Confederate Veterans of Stone Mountain, Chris Davis, 2000.

6   A descendant in Stone Mountain is believed to be Judge Marion Guess. The "Chero-
     kee Nation" was the first Indian newspaper published in the United States on
     February 21, 1828.

7   Etowah Mounds History: www.btinternet.com, Lewis Tumlin In 1838 Colonel
     Lewis Tumlin purchased the land that contained the mounds near Cartersville,
     Ga. The mounds would remain in his family for 125 years. Lewis Tumlin married
     Maria Goldsmith. Beginning in 1865, he also purchased an interest in
     Stone Mountain.

8   Dekalb Court House deeds.

9   Dekalb County deed book L page 278.

10   Augusta Chronicle & Sentinel June 25, 1852.

11   The short term for railroad. When automobiles came into use the term "automobile
     road" was used.

12   The second name for Atlanta, Terminus was the first, the name "Atlanta" was first
     suggested in 1845.

13   Atlanta Constitution, November 12, 1893 details the story of William Adair, Jr. and
     his railroad experience.

14   Stone Mountain Baptist Church records indicate the church was integrated
     until 1867.

15   History Stn Mtn Baptist Church, *Atlanta Journal and Constitution* November
     12, 1893.

16   Amount Andrew Johnson paid for the Mountain is unknown. Since Johnson bought
     the hotel from Meador, he probably purchased some of the mountain at that time
     from Meador.

17   GA Law 1838 page 10.

18   GA Legislature Act Nov-Dec 1839, Name changed to Stone Mountain by Act of Leg-
     islature in 1847.

19   *Carved in Stone*, Mercer Univ. Press, Macon, GA 1997, David Freeman, p 30. Photo
     on Supplementary Disc.

20   Andrew Johnson is buried in the Johnson-Goldsmith-Maddox cemetery located
     across Memorial Drive where it intercects with West Mountain Street in Stone
     Mountain, GA. This plot was part of one of the original Johnson properties.

21   Dekalb County map of Indian Trails. The History of Dekalb County GA 1822-1900.
     Chapter 6. The Trail ran east from the Chattahoochee River through modern day
     Cascade Road and Five Points in downtown Atlanta through the Decatur area and
     on to Stone Mountain.

CHAPTER 2: MEET THE NEW SHERIFF—SPRING 1853

22   Straps is the common name for suspenders.

23   Dekalb History Center records of Dekalb County Sheriffs.

24   History of Stone Mountain Record of Postmasters, DeKalb County.

25   Congressman Dent purchases the entire Mountain from the heirs of Andrew John-
     son for $25,000. Deed given 14 November 1853. Dekalb County Courthouse Deed

Records. Book P, pp 43, 44, 45. Joe E. and John T. Dent Exers. of W. B. W. Dent to Wm. B. Wood and John T. Meadow deeded Feb. 25, 1863. Bk P, pp 429, 430, 431.

26 Joshua Hill purchases interest in the Mountain beginning on January 6, 1866. Bk G p 263.

27 1860 census Stone Mountain.

28 The News-Herald April 27, 1850 Article interview by James C. Flanigan says Juhan was a surveyor.

29 1850 census Stone Mountain.

30 Pecans and American chestnut trees were common throughout the area. The American chestnut once graced eastern forests in mighty splendor forming the canopy for most of the Appalachian Mountains. Due to a blight this mighty giant all but disappeared over a century ago. It was often referred to as the "King of Trees" or "farmer's friend" in early tree references. Appalachian farmers used the straight-grained, rot resistant wood for split rail fences, fence posts, barns and building homes. ipm.ppws. vt.edu/griffin/accf.

31 Gin is the short term for cotton gin; also, called a "Ginny" not to be confused with the nickname for a mule.

32 Macon Telegraph April 3 1830.

33 Gleason's pictorial drawing room companion. April 8, 1854 page 217.

34 *A History of Coweta County From 1825 to 1880 W. U. Anderson*, The Newnan Coweta Historical Society, Inc., Newnan, Ga. 1977 The entire obituary is contained on the CD located in the back of the book.

35 See the supplemental disc for the full text.

CHAPTER 3: FIVE YEARS LATER—A QUEST FOR THE BEST

36 *Cradled in Glory* Georgia Military Institute 1851-1856 Caisson Press 1977 Gary Livingston p 12.

37 He was one of the founding professors at The South Carolina Military Academy, now known as The Citadel, in 1843. Capers taught there until 1847. *Cradled in Glory*, Georgia Military Institute, 1851-1865 Gary Livingston, Caisson Press, Cooperstown, NY 1977. p 9 -13. Herein after referred to as "*Cradled in Glory.*"

38 Georgia Military Institute 1858 Register, 21 Herein after referred to as "GMI."

39 Regulations Georgia Military Institute, page 16,*Cradled in Glory* p 21-30.

40 Regulation Georgia Military Institute pp 17-19 *Cradled in Glory* p 21-30.

41 *Ibid*, p 83 *Cradled in Glory.*

42 Rogers Sketch, page 83 *Cradled in Glory.*

43 Sarah B. G. Temple, The First Hundred Years, 1935 pp 154-156, 183 *Cradled in Glory, Ibid.*

44 Official Register of the Officers and Cadets, GMI, Marietta, Ga. page 21 *Cradled in Glory, Ibid.*

45 www.cwartillery.org/artequip.html.

46 GMI Regulations pp 9,10 1858 Register pp 19-21,*Cradled in Glory* p 11.

47   Patton 1989:10.
48   Wife of Editor and Judge,George K. Smith of Decatur
49   Freshman class was called the First Class.
50   See supplemental disc for full text of copy of a newspaper ad for the Seminary.

CHAPTER 4: ENDEARMENT, ADVANCEMENT AND PROGRESS

51   Quoted from the Mountain Banner of June 20, 1860.

CHAPTER 5: EMBRACING THE CHALLENGE

52   *Confederate Veterans of Stone Mountain*, Chris Davis 2000 p 21. Paul attended
     GMI going through the entire Civil War as a cadet in Company B. He is buried in the
     Stone Mountain City Cemetery.
53   Renamed Bartow County in honor of Francis Bartow, the first officer on either side
     to be killed in combat during the First Battle of Manassas in 1861.

CHAPTER 6: HONOR AND TRUST

54   Bartow County Court House Records.
55   Congressional record- Wilmot Proviso 1846, was an amendment to a bill before the
     U.S. House of Representatives during the Mexican War. The Bill provided an appro-
     priation of $2 million for President Polk to negotiate a territorial settlement with
     Mexico. Rep. David Wilmot introduced an amendment to the bill that none of the
     territory acquired in the Mexican War should be open to slavery. The amended bill
     was passed in the House, but the Senate adjourned without voting on the Bill.
56   *Ibid,* 1850, the 70-year-old Clay presented a Bill know as the Missouri compromise.
57   I. W. Avery,Further sited as "Avery"pp 30-32, 78, 826 The History of the State of
     Georgia 1850-1881.
58   Trammel Biography-GA Archives. During the Civil War he was a supply officer with
     the Confederacy. Afterwards, he was a state representative and before his career was
     over he was president of the Georgia Railroad Association. As a law maker, he was
     part of a group that plotted to make laws to keep the black man in a servitude status.
     Also, by a technicality, he was Governor of Georgia, for one day, in between Gover-
     nors. He is buried at West Hill Cemetery in Dalton, GA.
59   Constitutionalist, June 30, 1857.
60   Avery p 36.
61   Biography of Joseph E. Brown, Ga. State Archives. Bioguide.congress.gov/scripts/
     biodisplay.pl?index=B000936.
62   Supra chapter I, no. 56.
63   Confederate Record pp 229-30, 248-49.
64   A Short History of Georgia, E. Merton Coulter.
65   Wikipedia org/wiki/Warren_Akin,_Sr., (October 9, 1811–December 17, 1877) was a
     prominent Confederate politician. He was born Elbert County, Georgia. He served
     in the Georgia state legislature 1861 to 1863. He represented the state in the Second
     Confederate Congress from 1864 to 1865.

66   Sams nd:99. An advertisement for the Stone Mtn House ran in the Atlanta Weekly Constitution in 1856.

67   A Fool's Errand, 1879,New York, Ford, Howard & Hulbert,Author Unknown.

CHAPTER 7: EMOTIONS REIGN—NOVEMBER 1860

68   Senator Toombs entire speech may be read on the accompanying CD.

69   Senator Stephens entire speech may be read on the accompanying CD. Actually Robert Toombs said: "Fellow citizens we have just listened to a speech from one of the brightest intellects and purest patriots that now live. I move that this meeting now adjourn, with three cheers for Alexander H.Stephens." Herschel V. Jonhnson congratulated Toombs for his generous conduct toward Stephens, "with so large a majority of secessionist." Toombs replied, "I always behave myself at a funeral."

CHAPTER 8: JOE BROWN DRAWS THE SWORD

70   Alexander Stephens home in Crawfordville , Georgia and was named "Liberty Hall" by him. Alexander Stephens is mentioned several times in relations to Stone Mountain. Although there is no documentation that this building in Stone Mountain was owned by him or named by him. Also, it stands to reason that he knew Andrew Johnson since they both were politicians. Alexander Hamilton is mentioned in several records as being the surveyor and laying out the streets of the City of Stone Mountain (New Gibralter originally) in 1839. At that time Alexander Stephens was in the Georgia Legislature and he possibly could have had some influence in routing the Georgia Railroad through Stone Mountain from Madison. He pushed extremely hard to get the Atlantic and Western Railroad approved as a State of Georgia property. The author has been unable to find any of the records of the officers or stockholder of the Georgia Railroad and Banking Company to ascertain whether or not Alexander Stephens was a stockholder in the Company.

71   As additional evidence Alexander Stephens mentions Stone Mountain in his speech against secession to the Georgia Legislature on November 14, 1860 "…stands out bold, high, and prominent, like your Stone Mountain…." Also after the war Alexander Stephens brought approximately 180 acres and agreed to have a Joint Venture with the Stone Mountain Hotel Company owned by Thomas Johnson.

72   History of Dekalb Country. Dekalb History Center.

73   *Ibid.*

74   Commander Captain Francis Bartow in the Savannah press.

75   Sophomore class.

76   See supplemental disc for full text.

77   History of Dekalb County Georgia, Dekalb County History Center.

78   Confederate records of GA Vol 1 p 10.

79   *Ibid.*

CHAPTER 9: LOST ON THE MOUNTAIN

80   Dekalb History Center, History of Dekalb County Sheriff Roll of Dekalb County History.

ENDNOTE CORRECTIONS
1. #'s 70-71 SHOULD BE COMBINED AS #70. "ALEXANDER HAMILTON" SHOULD BE "ALEXANDER HAMILTON STEPHENS".
2. REDUCE #'s 72 THRU 97 BY 1, (72 CHANGES TO 71, ETC).
ALL OTHER ENDNOTES APPEAR TO BE IN CORRECT ORDER.

CHAPTER 10: THE SABER STRIKES

81   Temple, Years pp 238-241.

82   Excerpts from a letter from Volunteer, Tom Dowtin to his sister. *Cradled in Glory* p 50. Generally Letters written by Paul and Norman are excerpts from real letters written by other cadets.

83   Written by St. George Tucker. Song and Ballads of the Southern people p 14 186 Appleton.

84   History of Anaconda Plan, digitalhistory.uh.edu/database/article_display. cfm?HHID=95.

85   *Ibid.*

86   *Ibid.*

87   *Ibid.*

88   *Ibid.*

89   *Ibid.*

90   *Ibid.*

91   *Ibid.*

92   Born in 1821, Wilkes County,GA. Buried in Atlanta, Ga. 1891. Lawyer, US Congressman before war. 1861 raised 7th Georgia, May 1861 Col., First Manassas, January 1862 resigned to sit in Confederate Congress, returned to army, August 1864 Brig. Gen., recruited four regiments of Georgia reserves, opposed Sherman's march, Coosawhatchie (w). Post War Career Lawyer . A strong opponent of the Davis administration.

93   History of Seventh Regiment Georgia Volunteer Infantry.

94   Sara B. G. Temple. The First Hundred Years, 1935 pp 238-240.

95   Stone Mountain Seminary Advertisement- View supplemental disc for full text.

96   1850 census Stone Mountain District.

97   Confederate Veterans of Stone Mountain,by Chris Davis 2000.

CHAPTER 11: ADVANCED WEAPON TESTING

98   civilwarartillery.com/manufacturers.htm, Georgia Railroad Machine Shop: Augusta, GA. News article in the Columbus Daily Enquirer of August 31, 1861, announced that the mechanics at the above had built a "new styled cannon" called a Sumner Oscillating Breech Loading Rifled Gun. It was manufactured from the crank axle of a railroad engine. There were two breech loading rifles made by the Georgia Railroad Machine shop and issued through the Atlanta Arsenal on January 28 and April 11. The January 14 issue states however: "Maker: Rushton, Georgia Railroad, Atlanta, GA." Some 12-pounder Napoleons cast at the nearby Augusta Arsenal were finished at these shops.

99   Camp Kirkpatrick was located in Kirkpatrick's Grove, two miles west of Decatur and four miles east of Atlanta on the Ga. Railroad. Atlanta History Bulletin, War diary of Elma Kurtz., Hanleiter, Cornelius R., 1815-1897 (MSS426) Diaries, 1861-1865. Newspapers did not appear in Atlanta until the 1840s. Cornelius R. Hanleiter put down

the first permanent roots of Atlanta journalism when he moved his newspaper, the Southern Miscellany, there from Madison, Georgia, in 1847. Hanleiter moved because he believed the westward railroad expansion meant big things were in store for the hamlet, then called Marthasville.

100 *Ibid*, Wright's Legion, 9/17/1861-11/16/1861, Atlanta History Bulletin, War diary of Cornelius R. Hanleiter Elma S. Kurtz.

101 *Ibid.*

102 *Ibid.*

103 *Ibid.*

104 *Ibid.*

105 63 wine gallons to a hogshead.

106 History of Neosho,MO, Neosho.org.

107 History of the United States Navy November 1861, The first USS Sabine was a sailing frigate United States Navy in 1855. The ship was among the first ships to see action in the American Civil War. In 1862, a large portion of the Monitor crew were volunteers from the Sabine.

108 Biography of General Winfield Scott.

109 *Ibid.*

110 See color Photo on Supplemental disc. Photograph copied by permission from Larry Winslett. *Stone Mountain a Walk in the Park*. 2007, Bright Hawk Press, Dahlonega, GA.

111 Fares were five cents per mile on the Georgia Railroad at that time. Railga.com.

CHAPTER 12: A NEW DAWN

112 Postcard 1901.

113 History of Southern Baptist Convention Augusta, Ga. May 1845. friendsofnewstead. org/who_r_the_baptist_.

114 Augusta Museum of History.

115 Augusta Museum of History.

116 Built in 1753, known as the Pirates' House to serve the needs of sailors who visited the growing seaport. The Herb House, as it is now named, was erected in 1734 adjoins the Pirates' House. The Herb House is said to be the oldest house in Georgia.

117 The Gullah language, a Creole blend of Elizabethan English and African languages, was born of necessity on Africa's slave coast, and developed in the slave communities of the isolated plantations of the coastal South.

CHAPTER 13: A NEST ON THE RIVER

118 P 131-132 Confederate Records of GA. Vol II.

119 Confederate Records of Georgia app 132-133 Vol II.

120 Confederate Veterans of Stone Mountain,by Chris Davis. 2000.

121 Andrew Johnson's son.

CHAPTER 14: PANIC IN THE STREETS

122   History of Fort Pulaski, nps.gov/history/hps/abpp/battles/ga001.htm.
123   *Ibid.*
124   *Ibid.*
125   *Ibid*; Charles Olmstead and another GMI graduate George P. Harrison, Jr. were involved in the seizure of Fort Pulaski.
126   *Ibid.*

CHAPTER 15: MEDICINE, SURGERY AND HOPE

127   History of GMI, Temple Years.

CHAPTER 16: BACK IN STONE MOUNTAIN

128   The double cannon is located in front of city hall in Athens, Georgia; The historical marker next to the cannon details the history of the cannon's inventor and invention.
129   Georgia History Society, Savannah archives, Savannah Georgia.
130   Medical instruments during the civil war dictionary.
131   Materia Medica and Therapeutics, 1889, John shoemaker, F. A. Davis and Co. Alnuin is the name of the alcoholic extract, which is principally composed of resin. Materia Medica and Therapeutics, 1889, John shoemaker, F. A. Davis and Co.
132   Savannah History Center,Mayors of Savannah.
133   Savannah History Center, "Savannah Hospitals"Guyton General Hospital, established in May, 1862. Located on a nine-acre tract between the Central RR and Pine Street and Lynn Bonds Ave. Hospital had 270 Beds and 46 fireplaces.
134   Fireworks with a central explosion delivering multiple colorful streamers.

CHAPTER 18: DELIBERATING GEORGIA

135   O. R. Volume LII Series 1, Part 2,Page 527.
136   OR Series I Vol XXX part I, pp 55-58, 47, 38, 136.
137   *Ibid.*
138   Marietta Confederate and City cemetery. *Cradled in Glory* p 67.
139   militaryhistoryonline.
140   kwebb@alianet.alia.org.au.
141   *Cradled in Glory.*
142   In the 1700s colonial women from Boston to the Carolinas made the first breakfast cereal by pouring milk and sugar over popped pop corn.
143   Nellie Kinzie Gordon. Mother of Juliette Gordon Low.
144   CS Naval history.
145   Naval history of Confederate States.
146   *Ibid.*

147 *Everglade* is an elegant passenger ship purchased for $40,000 had two smooth bore cannons on her deck.

CHAPTER 19: HAPPY BIRTHDAY, LEGARE

148 Joshua Hill's wife real name.

149 *For He's A Jolly Good Fellow* is a British and American song which is sung to congratulate a person on a significant event. *Happy Birthday* was not written until 1893.

150 Giving spankings to the birthday person is another type of game that started as a superstition hundreds of years ago. Spankings are given one for each year and then one to to grow on, one to live on, one to eat on, one to be happy on, and finally one to get married on. It was once considered bad luck if the birthday person wasn't spanked because the spanks were supposed to "soften up the body for the tomb". No one is really sure if it was actually all just a joke but the superstition is no longer believed.

151 Now the location of a marina, located on the Wilmington River.

152 Elected Captain in the 63rd July 3, 1863. History of the GA. 63rd.

153 The historical figure Hugh Legare Hill mustered in on November 11, 1863 in Savannah, GA.

154 History of the 63rd genealogy.thehardens.net/PSO1_072.HTM. All of the individuals who introduced themselves are on the roster of the 63rd including John Dent.

155 Joseph V. H.. Allen roll for Sept. 14, 1864 last on file. Shows him absent, sick Roster Co. A 63rd.

156 History of the 63rd.

157 History of the 63rd.

158 Colonel Josiah Gorgas graduated from West Point 1841. Became the Confederate Chief of Ordnance.

159 Letter from a soldier.

160 Samuel Moore autobiography.

CHAPTER 20: THE SPIRIT OF MISTLETOE

161 *Ibid.*

162 *Ibid.*

163 History of Savannah.

CHAPTER 21: PLUM PUDDING

164 From the collection of the Cochran-Wells letter. Courtesy of the Stone Mountain Historic Society.

165 *Ibid.*

166 The marriage of W. T. Sherman to his step-sister Ellen Ewing was held at the Washington, D.C. Pennsylvania Avenue home of Honorable Thomas Ewing, and it was attended by many well know historical figures such as Daniel Webster, Henry Clay, President Taylor, and his entire cabinet.

CHAPTER 22: HOME TO RECOVER

167 Hardtack is thick cracker made of flour, water, and sometimes salt. When properly stored, it will last for years. Because it could be prepared cheaply and would last so long, hardtack was the most convenient food for soldiers. Hardtack was eaten by itself, or crumbled into coffee or soup. Probably more were eaten that way than in any other, as they were usually eaten as breakfast and supper.

CHAPTER 23: THE NOBLE AND THE VALIANT

168 Oatland Island is located North of Whitemarsh Island between the Savannah and Wilmington Rivers.

169 February 22, 1864 Skirmish at Whitemarsh Island, and Oatland Island, Ga. Report of B.G. Raleigh E. Colston, CSA. OR, Series 1, Vol 35, Part 1 Chapter 57,pp 361-364.

170 *Savannah (GA) Republican*, August 11, 1862, p. 2, c. 3.

CHAPTER 24: DALTON TO RESACA

171 General Sherman has his headquarters at the Clisby-Austin house in Tunnel Hill, GA.

172 History of Co A 63rd, genealogy.thehardens.net

173 The Union army consisted of 100,000 soldiers and the Confederate army consisted of 60,000 soldiers.

174 This is the earliest generally accepted date for the start of the Atlanta Campaign.

175 This is the latest date generally accepted as the start of the Atlanta Campaign.

176 Snake Creek Gap was well defended. Gen. Cleburne asked Mackall how Snake Gap Creek could have been left unguarded; Mackall answered that "it was the result of a flagrant disobedience of order; by whom he did not say." Clearly, however he had Gen Wheeler in mind. Cleburne to Sellers (Hood' AAG) 16 Aug '64. OR 1, 38 Part 3 p 721.

177 Wheeler was a young, dashing, but irresponsible Army cavalry commander. He disliked the routine activities of patrol and reconnaissance preferring dramatic cavalry assaults. Joseph E. Johnson, A Civil War Biography by Craig Symonds. Norton, pub 1992 p 235. Hereinafter referred to as "Symonds."

178 *Sherman's Memoirs.* When Gen Sherman heard that Gen. McPherson was safely through Snake Creek Gap, Gen. Sherman is supposed to have exclaimed: "I've got Joe Johnston dead!" From a later report Sherman was surprised at McPherson's decision to withdraw. Generals Thomas and Schofield were on the heels of Johnston's army. If McPherson had proceeded with his 23,000 men, Johnston's entire Confederate Army of Tennessee would have been trapped and the war in GA may have possibly come to an end.

179 Joseph E. Johnston, A Civil War Biography, Craig L. Symonds, W. W. Norton New York, London 1992 Hereafter noted as "Symonds."

180 The Georgia 1st is one of several units transferred to fill the ranks of the 63rd.

181 Brown to Wayne Correspondence GA. Archives. *Cradled in Glory* pp 87-88.

182 Symonds.

183 *Cradled in Glory* p 95.

184 Rodgers , Robert L., An Historical Sketch of the Georgia Military Institute. 1890 p 82 Hereafter referred to as "Rodgers" *Cradled in Glory* p 95.

185 *Ibid*

186 *Ibid*

187 GA State Archives. Capers to Adj. Gen. Henry C. Wayne May 16, 1864 Rodgers pp 82-83 *Cradled in Glory* p 97.

188 OR Series 1, Vol 38, Part 3, pp 978-979, Rodgers page 83.

189 The Grey Jackets p. 263, 1867.

190 History of the 63rd.

191 History of 63rd.

192 OR Vol 38, Series 1,Part 3 p 378.

193 OR Vol 38, Series 1, Part 3, pp 978-979 . Rodgers 82-83 *Cradled in Glory* p 98-99.

194 OR Series 1, Vol 38, Part 3, pp 978-979. Rodgers 82-83.

195 Diary of Union Lieutenant James Oaks.

CHAPTER 25: DEFIANT GENERALS

196 Rodgers page 83 OR Series 1 Vol 38, Part 3 pp 978-979 *Cradled in Glory* p 99.

197 Rodgers page 83 *Cradled in Glory* p 100.

198 Rodgers p 93.

199 OR 1, Vol 38, part 4, p 417. Symonds p 283.

200 Symonds p 283 OR 1, Vol 38, part 3 pp 980-1. In his postwar Narrative Johnston unnecessarily stressed the point that Hood had "exposed and abandoned" these guns. Hood responded in his own memoir "they were four old iron pieces not worth the sacrifice of the life of even one man."

201 Nephew of General Mackall, General Johnston's Chief of Staff.

202 Symonds p 283 OR 1, Vol 38, part 3 p 981. Johnston attributed the delay in canceling Stewart's orders to tardiness in Hood's headquarters.

203 Symonds page 283.

204 Symonds p 284. OR 1, Vol 38, Part 3 page 981.

205 Confederate losses are difficult to determine. From *Sherman's Memoirs* Sherman listed his own losses at 600 killed and 3375 wounded.

206 Battle of Resaca. History Center Resaca, GA.

207 *Sherman's Memoirs* Vol. 1 chapter 16.

208 Symonds p 298. OR 1, Vol 38, Part 3 p 982.

209 General Sherman does not press the issue because he wants to wait until his army is concentrated in order to commit to a full scale battle. OR 1, Vol 38, part 4 p 721.

210 Father of Douglas McArthur.

211 Name changed from Cassville to Manassas after Confederate victory July 1861.

212 Symonds p 290. OR series 1, Vol 38, part 3, p 982 In the published (O) version of the McKall Journal is the line: "Hood has been anxious to get from this place south of the Etowah."

213   Mackall Journal OR Series , Vol 38, Part 3 p:982.

214   Lydia Johnston to Polk 16 May 1864.

215   Leonidas Polk. The Fighting Bishop, Born April 10 1806, Raleigh , NC . Died June 14 1864, Pine Mountain GA. Third cousin of President Polk. He commanded Polk's Corps in the Atlanta campaign and was killed by artillery fire while observing Union positions at Pine Mountain. Gen. Sherman, who in a tersely worded statement sent to Gen. Halleck, "We killed Bishop Polk yesterday and have made good progress to-day…"Symonds, page 290, US Civil war Generals; sunsite.utk.edu/civil-war/generals.html.

216   *Sherman's Memoirs*, Vol 3 Chaper 16; Atlanta Campaign, March, April, May, 1864.

217   General Order dated 19 May 1864 OR Series 1, Vol 38, part 4 p 728.

218   Joseph E. Johnson to Pres. Davis 20 May 1864. OR series 1, Vol 38, part 4 p 728. Symonds p 293.

219   OR series 1, Vol 38, part 3, page 622. Symonds p 293.

220   History of the 3rd Texas Rangers.

221   *Sherman's Memoirs* Vol 2 Part 3 Chapter 16, Atlanta Campaign, March, April, May, 1864.

222   History roster of 63rd.

223   *Sherman's Memoirs* Vol 2, Part 3, Chapter 16, Atlanta Campaign-Nashville and Chattanooga to Kenesaw-March, April, May, 1864.

224   History of the Georgia 63rd . Alabama State Archives.

225   Alabama State Archives.

226   History Cassville, GA. City of Cassville, Georgia.

227   At the time, Johnston swallowed his disappointment. He and Hood continued to work well together on cordial terms. But years later, after the war, when Johnston discovered that Hood had been writing secretly to Davis contrasting his own aggressiveness with Johnston's caution, he looked back on Hood's action at Cassville as a deliberate attempt to undercut the campaign. MacKall Journal (O) OR series 1, Vol 38, part 3, p 984. In his Memoirs Hood claimed that he wanted to go on the offensive and he urged Johnston to attack. French, who was present, wrote that "whilst I was there Hood made no reference to being in a good position for acting on the aggressive and making an attack" French, Two Wars, 198. Symonds, page 288.

228   Joseph E. Johnston to Wheeler, 20 May 1864, OR Series 1, Vol 38, part 4, p 729.

CHAPTER 26: IN PURSUIT OF VICTORY IN WAR AND POLITICS

229   *Sherman's Memoirs* Vol 2, Part 3, Chapter 16; Atlanta Campaign-Nashville and Chattanooga to Kenesaw-March, April, May, 1864.

230   *Ibid.*

231   *Ibid.*

232   *Sherman Memories* ,Vol 2 Part 3 Chapter 16 Atlanta Campaign-Nashville and Chattanooga to Kenesaw-March, April, May, 1864.

233   *Ibid.*

234   *Ibid.*

235   *Ibid.*

236 *Ibid.*

237 *Sherman's Memoirs* ,Vol 1 Chapter 16A History of Bartow County, Georgia.

238 Allen P. Tankersley, *College Life at Old Oglethorpe*, University of GA. Press 1951. James C. Bonner, Ed, *The Journal of a Milledgeville Girl*, 1861-1867. University of GA. Press 1964, pp 49-50.

239 Rodgers p 83 *Cradled in Glory* p 106.

240 In 1864 a wing of the Republican party forms the Radical Democracy Party and nominated John C. Frémont as their candidate for president, until he withdrew.

241 Copperhead Party (Peace Democrats) A majority of Peace Democrats supported war to save the Union, but a strong and active minority asserted that the Republicans had provoked the South into secession; that the Republicans were waging the war in order to establish their own domination, suppress civil and states rights, and impose "racial equality"; and that military means had failed and would never restore the Union. "Historical Times Encyclopedia of the Civil War" Edited by Patricia L. Faust.

242 *The Life of John Charles Frémont*, By John Charles Frémont, Samuel Mosheim Smucker. Published 1856. FRÉMONT, John Charles, Born January 21 1813, Savannah GA. Died July 13 1890, New York NY. Before the Civil War he was a Teacher, 1838 appointed to US Army as topographical engineer, explorer, resigned 1848 following court martial for mutiny, US senator, Presidential candidate Civil War service. May 1861 appointed Maj. Gen. in Regular Army, commanded Dept of the West, relieved of duty after issuing an emancipation proclamation in 1861, 1862 Shenandoah Valley campaign, relieved at his own request when ordered to serve under Gen. Pope. Post Civil War Career, territorial governor of Arizona. sunsite.utk.edu/civil-war/generals.html, Kerry Webb.

243 *The Life of John Charles Frémont*, By John Charles Frémont, Samuel Mosheim Smucker. Published 1856.

244 *The Collected Works of Abraham Lincoln*, Roy P. Basler, Editor, 1953, the Abraham Lincoln Association.

245 *Sherman's Memoirs* Vol 2 part 3, Chapter 17, Battle about Kenesaw Mountain June 1864.

246 History of 1864 Convention.

247 *Ibid.*

Part II

CHAPTER 1: THE MESSENGERS

248 Letter Hill to James Crew.

249 *Ibid.*

250 *Ibid.*

251 There are three cadets of her surname in the cadet ranks, all from Burke County.

252 Address of Mary E Jones and Reply of Ensign J. R. McClesky on the Occasion of her Presentation of a Battle-flag to the Georgia Cadets. (Atlanta: Intelligencer Printing Office 1864. *Cradled in Glory* p 106-107.

253 *Ibid.* Georgia was called the "Empire State" during this period

254 *Ibid.*

255   1860 Dekalb County listing of Households and Occupations of Stone Mountain residence.

256   Rodgers pp 83-84. OR 1, Vol 38, Part 5 p 871 114-116.

257   *Ibid*, OR 1 Vol 38, Part 5, p 862.

258   Rodgers pp. 83-84 *Cradled in Glory* p 116-117.

259   *Sherman's Memoirs* Vol 2 part 3 Chapter 18, Battle about Atlanta, July, 1864.

260   OR Vol 38, Series 1, part 5 p. 89.

261   OR Series 1, Vol 38, part 5 p 99.

262   J. W.. Buchanan's residence stood on the Old Hightower Trail where Peachtree Rd. crosses was a landmark of Federal troop movement in July 1864. July 17th General Garrard's cavalry crossed the Chattahoochee at McAfee's Bridge and camped at the headwaters of Nancy Creek west of Buchanan's. Ga. The objective of these troops is the destruction of the Ga. Railroad. Historical Marker 044-4.

263   OR series 1, Vol 38, part 5 p 108.

CHAPTER 2: BRAGG'S DECEIT

264   The Baptist preacher, Feilding (sic) Maddox. The local Methodist preacher was Dr. Davies.

265   OR Vol 38, 1, 5 pg 89.

266   OR Vol 38, 1, 3, p 245.

267   OR Vol 38, 1, 1, pg 99.

268   OR Vol 38, 1, 3, p 237.

269   OR Series 1, Vol 38, part 5, Chapter 50,page 119.

270   OR Vol 38, 1, 5, pg 119.

271   OR Vol 38, 1, 5, pg 119.

272   OR Vol 38, 1, 5, pg 119.

273   OR Vol 38, 1, 5, p 122.

274   OR series 1, Vol 38, part 5 p 123.

275   OR series 1, Vol 38, part 5, p 8782 letter Bragg to Davis,Symonds p 322.

276   A stack of cannon balls, on 950 West Marietta Rd., marks the location of the marks the Dexter Niles House site, where Confederate Gen. Joseph Johnston learned he was replaced by Gen. John Bell Hood.

277   *Ibid*.

278   Johnston Narrative, 364, Symonds, p 324.

279   Bragg to Davis, OR series 1, Vol 39, part 2 pp 712-714 Bragg intentionally overstates figures for strength and losses.

280   OR Vol 38, 1, 5, pg 139-140.

281   OR Vol 38, 1, 5, pg 142-43

282   OR Vol 38, 1, 5, pg 147.

283   OR Series 1, Vol 38, part 5 page 150.

284   Symonds p 326, OR Series 1, Vol 38, part 5, pp 882-883 Davis letter to Joseph E. Johnston.

285   *Ibid*.

CHAPTER 3: SURPRISE

286 OR Vol 30, Part 5, p 166.

287 Sherman's spelling of "Peachtree."

288 OR Vol 30, 1, Part 5 , p 16.

289 OR Series 1 Vol 38, Part 5 p 165.

290 OR Vol 38, 1, 5, pg 168.

291 OR Vol 38, 1, 5, p 169.

292 OR series 1, Vol 38, part 5, page 175-179.

293 OR series 1, Vol 38, part 5, p 885.

294 OR Vol 38, 1 p 5, 888. Symonds, p 330 297 OR , I, 38 (5): pp 888-9.

295 OR Vol 38, 1, 5, pp 887-888.

296 Symonds p. 330-31.

297 *Sherman's Memoirs* Vol 1 Chapter 18 "Communications" refers to supply lines.

298 John Bell Hood. A rash fighter, he performed well in subordinate roles, but not as an army commander. sunsite.utk.edu/civil-war/generals.html

299 OR Vol 38, 1, 5, p 175-76.

300 OR Vol 38, 1, 5, p 181, 1, 3, p 185.

301 OR Vol 38, 3, p 20, 38, 101; Vol 52, p 1, 5, 569.

302 OR Vol 38, 1, 5, p 176-77; Vol 38, 2, 808.

303 OR Vol 38, 1, 5, p 177.

304 OR Vol 38, 1, 3, p 228.

305 OR Vol 38, 1, 3, p 121-22.

306 OR Vol 38, 1, 3, p 188.

307 OR Vol 38, 1, 3, p 210

308 OR Vol 38, 1, 3, p 235.

309 OR Vol 38, 1, 3, p 253.

310 OR Vol 38, 1, 3, p 298.

311 OR Vol 38, 1, 3, p 66.

312 OR Vol 38, 1, 3, p 260.

313 OR Vol 38, 1, 3, p 217.

314 OR Vol 38, 1, 3, p 205.

315 On a hot day in 1864 word came to the Tucker area that the Union Army was advancing. The army of Tennessee under the command of General James McPherson decided to come to the Southeast to cut off the Georgia railroad near Stone Mountain to isolate Atlanta from the east. The Federals 15th Army Corps under the command of General John Logan crossed the Chattahoochee River at Roswell and detoured to Browning's Courthouse in Tucker to give support to Garrard's Army in the destruction of the railroad. This courthouse was recently moved to the grounds of the Tucker Recreation Center on LaVista Road. Garrard's soldiers headed toward Stone Mountain along Fellow Ship Road on July 18, 1864. tuckergahistorical.org/history

316 John Herbert Kelly, Born 3/31/1840, Pickens Cty, AL. Died Sept. 4, 1864, Franklin TN. Student at West Point and resigned December 1860. Civil War- 1861 2nd Lt. of artillery, Capt. on Hardee's staff, Maj. in 14th Arkansas, Shiloh, Col. of 8th Arkansas, Perryville, Murfreesboro, Chickamauga, November 1863 Brig. Gen., cavalry

command under Wheeler, Atlanta campaign, mortally wounded during a raid on Sherman's communications. He was the youngest Confederate general at the time of his appointment. Signed Cleburne's memorandum concerning the emancipation of slaves willing to fight for the Confederacy. sunsite.utk.edu/civil-war/generals.html

317   OR Vol 38, Series 1 part 3 p 210.

318   In 1860 the population of Stone Mountain was around 750 people.

319   OR Vol 38, Series 1 part 3, pp 121-122.

320   OR Vol 38, Series 1 part 2 pp 808-809.

CHAPTER 4: SAVING THE HOSPITALS

321   OR Vol 38, series 1 part 3, pp 19-20.

322   OR Vol 38, series 1, part 5,page 176.

323   Vol 38. 1, 5, pg 179-8.

324   GA Historical Marker, Stone Mountain, GA.

325   A Parrott is a rifled cannon firing a ten pound projectile, highly prized by the Union and the Confederacy.

326   Bennett Rainey Jeffares, Private, Company D., McCullough Rifles 38th Ga. Regiment was in Stone Mountain recovering from his wounds he received at Gaines Mill. Arriving in Stone Mountain from Chimborazo Hospital #3, his orders read, "To recuperate in Stone Mountain Hospital" near his home. His assignment is with the ambulance and nurse detail for the hospital.

327   OR Vol 38, 2, 808.

328   OR Vol 38, Series 1, part 2 pp 803-804, 808.

329   OR Vol 38, 1,3, p 201.

330   OR Vol 38, 1, 3, p 210.

331   OR Vol 38, 1, 3, p 210.

332   OR Vol 38, 1, 3, p 210.

333   Vol 38, 1, 2, 808.

334   OR Vol 38, Series 1, part 5 page 209.

335   OR Vol 38, 1, 5, p 209, 139, 221.

336   OR Vol 38. 2, 5, p 221.

CHAPTER 5: THE BATTLE FOR DECATUR

337   "Life in Dixie" General Garrard's cavalry selected Mary Gay's place as their headquarters.

338   *Ibid.*

339   Mary Gay p 139-40.

340   Canister, a round of canister is a tin can filled with small projectiles turning the cannon into a giant sawed off shotgun obliterating anything in its path.

341   Mary Gay p 140.

342   *Sherman Memories* Vol 1 Chapter 18.

343   OR Vol 38, Series 1, part 1 pp 72-73, *Sherman's Memoirs*; *Ibid.*

344   OR Vol 38, Series 1, part 1 pp 73-74

345 General Oliver Otis Howard commanded IV Corps in Atlanta campaign, commanded Army of the Tennessee in March to the Sea, Carolinas campaign, December 1864 Brig. Gen. in Regular Army. *Brevet Promotions* Maj. Gen. U.S.A. March 13 1865.

346 Confederate armies were named for the geographic regions they operate in whereas Federal armies were named for the major rivers operation area. Thus the Confederate Army of Tennessee faces the Federal Army of The Tennessee (River).

347 OR Vol 38, series 1 part 2 p 809.

348 OR Vol 38, series 1 part 2, 809, 842, 843, 846.

349 THE PROMISED LAND being a Glimpse of Antebellum Ga. taken from the "Farm Journal" of Thomas Maguire. Complied by John M. Harrison Atlanta GA. Dec. 1949. Hereinafter, Maguire's diary.

350 Bee Gum is the local name for a bee hive.

351 OR Vol 38, p 2, pg 809, 843.

CHAPTER 6: IN DEFENSE OF...

352 OR Series 1, Vol 38, Part 2 p. 809. General Garrard stated this new unoccupied hospital consisted of over thirty buildings capable of housing 10,000 patients were burnt. This would have been the largest hospital in the South.

353 OR Vol 38, Series 1, part 2, P 809.

354 OR 38,series 1,pt 3 p 953.

355 Vol 38, series 1, part 2, p

356 Dixieoutfitters.com/p/gravestone-for-ga-hero?, Georgia Historical Marker, 107-1 in Covington GA., History of Newton County, GA 1988 p 349.

357 I soldiered for the Union, Civil War Diary of Wm Miller.

358 Rodgers 84, 92. Rodgers, Broadside. *Cradled in Glory*, excerpts from various letters of cadets.

359 *Cradled in Glory*, p 122. Goode was the first cadet to be wounded.

360 Breese is about to faint himself.

361 Broadside Roster 1905, History of GMI, p 30 Bowling C Yates. *Cradled in Glory* p 123.

362 Rodgers Sketch 84, 92, Rodgers Broadside.

363 1860 Census.

364 Derive from the Republicans because the Copperheads wear the three-cent copper Indian-head coin as badges. The Copperheads were also called the "Peace Democrats." The Copperheads are Southern sympathizers also known as the "Butternuts" named after the color of the Confederate uniforms. The Copperheads were a vocal group of Democrats in the North who oppose the Civil War. The copperheads want an immediate peace settlement with the Confederate states.

365 Lincoln banning the writ of habeas corpus. "Many of the Northern newspapers including the *Chicago Times*, and the Catholic paper, *Metropolitan Record*, supported peace and blamed the war on the abolitionists. The Editor, Edward G. Roddy, of the Uniontown, Pennsylvania paper, *Genius of Liberty,* states that 'black people are of an inferior race and Abraham Lincoln is a despot and dunce.'"

CHAPTER 7: THE FORTUNE OF WAR

366 From Franklin Garrett's *Atlanta And Environs* Vol 1 describing the Surrender of Atlanta (pages 633-638).
367 Now Buckhead Avenue.
368 A marker now stands at the corner of Peachtree Street and Alabama Street indicating where the surrender took place
369 OR Vol 38, s1, p5, p 796.
370 *Sherman's Memoirs* Part 3, Vol 1, Chapter 19.
371 The entire text of the correspondence between Sherman, Hood and Calhoun are contained on the supplemental CD incorporated with this book. Correspondence Pertaining to Sherman's Evacuation of Atlanta, *Sherman's Memoirs* , OR Vol XXXIX part 2, Series 1, [S# 78].

CHAPTER 8: COLLEAGUES FOR THE UNION

372 *Sherman's Memoirs*, Part 3, Chapter 19, Atlanta and After, Pursuit of Hood, September-October 1864.
373 *Ibid.*
374 *Ibid.*
375 *Ibid.*
376 *Ibid.*
377 *Ibid.*
378 *Ibid.*
379 *Ibid.*
380 *Sherman's Memoirs* Part 3, Vol 1, Chapter 19. The entire text of this document in contained in the CD incorporated with this book.
381 The exact date for Hugh Legare Hill's funeral is unknown.
382 Congressman Hill to Superintendent Crews letter.
383 *Sherman's Memoirs* Part 3, Chapter 19, The entire text of this document in contained in the CD incorporated with this book.

CHAPTER 9: A FRIEND'S TALE OF WOE

384 Life in Dixie Darby Printing Co. 1979 Fifth Edition Mary A. H. Gay. Published by Dekalb History Society.
385 *Ibid.*
386 *Ibid.*
387 Rodgers Sketch p 92 *Cradled in Glory* pp 127-133
388 O. R. Volume XXXIX Series 1 part 1, P 681.
389 Maguire's Diary.
390 *Ibid.*
391 Vol 39, Series 1, part 1 p 665.
392 *Ibid.*
393 *Ibid.*

CHAPTER 10: PREPARATION

394 Vol 39, Series 1 part 1, pp 660, 661, 665-667, 690.
395 *Ibid.*
396 Maguire's Diary.
397 Son of Andrew Johnson.
398 Vol 39, Series 1 part 1, pp 660,661, 665-667, 690.
399 Confederate Records of the State of GA. Candler 1909,Vol 2 , State papers of Gov. J. E.. Brown pp 773-774.
400 *Cradled in Glory*, p 134.
401 *Sherman's Memoirs* Part 4, Vol 2, Chapter 21 , OR Vol 39, series 1, part 3 p 701.
402 Maguire's Diary.
403 Election results 1864 Presidential Election.
404 *Sherman's Memoirs* Part 4, Vol 2, Chapter 21 p 171.
405 Excerpts from a letter General Henry Slocum wrote to his wife Clara dated November 12, 1864.
406 *Ibid.*
407 *Ibid.*
408 *Ibid.*
409 *Ibid.*
410 *Ibid.*
411 Sherman Memoirs Part 4, Vol 2, Chapter 21.
412 In fact, seizures of horses and mules far exceeded the amount needed. Those that were brought in were sorted and the best replaced weaker, broken-down animals in the wagon trains. The culling of horseflesh went on constantly so that at the end of the march, the army had better animals that it did when it left Atlanta. Sherman said," I have no doubt the State of Georgia has lost by our operation, 15,000 first-rate mules. We started with about 5,000 head of cattle, and arrived with over 10,000; of course, consuming mostly turkeys, chickens, sheep, hogs, and the cattle of the country. For Sherman to arrive in Savannah with one beef cow for every six men is an indication of just how rich the area he passed through had been. *Sherman's Memoirs*, Part 4, Chapter 21.
413 *Battles and Leaders*, IV, p 685.
414 *Sherman's Memoirs*, Part 4, Vol 2, Chapter 21 p 177.
415 *Sherman's Memoirs*, Part 4, Vol 2, Chapter 21 p 175-177.
416 *Sherman's Memoirs*, Part 4, Vol 2, Chapter 21 p 177.

CHAPTER 11: EYE WITNESS

417 *Sherman's Memoirs*, Vol 2, Ch 21, pg 171.
418 *Ibid.*
419 *Ibid.*
420 State Archives if Georgia, List of Mayors.
421 Part of the history of the Sycamore Grill (Dr. Hamilton's hospital) based on local legend.
422 Captain George W. Pepper of the 80th Regiment of the Ohio Infantry letter.

CHAPTER 12: WITHOUT RESISTANCE

423 OR Vol 44, 216-301.

424 State of Georgia Civil War Commission.

425 Grant married Julia Boggs Dent, from St. Louis, Missouri and a cousin of Congressman W. B. W.. Dent. When Grant became President, she changed the role of the First Lady taking an active leadership role in Washington society, and began the transition of the role of First Lady into one of national leadership. White Haven-Ulysses S. Grant National Historic Site.on his own.

426 The people of North Alabama were hill farmers of modest means and typical of southern unionists. In 1860, with only 2 percent of the families owned slaves. They are largely an isolated mountain people who had little influence on state government. They ask that the Confederacy on the one hand and the Union on the other, to leave them alone and unmolested. Instead, these hill farmers are branded as traitors or Tories and a systematic campaign of persecution was launched by the Confederate home guard. It is unclear how many Alabamians wore blue, because many, after secreting themselves to federal lines, simply joined other state regiments. More than 2,000 served in the 1st Alabama Cavalry.

427 OR The War of the Rebellion: A Compilation of the Official Records of the Union and Confederate Armies. Volume XLIV | Pages 216.

428 *Sherman's Memoirs* , Part 4, Vol 2, Chapter 21.

429 *Ibid.*

430 "The Wild Adventure of a Crazy Fool." p 40 March to the Sea, *Sherman's Memoirs* part 4, 178.

431 *Sherman's Memoirs* Part 4, Vol 2, Chapter 21, p. 179.

432 *Sherman's Memoirs* Part 4, Vol 2, Chapter 21, p. 179.

433 Original name of East Mountain Street. See City Map dated 1912.

CHAPTER 13: TÊTE-À-TÊTE

435 The nickname the Union troops had for General Sherman.

436 It was due to their strong influence with the Trustees that the right to purchase and use Negro slaves passed the Board of Trustees of the Charter.

437 *Sherman's Memoirs* Part 4, Vol 2, Chapter 21.

438 *Sherman's Memoirs* Part 4, Vol 2, Chapter 21.

439 On October 16, 1859, John Brown acting under the pseudonym Isaac Smith, and several followers seized the U.S. Armory and Arsenal at Harpers Ferry. Brown captured Lewis Washington, a great-grandnephew of George Washington and took from him a sword given to George Washington by Frederick the Great in 1794. of Marines to capture Brown. On the 18th, Lee ordered Lt. Israel Green's group to storm the engine house. At a signal from Lt. J.E.B. Sturat, the engine house door was knocked down . Green wounded Brown and brought him into submission with his sword. The raid by the Marines lasted less than three minutes and Lewis Washington retrieved his

Great-Grand-Uncle's sword. West Virginia Archives and History, *John Brown and the Harpers Ferry Raid.*

440 Harrison Riley had a very colorful history documented in the Lumpkin County records.

441 *Sherman's Memoirs* Part 4, Vol 2, Chapter 21.

442 The First Conscription Acts: In April 1862. The Confederate Congress passed the Conscription Act which drafted white men between 18 and 35 for three years' service. March 1983. Because of recruiting difficulties, The United States passed an act making all men between the ages of 20 and 45 liable to be called for military service. Service could be avoided by paying a fee or finding a substitute.

443 *Sherman's Memoirs* Part 4, Vol 2, Chapter 21.

444 *Ibid.*

445 *Ibid.*

446 *Ibid.*

447 *Ibid.*

448 Sherman's letters to his brother and daughter Minnie.

CHAPTER 14: PASSING THROUGH

449 *Sherman's Memoirs* Part 4, Vol 2, Chapter 21. *Savannah Newspaper Digest*, July 1-Dec.. 31, 1864 quotes the *Augusta Chronicle*: Nov. 18, 1864, learns that the last Yankee foraging party went out of Atlanta two weeks since, foraging in the vicinity of Stone Mountain, and Gwinnett County. They carried off large numbers of cattle, hogs, sheep and other provisions.

450 Maguire's Diary.

451 Maguire's Diary.

452 *Sherman's Memoirs* Part 4, Vol 2, Chapter 21.

453 Maguire's Diary.

454 *Sherman's Memoirs* Part 4, Vol 2, Chapter 21.

455 *Ibid.*

456 Rambles Through Morgan County: Her History, Century Old Houses and Churches and Tales to Remember. Hicky, Louise McHenry Morgan County Historical Society, Georgia, 1989.

457 *Temple Years* 322-323 *Sherman's Memoirs* Part 4, Vol 2, Chapter 21 p 177.

458 Georgia.org/travel/legends+and+lore.

459 sharpsguides\ga\civilwar\griswoldvilleclinton area.

460 Georgia.org/travel/legends+and+lore.

461 Rodgers, Sketch 93-94, *Sherman's Memoirs* part 4 Chp 21, OR Part 1, Vol 53, p 32.

462 *Ibid*, History of Kentucky 4th.

463 *Ibid.*

464 *Ibid.*

465 Georgia.org/travel/legends+and+lore.

466 Rodgers Sketch p 93-94 *Cradled in Glory* pp 139-152.

CHAPTER 15: PROUD AND STRONG

467   Rodgers Sketch 85-85 OR series 1, Vol 44,147. OR Series 1, Vol 53, p 33 pp 139-152. *Cradled in Glory* pp 139-152.

468   OR Series 1, Vol 44,p 147. Rodgers 85-86. *Cradled in Glory* pp 139-152.

469   Rodgers p 94, OR Series 1, Vol 44, p 154 *Cradled in Glory* pp 139-152.

470   Cadet Marsh was mortally wounded in the groin on November 24 and died on November 26, 1864. *Cradled in Glory* pp 139-152 p 143.

471   Rodgers Sketch 85-86. OR Series 1,Vol ,53 p 34 OR Series 1 Vol 44, p 147, 154. *Cradled in Glory* pp 139-152.

472   *Cradled in Glory* p 155.

473   *Cradled in Glory* pp 156-158.

474   Journal Confederate Historical Society 1962 p 12.

475   *Cradled in Glory* pp 156-158.

476   Rodgers Sketch 87, 95 OR Series 1 Vol 44 pp 621-622.

477   *Cradled in Glory* p 158-160.

478   OR Series 1 Vol 44 p 328 Rodgers p 96.

CHAPTER 16: AGAINST ALL ODDS

479   OR Vol 44 Part 1 page 942; "city" refers to Savannah.

480   *Sherman's Memoirs* part 4 chpt 21.

481   Robert Niepert; Samuel Moore, CSA Excerpts from Moore's Autobiography.

482   *Ibid.*

483   Robert Niepert; Samuel Moore,CSA Excerpts from Moore's Autobiography.

484   *Ibid.*

485   Robert Niepert; Samuel Moore,CSA Excerpts from Moore's Autobiography.

486   *Sherman's Memoirs*, Part 4 Chapter 21.

487   *Ibid.*

488   *Sherman's Memoirs*, Part 4 Chapter 21.

489   *Sherman's Memoirs*, Part 4 Chapter 21.

490   OR Vol 44 Pg 110, 357.

491   OR Vol 44 Pg 110, 357.

492   Robert Niepert; Samuel Moore,CSA Excerpts from Moore's Autobiography.

493   *Sherman's Memoirs* Part 4, Chapter 21.

494   *Ibid.*

495   *Ibid.*

496   OR Series 1 Vol 44, pp 109-111, 357.

497   OR Series 1 Vol 44, pp 109-111, 357.

498   *Ibid.*

499   Robert Niepert; Samuel Moore, CSA Excerpts from Moore's Autobiography.

500   GA Archives battle summaries.

501   *Sherman's Memoirs* Part 4, Chapter 21.

502   Moore's Diary.

503   *Sherman's Memoirs* Part 4, Chapter 21.

504   *Sherman's Memoirs* Part 4, Chapter 21.

505   *Ibid.*

506   *Sherman's Memoirs* Part 4, Chapter 21.

507   *Sherman's Memoirs* Part 4, Chapter 21.

508   *Sherman's Memoirs* Part 4, Chapter 21.

509   *Sherman's Memoirs* Part 4, Vol 2, Chapter 21.

510   Robert Niepert; Samuel Moore, CSA Excerpts from Moore's Autobiography.

511   *Ibid.*

512   *Ibid.*

513   *Ibid.*

CHAPTER 17: SURRENDER OR DIE

514   OR Vol 44 page 737.

515   OR Vol 44 page 737.

516   OR Vol 44 page 737.

517   OR Vol 44 Part 1 page 942.

518   Confederate Brig. Gen. Nathan "Shanks" Evans stopped a badly coordinated at-
       tempt by Union forces under Brig. Gen. Charles P. Stone to cross the Potomac at
       Harrison's Island and capture Leesburg. A timely Confederate counterattack drove
       the Federals over the bluff and into the river. More than 700 Federals were captured.
       Col. Edward D. Baker (a U.S. Senator) was killed. This Union rout had severe politi-
       cal ramifications in Washington and led to the establishment of the Congressional
       Joint Committee on the Conduct of the War. Forces Engaged: 3,600 total (US
       2,000; CS 1,600)Estimated Casualties: 1,070 total (US 921; CS 149).

519   *Sherman's Memoirs* Part 4, Chapter 21.

520   OR Vol 44, p 960.

521   Reminiscences of Reverend George Blount May 25, 1903. Also states that there were
       no acts of vandalism was committed by the Negroes.

522   OR Series 1 Vol 44 p 792.

523   Gustavus W. Smith.

524   *Cradled in Glory* p 161.

525   Excerpt from *The Evacuation of the City of Savannah*, December 1864, Written by
       Rev George Adams Blount on May 25, 1903.

526   *Ibid.*

527   *Excerpt from The Evacuation of the City of Savannah*, December 1864, Written by
       Rev George Adams Blount on May 25, 1903.

528   *Excerpt from The Evacuation of the City of Savannah*, December 1864, Written by
       Rev George Adams Blount on May 25, 1903.

529   Excerpt from *The Evacuation of the City of Savannah*, December 1864, Written by
       Rev George Adams Blount on May 25, 1903.

530   Rodgers p 96. OR Series 1 Vol 44, p 57 *Cradled in Glory* p 161. Blount excerpts.

531   OR Vol 44 pg 974.

532   An old worn out horse for hire.

533   OR Vol 44, p 804.

534   James Sneed departed with General Hardee, but arranged for a newspaper to appear on December 21.

535   OR Series 1 Vol 44, p 280 Minutes of Solomon's Lodge Number 1.

536   *Sherman's Memoirs* Vol 2 part 4 Chapter 20.

537   *Ibid.*

538   Letter from Sherman to Douglass Green 3 Mar 1888.

539   Albert Gallatin Browne. During the Civil War, Browne served as the special supervising agent, 5th Special Agency of the U.S. Treasury Department in Beaufort, Port Royal, Charleston, S.C., and Savannah, Ga. He was in charge of seizing supplies and goods left behind by the Confederate Army for shipment to the North and supervising trade and commerce in areas of the Confederacy occupied by U.S. forces. Under certain acts, the agency received and collected abandoned, captured, and sizeable property.

540   OR Vol 44, p. 809

541   *Sherman's Memoirs* Vol 2 part 4 Chapter 21.

CHAPTER 18: REFLECTIONS

542   *Sherman's Memoirs* Vol 2, part 4 Chapter 21.

543   Sherman Family History.

544   *Ibid.*

545   Mother of Juliette Gordon Low. Founder of the Girl Scouts.

546   OR Series 1 Vol 44, p 793.

547   OR Series 1, Vol 53, p 306, p 166. Excerpts from Mayor Arnold's address to the citizens of Savannah. *Sherman's Memoirs* Part 4, Chapter 22.

548   Blount, The Evacuation of the City of Savannah, May 25, 1903.

549   General Orders No. 2 12/24/1864, Special Field Order N. 141 12/24/1864 p. 801, 805.

550   *Sherman Memoirs*, Part 4, Chapter 22, OR Series 1 Vol 44, pp 841-842.

551   *Sherman's Memoirs* Part 4 Chapter 21.

CHAPTER 19: CHRISTMAS 1864

552   General Orders No. 2 December 24, 1864 and Special Field Order No. 141 same date.

553   Christmas during the Civil War.

554   OR Series 1 Vol 47 part 2, p 1105. OR Series 1 Vol 53 p 412

555   P 258 *Life in Dixie*, Mary Gay.

556   *Ibid.*

557   *Ibid.*

558   Maguire's Diary.

559   *Cradled in Glory* pp 162-163.

560   Rodgers, 87, 97 *Cradled in Glory, Ibid.*

CHAPTER 20: QUESTIONS AND ANSWERS

561   Rodgers, 96-97 *Cradled in Glory* p 163-164.
562   Rogers, 96, 97. *Cradled in Glory* 163-164.
563   *Relief for Savannah* p 461, OR Vol 47, p 166.
564   Savannah City minutes Mayor Arnold, OR Vol 47 p 166.
565   Casimir Pulaski was a Polish military officer who fought on the side of the American colonists against the British in the Revolutionary War. The "father of the American cavalry," he was mortally wounded during the 1779 siege of Savannah, Georgia.
566   Woodbridge Pamphlet. Georgia History Society.
567   *Sherman Memoirs* Part 4 Chapter 22. Excerpts Mayor Arnold Vol 47 p 166.
568   *Sherman's Memories*, Part 4, Chapter 22 March to the Sea-Atlanta to Savannah.
569   *Sherman's Memoirs* Part 4 Chapter 22.
570   *Ibid.*
571   *Ibid*, OR Vol 44 p 80.
572   *Ibid.*
573   *Ibid.*
574   *Ibid.*
575   *Ibid.*
576   *Ibid.*
577   *Ibid.*
578   Sharing the name of the Confederate President, the Union General Jefferson Davis was a Mexican War veteran and was present during the bombardment of Fort Sumter. He served throughout the Civil War and was XIV corps commander during the march to the sea.
579   *Ibid.*
580   *Ibid.*
581   OR Series 1, Vol 44,p 406 Wheelers report.

CHAPTER 21: WHAT DO YOU THINK?

582   *Ibid.*
583   *Ibid.*
584   *Ibid.*
585   *Ibid.*
586   The entire biography text of each individual is contain on the CD.
587   *Ibid.*
588   Clipping from *New-York Daily Tribune*, [13 Feb. 1865], "Negroes of Savannah," Consolidated Correspondence File, ser. 225, Central Records, Quartermaster General, Record Group 92, National Archives.
589   297 *Sherman's Memoirs* Part 4 Chapter 22.
590   *Ibid.*

591   *Ibid.*
592   *Ibid.*
593   *Ibid.*
594   *Ibid.*
595   *Ibid.*
596   *Ibid.*
597   *Ibid.*
598   *Ibid.*

CHAPTER 22: POLITICS AND GENERALS

599   *Ibid.*
600   *Ibid.*
601   *Ibid.*
602   *Ibid.*
603   *Ibid.*
604   *New York Times*, January 15 1865.
605   Minutes of City Council.
606   Philadelphia *Public Ledger*, Jan. 11, 1865.
607   Savannah *Republican* January 10 1865.
608   Savannah *Republican* Jam 20, 21, 22, 1865.
609   Savannah and Boston pamphlet Woodbridge Family Ga. Historical Society.
610   Mayor F. W. Lincoln to Arnold 1/13/1865, in Minutes of Council 137-138.
611   Original article appeared in the New York Times and was reprinted in *Frank Leslie's*; Illustrated Newspaper, 2/25/1865.
612   Lee and Agnew, Historical Records of the Savannah, 133 n.
613   Savannah *Republican* 1/26/65.

CHAPTER 23: SUDDENLY

614   *Southern Recorder*, May 9, 1865.
615   *Confederate Records of the State of Georgia* 3:714.
616   *Cradled in Glory* p 168-169.
617   *Ibid.*
618   …it is hoped that the Georgia Railroad will be extended to Stone Mountain in order to afford them relief. *Savannah Newspaper Digest* . July 1 to Dec. 31, 1864.
619   *A Fools Errand*, 1880.

CHAPTER 24: HOMEWARD BOUND

620   *A Fools Errand.*, 1880.
621   Sweeping cotton-term used for sweeping cotton lint off of the floors.
622   *History of Newnan County.*
623   *History of Newnan County* p 694-697 and *History of Fort Stedman.*
624   *History of Bartow County.*

625 Dent genealogy.

626 *Atlanta and Environs*, p 558.

627 *Ibid.*

628 *Confederate Veterans of Stone Mountain*, Chris Davis.

629 Josiah (Joseph) Livsey is one of the descendants of Green H. Livsey. Joe married Mary Frances Camp the daughter of Merit Camp, a Gwinnett County pioneer. The Livsey plantation house is still standing on Mink-Livsey Road in Gwinnett County, Georgia. Personal records of Mrs. Lola Belle Livsey Kennedy and Mrs. Dixie Elizabeth Livsey Ray.

630 *A Fool's Errand*, 1880. Author unknown.

631 *Ibid.*

632 *Ibid.*

633 *Ibid.*

634 *Ibid.*

635 *Ibid.*

CHAPTER 25: IN THE SHADOW OF THE GRANITE SENTINEL

636 Fielding Maddox was the Pastor of the Stone Mountain First Baptist Church in 1865.

637 Roster of members of Stone Mountain Lodge.

notes

NOTES